# Leadership
## Research Findings, Practice, and Skills

Fifth Edition

ANDREW J. DUBRIN
Rochester Institute of Technology

Houghton Mifflin Company   *Boston   New York*

To Camila and Sofia

Publisher: George Hoffman
Senior Sponsoring Editor: Lise Johnson
Development Editor: Jessica Carlisle
Editorial Assistant: Amy Galvin
Project Editor: Patricia English
Editorial Assistant: Katherine Roz
Senior Art/Design Coordinator: Jill Haber
Senior Photo Editor: Jennifer Meyer Dare
Composition Buyer: Chuck Dutton
Associate Manufacturing Buyer: Brian Pieragostini
Executive Marketing Manager: Steven Mikels
Marketing Specialist: Lisa E. Boden

Cover image: © Dr. Pott/age footstock

Printed in the U.S.A.

Library of Congress Control Number: 2005935739

Instructor's exam copy:          658.4
ISBN 13: 978-0-618-73137-4        DUB
ISBN 10: 0-618-73137-7

For orders, use student text ISBNs:
ISBN: 13: 978-0-618-62328-0
ISBN 10: 0-618-62328-0

6789-CRS-10 09 08

# Brief Contents

# Contents

# Preface

Welcome to the Fifth Edition of *Leadership: Research Findings, Practice, and Skills*. The new edition of this text is a thorough update of the Fourth Edition that has been used widely in both graduate and undergraduate courses in leadership.

Leadership has emerged as a course by itself after long having been a key topic in several disciplines. Many scholars and managers alike are convinced that effective leadership is required to meet most organizational challenges. Today organizations recognize that leadership transcends senior executives. As a result, organizations require people with appropriate leadership skills to inspire and influence others in small teams, task forces, and units at all organizational levels.

Without effective leadership at all levels in organizations, it is difficult to sustain profitability, productivity, and good customer service. In dozens of different ways, researchers and teachers have demonstrated that leadership does make a difference. Many curricula in business schools and other fields, therefore, now emphasize the development of leadership skills. With the recent exposures of the dark side of business leadership, such as CEOs finding ways to create fortunes for themselves at the expense of employees and stockholders, more attention than ever is being paid to the values and personal characteristics of leaders. Toward that end, this text continues its emphasis on the qualities of effective leaders, including an entire chapter on leadership ethics and social responsibilities.

## Purpose of the Text

The purpose of this text is implied by its title—*Leadership: Research Findings, Practice, and Skills,* Fifth Edition. It is designed for undergraduate and graduate courses in leadership that give attention to research findings about leadership, leadership practice, and skill development. The text best fits courses in leadership that emphasize application and skill building. *Leadership* is also designed to fit courses in management development that emphasize the leadership aspect of management. In addition, it can serve as a supplement to organizational behavior or introductory management courses that emphasize leadership.

The student who masters this text will acquire an overview of the voluminous leadership literature that is based both on research and experience. Information in this text is not restricted to research studies and syntheses of research and theories; it also includes the opinions of practitioners, consultants, and authors who base their conclusions on observations rather than empirical research.

What the text is *not* also helps define its nature and scope. This book does not attempt to duplicate the scope and purpose of a leadership handbook by integrating theory and research from several thousand studies. At the other extreme, it is not an evangelical approach to leadership espousing one leadership technique. I have attempted to find a midpoint between a massive synthesis of the literature and a trade book promoting a current leadership fad. *Leadership: Research Findings, Practice, and Skills,* Fifth Edition, is designed to be a mixture of scholarly integrity, examples of effective leadership in action, and skill development.

*Leadership* is not intended to duplicate or substitute for an organizational behavior text. Because almost all organizational behavior texts are survey texts, they will mention many of the topics covered here. My approach, however, is to emphasize skill development and prescription rather than to duplicate basic descriptions of concepts and theories. I have tried to minimize overlap by emphasizing the leadership aspects of any concept presented here that might also be found in an organizational behavior or management text. Often when overlap of a topic exists, the presentation here focuses more on skill development than on a review of theory and research. For example, the section on motivation emphasizes how to apply basic explanations of motivation such as expectancy theory.

One area of intentional overlap with organizational behavior and management texts does exist: a review of all basic leadership theories. In such instances, however, I emphasize skill development and ideas for leadership practice stemming from these older theories.

## Features of the Book

To accomplish its purpose, this text incorporates many features into each chapter in addition to summarizing and synthesizing relevant information about leadership:

- **Chapter Outlines** giving the reader a quick overview of the topics covered

- **Learning Objectives** to help focus the reader's attention on major outcomes

- Boldfaced **key terms,** listed at the end of the chapter and defined in a **Glossary** at the back of the text

- Real-life and hypothetical **examples** throughout the text

- **Leader in Action** inserts describing the leadership practices, behaviors, and personal attributes of real-life leaders

- **Leadership Self-Assessment Exercises** relating to both skills and personal characteristics

- **Leadership Skill-Building Exercises,** including role-plays, to emphasize the activities and skills of effective leaders

- End-of-chapter **Summaries** that integrate all key topics and concepts

- End-of-chapter **Guidelines for Action and Skill Development**, giving additional suggestions for improving leadership skill and practice

- **Discussion Questions and Activities** suited for individual or group analysis

- Two **Leadership Case Problems** per chapter, which illustrate the major theme of the chapter and contain questions for individual or group analysis

- A **Leadership Portfolio** skill-building exercise in each chapter that instructs the student to record progress in developing leadership skills and behaviors.

- **Internet Skill-Building Exercises** that reinforce the Internet as another source of useful information about leadership. Where possible, the student is directed toward an interactive exercise.

- A **Knowledge Bank** section in each chapter that directs the student toward the textbook web site to access supplementary information, such as additional research or knowledge from organizational behavior that fits the subject at hand.

## Framework of the Text

The text is a blend of description, skill development, insight development, and prescription. Chapter 1 describes the meaning, importance, and nature of leadership, including leadership roles and the importance of followership. Chapter 2 identifies personal attributes associated with effective leaders, a subject that has experienced renewed importance in recent years. Charismatic and transformational leadership, an extension of understanding the personal attributes of leadership, is the subject of Chapter 3.

Chapter 4 surveys behaviors and practices associated with effective leadership in a variety of situations, and describes leadership styles. Chapter 5 extends the study of styles by describing the contingency and situational aspects of leadership. Chapter 6 focuses on leadership ethics and social responsibility. Chapter 7 describes how leaders use power and politics. Chapter 8 extends this topic by analyzing the tactics leaders use to influence people. Chapter 9 describes how leaders foster teamwork and empower team members.

The next five chapters deal with specific leadership skills: motivating and coaching skills (Chapter 10), which constitute the basis of many leadership positions; creativity and innovation (Chapter 11); communication (including nonverbal and cross-cultural communication) and conflict resolution skills (Chapter 12); vision and strategy creation and knowledge management (Chapter 13); and effective leadership in international and culturally diverse settings (Chapter 14).

Chapter 15 concludes the book with an overview of approaches to leadership development and learning. In addition, there is a discussion of leadership succession.

## Changes in the Fifth Edition

The Fifth Edition of *Leadership: Research Findings, Practice, and Skills* is a thorough update of the Fourth Edition. Some of the changes in this edition reflect the recent leadership information I felt should be included in the new edition. Many changes, though, reflect suggestions made by adopters and reviewers. For example, one reviewer suggested that I include a leadership portfolio skill-building exercise in each chapter. (Such an exercise was found in Chapter 15 of the Fourth Edition.) To make way for the new material, I have selectively pruned older examples and research findings, and shifted some information to the online Knowledge Bank. A comprehensive list of changes appears in the "Transition Guide" at the beginning of the *Instructor's Resource Manual*. The following list highlights the changes in the Fifth Edition:

## Changes Throughout the Text

- Several new Internet exercises at the end of each chapter
- Fourteen new chapter introductions
- Fourteen new Leader in Action boxes
- Sixteen new cases and three updated cases from the Third Edition
- More emphasis on leaders of less well-known firms, middle managers in larger firms, and small-business owners, and sports leaders
- New examples throughout
- Several new Guidelines for Action and Skill Development
- Six new Leadership Self-Assessment Quizzes

## Content Changes Within Chapters

Chapter 1 now contains the information about followership that was in Chapter 15. Chapter 2 presents information about tenacity and resilience as a leadership trait, as well as the WICS model of leadership in organizations. Chapter 3 presents a few new company visions, as well as research about training about certain aspects of charisma. Chapter 5 now includes disaster planning as part of crisis management. Chapter 6 includes strategic leadership for ethics and social responsibility, working with suppliers to improve working conditions, and placing company interests over personal interests. Chapter 7 presents a table on the symptoms of dysfunctional office politics.

Chapter 8 includes implicit leadership theories and influence. Chapter 9 includes a table of leadership behaviors and thoughts that enhance cooperation within the group. Chapter 10 includes a section on appealing to pride as a motivational technique. Chapter 11 includes two new business examples of thinking outside the box, as well as enhancing innovation by integrating production and development, and encouraging people across divisions to share ideas.

Chapter 12 contains a description of how to resolve conflict between two group members. Chapter 13 adds the strategies of product and global diversification, and creating demand by solving problems. Chapter 14 adds the leadership style of Malaysian managers, cultural intelligence, and intercultural training. Chapter 15 includes coaching and psychotherapy as an approach to leadership development, and a new formulation of domains of impact for leadership development.

## Supplements

Several supplements that facilitate teaching accompany this edition.

***Instructor's Resource Manual with Test Bank.*** This manual features chapter outlines and lecture notes, possible answers to discussion questions and case questions, and comments on exercises in the text. The test bank portion includes 25 multiple-choice and 25 true–false questions for each chapter. The instructor's manual also describes how to use Computer-Assisted Scenario Analysis (CASA). Especially designed for helping students develop a contingency point of view, CASA is a user-friendly technique that can be used with any word processing software. It allows the student to insert a new scenario into the case and then re-answer the questions based on the new scenario. CASA helps to develop an awareness of contingency factors in making leadership decisions, as well as develop creative thinking. A brief version of CASA was published in the October 1992 issue of *The Journal of Management Education.*

*HMTesting.* This computerized version of the *Test Bank* allows instructors to select, edit, and add questions, or generate randomly selected questions to produce a test master for easy duplication. Online Testing and Gradebook functions allow instructors to administer tests via their local area network or the World Wide Web, set up classes, record grades from tests or assignments, analyze grades, and compile class and individual statistics. This program can be used on both PCs and Macintosh computers.

*Videos.* The video package focuses on important leadership and teamwork skills and concepts found throughout the text. A Video Guide with segment overviews and discussion questions is included.

*Web Site.* The fifth edition of *Leadership* offers a web site. The **student site** contains new ACE Self-Tests, chapter links to companies highlighted in the text, a Knowledge Bank, and a Resource Center with links to professional organizations and other sites related to leadership. The password-protected **instructor site** provides electronic lecture notes from the *Instructor's Resource Manual,* CRS clicker content, and PowerPoint® slides for downloading. These slides include summaries of key concepts, concise text, art, and other supplementary information to create a total presentation package. The web site also includes **Overhead Transparencies,** a set of nearly 70 downloadable PDFs that offer visual teaching assistance to the instructor. Figures, tables, diagrams, and illustrations from the text are included.

## Acknowledgments

Any project as complex as this one requires a team of dedicated and talented people to see that it achieves its goals. First, I thank the many effective leaders whom I have observed in action for improving my understanding of leadership. Second, I thank the following professors who offered suggestions for improving this and previous editions:

Steven Barry
*University of Colorado–Boulder*
John Bigelow
*Boise State University*
Bruce T. Caine
*Vanderbilt University*
Felipe Chia
*Harrisburg Area Community College*
Conna Condon
*Upper Iowa University*
Emily J. Creighton
*University of New Hampshire*

Rawlin Fairbough
*Sacred Heart University*
Justin Frimmer
*Jacksonville University*
Barry Gold
*Pace University*
George B. Graen
*University of Cincinnati*
Stephen G. Green
*Purdue University*
James R. Harris
*North Carolina Agricultural and Technical State University*

Paul Harris
*Lee College*
Nell Hartley
*Robert Morris College*
Linda Hefferin
*Elgin Community College*
Winston Hill
*California State University, Chico*
Avis L. Johnson
*University of Akron*
Marvin Karlins
*University of South Florida*
Nelly Kazman
*University of La Verne*
David Lee
*University of Dayton*
Brian McNatt
*University of Georgia*
Ralph Mullin
*Central Missouri State University*
Linda L. Neider
*University of Miami*
Rhonda S. Palladi
*Georgia State University*

Joseph Petrick
*Wright State University*
Mark Phillips
*University of Texas at San Antonio*
Judy Quinn
*Kutztown University*
Clint Relyea
*Arkansas State University*
Howard F. Rudd
*College of Charleston*
Robert Scherer
*Wright State University*
Marianne Sebok
*Community College of Southern Nevada*
Charles Seifert
*Siena College*
Randall G. Sleeth
*Virginia Commonwealth University*
Ahmad Tootoonchi
*Frostburg State University*
David Van Fleet
*Arizona State University West*
John Warner
*University of New Mexico*

The editorial and production team at Houghton Mifflin Company also receives my gratitude. By name they are Lise Johnson, Jessica Carlisle, Amy Galvin, Patricia English, and Katherine Roz. Writing without loved ones would be a lonely task. My thanks, therefore, also go to my family members—Drew, Douglas and Gizella, Melanie and Will, Rosie, Clare, Camila, and Sofia.

A.J.D.

# About the Author

Andrew J. DuBrin is a Professor of Management emeritus in the College of Business at the Rochester Institute of Technology, where he teaches courses and conducts research in leadership, organizational behavior, and career management. He also served as department chairman and team leader in previous years. He received his Ph.D. in Industrial Psychology from Michigan State University.

DuBrin has business experience in human resource management, and consults with organizations and individuals. His specialties include leadership, influence tactics, and career development. DuBrin is an established author of both textbooks and trade books, and contributes to professional journals, magazines, newspapers, and online shows. He has written textbooks on organizational behavior, management, and human relations. His trade books cover many topics including charisma, team play, coaching and mentoring, office politics, and self-discipline.

Chapter

1

# The Nature and Importance of Leadership

1

As a former ROTC scholar and six-year navy officer, the CEO and president of Bcc Software, Inc. might be expected to be somewhat of a drill sergeant at work. Instead, employees at Jon Runstrom's mailing software design firm describe the 57-year-old as a kind and understanding manager, ready to pitch in at any level—even helping his staff stuff envelopes.

"I think we had just moved in and we didn't have things set up. We didn't have tables. I remember sitting on the floor. There were about ten of us just stuffing. He came over, sat down, and worked right along with us," says James Mann, Bcc Software vice president for customer support. "I can remember a support technician saying, 'That's a great thing to see.' It was a great opportunity. We were able to sit down with Jon and talk with him and have fun and joke around."

Runstrom's down-to-earth management style, which has helped maintain a 2 percent turnover rate over the last five years at Bcc Software, is partly due to his degree in industrial psychology. It also stems from his humbling experience in launching an information technology startup some twenty-six years ago that eventually became Bcc. The company has grown from a two-person startup to a staff of fifty-eight with thousands of software customers in all fifty states, Puerto Rico, and Canada.

Runstrom says, "For any business, I don't care what you're doing, you've got to treat employees as if they're your own customers." Bcc's Software's facilities were designed to give employees maximum personal space. Runstrom also advocates flexible working schedules and organizes golf tournaments for employees and trips to amusement parks.

"The culture here at Bcc is a very open environment, very flexible environment. People here appear to be happy. Customer support, for example, you can have a turnover rate of say 50 to 60 percent, and at this point we're at zero percent. No one has left this department in a year," says Mann.

Runstrom says he's never been a top-down kind of boss. "Those things in my mind never did work, never do work, never will work." He adds that flexibility is fundamental to good management, and that you have to trust people.[1]

---

The characterization of Jon Runstrom touches on many leadership topics to be covered in this book, including the ideas that caring leadership can make a difference in an organization's success, that a successful leader works well with his or her team, and that many effective leaders are visible and approachable. Our introductory chapter begins with an explanation of what leadership is and is not. We then examine how leaders make a difference, the various roles they play, and the major satisfactions and frustrations they experience. The chapter also includes an explanation of how reading this book and doing the various quizzes and exercises will enhance your own leadership skills. It concludes with a discussion of "followership"—giving leaders good material to work with.

## The Meaning of Leadership

You will read about many effective organizational leaders throughout this text. The common characteristic of these leaders is their ability to inspire and stimulate others to achieve worthwhile goals. Thus we can define **leadership** as the ability to inspire confidence and support among the people who are needed to achieve organizational goals.[2]

A Google search of articles and books about leadership indicates 533 million entries. In all those entries, leadership has probably been defined in many ways. Here are several other representative definitions of leadership:

■ Interpersonal influence, directed through communication toward goal attainment

■ The influential increment over and above mechanical compliance with directions and orders

■ An act that causes others to act or respond in a shared direction

■ The art of influencing people by persuasion or example to follow a line of action

■ The principal dynamic force that motivates and coordinates the organization in the accomplishment of its objectives[3]

■ A willingness to take the blame (as defined by legendary football quarterback Joe Montana)[4]

A major point about leadership is that it is not found only among people in high-level positions. Leadership is needed at all levels in an organization and can be practiced to some extent even by a person not assigned to a formal leadership position. For example, working as a junior accountant, a person might take the initiative to suggest to management that they need to be more careful about what they classify as a true sale. An extreme example of the importance of workers exercising leadership is Roadway Express, Inc. After implementing a program of employee involvement in productivity improvement, Roadway management concluded that if Roadway is to compete in an industry in which net profit margins are less than 5 percent in a good year, every one of its 28,000 employees must be a leader.[5]

The ability to lead others effectively is a rare quality. It becomes even more rare at the highest levels in an organization because the complexity of such positions requires a vast range of leadership skills. This is one reason that firms in search of new leadership seek out a select group of brand-name executives.[6] It is also why companies now emphasize leadership training and development to create a new supply of leaders throughout the firm.

## Leadership as a Partnership

The current understanding of leadership is that it is a long-term relationship, or partnership, between leaders and group members. According to Peter Block, in a **partnership** the leader and the group members are connected in such a way that the power between them is approximately balanced. Block also describes partnership as the opposite of parenting (in which one person—the parent—takes responsibility for the welfare of the other—the child). Partnership occurs when control shifts from the leader to the group member, in a move away from authoritarianism and toward shared decision making.[7] Four things are necessary for a valid partnership to exist:

1. *Exchange of purpose.* In a partnership, every worker at every level is responsible for defining vision and values. Through dialogue with people at many levels, the leader helps articulate a widely accepted vision.

2. *A right to say no.* The belief that people who express a contrary opinion will be punished runs contrary to a partnership. Rather, a person can lose an argument but never a voice.

3. *Joint accountability*. In a partnership, each person is responsible for outcomes and the current situation. In practice, this means that each person takes personal accountability for the success and failure of the organizational unit.

4. *Absolute honesty*. In a partnership, not telling the truth to one another is an act of betrayal. When power is distributed, people are more likely to tell the truth because they feel less vulnerable.[8]

Block's conception of leadership as a partnership is an ideal to strive toward. Empowerment and team building—two major topics in this book—support the idea of a partnership.

Looking at leadership as a partnership is also important because it is linked to an optimistic view of group members, referred to as **stewardship theory**. This theory depicts group members (or followers) as being collectivists, pro-organizational, and trustworthy.[9] A collectivist is a person who is more concerned about the welfare of the group than about his or her personal welfare. Have you met many collectivists in the workplace?

## Leadership as a Relationship

A modern study of leadership emphasizes that leadership is a relationship between the leader and the people being led. Research indicates that having good relationships with group members is a major success factor for the three top positions in large organizations. James Kouzes and Barry Posner conducted an online survey asking respondents to indicate, among other questions, which would be more essential to business success in five years: social skills or Internet skills. Seventy-two percent indicated social skills, and 28 percent Internet skills. The authors concluded that the web of people matters more than the web of technology.[10] (Yet a person who lacks Internet skills may not have the opportunity to be in a position to manage relationships.) Building relationships with people is such an important part of leadership that the theme will be introduced at various points in this text.

## Leadership Versus Management

To understand leadership, it is important to grasp the difference between leadership and management. We get a clue from the standard conceptualization of the functions of management: planning, organizing, directing (or leading), and controlling. Leading is a major part of a manager's job, yet a manager must also plan, organize, and control.

Broadly speaking, leadership deals with the interpersonal aspects of a manager's job, whereas planning, organizing, and controlling deal with the administrative aspects. Leadership deals with change, inspiration, motivation, and influence. Table 1-1 presents a stereotype of the differences between leadership and management. As is the case with most stereotypes, the differences tend to be exaggerated.

According to John P. Kotter, a prominent leadership theorist, managers must know how to lead as well as manage. Without being led as well as managed, organizations face the threat of extinction. Following are several key distinctions between management and leadership:

| TABLE 1-1 | Leaders Versus Managers |
| --- | --- |

| LEADER | MANAGER |
| --- | --- |
| Visionary | Rational |
| Passionate | Business-like |
| Creative | Persistent |
| Inspiring | Tough-minded |
| Innovative | Analytical |
| Courageous | Structured |
| Imaginative | Deliberative |
| Experimental | Authoritative |
| Independent | Stabilizing |
| Shares knowledge | Centralizes knowledge |
| Trusting | Guarded |
| Warm and radiant | Cool and reserved |
| Expresses humility | Rarely admits to being wrong |
| Initiator | Implementer |
| Acts as coach, consultant, teacher | Acts as a boss |
| Does the right things | Does things right |

Source: Genevieve Capowski, "Anatomy of a Leader: Where Are the Leaders of Tomorrow?" *Management Review*, March 1994, p. 12; David Fagiano, "Managers Versus Leaders: A Corporate Fable," *Management Review*, November 1997, p. 5; Keki R. Bhote, *The Ultimate Six Sigma* (New York: AMACOM, 2002).

- Management produces order, consistency, and predictability.
- Leadership produces change and adaptability to new products, new markets, new competitors, new customers, and new work processes.
- Leadership, in contrast to management, involves having a vision of what the organization can become and mobilizing people to accomplish it.
- Leadership requires eliciting cooperation and teamwork from a large network of people and keeping the key people in that network motivated by using every manner of persuasion.
- Leadership produces change, often to a dramatic degree, such as by spearheading the launch of a new product or opening a new market for an old product. Management is more likely to produce a degree of predictability and order.
- Top-level leaders are likely to transform their organizations, whereas top-level managers just manage (or maintain) organizations.
- A leader creates a vision (lofty goal) to direct the organization. In contrast, the key function of the manager is to implement the vision. The manager and his or her team thus choose the means to achieve the end that the leader formulates.[11]

If these views are taken to their extreme, the leader is an inspirational figure and the manager is a stodgy bureaucrat mired in the status quo. But we must be careful not to downplay the importance of management. Effective leaders have to be good managers themselves, or be supported by effective managers. A germane example is the inspirational entrepreneur who is so preoccupied with motivating employees and captivating customers that he or she neglects internal administration. As a result, costs skyrocket beyond income, and such matters as funding the employee pension plan and paying bills and taxes on time are overlooked. In short, the difference between leadership and management is one of emphasis. Effective leaders also manage, and effective managers also lead.

## The Impact of Leadership on Organizational Performance

An assumption underlying the study of leadership is that leaders affect organizational performance. Boards of directors—the highest-level executives of an organization—make the same assumption. A frequent antidote to major organizational problems is to replace the leader in the hope that the newly appointed leader will reverse performance problems. Here we will review some of the evidence and opinion, pro and con, about the ability of leaders to affect organizational performance. The Leader in Action profile provides a positive example of the importance of effective leadership.

 **LEADER IN ACTION**

### ROSE MARIE BRAVO OF BURBERRY GROUP PLC

When Rose Marie Bravo took over as chief executive of Burberry Group plc in 1997, the company was a staid British raincoat maker, far off the radar screens of the fashion world. Today, Burberry's turnaround is legendary, and its tartan bedecks everything from hats to luggage to bikinis, in a riot of colors from pink to blue to purple.

Most notably, Burberry has been able to sustain its new momentum, consistently posting gains in an industry notorious for passing trends and fickle consumers. The company has had five straight years of annual sales increases, with annual volumes of about $1.2 billion (676 pounds sterling).

The Bronx-born Ms. Bravo, 53, began as a cosmetics and fragrance buyer at Macy's before jumping to the now defunct upscale retailer, I. Magnin, where she rose to chairman and CEO. In 1992, she was named president of Saks Fifth Avenue,

which she ran for five years until leaving to join London-based Burberry. She sat down with *The Wall Street Journal* to talk about how she plans to keep Burberry flourishing without diluting the brand's exclusive image. Excerpts showing Bravo's leadership practice and attitudes follow:

**WSJ:** How do you keep the brand hot and fresh season after season when fashion always changes?

**Bravo:** This is the biggest question facing any brand, whether it is Coca-Cola or Mercedes Benz. Constant creativity and innovation are required. You just can never stop. Our new motto at Burberry is we never stop designing. And creativity doesn't just come from the designers.

For example, we did an ad campaign . . . they did flashes of color, literally thrown onto a black and white picture. It almost looked like a kid had spilled color onto the photograph. We looked at it and said, this should be scarves. We did a whole series of scarves that became bestsellers. This idea came from our [advertising] agency.

Ideas can come from the sales floor, the marketing department, even from accountants, believe it or not. So keeping that open attitude that you can get an idea that can be a business idea from just about anywhere is important. It is not just the ownership of one person or two people.

**WSJ:** What do you do specifically to motivate and inspire people?

**Bravo:** We like management to visit the stores, talk to the salespeople. People at whatever level they are working have a point of view and have something to say that is worth listening to. We try to set an agenda throughout the company where everyone's opinion counts, and it's nice to be asked.

**WSJ:** Star designers have become more common today. But it sounds like you believe in a team approach.

**Bravo:** Some people like a lot of confrontation. I don't. I like people to get along. I like to have everybody contribute. But I don't necessarily believe in consensus, because then you can end up with mediocrity.

**WSJ:** For example?

**Bravo:** The plaid shopping bag. Everybody wanted to go neutral—solid beige or black. I felt instinctively, it was too subtle. In fact, we could have the only shopping bag that didn't have a logo on it, and we didn't have to write our name across it. I called Geraldine Stutz, the retired head of Henri Bendel (the New York specialty retailer famous for its brown striped bags). I said, "We need to do a shopping bag, what do you think?" She said, "Come on, it has to be plaid."

Bravo offers five lessons for rebuilding and sustaining a hot brand:

- Lesson 1: Don't rest on your laurels—reinvent yourself every day and never stop thinking of new ways to wow the customer.

- Lesson 2: Maintain your core customer while pursuing a new one.

- Lesson 3: Don't worry about where a new idea comes from. Execution is the key.

- Lesson 4: Don't rely on a formula. Just because something works for one company doesn't mean it will work for another.

- Lesson 5: Surround yourself with great people. It's all about teamwork.

### QUESTIONS

1. In what way does Bravo bring technical expertise to her leadership position?
2. In what way does Bravo emphasize listening to workers in her leadership approach?

SOURCE: Excerpted from Sally Beatty, "Plotting Plaid's Future: Burberry's Rose Marie Bravo Designs Ways to Keep Brand Growing and Still Exclusive," *The Wall Street Journal*, September 9, 2004, pp. B1, B8. Copyright 2004 by Dow Jones & Co., Inc. Reprinted with permission of Dow Jones & Co. Inc. in the format Textbook via Copyright Clearance Center.

## *Research and Opinion: Leadership Does Make a Difference*

The idea that leaders actually influence organizational performance and morale is so plausible that there is not an abundance of research and opinion that deals with this issue. (Nor do we have loads of studies demonstrating that sleeping reduces fatigue.) Here we look at a sample of the existing research and opinion.

A team of researchers investigated the impact of transactional (routine) and charismatic (inspirational) leadership on financial performance.[12] The researchers analyzed 210 surveys completed by senior managers from 131 *Fortune 500* firms. Transactional and charismatic leadership styles were measured with a leadership questionnaire. Each participant was asked to think about the CEO of his or her company and rate that individual on the leadership scale. Because an uncertain environment often makes having a strong leader more important, participants also completed a questionnaire that measured perceived environmental uncertainty. Organizational performance was measured as net profit margin (NPM), computed as net income divided by net sales. The performance data were gathered from public information about the companies.

The results of the study disclosed that (1) transactional leadership was not significantly related to performance, (2) charismatic leadership showed a slight positive relationship with performance, and (3) when the environment is uncertain, charismatic leadership is more strongly related to performance.

In another study, a group of researchers analyzed 200 management techniques as employed by 150 companies over ten years. The aspect of the study evaluating the effects of leadership found that CEOs influence 15 percent of the total variance (influencing factors) in a company's profitability or total return to shareholders. The same study also found that the industry in which a company operates also accounts for 15 percent of the variance in profitability. So the choice of a CEO leader is as important as the choice of whether to remain in the same industry or enter a different one.[13]

In addition to tangible evidence that leadership makes a difference, the perception of these differences is also meaningful. An understanding of these perceptions derives from **attribution theory**, the theory of how we explain the causes of events. Gary Yukl explains that organizations are complex social systems of patterned interactions among people. In their efforts to understand (and simplify) organizational events, people interpret these events in simple human terms. One especially strong and prevalent approach is to attribute causality to leaders. They are viewed as heroes and heroines who determine the fates of their organizations.[14] The extraordinary success of Southwest Airlines Co. during the 1990s is thus attributed to Herb Kelleher, its flamboyant chief executive. Kelleher initiated no-frills, low-cost air service and built Southwest into a highly profitable airline. (Ultimately, new competitors modeled after Southwest, such as JetBlue Airlines, took away some of Southwest's profitability.) Most organizational successes are attributed to heroic leaders—according to attribution theory.

## *Research and Opinion: Formal Leadership Does Not Make a Difference*

In contrast to the previous argument, the antileadership argument holds that leadership has a smaller impact on organizational outcomes than do forces in the situation. To personalize this perspective, imagine yourself appointed as the manager of a group of highly skilled investment bankers. How well your group performs could be attributed as much to their talent and to economic conditions as to your leadership. The three major arguments against the importance of leadership are substitutes for leadership, leadership irrelevance, and complexity theory.

**FIGURE 1-1** Substitutes for Leadership

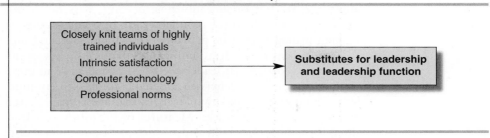

**Substitutes for Leadership** At times competent leadership is not necessary, and incompetent leadership can be counterbalanced by certain factors in the work situation. Under these circumstances, leadership itself is of little consequence to the performance and satisfaction of team members. According to this viewpoint, many organizations have **substitutes for leadership**. Such substitutes are factors in the work environment that provide guidance and incentives to perform, making the leader's role almost superfluous.[15] Figure 1-1 shows four leadership substitutes: closely knit teams, intrinsic satisfaction, computer technology, and professional norms.

*Closely knit teams of highly trained individuals.* When members of a cohesive, highly trained group are focused on a goal, they may require almost no leadership to accomplish their task. Several researchers have studied air traffic controllers who direct traffic into San Francisco and pilots who land jet fighters on a nuclear aircraft carrier. With such groups, directive (decisive and task-oriented) leadership is seemingly unimportant. When danger is the highest, these groups rely more on each other than on a leader.

*Intrinsic satisfaction.* Employees who are engaged in work they find strongly self-motivating, or intrinsically satisfying, require a minimum of leadership. Part of the reason is that the task itself grabs the worker's attention and energy. The worker may require little leadership as long as the task is proceeding smoothly. Many information technology firms provide a minimum of leadership and management to computer professionals, who may be totally absorbed in such tasks as combating the latest computer virus.

*Computer technology.* Some companies today use computer-aided monitoring and computer networking to take over many of the supervisor's leadership functions. The computer provides productivity and quality data, and directions for certain tasks are entered into the information system. Even error detection and goal setting are incorporated into some interaction systems. Instead of asking a supervisor for assistance, some employees use the computer network to ask for assistance from other workers. (We could argue here that the computer is being used to control rather than to lead workers.)

*Professional norms.* Workers who incorporate strong professional norms often require a minimum of supervision and leadership. A group of certified professional accountants may not need visionary leadership to inspire them to do an honest job of auditing the books of a client or advising against tax fraud.

Although the leadership substitute concept has some merit, it reflects naiveté about the role of organizational leadership. Bass notes that self-management by groups and individuals requires delegation by a higher authority. In addition, higher-ranking managers provide guidance, encouragement, and support.[16]

More recent research study suggests that the theory of substitutes for leadership may be flawed and that leadership does indeed have an impact on group effectiveness. A team of researchers conducted a study of forty-nine organizations with at least 50 employees and two levels of management. The sample consisted of 940 employees and 156 leaders. Measures of substitutes for leadership were similar to the information presented above, such as "I am a member of a professional group whose standards and values guide me in my work." In short, the study suggested that "leadership matters." The likeability of the leader and whether the leader provides rewards for good performance were found to be the major correlates of performance.[17]

***Leader Irrelevance*** According to the theorizing of Jeffrey Pfeffer, leadership is irrelevant to most organizational outcomes. Rather, it is the situation that must be carefully analyzed. Pfeffer argues that factors outside the leader's control have a larger impact on business outcomes than do leadership actions.[18] During the late 1990s and early 2000s cell phone ownership surged throughout the world, with 80 percent of adults in the United States owning cell phones. The sales boom in this electronic equipment could be better attributed to an outside force than to inspirational leadership within telecommunications companies.

Another aspect of the leader irrelevance argument is that high-level leaders have unilateral control over only a few resources. Furthermore, the leader's control of these resources is limited by obligations to stakeholders like consumers and stockholders. Finally, firms tend to choose new organizational leaders whose values are compatible with those of the firm. The leaders therefore act in ways similar to previous leaders.

Jim Collins, who has extensively researched how companies endure and how they shift from average to superior performance, also doubts the relevance of leadership. According to his earlier research, corporate leaders are slaves of much larger organizational forces. Collins makes the analogy of children holding a pair of ribbons inside a coach and imagining they are driving the horse. It is not the leader's personality that makes a difference; more important is the organization's personality. For example, Collins notes that Jack Welch was the product rather than the producer of GE's success during his long reign.[19]

The leader irrelevance argument would have greater practical value if it were recast as a *leader constraint theory,* which would hold that leaders are constrained in what they can do but still have plenty of room to influence others.

***Complexity Theory*** Similar to the pessimistic outlook of leader irrelevance is the perspective of *complexity theory,* which holds that organizations are complex systems that cannot be explained by the usual rules of nature. Leaders and managers can do little to alter the course of the complex organizational system. The same view holds that forces outside the leader or manager's control determine a company's fate. Managers cannot predict which business strategies or product mixes will survive. The best they can hope for is to scramble or innovate in order to adapt to outside forces. Ultimately all companies will die but at different times, because it is the system, not leadership and management, that dominates.[20]

## Leadership Roles

Another way to gain an understanding of leadership is to examine the various roles carried out by leaders. A *role* in this context is an expected set of activities or behaviors stemming from one's job. Leadership roles are a subset of the managerial roles studied by Henry Mintzberg and others.[21] Before reading ahead to the summary of leadership roles, you are invited to complete Leadership Self-Assessment Quiz 1-1.

**LEADERSHIP SELF-ASSESSMENT QUIZ 1-1**

### READINESS FOR THE LEADERSHIP ROLE

INSTRUCTIONS Indicate the extent to which you agree with each of the following statements, using the following scale: 1, disagree strongly; 2, disagree; 3, neutral; 4, agree; 5, agree strongly.

1. It is enjoyable to have people count on me for ideas and suggestions.

   1    (2)    (3)    4    5

2. It would be accurate to say that I have inspired other people.

   1    2    (3)    4    (5)

3. It's a good practice to ask people provocative questions about their work.

   1    2    3    (4)    5

4. It's easy for me to compliment others.

   1    2    3    4    (5)

5. I like to cheer people up even when my own spirits are down.

   1    2    (3)    4    5

6. What my team accomplishes is more important than my personal glory.

   1    2    (3)    4    5

7. Many people imitate my ideas.

   1    (2)    3    4    5

8. Building team spirit is important to me.

   1    (2)    3    4    5

*(continued)*

9. I would enjoy coaching other members of the team.

1           2           3           (4)          5

10. It is important to me to recognize others for their accomplishments.

1           2           3           4           (5)

11. I would enjoy entertaining visitors to my firm even if it interfered with my completing a report.

1           (2)          3           4           5

12. It would be fun for me to represent my team at gatherings outside our department.

1           (2)          3           4           5

13. The problems of my teammates are my problems too.

1           2           (3)          4           5

14. Resolving conflict is an activity I enjoy.

1           (2)          3           4           5

15. I would cooperate with another unit in the organization even if I disagreed with the position taken by its members.

1           2           (3)          4           5

16. I am an idea generator on the job.

1           2           (3)          4           5

17. It is fun for me to bargain whenever I have the opportunity.

1           2           (3)          4           5

18. Team members listen to me when I speak.

1           2           3           (4)          5

19. People have asked me to assume the leadership of an activity several times in my life.

1           2           3           (4)          5

20. I have always been a convincing person.

1           2           (3)          4           5

*Total score:* 63

SCORING AND INTERPRETATION Calculate your total score by adding the numbers circled. A tentative interpretation of the scoring is as follows:

- 90–100: High readiness for the leadership role
- 60–89: Moderate readiness for the leadership role
- 40–59: Some uneasiness with the leadership role
- 39 or less: Low readiness for the leadership role

If you are already a successful leader and you scored low on this questionnaire, ignore your score. If you scored surprisingly low and you are not yet a leader, or are currently performing poorly as a leader, study the statements carefully. Consider changing your attitude or your behavior so that you can legitimately answer more of the statements with a 4 or a 5. Studying the rest of this text will give you additional insights that may be helpful in your development as a leader.

Leading is a complex activity, so it is not surprising that Mintzberg and other researchers identified nine roles that can be classified as part of the leadership function of management.

1. *Figurehead*. Leaders, particularly high-ranking managers, spend some part of their time engaging in ceremonial activities, or acting as a figurehead. Four specific behaviors fit the figurehead role of a leader:
   a. entertaining clients or customers as an official representative of the organization
   b. making oneself available to outsiders as a representative of the organization
   c. serving as an official representative of the organization at gatherings outside the organization
   d. escorting official visitors

2. *Spokesperson*. When a manager acts as a spokesperson, the emphasis is on answering letters or inquiries and formally reporting to individuals and groups outside the manager's direct organizational unit. As a spokesperson, the managerial leader keeps five groups of people informed about the unit's activities, plans, capabilities, and possibilities (vision):
   a. upper-level management
   b. clients or customers
   c. other important outsiders such as labor unions
   d. professional colleagues
   e. the general public

Dealing with outside groups and the general public is usually the responsibility of top-level managers.

3. *Negotiator.* Part of almost any manager's job description is trying to make deals with others for needed resources. Researchers have identified three specific negotiating activities:

   a. bargaining with superiors for funds, facilities, equipment, or other forms of support
   b. bargaining with other units in the organization for the use of staff, facilities, equipment, or other forms of support
   c. bargaining with suppliers and vendors for services, schedules, and delivery times

4. *Coach and motivator.* An effective leader takes the time to coach and motivate team members. This role includes four specific behaviors:

   a. informally recognizing team members' achievements
   b. providing team members with feedback concerning ineffective performance
   c. ensuring that team members are informed of steps that can improve their performance
   d. implementing rewards and punishments to encourage and sustain good performance

5. *Team builder.* A key aspect of a leader's role is to build an effective team. Activities contributing to this role include:

   a. ensuring that team members are recognized for their accomplishments, such as through letters of appreciation
   b. initiating activities that contribute to group morale, such as giving parties and sponsoring sports teams
   c. holding periodic staff meetings to encourage team members to talk about their accomplishments, problems, and concerns

6. *Team player.* Related to the team-builder role is that of the team player. Three behaviors of team players are:

   a. displaying appropriate personal conduct
   b. cooperating with other units in the organization
   c. displaying loyalty to superiors by supporting their plans and decisions fully

7. *Technical problem solver.* It is particularly important for supervisors and middle managers to help team members solve technical problems. Two activities contributing to this role are:

   a. serving as a technical expert or adviser
   b. performing individual contributor tasks on a regular basis, such as making sales calls or repairing machinery

8. *Entrepreneur.* Although not self-employed, managers who work in large organizations have some responsibility for suggesting innovative ideas or furthering the business aspects of the firm. Three entrepreneurial leadership role activities are:

   a. reading trade publications and professional journals to keep up with what is happening in the industry and profession
   b. talking with customers or others in the organization to keep aware of changing needs and requirements
   c. getting involved in situations outside the unit that could suggest ways of improving the unit's performance, such as visiting other firms, attending professional meetings or trade shows, and participating in educational programs

9. *Strategic planner.* Top-level managers engage in strategic planning, usually assisted by input from others throughout the organization. Carrying out the strategic-planner role enables the manager to practice strategic leadership. Specific activities involved in this role include:

a. setting a vision and direction for the organization
b. helping the firm deal with the external environment
c. helping develop organizational policies

A common thread in the leadership roles of a manager is that the managerial leader in some way inspires or influences others. An analysis in the *Harvard Business Review* concluded that the most basic role for corporate leaders is to release the human spirit that makes initiative, creativity, and entrepreneurship possible.[22] An important practical implication is that managers at every level can exercise leadership. For example, a team leader can make an important contribution to the firm's thrust for quality by explaining to team members how to minimize duplications in a mailing list. Leadership Skill-Building Exercise 1-1 provides additional insights into the various leadership roles.

Up to this point we have described the meaning of leadership, how leadership affects organizational performance, and the many activities carried out by leaders. You have had an opportunity to explore your attitudes toward occupying the leadership role. We now further personalize information about leadership.

**LEADERSHIP SKILL-BUILDING EXERCISE 1-1**

### IDENTIFYING LEADERSHIP ROLES

Three months into his job at J.C. Penney Company, Inc., Allen Questrom delivered a spiel and stuck to it. It is the Questrom way: dole out the broad vision and repeat it until everyone gets it right. He gave J.C. Penney employees two to five years to turn the ship around. He did not plan to do it alone. He was not taking any guarantees, but he was comfortable being captain. He asked employees who were helping to rebuild the J.C. Penney organization to rethink everything. "A business isn't run by one person. It's run by teams," said J.C. Penney's chairman and chief executive officer during an interview at the company's Plano, Texas, headquarters. "My job is to set the objectives and get people to understand them and execute them."

Questrom joined J.C. Penney in September 2000 from Barneys New York, but he is best known for his long tenure at Federated Department Stores, Inc. He brought that company out of bankruptcy and acquired the Macy's and Broadway chains, which gave Federated a strong market share up and down both coasts. The veteran retailer has been charming employees, customers, and creditors for years. Particularly impressive has been his ability to turn around prestigious stores that have fallen on hard times. In addition to Federated, Questrom helped revive Neiman Marcus and Barneys.

A major challenge Questrom faced on joining J.C. Penney is that some critics thought that its fashions were tired and its prices were too high. Retail analysts felt that the biggest challenge at Penney was to redefine what the brand was

*(continued)*

about. Questrom emphasized that the company caters to the broad middle market, where the bulk of consumers are found. Penney's national presence, a good catalog, and an online business are also assets. But analysts at Morningstar.com were particularly harsh about the problems facing Penney and Questrom: "The company's problems are nothing short of humongous, and include an inefficient supply chain, outdated apparel offerings, a stodgy brand name, and a money-losing drugstore operation."

Questrom *said* he believed in the J.C. Penney brand and was trying to get back to J.C. Penney's roots as the department store of choice for middle-income Americans. (J.C. Penney also owned the Eckerd drugstore chain before selling all the stores in 2004.) But he was not sentimental, and he was not wedded to ideas that had not worked. In November 2000, J.C. Penney reported its first loss from operations in the history of the company. The retailer, which was almost 100 years old, was being called a dinosaur. Questrom had this to say about the task he faced:

> I spend time thinking about getting this company in order. What difference does it make if it's 100 or 10 or 20? What's meaningful to me is whether our stores are current. I would like this company to be successful on its 100th anniversary. I've only been here a few months, and I see a very loyal but an unhappy group of people.

Questrom said the only way to boost morale was to start making money again. Profit would take care of the stock price as well. Since the mid-1990s, the retailer had lost customers to discount chains such as Target and Wal-Mart and to moderate-priced retailers, including Kohl's and Old Navy, as they had expanded nationwide. Becoming profitable was going to be painful because it would mean change, Questrom said. To offer competitive prices to shoppers, the company needed a more competitive cost structure, which meant cutting costs.

J.C. Penney's department stores had to have the right assortment of merchandise at competitive prices. The only way to do that was to centralize the buying decisions. Headquarters would pick and deliver the merchandise, and store personnel would focus on running the stores. Questrom said that J.C. Penney fell behind its competitors when it did not centralize sooner. It was no longer efficient to have 1,150 stores each making that many decisions about merchandise. It was slow, expensive, and confusing to the customers. It also prevented the company from developing a national message.

Questrom said that some of the immediacy of having vendors knocking on your door every day was lost when the company moved to Dallas from New York in 1988. "We have to be aware of what's happening in the fashion world and bring that to middle America at great values." He considered adding offices in New York and Los Angeles to put J.C. Penney merchandisers closer to the biggest concentration of vendors.

One of Questrom's first moves was to close 44 of J.C. Penney's 1,000 stores and lay off some 5,000 staff, taking a restructuring charge of $275 million. "We're looking at the entire organization and looking at getting rid of things we wouldn't have if we were just starting out as a new company." Another part of Questrom's turnaround plan was to recruit outsiders to key positions, to help enliven the J.C. Penney corporate culture. He also remodeled stores to make them less cluttered and better lit. Questrom looked forward to the challenge of helping revive J.C. Penney. He said, "I've been involved most of my life in turn-around situations. I look at this as another mountain to climb."

Among the key players on the Questrom team is Vanessa Dingledine Castagna, the chairperson and CEO of J.C. Penney stores, catalog, and Internet. She sees her operation as part of a bold, multifaceted marketing plan designed to inject new life and financial strength into one of the nation's longest-standing companies. Castagna believes that the discipline she learned in the Purdue University Marching Band has helped her achieve success in the competitive retail world. She comments:

> It's very stimulating to be part of a dynamic organization with associates who care so much about the store's heritage that they will go through a difficult time to turn it around. My inspiration comes from our associates in the stores and distribution centers, and secondly from young people I'm involved with in an after-school program.

Department stores have not been viewed in the retail industry as a growth business. But even this mature concept can operate in a profitable way, Questrom said. "Federated and May [Department Stores] can grow earnings of 12 percent to 15 percent a year, which is a lot more money than the Amazon.coms can do." By 2004, Questrom and his team were achieving their goal of creating a profitable enterprise: the company had a one-year sales growth of 45 percent, with a net income of $928 million. By September 2005, the results appeared even more promising.

---

SKILL DEVELOPMENT Jot down all the leadership roles you perceived in the case history just presented. Specify the activity and the role it reflects. Refer to the nine leadership roles described previously. You might also want to visit *www.jcpenney.com* to see how well the store is doing. Go beyond the advertising to search the page for investor information.

SOURCE: "Penney's Chief Ready to Rebuild," *Knight Ridder*, January 2, 2001; Stephanie Anderson, "Can an Outsider Fix J.C. Penney?" *BusinessWeek*, February 12, 2001, pp. 56–58; www.jcpenney.com; http://news/Wire/O.12302837.00.html; J.C. Penney Company, Inc.; www.hoovers.com, October 10, 2004; "Discipline Learned in Band Brings Success to J. C. Penney CEO," www.purdue.edu/BANDS/News, 2003; Mark Albright, "It's Official: J.C. Penney Will Sell Eckerd Stores," *St. Petersburg Times Online Business*, February 27, 2004.

# The Satisfactions and Frustrations of Being a Leader

The term *leader* has a positive connotation for most people. To be called a leader is generally better than to be called a follower or a subordinate. (The term *follower* has virtually disappeared in organizations, and the term *subordinate* has fallen out of favor. The preferred term for a person who reports to a leader or manager is *team member, group member,* or *associate.* Researchers, however, continue to use the terms *subordinate* and *follower* for technical purposes.) Yet being a leader, such as a team leader, vice president, or COO (chief operating officer), does not always bring personal satisfaction. Some leadership jobs are more fun than others, such as being the leader of a successful group with cheerful team members.

Because most of you are contemplating becoming a leader or moving further into a leadership role, it is worthwhile to examine some of the potential satisfactions and frustrations many people find in being an organizational leader.

## Satisfactions of Leaders

The types of satisfactions that you might obtain from being a formal leader depend on your particular leadership position. Factors such as the amount of money you are paid and the type of people in your group influence your satisfaction. There are seven sources of satisfaction that leaders often experience.

1. *A feeling of power and prestige.* Being a leader automatically grants you some power. Prestige is forthcoming because many people think highly of people who are leaders. In some organizations, top-level leaders are addressed as Mr., Mrs., or Ms., whereas lower-ranking people are referred to by their surnames. Yet many leaders encourage others to call them by their first name.
2. *A chance to help others grow and develop.* A leader works directly with people, often teaching them job skills, serving as a mentor, and listening to personal problems. Part of a leader's job is to help other people become managers and leaders. A leader often feels as much of a "people helper" as does a human resource manager or a counselor.
3. *High income.* Leaders, in general, receive higher pay than team members, and executive leaders in major business corporations typically earn several million dollars per year. A handful of business executives receive compensation of over $100 million per year. If money is an important motivator or satisfier, being a leader has a built-in satisfaction. In some situations a team leader earns virtually the same amount of money as other team members. Occupying a leadership position, however, is a starting point on the path to high-paying leadership positions.
4. *Respect and status.* A leader frequently receives respect from group members. He or she also enjoys a higher status than people who are not occupying a leadership role. Status accompanies being appointed to a leadership position on or off the job. When an individual's personal qualifications match the position, his or her status is even higher.
5. *Good opportunities for advancement.* Once you become a leader, your advancement opportunities increase. Obtaining a leadership position is a vital first step for career advancement in many organizations. Staff or individual contributor positions help

broaden a person's professional experience, but most executives rise through a managerial path.

6. *A feeling of "being in on" things.* A side benefit of being a leader is that you receive more inside information. For instance, as a manager you are invited to attend management meetings. In those meetings you are given information not passed along to individual contributors. One such tidbit might be plans for expansion or downsizing.

7. *An opportunity to control money and other resources.* A leader is often in the position of helping to prepare a department budget and authorize expenses. Even though you cannot spend this money personally, knowing that your judgment on financial matters is trusted does provide some satisfaction. Many leaders in both private and public organizations control annual budgets of several million dollars.

## Dissatisfactions and Frustrations of Leaders

About one out of ten people in the work force is classified as a supervisor, administrator, or manager. Not every one of these people is a true leader. Yet the problems these people experience often stem from the leadership portions of their job. Many individual contributors refuse to accept a leadership role because of the frustrations they have seen leaders endure. These frustrations include the following:

1. *Too much uncompensated overtime.* People in leadership jobs are usually expected to work longer hours than other employees. Such unpaid hours are called casual overtime. People in organizational leadership positions typically spend about fifty-five hours per week working. During peak periods of peak demands, this figure can surge to eighty hours per week.

2. *Too many "headaches."* It would take several pages to list all the potential problems leaders face. Being a leader is a good way to discover the validity of Murphy's law: "If anything can go wrong, it will." A leader is subject to a batch of problems involving people and things. Many people find that a leadership position is a source of stress, and many managers experience burnout.

3. *Not enough authority to carry out responsibility.* People in managerial positions complain repeatedly that they are held responsible for things over which they have little control. As a leader, you might be expected to work with an ill-performing team member, yet you lack the power to fire him or her. Or you might be expected to produce high-quality service with too small a staff and no authority to become fully staffed.

4. *Loneliness.* As Secretary of State and former five-star general Colin Powell says, "Command is lonely." The higher you rise as a leader, the lonelier you will be in a certain sense. Leadership limits the number of people in whom you can confide. It is awkward to confide negative feelings about your employer to a team member. It is equally awkward to complain about one group member to another. Some people in leadership positions feel lonely because they miss being "one of the gang."

5. *Too many problems involving people.* A major frustration facing a leader is the number of human resource problems requiring action. The lower your leadership

position, the more such problems you face. For example, the office supervisor spends more time dealing with problem employees than does the chief information officer.

6. *Too much organizational politics.* People at all levels of an organization, from the office assistant to the chairperson of the board, must be aware of political factors. Yet you can avoid politics more easily as an individual contributor than you can as a leader. As a leader you have to engage in political byplay from three directions: below, sideways, and upward. Political tactics such as forming alliances and coalitions are a necessary part of a leader's role. Another troublesome aspect of organizational politics is that there are people lurking to take you out of the game, particularly if you are changing the status quo. These enemies within might attack you directly in an attempt to shift the issue to your character and style and avoid discussing the changes you are attempting to implement. Or, your superiors might divert you from your goals by keeping you overwhelmed with the details of your change effort.[23] In addition, backstabbers may agree with you in person but badmouth you to others.

7. *The pursuit of conflicting goals.* A major challenge leaders face is to navigate among conflicting goals. The central theme of these dilemmas is attempting to grant others the authority to act independently, yet still getting them aligned or pulling together for a common purpose.[24] Many of the topics relating to these conflicting goals are discussed at later points in the text.

college.hmco.com/pic/
dubrin5e

🆒 **@ KNOWLEDGE BANK:** A table of these dilemmas as identified by a group of bank executives can be found online in the Knowledge Bank section of the web site for this text.

8. *Being perceived as unethical, especially if you are a corporate executive.* The many corporate financial scandals made public in recent years have led to extreme perceptions that CEOs, in particular, are dishonest, unethical, and almost criminal in their behavior. Even if 95 percent of corporate leaders are honest and devoted to their constituents, the leader still has to deal with the possibility of being perceived as dishonest.

## A Framework for Understanding Leadership

Many different theories and explanations of leadership have been developed because of the interest in leadership as a practice and as a research topic. Several attempts have been made to integrate the large number of leadership theories into one comprehensive framework.[25] The framework presented here focuses on the major sets of variables that influence leadership effectiveness. The basic assumption underlying the framework can be expressed in terms of a simple formula with a profound meaning:

$$L = f (l, gm, s)$$

The formula means that the leadership process is a function of the leader, group members (or followers), and other situational variables.[26] In other words, leadership does not exist in the abstract but takes into account factors related to the leader, the person or persons being led, and a variety of forces in the environment. A charismatic

## FIGURE 1-2  A Framework for Understanding Leadership

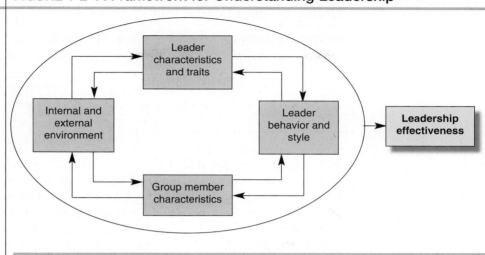

Source: *Managing Today!* by Stephen P. Robbins, © 1997. Reprinted by permission of Prentice-Hall, Inc. Upper Saddle River, N.J.

and visionary leader might be just what a troubled organization needs to help it achieve world-class success. Yet a group of part-time telemarketers might need a more direct and focused type of leader to help them when their telephone calls mostly meet with abrupt rejection from the people solicited.

The model presented in Figure 1-2 extends this situational perspective.[27] According to this model, leadership can best be understood by examining its key variables: leader characteristics and traits, leader behavior and style, group member characteristics, and the internal and external environment. At the right side of the framework, **leadership effectiveness** refers to attaining desirable outcomes such as productivity, quality, and satisfaction in a given situation. Whether or not the leader is effective depends on the four sets of variables in the box.

Beginning at the top of the circle, *leader characteristics and traits* refers to the inner qualities, such as self-confidence and problem-solving ability, that help a leader function effectively in many situations. *Leader behavior and style* refers to the activities engaged in by the leader, including his or her characteristic approach, that relate to his or her effectiveness. A leader who frequently coaches group members and practices participative leadership, for example, might be effective in many circumstances.

*Group member characteristics* refers to attributes of the group members that could have a bearing on how effective the leadership attempt will be. Intelligent and well-motivated group members, for example, help the leader do an outstanding job. The *internal and external environment* also influences leadership effectiveness. A leader in a culturally diverse environment, for example, will need to have multicultural skills to be effective. All of the topics in this text fit somewhere into this model, and the fit will be more obvious at some places than at others. Table 1-2, on the following page, outlines how the elements of the leadership model line up with chapters in the text.

**TABLE 1-2**    Relationship Between Chapter Topics and the Framework for Understanding Leadership

| COMPONENT OF THE MODEL | RELEVANT CHAPTER OR CHAPTERS |
|---|---|
| Leader characteristics and traits | Chapter 2, "Traits, Motives, and Characteristics of Leaders" |
| | Chapter 3, "Charismatic and Transformational Leadership" |
| | Chapter 6, "Leadership Ethics and Social Responsibility" |
| | Chapter 11, "Creativity, Innovation, and Leadership" |
| | Chapter 12, "Communication and Conflict Resolution Skills" |
| Leader behavior and style | Chapter 4, "Leadership Behaviors, Attitudes, and Styles" |
| | Chapter 6, "Leadership Ethics and Social Responsibility" |
| | Chapter 8, "Influence Tactics of Leaders" |
| | Chapter 9, "Developing Teamwork" |
| Group member characteristics | Chapter 5, "Contingency and Situational Leadership" |
| | Chapter 10, "Motivation and Coaching Skills" |
| Internal and external environment | Chapter 13, "Strategic Leadership and Knowledge Management" |
| | Chapter 14, "International and Culturally Diverse Aspects of Leadership" |
| | Chapter 7, "Power, Politics, and Leadership" |
| | Chapter 15, "Leadership Development and Succession" |

The arrows connecting the four sets of variables in Figure 1-2 suggest a reciprocal influence among them. Some of these linkages are stronger than others. The most pronounced linkage is that a leader's characteristics and traits will typically influence the leader's style. If a given individual is extroverted, warm, and caring, it will be natural for him or her to adopt a people-oriented leadership style. Another linkage is that the group members' characteristics might influence the leader's style. If the members are capable and self-sufficient, the leader is likely to choose a leadership style that grants freedom to the group. It will be easier for the leader to empower these people. A final linkage is that the internal and external environment can influence or mediate the leader's traits to some extent. In an environment in which creativity and risk taking are fostered, leaders are more likely to give expression to their tendencies toward creative problem solving and risk taking.

## Skill Development in Leadership

Leadership skills are in high demand. Executives seeking candidates for high-level management jobs list leadership skills as the top attributes they want. After these come industry-specific experience and functional/technical expertise.[28] Leadership skills are also sought in candidates for entry-level professional positions. Although students of leadership will find this information encouraging, developing leadership skills is more complex than developing a structured skill such as sending photos over the Internet. Nevertheless, you can develop leadership skills by studying this text, which follows a general learning model:

1. *Conceptual knowledge and behavioral guidelines.* Each chapter in this text presents useful information about leadership, including a section titled "Guidelines for Action and Skill Development."
2. *Conceptual information demonstrated by examples and brief descriptions of leaders in action.* Much can be learned by reading about how effective (or ineffective) leaders operate.
3. *Experiential exercises.* The text provides an opportunity for practice and personalization through cases, role plays, and self-assessment quizzes. Self-quizzes are emphasized here because they are an effective method of helping you personalize the information, thereby linking conceptual information to yourself. For example, you will read about the importance of assertiveness in leadership and also complete an assertiveness quiz.
4. *Feedback on skill utilization, or performance, from others.* Feedback exercises appear at several places in the text. Implementing some of the skills outside of the classroom will provide additional opportunities for feedback.
5. *Practice in natural settings.* As just implied, skill development requires active practice. A given skill has to be practiced many times in natural settings before it becomes integrated comfortably into a leader's mode of operation. A basic principle of learning is that practice is necessary to develop and improve skills. Suppose, for example, that you read about giving advice in the form of questions, as described in Chapter 10. If you practice this skill at least six times in live settings, you will probably have acquired an important new skill for coaching others.

Leadership Skill-Building Exercise 1-2 gives you the opportunity to begin developing your leadership skills systematically.

**LEADERSHIP SKILL-BUILDING EXERCISE 1-2**

### MY LEADERSHIP PORTFOLIO

Here, we ask you to begin developing a leadership portfolio that will be a personal document of your leadership capabilities and experiences. In each chapter, we will recommend new entries for your portfolio. At the same time, you are encouraged to use your imagination in determining what constitutes a suitable addition to your leadership portfolio.

We suggest you begin your portfolio with a personal mission statement that explains the type of leadership you plan to practice. An example might be, "I intend to become a well-respected corporate professional, a key member of a happy and healthy family, and a contributor to my community. I aspire to lead many people toward constructive activities." Include your job résumé in your portfolio, and devote a special section to leadership experiences. These experiences can be from the job, community and religious activities, and sports. (See Leadership Self-Assessment Quiz 1-2.)

**LEADERSHIP SELF-ASSESSMENT QUIZ 1-2**

## THE LEADERSHIP EXPERIENCE AUDIT

Readers of this book vary considerably in their leadership, managerial, and supervisory experience. Yet even readers who have not yet occupied a formal leadership position may have had at least a taste of being a leader. Use the following checklist to record any possible leadership experiences you might have had in the past or have now.

☑ Held a formal leadership position, such as vice president, department head, manager, assistant manager, team leader, group leader, or crew chief

☐ Seized the opportunity on the job to take care of a problem, although I was not assigned such responsibility

☑ Headed a committee or task force

☐ Was captain or cocaptain of an athletic team

☐ Held office in a club at high school, career school, or college

☐ Was editor of a campus newspaper or section of the newspaper such as sports

☐ Organized a study group for a course

☐ Organized an ongoing activity to sell merchandise at people's homes, such as for Avon, Mary Kay, or Tupperware

☐ Worked in multilevel sales and recruited and guided new members

☐ Organized a charity drive for a school or religious organization

☑ Organized a vacation trip for friends or family

☐ Took charge during a crisis, such as by helping people out of a burning building or a flooded house

☐ Was head of a choir or a band

☐ Headed a citizens' group making demands on a company or the government

☐ Organized a group of friends to help out people in need, such as physically disabled senior citizens

☐ Other:

INTERPRETATION The more experiences you checked, the more leadership experience you already have under your belt. Leadership experience of any type can be valuable in learning to work well with people and coordinate their efforts. Many CEOs in a variety of fields got their start as assistant fast-food restaurant managers.

college.hmco.com/pic/
dubrin5e

**KB @ KNOWLEDGE BANK:** contains a Leadership Skill-Building Exercise that will give you more insight into the multidimensional nature of effective group membership.

## Followership: Being an Effective Group Member

To be an effective leader, one needs good followers. Leaders cannot exist without followers.[29] As we mentioned at the outset of this book, the word *followers* suffers from political incorrectness, yet it is a neutral term as used by leadership researchers. Most of the topics in our study of leadership are aimed at inspiring, motivating, and influencing group members to want to achieve organizational goals. It is also valuable, however, to focus on two key aspects of being an effective group member: the personal characteristics of productive followers and the importance of collaboration between leaders and followers.

### Essential Qualities of Effective Followers

As observed by Robert E. Kelley, effective followers share four essential qualities:[30]

1. *Self-management.* The key to being a good follower is to think for oneself and to work well without close supervision. Effective group members see themselves as being as capable as their leaders.
2. *Commitment.* Effective followers are committed to something beyond themselves, be it a cause, product, department, organization, idea, or value. To a committed group member, the leader facilitates progress toward achieving a goal.
3. *Competence and focus.* Effective followers build their competence and focus their efforts for maximum impact. Competence centers on mastering skills that will be useful to the organization. Less effective group members rarely take the initiative to engage in training and development.
4. *Courage.* Effective followers establish themselves as independent, critical thinkers and fight for what they believe is right. A good follower, for example, might challenge the company's policy of taking ninety days to make good on accounts payable, or of recruiting key people almost exclusively from people with demographic characteristics similar to those of top management.

The above list is illustrative, since almost any positive human quality would contribute directly or indirectly to being an effective group member or follower. Another way of framing the qualities of effective followers is to say that such followers display the personal characteristics and qualities of leaders. Although leaders cannot be expected to change the personalities of group members, they can take steps to encourage the above qualities. Interventions such as coaching, empowerment, supportive communication, and frequent feedback would support effective followership.

### Collaboration Between Leaders and Followers

A key role for followers is to collaborate with leaders in achieving organizational goals. As described by leadership guru Warren Bennis, the postbureaucratic organization (a type of organization that came after the bureaucratic era, such as team-based organizations) requires a new kind of alliance between leaders and the led. When high-level leaders do not make all of the decisions but solicit input from knowledgeable group members, leaders and followers work together more closely. In the words of Bennis:[31]

> Today's organizations are evolving into federations of networks, clusters, cross-functional teams, temporary systems, ad hoc task forces, lattices, modules, matrices—almost anything but pyramids with their obsolete TOPdown leadership. The new leader will encourage healthy dissent and values those followers courageous enough to say no.

A related point here is that the new leader and the led are close allies. Great leaders are made by great groups, every organizational member to contribute energy and talent to help leaders carry out their roles successfully.

## Summary

college.hmco.com/pic/dubrin5e

Leadership is the ability to inspire confidence in and support among the people who are needed to achieve organizational goals. Leading is a major part of a manager's job, but a manager also plans, organizes, and controls. Leadership is said to deal with change, inspiration, motivation, and influence. In contrast, management deals more with maintaining equilibrium and the status quo. An important current development is to regard leadership as a long-term relationship, or partnership, between leaders and group members.

Many people attribute organizational performance to leadership actions. Some research evidence supports this widely accepted view. Others argue that certain factors in the work environment, called substitutes for leadership, make the leader's role almost superfluous. Among these factors are closely knit teams of highly trained workers, intrinsic satisfaction with work, computer technology, and professional norms. Another antileadership argument is that the leader is irrelevant in most organizational outcomes because the situation is more important and the leader has unilateral control over only a few resources. Moreover, since new leaders are chosen whose values are compatible with those of the firm, those values actually are more important.

Complexity theory argues that leaders and managers can do little to alter the course of the complex organizational system. The system, rather than the leader, dictates that all companies ultimately die.

Examining the roles carried out by leaders contributes to an understanding of the leadership function. Nine such leadership roles are the figurehead, spokesperson, negotiator, coach and motivator, team builder, team player, technical problem solver, entrepreneur, and strategic planner. An important implication of these roles is that managers at every level can exert leadership.

Leadership positions often are satisfying because they offer such things as power, prestige, the opportunity to help others, high income, and the opportunity to control resources. At other times being a leader carries with it a number of frustrations, such as insufficient authority, having to deal with human problems, and too much organizational politics. The leader also has the difficult task of balancing workers' need to be independent with their need to commit to a common purpose.

The framework for understanding leadership presented here is based on the idea that the leadership process is a function of the leader, group members, and other situational variables. According to the model, leadership can best be understood by examining its key variables: leader characteristics and traits, leader behavior and style, group member characteristics, and the internal and external environment. Leadership effectiveness is dependent on all four sets of variables.

Leadership skills can be developed by following a general learning model that involves acquiring conceptual knowledge, reading examples, doing experiential exercises, obtaining feedback, and practicing in natural settings.

To be an effective leader, one needs good followers with characteristics such as self-management, commitment, competence and focus, and courage. A key role for followers is to collaborate with leaders in achieving organizational goals. The postbureaucratic organization requires a new kind of alliance between leaders and the led.

## Key Terms

Leadership

Partnership

Stewardship theory

Attribution theory

Substitutes for leadership

Leadership effectiveness

##  Guidelines for Action and Skill Development

Vast amounts of information have been gathered about leaders and leadership, and many different leadership theories have been developed. Many leadership research findings and theories are confusing and contradictory. Nevertheless, from this thicket of information emerge many useful leadership concepts and techniques to guide you toward becoming a more effective leader.

As you work toward leadership effectiveness, first be familiar with the approaches to leadership described in this text. Then choose the formulation that seems best to fit the leadership situation you face. For example, if you are leading a team, review the information about team leadership. Typically an effective leader needs to combine several leadership approaches to meet the demands of a given situation. For instance, a leader might need to combine creative problem solving and emotional support to members to help the team rebound from a crisis.

## Discussion Questions and Activities

1. What forces in the environment or in society have led to the surge in interest in the subject of leadership in recent years?
2. In recent years, there have been dozens of financial scandals involving business executives (such as the problems at Enron and Global Crossing). What impact has this information had on your interest in becoming, or remaining, a leader in a business setting?
3. Give an example of how you have exerted leadership on or off the job in a situation in which you did not have a formal leadership position. Explain why you describe your activity as leadership.
4. What would a boss of yours have to do to demonstrate that he or she is an effective leader and an effective manager?
5. Identify a business or sports leader who you think is highly effective. Present your observations to the class.
6. Based on an informal survey, many people who were voted "the most likely to succeed" in their high school yearbooks became leaders later on in their career. How can you explain this finding?

7. After reading this chapter, do you believe that a person who is not a "born leader" still has a good chance of becoming an effective leader? Explain.
8. Top-level leaders of major business corporations receive some of the highest compensation packages in the work force. Why are business leaders paid so much?
9. Which of the nine leadership roles do you think you are the most suited for at this stage in your career? Explain your reasoning.
10. In what way might being an effective follower help prepare a person for becoming an effective leader?

## LEADERSHIP CASE PROBLEM A

### CAN WAYNE INOUYE REBOOT GATEWAY?

After four years of selling big-screen TVs, DVD recorders, and digital cameras, Gateway, Inc. announced that it is retreating from the consumer electronics world and returning to its original mission of marketing personal computers.

"Our first objective is to fix our core business," says Wayne R. Inouye, who recently assumed the role of chief executive. "People talk about multitasking, but in real life you have to focus on one thing at a time." Inouye says that new deals with PC retailers Best Buy Co., Inc. and CompUSA Inc., as well as a greater focus on fast-growing notebook PCs, should allow the money-losing company to earn consistent profits beginning next year.

The move is a huge gamble for Gateway, which has relied on consumer electronics to prop up profit margins at its once thriving PC business. But Gateway's consumer electronics sales never overcame the drag from its PC business, which still accounted for 72 percent of its revenue last year. Gateway lost a cumulative $2.4 billion in the last four years, as sales dropped to $3.4 billion from a one-year high of $6.1 billion.

Gateway has suffered four failed restructurings in the past three years, all under the auspices of former chief executive Ted Waitt, who stepped down as CEO in 2004. This time around, Inouye, a veteran retailing executive, hopes to revive Gateway by applying the same Spartan approach that he successfully used to turn around PC maker eMachines, Inc., which Gateway acquired in 2004. There, he slashed expenses by consolidating component suppliers, boosting quality, and filling retail orders on time. At the time of its acquisition, eMachines employed only 138 workers but was consistently profitable and had $1 billion in annual sales.

So far at Gateway, Inouye has closed the last 188 of its loss-plagued Gateway Country stores and outsourced manufacturing and customer service. Gateway will continue to market PCs and related products via the Internet and telephone sales, in addition to managing its new deals with big retailers.

The changes were made with two lofty goals in mind: (1) eventually to unseat Hewlett-Packard Co. as the leading seller of home PCs, and (2) to become a $10 billion business in the next three to five years. "I don't think it's a big stretch," the CEO insists.

Yet Gateway's new direction represents a complete turnaround from just four years ago, when Waitt plunged into consumer electronics as Gateway's business fell victim to price wars ignited by Dell Inc. and Hewlett-Packard Company (HP). Like Dell, Gateway was founded as a direct seller. But by the mid-1990s, the company had launched its own chain of showrooms to demonstrate its products and provide software training and repairs. Over time, those Gateway Country stores morphed into sales of computers and high-end consumer electronics. But Gateway was never able to make its retail outlets profitable, and as revenue plummeted the expense of the stores proved too steep to maintain.

Inouye's plan now calls for expanding U.S. retail and overseas sales to achieve at least 1 million PC sales a quarter, up from the recent number of 750,000. Inouye also expects to slash overhead costs—once the highest in the industry at 26 percent of revenue—to below Dell's 9.5 percent. Gateway now employs about 1,800 workers, down from 7,500 when Inouye took over. Much of the lower head count comes from closing the Gateway Country stores. Inouye explains that lower expenses will allow the company to be profitable even with thin margins of about 8 percent.

Famously frugal, Inouye never spends more than $6 for lunch, buys the cheapest gas for his car, and has been known to clip coupons for staples such as soap. His father was a tomato and peach farmer in Yuba City, California. An uncanny ability to extract key financial details from operating reports earned Inouye the nickname "Wayne Man," after the human calculator in the film *Rain Man.*

His talents and quirks not withstanding, some business analysts characterize the CEO's plan to displace HP as quixotic (far-fetched). The shift away from higher-margin consumer electronics could also leave Gateway even less apt to earn a profit.

Inouye says that Gateway already surpasses HP in customer satisfaction surveys and its new low-overhead approach will allow it to profitably undercut the much bigger PC and printer maker in the retail market. He expects to best HP by grabbing an "over 50 percent" share of the U.S. retail sales as soon as the first quarter of 2005. HP currently holds a 60 percent share of retail sales, compared with Gateway's 30 percent share.

## QUESTIONS

1. Which leadership roles is Inouye occupying in his plans to revitalize Gateway?
2. How realistic are the growth goals that Inouye has established for Gateway?
3. What impact do you think Inouye's personal frugality will have on his credibility as a leader during Gateway's transition?
4. What leadership challenges face Inouye as he attempts to implement his turnaround of Gateway?

SOURCE: Gary McWilliams, "Gateway CEO Presses Restart: Back to PCs," *Wall Street Journal*, September 13, 2004, pp. B1, B5. *Wall Street Journal*. Eastern Edition (only staff-produced materials may be used) by Gary McWilliams. Copyright 2004 by Dow Jones & Company, Inc. Reproduced with permission of Dow Jones & Company, Inc. in the format Textbook via Copyright Clearance Center.

# LEADERSHIP CASE PROBLEM B

## JEN LEE WANTS THE FAST TRACK

At age 25, Jen Lee already had impressive leadership experience. She was the head of her Girl Scout troop at age 11, the president of the Asian Student Association in high school, and the captain of her soccer team in both high school and college. She also organized a food drive for homeless people in her hometown for three consecutive summers. So Lee believed that these experiences, in addition to her formal education, were preparing her to be a corporate leader. At college Lee majored in information systems and business administration.

*(continued)*

Lee's first position in industry was a business analyst at a medium-size consulting firm that helped clients implement large-scale systems such as enterprise software. She explained to her team leader at the outset that she wanted to be placed on a management track rather than a technical track because she aspired to becoming a corporate executive. Lee's team leader explained, "Jen, I know you are in a hurry to get ahead. Lots of capable people are looking to climb the ladder. But you first have to build your career by proving that you are an outstanding analyst."

Lee thought, "It looks like the company may need a little convincing that I'm leadership material, so I'm going to dig in and perform like a star." And Lee did dig in, much to the pleasure of her clients, her team leader, and her coworkers. Her first few performance appraisals were outstanding, yet the company was still not ready to promote Jen to a team leader position. Lee's team leader explained, "Bob [the team leader's manager] and I both agree that you are doing an outstanding job, but promotions are hard to come by in our company these days. The company is shrinking more than expanding, so talks about promotion are a little futile right now."

Lee decided that it would take a long time to be promoted to team leader or manager in her present company, so she began to quietly look for a new position in her field. Her job hunt proceeded more swiftly than she anticipated. Through a sports club contact, Lee was granted a job interview with a partner in a larger consulting firm offering similar services. After a series of four interviews, Lee was hired as a senior business analyst performing work on a system similar to the one she had been working with for two years. During her interviews, Lee emphasized her goal of occupying a leadership position as soon as the company believed that she was ready for such a role. Her first client assignment was helping a team of consultants install a state income tax call center.

After a one-month-long orientation and training program, Lee was performing billable work at her new employer. At the outset, she reminded her new manager and team leader that she preferred the managerial route to remaining in a technical position. After six months of hard work, Lee looked forward to her first formal performance evaluation. Her team leader informed her that her performance was better than average, but short of outstanding. Lee asked for an explanation of why her performance was not considered outstanding. She informed her team leader and manager, "I need an outstanding rating to help me achieve my goal of becoming a leader in our company."

The manager replied, "Our performance evaluations are based on your contribution to the company. We care much less about writing performance evaluations to help a senior business analyst reach her career goals. Besides, Jen, you've made your point enough about wanting to be a leader in our firm. Let your performance speak for itself."

That evening, Jen met with her fiancé, Kenneth, to discuss her dilemma. "The problem, Ken, is that they don't get it. I'm leadership material, and they don't see it yet. I'm performing well and letting my intentions be known, but my strategy isn't working. The company is missing out on a golden opportunity by not putting me on a fast leadership track. I have to convince them of their error in judgment."

Kenneth, a human resource specialist, replied, "I'm listening to you, and I want to give you good advice. Let me be objective here despite the fact that I love you. What have you done lately to prove to the company that you are leadership material?"

## QUESTIONS

1. Who has the problem here: Jen or the consulting firm in question?
2. What advice can you offer Jen to help her increase her chances of occupying a formal leadership position in the company?
3. What is your evaluation of the advice Ken offered Jen?

## INTERNET SKILL-BUILDING EXERCISE

Apply the chapter concepts! Visit the Web and complete this Internet skill-building exercise to learn more about current leadership topics and trends.

### KEY LEADERSHIP TOPICS

Visit the Center for Creative Leadership (CCL), *www.ccl.org,* to develop additional insight into major topics in leadership. Glance at the titles of articles about leadership to become sensitive to some of the major issues. Note the topics of three articles or books, and check the index to this textbook to see if the same topics are considered important here; make the same check at the Center for Creative Leadership site. While visiting CCL, think through whether the leadership courses offered by the center would interest you.

# Traits, Motives, and Characteristics of Leaders

From the New York Yankees dugout the grass looks greener than it does on TV. The players seem taller and the baseline gravel seems coarser. But one image that appears the same from this on-field perspective is Joe Torre's cool game face. The Yankees' manager prides himself on his calm, on and off the field. It is key to an understated management style that enabled him since he took charge in 1996 to lead a culturally diverse team of players—with huge salaries and egos—to eight consecutive postseason appearances and six World Series appearances.

"My greatest talent is calmness and being positive," says Torre, 64. "I concentrate on what you can do even in the worst of times. You don't judge by last week's errors or lost opportunity." He keeps that attitude throughout the season.

"He never panics," says team captain and all-star shortstop Derek Jeter. Even when Jeter went hitless in thirty-two at-bats in the early 2004 season, Torre said Jeter was "still the one I trust. It's a long season."

Torre pushes his players for results, but only, he says, by treating them as he would wish to be treated—with fairness and honesty.[1]

---

The vignette just presented describes a well-known manager who has several of the leadership traits discussed in this chapter, particularly stability under pressure and honesty. When people evaluate managers in terms of their leadership effectiveness, they often scrutinize the managers' traits and personal characteristics. Instead of focusing only on the results the managers achieve, those making the evaluation assign considerable weight to the manager's attributes, such as adherence to high standards. Many people believe intuitively that personal characteristics strongly determine leadership effectiveness.

The belief that certain personal characteristics and skills contribute to leadership effectiveness in many situations is the **universal theory of leadership**. According to this theory, certain leadership traits are universally important; that is, they apply in all situations. This and the following chapter concentrate on personal characteristics; Chapter 4 describes the behaviors and skills that are part of the universal theory. Of course, personal characteristics are closely associated with leadership skills and behaviors. For example, creative thinking ability (a characteristic) helps a leader formulate an exciting vision (leadership behavior).

Characteristics associated with leadership can be classified into three broad categories: personality traits, motives, and cognitive factors. These categories of behavior serve as helpful guides. However, they are not definitive: a convincing argument can often be made that an aspect of leadership placed in one category could be placed in another. Nevertheless, no matter how personal characteristics are classified, they point toward the conclusion that effective leaders are made of the *right stuff*. Published research about the trait (*great person*) approach first appeared at the turn of the century, and it continues today. Since a full listing of every personal characteristic ever found to be associated with leadership would take several hundred pages, this chapter discusses only the major and most consistently found characteristics related to leadership effectiveness.

## Personality Traits of Effective Leaders

Observations by managers and human resource specialists, as well as dozens of research studies, indicate that leaders have certain personality traits.[2] These characteristics contribute to leadership effectiveness in many situations as long as the leader's style fits the situation reasonably well. For example, an executive might perform admirably as a leader in several different high-technology companies with different organizational cultures. However, his intellectual style might make him a poor fit with production workers. Leaders' personality traits can be divided into two groups: general personality traits, such as self-confidence and trustworthiness, and task-related traits, such as an internal locus of control.

### General Personality Traits

We define a general personality trait as a trait that is observable both within and outside the context of work. That is, the same general traits are related to success and satisfaction in both work and personal life. Figure 2-1 lists the general personality traits that contribute to successful leadership.

***Self-Confidence*** Self-confidence improves one's performance in a variety of tasks, including leadership.[3] A leader who is self-assured without being bombastic or overbearing instills self-confidence in team members. A self-confident team leader of a group facing a seemingly impossible deadline might tell the group, "We are understaffed and overworked, but I know we can get this project done on time. I've been through tough demands like this before. If we work like a true team, we can pull it off."

Self-confidence was among the first leadership traits researchers identified, and it has recently received considerable attention as a major contributor to leadership effectiveness.[4] In addition to being self-confident, the leader must project that self-confidence to the group. He or she may do so by using unequivocal wording, main-

### FIGURE 2-1 General Personality Traits of Effective Leaders

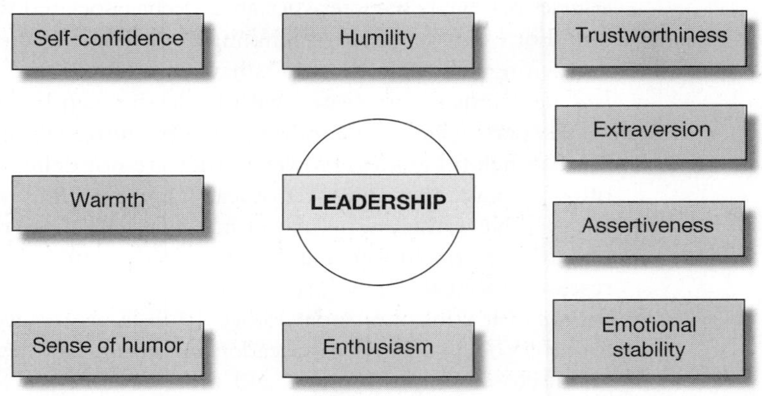

taining good posture, and making appropriate gestures such as pointing an index finger outward.

Self-confidence is not only a personality trait. It also refers to a behavior and an interpersonal skill that a person exhibits in a number of situations. It is akin to being cool under pressure. We can conclude that a person is a self-confident leader when he or she maintains composure when dealing with a crisis, such as while managing a large product recall. The interpersonal skill comes in being able to keep others calm during turmoil.

college.hmco.com/pic/dubrin5e

**@ KNOWLEDGE BANK:** The Knowledge Bank for this chapter includes suggestions for developing self-confidence as required for leadership effectiveness.

*Humility* Although self-confidence is a key leadership trait, so is humility, or being humble at the right times. Part of humility is admitting that you do not know everything and cannot do everything, as well as admitting your mistakes to team members and outsiders. A leader, upon receiving a compliment for an accomplishment, may explain that the group deserves the credit. The case for humility as a leadership trait is made strongly by Stephen G. Harrison, the president of a consulting firm, in his comment about how the definition of great leadership has changed: "Great leadership is manifested or articulated by people who know how to understate it. There is leadership value in humility, the leadership that comes from putting people in the limelight, not yourself. Great leadership comes from entirely unexpected places. It's understatement, it's dignity, it's service, it's selflessness."[5]

Research by Jim Collins on what makes companies endure and dramatically improve their performance supports the importance of humility. He uses the term *Level 5 Leader* to describe the most accomplished leaders. Level 5 Leaders are modest yet determined to accomplish their objectives.[6]

*Trustworthiness* Evidence and opinion continue to mount that being trustworthy and/or honest contributes to leadership effectiveness.[7] An effective leader or manager is supposed to *walk the talk,* thereby showing a consistency between deeds (walking) and words (talk). In this context, **trust** is defined as a person's confidence in another individual's intentions and motives and in the sincerity of that individual's word.[8] Leaders must be trustworthy, and they must also trust group members. Given that so many people distrust top-level business leaders, as well as political leaders, gaining and maintaining trust is a substantial challenge. The following trust builders are worthy of a prospective leader's attention and implementation:[9]

- Make your behavior consistent with your intentions. Practice what you preach and set the example. Let others know of your intentions and invite feedback on how well you are achieving them.

- When your organization or organizational unit encounters a problem, move into a problem-solving mode instead of looking to blame others for what went wrong.

- Honor confidences. One incident of passing along confidential information results in a permanent loss of trust by the person whose confidence was violated.

- Maintain a high level of integrity. Build a reputation for doing what you think is morally right in spite of the political consequences.
- Tell the truth. It is much easier to be consistent when you do not have to keep patching up your story to conform to an earlier lie.
- Make trust pay in terms of receiving rewards. Trust needs to be seen as a way of gaining advantage.

It takes a leader a long time to build trust, yet one brief incident of untrustworthy behavior can permanently destroy it. Leaders are usually allowed a fair share of honest mistakes. In contrast, dishonest mistakes quickly erode leadership effectiveness.

When a leader is perceived as trustworthy, the organization benefits. Kurt T. Dirks and Donald L. Ferrin examined the findings and implications of research during the last four decades about trust in leadership. The review involved 106 studies and 27,103 individuals. The meta-analysis (quantitative synthesis of studies) emphasized supervisory leadership based on the importance of trust in day-to-day interactions with group members. Trusting a leader was more highly associated with a variety of work attitudes of group members. The highest specific relationships with trust were as follows:[10]

- Job satisfaction ($r = .51$)
- Organizational commitment ($r = .49$)
- Turnover intentions ($r = -.40$) (If you trust your leader, you are less likely to intend to leave.)
- Belief in information provided by the leader ($r = .35$)
- Commitment to decisions ($r = .24$)
- Satisfaction with the leader ($r = .73$)
- LMX ($r = .69$) (LMX refers to favorable exchanges with the leader.)

The relationship of trust to job performance was statistically significant but quite low ($r = .16$). One reason may be that many people perform well for a leader they distrust out of fear of being fired or bad-listed.

Being trustworthy and earning trust are considered so essential to effective leadership that some companies use these factors to evaluate leaders and managers. For example, IBM evaluates its leaders on ten key factors, one of which is *earning trust*. A leader who earns trusts "does what is right for the long-term good of relationships inside and outside of IBM." As with the other traits (some of which are really behaviors), the relevance of earning trust was uncovered from interviews with thirty-three IBM executives who had been regarded as outstanding leaders within the company.[11]

Leadership Self-Assessment Quiz 2-1 gives you the opportunity to examine your own tendencies toward trustworthiness.

**Extraversion** Extraversion (the scientific spelling for *extroversion*) has been recognized for its contribution to leadership effectiveness because it is helpful for leaders to be gregarious and outgoing in most situations. Also, extraverts are more likely to want to assume a leadership role and participate in group activities. A meta-analysis of seventy-three studies involving 11,705 subjects found that extraversion was the most consistent personality factor related to leadership effectiveness and leadership emergence[12] (*Emergence* refers to someone being perceived as having leadership qualities.)

# BEHAVIORS AND ATTITUDES OF A TRUSTWORTHY LEADER

**INSTRUCTIONS** Listed below are behaviors and attitudes of leaders who are generally trusted by their group members and other constituents. After you read each characteristic, check to the right whether this is a behavior or attitude that you appear to have developed already, or whether it does not fit you at present.

|  | Fits Me | Does Not Fit Me |
|---|:---:|:---:|
| 1. Tells people he or she is going to do something, and then always follows through and gets it done | ☒ | ☐ |
| 2. Is described by others as being reliable | ☒ | ☐ |
| 3. Is good at keeping secrets and confidences | ☒ | ☐ |
| 4. Tells the truth consistently | ☒ | ☐ |
| 5. Minimizes telling people what they want to hear | ☐ | ☒ |
| 6. Is described by others as "walking the talk" | ☐ | ☒ |
| 7. Delivers consistent messages to others in terms of matching words and deeds | ☒ | ☐ |
| 8. Does what he or she expects others to do | ☒ | ☐ |
| 9. Minimizes hypocrisy by not engaging in activities he or she tells others are wrong | ☒ | ☐ |
| 10. Readily accepts feedback on behavior from others | ☐ | ☒ |
| 11. Maintains eye contact with people when talking to them | ☐ | ☒ |
| 12. Appears relaxed and confident when explaining his or her side of a story | ☐ | ☒ |
| 13. Individualizes compliments to others rather than saying something like "You look great" to many people | ☒ | ☐ |
| 14. Does not expect lavish perks for himself or herself while expecting others to go on an austerity diet | ☒ | ☐ |
| 15. Does not tell others a crisis is pending (when it is not) just to gain their cooperation | ☒ | ☐ |
| 16. Collaborates with others to make creative decisions | ☒ | ☐ |
| 17. Communicates information to people at all organizational levels | ☐ | ☒ |
| 18. Readily shares financial information with others | ☐ | ☒ |
| 19. Listens to people and then acts on many of their suggestions | ☐ | ☒ |
| 20. Generally engages in predictable behavior | ☒ | ☐ |

*(continued)*

SCORING AND INTERPRETATION These statements are mostly for self-reflection, so no specific scoring key exists. However, the more of the above statements that fit you, the more trustworthy you are—assuming you are answering truthfully. The usefulness of this self-quiz increases, if somebody who knows you well also answers it. Your ability and willingness to carry out some of the behaviors specified in this quiz could have an enormous impact on your career because so many business leaders in recent years have not been perceived as trustworthy. Being trustworthy is therefore a career asset.

Even though it is logical to think that extraversion is related to leadership, many effective leaders are laid-back and even introverted. Michael Dell, the famous founder of Dell Inc., is a reserved individual who is sometimes described as having a vanilla personality. Yet Dell has been working to become more extraverted in recent years.

*Assertiveness* Letting others know where you stand contributes to leadership effectiveness. **Assertiveness** refers to being forthright in expressing demands, opinions, feelings, and attitudes. Being assertive helps leaders perform many tasks and achieve goals. Among them are confronting group members about their mistakes, demanding higher performance, setting high expectations, and making legitimate demands on higher management. A director of her company's cell phone service unit was assertive when she said to her staff, "Our cell service is the worst in the industry. We have to improve." An assertive person is reasonably tactful rather than being aggressive and obnoxious.

Leadership Self-Assessment Quiz 2-2 gives you the opportunity to determine how assertive you are.

**LEADERSHIP SELF-ASSESSMENT QUIZ 2-2**

### THE ASSERTIVENESS SCALE

INSTRUCTIONS Indicate whether each of the following statements is mostly true or mostly false as it applies to you. If in doubt about your reaction to a particular statement, think of how you would *generally* respond.

| | Mostly True | Mostly False |
|---|---|---|
| 1. It is extremely difficult for me to turn down a sales representative when he or she is a nice person. | ☐ | ☒ |
| 2. I express criticism freely. | ☒ | ☐ |
| 3. If another person is being very unfair, I bring it to that person's attention. | ☒ | ☐ |
| 4. Work is no place to let your feelings show. | ☒ | ☒ |
| 5. It is no use asking for favors; people get what they deserve. | ☐ | ☒ |

6. Business is not the place for tact; say what you think. ☐ ☒

7. If a person looks as if he or she is in a hurry, I let that person in front of me in a supermarket line. ☒ ☐

8. A weakness of mine is that I am too nice a person. ☐ ☒

9. If my restaurant bill is even 50 cents more than it should be, I demand that the mistake be corrected. ☒ ☐

10. If the mood strikes me, I will laugh out loud in public. ☒ ☐

11. People would describe me as too outspoken. ☒ ☐

12. I am quite willing to have the store take back a piece of furniture that was scratched upon delivery. ☒ ☐

13. I dread having to express anger toward a coworker. ☒ ☒

14. People often say that I am too reserved and emotionally controlled. ☐ ☒

15. I have told friends and work associates exactly what it is about their behavior that irritates or displeases me. ☐ ☒

16. I fight for my rights down to the last detail. ☒ ☐

17. I have no misgivings about returning an overcoat to the store if it does not fit me right. ☒ ☐

18. After I have an argument with a person, I try to avoid him or her. ☒ ☐

19. I insist that my spouse (or roommate or partner) do his or her fair share of undesirable chores. ☒ ☐

20. It is difficult for me to look directly at another person when the two of us are in disagreement. ☐ ☒

21. I have cried among friends more than once. ☒ ☐

22. If someone near me at a movie keeps up a conversation with another person, I ask him or her to stop. ☒ ☐

23. I am able to turn down social engagements with people I do not particularly care for. ☒ ☐

24. It is in poor taste to express what you really feel about another individual. ☐ ☒

25. I sometimes show my anger by swearing at or belittling another person. ☐ ☒

26. I am reluctant to speak up at a meeting. ☐ ☒

*(continued)*

27. I find it relatively easy to ask friends for small favors such ☒ ☐
as giving me a ride to work while my car is being repaired.

28. If another person is talking very loudly in a restaurant ☐ ☒
and it bothers me, I inform that person.

29. I often finish other people's sentences for them. ☐ ☒

30. It is relatively easy for me to express love and affection ☒ ☐
toward another person.

SCORING KEY

| | | |
|---|---|---|
| 1. Mostly false | 11. Mostly true | 21. Mostly true |
| 2. Mostly true | 12. Mostly true | 22. Mostly true |
| 3. Mostly true | 13. Mostly false | 23. Mostly true |
| 4. Mostly false | 14. Mostly false | 24. Mostly true |
| 5. Mostly false | 15. Mostly true | 25. Mostly true |
| 6. Mostly true | 16. Mostly true | 26. Mostly false |
| 7. Mostly false | 17. Mostly true | 27. Mostly true |
| 8. Mostly false | 18. Mostly false | 28. Mostly true |
| 9. Mostly true | 19. Mostly true | 29. Mostly true |
| 10. Mostly true | 20. Mostly false | 30. Mostly true |

SCORING AND INTERPRETATION Score 1 for each of your answers that agrees with the scoring key.

- 0–15: Nonassertive
- 16–24: Assertive
- 25+: Aggressive

Do this exercise again about thirty days from now to see how stabile your answers are. You might also discuss your answers with a close friend to determine if that person has a similar perception of your assertiveness.

A score in the nonassertive range could suggest that you need to develop your assertiveness and self-confidence and become less shy to enhance those aspects of your leadership that involve face-to-face interaction with people. To help verify the accuracy of this score, ask a current or former boss whether he or she agrees that you are nonassertive.

*Emotional Stability* Anyone who has ever worked for an unstable boss will attest to the importance of emotional stability as a leadership trait. **Emotional stability** refers to the ability to control emotions to the point that one's emotional responses are appropriate to the occasion. Emotions associated with low emotional stability include anxiety, depression, anger, embarrassment, and worry.

Emotional stability is an important leadership trait because group members expect and need consistency in the way they are treated. A sales manager had this to say about her boss, the vice president of marketing: "It was difficult to know whether to bring problems to Larry's attention. Some days he would compliment me for taking customer problems seriously. Other times he would rant and rave about the ineffectiveness of the sales department. We all worry about having our performance appraised on one of Larry's crazy days." In contrast, you will recall that calmness and stability contribute to the leadership of Joe Torre, the New York Yankees manager.

One study found that executive leaders who are emotionally unstable and lack composure are more likely to handle pressure poorly and give in to moodiness, outbursts of anger, and inconsistent behavior. Such inconsistency undermines their relationships with group members, peers, and superiors. In contrast, effective leaders are generally calm, confident, and predictable during a crisis.[13]

*Enthusiasm* In almost all leadership situations, it is desirable for the leader to be enthusiastic. Group members tend to respond positively to enthusiasm, partly because enthusiasm may be perceived as a reward for constructive behavior. Enthusiasm is also a desirable leadership trait because it helps build good relationships with team members. A leader can express enthusiasm both verbally ("Great job"; "I love it") and nonverbally (making a "high five" gesture). An executive newsletter made an enthusiastic comment about enthusiasm as a leadership trait:

> People look to you for [enthusiasm] to inspire them. It is the greatest tool for motivating others and for getting things done. As a leader, you have to get out in front of your people. Even the most enthusiastic employee is loath to show more of it than his or her boss. If you don't project a gung-ho attitude, everybody else will hold back.[14]

*Sense of Humor* Whether humor is a trait or a behavior, the effective use of humor is an important part of the leader's role. Humor adds to the approachability and people orientation of a leader. Claudia Kennedy, as a three-star army general and the army's senior intelligence official, occupied a key leadership position. During an interview for a magazine article, she mentioned that although she had no regrets, her demanding career had not allowed for having a husband and children. The reporter commented, "You could still get married." Kennedy retorted, "Well certainly—put my phone number in this article."[15]

Laughter and humor serve such functions in the workplace as relieving tension and boredom and defusing hostility. Because humor helps the leader dissolve tension and defuse conflict, it helps him or her exert power over the group. Self-effacing humor is the choice of comedians and organizational leaders alike. By being self-effacing, the leader makes a point without insulting or slighting anybody. Instead of criticizing a staff member for being too technical, the leader might say, "Wait, I need your help. Please explain how this new product works in terms that even I can understand." Notice that General Kennedy's comments were slightly self-effacing by implying that she needed to have her phone number widely disseminated in order to obtain dates.

Leadership Skill-Building Exercise 2-1 provides an opportunity to use humor effectively.

### A SENSE OF HUMOR ON THE JOB

This is an exercise for six persons. One person plays the role of the company president, who has scheduled a staff meeting. The president's task is to inform employees that the seventh top manager in the last year has just resigned. He or she should make a few humorous introductory comments that will relieve some of the tension and worry. The five other people, who play the roles of the remaining staff members, should also make effective use of humor in responding to the president's comments.

***Warmth*** Being a warm person and projecting that warmth contribute to leadership effectiveness in several ways. First, warmth helps establish rapport with group members. Second, the projection of warmth is a key component of charisma. Third, warmth is a trait that helps provide emotional support to group members. Giving such support is an important leadership behavior. Fourth, in the words of Kogan Page, "Warmth comes with the territory. Cold fish don't make good leaders because they turn people off."[16]

### Task-Related Personality Traits

Certain personality traits of effective leaders are closely associated with task accomplishment. The task-related traits described here are outlined in Figure 2-2.

***Passion for the Work and the People*** A dominant characteristic of effective leaders is their passion for their work and to some extent for the people who help them accomplish the work. The passion goes beyond enthusiasm and often expresses itself as an obsession for achieving company goals. Many leaders begin their workday at 6:00 A.M. and return to their homes at 7:00 P.M. After dinner they retreat to their home offices to conduct business for about two more hours. Information technology devices, such as personal digital assistants and cell phones, feed the passion for work, making it possible to be in touch with the office even during golf or a family picnic. The downside to extreme passion for work is that it can lead to work addiction, thereby interfering with other joys in life.

Passion for their work is especially evident in entrepreneurial leaders, no matter what size and type of business. A given business, such as refurbishing engines, might appear mundane to outsiders. The leader of such a business, however, is willing to talk for hours about tearing down old engines and about the wonderful people who help do the job. Jeff Bezos, the founder of Amazon.com and one of the world's best-known entrepreneurs, exemplifies passion for work. Asked if running Amazon was as much fun as it used to be, he replied:

The truth is yes. Sure I like being the poster child instead of the *piñata* a little bit more. But I'm a change junkie. I love the rate of change. I love the intellectual challenge of what we're doing. I love the people I work with. It's not like me against the world. We've got a big team of people. It's fun.[17]

Being passionate about the nature of the business can be a major success factor in its survival. Randy Komisar, a strategy consultant to many dot-com business firms, argues that the purpose of business cannot be simply to make lots of money. He says that too many business start-ups lack a deep foundation in values and are managed by a drive for success, not by passion. "Drive pushes you toward an objective, and you can deny part of yourself by sheer will to achieve a goal," Komisar explains. "Passion irresistibly pulls you toward the need to express yourself and has to come from within and be nurtured." A problem with drive alone is that the end justifies the means.[18]

*Emotional Intelligence* Leadership researchers and experienced workers have long known that how well a person manages his or her emotions and those of others influences leadership effectiveness. For example, recognizing anger in yourself and others, as well as being able to empathize with people, can help you be more effective at exerting influence. In recent years, many different aspects of emotions, motives, and personality that help determine interpersonal effectiveness and leadership skill have been placed under the comprehensive label of *emotional intelligence*. **Emotional intelligence** refers to the ability to do such things as understand one's feelings, have empathy for others, and regulate one's emotions to enhance one's quality of life. This type of intelligence generally has to do with the ability to connect with people and understand their emotions. Many of the topics in this chapter (such as warmth) and throughout the text (such as political skill) can be considered related to emotional intelligence.

## FIGURE 2-2 Task-Related Personality Traits of Leaders

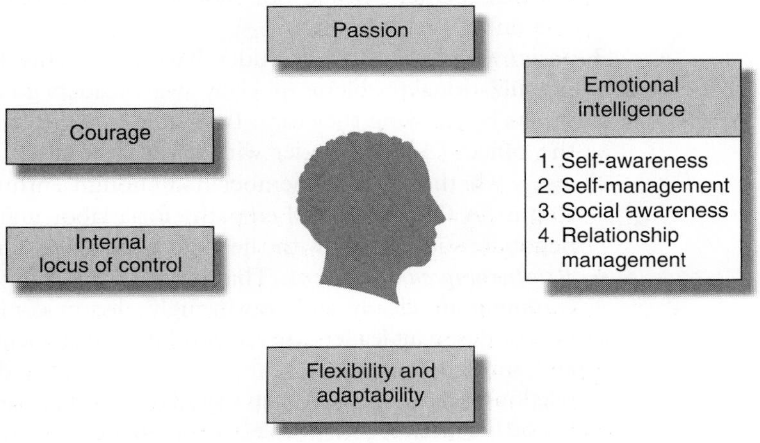

Based on research in dozens of companies, Daniel Goleman discovered that the most effective leaders are alike in one essential way: they all have a high degree of emotional intelligence. Cognitive intelligence (or general mental ability) and technical skills are considered threshold capabilities for success in executive positions. Yet, according to Goleman, without a high degree of emotional intelligence, a person can have excellent training, superior analytical skills, and loads of innovative suggestions, but he or she still will not make a great leader. His analysis also revealed that emotional intelligence played an increasingly important role in high-level management positions, where differences in technical skills are of negligible importance. Furthermore, when star performers were compared with average ones in senior leadership positions, differences in emotional intelligence were more pronounced than differences in cognitive abilities.[19]

Four key factors in emotional intelligence are described next, along with a brief explanation of how each factor links to leadership effectiveness. The components of emotional intelligence have gone through several versions, and the version presented here is tied closely to leadership and interpersonal skills. The leader who scores high in emotional intelligence is described as *resonant*.[20]

1. *Self-awareness.* The ability to understand your own emotions is the most essential of the four emotional intelligence competencies. Having high self-awareness allows people to know their strengths and limitations and have high self-esteem. Resonant leaders use self-awareness to accurately measure their own moods, and they intuitively understand how their moods affect others. (Effective leaders seek feedback to see how well their actions are received by others. A leader with good self-awareness would recognize such factors as whether he or she was liked or was exerting the right amount of pressure on people.)

2. *Self-management.* This is the ability to control one's emotions and act with honesty and integrity in a consistent and adaptable manner. The right degree of self-management helps prevent a person from throwing temper tantrums when activities do not go as planned. Resonant leaders do not let their occasional bad moods ruin their day. If they cannot overcome the bad mood, they let work associates know of the problem and how long it might last. (A leader with high self-management would not suddenly decide to fire a group member because of one difference of opinion.)

3. *Social awareness.* This includes having empathy for others and intuition about organizational problems. Socially aware leaders go beyond sensing the emotions of others by showing they care. In addition, they accurately size up political forces in the office. (A team leader with social awareness, or empathy, would be able to assess whether a team member had enough enthusiasm for a project to assign it to him. A CEO who had empathy for a labor union's demands might be able to negotiate successfully with the head of the labor union to avoid a costly strike.)

4. *Relationship management.* This includes the interpersonal skills of being able to communicate clearly and convincingly, disarm conflicts, and build strong personal bonds. Resonant leaders use relationship management skills to spread their enthusiasm and solve disagreements, often with kindness and humor. (A leader with good relationship management skills would not burn bridges and would continue to enlarge his or her network of people to win support when support is needed. A leader or manager with good relationship management skills is more likely to be invited by headhunters to explore new career opportunities.)

If leaders do not have emotional intelligence, they may not achieve their full potential. Steve Heyer, a former high-level executive at Coca-Cola, is a case in point. He was hired into Coca-Cola as a person with the potential to become the next CEO. But Heyer's personality ran against the company's ingrained culture, and he did not pick up on the subtle cues about how he should behave (part of emotional intelligence). He was harsh with people and flaunted his position. Because Coke depends on its bottlers, company executives have a saying: "If your bottler drives a Cadillac, *you* drive a Buick. If your bottler drives a Buick, *you* drive a Ford. If your bottler drives a Ford, *you* walk." Heyer drove a Mercedes. Furthermore, he purchased a house on the same street as Coke's patriarch, Robert Woodruff.[21] Heyer was denied promotion to CEO, and he left the company in June 2004. He also clashed with key people in his next executive position, as key executive in an investment banking firm. In contrast to Heyer, many of the leaders described in this text have high emotional intelligence.

Research on emotional intelligence and leadership has also focused on the importance of the leader's mood in influencing performance. Daniel Goleman, Richard Boyatzis, and Annie McKee believe that the leader's mood and his or her associated behaviors greatly influence bottom-line performance. One reason is that moods are contagious. A cranky and ruthless leader creates a toxic organization of underachievers (who perform at less than their potential). In contrast, an upbeat and inspirational leader breeds followers who can surmount most challenges. Thus mood finally affects profit and loss. The implication for leaders is that they have to develop emotional intelligence regarding their moods. It is also helpful to develop a sense of humor, because lightheartedness is the most contagious of moods.[22]

Despite all the attention paid to emotional intelligence, it is a supplement to, not a substitute for, mental ability. A person cannot be an effective leader on the basis of emotional intelligence alone.

*Flexibility and Adaptability* A leader is someone who facilitates change. It therefore follows that a leader must be flexible enough to cope with such changes as technological advances, downsizings, outsourcing, a shifting customer base, and a changing work force. **Flexibility**, or the ability to adjust to different situations, has long been recognized as an important leadership characteristic. Leaders who are flexible are able to adjust to the demands of changing conditions, much as antilock brakes enable an automobile to adjust to changes in road conditions. Without the underlying trait of flexibility, a person could be an effective leader in only one or two situations. The manufacturing industry exemplifies a field in which situation adaptability is particularly important because top executives are required to provide leadership for both traditional production employees as well as highly-skilled professionals.

*Internal Locus of Control* People with an **internal locus of control** believe that they are the prime mover behind events. Thus, an internal locus of control helps a leader in the role of a take-charge person because the leader believes fundamentally in his or her innate capacity to take charge. An internal locus of control is closely related to self-confidence. A strong internal locus facilitates self-confidence because the person perceives that he or she can control circumstances enough to perform well.

A leader with an internal locus of control is likely to be favored by group members. One reason is that an "internal" person is perceived as more powerful than an "external" person because he or she takes responsibility for events. The leader with an internal locus of control would emphasize that he or she can change unfavorable conditions, as did Allen Questrom during his time at J.C. Penney (Chapter 1). You may recall that he also encouraged the managers reporting to him to also take responsibility for their part in Penney's turnaround.

Leadership Skill-Building Exercise 2-2 provides you with an opportunity to begin strengthening your internal locus of control. Considerable further work would be required to shift from an external to an internal locus of control.

LEADERSHIP SKILL-BUILDING EXERCISE 2-2

### DEVELOPING AN INTERNAL LOCUS OF CONTROL

A person's locus of control is usually a deeply ingrained thinking pattern that develops over a period of many years. Nevertheless, you can begin developing a stronger internal locus of control by analyzing past successes and failures to determine how much influence you had on the outcome of these events. By repeatedly analyzing the relative contribution of internal versus external factors in shaping events, you may learn to feel more in charge of key events in your life. The events listed below are a good starting point.

1. *A contest or athletic event that you either won or made a good showing in*
   What were the factors within your control that led to your winning or making a good showing?

   _____

   _____

   _____

   What were the factors beyond your control that led to your winning or making a good showing?

   _____

   _____

   _____

2. *A course in which you received a poor grade*
   What were the factors within your control that led to this poor grade?

   _____

   _____

   _____

   What were the factors beyond your control that led to this poor grade?

   _____

   _____

   _____

**3.** *A group project to which you were assigned that worked out poorly*
What were the factors within your control that led to this poor result?

_____

_____

_____

What were the factors beyond your control that led to this poor result?

_____

_____

_____

After you have prepared your individual analysis, you may find it helpful to discuss your observations in small groups. Focus on how people could have profited from a stronger internal locus of control in the situations analyzed.

*Courage* Leaders need courage to face the challenges of taking prudent risks and taking initiative in general. Courage comes from the heart, as suggested by the French word for heart, *coeur*. Leaders must face up to responsibility and be willing to put their reputations on the line. It takes courage for a leader to suggest a new undertaking, because if the undertaking fails, the leader is often seen as having failed. The more faith people place in the power of leaders to cause events, the more strongly they blame leaders when outcomes are unfavorable.

It also takes courage to take a stand that could backfire. David Dorman, the chairman and chief executive of AT&T, made a courageous decision several years ago when he announced that AT&T would stop promoting its local and long-distance services to home consumers and focus exclusively on big business customers. AT&T had been providing long-distance services since 1885, and at one time the company served virtually every U.S. home with a phone. Thus Dorman's decision marked the end of an era. Dorman said the decision to pull the plug on the consumer business was painful but necessary because revenues from consumer services were falling 20 percent per year.[23] But this decision, if wrong, could lead to the total demise of AT&T as a free-standing company.

## Leadership Motives

Effective leaders, as opposed to nonleaders and less effective leaders, have frequently been distinguished by their motives and needs. In general, leaders have an intense desire to occupy a position of responsibility for others and to control them. Figure 2-3 outlines four specific leadership motives or needs. All four motives can be considered task related.

### The Power Motive

Effective leaders have a strong need to control resources. Leaders with high power motives have three dominant characteristics: (1) they act with vigor and determination

**FIGURE 2-3** Leadership Motives

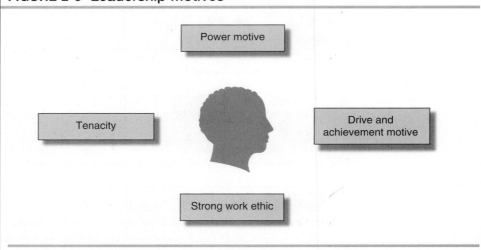

to exert their power; (2) they invest much time in thinking about ways to alter the behavior and thinking of others; and (3) they care about their personal standing with those around them.[24] The power motive is important because it means that the leader is interested in influencing others. Without power, it is much more difficult to influence others. Power is not necessarily good or evil; it can be used for the sake of the power holder (personalized power motive) or for helping others (socialized power motive).[25]

***Personalized Power Motive*** Leaders with a personalized power motive seek power mostly to further their own interests. They crave the trappings of power, such as status symbols, luxury, and money. In recent years, some leaders have taken up power boating, or racing powerful, high-speed boats. When asked how he liked his power-boating experience, an entrepreneurial leader replied, "It's fun, but the startup costs are about $350,000."

Because of his love for the trappings of power, Donald Trump® is seen as a leader with a strong personalized power motive. Even the name *Donald Trump* is registered; that is, it is supposed to be written with the "registered" symbol upon first mention. Trump has a penchant for naming yachts, hotels, and office buildings after himself. His drive for power is intertwined with his immodesty and lack of humility. Trump's television show, *The Apprentice,* helped make him a national symbol of power, and his firm even tried to make the term *"You're fired"* a registered trademark.

Despite Trump's elevated personalized power motive, he does not fit all three characteristics stated above. Trump gives his financial managers considerable latitude in managing his enterprises. In contrast to Trump, some leaders with strong personalized power motives typically enjoy dominating others. Their need for dominance can lead to submissive subordinates who are frequently sycophants and yes-persons.

***Socialized Power Motive*** Leaders with a socialized power motive use power primarily to achieve organizational goals or a vision. In this context, the term *socialized* means that the leader uses power primarily to help others. As a result, he or she is likely to provide more effective leadership. Leaders with socialized power motives tend to be more emotionally mature than leaders with personalized power motives. They exercise power more for the benefit of the entire organization and are less likely to manipulate others through the use of power. Leaders with socialized power motives are also less defensive and more willing to accept expert advice. Finally, they have longer-range perspectives.[26]

It is important not to draw a rigid line between leaders with personalized power motives and those with socialized power motives. The distinction between doing good for others and doing good for oneself is often made on the basis of very subjective criteria. A case in point is H. Ross Perot, the highly successful business founder, social activist, and two-time candidate for U.S. president. Perot supporters attest to his genuine desire to create a good life for others and to serve the public. His detractors, however, regard Perot as a leader obsessed with power and self-importance.

## The Drive and Achievement Motive

Leaders are known for working hard to achieve their goals. **Drive** refers to a propensity to put forth high energy into achieving goals and to a persistence in applying that energy. Drive also includes **achievement motivation**—finding joy in accomplishment for its own sake. Entrepreneurs and high-level corporate managers usually have strong achievement motivation. Such people have a consistent desire to:

1. Achieve through their own efforts and take responsibility for success or failure
2. Take moderate risks that can be handled through their own efforts
3. Receive feedback on their level of performance
4. Introduce novel, innovative, or creative solutions
5. Plan and set goals[27]

## A Strong Work Ethic

Effective leaders typically have a strong **work ethic**, a firm belief in the dignity of work. People with a strong work ethic are well motivated because they value hard work. Most leaders need this quality because they have a heavy workload. A strong work ethic helps the organizational leader believe that the group task is worthwhile. For example, the outside world might not think that the production of specialty soft drinks (such as high-caffeine cola) and bottled spring water is important. Yet the founder of one such company said that he delights in the pleasure his company brings to so many people. He also added, "A lot of IT [information technology] specialists wouldn't be nearly as productive without getting energized by our cola."

## Tenacity and Resilience

A final observation about the motivational characteristics of organizational leaders is that they are *tenacious*. Leaders are better at overcoming obstacles than are nonleaders. Tenacity multiplies in importance for organizational leaders because it takes a long time to implement a new program or to consummate a business deal, such as acquiring another company. A study of 150 leaders conducted by Warren Bennis reinforces the link between leadership effectiveness and tenacity. All interviewees embodied a strongly developed sense of purpose and a willful determination to achieve what

## LEADER IN ACTION

### THE PERSEVERING AND RESILIENT ED BREEN, NOW OF TYCO

When Motorola acquired General Instrument Corporation in January 2000, Edward D. Breen lost his CEO job and became a division head. Many executives would have quit to avoid living with a bruised ego from shrunken power and reduced visibility, especially if they were independently wealthy. Breen not only stayed, but he also flourished in the new company. Breen's strategy was to retain nearly all his former management team, make fast decisions, and pursue top posts elsewhere.

The 46-year-old executive, a former college wrestler, had made a rapid rise to president and chief operating officer of General Instrument Corporation. He became a General Instrument salesman after college and joined senior management just ten years later. In 2001 he was the only top officer to earn a raise or restricted shares. He also garnered more stock options than Christopher Galvin, the chairman, CEO, and founder's grandson.

While a division head, the loyalty Breen fostered with fifty former General Instrument vice presidents paid off. All but one followed him to Motorola. "Everybody was pretty loyal to the team," said one insider. "A lot of them thought he would move up in the company."

Breen and his team represented the kind of talent Motorola needed, and he soon emerged as a key architect of Motorola's recovery effort. He agreed to remain for one year, and Motorola promised him a $1.7 million bonus if he stayed for two. As head of Motorola's new broadband communications division, Breen refused to act demoted. He insisted on continuing to use a leased Gulfstream jet so he could visit distant customers, even while the company was making deep budget cuts that included many jobs. And he worked fast. He integrated the two companies' cable-gear businesses in two months instead of

the six months demanded by Galvin. He also consolidated sales forces and drafted a strategic plan.

In the fall of 2000 the departure of a veteran once viewed as Motorola's next president created a horse race between Breen and two others for the number 2 position. In the past, Motorola had picked longtime insiders for its top spots. Afraid of losing Breen, however, in January 2001 Motorola named him head of its network sector and gave him several rewards, including restricted shares initially valued at $10.3 million. Breen was offered the number 2 spot just before Labor Day and took his seat four months later.

Then, in July of 2002, he abruptly stepped down as president and chief operating officer of Motorola and moved into the position of chairman and chief operating officer of Tyco International Ltd., a giant conglomerate plagued with financial scandal in the ranks of top management.

At Tyco Breen viewed his opulent office as an embarrassment. Dennis Kozlowski, the former Tyco CEO, had spared no expense in using company funds to adorn his corporate offices and his numerous personal residences. His ten-year reign of greed and extravagance had left the conglomerate's reputation in tatters. In 2005, Kozlowski was sentenced to up to 25 years in prison for stealing hundreds of millions of dollars from the company. However, over an eight-year period Tyco management had acquired 1,000 businesses, and many of these were relatively unharmed by the financial excesses of the former regime.

While auditors were still digging into Tyco's accounting ledgers for indicators of fraud and deception, Breen wanted to make sure no financial malfeasance happened on his watch. In his first five months on the job he replaced Tyco's entire executive team and its entire board, something no one can recall a major U.S. company ever having done before. Everyone who worked in the company's

57th Street (Manhattan) offices was fired except for one receptionist and two assistants. Breen also slashed the generous executive compensation.

To help reduce costs, Breen also assembled a team of 270 people charged with eliminating redundant factories, storage facilities, and offices all across the company. In addition, many purchasing contracts will be renegotiated. Breen hopes to save $1 billion in reduced costs. Furthermore, he is looking to move to modest headquarters in Princeton, New Jersey.

Breen is confident he can restore Tyco's reputation. In 2002, Tyco lost more than $9 billion on revenues of $36 billion. But Breen believed that by managing the conglomerate properly, such as by rolling out centralized efficiency programs, he could create healthy growth at Tyco. For 2004, Tyco earned $3 billion from sales of $40 billion. Breen has plenty of supporters who think that if anyone can pull off such a turnaround,

he can. Breen is known as a down-to-earth, practical collaborator who believes in accomplishing tasks and achieving goals. "Ed is full of energy and has impeccable integrity," says Ralph Whitworth, a shareholder activist who added more shares to his Tyco holdings after Breen joined. By 2003, Tyco had generated close to $1 billion in profits with $38 billion in sales, and the positive results were still in place two years later.

### QUESTIONS

1. In what way is Breen courageous and resilient?
2. If Breen is so ethical, why did he leave Motorola so soon after receiving a promotion to CEO?
3. Identify several of Breen's leadership traits, motives, and characteristics.

SOURCE: Joann S. Lublin, "CEO Remains Loyal After an Acquisition and Is Now Rewarded," *Wall Street Journal*, June 4, 2002, p. B1; Melanie Warner, "Exorcism at Tyco," *Fortune*, April 28, 2003, pp. 106–110; Spencer Chin, "Breen Leaves Motorola to Tackle Troubled Tyco," *ebn* (High Beam Research), July 29, 2002, **p. 1.**

they wanted. "Without that," said Bennis, "organizations and individuals are not powerful. The central ingredient of power is purpose."[28]

The preceding Leader in Action describes a business leader who is both tenacious and resilient. Leadership Self-Assessment Quiz 2-3 gives you the opportunity to obtain a tentative measure of your resilience.

---

**LEADERSHIP SELF-ASSESSMENT QUIZ 2-3**

### THE PERSONAL RESILIENCY QUIZ

INSTRUCTIONS Answer each of the following statements *mostly agree* or *mostly disagree* as it applies to yourself. In taking a questionnaire such as this, it can always be argued that the true answer to any one particular statement is "It depends on the situation." Despite the validity of this observation, do your best to indicate whether you would mostly agree or disagree with the statement.

| | Mostly Agree | Mostly Disagree | Score (see key) |
|---|---|---|---|
| 1. Winning is everything. | ☐ | ☒ | 1 |
| 2. If I have had a bad day at work or school, it tends to ruin my evening. | ☒ | ☐ | |

*(continued)*

3. If I just keep trying, I will get my
share of good breaks. ☒ ☐ _1_

4. It takes me much longer than most
people to shake the flu or a cold. ☒ ☐ _____

5. If it were not for a few bad breaks I have
received, I would be much further
ahead in my career. ☐ ☒ _1_

6. There is no disgrace in losing. ☒ ☐ _1_

7. I am a generally self-confident person. ☐ ☒ _____

8. Finishing last beats not competing at all. ☒ ☐ _1_

9. I like to take a chance, even if the
probability of winning is small. ☒ ☐ _1_

10. If I have two reversals in a row, I do
not worry about it being part of a losing
streak. ☐ ☒ _____

11. I am a sore loser. ☐ ☒ _1_

12. It takes a lot to get me discouraged. ☐ ☒ _____

13. Every "no" I encounter is one step
closer to a "yes." ☐ ☒ _____

14. I doubt I could stand the shame of being
fired or being downsized. ☐ ☒ _1_

15. I enjoy being the underdog once in
a while. ☒ ☐ _1_

SCORING KEY Give yourself 1 point for each statement you responded to that is in agreement with the answer key below. If your response does not agree with the key, give yourself a zero. Add your points for the 15 statements to obtain your total score.

| | | |
|---|---|---|
| 1. Mostly disagree | 6. Mostly agree | 11. Mostly disagree |
| 2. Mostly disagree | 7. Mostly agree | 12. Mostly agree |
| 3. Mostly agree | 8. Mostly agree | 13. Mostly agree |
| 4. Mostly disagree | 9. Mostly agree | 14. Mostly disagree |
| 5. Mostly disagree | 10. Mostly agree | 15. Mostly agree |

SCORING AND INTERPRETATION Your score on the Personal Resiliency Quiz gives you a rough index of your overall tendencies toward being able to back bounce from adversity. The higher your score, the more resilient you are in handling disappointment, setbacks, and frustration. The following breakdown of scores will help you determine your degree of resiliency.

- 13+ *Very Resilient:* You are remarkably effective in bouncing back from setback, or being resilient. Your resiliency should help you lead others when setbacks arise.
- 4–12 *Moderately Resilient:* Like most people, you probably cope well with some type of adversity but not others.
- 0–3 *Not Resilient:* You are the type of individual who has difficulty coping with adversity. Focusing on learning how to cope with setbacks and maintain a courageous outlook could help you in your development as a leader.

## Cognitive Factors and Leadership

Mental ability as well as personality is important for leadership success. To inspire people, bring about constructive change, and solve problems creatively, leaders need to be mentally sharp. Another mental requirement is the ability to sort out essential information from less essential information and then store the most important information in memory. Problem-solving and intellectual skills are referred to collectively as **cognitive factors**. The term *cognition* refers to the mental process or faculty by which knowledge is gathered. We discuss six cognitive factors that are closely related to cognitive intelligence, as shown in Figure 2-4. The descriptor *cognitive* is somewhat necessary to differentiate traditional mental ability from emotional intelligence.

### General Mental Ability (Cognitive Intelligence)

Being very good at solving problems is a fundamental characteristic of effective leaders in all fields. Business leaders, for example, need to understand how to analyze

**FIGURE 2-4** **Cognitive Factors and Leadership**

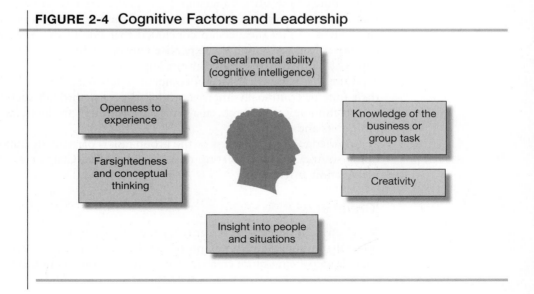

company finances, use advanced software, manage inventory, and deal with international trade regulations. Research spanning 100 years has demonstrated that leaders receive higher scores than most people on mental ability tests, including IQ (a term for a test score that for many people is synonymous with intelligence). A meta-analysis of 151 studies found a positive relationship between intelligence and job performance of leaders in many different settings. The relationship is likely to be higher when the leader plays an active role in decision making and is not overly stressed. The researchers also found support for the old idea that intelligence contributes the most to leadership effectiveness when the leader is not vastly smarter than most group members.[29]

## Knowledge of the Business or Group Task

Intellectual ability is closely related to having knowledge of the business or the key task the group is performing. An effective leader has to be technically competent in some discipline, particularly when leading a group of specialists. It is difficult for the leader to establish rapport with group members when he or she does not know what they are doing and when the group does not respect the leader's technical skills.

A representative example of the contribution of knowledge of the business to leadership effectiveness is the situation of Jim Press, the executive vice president and chief operating officer of Toyota Motor Sales, U.S.A., Inc. Press is considered to be one of the most influential executives in the American auto industry. A middle-aged man, he conducts regular pep rallies with Toyota employees. Press has a rare blend of attributes. He is a thirty-four-year Toyota veteran who has mastered the company's highly regarded engineering and manufacturing systems. His interpersonal skills combined with his intimate knowledge of auto manufacturing give him enormous clout within Toyota, and within the U.S. automotive industry in general.[30]

The importance of knowledge of the business is increasingly being recognized as an attribute of executive leadership. Leaders at every level are expected to bring forth useful ideas for carrying out the mission of the organization or organizational unit. An analysis of CEO leadership concluded that one of the basic ways in which top executives lead is through the **expertise approach**. Executives who lead by using this approach think that the leader's most important responsibility is providing an area of expertise that will be a source of competitive advantage. Such CEOs devote most of their time to continually improving their expertise through such means as studying new technological research, analyzing competitors' products, and conferring with customers and engineers.[31]

Knowledge of the business or the group task is particularly important when developing strategy and formulating mission statements. Chapter 13 deals with strategy formulation at length.

## Creativity

Many effective leaders are creative in the sense that they arrive at imaginative and original solutions to complex problems. Creative ability lies on a continuum, with some leaders being more creative than others. At one end of the creative continuum are business leaders who think of innovative products and services. One example is Steve Jobs of Apple Computer, Inc., and Pixar Animation Studios. Jobs has contributed creative product ideas to both firms, including endorsing the development of the iPod. At the middle of the creativity continuum are leaders who explore imaginative—but not breakthrough—solutions to business problems. At the low end of the creativity continuum are leaders who inspire group members to push forward with standard solutions to organizational problems. Creativity is such an important aspect of the leader's role in the modern organization that the development of creative problem-solving skills receives separate attention in Chapter 11.

## Insight into People and Situations

Another important cognitive trait of leaders is **insight**, a depth of understanding that requires considerable intuition and common sense. Intuition is often the mental process used to provide the understanding of a problem. Insight helps speed decision making. Lawrence Weinbach, chairman, president, and CEO of Unisys, puts it this way: "If we want to be leaders, we're going to have to make decisions with maybe 75 percent of the facts. If you wait for 95 percent, you are going to be a follower."[32] Jeff Bezos of Amazon.com believes that the bigger the decision, such as whether or not to enter a particular business, the greater the role of insight and intuition.

Michael Dell endorses the importance of insight and hunches in making major decisions, yet he emphasizes that one cannot neglect hard data. Dell says, "In leadership, it's important to be intuitive—but not at the expense of facts. Without the right data to back it up, emotional decision making during difficult times will inevitably lead a company into great danger."[33]

Insight into people and situations involving people is an essential characteristic of managerial leaders because it helps them make the best use of both their own and others' talents. For example, it helps them make wise choices in selecting people for key assignments. Insight also enables managers to do a better job of training and developing team members because they can wisely assess the members' strengths and weaknesses. Another major advantage of being insightful is that the leader can size up a situation and adapt his or her leadership approach accordingly. For instance, in a crisis situation, group members welcome directive and decisive leadership. Being able to read people helps the manager provide this leadership.

Insight also helps one perceive trends in the environment. Leaders must be able to process many different types of information and use their perceptions to predict the direction of environmental forces. For example, many human resource managers size up the environment to identify factors that will attract talented professionals to their firm during a labor shortage. Among the key factors are opportunity for continuous learning, flexible work schedules, and stock options. A more traditional approach might emphasize high starting salaries and opportunity for promotion.

You can gauge your insight by charting the accuracy of your hunches and predictions about people and business situations. For example, size up a new coworker or manager as best you can. Record your observations and test them against how that person performs or behaves many months later. The feedback from this type of exercise will help sharpen your insights.

### Farsightedness and Conceptual Thinking

To develop visions and corporate strategy, a leader needs **farsightedness**, the ability to understand the long-range implications of actions and policies. A farsighted leader recognizes that hiring talented workers today will give the firm a long-range competitive advantage. A more shortsighted view would be to hire less-talented workers to satisfy immediate employment needs. The farsighted leader/manager is not oblivious to short-range needs but will devise an intermediate solution, such as hiring temporary workers until people with the right talents are found.

Conceptual thinking refers to the ability to see the overall perspective, and it makes farsightedness possible. A conceptual thinker is also a *systems thinker* because he or she understands how the external environment influences the organization and how different parts of the organization influence each other. A good conceptual thinker recognizes how his or her organizational unit contributes to the firm or how the firm meshes with the outside world.

Being farsighted benefits the leadership of basic businesses as well as that of high-technology firms. Two twin brothers, Norman Leenhouts and Nelson Leenhouts, started a real estate business fifty-three years ago that is now called Home Properties. Today their total properties are valued at $2.9 billion and include 49,000 apartments in twelve states and more than 1 million square feet of commercial space. The Leenhouts have been able to see the possibilities in properties that others might consider undesirable. Their basic concept is to buy older, mostly brick complexes with deteriorating kitchens and bathrooms. Home Properties then fixes up the kitchens and bathrooms, raises the rents, and turns a profit.[34]

### Openness to Experience

Yet another important cognitive characteristic of leaders is their openness to experience, or their positive orientation toward learning. People who have a great deal of openness to experience have well-developed intellects. Traits commonly associated with this dimension of the intellect include being imaginative, cultured, curious, original, broad-minded, intelligent, and artistically sensitive.

### The WICS Model of Leadership in Organizations

Robert J. Sternberg has developed a new approach to understanding leadership based on cognitive factors. The **WICS model of leadership** encompasses and synthesizes wisdom, creativity, and intelligence to explain leadership effectiveness. To be a highly effective leader, one needs these three components working together or synthesized, as diagrammed in Figure 2-5. Intelligence in this model includes both the traditional and analytical intelligence, as well as practical intelligence. The last-mentioned attribute refers to the ability to solve everyday problems by using experience-based knowledge to adapt to and shape the environment—sometimes referred to as *street smarts*. Creativity is the same type of creativity mentioned in this chapter. Wisdom is the most important quality a leader can have, but it is relatively rare. The insight and intuition referred to earlier in the chapter are much like wisdom. A leader with wisdom would use intelligence, creativity, and experience for a common good.[35]

According to the WICS model, a leader needs the following for the successful utilization of intelligence:

**FIGURE 2-5** The WICS Model of Leadership

Source: Robert J. Sternberg, "WICS: A Model of Leadership in Organizations," *Academy of Management Learning and Education*, December 2003, p. 387. *Academy of Management Learning and Education* by Robert J. Sternberg. Copyright 2003 by *Academy of Management Learning and Education.* Reproduced with permission of *Academy of Management Learning and Education* in the format Textbook via Copyright Clearance Center.

- Creative skills to generate new ideas
- Analytical skills to evaluate whether the ideas are good ones
- Practical skills to implement the ideas and to persuade others of their value

Jim Press of Toyota, described earlier, might classify as a leader with intelligence, creativity, and wisdom because he has contributed to the design and manufacture of high-quality vehicles and to the creation of thousands of jobs. The WICS model emphasizes that cognitive factors are indeed useful for leadership. Personality factors, however, are still a key part of being an effective leader.

To help personalize the information about key leadership traits presented so far, do Leadership Skill-Building Exercise 2-3.

LEADERSHIP SKILL-BUILDING EXERCISE 2-3

### GROUP FEEDBACK ON LEADERSHIP TRAITS

The class organizes into groups of about seven people. A volunteer sits in the middle of each group. Each group member looks directly at the person in the "hot seat" and tells him or her what leadership trait, characteristic, or motive he or she seems to possess. It will help if the feedback providers offer a few words of explanation for their observations. For example, a participant who is told that he or she has self-confidence might also be told, "I notice how confidently you have told the class about your success on the job." The group next moves on to the second person, and so forth. (We assume that you have had some opportunity to observe your classmates prior to this exercise.)

Each member thus receives positive feedback about leadership traits and characteristics from all the other members in the group. After all members have had their turn at receiving feedback, discuss as a group the value of the exercise.

## The Influence of Heredity and Environment on Leadership

Does heredity or environment contribute more to leadership effectiveness? Are leaders born or made? Do you have to have the right stuff to be a leader? Many people ponder these issues now that the study of leadership is more in vogue than ever. The most sensible answer is that the traits, motives, and characteristics required for leadership effectiveness are caused by a combination of heredity and environment. Personality traits and mental ability traits are based on certain inherited predispositions and aptitudes that require the right opportunity to develop. Mental ability is a good example. We inherit a basic capacity that sets an outer limit to how much mental horsepower we will have. Yet people need the right opportunity to develop their mental ability so that they can behave brightly enough to be chosen for a leadership position.

The physical factor of energy also sheds light on the nature-versus-nurture issue. Some people are born with a biological propensity for being more energetic than others. Yet unless that energy is properly channeled, it will not help a person become an effective leader.

The nature-versus-nurture issue also surfaces in relation to the leadership characteristic of creativity and innovation. Important genetic contributors to imaginative thinking include brainpower and emotional expressiveness. Yet these traits require the right environment to flourish. Such an environment would include encouragement from others and ample opportunity to experiment with ideas.

Research about emotional intelligence reinforces the statements made so far about leadership being a combination of inherited and learned factors. The outermost areas of the brain, known as the neocortex, govern analytical thinking and technical skill, which are associated with cognitive or traditional intelligence. The innermost areas of the brain govern emotions, such as the rage one feels when being criticized by a customer. Emotional intelligence originates in the neurotransmitters of the limbic system of the brain, which governs feelings, impulses, and drives.

A person therefore has genes that influence the emotional intelligence necessary for leadership. However, experience is important for emotional intelligence because it increases with age,[36] and a person usually becomes better at managing relationships the more practice he or she has. As one turnaround manager said, "I've restructured five different companies, and I've learned to do it without completely destroying morale."

The case histories of six sets of brothers highlight the complexity of sorting out the influences of heredity versus environment on leadership. All twelve achieved the title of president or higher at companies of at least 100 employees or $10 million in annual revenues. For example, the Leiwekes became CEOs of hockey teams: Tod is the president of the Minnesota Wild, and Tim is the president of the Los Angeles Kings. The reporter who gathered these case histories presented them as evidence of "CEO DNA."[37] Whether or not the author was totally serious, the implication is that heredity was the primary reason that these brothers had similar successes. However, they also had quite similar environments: same parents, primary and secondary school study in the same neighborhood, similar education, similar learned values, and so forth. Thus this issue is far from settled.

## The Strengths and Limitations of the Trait Approach

A compelling argument for the trait approach is that the evidence is convincing that leaders possess personal characteristics that differ from those of nonleaders. Based on their review of the type of research reported in this chapter, Kirkpatrick and Locke concluded: "Leaders do not have to be great men or women by being intellectual geniuses or omniscient prophets to succeed. But they do need to have the 'right stuff' and this stuff is not equally present in all people."[38] The current emphasis on emotional intelligence and ethical conduct, which are really traits, attitudes, and behaviors, reinforces the importance of the trait approach.

Understanding the traits of effective leaders serves as an important guide to leadership selection. If we are confident that honesty and integrity, as well as creativity and imagination, are essential leadership traits, then we can concentrate on selecting leaders with those characteristics. Another important strength of the trait approach is that it can help people prepare for leadership responsibility and all of the issues that accompany it. A person might seek experiences that enable him or her to develop vital characteristics such as self-confidence, good problem-solving ability, and assertiveness.

A limitation to the trait approach is that it does not tell us which traits are absolutely needed in which leadership situations. We also do not know how much of a trait, characteristic, or motive is the right amount. For example, some leaders get into ethical and legal trouble because they allow their ambition to cross the border-line into greed and gluttony. In addition, too much focus on the trait approach can breed an elitist conception of leadership. People who are not outstanding on key leadership traits and characteristics might be discouraged from seeking leadership positions.

The late Peter Drucker, a key figure in the modern management movement, was skeptical about studying the qualities of leaders. He believed that a leader cannot be categorized by a particular personality type, style, or set of traits. Instead, a leader should be understood in terms of his or her constituents, results, behaviors, and responsibilities. A leader must look in the mirror and ask if the image there is the kind of person he or she wants to be. (However, Drucker in this instance may have been alluding to the leader's traits and values!)[39]

A balanced perspective on the trait approach is that certain traits, motives, and characteristics increase the probability that a leader will be effective, but they do not guarantee effectiveness. The leadership situation often influences which traits will be the most important.[40]

**READER'S ROADMAP**

In this chapter we focused on the traits, motives, and characteristics of the leader—his or her inner qualities. In the next chapter we dig further into leadership qualities by studying charismatic and transformational leadership.

## Summary

A universal theory of leadership contends that certain personal characteristics and skills contribute to leadership effectiveness in many situations. The trait approach to leadership studies the traits, motives, and other characteristics of leaders. General personality traits associated with effective leadership include (1) self-confidence, (2) humility, (3) trustworthiness, (4) extraversion, (5) assertiveness, (6) emotional stability, (7) enthusiasm, (8) sense of humor, and (9) warmth.

Some personality traits of effective leaders are closely associated with task accomplishment. Among them are (1) passion for the work and the people, (2) emotional intelligence, (3) flexibility and adaptability, (4) internal locus of control, and (5) courage. Emotional intelligence is composed of four traits: self-awareness, self-management, social awareness, and relationship management.

Certain motives and needs associated with leadership effectiveness are closely related to task accomplishment. Among them are (1) the power motive, (2) the drive and achievement motive, (3) a strong work ethic, and (4) tenacity and resilience.

Cognitive factors are also important for leadership success. They include general mental ability and knowledge of the business or group task: that is,

technical competence. Creativity is another important cognitive skill for leaders, but effective leaders vary widely in their creative contributions. Insight into people and situations, including the ability to make effective judgments about business opportunities, also contributes to leadership effectiveness. Farsightedness and conceptual thinking help leaders to understand the long-range implications of actions and policies and to take an overall perspective. Being open to experience is yet another cognitive characteristic associated with effective leaders. The WICS theory of leadership in organizations emphasizes that leaders must synthesize wisdom, intelligence, and creativity (all cognitive factors).

The issue of whether leaders are born or bred frequently surfaces. A sensible answer is that the traits, motives, and characteristics required for leadership effectiveness are a combination of heredity and environment.

The trait approach to leadership is supported by many studies showing that leaders are different from nonleaders and that effective leaders are different from less effective leaders. Nevertheless, the trait approach does not tell us which traits are most important in which situations or how much of a trait is required.

## Key Terms

Universal theory of leadership

Trust

Assertiveness

Emotional stability

Emotional intelligence

Flexibility

Internal locus of control

Drive

Achievement motivation

Work ethic

Cognitive factors

Expertise approach

Insight

Farsightedness

WICS model of leadership

## ✔ Guidelines for Action and Skill Development

Because emotional intelligence is so important for leadership success, many organizations sponsor emotional intelligence training for managers. One way to get started on improving emotional intelligence would be to attend such a training program. However, like all forms of training, emotional intelligence training must be followed up with consistent and determined practice. A realistic starting point in improving your emotional intelligence is to work with one of its four components at a time, such as the empathy aspect of social awareness.

Begin by obtaining as much feedback as you can from people who know you. Ask them if they think you understand their emotional reactions and how well they think you understand them. It is also helpful to ask someone from another culture or someone who has a severe disability how well you communicate with him or her. (A higher level of empathy is required to communicate well with somebody much different from you.) If you have external or internal customers, ask them how well you appear to understand their position.

If you find any area of deficiency, work on that deficiency steadily. For example, perhaps you are not perceived as taking the time to understand a point of view quite different from your own. Attempt to understand other points of view. Suppose you believe strongly that money is the most important motivator for practically everybody. Speak to a person with a different opinion and listen carefully until you understand that person's perspective.

A few months later, obtain more feedback about your ability to empathize. If you are making progress, continue to practice. Then, repeat these steps for another facet of emotional intelligence. As a result of this practice, you will have developed another valuable interpersonal skill.

## Discussion Questions and Activities

1. How much faith do voters place in the trait theory of leadership when they elect public officials?
2. Suppose a college student graduates with a major for which he or she lacks enthusiasm. What might this person do about becoming a passionate leader?
3. What would a manager to whom you report have to do to convince you that he or she has emotional intelligence?
4. What would a manager to whom you report have to do to convince you that he or she has humility?
5. Describe any leader or manager whom you know personally or have watched on television who is unenthusiastic. What effect did the lack of enthusiasm have on group members?
6. If emotional intelligence is considered to be so important for high-level leadership, where does traditional or cognitive intelligence fit as an important characteristic of executive leaders?
7. What are your best-developed leadership traits, motives, and characteristics? How do you know?
8. A disproportionate number of people who received an M.B.A. at Harvard Business School are top executives in *Fortune* 500 business firms. How does this fact fit into the evidence about the roles of heredity and environment in creating leaders?
9. Visualize the least effective leader you know. Identify the traits, motives, and personal characteristics in which that person might be deficient.
10. Many people who disagree with the trait approach to leadership nevertheless still conduct interviews when hiring a person for a leadership position. Why is conducting such interviews inconsistent with their attitude toward the trait approach?

## LEADERSHIP CASE PROBLEM A

## THE RESILIENT SCOTT MCNEALY

Scott McNealy is the CEO of Sun Micro-systems, Inc., a company he helped to found. Talk with the ever-voluble McNealy, and you may hear one of his favorite quips: "Conventional wisdom doesn't contain a whole lot of wisdom." He believes it because of his own experience. In 1995, when Sun's major competitors were busy developing new servers to run Microsoft Corporation's Windows software, instead of showing common sense, McNealy increased his investment in Sun's own software called Solaris. What happened next made McNealy look brilliant. Rivals could not match the speed, reliability, and security of Sun's servers, and as the tech boom took off, they became the must-have gear for thousands of Internet startups and financial firms. Sales soared and profits exploded.

Five years later, as the boom of the late 1990s came to a crashing end, Wall Street had more advice for McNealy: batten down the hatches for the storm ahead, slash research, lay off staffers, and get serious about low-cost products. Once again, McNealy held his ground, but this time he was dreadfully wrong. Sun's sales have tumbled 48 percent in the last three years, it has lost a third of its market share, and it continues to head south even as its rivals ride the economic recovery. No other major player has been weakened as much during the tech downturn.

Through interviews with thirty-eight current and former Sun executives, including nine departees on the record, *BusinessWeek* learned that, as Sun's situation deteriorated, McNealy was bucking not just the counsel of outsiders but also that of his own lieutenants. After the tech industry went into its long slide in 2000, virtually his entire management team pleaded with McNealy to scale back his vision and adjust to leaner times.

By 2004, McNealy had cut back somewhat by laying off 10 percent of the workforce.

Time and time again, McNealy refused. An economics major from Harvard University, he was convinced that the economy would snap back quickly from its slump. He also believed that the Internet was so critical to companies that they could not hold off buying gear for long. "The Internet is still wildly underhyped, underutilized, and underimplemented," he said in early 2001. "I think we're looking at the largest equipment business in the history of anything. The growth opportunities are stunning" (*BusinessWeek*, p. 66). Preparing for the next upturn, he felt, was much more important than whittling expenses for a brief lull.

**"I'M NOT GOING AWAY"** As the tech wreck went from bad to worse, McNealy's contrary instincts kicked in. After all, he had been right to ignore the consequences within Sun's ranks before. In the 1980s, he overruled execs who were skittish about dropping Motorola, Inc.'s microprocessors for chips developed by Sun—a move that paid off in a big way. This time, as his team urged him to cut back, he felt the stakes were even higher. He was determined to fight off what he thought were short-term thinkers, particularly on Wall Street, so that Sun could be preserved as an innovative force.

Although he had thought about quitting during the boom, McNealy committed himself to Sun in late 2001, convinced that his credibility, experience, and sheer nerve were what the company needed during its darkest days. "I'm here and I'm not going away. This is a really tough situation, and we're going to get through this," he told staffers (*BusinessWeek*, p. 66). But McNealy badly underestimated the severity of the downturn and dismissed customers' desire for low-end servers. As time wore on, the losses piled up, and McNealy's high-minded resolve began to look to others like simple-minded obstinacy. One by one, his team lost faith and departed. All told, almost a dozen of McNealy's most trusted lieutenants have left in the past three years, including the chief of the server business.

Like many others, Masood Jabbar, Sun's long-time sales chief who retired in 2002, says he admires McNealy's courage. But the standoff became counterproductive. "The fight just didn't seem worth it anymore," says Jabbar. "It was an untenable situation" (*BusinessWeek*, p. 66). Yet the Sun board has no plan for McNealy to step down, and board members perceive him as a great leader.

McNealy says he still has what it takes to bring Sun back. "Maybe it's time to get rid of me," he says. "But this company has a lot invested in training and developing me. I have twenty years' experience. I'm 49 years old. I'm in good shape. Healthy. Lot of energy. Lot of wisdom. Relationships around the world" (*BusinessWeek*, p. 67). He seems remarkably unperturbed by the withering criticism of the past few years. Although he admits to some mistakes, he is just as acerbic and cocky as ever. He is not prone to self-doubt, or even much self-reflection.

Instead, McNealy is focused on turning Sun around with what he calls *disruptive innovation*, the same approach that has saved it so many times before. While most rivals make plain-vanilla computers and slug it out on price, Sun's plan is to change the rules of the game. At the high end of the server market, Sun is developing chips that can handle dozens of tasks at the same time. At the low end, Sun servers built around inexpensive chips will handle not only processing tasks but also the basic networking that rivals' boxes cannot handle. And Sun's pricing approach is something no server company has dared to try: it is planning to give away low-end servers to customers who agree to buy its software for several years. "We have a maverick strategy," says McNealy. "I think there's a huge opportunity right now" (*BusinessWeek*, p. 67).

McNealy contends that Sun is more focused than major rivals. Dell Inc., for instance, sells printers and digital music players, while IBM gets half its revenues from services. "We're not doing digital cameras. We're not doing printers," says McNealy. "We're fundamentally focused, much more so than any company I see out there."

## QUESTIONS

1. What is your opinion of Scott McNealy's courage and resiliency?

2. What personality trait or traits does McNealy possess that could be creating problems for him?

3. What do you recommend McNealy and his executive team do to restore their former glory?

SOURCE: Adapted from Jim Kersetter and Peter Burrows, "A CEO's Last Stand: Scott McNealy Knows He Made Many Mistakes. Is It Too Late to Recover?" *BusinessWeek*, July 26, 2004, pp. 64–70.

## LEADERSHIP CASE PROBLEM B

## THE URBAN IMPROVEMENT GUYS

Larry Glazer admits his latest project is a bit of an experiment. Along with partner Harold Samloff, Glazer is in the middle of rehabilitating the long-vacant Michael-Sterns building on North Clinton Avenue in Rochester, New York. After purchasing the building in March 2004, Glazer and Samloff upgraded the décor in both the common areas and individual apartments. For higher-rent lofts, tenants can have exposed brick walls and higher-quality countertops. Part of the building is dedicated to office space.

It is a project that is a bit out of character for Glazer and Samloff's Buckingham Properties. "We're gambling a bit," Glazer says. "If it works, we might try it again." That willingness to branch out into different areas has turned Buckingham Properties into one of Rochester's top developers. Buckingham has made its name by piecing together assemblages of properties— first residential, then industrial, Glazer likes to say.

Now Glazer, 59, and Samloff, 68, have turned their attention to an eclectic mix of properties in the Inner Loop, a highway around the downtown area. They are hoping to find a profit in the growing demand for fashionable office space. They say they have a firm commitment to improving life in the city. "We've always said that just like urban blight spreads, urban improvement spreads too."

Glazer and Samloff credit an even division of labor with helping them succeed. Glazer's title is chief executive officer; Samloff is chief operating officer. Samloff tackles management issues while Glazer pores over new prospects for the company. The staff members they have assembled have allowed Glazer and Samloff to focus more on the strategic future of the company than on the day-to-day intricacies of managing properties. "When we started out, we were doing everything," Glazer says. But the two still keep close tabs on their holdings. "We're tire-kickers," Samloff says. "We like to visit our projects on a regular basis."

The partnership is more than thirty-five years old. Glazer and Samloff met each other in 1970 during a Sunday morning tennis game organized by some friends. Samloff decided to ask Glazer if he wanted to partner on a rental property. Soon they were buying more houses together. At the time, Samloff was a full-time attorney and Glazer was working in the printing industry. Gradually, the real estate venture became a full-time job.

They continued to expand their holdings, buying houses and stores in the city not far from downtown. Then an opportunity to renovate an old industrial site presented itself—and Samloff and Glazer found they liked managing industrial properties. "We never really did have a game plan," Samloff says. "We just reviewed opportunities as they came to us."

The Michael-Sterns building was formerly a men's clothing plant that closed in 1977. Buckingham has spent about $6.5 million on renovation; but that price tag is not so bad considering the company bought the building from the city for $10,000.

One of the tenants in the building is the Catholic Family Center. Carolyn Portanova, the CEO of the center, says that she has great admiration for her new landlords. She says the project could be a catalyst for rehabilitating the whole neighborhood. "There's an energy there when you work with someone who has a vision about what something can be." Another tenant says he appreciates the fact that the Buckingham partners strike a deal and stick by it.

Both Glazer and Samloff enjoy the hands-on nature of their work and are also active in the community. The two men are now looking to the future. Both admit they are looking at life for their company after they leave. "We've got a business plan that we think should be continued," Samloff says. "We take something and say, this is pretty raw, but is there a gem in this ore we can extract?"

## QUESTIONS

1. Explain whether or not Glazer and Samloff qualify as leaders.

2. In what ways do the traits and characteristics of Glazer and Samloff complement each other?
3. What evidence do you find that Glazer and Samloff are farsighted?
4. What cognitive skills are reflected in the leadership of Buckingham Properties?

SOURCE: David Tyler, "Buckingham to Broadway," Rochester, New York, *Democrat and Chronicle,* April 11, 2002, pp. 1E, 8E; personal interview with Harold Samloff, June 21, 2002; October 5, 2004.

**LEADERSHIP SKILL-BUILDING EXERCISE 2-4**

### MY LEADERSHIP PORTFOLIO

For this addition to your leadership portfolio, first select five of the traits, motives, and characteristics described in this chapter that you think you have already exhibited. For each of these attributes, explain why you think you have it. An example would be as follows:

*Insight into people and situations:* As a restaurant manager, my job was to help hire an assistant manager who would share some of the responsibilities of running the restaurant. I invited a friend of mine, Laura, to apply for the position even though she had never worked in a restaurant. I noticed that she was businesslike and also had a good touch with people. Laura was hired, and she proved to be a fantastic assistant manager. I obviously sized her up correctly.

Second, select several leadership traits, motives, or characteristics that you think you need to develop to enhance your leadership skills. Explain why you think you need this development and how you think you might obtain it. An example would be as follows:

*Passion*: So far I am not particularly passionate about any aspect of work or any cause, so it is hard for me to get very excited about being a leader. I plan to read more about my field and then interview a couple of successful people in this field to find some aspect of it that would be a joy for me to get involved in.

## INTERNET SKILL-BUILDING EXERCISE

Apply the chapter concepts! Visit the Web and complete this Internet skill-building exercise to learn more about current leadership topics and trends.

### MEASURING YOUR EMOTIONAL INTELLIGENCE

Go to *www.eqhelp.com/saelfimp2.htm*, and choose one of the following two alternatives. (1) Obtain a scientific measurement of your emotional intelligence for about the price of a fully loaded pizza or fancy T-shirt. (Choose the option for the Simmons EQ Insights.) Compare your score on the test with your self-evaluation of your emotional intelligence. (2) For free, rate yourself on the thirteen key areas of emotional intelligence mentioned in the web site. Which of these areas are closely related to the traits, motives, and characteristics of leaders presented in this chapter?

# Charismatic and Transformational Leadership

In July 2004, Steve Jobs said he expected a full recovery from cancer surgery. Nevertheless, news of his illness raised the question of how his companies, Apple Computer, Inc., and Pixar Animation Studios, would fare without Steve—who some consider the companies' soul—at the helm. "What makes him very hard to replace is his charisma," said industry analyst Rob Enderle.

Jobs sent an email message from his hospital bed to Apple and Pixar employees announcing that he had had successful surgery to treat a form of pancreatic cancer, an islet cell neuroendocrine tumor. The can-cer is extremely rare and easily cured if diagnosed early, as Jobs says it was in his case. Jobs, 49, assured employees and investors that he expected a full recovery and planned to return to work by the next month.

Apple and Pixar both have leadership succession plans, according to Apple spokeswoman Katie Cotton. But analysts are uncertain who would—or could—lead Apple. "He's iconic. He's very much tied to the Apple name and the driving force behind Apple's reemergence," said analyst Michelle Gutierrez. "If anything happens to him, it'll be a big blow to the company."[1]

T he concerns about Steve Jobs discontinuing his leadership roles at Apple and Pixar illustrate how much importance many people attach to having a charismatic at the head of an organization. The study of charismatic and transformational leadership, an extension of the trait theory, has become an important way of understanding leadership.

In this chapter we examine the meaning and effects of charismatic leadership, the characteristics of charismatic leaders, how such leaders form visions, and how one develops charisma. We also describe the closely related and overlapping subject of transformational leadership. Finally, we look at the dark side of charismatic leadership.

## The Meanings of Charisma

Charisma, like leadership itself, has been defined in various ways. Nevertheless, there is enough consistency among these definitions to make charisma a useful concept in understanding and practicing leadership. *Charisma* is a Greek word meaning "divinely inspired gift." In the study of leadership, **charisma** is a special quality of leaders whose purposes, powers, and extraordinary determination differentiate them from others.[2] In general use, the term *charismatic* means to have a charming and colorful personality, such as that shown by basketball sensation Yao Ming or soccer star Mia Hamm.

college.hmco.com/pic/ dubrin5e

(KB) @ **KNOWLEDGE BANK:** contains a sampling of additional definitions of charisma.

The various definitions of charisma have a unifying theme. Charisma is a positive and compelling quality of a person that makes many others want to be led by that person. The phrase *many others* is chosen carefully. Few leaders are perceived as charismatic by *all* of their constituents. A case in point is Bill Gates, the chairman and cofounder of Microsoft Corporation, whose name surfaces frequently in discussions of charisma. Despite his wide appeal, many people consider Gates to be brash, out-spoken, too all-controlling, and obsessed with demolishing the competition—hardly characteristics of an inspiring leader.

Given that charisma is based on perceptions, an important element of charismatic leadership involves the *attributions* made by group members about the characteristics of leaders and the results they achieve. According to attribution theory, if people perceive a leader to have a certain characteristic, such as being visionary, the leader will more likely be perceived as charismatic. Attributions of charisma are important because they lead to other behavioral outcomes, such as commitment to leaders, self-sacrifice, and high performance.

A study of attributions and charisma found that the network a person belongs to influences the attributions he or she makes. The subjects in the study were police workers who rated the director of a police organization and students in an introductory business course who rated the charisma of their professors. The study found that network members influenced to some extent whether the study participants perceived their leader or professor to be charismatic and that perceptions of charisma were the closest among friends within networks.[3] What about you? Are your perceptions of the charisma of your professors influenced by the opinions of your network members?

### Charisma: A Relationship Between the Leader and Group Members

A key dimension of charismatic leadership is that, like all leadership, it involves a relationship or interaction between the leader and the people being led. Furthermore, the people accepting the leadership must attribute charismatic qualities to the leader. John Gardner believes that charisma applies to leader–constituent relationships in which the leader has an exceptional gift for inspiration and nonrational communication. At the same time the constituents' response is characterized by awe, reverence, devotion, or emotional dependence.[4] The late Sam Walton, founder of Wal-Mart Stores, had this type of relationship with many of his employees. Walton's most avid supporters believed he was an inspired executive to whom they could trust their careers.

Charismatic leaders use impression management to deliberately cultivate a certain relationship with group members. In other words, they take steps to create a favorable, successful impression, recognizing that the perceptions of constituents determine whether they function as charismatic leaders. Following are two of the many propositions (or conclusions and interpretations) offered by William L. Gardner and Bruce J. Avolio to explain how charismatic leaders use impression management:[5]

1. Charismatic leaders, more than noncharismatic leaders, value and pursue an interrelated set of images to convey the impression that they are trustworthy, credible, morally worthy, innovative, esteemed, and powerful. The leader's overall impression as a charismatic person depends on constructing and maintaining these images in the minds of followers.
2. Charismatic leaders, more than noncharismatic leaders, use the assertive impression management strategies of exemplification and promotion to secure and maintain desired images of their selves, their vision, and their organization.

Impression management seems to imply that these leaders are skillful actors in presenting a charismatic face to the world. But the behaviors and attitudes of truly charismatic leaders go well beyond superficial aspects of impression management, such as wearing fashionable clothing or speaking well. For example, a truly charismatic leader will work hard to create positive visions for group members.

Charismatic leadership is possible under certain conditions. The constituents must share the leader's beliefs and must have unquestioning acceptance of and affection for the leader. The group members must willingly obey the leader, and they must be emotionally involved both in the mission of the charismatic leader and in their own goals. Finally, the constituents must have a strong desire to identify with the leader.[6]

### The Effects of Charisma

Robert J. House developed a theory of charismatic leadership that defines charisma in terms of its effects. A charismatic leader, according to House, is any person who brings about certain outcomes to an unusually high degree. Charismatic leadership has taken place when extraordinary levels of devotion, identification, and emulation are aroused in group members—specifically, when the leader has produced the following nine effects:[7]

1. Group members' trust in the correctness of the leader's beliefs
2. Similarity of group members' beliefs to those of the leader
3. Unquestioning acceptance of the leader
4. Affection for the leader
5. Willing obedience to the leader
6. Identification with and emulation of the leader
7. Emotional involvement of the group members or constituents in the mission
8. Heightened goals of the group members
9. Feeling on the part of group members that they will be able to accomplish, or contribute to, the accomplishment of the mission

In practice, few charismatic leaders would have all nine of these effects on people, yet many of them might take place. Few professionals today, for example, are likely to have unquestioning acceptance of the leader because most professionals today expect leadership to be somewhat shared.

Jane A. Halpert factor-analyzed (statistically clustered) these nine hypothesized outcomes into three groups or dimensions, as outlined in Figure 3-1.[8] The first six effects refer to the power exerted by the leader. Three of them (similarity of beliefs, affection for the leader, identification with and emulation of the leader) are related to **referent power**, the ability to influence others because of one's desirable traits and characteristics. Three other effects (group member trust, unquestioning acceptance, and willing obedience) are related to **expert power**, the ability to influence others because of one's specialized knowledge, skills, or abilities.

The last three effects are perceptions related to the task or mission. Halpert notes that these effects (emotional involvement, heightened goals, and perceived ability to contribute) are concerned with *job involvement:* charismatic leaders encourage group members to be involved in their jobs. Job involvement is a key component of job satisfaction, and one empirical study has provided evidence of the relationship between charismatic leadership and job satisfaction. Using a sample of state government employees, the researchers found that managers who rated their own managers as high on charisma tended to have high job satisfaction with supervision. The study

**FIGURE 3-1** Halpert's Dimensions of Charisma

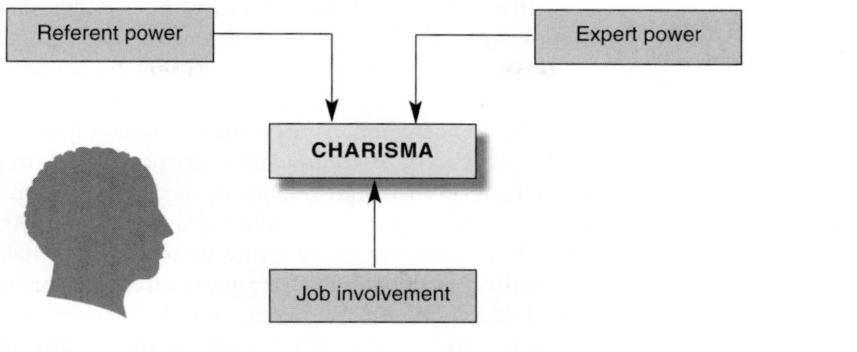

also found that working for a charismatic leader enhanced commitment to the organization.[9]

In summary, the nine charismatic effects in House's theory can be reduced to three dimensions: referent power, expert power, and job involvement. Such information is useful for the aspiring charismatic leader. To be charismatic, one must exercise referent power and expert power and must get people involved in their jobs.

## Types of Charismatic Leaders

The everyday use of the term *charisma* suggests that it is a straightforward and readily understood trait. As already explained, however, charisma has different meanings and dimensions. As a result, charismatic leaders can be categorized into five types: socialized charismatics, personalized charismatics, office-holder charismatics, personal charismatics, and divine charismatics.[10]

Following the distinction made for the power motive, some charismatic leaders use their power for the good of others. A **socialized charismatic** is a leader who restrains the use of power in order to benefit others. This type of leader also attempts to bring group members' values in line with his or her own values. The socialized charismatic formulates and pursues goals that fulfill the needs of group members and provide intellectual stimulation to them. Followers of socialized charismatics are autonomous, empowered, and responsible.

A second type of charismatic leader is the **personalized charismatic**. Such individuals serve primarily their own interests and so exercise few restraints on their use of power. Personalized charismatics impose self-serving goals on constituents, and they offer consideration and support to group members only when it facilitates their own goals. Followers of personalized charismatics are typically obedient, submissive, and dependent.

Another type of charismatic leader is the *office-holder charismatic*. For this type of leader, charismatic leadership is more a property of the office occupied than of his or her personal characteristics. The chief executive officer of the Procter & Gamble Company, for example, might have considerable luster but would lose much of it immediately after leaving office. Office-holder charismatics attain high status by occupying a valuable role.

In contrast to office-holder charismatics, *personal* (not *personalized*) *charismatics* gain very high esteem through the faith others have in them. A personal charismatic exerts influence whether he or she occupies a low- or high-status position because he or she has the right traits, characteristics, and behaviors. Former Secretary of State Colin H. Powell would qualify in the eyes of many as a personal charismatic. After retiring from his position as the top-ranking U.S. Army general, Powell was deluged with offers to serve on corporate boards and to make speaking appearances. He was eventually appointed as secretary of state in the George W. Bush administration and served during Bush's first term.

An historically important type of charismatic leader is the *divine charismatic*. Originally, charismatic leadership was a theological concept: a divine charismatic was someone endowed with a gift of divine grace. In 1924 Max Weber defined a charismatic leader as a mystical, narcissistic, and personally magnetic savior who would arise to lead people through a crisis. When Steven Jobs helped lead Apple Computer back to profitability and acclaim in the late 1990s, and when he spearheaded the iPod several years later, many company employees and Apple Computer fans reacted to him as if he were a divine charismatic. At stockholder meetings, some stockholders screeched and cheered as if Jobs were a famous rock star.

## Characteristics of Charismatic Leaders

The outstanding characteristic of charismatic leaders is that they are charismatic! They also have other distinguishing characteristics. Because charisma is a key component of transformational leadership, many of these characteristics also apply to transformational leaders. A **transformational leader** is one who brings about positive, major changes in an organization. Many charismatic leaders, however, are not transformational. Although they inspire people, they may not bring about major organizational changes. As we look at the characteristics of charismatic leaders,[11] you will note that many of these characteristics apply to leaders in general.

First, charismatic leaders are *visionary* because they offer an exciting image of where the organization is headed and how to get there. A vision is more than a forecast; it describes an ideal version of the future of an entire organization or an organizational unit. The next section provides additional information about vision in leadership, including guidelines on how to develop a vision. Chapter 13, in discussing the leadership aspects of business strategy, also contains information about formulating visions.

Charismatic leaders also have *masterful communication skills.* To inspire people, the charismatic leader uses colorful language and exciting metaphors and analogies. (More about the communication skills of charismatic leaders is presented later in this chapter.) Another key characteristic is the *ability to inspire trust.* Constituents believe so strongly in the integrity of charismatic leaders that they will risk their careers to pursue the chief's vision. Charismatic leaders are also *able to make group members feel capable*. Sometimes they do this by enabling group members to achieve success on relatively easy projects. They then praise the group members and give them more demanding assignments.

In addition, charismatic leaders have an *energy and action orientation*. Like entrepreneurs, most charismatic leaders are energetic and serve as role models for getting things done on time. *Emotional expressiveness and warmth* are also notable. A key characteristic of charismatic leaders is the ability to express feelings openly. A bank vice president claims that much of the charisma people attribute to her can be explained very simply: "I'm up front about expressing positive feelings. I praise people, I hug them, and I cheer if necessary. I also express my negative feelings, but to a lesser extent." Nonverbal emotional expressiveness, such as warm gestures and frequent (nonsexual) touching of group members, is also characteristic of charismatic leaders.

Because emotional expressiveness is such an important part of being and becoming charismatic, you are invited to take Leadership Self-Assessment Quiz 3-1 on page 74. It will help you think about a practical way of developing charismatic appeal.

Another trait of charismatic leaders is that they *romanticize risk*. They enjoy risk so much that they feel empty in its absence. Jim Barksdale, now a venture capitalist for online startup companies and former CEO of Netscape, says that the fear of failure is what increases your heart rate. As great opportunists, charismatic people yearn to accomplish activities others have never done before. Risk taking adds to a person's charisma because others admire such courage. In addition to treasuring risk, charismatic leaders use *unconventional strategies* to achieve success. The charismatic leader inspires others by formulating unusual strategies to achieve important goals. Anita Roddick, the founder of the worldwide chain of cosmetic stores called The Body Shop, accomplishes her goals unconventionally: she travels around the world into native villages, searching out natural beauty products that in the manufacturing process do not harm the environment or animals.

Charismatic leaders often have a *self-promoting personality*. They frequently toot their own horn and allow others to know how important they are. Richard Branson, the colorful chairman of the Virgin Group, has relied on self-promotion to build his empire, a collection of about 200 companies with the Virgin trademark. Among his antics have been flying around the world in a balloon and sliding down the side of a silver ball attached to a New York City building. He also conducts much of his business electronically from his private island in the Virgin Islands.

Another characteristic observed in many charismatic leaders is that they challenge, prod, and poke. They test your courage and your self-confidence by asking questions like "Do your employees really need you?" Donald Trump regularly asks his builders why they cannot construct a part of a building to look better, yet at lower cost.

A final strategy for becoming more charismatic is really an amalgam of the ideas already introduced: being *dramatic and unique* in significant, positive ways is a major contributor to charisma. This quality stems from a combination of factors, such as being energetic, promoting yourself, romanticizing risk, and being emotionally expressive. Andrea Jung, the chief executive of Avon Products, Inc., is dramatic and unique in the sense that she expresses love for all the Avon ladies.

## THE EMOTIONAL EXPRESSIVENESS SCALE

**INSTRUCTIONS** Indicate how well each of the following statements describes you by circling the best answer: very inaccurately (VI), inaccurately (I), neutral (N), accurately (A), very accurately (VA).

|  | VI | I | N | A | VA |
|---|---|---|---|---|---|
| 1. While watching a movie I sometimes shout in laughter or approval. | 1 | (2) | 3 | 4 | 5 |
| 2. During a group meeting, I have occasionally shouted my approval with a statement such as "Yes" or "Fantastic." | 1 | 2 | (3) | 4 | 5 |
| 3. During a group meeting, I have occasionally expressed disapproval by shouting an expression such as "absolutely not" or "horrible." | 1 | (2) | 3 | 4 | 5 |
| 4. Several times, while attending a meeting, someone has said to me, "You look bored." | 5 | (4) | 3 | 2 | 1 |
| 5. Several times while attending a social gathering, someone has said to me, "You look bored." | 5 | 4 | (3) | 2 | 1 |
| 6. Many times at social gatherings or business meetings, people have asked me, "Are you falling asleep?" | 5 | 4 | (3) | 2 | 1 |
| 7. I thank people profusely when they do me a favor. | 1 | 2 | 3 | (4) | 5 |
| 8. It is not unusual for me to cry at an event such as a wedding, graduation ceremony, or engagement party. | 1 | 2 | 3 | (4) | 5 |
| 9. Reading about or watching news events, such as an airplane crash, brings tears to my eyes. | 1 | 2 | (3) | 4 | 5 |
| 10. When I was younger, I got into more than my share of physical fights or shouting matches. | 1 | (2) | 3 | 4 | 5 |
| 11. I dread having to express anger toward a coworker. | 5 | 4 | 3 | (2) | 1 |
| 12. I have cried among friends more than once. | 1 | 2 | (3) | 4 | 5 |

| | | VI | I | N | A | VA |
|---|---|---|---|---|---|---|
| **13.** | Other people have told me that I am affectionate. | 1 | ②| 3 | 4 | 5 |
| **14.** | Other people have told me that I am cold and distant. | 5 | 4 | 3 | ② | 1 |
| **15.** | I get so excited watching a sporting event that my voice is hoarse the next day. | 1 | ② | 3 | 4 | 5 |
| **16.** | It is difficult for me to express love toward another person. | 5 | 4 | 3 | ② | 1 |
| **17.** | Even when alone, I will sometimes shout in joy or anguish. | 1 | ② | 3 | 4 | 5 |
| **18.** | Many people have complimented me on my smile. | 1 | ② | 3 | 4 | 5 |
| **19.** | People who know me well can easily tell what I am feeling by the expression on my face. | 1 | 2 | 3 | ④ | 5 |
| **20.** | More than once, people have said to me, "I don't know how to read you." | 5 | 4 | 3 | ② | 1 |

SCORING AND INTERPRETATION Add the numbers you circled, and use the following as a guide to your level of emotionality with respect to being charismatic and dynamic.

- **90–100:** Your level of emotionality could be interfering with your charisma. Many others interpret your behavior as being out of control.
- **70–89:** Your level of emotionality is about right for a charismatic individual. You are emotionally expressive, yet your level of emotional expression is not so intense as to be bothersome.
- **20–69:** Your level of emotionality is probably too low to enhance your charisma. To become more charismatic and dynamic, you must work hard at expressing your feelings.

If you believe that emotional expressiveness is a trait and behavior out of your reach or inclination, direct your efforts toward developing other traits and behaviors associated with charisma. For example, you could work on developing vision and taking risks.

## The Vision Component of Charismatic Leadership

A major buzzword in leadership and management is **vision**, the ability to imagine different and better conditions and ways to achieve them. A vision is a lofty, long-term goal. An effective leader is supposed to have a vision, whereas an ineffective leader either lacks a vision or has an unclear one. Creating a vision is one of the major tasks of top management. According to Jim Collins, a vision statement is likely to be more inspirational when it combines three elements:

1. A reason for being beyond making money
2. Timeless, unchanging core values
3. Ambitious but achievable goals

Mechanisms should then be established that set the values into action. A well-known example is that 3M encourages scientists to spend 15 percent of their time on whatever they want; this policy supports the company vision of being a world-class innovator.[12]

A vision is also considered an important part of strategy implementation. Implementing the vision (or ensuring that the vision is executed) is part of the leader's role. This is true despite the opinion that the leader creates the vision and the manager implements it. Jürgen Schrempp, the former chairman of DaimlerChrysler, believes strongly that the leader must also help execute his or her vision. "The chief should not be the one who just sort of guides the board on vision and strategy. You should also know what you are talking about. I go to the factories and we have debates on how cars should look five years from now."[13]

Visions have become so popular that some companies have them reproduced on wallet-size plastic cards, key rings, and coffee mugs. It has been said than an effective vision fits on a T-shirt. Here are several sample vision statements:

*Avon Products, Inc.:* The ultimate relationship marketer of products and services for women.

*Microsoft Corporation:* To enable people throughout the word to realize their potential.

*Vietnam Airlines:* The strategic vision for Vietnam Airlines in the next 10 to 20 years is to become one of the best airlines in the region, to operate efficiently, and to become even better at meeting the increasing requirements of the society for air transportation.

*Tommy Hilfiger Corporation:* Be whatever our customers want us to be.

Although many vision statements appear as if they could be formulated in fifteen minutes, managers invest considerable time in their preparation and often use many sources of data. To create a vision, obtain as much information from as many of the following sources as necessary:

- Your own intuition about developments in your field, the market you serve, demographic trends in your region, and the preferences of your constituents.
- The work of futurists (specialists in making predictions about the future) as it relates to your type of work.
- A group discussion of what it takes to delight the people your group serves.
- Annual reports, management books, and business magazines to uncover the type of vision statements formulated by others.
- Group members and friends; speak to them individually and collectively to learn of their hopes and dreams for the future.
- For a vision for an organizational unit, the organization's vision. You might get some ideas for matching your unit's vision with that of the organization.

Leadership Skill-Building Exercise 3-1 gives you an opportunity to practice vision formulation. Keep in mind that a critic of vision statements once said that it is often difficult to tell the difference between a vision and a hallucination.

---

**LEADERSHIP SKILL-BUILDING EXERCISE 3-1**

### FORMULATING A VISION

Along with your teammates, assume the role of the top management group of an organization or organizational unit that is in need of revitalization. Your revitalization tactic is to create a vision for the organization. Express the vision in not more than twenty-five words, using the guidelines for developing a vision described in the text. Come to an agreement quickly on the organization or large organizational unit that needs a vision. Or choose one of the following:

- The manufacturer of an electric-powered automobile
- A distributor of paid-for online music
- A waste disposal company
- The human resources department of a large company
- A manufacturer of watches retailing for a minimum of $25,000

---

## The Communication Style of Charismatic Leaders

Charismatic and transformational leaders communicate their visions, goals, and directives in a colorful, imaginative, and expressive manner. In addition, they communicate openly with group members and create a comfortable communication climate. To set agendas that represent the interests of their constituents, charismatic leaders regularly solicit constituents' viewpoints on critical issues. They encourage two-way communication with team members while still promoting a sense of confidence.[14] Here we describe two related aspects of the communication style of charismatic leaders: management by inspiration and management by anecdote.

### Management by Inspiration

According to Jay A. Conger, the era of managing by dictate is being replaced by an era of managing by inspiration. An important way to inspire others is to articulate a highly emotional message. Roger Enrico, the long-time dynamic CEO of PepsiCo, Inc., directed a leadership development program for selected company managers. At the outset of the program, he knocked participants off balance by telling them "nobody in this room can look at the company's problems and blame the turkeys at the top. You're now one of them."[15] Conger has observed two major rhetorical techniques of inspirational leaders: the use of metaphors and analogies, and the ability to gear language to different audiences.[16]

**Using Metaphors and Analogies** A well-chosen analogy or metaphor appeals to the intellect, to the imagination, and to values. The charismatic Mary Kay Ash (now deceased), founder of the cosmetics company Mary Kay Inc., made frequent use of metaphors during her career. To inspire her associates to higher performance, she often said: "You see, a bee shouldn't be able to fly; its body is too heavy for its wings. But the bumblebee doesn't know that and it flies very well." Mary Kay explained the message of the bumblebee metaphor in these terms: "Women come to us not knowing they can fly. Finally, with help and encouragement, they find their wings—and then they fly very well indeed."[17]

***Gearing Language to Different Audiences*** Metaphors and analogies are inspiring, but effective leaders must also choose the level of language that will suit their audience. This is important because constituents vary widely in verbal sophistication. One day, for example, a CEO might be attempting to inspire a group of Wall Street financial analysts, and the next day she or he might be attempting to inspire first-level employees to keep working hard despite limited salary increases.

An executive's ability to speak on a colloquial level helps create appeal. A person with the high status of an executive is expected to use an elevated language style. When the person unexpectedly uses the everyday language of an operative employee, it may create a special positive response. One of the many reasons Donald Trump is so popular with construction workers and tradespeople is that he often speaks to them in a tough-guy language familiar to them.

## *Management by Anecdote*

Another significant aspect of the communication style of charismatic and transformational leaders is that they make extensive use of memorable anecdotes to get messages across. **Management by anecdote** is the technique of inspiring and instructing team members by telling fascinating stories. The technique is a major contributor to building a strong company culture. When David Armstrong was an executive at Armstrong International, he used the following anecdote to reinforce the importance of listening to customers:

> Bill, our sales manager, wanted to add an obsolete feature to our company's new fish finder. We thought he was crazy. Bill knew that we preferred only to offer high-end, advanced products in order to hold on to our market share. The "flasher mode" he wanted to add to our fish finders was outdated, since it only told the fishers that fish were nearby—while our new computerized models would also indicate the fish's location and size.
>
> Who on earth would want the old-fashioned fish finder? Our customers, as it turned out. Many of them were old-time fishermen and didn't feel comfortable with the newfangled model, which confused them. They wanted the kind of machine they were used to.
>
> Nobody agreed with Bill at first, but eventually he got his way. We put the "flasher" back on the fish finder. Customers are still calling us to tell us how much they like this feature. We've sold a lot more units, because we listened to the market.[18]

After Armstrong tells this story, he explains the lessons illustrated by the story. One is, "Listen, listen, listen to your salespeople and your customers. Get direct feedback and don't second-guess them." Another is, "Ask yourself if this feature is necessary. Technology is not an end in itself." The third lesson is that classic products can out-sell new products. Experts told the Coca-Cola Company to change its formula, but Coca-Cola drinkers did not agree.[19]

Storytelling as a leadership tool has been elevated to such a level that some companies hire corporate storytelling consultants to help their executives develop the art. Storytelling is also useful for consultants who have to develop good connections with their clients.[20] Being charismatic helps the consultant attract and retain clients.

To get started developing the skill of management by anecdote (or storytelling), do Leadership Skill-Building Exercise 3-2.

**LEADERSHIP SKILL-BUILDING EXERCISE 3-2**

## CHARISMATIC LEADERSHIP BY ANECDOTE

INSTRUCTIONS Gather in a small problem-solving group to develop an inspiring anecdote about something that actually happened, or might have happened, at a present or former employer. Here are some guidelines:

1. Make up a list of core values the firm holds dear, such as quality, service, or innovation.

2. Think of an incident in which an employee strikingly lived up to (or violated) one of these values. Write it up as a story with a moral.

3. Share your stories with other members of the class, and discuss whether this exercise could make a contribution to leadership development.

SOURCE: From "Management by Anecdote," *SUCCESS*, December 1992, p. 35. Copyright © 1992 SUCCESS Publishing Inc. Reprinted by permission.

## The Development of Charisma

A person can increase his or her charisma by developing some of the traits, characteristics, and behaviors of charismatic people. Several of the charismatic characteristics described earlier in the chapter are capable of development. For example, most people can enhance their communication skills, become more emotionally expressive, take more risks, and become more self-promoting. In this section we examine several behaviors of charismatic people that can be developed through practice and self-discipline. We also look at evidence that charisma can be taught. The Leadership Self-Assessment Quiz 3.2 gives you an opportunity to think through how much development you might need in terms of *personal magnetism*, a type of sparkle that attracts other people to you and that adds to your charisma.

# THE PERSONAL MAGNETISM DEFICIT INVENTORY

**INSTRUCTIONS** Insufficient personal magnetism could be blocking your career growth, assuming you are already technically competent and hard working. To test how much magnetism you have, respond to the following statements in terms of Yes, No, or Not Applicable (NA).

| | Yes | No | NA |
|---|:---:|:---:|:---:|
| 1. It has been a long time since you received new assignments and/or promotions in your job. | ☐ | ☒ | ☐ |
| 2. You have been a downsizing victim at two or more firms. | ☐ | ☒ | ☐ |
| 3. People rarely ask for your opinion during a meeting. | ☐ | ☒ | ☐ |
| 4. You were absent from a meeting and nobody commented later that you were missed. | ☐ | ☒ | ☐ |
| 5. Almost nobody wants you to become a member of his or her network. | ☐ | ☒ | ☐ |
| 6. When you join a new team, you are rarely nominated to be the leader. | ☒ | ☐ | ☐ |
| 7. Your jokes and witty comments rarely receive much of a reaction from others. | ☐ | ☒ | ☐ |
| 8. Coworkers or fellow students seldom mention your name during meetings or other gatherings. | ☐ | ☒ | ☐ |
| 9. Other people rarely quote statements that you make. | ☐ | ☒ | ☐ |
| 10. You frequently make a statement or volunteer your opinion during a meeting, and you barely receive a reaction. | ☐ | ☒ | ☐ |
| 11. A person you know received a compliment for wearing a certain outfit, yet nobody complimented you when you wore almost the identical outfit. | ☐ | ☒ | ☐ |
| 12. People you attempt to lead rarely act inspired. | ☒ | ☐ | ☐ |
| 13. You rarely receive email messages or instant messages from contacts unless they are in response to your message. | ☐ | ☒ | ☐ |
| 14. In school, you were never (or are never) nominated to be the captain of a team or the head of a club. | ☒ | ☐ | ☐ |
| 15. Strangers rarely smile at you. | ☐ | ☒ | ☐ |

16. When in a public building or airport, a stranger rarely opens the door for you. ☒ ☐ ☐

17. When at a social gathering, you usually have to initiate conversations because few people start talking to you spontaneously. ☐ ☒ ☐

18. You receive few compliments on the job, in school, or in personal life. ☐ ☒ ☐

19. People tend to yawn frequently in face-to-face interactions with you. ☐ ☒ ☐

20. You cannot recall anyone ever saying that you are dynamic or that you have a sparkling personality. ☒ ☐ ☐

---

INTERPRETATION Very few people would be able to say that they have had none or only one of the twenty experiences just listed. But you may need to develop your personal magnetism and your charisma if you have had five or more of these experiences. The information in this section of the chapter and in the corresponding references could help you become more magnetic and charismatic.

## Techniques for Developing Charisma

**Create Visions for Others** Being able to create visions for others will be a major factor in your being perceived as charismatic. A vision uplifts and attracts others. To form a vision, use the guidelines presented previously in the chapter. The visionary person looks beyond the immediate future to create an image of what the organization or unit is capable of becoming. A vision is designed to close the discrepancy between current and ideal conditions. The vision thus sees beyond current realities.

Another characteristic of an effective vision formulated by the leader is that it connects with the goals and dreams of constituents.[21] For example, the leader of a group that is manufacturing fuel cells for electric cars might listen to team members talk about their desires to help reduce pollution in the atmosphere and then base the vision statement on a "desire to save the planet" or "reduce global warming."

**Be Enthusiastic, Optimistic, and Energetic** A major behavior pattern of charismatic people is their combination of enthusiasm, optimism, and high energy. Without a great amount of all three characteristics, a person is unlikely to be perceived as charismatic by many people. A remarkable quality of charismatic people is that they maintain high enthusiasm, optimism, and energy throughout their entire workday and beyond. Elevating your energy level takes considerable work, but here are a few feasible suggestions:

1. Get ample rest at night, and sneak in a fifteen-minute nap during the day when possible. If you have a dinner meeting where you want to shine, take a shower and nap before the meeting.

2. Exercise every day for at least ten minutes, including walking. No excuses are allowed, such as being too busy or too tired, or the weather being a handicap.
3. Switch to a healthy, energy-enhancing diet.
4. Keep chopping away at your To Do list so you do not have unfinished tasks on your mind, because they will drain your energy.

An action orientation helps you be enthusiastic, optimistic, and energetic. "Let's do it" is the battle cry of the charismatic person. An action orientation also means that the charismatic person prefers not to agonize over dozens of facts and nuances before making a decision.

**Be Sensibly Persistent** Closely related to the high energy level of charismatics is their almost-never-accept-no attitude. I emphasize the word *almost* because outstanding leaders and individual contributors also know when to cut their losses. If an idea or a product will not work, the sensible charismatic absorbs the loss and moves in another, more profitable direction. An executive at a telecom company said, "A test of executive material in our company is whether the middle manager has the guts to kill a failed project. Some managers become so ego-involved in a product they sponsored, they fight to keep it alive long after it should have died. They twist and distort financial information to prove that there is still life left in their pet product. A person with executive potential knows when to fold his or her tent."

**Remember Names of People** Charismatic leaders, as well as other successful people, can usually remember the names of people they have seen only a few times. (Sorry, no charisma credits for remembering the names of everyday work associates.) This ability is partly due to the strong personal interest charismatic leaders take in other people.

The surest way to remember names, therefore, is to really care about people. Failing that, the best way to remember a name is to listen carefully to the name, repeat it immediately, and study the person's face. You can also use the many systems and gimmicks available for remembering names, such as associating a person's name with a visual image. For example, if you meet a woman named Betsy Applewhite, you can visualize her with an apple (or a white personal computer) on her head. The best system of name retention remains to listen carefully to the name, repeat it immediately, and study the person's face.

**Make an Impressive Appearance** By creating a polished appearance, a person can make slight gains in projecting a charismatic image. A few people can make great gains by looking good. Ralph Lauren, the most successful fashion designer in American history,[22] is a leader who has enhanced his charisma through his impeccable physical appearance. Given that he is in the fashion business, a "Ralph Lauren–like" appearance is important for his personal image as well as to help build a brand image.

However, in most cases the effect of appearance depends on the context. If exquisite clothing and good looks alone made a person a charismatic leader, those impressive-looking store associates in upscale department stores would all be charismatic leaders. Therefore, in attempting to enhance your charisma through appearance, it is necessary to analyze your work environment to assess what type of appearance is impressive. Ralph Lauren, with his exquisite suits, cuff links, and pocket handkerchief, would create a negative image at a Silicon Valley firm: his carefully cultivated appearance would detract from his charisma. (Of course, Lauren could enhance his charisma by wearing clothing from his sporty Polo line.)

Despite these caveats, there is much you can do to enhance your appearance. In recent years there has been a surge of image consultants who help businesspeople develop an appearance that is useful in influencing people and getting hired. These consultants perform such services as helping you shop for a new wardrobe, suggesting a new hairstyle, or helping you revamp your slouching posture.[23]

**Be Candid** Charismatic people, especially effective leaders, are remarkably candid with people. Although not insensitive, the charismatic person is typically explicit in giving his or her assessment of a situation, whether the assessment is positive or negative. Charismatic people speak directly rather than indirectly, so that people know where they stand. Instead of asking a worker, "Are you terribly busy this afternoon?" the charismatic leader will ask, "I need your help this afternoon. Are you available?"

**Display an In-Your-Face Attitude** The preferred route to being perceived as charismatic is to be a positive, warm, and humanistic person. Yet some people earn their reputation for charisma by being tough and nasty. An in-your-face attitude may bring you some devoted supporters, although it will also bring you many detractors. The tough attitude is attractive to people who themselves would like to be mean and aggressive.

### Instruction in Charisma: Research Evidence

Research with a group of German managers demonstrates that certain aspects of charisma can be taught and learned. A one-and-one-half-day training program that teaches inspirational communication as part of charismatic leadership was evaluated in two studies with a total of forty-seven managers. A research design was developed to compare public speakers who had received training in the behaviors of inspirational communication with public speakers who had not received such training. Measurements of charismatic behaviors were made before and after training.

The training consisted of teaching managers about the verbal (spoken) aspects of inspiring workers, as well as the paralinguistic (nonverbal) aspects. As part of the training, participants were presented with principles of an inspirational speech; they were then videotaped as they spoke and received feedback on their performance. Role-playing was also used. The training produced several good results as measured by raters who listened to the inspirational speeches—in the use of gestures, metaphors, and emotional appeals. Similar results were not found for untrained behaviors.[24]

college.hmco.com/pic/
dubrin5e

**☯ @ KNOWLEDGE BANK:** Details of the study are presented in the Knowledge Bank.

## Transformational Leadership

Transformational leadership focuses on what the leader accomplishes rather than on the leader's personal characteristics and his or her relationship with group members.

As mentioned previously, the transformational leader helps bring about major, positive changes by moving group members beyond their self-interests and toward the good of the group, organization, or society. The essence of transformational leadership, according to a recent view, is developing and transforming people.[25] In contrast, the *transactional* leader focuses on more routine transactions rewarding group members for meeting standards (contingent reinforcement). Extensive research by Bernard M. Bass indicates that the transformational-versus-transactional distinction has been observed in a wide variety of organizations and cultures.[26]

So who is a transformational leader? One example is Greg Brenneman, the chairman and CEO of Burger King Corporation who is attempting to revitalize the company's declining market share. Brenneman is credited with previously helping turn around Continental Airlines, Inc., and the consulting arm of PricewaterhouseCoopers International Limited. In his savior role at Burger King, he is adding new domestic units as well as focusing on menu development to enhance same-store revenues. Shortly after Brenneman arrived, to boost morale he gave corporate staff members bonuses worth three times more than what they received the previous year. Because of his ability to revive a troubled company, Brenneman has been sought by several other companies, including Waste Management, Inc., to be their CEO.[27]

## How Transformations Take Place

Leaders often encounter the need to transform organizations from low performance to acceptable performance or from acceptable performance to high performance. At other times, a leader is expected to move a firm from a crisis mode to high ground. To accomplish these lofty purposes, the transformational leader attempts to overhaul the organizational culture or subculture. His or her task can be as immense as the process

**FIGURE 3-2  How Transformations Take Place**

**THE LEADER:**

1. Raises people's awareness
2. Helps people look beyond self-interest
3. Helps people search for self-fulfillment
4. Helps people understand need for change
5. Invests managers with sense of urgency
6. Is committed to greatness
7. Adopts a long-range, broad perspective
8. Builds trust
9. Concentrates resources where most needed

→ **TRANSFORMATIONS**

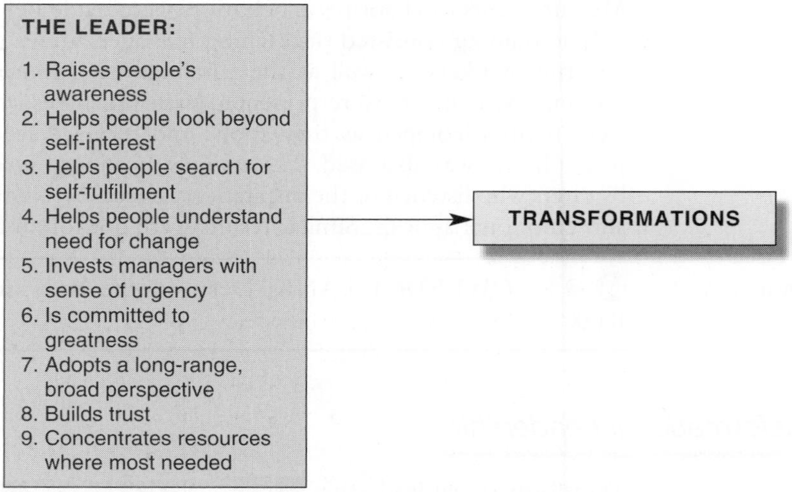

of organizational change. To focus our discussion specifically on the leader's role, we look at several ways in which transformations take place.[28] (See also Figure 3-2.)

1. *Raising people's awareness.* The transformational leader makes group members aware of the importance and values of certain rewards and how to achieve them. He or she might point to the pride workers would experience should the firm become number 1 in its field. At the same time, the leader should point to the financial rewards accompanying such success.

2. *Helping people look beyond self-interest.* The transformational leader helps group members look to "the big picture" for the sake of the team and the organization. The executive vice president of a bank told her staff members, "I know most of you dislike doing your own support work. Yet if we hire enough staff to make life more convenient for you, we'll be losing money. Then the government might force us to be taken over by a larger bank. Who knows how many management jobs would then have to be cut."

3. *Helping people search for self-fulfillment.* The transformational leader helps people go beyond a focus on minor satisfactions to a quest for self-fulfillment. The leader might explain, "I know that making sure you take every vacation day owed you is important. Yet if we get this proposal out on time, we might land a contract that will make us the envy of the industry." (Being the envy of the industry satisfies the need for self-fulfillment.)

4. *Helping people understand the need for change.* The transformational leader must help group members understand the need for change both emotionally and intellectually. The problem is that change involves dislocation and discomfort. An effective transformational leader recognizes this emotional component to resisting change and deals with it openly. Organizational change is much like a life transition. Endings must be successfully worked through before new beginnings are possible. People must become unhooked from their pasts.

   Dealing with the emotional conflicts of large numbers of staffers is obviously an immense task. One approach taken by successful leaders is to conduct discussion groups in which managers and workers are free to discuss their feelings about the changes. This approach has been used quite effectively when firms are downsized. Many of the "survivors" feel guilty that they are still employed while many competent coworkers have lost their jobs. Clearly, conducting these sessions requires considerable listening skill on the manager's part.

5. *Investing managers with a sense of urgency.* To create the transformation, the leader assembles a critical mass of managers and imbues in them the urgency of change. The managers must also share the top leader's vision of what is both necessary and achievable. To sell this vision of an improved organization, the transformational leader must capitalize on available opportunities.

6. *Committing to greatness.* Peter Koestenbaum argues that business can be an opportunity for individual and organizational greatness. By adopting this greatness attitude, leaders can ennoble human nature and strengthen societies. Greatness encompasses striving for business effectiveness such as profits and high stock value, as well as impeccable ethics. An emphasis on ethical leadership instills a desire for customer service and quality and fosters feelings of proprietorship and involvement.[29] (A commitment to greatness is, of course, important for all leaders, not just those who are charismatic.)

7. *Adopting a long-range perspective and at the same time observing organizational issues from a broad rather than a narrow perspective.* Such thinking on the part of the transformational leader encourages many group members to do likewise. Unless many people think with a future orientation, and broadly, an organization cannot be transformed.[30]

8. *Building trust.* Another useful process for transforming a firm is to build trust between leaders and group members, particularly because distrust and suspicion are rampant during a company revival. Executive Carlos Ghosn found that building trust was an essential ingredient of his turnaround efforts at Nissan Motors in Japan. One component of building trust was to impose transparency on the entire organization. In this way everyone knew what everyone else was doing.[31]

9. *Concentrating resources on areas that need the most change.* The turnaround artist or transformational leader cannot take care of all problems at once in a troubled organization. A practical strategy is to get around limitations on funds, staff, or equipment by concentrating resources on problem areas that are most in need of change and have the biggest potential payoff. For example, when police chief Bill Bratton turned around the much-maligned New York Police Department in the mid-1990s, he concentrated resources on the narcotics squad because so much crime is related to narcotics.[32] And Bill Brenneman added an Enormous Omelette Sandwich to the Burger King menu shortly after beginning his turnaround.

## Attributes of Transformational Leaders

Transformational leaders possess the personal characteristics of other effective leaders, especially charismatic leaders. In addition, a compilation of studies suggests that nine qualities are particularly helpful in enabling leaders to bring about transformations.[33]

Above all, transformational leaders are *charismatic.* Two key personality factors enhancing their charisma are agreeableness and extraversion, which combine to enhance their interpersonal relationships. Of these, extraversion had the biggest impact.[34] Unless they are the brutal slash-and-burn type of turnaround manager, transformational leaders have the respect, confidence, and loyalty of group members. One reason is that managers who use the transformational leadership style tend to score higher on *emotional intelligence.*[35]

Charismatic, transformational leaders create a *vision.* By communicating a vision, they convey a set of values that guide and motivate employees. Moreover, although transformational leaders are often greatly concerned with organizational survival, they also take the time to *encourage the personal development of their staff.* As group members develop, their performance is likely to increase. Transformational leaders also give *supportive leadership,* such as by giving positive feedback to group members and recognizing individual achievements. Supportive leadership also contributes to the development of group members.

Transformational leaders, like most effective leaders and managers, practice *empowerment* by involving team members in decision making. John Chambers of Cisco, who is somewhat of a transformational leader, regards empowerment as the distinguishing feature of his leadership. *Innovative thinking,* another important characteristic, helps transformational leaders achieve their goals; for example, they might develop innovative ways to raise cash and cut costs quickly. Transformational leaders encourage their staff to think innovatively as well and give them challenging assignments. As with other effective leaders and managers, they also *lead by example.* During a period of cost cutting, for example, a transformational leader might fly business coach and eat in the company cafeteria instead of having gourmet food catered to his or her office.

A study conducted with 132 managers and 407 subordinates indicated that managers who are perceived to be transformational score higher on a test of *moral reasoning* than do transactional leaders.[36] In contrast to the type of transformational leaders in the study just mentioned, those who specialize in rescuing failed corporations do not appear to score high in moral reasoning. Such actions include shutting down many company facilities, laying off much of the work force, and canceling contracts with various vendors.

Not every leader classified as transformational will have the nine characteristics just described. For example, some transformational leaders are brusque with people rather than agreeable. Furthermore, it is not always easy to determine whether a given leader can be accurately described as transformational.

The accompanying Leader in Action tells a story about a transformational leader. As you read the sketch, look for the leader's transformational behaviors and attributes.

## LEADER IN ACTION

### THE TRANSFORMATIONAL JOHN THOMPSON OF SYMANTEC

As chairman and CEO of Symantec Corporation, 55-year-old John Thompson trolls the waters of Silicon Valley to determine the hottest growth areas within the network security software industry and to identify potential acquisition targets with products that complement his company's software portfolio. He's good at it.

One of Symantec's recent deals, the $370 million acquisition of Brightmail Incorporated, gave it access to a suite of antispam technologies. Before that was the $100 million buyout of ON Technology Corporation, a provider of software used to rapidly deploy applications and operating systems. Deals such as these are all in a day's work for Thompson, who has spearheaded dozens of acquisitions since taking the helm in 1999. "Those [acquisitions] were, in essence, about expanding us and moving us into adjacent mar-

kets—adjacent to the security space—and expanding the opportunity pool for the company to compete in," Thompson said from the company's Cupertino, California, headquarters. "So our business opportunity or addressable market went from about $16 billion to almost $32 billion."

Thompson successfully has transformed Symantec from a $632 million consumer software company into a multinational market leader in enterprise security software with 5,600 employees and projected revenues of $2.41 billion for fiscal 2005. Under his leadership, the company's stock has risen more than 500 percent (compared with about a 40 percent loss for the tech-laden NASDAQ over the same period of time). In fact, during the five years since Thompson took over, Symantec stock has outperformed not only the stock of its chief competitors but also that of

*(continued)*

nearly every other major technology firm. These results make a powerful case for Thompson to be recognized as "the best CEO in Silicon Valley." For Symantec's explosive growth in the fast-paced and ever-changing world of network security, *Black Enterprise* selected Thompson to be Corporate Executive of the Year for 2004.

## MASTER OF THE TURNAROUND

Thompson's road to the executive suite of a company best known to consumers for its Norton AntiVirus product was a lengthy one. He grew up in South Florida, where his parents instilled in him a set of blue-collar values that he still applies today. He worked at odd jobs such as cutting grass, but even at an early age he wanted to go into business. "I always had this aspiration of someday being a businessman," Thompson recalls. "Now I don't know what that meant, because back in those days—in the early to mid-sixties—a business leader in the black community ran the local grocery store or might very well have had a dry cleaning service. A business in the black community back then was fairly localized, not something that had national or global scale."

After graduating with a business degree from Florida A & M University, Thompson joined IBM in 1971 as a sales representative. After ten years at IBM, he became a regional sales manager. One of Thompson's challenges at IBM was to turn around the company's failing Midwest region. The division had a high cost of sales and declining revenues, and the solution of Thompson's predecessors had been to cut a percentage of the sales force each year and hope that the cuts were deep enough to offset the declining revenue balance. So Thompson brought together a group of people who would remain responsible for customer relationships. Behind this group was a team of product specialists who would service accounts based on existing demand. The new model lowered costs, improved customer satisfaction, and allowed the business to stabilize its revenue performance while reducing the head count from roughly 9,000 to 4,400.

Shortly thereafter, Thompson ran IBM Americas, a $37-billion-a-year division, where he helped integrate ecommerce into the businesses and services of corporate and government clients throughout North America. While in this role, Thompson began to realize that he wanted a shot at running a company as CEO.

## BIGGER FISH IN A SMALLER POND

Unknown to Thompson at the time, the board of Symantec felt the company needed to go in a new direction, and a search was under way to find a replacement for the founder and CEO. After a series of interviews, Thompson felt Symantec was a perfect fit for him, and it allowed him to move from a corporate behemoth to a smaller, more nimble company.

In 1999, Symantec was a sort of mid-cap conglomerate in the software business, a company that managed brands, not technology and channels or customer relationships. (*Mid*-cap refers to middle-size value, such as $200 million of all the company stock outstanding.) Thompson decided to change all that and opted to focus on one technology category: security. And so two years before 9/11 brought security—including network security—to the forefront of the minds of Americans and the global community, Thompson and company jettisoned all technologies that were not relevant to securing the Internet infrastructure.

With the blessing of the board, Thompson had free rein to work his transformation. To this end, many of the firm's top managers were replaced. Even board members were replaced. According to Thompson, only two of the directors that were at Symantec when he arrived are still on board.

The turnaround plan was simple but effective: focus on a set of core technologies that target both the consumer and corporate/government entities. "By saying, 'We're going to become the leader in Internet security,' [we made] clear to everybody inside the company and outside what we were trying to get done," Thompson recalls.

Thompson's team spent over $2 billion on a series of acquisitions "all oriented around building up the portfolio or the capacity we have to do a better job of securing the transactions and the Internet infrastructure that customers have put in place," says Thompson. The company quickly began to emerge as the leading player in network security.

Analysts remain positive about the direction in which Thompson has taken the company. "The strategy, the vision, . . . is just really effective," says financial analyst Daniel Cummins. "If I got John right, I think he likes to keep everybody around him running scared and not complacent. He's obviously a good executor and manager, and he's been able to recruit similarly effective managers—some of whom have also come from IBM."

Richard A. Clarke, chairman of a homeland and cyber security advisory firm, says that "Thompson has the ability to make everybody like him and want to be with him in that sort of winning salesman personality, which is what he was—a salesman. But he combines that with a hard-nosed, make-it-happen determination, and a real understating of the detail and technology."

### QUESTIONS

1. In what way has John Thompson been a transformational leader?
2. What evidence do you find that John Thompson is charismatic?
3. What criticisms might you make of the way John Thompson brings about transformations?

SOURCE: Excerpted and adapted from Alan Hughes, "The Best CEO in Silicon Valley," *Black Enterprise*, September 2004, pp. 108–117. Copyright 2004. Reprinted with permission *Black Enterprise* magazine, New York, NY.

## The Impact of Transformational and Charismatic Leadership on Performance

Although the present discussion deals primarily with transformational leadership, it would be artificial to separate its impact on performance from that of charismatic leadership. An important reason is that charismatic leadership, as already discussed, is a component of transformational leadership. A concern some scholars have about transformational leadership is that it sounds too mystical and "soft." Fortunately, several empirical studies have been conducted on the effects of charismatic and transformational leadership in work settings. We review an overall analysis of the impact of transformational leadership and a specific study.

**Overall Validity of Transformational Leadership** Timothy A. Judge and Ronald F. Piccolo reviewed eighty-seven studies to examine the impact of transformational leadership on various measures of performance. The researchers also evaluated the impact of transactional leadership and laissez-faire leadership on performance. Laissez-faire leadership is a style that gives group members the freedom to do basically what they want with a minimum of direction. The three approaches to leadership were measured by questionnaires based on subordinates' perceptions.

Transformational leadership showed the highest overall relationships on six criteria: (a) follower job satisfaction, (b) follower leader satisfaction, (c) follower motivation, (d) leader job performance, (e) group or organization performance, and (f) rated leader effectiveness. Interestingly, transactional leadership was also shown to produce good results, and laissez-faire leadership was associated with negative results. Unlike previous studies, transactional leadership showed a strong positive relationship to transformational leadership. (Ordinarily, transformational leadership and transactional leadership are negatively related because transformational leaders are said not to engage in routine transactions with group members.) Transformational leadership was negatively related to laissez-faire leadership.[37] The explanation is most likely that transformational leaders are actively involved with group members.

**Business Unit Performance** As part of a larger study, Jane M. Howell and Bruce J. Avolio investigated the relationship of transformational leadership to business unit performance. The sample included seventy-eight managers from the highest four levels of management in a large Canadian financial institution. At the time of the study, the firm was facing a turbulent external environment because of increased competition. A modification of the MLQ Charismatic Leadership Scale was developed to measure three aspects of transformational leadership: charisma, intellectual stimulation, and individual consideration. The measure of business unit performance represented the degree to which the manager reached goals for the year, calculated in terms of the percentage of goals met. Each goal was measured against criteria for expected, superior, and outstanding performance.

Data analysis revealed that leaders who displayed more individualized consideration, intellectual stimulation, and charisma positively contributed to business unit performance. Leaders who used the techniques of management by exception and contingent rewards (positive reinforcement) were less likely to increase unit performance. The authors concluded that the more positive contribution to business unit performance came from behaviors associated with transformational leadership.[38]

## Concerns About Charismatic Leadership

Up to this point, an optimistic picture has been painted of both the concept of charisma and charismatic leaders. For the sake of fairness and scientific integrity, contrary points of view must also be presented. The topic of charismatic leadership has been challenged from two major standpoints: the validity of the concept, and the misdeeds of charismatic leaders.

### Challenges to the Validity of Charismatic Leadership

Some leadership researchers doubt that charisma can be accurately defined and measured. Conducting research about charisma is akin to conducting research about high quality: you know it when you see it, but it is difficult to define in operational terms. Furthermore, even when one leader is deemed to be charismatic, he or she has many detractors. According to the concept of **leadership polarity**, leaders are often either revered or vastly unpopular. People rarely feel neutral about them. Bill Gates is a prime example of leadership polarity. Thousands of people are almost mesmerized by Gates, but thousands of other people dislike him intensely (or are envious). About 200 web sites have accumulated of the nature "*www.ihatebillgates.com*" (a generic site not directing the reader to a specific site). Martha Stewart is another popular leader who experiences leadership polarity. Many of her fans are mesmerized by her personality and accomplishments. Many of her detractors detest her (perhaps based on envy) and were gleeful when Stewart was accused of insider trading and sent to prison.

Another problem with the concept of charisma is that it may not be necessary for leadership effectiveness. Warren Bennis and Burt Nanus have observed that very few leaders can accurately be described as charismatic. The organizational leaders the two researchers studied were "short and tall, articulate and inarticulate, dressed for success and dressed for failure, and there was virtually nothing in terms of physical appearance, personality, or style that set them apart from followers."

Based on these observations, Bennis and Nanus hypothesized that instead of charisma resulting in effective leadership, the reverse may be true: people who are outstanding leaders are granted charisma (perceived as charismatic) by their constituents as a result of their success.[39] A case in point is that as Steve Jobs of Apple Computer succeeded in making a major impact on the world of online music, his popularity surged again. During the period when Apple was not performing as well, attitudes toward Jobs were less positive.

## The Dark Side of Charismatic Leadership

Some people believe that charismatic leadership can be exercised for evil purposes. This argument was introduced previously in relation to personalized charismatic leaders. Years ago, Robert Tucker warned about the dark side of charisma, particularly with respect to political leaders:

> The magical message which mesmerizes the unthinking (and which can often be supplied by skilled phrase makers) promises that things will become not just better but perfect. Charismatic leaders are experts at promising Utopia. Since perfection is the end, often the most heinous actions can be tolerated as seemingly necessary means to that end.[40]

Some charismatic leaders are unethical and lead their organizations toward illegal and immoral ends. People are willing to follow the charismatic leader down a quasi-legal path because of his or her personal magnetism. Garry Winnick, the former chairman of Global Crossing Ltd., is a modern-day symbol of how gluttonous and destructive a charismatic leader can be. Winnick, a former junk bond broker, charmed thousands with his affable personality. He purchased several Rolls Royce automobiles as gifts for social friends and work associates. On the way to leading Global Crossing toward bankruptcy, he sold about $730 million of his own company stock. His workspace was a replica of the White House Oval Office. While thousands of workers were being laid off, Winnick was building the most expensive private residence in the world for himself and his family. With renovations, the property in Bel Air, California, was valued at about $90 million.

**READER'S ROADMAP**

In Chapter 2 we focus on the traits, motives, and characteristics of the leader—or the inner qualities of him or her. Here we dug further into leadership qualities by studying charismatic and transformational leadership. In the next chapter we focus more sharply on the actions of leaders in terms of their behaviors, attitudes, and styles.

## Summary

college.hmco.com/pic/dubrin5e

Charisma is a special quality of leaders whose purposes, powers, and extraordinary determination differentiate them from others. It is also a positive and compelling quality of a person that makes many others want to be led by that person. An important element of charismatic leadership involves the attributions made by group members about the characteristics of leaders and the results they achieve. Social network members often influence a person's attributions of charisma. The relationship between group members and the leader is important because of these attributions. Charismatic leaders frequently manage their impressions to cultivate relationships with group members.

Charismatic leadership can be understood in terms of its effects, such as group members' trust in the correctness of the leader's beliefs. One study showed that the effects of charismatic leadership can be organized into three dimensions: referent power, expert power, and job involvement. Charismatic leadership enhances job satisfaction.

Charismatic leaders can be subdivided into five types: socialized, personalized (self-interested), office-holder, personal (outstanding characteristics), and divine. Charismatic leaders have characteristics that set them apart from noncharismatic leaders: they have a vision, masterful communication skills, the ability to inspire trust, and the ability to make group members feel capable. They also have an energy and action orientation, are emotionally expressive and warm, romanticize risk, use unconventional strategies, have a self-promoting personality, and emphasize being dramatic and unique.

The idea of vision is closely linked to charisma because charismatic leaders inspire others with an uplifting and attractive vision. In formulating a vision, it is helpful to gather information from a variety of sources, including one's own intuition, futurists, and group members.

Charismatic and transformational leaders communicate their visions, goals, and directives in a colorful, imaginative, and expressive manner.

Communication effectiveness allows for management by inspiration. One technique for inspiring others is to use metaphors, analogies, and organizational stories. Another is gearing language to different audiences. Charismatic and transformational leaders also extensively use memorable anecdotes to get messages across.

A person can increase his or her charisma by developing some of the traits, characteristics, and behaviors of charismatic people. The suggestions presented here include creating visions for others; being enthusiastic, optimistic, and energetic; being sensibly persistent; remembering names of people; making an impressive appearance; being candid; and displaying an in-your-face attitude.

To bring about change, the transformational leader attempts to overhaul the organizational culture or subculture. Specific change techniques include raising people's awareness of the importance of certain rewards and getting people to look beyond their self-interests for the sake of the team and the organization. Transformational leaders help people search for self-fulfillment and understand the need for change, and they invest managers with a sense of urgency. The transformational leader also commits to greatness, adopts a long-range perspective, builds trust, and concentrates resources where change is needed the most.

Transformational leaders have characteristics similar to those of other effective leaders. In addition, they are charismatic, create a vision, encourage personal development of the staff, and give supportive leadership. Emphasis is also placed on empowerment, innovative thinking, and leading by example. Transformational leaders are likely to be strong on moral reasoning.

Transformational leadership is positively related to the criteria of follower job satisfaction, leader satisfaction, follower motivation, leader job performance, group or organization performance, and rated leader effectiveness. Transactional leadership attains the same results to a lesser degree, whereas laissez-faire leadership is negatively related to such criteria. Empirical research indicates that leaders who display more individualized consideration, intellectual stimulation, and charisma (transformational leaders) have high business unit performance.

One concern about charismatic and transformational leadership is that the concept is murky. Many noncharismatic leaders are effective. Another concern is that some charismatic leaders are unethical and devious, suggesting that being charismatic does not necessarily help the organization. By behaving in a socially responsible manner, charismatic leaders can avoid abusing their influence over others.

## Key Terms

Charisma

Referent power

Expert power

Socialized charismatic

Personalized charismatic

Transformational leader

Vision

Management by anecdote

Leadership polarity

## Guidelines for Action and Skill Development

Following are suggestions to help a person act in a charismatic manner. All of them relate to well-accepted interpersonal skill techniques.

1. **Be sure to treat everyone you meet as the most important person you will meet that day.** For example, when at a company meeting, shake the hand of every person you meet.

2. **Multiply the effectiveness of your handshake.** Shake firmly without creating pain, and make enough eye contact to notice the color of the other person's eyes. When you take that much trouble, you project care and concern. Think a positive thought about the person whose hand you shake.

3. **Give sincere compliments.** Most people thrive on flattery, particularly when it is plausible. Attempt to compliment only those behaviors, thoughts, and attitudes you genuinely believe merit praise. At times you may have to dig to find something praiseworthy, but it will be a good investment of your time.

4. **Thank people frequently, especially your own group members.** Thanking others is still so infrequently practiced that it gives you a charismatic edge.

5. **Smile frequently, even if you are not in a happy mood.** A warm smile seems to indicate a confident, caring person, which contributes to a perception of charisma. A smile generally says, "I like you. I trust you. I'm glad we're together."

6. **Maintain a childlike fascination for your world.** Express enthusiasm for and interest in the thoughts, actions, plans, dreams, and material objects of other people. Your enthusiasm directed toward others will engender enthusiasm in you.

7. **Be more animated than others.** People who are perceived to be more charismatic are simply more animated than others. They smile more frequently, speak faster, articulate better, and move their heads and bodies more often.[41]

## Discussion Questions and Activities

1. Athletes and other celebrities who smile frequently and wave to the audience are often described as being "charismatic." What is wrong or incomplete about this use of the term *charisma?*

2. Identify a business, government, education, or sports leader whom you perceive to be charismatic. Explain the basis for your judgment.

3. Identify a well-known leader who is *not* charismatic. Explain what other qualities might have helped this leader succeed.

4. Steve Jobs of Apple Computer, Inc., and many fashion designers wear the same outfit most of the time, even for press interviews and trade shows or fashion shows. The outfit consists of a long-sleeve or short-sleeve T-shirt and blue jeans without a belt. How does this costume affect their projection of charisma?

5. Describe how a person might write email messages to give an impression of being charismatic.

6. Aside from contributing to leadership effectiveness, for what other types of jobs might charisma be an asset?

7. Explain why the presence of a charismatic leader tends to enhance the job satisfaction of group members.

8. What opportunities might a first-level supervisor or team leader have to be a transformational leader?

9. A concern has been expressed that leaders who are charismatic are often incompetent. They simply get placed into key positions because they create such a good impression. What do you think of this argument?

10. Design a research study or survey to determine if being perceived as charismatic really helps a person advance in a managerial career.

 ## LEADERSHIP CASE PROBLEM A

### CAN ED ZANDER REINVENT MOTOROLA?

Ed Zander, a former Sun Microsystems executive and director of an investment firm, was appointed as the chairman and chief executive officer of Motorola, Inc., in January 2004. The talkative and affable Zander devoted his first three months on the job to listening. He heard an earful. For example, the chairman of an Egyptian telecom firm complained that year after year Motorola had not delivered on its promises, such as turning out cell phones on time.

**MOTOROLA'S BUSINESS SITUATION** In the span of a decade, Motorola has gone from technology titan to industry doormat. A wireless pioneer, it missed the shift from analog to digital cell phones and thus had to give up its number 1 market share to Nokia. It was once equal to Intel in microprocessors, but its semiconductor business dropped out of the upper echelon in that industry.

Signaling a need to break with the past, the company's board passed over popular internal candidate Mike Zafirovski, a General Electric veteran and Motorola's president and chief operating officer. In going to the outsider Zander, Motorola chose an executive with operational smarts and marketing savvy—he dreamed up the company-unifying message that Sun "put the dot in dot-com"—but no experience in wireless or consumer marketing. Zander was chosen in part because of his extraordinary energy and his focus on getting things done.

As Zander began his Motorola job, it was clear that his mission was nothing less than saving an iconic company that had lost its way. His first task was figuring out what Motorola really is. After Zander visited the corporate research and development labs, he remarked, "I didn't know we have all this." By the end of the day, he said, "I have a migraine" (*Fortune*, p. 128). In addition to products clearly related to communications, Motorola's researchers are working on projects as far afield as a device to test for cystic fibrosis and breakthrough technology in cathode-ray-tube televisions.

"One thing I've learned Motorola does really well is that it loves complex problems," Zander says. "The more things are gnarly, the better folks understand how to do it. I said, 'Look folks, we've got an arsenal here, a war chest of technology. But we've got to pick out big bets. We've got to narrow this list down'" (*Fortune*, p. 128).

For years, Motorola was defined by big bets that paid off, with the big bets landing it on every *Fortune* 500 list in the ranking's fifty-year history. Motorola rode up the list on the legacy of its leadership in car radios, path-breaking walkie-talkies for the U.S. Army in World War II, semiconductors wedged into everything from automobiles to washing machines, and finally cellular telephones, a business Motorola dominated in the mid-1990s. Since those days, Motorola has slipped considerably in sales in comparison to other companies on the *Fortune* 500 list.

Motorola's slide is explained by one flop after another from the mid-1990s forward. First it failed to anticipate the worldwide shift to digital cell phones and allowed Nokia to overtake it as the world's number 1 cell phone maker. Once a leader in wireless infrastructure equipment, Motorola's market share slid to 10 percent in 2003. The cable unit's revenues declined 49 percent since the cable companies slowed purchases and Motorola fell behind to competitors in delivering new products. Motorola's biggest blunder was the ten-plus years and $2.6 billion it lost in now-bankrupt Iridium, the satellite network famous for its brick-sized phones and dollars-per-minute international calls.

Motorola developed a reputation for owning killer technology that got stuck in the labs. Says Tom Lynch, a General Instrument Corporation veteran who now runs Motorola's cell phone business: "There are endless examples of instances where the company has blazed a trail and someone else has reaped the benefits" (*Fortune*, p. 130).

In recent years, Motorola mistakes have continued. An analyst from a market research firm, the Yankee Group, said that Motorola has missed out on just about every window that has opened. For example, when color-screen phones became hot in 2002, Motorola could not produce them in large volumes, and Samsung moved in to become the number 2 cell phone player by revenue.

Before hiring Zander, Motorola exited the chip business, whose boom-and-bust cycles did not fit well with the rest of the company. Motorola now has five businesses: cell phones, infrastructure equipment, two-way radio systems, electronic equipment for automobiles, and cable TV. Employment has dropped from 147,000 at the peak to 88,000 in 2004. Profits are about $890 million on sales of $27 billion. Since Zander has been in charge, sales and profits have climbed substantially.

**ZANDER AS A LEADER AND MANAGER** Zander grasps that repairing the company's image is his first order of business. He says he will judge his success when critics stop asking if Motorola is a disparate collection of standalone businesses. Zander is searching for a mission statement. He says, "The world wants me to come up with this grand vision, but what I'm hearing from customers right now is to execute and deliver products, and make the company more efficient" (*Fortune*, p. 132). So while Motorola may need a master plan, simply keeping promises is an equally urgent concern.

Zander says he needs a little more time to figure out what the mission statement should be. "I mean we're a communications company. But we still need to get what we want to identify with in this new millennium" (*Fortune*, p. 132).

Zander is enlisting help by visiting investors and Wall Street analysts to get their thoughts. He also asked a former electrical engineering professor to conduct investigations into Motorola's technology, and is visiting telephone companies around the world.

*(continued)*

To get a sense of the company, he uses his "common touch": he talks to key employees and listens to customers, trying to understand his new company's inner workings.

Whereas Zander's predecessor, Christopher B. Galvin, was reserved, polite, and genteel, Zander is a brash Brooklynite, incessantly pumping hands and flashing his trademark milewide smile. He uses his style to get results. In the past, employee bonuses were based on the performance of individual business units. But now Zander has made collaborating across the company a key factor in raises and bonuses. "If you don't cooperate and work together, I will kill you," Zander said (*BusinessWeek*, p. 82). He laughs and says that it is his way of explaining to people that they are going to fix things. He has been relentless in trying to get the most out of his staff. When the heads of each business unit first laid out their targets, Zander barked that they were sandbagging.

Zander's most dramatic effort to date is a plan to dismantle Motorola's debilitating bureaucracy and end a culture of internal rivalries so intense that employees have referred to its business units as "warring tribes." Zander has given early indication of wanting to reorganize the company around customer markets instead of product divisions.

Zander has begun to articulate a vision of the company in terms of its four big end markets: the individual, the home, the auto, and the big organization, including governments. He has also picked up on a theme the company had been pursuing before his arrival: seamless mobility, the unrealized opportunity for users to transfer their calls and data easily from office to car to home and back again. Videos could also be transferred from television to the phone and to the car. "If we declare that's the big five-year bet, then everybody in the company's got to get galvanized around it," Zander says (*Fortune*, p. 133).

By fall 2005 Zander was receiving credit for revitalizing Motorola as one of America's hottest big companies. Market share in cell phones was up 18 percent, and much of this growth was attributed to the ultrathin RAZR flip-top phone. The RAZR was in the works when Zander arrived, yet Zander became its champion and insisted that the phone have a catchy name.

## QUESTIONS

1. What would be an effective vision statement for Motorola?
2. Which types of transformations is Zander attempting to bring about?
3. What evidence do you find that Ed Zander has some charismatic qualities?
4. What criticisms might you make of Zander's leadership approach?

SOURCE: Adam Lashinsky, "Can Moto Find Its Mojo?" *Fortune*, April 5, 2004, pp. 126–132; Roger O. Crockett, "Reinventing Motorola," *BusinessWeek*, August 2, 2004, pp. 82–83; "Motorola Names Former Sun Chief," Rochester, New York, *Democrat and Chronicle*, December 17, 2003, p. 6D; "Management 101: Moto's Zander: Brilliant or Lucky?" *Fortune*, August 22, 2005, p. 20.

## LEADERSHIP CASE PROBLEM B

### CHARISMATICALLY CHALLENGED CHAD

Twenty-seven-year-old Chad McAllister worked as a merchandising specialist for ValuMart, one of the largest international retail chains. Based in the United States, ValuMart also has a strong presence in Canada, Europe, Japan, and Hong Kong. Chad began his employment with ValuMart as an assistant store manager, and two years later he was invited into the training program for merchandising specialists.

Chad performed well as a merchandising trainee in the soft-goods line. His specialty areas included men's, women's, and children's clothing, linens and bedding, men's and women's jewelry, and home decorations. For several years in a row, Chad received performance evaluation ratings of above average or outstanding. Among the write-in comments made by his supervisors were "diligent worker," "knows the tricks of merchandising," "good flair for buying the right products at the right price," and "fits right into the team."

Despite the positive performance evaluations supported with positive comments, Chad had a gnawing discontent about his career at ValuMart. Although he had five years of good performance, he was still not invited to become a member of the "ValuTrackers," a group of merchandising and operations specialists who are regarded as being on the fast track to becoming future ValuMart leaders. The leaders hold high-level positions such as head merchandiser, regional vice president, and store manager.

Several times when Chad inquired as to why he was not invited to join the ValuTrackers, he was told that he was not quite ready to be included in this elite group. He was also told to not be discouraged because the company still valued his contribution.

One day Chad thought to himself, "I'm headed toward age 30, and I want a great future in the retail business now." So he convinced his boss, the merchandising supervisor (Evan Tyler), to set up a career conference with three people: Chad, his boss, and his boss's boss (Heather Bridges), the area merchandising manager. He let Evan know in advance that he wanted to talk about his potential for promotion.

Evan started the meeting by saying, "Chad, perhaps you can tell Heather and me again why you requested this meeting."

Chad responded, "Thanks for asking, Evan. As I mentioned before, I'm wondering what you think is wrong with me. I receive a lot of positive feedback about my performance, but I'm not a ValuTracker. Also, you seem to change the subject when I talk about wanting to become a merchandising supervisor, and eventually a merchandising executive. What am I doing wrong?"

Heather responded, "Evan and I frequently talk about the performance and potential of all our merchandising specialists. You're a good performer, Chad, but you lack that little spark that makes a person a leader. You go about your job efficiently and quietly, but that's not enough. We want future leaders of ValuMart to make an impact."

Evan added, "I go along with Heather's comments. Another point, Chad, is that you rarely take the initiative to suggest ideas. I was a little shocked by your request for a three-way career interview because it's one of the few initiatives you have taken. You're generally pretty laid back."

"Then what do I have to do to convince you two that I should be a ValuTracker?" asked Chad.

Heather replied, "Start acting more like a leader. Be more charismatic. Be more personally magnetic." Evan nodded in agreement.

## QUESTIONS

1. What career advice can you offer Chad McAllister?
2. What might Chad McAllister do to develop more charisma?
3. What is your opinion of the fairness of the ValuTracker program?

## MY LEADERSHIP PORTFOLIO

How much charisma, or charismatic behaviors, have you exhibited this week? Think back to all your interactions with people in this last week or two. What have you done that might have been interpreted as charismatic? Review the characteristics of a charismatic leader described in the text and in the Guidelines for Action and Skill Development. For example, did you smile warmly at someone, did you wave to a person you see infrequently and address him or her by name? Did you help your team, club, or group think seriously about its future? As part of this same exercise, record your charismatic behaviors for the upcoming week. Be alert to opportunities for displaying charisma.

## INTERNET SKILL-BUILDING EXERCISE

Apply the chapter concepts! Visit the Web and complete this Internet skill-building exercise to learn more about current leadership topics and trends.

### CHARISMA TIPS FROM THE NET

A section in this chapter offered suggestions for becoming more charismatic. Search the Internet for additional suggestions and compare them to the suggestions in the text. A good starting point is *http://www.workstar.net/library/charisma.htm*. Be alert to contradictions, and offer a possible explanation for each contradiction. You might want to classify the suggestions into two categories: those dealing with the inner person, and those dealing with more superficial aspects of behavior. A suggestion of more depth would be to become a visionary, and a suggestion of less depth would be to wear eye-catching clothing.

# Leadership Behaviors, Attitudes, and Styles

In the buttoned-up, male-dominated world of automotive chieftains, Tower Automotive, Inc., CEO Kathleen Ligocki is an oddity. She had no intention of making a career in the automotive business when, twenty-five years ago, she took a job as a factory foreman at a General Motors Company plant in Kokomo, Indiana. Ligocki grew to love the pace and culture of the factory, and she moved a few years later to a GM sales job in Boston. For the past two decades, she has spent much of her career ascending the ranks at GM and then at Ford.

Ligocki then left her job as Ford's vice president of customer service to become president and chief executive of Tower, a growing but debt-laden auto supplier. The eleven-year-old Tower produces components and assemblies for every major automaker. Its primary product is metal body structures—the part of the car or truck beneath the "skin"—but it also makes power-train modules, suspension components, and other parts. Tower has more than 12,000 employees in fourteen countries and approximately sixty manufacturing, product development, and administrative sites around the world.

Ligocki, 47, said the decision to leave Ford was difficult, and she discussed it at length with Chairman Bill Ford. But it was a move that elevated Ligocki, who once ran Ford of Mexico, to what many consider the highest perch of any woman in the industry.

After traveling to 180 countries, Logocki believes that, while challenges exist for women in the male-dominated business, a female perspective can provide a competitive edge. "Women don't really separate work from home," she said. "If this were a group of women executives, in the same sentence we could be talking about the challenges of steel prices and the fact that I love your suit. Most international executives operate the same way. If you're in Mexico, you have to get to know people—their families, their interests—before you start talking business. That's natural for a woman."[1]

The brief statements made by the newly appointed CEO illustrate the possibility that gender differences exist in leadership style. At the same time, her insights point to the importance of relationship-oriented behaviors and attitudes—including having empathy for others—for achieving success as a leader. This chapter describes a number of key behaviors and attitudes that help a manager function as a leader. We also describe the closely related topic of leadership styles.

Frequent reference is made in this chapter, and at other places in the text, to leadership effectiveness. A working definition of an **effective leader** is one who helps group members attain productivity, including high quality and customer satisfaction.

## The Classic Dimensions of Consideration and Initiating Structure

Studies conducted at Ohio State University in the 1950s identified 1,800 specific examples of leadership behavior that were reduced to 150 questionnaire items on leadership functions.[2] The functions are also referred to as *dimensions of leadership behavior*. This research became the foundation for most of future research about leadership behavior, attitudes, and styles. The researchers asked team members to describe their supervisors by responding to the questionnaires. Leaders were also asked to rate themselves on leadership dimensions.

Two leadership dimensions accounted for 85 percent of the descriptions of leadership behavior: "consideration" and "initiating structure."

**Consideration** is the degree to which the leader creates an environment of emotional support, warmth, friendliness, and trust. The leader creates this environment by being friendly and approachable, looking out for the personal welfare of the group, keeping the group abreast of new developments, and doing small favors for the group.

Leaders who score high on the consideration factor typically are friendly and trustful, earn respect, and have a warm relationship with team members. Leaders with low scores on the consideration factor typically are authoritarian and impersonal in their relationships with group members. Five questionnaire items measuring the consideration factor are as follows:

1. Do personal favors for people in the work group.
2. Treat all people in the work group as your equal.
3. Be willing to make changes.
4. Back up what people under you do.
5. Do little things to make it pleasant to be a member of the staff.

The relationship-oriented behaviors described later in this chapter are specific aspects of consideration. Another key example of consideration is *making connections* with people. Julia Stewart, president of the Applebee's division of Applebee's International, Inc., believes that making connections is one of her most essential leadership functions. She spends about five minutes every day checking in with each of the nine managers who directly report to her. They talk about such social topics as where they ate over the weekend (even if it was not Applebee's). Stewart says that leaders cannot afford *not* to take time to chitchat. "I worry about the bosses who are in the crisis mode 80 or 90 percent of the time. By spending the first couple of minutes each day with the employees, I have more of an understanding of what makes them tick."[3]

Making connections with people is also important in today's globalized environment, where you have to work with a wide range of people and opinions. Jean Lipman-Blumen explains that leaders who can connect with a broad group of people will be the most successful.[4]

**Initiating structure** means organizing and defining relationships in the group by engaging in such activities as assigning specific tasks, specifying procedures to be followed, scheduling work, and clarifying expectations for team members. A team leader who helped group members establish realistic goals would be engaged in initiating structure. Other concepts that refer to the same idea include *production emphasis, task orientation,* and *task motivation.* The task-related leadership behaviors and attitudes described later in this chapter are specific aspects of initiating structure.

Leaders who score high on this dimension define the relationship between themselves and their staff members, as well as the role that they expect each staff member to assume. Such leaders also endeavor to establish well-defined channels of communication and ways of getting the job done. Five self-assessment items measuring initiating structure are as follows:

1. Try out your own new ideas in the work group.
2. Encourage the slow-working people in the group to work harder.

3. Emphasize meeting deadlines.
4. Meet with the group at regularly scheduled times.
5. See to it that people in the work group are working up to capacity.

A positive example of a leader who emphasizes initiating structure is James Albaugh, the defense chief at The Boeing Company. While managing at Rocketdyne, a rocket engine division, Albaugh reorganized the assembly line and trained workers to improve their efficiency. Colleagues remember him as somewhat of an obsessive manager. For example, Albaugh once left a manager a Post-it® note with a cigarette butt stuck to it—a reminder that efficiency includes sweeping the floor.[5]

Leaders have been categorized with respect to how much emphasis they place on the two dimensions of consideration and initiating structure. As implied by Figure 4-1, the two dimensions are not mutually exclusive. A leader can achieve high or low status on both dimensions. For example, an effective leader might contribute to high productivity and still place considerable emphasis on warm human relationships. The four-cell grid of Figure 4-1 is a key component of several approaches to describing leadership style. We return to this topic later in this chapter and in Chapter 5.

A new study of the validity of consideration and initiating structure indicates that these classic dimensions do indeed contribute to an understanding of leadership because they are related to leadership outcomes. A meta-analysis showed that consideration is strongly related to the job satisfaction of group members, satisfaction with the leader, worker motivation, and leader effectiveness. Initiating structure was slightly more strongly related to job performance, group performance, and organization performance. However, initiating structure was also associated with satisfaction and performance.[6] These results are encouraging because they reinforce the importance of this pioneering research.

**FIGURE 4-1 Four Combinations of Initiating Structure and Consideration**

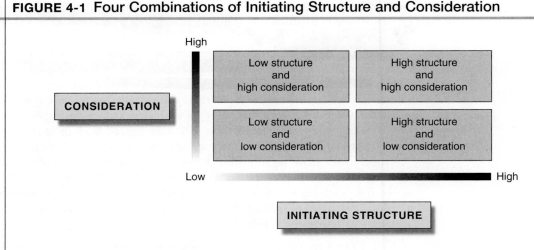

## Task-Related Attitudes and Behaviors

The task-related versus relationship-related classification remains a useful framework for understanding leadership attitudes, behaviors, and practices. This section identifies and describes task-related attitudes and behaviors that are characteristic of effective leaders, as outlined in Table 4-1. *Task-related* in this context means that the behavior, attitude, or skill focuses more on the task to be performed than on the interpersonal aspect of leadership.

1. *Adaptability to the situation.* Effective leaders adapt to the situation. Adaptability reflects the contingency viewpoint: a tactic is chosen based on the unique circumstances at hand. A leader who is responsible for psychologically immature group members will find it necessary to supervise them closely. If the group members are mature and self-reliant, the leader will use less supervision. The adaptive leader also selects an organization structure that is best suited to the demands of the situation, such as choosing between a brainstorming group and a committee.

2. *Direction setting.* Given that a major responsibility of leadership is to produce change, the leader must set the direction of that change. Direction setting is part of creating a vision and a component of strategy. The strategy describes a feasible way of achieving the vision. One of the most dramatic examples of this behavior took place at IBM Corporation in 1993 when Louis Gerstner, Jr., the new chairman and CEO at the time, pointed the company in a new direction. Instead of emphasizing the manufacture and sale of hardware, the new IBM concentrated on selling services and software. Similarly, shortly after John Thompson took over as CEO of Symantec, he pointed the company in the direction of concentrating on Internet security software (including Norton AntiVirus software).

3. *High performance standards.* Effective leaders consistently hold group members to high standards of performance. When performance is measured against these high standards, productivity is likely to increase, since people tend to live up to the expectations of their superiors. This is called the **Pygmalion effect**, and it works in a subtle, almost unconscious way. When a managerial leader believes that a group member will succeed, the manager communicates this belief without realizing it. Conversely, when a leader expects a group member to fail, that person will not disappoint the manager. The manager's expectation of success or failure

---

| **TABLE 4-1** | Task-Related Leadership Attitudes and Behaviors |
|---|---|
| 1. Adaptability to the situation | |
| 2. Direction setting | |
| 3. High performance standards | |
| 4. Risk taking and a bias for action | |
| 5. Hands-on guidance and feedback | |
| 6. Stability of performance | |
| 7. Ability to ask tough questions | |

becomes a self-fulfilling prophecy because the perceptions contribute to success or failure.

4. *Risk taking and a bias for action.* A bias for action rather than contemplation has been identified as a characteristic of a successful organization.[7] Combined with sensible risk taking, it is also an important leadership behavior. To bring about constructive change, the leader must take risks and be willing to implement those risky decisions. A bias for action is a desire to execute a plan, rather than a tendency to create visions without following through on them. Larry Bossidy, who held high-level positions at GE and Allied Signal, Inc., has this to say about the importance of execution: "I'm an impatient person, and I get more satisfaction from seeing things get done than I do about philosophizing or building sand castles. Many people regard execution as detail work that's beneath the dignity of a business leader. That's wrong. It's a leader's most important job."[8]

5. *Hands-on guidance and feedback.* You will recall that technical competence and knowledge of the business are important leadership characteristics. They enable the leader to provide group members with hands-on guidance about how to accomplish important work. The leader who provides such guidance helps the group accomplish important tasks; at the same time, group members learn important skills. Too much guidance of this nature, however, can be a symptom of poor delegation and micromanagement (managing too closely).

The hands-on leader stays close to the group task so he or she can provide guidance. Darryl B. Moody is the head of homeland security and intelligence for the consultancy BearingPoint, Inc. He enjoys getting out, meeting clients, and developing new business. "I like to roll up my sleeves and get my hands dirty doing technical work on the products that my team is delivering," he says.[9]

### FEEDBACK SKILLS

After small groups have completed an assignment such as answering the case questions or discussion questions, hold a performance feedback session. Also use observations you have made in previous problem-solving activities as the basis for your feedback. Each group member provides some feedback to each other member about how well he or she thinks the other person performed. Use only volunteers, because this type of feedback may be uncomfortable and disturbing to some individuals. Students not receiving the feedback can serve as observers and later present their feedback on what took place during the exercise. To increase the probability of benefiting from this experience, feedback recipients must listen actively. Refer to the section in Chapter 10 on coaching skills and techniques for more information on feedback and active listening.

A convenient way to do this exercise is for everyone to sit in a circle. Choose one feedback recipient to begin. Going clockwise around the circle, each group member gives that person feedback. After all people have spoken, the feedback recipient gives his or her reactions. The person to the left of the first recipient is the next one to get feedback.

After everyone has had a turn receiving performance feedback, hold a general discussion. Be sure to discuss three key issues:

**1.** How helpful was the feedback?

**2.** What was the relative effectiveness of positive versus negative feedback?

**3.** Were some group members better than others in giving feedback?

Closely related to guidance is giving frequent feedback on performance. The leader can rarely influence the actions of group members without appropriate performance feedback. This feedback tells group members how well they are doing so that they can take corrective action if needed. It also serves as a reinforcer that prompts group members to continue favorable activities. Leadership Skill-Building Exercise 4-1 provides practice in developing feedback skills.

6. *Stability of performance.* Effective leaders are steady performers, even under heavy workloads and uncertain conditions. Remaining steady under conditions of uncertainty contributes to effectiveness because it helps team members cope with the situation. When the leader remains calm, group members are reassured that things will work out. Stability also helps the managerial leader appear professional and cool under pressure. Many business leaders displayed enormous stability of performance after the September 11, 2001, attacks on the World Trade Center. Among the many heroes and heroines emerging from the crisis were leaders at Morgan Stanley, the World Trade Center's largest tenant. The firm was fully operational forty-eight hours after the tragedy. As Morgan Stanley leaders assured workers that the company would survive, employees were routed to backup facilities in New Jersey and Brooklyn.[10]

7. *Ability to ask tough questions.* There are many times when leaders can be effective by asking tough questions rather than providing answers. A **tough question** is one that makes a person or group stop and think about why they are doing or not doing something. (A tough question might also be considered the *right* question.) In this way, group members are forced to think about the effectiveness of their activities. They might ask themselves, "Why didn't I think of that? It seems so obvious." Asking questions is important because quite often group members may have the solutions to difficult problems facing the organization.[11]

Here is an example of a tough question: The division general manager says to the marketing manager, "The sales forecast you made for the next four years assumes that teenagers will continue to purchase jeans at the same rate. Suppose jeans suddenly fall out of fashion with teenagers? Why do you depend so heavily on one product? What can you do to prevent a crisis?"

Now that you have studied various components of task-oriented attitudes and behaviors, do Leadership Self-Assessment Quiz 4-1. It will further sensitize you to the task activities of leaders and managers.

## TASK-ORIENTED ATTITUDES AND BEHAVIORS

**INSTRUCTIONS** Indicate whether you mostly agree or mostly disagree with the following statements. Relate the statements to any work situation, including sports, community activities, and school activities, in which you have been responsible for the work of others. If a work situation does not come to mind, imagine how you would act or think.

|  | Mostly agree | Mostly disagree |
|---|---|---|
| 1. I keep close tabs on productivity figures and interpret them to the group. | ____ | ____ |
| 2. I send frequent email messages to group members, giving them information about work procedures. | ____ | ____ |
| 3. I clearly specify the quality goals our group needs to achieve. | ____ | ____ |
| 4. I maintain clear-cut standards of performance. | ____ | ____ |
| 5. When I conduct a meeting, the participants can count on a clear-cut agenda. | ____ | ____ |
| 6. I feel good about my workweek only if our team has met or exceeded its productivity goals. | ____ | ____ |
| 7. People should not be spending time with computers in the office unless the computers are actually increasing productivity. | ____ | ____ |
| 8. I freely criticize work that does not meet standards. | ____ | ____ |
| 9. I spend at least 20 percent of my workweek either planning myself or helping team members with their planning. | ____ | ____ |
| 10. I spend a good deal of time solving technical or business problems myself, or helping group members do the same. | ____ | ____ |

**INTERPRETATION** If you responded "mostly agree" to eight, nine, or ten of the above statements, you have a strong task orientation. If you responded "mostly disagree" to four or more of the statements, you have below-average task-oriented behaviors and attitudes.

**SKILL DEVELOPMENT** A task orientation is important because it can lead directly to goal attainment and productivity. Nevertheless, a task orientation must be balanced with a strong people orientation and interpersonal skills for maximum effectiveness.

## Relationship-Oriented Attitudes and Behaviors

Leadership involves influencing people, so it follows that many effective leadership attitudes, behaviors, and practices deal with interpersonal relationships and are the basis for effective interpersonal skills. Randy Komisar, known as a "virtual CEO" because he helps launch startup technology firms, presents a strong case for building interpersonal relationships. Asked how he sweeps into companies and manages employees effectively, Komisar replied: "I rely on relationship power, not traditional position power that comes from my title. I find that building relationships with people and inspiring them are the key to my leadership. That's how I think any manager becomes a leader."[12]

Table 4-2 lists the seven relationship-oriented attitudes and behaviors that we will discuss next. (Most other parts of this book describe the interpersonal skill aspects of leadership.)

1. *Aligning people.* Getting people pulling in the same direction and working together smoothly is a major interpersonal challenge. To get people pulling together, it is necessary to speak to many people. The target population can involve many different stakeholders. Among them are managers and team leaders, higher-ups, peers, and workers in other parts of the organization, as well as suppliers, government officials, and customers. Anyone who can implement the vision and strategies or who can block implementation must be aligned.[13] Once aligned, organizational members can pull together toward a higher purpose. Alignment of people also incorporates getting the group working together smoothly.

   Alignment is easier when the group has an agreed-upon mission or purpose. Paul Tagliabue, the CEO of the National Football League (NFL), is noted for his ability to create harmony among players and owners. Gene Upshaw, the head of the Players Association, made this comment about the mission Tagliabue has helped develop: "I don't see this as us versus the owners, but instead it's us versus all the other entertainment choices out there: the movies, music, theater."[14]

2. *Concert building and collaboration.* The leader's role of **concert building** involves both aligning and mobilizing in a manner similar to an orchestra leader. The concert

| **TABLE 4-2** | Relationship-Oriented Attitudes and Behaviors |
|---|---|
| | 1. Aligning people |
| | 2. Concert building and collaboration |
| | 3. Creating inspiration and visibility |
| | 4. Satisfying higher-level needs |
| | 5. Giving emotional support and encouragement |
| | 6. Promoting principles and values |
| | 7. Being a servant leader |

builder's goal is to produce a system that is self-evaluating, self-correcting, self-renewing, and ongoing. David S. Brown describes concert-building leadership in these terms:

> The system can be thought of as a large modern orchestra with a number of professionals playing quite different instruments and performing separate—and often very difficult—tasks. Each instrumentalist, like so many in large organizations, is indeed a specialist in a particular field whose work must be integrated with the work of others to make up a whole.[15]

Concert building is a specific case of the importance of attaining collaboration to make leadership possible. Leadership is based on collaboration. As Kouzes and Posner observe, "Throughout the years, leaders from all economic sectors, and from around the globe continue to tell us, 'You can't do it alone.' Leadership is not a solo act, it's a team effort."[16]

Becoming an organizational concert builder requires many of the skills and insights described throughout this book. Building teamwork, as described in Chapter 9, is particularly relevant.

3. *Creating inspiration and visibility.* As described in the discussion of charismatic and transformational leadership, inspiring others is an essential leadership practice. Inspiring people usually involves appealing to their emotions and values, such as when the head of a snowmobile business unit encourages workers to believe that they are making winters more enjoyable for people who live in regions that accumulate snow.

Because human contact and connections reinforce inspiration, another part of being inspirational is being visible and available. One of the many ways in which Sam Palmisano, the CEO of IBM, inspires people is through his visibility. He frequently interacts face-to-face with workers at all levels in the company. His ability to chat with almost anybody he meets makes him approachable to employees and customers. Many people at different ranks have stories of Palmisano pulling them aside and asking wide-eyed through his Harry Potter glasses, "How do you think we're doing?"[17]

Becoming inspired is an emotional process that is triggered by a variety of behaviors on the part of the leader. The next few sections describe some of the things leaders try to achieve with group members that include an element of inspiration.

4. *Satisfying higher-level needs.* To inspire people, effective leaders motivate people by satisfying higher-level needs, such as needs for achievement, a sense of belonging, recognition, self-esteem, and a feeling of control over one's life. Many leaders in organizations express an awareness of the importance of need satisfaction for building good relationships with workers. Doug DeVos, the chief executive of Amway Corporation, the multilevel seller of personal and home products, sees need satisfaction as being part of having a genuine regard for workers. He notes:

> My father [the company founder] always looked at his job as being that of a cheerleader, and the more I have been here, the more I appreciate his observation. If the person who ultimately delivers the Amway product doesn't get the job done right because of some need that I have neglected, then I have failed as a CEO. If

that person has needs, I have to have compassion enough to recognize and respond to them.[18]

5. *Giving emotional support and encouragement.* Supportive behavior toward team members usually increases leadership effectiveness. A supportive leader gives frequent encouragement and praise. One of the many work-related ways of encouraging people is to allow them to participate in decision making. Emotional support generally improves morale and sometimes improves productivity. In the long term, emotional support and encouragement may bolster a person's self-esteem.[19] Being emotionally supportive comes naturally to the leader who has empathy for people and who is a warm person.

6. *Promoting principles and values.* A major part of a top leader's role is to help promote values and principles that contribute to the welfare of individuals and organizations. This promotion can be classified as relationship-oriented because it deals directly with the emotions and attitudes of people, and indirectly with the task. Steven Covey, who is widely quoted for his uplifting messages, advises that an organization's mission statement must be for all good causes.[20] Leaders who believe in these good causes will then espouse principles and values that lead people toward good deeds in the workplace.

Almost every leader or manager—even the most devious among them—claims to harbor values and principles that promote human welfare and the general good. Yet not all leaders and managers actually implement such values and principles. John Thompson, the CEO of Symantec Corporation, provides a positive example of translating values into action. A reporter asked Thompson if he recruited members of the hacker community (because of their superior knowledge of computer viruses). Thompson replied:

> No, we don't. We have people who are every bit as capable but they live by a moral compass or an ethical standard that is consistent with our brand. We trade on trust. And so if customers ever thought that Symantec was at the root of some of this because we've had people who didn't live by the same ethical code or moral code that we believe in, that wouldn't be a good thing.[21]

To encourage managers and all other employees to conduct their work affairs at a high moral level, many companies put their values in written form. The values might be placed in employee handbooks, on company intranets, or on company web sites.

What constitutes the right values depends on the leader's core beliefs. The thinking of Bill George, the former chairman and CEO of Medtronic, Inc., has inspired many managers. As described in his book, *Authentic Leadership*, the welfare of customers and employees should be placed above those of shareholders in the corporate hierarchy. Another key value is to help employees achieve a fair balance between work and family life.[22] More will be said about values and ethics in Chapter 6.

Providing moral leadership begins with understanding one's own values. Leadership Skill-Building Exercise 4-2 gives you an opportunity to think through your work-related values so that you can better provide moral leadership to others.

**LEADERSHIP SKILL-BUILDING EXERCISE 4-2**

## CLARIFYING YOUR WORK VALUES

**INSTRUCTIONS** To provide effective value leadership, it is essential that you first understand your own values with respect to dealing with others. Rank from 1 to 12 the importance of the following values to you as a person. The most important value on the list receives a rank of 1; the least important, a rank of 12. Use the space next to "Other" if we have left out an important value in your life.

\_\_\_ Having respect for the dignity of others

\_\_\_ Ensuring that others have interesting work to perform

\_\_\_ Earning the trust of others

\_\_\_ Earning the respect of others

\_\_\_ Impressing others with how well my group performs

\_\_\_ Giving others proper credit for their work

\_\_\_ Inspiring continuous learning on the part of each member in our group, myself included

\_\_\_ Holding myself and others accountable for delivering on commitments

\_\_\_ Helping others grow and develop

\_\_\_ Inspiring others to achieve high productivity and quality

\_\_\_ Developing the reputation of being a trustworthy person

\_\_\_ Other

1. Compare your ranking of these values with that of the person next to you, and discuss.

2. Perhaps your class, assisted by your instructor, might arrive at a class average on each of these values. How does your ranking compare to the class ranking?

3. Look back at your own ranking. Does your ranking surprise you?

4. Are there any surprises in the class ranking? Which values did you think would be highest and lowest?

Clarifying your values for leadership is far more than a pleasant exercise. Many business leaders have fallen into disgrace and brought their companies into bankruptcy because of values that are unacceptable to employees, stockholders, outside investigators, and the legal system. For example, a CEO who valued "developing the reputation of being a trustworthy person," would not borrow $400 million from the company while paying thousands of employees close to the minimum wage.

7. *Being a servant leader.* Your desire to help others is another important workplace value. A **servant leader** serves constituents by working on their behalf to help them achieve their goals, not the leader's own goals. The idea behind servant leadership, as formulated by Robert K. Greenleaf, is that leadership derives naturally from a commitment to service.[23] Serving others, including employees, customers, and community, is the primary motivation for the servant leader. A servant leader is therefore a moral leader. Servant leadership has been accomplished when group members become wiser, healthier, and more autonomous. The following are key aspects of servant leadership.[24]

- *Place service before self-interest.* A servant leader is more concerned with helping others than with acquiring power, prestige, financial reward, and status. The servant leader seeks to do what is morally right, even if it is not financially rewarding. He or she is conscious of the needs of others and is driven by a desire to satisfy them. (You will recall that wanting to satisfy the needs of others is a basic relationship behavior.)

- *Listen first to express confidence in others.* The servant leader emphasizes listening in order to get to know the concerns, requirements, and problems of group members. Instead of attempting to impose his or her will on others, the servant leader listens carefully to understand what course of action will help others accomplish their goals. After understanding others, the best course of action can be chosen. Through listening, for example, a servant leader might learn that the group is more concerned about team spirit and harmony than striving for companywide recognition. The leader would then concentrate more on building teamwork than searching for ways to increase the visibility of the team.

- *Inspire trust by being trustworthy.* Being trustworthy is a foundation behavior of the servant leader. He or she is scrupulously honest with others, gives up control, and focuses on the well-being of others. Usually such leaders do not have to work hard at being trustworthy because they are already quite moral.

- *Focus on what is feasible to accomplish.* Even though the servant leader is idealistic, he or she recognizes that one individual cannot accomplish everything. So the leader listens carefully to the array of problems facing group members and then concentrates on a few. The servant leader thus systematically neglects certain problems. A labor union official might carefully listen to all the concerns and complaints of the constituents and then proceed to work on the most pressing issue.

- *Lend a hand.* A servant leader looks for opportunities to play the Good Samaritan. As a supermarket manager, he or she might help out by bagging groceries during a busy period. Or a servant leader might help dig up mud in the company lobby after a hurricane.

At clothing retailer Men's Warehouse, Inc., servant leadership is in style. A district manager at the Warehouse may want to go home and be with his family, but he will tell a store manager that he will stay and cover the store, so the store manager can spend time with *his* or *her* family at a son's baseball game. The underlying idea is for managers to give top priority to helping others.[25]

## *360-Degree Feedback for Fine-Tuning a Leadership Approach*

In most large organizations, leaders not only provide feedback to group members, but they also receive feedback that gives them insight into the effects of their attitudes and behaviors. The feedback is systematically derived from a full sampling of parties who interact with the leader. In particular, **360-degree feedback** is a formal evaluation of superiors based on input from people who work for and with them, sometimes including customers and suppliers. It is also referred to as multisource feedback or multirater feedback. The process is also called 360-degree survey, because the input stems from a survey of a handful of people. One variation of the method is to build a 360-degree feedback system accessed via the Internet and the company's intranet. The Internet systems reduce some of the burdensome amount of paper involved in most 360-degree feedback systems, yet the participants must still fill out electronic forms.

Three hundred and sixty–degree feedback is more frequently used for leadership and management development than for performance evaluation. Particularly when used for development, 360-degree feedback includes self-evaluation. When self-evaluation is included, the individual completes the same form that all others used to describe his or her behavior. The feedback is communicated to the leader (as well as others receiving 360-degree feedback) and interpreted with the assistance of a human resources professional or an external consultant.

Specialists in the field view 360-degree feedback as more suited for its original purpose of development for a manager or leader than for administrative purposes such as performance evaluation and salary administration. When used for development, 360-degree feedback should emphasize qualitative comments rather than strictly quantitative ratings.[26] For example, being told, "You do not maintain eye contact with me during meetings," is more helpful than simply receiving a low rating on "Makes others feel comfortable."

The data from the survey can be used to help leaders fine-tune their attitudes and behavior. For example, if all the interested parties gave the leader low ratings on "empathy toward others," the leader might be prompted to improve his or her ability to empathize, such as by reading about empathy, attending a seminar, and simply making a conscious attempt to empathize when involved in a conflict of opinion with another person.

A few years ago the two top executives at Dell Inc., Michael Dell and Kevin Rollins, implemented a 360-degree evaluation process to improve their leadership effectiveness. All the direct reports were invited to evaluate the two executives. (A *direct report* is a worker who reports directly to a manager.) Results of the survey indicated that the managers wanted more feedback and more opportunity to participate in decision making. They also wanted Dell and Rollins to be more open and friendly and to make a better emotional connection with them.[27]

An example of a 360-degree feedback form is shown in Figure 4-2. The example shows the gaps between the leader's self-perceptions and the perceptions of the group. When such gaps occur, sometimes professionally trained counselors should be involved in 360-degree feedback. Some people feel emotionally crushed when they find a wide discrepancy between their self-perception on an interpersonal skill dimension and the perception of others. A middle manager involved in a 360-degree evaluation prided herself on how well she was liked by others. The feedback that

**FIGURE 4-2  A 360-Degree Feedback Chart**

Manager evaluated: *Bob Germane*

Ratings *(10 is highest)*

| Behavior or Attitude | Self Rating | Average Group Rating | Gap |
|---|---|---|---|
| 1. Gives right amount of structure | 9 | 7.5 | –1.5 |
| 2. Considerate of people | 10 | 6.2 | –3.8 |
| 3. Sets a direction | 9 | 3.9 | –5.1 |
| 4. Sets high standards | 7 | 9.0 | +2.0 |
| 5. Gives frequent feedback | 10 | 6.3 | –3.7 |
| 6. Gets people pulling together | 9 | 5.1 | –3.9 |
| 7. Inspires people | 10 | 2.8 | –7.2 |
| 8. Gives emotional support | 8 | 3.7 | –4.3 |
| 9. Is a helpful coach | 10 | 4.5 | –5.5 |
| 10. Encourages people to be self-reliant | 6 | 9.4 | +3.4 |

NOTE: A negative gap means you rate yourself higher on the behavior or attitude than does your group. A positive gap means the group rates you higher than you rate yourself.

emerged, however, depicted her as intimidating, hostile, and manipulative. Upon receiving the feedback, the woman went into a rage (proving the feedback true!) and then into despondency. Professional counseling can sometimes help a person benefit from critical feedback and place it in perspective.

For best results, it is extremely important that 360-degree surveys reflect those behaviors and attitudes that the organization values most highly. Care should also be taken that the dimensions measured reflect important aspects of leadership functioning. Following are some suggestions for making better use of 360-degree surveys.[28]

- Focus on business goals and strategy. Feedback should provide leaders and managers with insight into the skills they need to help the organization meet its goals.
- Ensure that the feedback dimensions reflect important aspects of leadership functioning.
- Train workers in giving and receiving feedback. Providing constructive feedback takes coaching, training, and practice. One study showed that negative feedback received from a 360-degree survey is perceived as less useful than positive feedback.[29]

- Create an action plan for improvement for each leader based on the feedback. For example, a leader rated low on interpersonal skills might benefit from training in emotional intelligence.

- Ensure that the managers rated have full ownership of the feedback information so that they will perceive the feedback as being geared toward personal development rather than administrative control.

# Leadership Styles

A leader's combination of attitudes and behaviors leads to a certain regularity and predictability in dealing with group members. **Leadership style** is the relatively consistent pattern of behavior that characterizes a leader. The study of leadership style is an extension of understanding leadership behaviors and attitudes. Most classifications of leadership style are based on the dimensions of consideration and initiating structure. Phrases such as "he's a real command-and-control-type," and "she's a consensus leader" have become commonplace.

Here we describe the participative leadership style, the autocratic leadership style, the Leadership Grid®, the entrepreneurial leadership style, gender differences in leadership style, and choosing the best style. Chapter 5 continues the exploration of leadership styles by presenting several contingency leadership theories.

## Participative Leadership

Sharing decision making with group members and working with them side by side has become the generally accepted leadership approach in the modern organization. **Participative leaders** share decision making with group members. Participative leadership encompasses so many behaviors that it can be divided into three subtypes: consultative, consensus, and democratic.

**Consultative leaders** confer with group members before making a decision. However, they retain the final authority to make decisions. **Consensus leaders** strive for consensus. They encourage group discussion about an issue and then make a decision that reflects general agreement and that group members will support. All workers who will be involved in the consequences of a decision have an opportunity to provide input. A decision is not considered final until it appears that all parties involved will at least support the decision. **Democratic leaders** confer final authority on the group. They function as collectors of group opinion and take a vote before making a decision.

The participative style has also been referred to as *trickle-up leadership* because the leader accepts suggestions for managing the operation from group members. Welcoming ideas from below is considered crucial because as technology evolves and organizations decentralize, front-line workers have more independence and responsibility. These workers are closer to the market, closer to seeing how the product is used, and closer to many human resource problems. Front-line knowledge can provide useful input to leaders for such purposes as developing marketing strategy and retaining employees.[30]

The participative style encompasses the teamwork approach. Predominant behaviors of participative leaders include coaching team members, negotiating their demands, and collaborating with others. Often the team member who has the most relevant knowledge for the task at hand slips into a leadership role. Research indicates that poor-performing teams are often dominated by the team leader, whereas high-performing teams are characterized by shared leadership.[31]

The participative style is well suited to managing competent people who are eager to assume responsibility. Such people want to get involved in making decisions and giving feedback to management. Since most graduates from business and professional programs expect to be involved in decision making, participative leadership works well with the new breed of managers and professionals.

The leadership approach of A. G. Lafley, the chief executive of Procter & Gamble, provides some insight into the nuances of being a participative leader. In the following commentary, he is compared to his predecessor, Durk L. Jager:

> So how has Lafley succeeded where Jager so spectacularly failed? In a word, style. Where Jager was gruff, Lafley is soothing. Where Jager bullied, Lafley persuades. He listens more than he talks. He is living proof that the messenger is just as important as the message. As he says, "I'm not a screamer, not a yeller. But don't get confused by my style, I am very decisive." The head of P&G's global fabric and home-care division says, "People want to follow him. I frankly love him like my brother."[32]

Participative leadership does have some problems. It often results in extensive and time-consuming team meetings and committee work. Also, consensus and democratic leaders are sometimes accused of providing too little direction. A case in point is Alan Hassenfeld, the former CEO at toy maker Hasbro, Inc. A consultant noted that his "leadership style was hands-off and consensus-building to the point of paralysis."[33] Sometimes participative leadership is carried to extremes. Team members are consulted about trivial things that management could easily handle independently. Another problem is that many managers still believe that sharing decision making with members reduces their power.

## Autocratic Leadership

In contrast to participative leaders are **autocratic leaders** who retain most of the authority. They make decisions confidently, assume that group members will comply, and are not overly concerned with group members' attitudes toward a decision. Autocratic leaders are considered task-oriented because they place heavy emphasis on getting tasks accomplished. Typical autocratic behaviors include telling people what to do, asserting themselves, and serving as a model for team members. A positive example of a famous business leader who was usually autocratic is Louis Gerstner, Jr., of IBM. A highly decisive and intelligent person, he would move quickly on major decisions without receiving much input from others.

The leadership behavior of Jerry Sanders, the flamboyant founder of Advanced Micro Devices (AMD), helps us understand how domineering an autocratic leader can be. During the management committee meetings, Sanders would talk the entire forty-five minutes. Sanders's replacement, Hector Ruiz, speaks for twenty minutes. "Under Jerry, frankly, the company was very autocratic and power-centric," says Ruiz.[34]

Part of your skill development as a leader involves gaining insight into your own leadership style or potential style. To this end, you can take Leadership Self-Assessment Quiz 4-2.

?

## WHAT STYLE OF LEADER ARE YOU OR WOULD YOU BE?

**INSTRUCTIONS** Answer the following questions, keeping in mind what you have done, or think you would do, in the scenarios and attitudes described.

|  | Mostly true | Mostly false |
|---|---|---|
| 1. I am more likely to take care of a high-impact assignment myself than turn it over to a group member. | ✓ | |
| 2. I would prefer the analytical aspects of a manager's job to working directly with group members. | ✓ | |
| 3. An important part of my approach to managing a group is to keep the members informed almost daily of any information that could affect their work. | ✓ | |
| 4. It is a good idea to give two people in the group the same problem and then choose what appears to be the best solution. | ✓ | |
| 5. It makes good sense for the leader or manager to stay somewhat aloof from the group so that you can make a tough decision when necessary. | | ✓ |
| 6. I look for opportunities to obtain group input before making a decision, even on straightforward issues. | | ✓ |
| 7. I would reverse a decision if several of the group members presented evidence that I was wrong. | ✓ | |
| 8. Differences of opinion in the work group are healthy. | ✓ | |
| 9. I think that activities to build team spirit, like fixing up a poor family's house on a Saturday, are an excellent investment of time. | ✓ | |
| 10. If my group were hiring a new member, I would like the person to be interviewed by the entire group. | ✓ | |
| 11. An effective team leader today uses email for about 98 percent of communication with team members. | | ✓ |

12. Some of the best ideas are likely to come from the group members rather than from the manager.

13. If our group were going to have a banquet, I would get input from each member on what type of food should be served.

14. I have never seen a statue of a committee in a museum or park, so why bother making decisions by a committee if you want to be recognized?

15. I dislike it intensely when a group member challenges my position on an issue.

16. I typically explain to group members how (what method) they should use to accomplish an assigned task.

17. If I were out of the office for a week, most of the important work in the department would get accomplished anyway.

18. Delegation of important tasks is something that would be (or is) very difficult for me.

19. When a group member comes to me with a problem, I tend to jump right in with a proposed solution.

20. When a group member comes to me with a problem, I typically ask that person something like, "What alternative solutions have you thought of so far?"

---

SCORING AND INTERPRETATION The answers for a participative leader are as follows:

| | | |
|---|---|---|
| 1. Mostly False | 8. Mostly True | 15. Mostly False |
| 2. Mostly False | 9. Mostly True | 16. Mostly False |
| 3. Mostly True | 10. Mostly True | 17. Mostly True |
| 4. Mostly False | 11. Mostly False | 18. Mostly False |
| 5. Mostly False | 12. Mostly True | 19. Mostly False |
| 6. Mostly True | 13. Mostly True | 20. Mostly True |
| 7. Mostly True | 14. Mostly False | |

---

If your score is 15 or higher, you are most likely (or would be) a participative leader. If your score is 5 or lower, you are most likely (or would be) an authoritarian leader.

*(continued)*

SKILL DEVELOPMENT The quiz you just completed is also an opportunity for skill development. Review the twenty questions and look for implied suggestions for engaging in participative leadership. For example, question 20 suggests that you encourage group members to work through their own solutions to problems. If your goal is to become an authoritarian leader, the questions can also serve as useful guidelines. For example, question 19 suggests that an authoritarian leader looks first to solve problems for group members.

## Leadership Grid® Styles

A classic method of classifying leadership styles suggests that the best way to achieve effective leadership is to integrate the task and relationship orientations. The **Leadership Grid®** is a framework for specifying the extent of a leader's concern for production and people.[35]

college.hmco.com/pic/
dubrin5e

🐙 @ **KNOWLEDGE BANK:** contains a diagram of the Leadership Grid.

Concern for production, rated on the horizontal axis, includes such matters as results (including high quality), the bottom line, performance, profits, and mission. Concern for people, rated on the vertical axis, is reflected in such matters as showing support for team members, getting results based on trust and respect, and worrying about employees' job security. Each concern is rated on a 1–9 scale. The benchmark styles on the Leadership Grid are as follows:

*Authority-Compliance (9,1).* The authority-compliance style is characterized by a maximum concern for production combined with a minimum concern for people. A leader with this orientation concentrates on maximizing production by exercising power and authority and by dictating to people.

*Country Club Management (1,9).* The "country club" style shows a minimum concern for production and a maximum concern for people. Primary attention is placed on good feelings among team members and coworkers, even at the expense of achieving results.

*Impoverished Management (1,1).* The impoverished management style shows a minimum concern for both production and people. Such a leader does only the minimum required to remain a member of the firm. (According to the current definition of leadership, this type of manager does not qualify as a leader.)

*Middle-of-the-Road Management (5,5).* In the center is the 5,5 orientation. Leaders with this middle-of-the-road style do their job but avoid making waves and conform to the status quo.

*Team Management (9,9).* The team management style integrates concern for production and people. It is a goal-directed team approach that seeks to gain optimum results through participation, involvement, and commitment.

| Managers generally have one dominant leadership style and a backup style. Leaders tend to use the backup style when the dominant style does not achieve the desired results. For instance, you might use the 9,9 approach, only to find that most team members are unenthusiastic about implementing a total quality program. It might then be necessary to shift to a 9,1 approach.

The creators of the grid argue strongly for the value of team management (9,9). They present evidence that the team management orientation usually results in improved performance, low absenteeism and turnover, and high employee satisfaction. However, the Leadership Grid does not dictate that the manager rely mechanically on one style in trying to lead very different groups. Instead, he or she should use principles of human behavior to size up the situation.

## Entrepreneurial Leadership

Many entrepreneurs use a similar leadership style that stems from their personality characteristics and circumstances. Although there are different types of entrepreneurs, in general an entrepreneur is a person who founds and operates an innovative business. Not all business owners, including franchise operators, are therefore entrepreneurial leaders. The general picture that emerges of an entrepreneur is a task-oriented and charismatic person. Entrepreneurs drive themselves and others relentlessly, yet their personalities also inspire others.

This entrepreneurial leadership style often incorporates the behaviors described in the following paragraphs.[36] However, authorities disagree about whether an entrepreneurial personality exists.

1. *Strong achievement drive and sensible risk taking.* Entrepreneurs have stronger achievement motives than most leaders (see Chapter 2). Building a business is an excellent vehicle for accomplishment and risk taking. To accomplish what they think needs to be accomplished, entrepreneurs are willing to work extraordinary hours, with twelve-hour days, seven days a week not being unusual. Because entrepreneurs take sensible risks, many do not perceive themselves as being risk takers—just as many tightrope walkers believe they are not taking risks because they are in control. Leadership Self-Assessment Quiz 4-3, on page 122, gives you the opportunity to think about your risk-taking tendencies.

2. *High degree of enthusiasm and creativity.* Entrepreneurs are highly enthusiastic, partially because they are so excited about their achievements. As *Entrepreneur* magazine puts it, "Something about being an entrepreneur is, for them, a five-star, butt-kicking, rocket-boosting blast." Entrepreneurs' enthusiasm, in turn, makes them persuasive. As a result, they are often perceived as charismatic. Some entrepreneurs are so emotional that they are regarded as eccentric.

3. *Tendency to act quickly when opportunity arises.* Entrepreneurs are noted for seizing upon opportunity. When a deal is on the horizon, they push themselves and those around them extra hard. The accompanying Leader-in-Action insert illustrates how an entrepreneur finds an opportunity.

## LEADER IN ACTION

### DIANE CORRIGAN OF UNIQUE CRITIQUE CREATES A GOOD IMPRESSION

It is not easy to start a business that no one has ever heard of, but Diane Corrigan is convinced persistence will pay off. A few years ago, Corrigan started a business image consulting firm called Unique Critique to show businesses how they can improve their physical appearance to create the best possible impression on customers and the general public.

Using a checklist with more than forty items, she or one of her four part-time inspectors looks for anything that could leave a bad impression. Usually it is a janitorial or landscaping task that needs to be done better, but Corrigan also notices when the décor is outdated or uncoordinated. An initial inspection usually takes an hour or two, and Corrigan recommends follow-up visits. She can work directly with janitorial and landscaping services to get the problems corrected or find a qualified contractor to do a specific job.

The problem Corrigan finds is that potential clients do not know what a business image consultant does. "People think an image consultant talks about how to dress and what colors you should wear," she said. "People don't understand what I do at first, but once they get it, they're very enthusiastic."

Corrigan became an entrepreneur after a car accident forced her to change careers. For almost twenty years she had owned You Have It Maid, a residential and commercial cleaning service, but recurring neck and back pain prevented her from standing for very long or working alongside her cleaning crews. She thought about becoming a nurse practitioner, but she finally decided to capitalize on the knowledge she gained by running her cleaning service and managing a restaurant. "I had all this experience, and it was a revelation to realize that I could use it in a new way," she said.

With her keen eye for detail, Corrigan could tell when the walls had not been scrubbed in the bathroom for a long time. She noticed things that should not be there, such as toilet brushes, and things that were missing, such as coat hooks. She found that many businesses were not aware of the bad impression they were making on their customers and decided they needed someone to point out those details. But there was no model to follow because she could not find anyone who provided such a service.

Many people doubted her business idea would work. "I've had to overcome a lot of pessimism," Corrigan said. "People said there must be a reason why no one else had done it." Those objections helped motivate Corrigan to become better prepared. She earned her business entrepreneur certification at Macomb Community College and took a master gardening class at Michigan State University. She surveyed more than 200 businesspeople and professionals. She is currently taking a sales course.

Whenever she encounters setbacks or delays, Corrigan likes to refer to a quote from former President Calvin Coolidge: "Nothing in the world can take the place of persistence. Talent will not; nothing is more common than unsuccessful men [people] with talent. Genius will not; unrewarded genius is almost a proverb. Education will not; the world is full of educated derelicts. Persistent and determination alone are omnipotent."

### QUESTIONS

1. Which entrepreneurial leadership traits, behaviors, and attitudes does Diane Corrigan appear to display?
2. How valid is Calvin Coolidge's analysis of the importance of persistence?

SOURCE: Eric Pope, "Image Consultant Credits Her Success to Persistence," *Detroit News* (*detnews.com*), June 13, 2004, pp. 1–2. Reprinted with permission from the *Detroit News*.

4. *Constant hurry combined with impatience.* Entrepreneurs are always in a hurry. While engaged in one meeting, their minds typically begin to focus on the next meeting. Their flurry of activity rubs off on group members and those around them. Entrepreneurs often adopt a simple dress style in order to save time, and they typically allow little slack time between appointments.

5. *Visionary perspective combined with tenacity.* Entrepreneurs, at their best, are visionaries. As with other types of effective leaders, they see opportunities others fail to observe. Specifically, they have the ability to identify a problem and arrive at a solution. Ted Turner of CNN is a legendary example of an entrepreneurial visionary. Turner picked up on a trend that people wanted—an all-news cable channel that they could access anytime. Not only is CNN, including Headline News, a commercial success, but it also revolutionized the way people get their news all over the globe. After the vision is established, the entrepreneur tenaciously implements the vision, working an eighty-hour week if need be.

6. *Dislike of hierarchy and bureaucracy.* Entrepreneurs are not ideally suited by temperament to working within the mainstream of a bureaucracy. Many successful entrepreneurs are people who were frustrated by the constraints of a bureaucratic system. The implication for leadership style is that entrepreneurs deemphasize rules and regulations when managing people.

7. *Preference for dealing with external customers.* One reason that entrepreneurs have difficulty with bureaucracy is that they focus their energies on products, services, and customers, rather than on employees. Some entrepreneurs are gracious to customers and moneylenders but brusque with company insiders. A blind spot many entrepreneurs have is that they cannot understand why their employees do not share their passion for work and customer focus. As a result, they may be brusque with employees who do not share their dedication to the firm.

8. *Eye on the future.* Entrepreneurs have the pronounced characteristic of thinking about future deals and business opportunities even before a current business is running smoothly. "Where is my next deal coming from?" is the mantra of the true entrepreneur. Even after accumulating great wealth from a present business activity, the entrepreneurial leader looks toward future opportunities. A good example is Richard Branson of the Virgin Group. His empire contains about 250 companies with the Virgin label, yet he continues to look for the next company to start or acquire.

college.hmco.com/pic/ dubrin5e

**KB** **@ KNOWLEDGE BANK:** contains additional information about the entrepreneurial personality.

As explained in the accompanying Knowledge Bank, the entrepreneurial personality, if carried to an extreme, can lead to addictive behavior, including substance abuse. To practice one aspect of entrepreneurial leadership, do Leadership Skill-Building Exercise 4-3 on page 123.

**LEADERSHIP SELF-ASSESSMENT QUIZ 4-3**

## WHAT IS YOUR PROPENSITY FOR TAKING RISKS?

INSTRUCTIONS Indicate how well each of the following statements reflects your attitudes or behavior, using this scale: very inaccurately (VI); inaccurately (I); moderately well (MW); accurately (A); very accurately (VA).

| | VI | I | MW | A | VA |
|---|---|---|---|---|---|
| 1. If I had a serious illness, I would purchase generic instead of brand-name drugs. | 1 | ②  | 3 | 4 | 5 |
| 2. I invest (or would invest) much more money in bonds or CDs (certificates of deposit) than in stocks. | 5 | ④ | 3 | 2 | 1 |
| 3. The thought of starting my own business appeals to me. | ① | 2 | 3 | 4 | 5 |
| 4. I am (or was) willing to go on blind dates frequently. | 1 | 2 | ③ | 4 | 5 |
| 5. My career advice to young people is to pursue a well-established occupation with a high demand for newcomers to the field. | 5 | ④ | 3 | 2 | 1 |
| 6. I would be willing to relocate to a city where I had no family or friends. | 1 | 2 | 3 | ④ | 5 |
| 7. During the last few years, I have taken up a new sport, dance, or foreign language on my own. | 1 | 2 | ③ | 4 | 5 |
| 8. My preference is to have at least 90 percent of my compensation based on guaranteed salary. | 5 | 4 | 3 | ② | 1 |
| 9. From time to time I buy jewelry, clothing, or food from street vendors. | 1 | 2 | ③ | 4 | 5 |
| 10. The idea of piloting my own single-engine plane over the ocean appeals to me. | 1 | ② | 3 | 4 | 5 |

*Total score* _____

SCORING AND INTERPRETATION Obtain your score by adding the numbers you have circled.

- 46–50: You are a heavy risk taker, bordering on reckless at times. You are most likely not assessing risk carefully enough before proceeding.
- 38–45: You probably are a sensible risk taker and an adventuresome person in a way that enhances your leadership appeal to others.
- 5–37: You have a propensity to avoid risks. Your conservatism in this regard could detract from an entrepreneurial leadership style.

Risk taking is important for leadership because both charismatic and entrepreneurial leaders are noted for their risk taking. In addition, it is difficult to bring about change (a vital leadership function) if you are averse to taking risks.

## ENTREPRENEURIAL LEADERSHIP

An important part of the entrepreneurial role is to convince others of the merit of your idea so that they will invest in your company or lend you money. Two students play the role of a team of entrepreneurs who have a new product or service and want to launch a business. (The two entrepreneurs choose the product or service.) About five other students play the role of a group of venture capitalists or bankers listening to the presentation to decide whether to invest or lend money. The entrepreneurs will communicate excitement and commitment about their product, along with a good business plan. (You might want to quickly review the material about persuasive communication in Chapter 12.) The students who are not participating will evaluate how well the two entrepreneurs displayed aspects of the entrepreneurial leadership style.

## *Gender Differences in Leadership Style*

Controversy over whether men and women have different leadership styles continues. Several researchers and observers argue that women have certain acquired traits and behaviors that suit them for relations-oriented leadership. Consequently, women leaders frequently exhibit a cooperative, empowering style that includes nurturing team members. According to this same perspective, men are inclined toward a command-and-control, militaristic leadership style. Women find participative management more natural than do men because they feel more comfortable interacting with people. Furthermore, it is argued that women's natural sensitivity to people gives them an edge over men in encouraging group members to participate in decision making. Here we look briefly at some of the evidence and reasoning showing that gender differences do and do not exist between the leadership styles of today's organizational leaders.

As many researchers use the term, *gender* refers to perceptions about the differences among males and females. An example would be believing that women managers tend to be better listeners than their male peers. Gender differences refer to roles that men and women occupy. Sex differences, however, refer to actual (objective and quantitative) differences, such as the fact that the mean height of men exceeds that of women. Nevertheless, the terms *gender* and *sex* are still used interchangeably in general usage and to some extent in scholarly writings.

***The Argument for Male–Female Differences in Leadership Style*** Judy Rosener concluded that men and women do tend toward opposite styles. Based on self-reports, she found that men tended toward a command-and-control style. In contrast, women tended toward a transformational style, relying heavily on interpersonal skills.[37] Bernard M. Bass has found some specific male–female differences in leadership style. Data collected from subordinates suggest that women are less likely to practice management-by-exception (intervening only when something goes wrong). Even when the women leaders studied did practice management-by-exception, they typically tempered criticism with positive feedback. Bass also found that women leaders are slightly more likely to be described as charismatic. In a survey of sixty-nine world-class leaders (nine women included), women scored higher on the transformation factor than did men.[38]

Another perspective on gender differences is that women entrepreneurs are more likely than their male counterparts to perceive their business as a family. As corporate managers, women tend to place greater emphasis on forming caring, nurturing relationships with employees. Women are also more likely than men to praise group members. And when an employee falls short of expectations, women are more likely to buffer criticism by finding something praiseworthy.[39]

One question relating to gender differences is whether men or women are more effective as leaders. Eighteen hundred men and women managers from the United States and Canada were matched on organization level, job function, and management experience. Each manager completed a self-evaluation and was also evaluated by an average of one boss, four peers, and four direct reports who used the observer version of the same questionnaire. Leadership differences between men and women leaders were perceived in a similar way by the four groups (self, boss, peers, and direct reports), as follows:

- Women scored higher on leadership scales measuring orientation toward production and obtaining results, whereas men scored higher on scales assessing an orientation toward strategic planning and organizational vision.

- Women were perceived as functioning with more energy, intensity, and emotional expression and a greater capacity to keeps workers enthused. Men were seen as more likely to maintain a low-key style through the control of emotional expression.

- Women were rated higher on relationship-oriented leadership skills by all groups, whereas men were rated higher on task-oriented leadership skills by superiors and peers, but not by direct reports.

Despite these differences, on the dimension of overall effectiveness, the sexes were perceived the same. Superiors gave equal effectiveness ratings to men and women. However, peers and direct reports perceive women as slightly more effective than men. The researchers recommended that women may benefit from additional training in strategic analysis and men may benefit from additional training in interpersonal skills.[40]

Fundamental differences in the biological and psychological makeup of men and women have also been used as evidence that the two sexes are likely to manifest different leadership styles. Brain researchers Raquel Gur and Ruben Gur uncovered one such set of differences. They found that women may be far more sensitive to emotional cues and verbal nuances than men. Women leaders would therefore be more suited to responding to the feelings of group members and understanding what they really mean by certain statements.[41] Gender differences in communication also are reflected in leadership style. Above all, women are more likely than men to use spoken communication for building relationships and giving emotional support.[42] Men focus more on disseminating information and demonstrating competence. Women are therefore more likely to choose a relationship-oriented leadership style.

**The Argument Against Gender Differences in Leadership Style** Based on a literature review, Jan Grant concluded that there are apparently few, if any, personality or behavioral differences between men and women managers. Also, as women move up the corporate ladder, their identification with the male model of managerial success becomes important; they consequently reject even the few managerial feminine traits they may have earlier endorsed.[43]

To what extent the stereotypes of men and women leaders are true is difficult to judge. Even if male and female differences in leadership style do exist, they must be placed in proper perspective. Both men and women leaders differ among themselves in leadership style. Plenty of male leaders are relationship oriented, and plenty of women practice command and control (the extreme task orientation). Many women believe that women managers can be more hostile and vindictive than men managers.

A more important issue is how to capitalize on both male and female leadership tendencies. Connie Glaser believes that the best approach to leadership takes advantage of the positive traits of both men and women. She sees a new management style that blends the male and female sides:

> While the female may impart that sense of nurturing, the sensitivity to individual and family needs, that's offset by certain traits that the male brings to the table. The ability to make decisions quickly, the sense of humor, the risk-taking—those are qualities that traditionally have been associated with the male style of management.[44]

## Selecting the Best Leadership Style

An underlying theme of our discussion of leadership styles, and the next chapter, is that there is no one best or most effective leadership style. A study with 3,000 executives revealed that leaders who get the best results do not rely on one style. Instead, they use several different styles in one week, such as by being autocratic in some situations and democratic in others.[45] Another consideration is the culture in which the leadership takes place. For example, an effective leadership style for most German workers would be a high performance (task) orientation and a modest amount of compassion (consideration).[46] Thirty-five years ago pioneering researcher Ralph Stogdill made a statement about selecting a leadership style that still holds today: "The most effective leaders appear to exhibit a degree of versatility and flexibility that enables them to adapt their behavior to the changing and contradictory demands made on them."[47]

Table 4-3 presents useful information for choosing between the participative and autocratic styles, depending on the needs of the group members and other forces in the situation. The most successful leaders typically find the right blend of task and relationship orientations.

Leadership Self-Assessment Quiz 4-4 gives you an opportunity to think about your own willingness to adapt to circumstances as a leader. By developing such flexibility, you increase your chances of becoming an effective leader—one who achieves high productivity, quality, and satisfaction. Finally, before moving on to the end-of-chapter activities, do Leadership Skill-Building Exercise 4-4.

| TABLE 4-3 | Choosing a Leadership Style to Fit the Situation |

| **CONSIDER BEING PARTICIPATIVE UNDER THESE CONDITIONS:** | |
|---|---|
| LEADER/MANAGER | Has limited power and limited authority to use it |
| | Needs input from valuable employees |
| | Risks rejection of his or her authority |
| | Has few existing time pressures |
| | Has limited sanctions that he or she can exert |
| GROUP MEMBERS | Expect to have some control over methods used |
| | Have predominantly middle-class values |
| | Possess relatively scarce skills |
| | Like the system, but not authority |
| WORK SITUATION | Encourages consensus building |
| | Is characterized by overall organizational objectives |
| | Involves shared responsibility for control |
| | Has some time pressures |
| | Consists of gradual changes or regularly spaced changes |
| | Occasionally involves actual or potential hazards |
| | Values teamwork skills |
| **CONSIDER BEING AUTOCRATIC UNDER THESE CONDITIONS:** | |
| LEADER/MANAGER | Has lots of power and limited restraints on its use |
| | Has a way of saving matters in an emergency |
| | Has some unique knowledge useful to the group |
| | Is firmly entrenched in his or her position |
| GROUP MEMBERS | Are dependent on the leader |
| | Are rarely asked for an opinion |
| | Are readily replaced by other workers |
| | Recognize emergencies |
| | Are autocrats themselves |
| | Have little need for independence |
| WORK SITUATION | Requires a clear direction |
| | Requires a new vision because of changes |
| | Is characterized by strong controls |
| | Is marked by low profit margins or tight cost controls |
| | Includes physical dangers |
| | Requires low-level skills from workers |
| | Requires that changes be made frequently and quickly |

Source: *Personnel* by Robert W. Johnston. Copyright 1981 by *American Management Association (J)*. Reproduced with permission of *American Management Association (J)* in the format Textbook via Copyright Clearance Center. Updated with information from Daniel Goleman, "Leadership That Gets Results," *Harvard Business Review*, March–April 2000, pp. 82, 83.

**HOW FLEXIBLE ARE YOU?**

INSTRUCTIONS To succeed as a managerial leader, a person needs a flexible style: an ability to be open to others and a willingness to listen. Where do you stand on being flexible? Test yourself by answering "often," "sometimes," or "rarely" to the following questions.

1. Do you tend to seek out only those people who agree with your analysis of issues?   _S_

2. Do you ignore most of the advice from coworkers about process improvements?   _S_

3. Do your team members go along with what you say just to avoid an argument?   _S_

4. Have people referred to you as "rigid" or "close minded" on several occasions?   _S_

5. When presented with a new method, do you immediately look for a flaw?   _O_

6. Do you make up your mind early on with respect to an issue, and then hold firmly to your opinion?   _O_

7. When people disagree with you, do you tend to belittle them or become argumentative?   _r_

8. Do you often feel you are the only person in the group who really understands the problem?   _r_

CHECK YOUR SCORE If you answered "rarely" to seven or eight questions, you are unusually adaptable. If you answered "sometimes" to at least five questions, you are on the right track, but more flexibility would benefit your leadership. If you answered "often" to more than four questions, you have a long way to go to improve your flexibility and adaptability. You are also brutally honest about your faults, which could be an asset.

## CONTRASTING LEADERSHIP STYLES

One student plays the role of a new associate working for a financial services firm that sells life insurance and other investments. The associate has completed a six-week training program and is now working full time. Four weeks have passed, and the associate still has not made a sale. The associate's boss is going to meet with him or her today to discuss progress. Another student plays the role of a task-oriented leader. The two people participate in the review session.

Before playing (or assuming) the role of the associate or the boss, think for a few minutes how you would behave if you were placed in that role in real life. Empathize with the frustrated associate or the task-oriented leader. A good role player is both a scriptwriter and an actor.

Another two students repeat the same scenario except that this time the manager is a strongly relationship-oriented leader. Two more pairs of students then have their turn at acting out the task-oriented and relationship-oriented performance reviews. Another variation of this role play is for one person to play the roles of both the task-oriented and the relationship-oriented boss. Other class members observe and provide feedback on the effectiveness of the two styles of leadership.

## READER'S ROADMAP

So far in this book, we have examined the nature of leadership and the inner qualities of leaders, along with their behaviors, attitudes, and styles. In the next chapter, we describe some of the specific approaches to adapting one's leadership approach to the situation.

## Summary

college.hmco.com/pic/dubrin5e

Effective leadership requires the right behaviors, skills, and attitudes, as emphasized in the classic Ohio State University studies. Two major dimensions of leadership behavior were identified: consideration and initiating structure. Consideration is the degree to which the leader creates an environment of emotional support, warmth, friendliness, and trust. Making connections with people is a current aspect of consideration. Initiating structure is the degree to which the leader organizes and defines relationships in the group by such activities as

assigning tasks and specifying procedures. Both consideration and initiating structure are related to important leadership outcomes such as job satisfaction and performance.

Many task-related attitudes and behaviors of effective leaders have been identified. Among them are (1) adaptability to the situation, (2) direction setting, (3) high performance standards, (4) risk taking and a bias for action, (5) hands-on guidance and feedback, (6) stability of performance, and (7) ability to ask tough questions.

Many relationship-oriented attitudes and behaviors of leaders have also been identified. Among them are (1) aligning people, (2) concert building and collaboration, (3) creating inspiration and visibility, (4) satisfying higher-level needs, (5) giving emotional support and encouragement, (6) promoting principles and values, and (7) being a servant leader.

Servant leaders are committed to serving others rather than achieving their own goals. Aspects of servant leadership include placing service before self-interest, listening to others, inspiring trust by being trustworthy, focusing on what is feasible to accomplish, and lending a hand.

Many leaders today are receiving extensive feedback on their behaviors and attitudes in the form of 360-degree feedback, whereby people who work for or with the leader provide feedback on the leader's performance. Such feedback is likely to be useful when the feedback relates to business goals and strategy and to important aspects of leadership, when training is provided in giving and receiving feedback, when action plans are developed, and when managers own the feedback evaluation.

Understanding leadership style is an extension of understanding leadership attitudes and behavior. Participative leaders share decision making with group members. The participative style can be subdivided into consultative, consensus, and democratic leadership. The participative style is well suited to managing competent people who are eager to assume responsibility. Yet the process can be time consuming, and some managers perceive it to be a threat to their power. Autocratic leaders retain most of the authority for themselves. The Leadership Grid classifies leaders according to their concern for both production (task accomplishment) and people.

Another important style of leader is the entrepreneur. The entrepreneurial style stems from the leader's personal characteristics and the circumstances of self-employment. It includes a strong achievement drive and sensible risk taking; a high degree of enthusiasm and creativity; the tendency to act quickly on opportunities; hurriedness and impatience; a visionary perspective; a dislike of hierarchy and bureaucracy; a preference for dealing with external customers; and an eye on the future.

Male–female differences in leadership style have been observed. Women have a tendency toward relationship-oriented leadership, whereas men tend toward command and control. A major study showed that men and women leaders are perceived to be about equally effective. Some people argue that male–female differences in leadership are inconsistent and not significant.

Rather than searching for the one best style of leadership, managers are advised to diagnose the situation and then choose an appropriate leadership style to match. To be effective, a leader must be able to adapt his or her style to the circumstances.

## Key Terms

Effective leader

Consideration

Initiating structure

Pygmalion effect

Tough question

Concert building

Servant leader

360-degree feedback

Leadership style

Participative leaders

Consultative leaders

Consensus leaders

Democratic leaders

Autocratic leaders

Leadership Grid®

## ✔ Guidelines for Action and Skill Development

Most leadership style classifications are based on the directive (task-oriented) dimension versus the nondirective (relationship-oriented) dimension. In deciding which of these two styles is best, consider the following questions:

1. **What is the structure of your organization and the nature of your work?** You might decide, for example, that stricter control is necessary for some types of work, such as dealing with proprietary information.
2. **Which style suits you best?** Your personality, values, and beliefs influence how readily you can turn over responsibility to others.

3. **Which style suits your boss and organization?** For example, a boss who is highly directive may perceive you as weak if you are too nondirective.
4. **How readily will you be able to change your style if good results are not forthcoming?** Morale can suffer if you grant too much latitude today and have to tighten control in the future.
5. **Is there high potential for conflict in the work unit?** A directive leadership style can trigger conflict with independent, strong-willed people. A more nondirective style allows for more freedom of discussion, which defuses conflict.[48]

## Discussion Questions and Activities

1. How is initiating structure related to the cognitive skills of a leader?
2. Give an example of a high-consideration behavior that a supervisor of yours showed on your behalf. What was your reaction to his or her behavior?
3. Why is direction setting still an important leadership behavior in an era of empowerment?
4. Why is an effective leader supposed to provide emotional support to team members, even when they are mature adults?
5. In what ways might a *personalized charismatic leader* have quite different motives than a servant leader?
6. How might a manager use email to help carry out both task-oriented and relationship-oriented behaviors?

7. How would you characterize the leadership style of your favorite executive, athletic coach, or television character who plays a boss?
8. Why is the consensus leadership style widely recommended for providing leadership to workers under age 35?
9. Find a printed or Internet article on a business entrepreneur (or think of one from personal experience). How well does that person fit the entrepreneurial leadership style?
10. What can a man do to overcome the stereotype that people expect him to be a command-and-control style leader?

## LEADERSHIP CASE PROBLEM A

### THE CONFUSING 360-DEGREE FEEDBACK

Calvin Haskins, age 33, is the information systems manager for National Auto Supply Inc., a major supplier to auto parts and supply stores. National is a distributor whose customers include several of the larger chains of auto supply stores, as well as hundreds of smaller, independent stores. The company thus works as an intermediary between manufacturers and retailers. Founded in 1952, National has prospered even during business recessions.

CEO Troy Wentworth explains that National does particularly well during downturns in the economy because people are likely to hold on to their vehicles longer, making the purchase of auto parts and tires more necessary. Also, during the downturn more people purchase used vehicles, which require more replacement parts than do newer cars.

During the last several years, ecommerce has created new challenges for National Auto Supply, and company managers and professionals are working hard to develop a business model that will enable National to prosper as a distributor in this climate. One challenge they face is that many auto parts manufacturers are selling directly to auto parts stores over the Internet. National Auto Supply sells over the Web selectively because it does not want to alienate its customers, the auto supply stores, by going directly to consumers.

Wentworth has been acutely aware that National is undergoing a major transition in adapting to ecommerce and that many employees are confused and worried about the transition. Although he talks confidently to employees, stockholders, and research analysts about the future of the company, Wentworth has some concerns about National's ability to survive. In discussing the challenges with a management consultant, he said: "I guess the right term is *disintermediarization*. Some intermediaries, or distributors, are vanishing in the era of the Net. On the other hand, other distributors are prospering better than ever. I'm not sure yet which group we will fall into."

One action Wentworth took to help support the company during the transition was to look toward strengthening its leadership and management. Based on articles he had read in management magazines and on discussions with his consultant, Wentworth thought that a good starting point would be to conduct 360-degree surveys for the entire management team, including himself.

He noted, "We're big enough men and women here to find out what our internal and external customers think of us. If we are making any major errors in dealing with people, we need to know about it in a hurry. National will not survive this industry shakeout without all our leaders performing at their best."

National Auto Supply hired one of the leading firms in the field to conduct 360-degree surveys for seven key people. Contributors to the survey included the other managers in the company, a large group of employees, a handful of major customers, and self-evaluations. Five people receiving the feedback thought the activity was beneficial, in that it would help them fine-tune their approach to leading and managing workers. The finance vice president said the activity was a total waste of time. He noted, "My wife and children have been telling me the same thing for years. Why pay a consultant to gather that type of information when I can get it for free at home? Besides, my job is to manage the company's financial resources, not run a happiness camp."

Calvin Haskins had a different problem, saying that he wanted to improve as a leader and a manager but that the feedback was pulling him in different directions. He had one feedback session with Nancy Gonzalez, the organizational psychologist who conducted the 360-degree survey for National. Still confused as to what changes he should make, Haskins had another session planned with Gonzalez.

Haskins explained his dilemma in these terms: "I'm getting feedback that is contradictory and confusing. I realize that high-tech professionals do not all have the same personality and needs, but the feedback still has me baffled. This chart is a little wacky [referring to the feedback form shown in Exhibit 1]. It looks like I'm not giving the right amount of structure, and I'm not doing a good job of setting direction. Yet I have good ratings for setting high standards and inspiring people. Also, I give enough feedback, but I'm not a very good coach. Are they talking about the same person?

*(continued)*

"The written comments that I received in addition to the ratings also leave me puzzled as to what improvements I should make. Here's a sampling of them:

- Gets too bogged down in technology at times to do a good job as a leader.
- Tends to leave me on my own too much without giving me enough direction.
- Can be a real micromanager.
- Calvin is a little heavy-handed in his feedback.

- I appreciate Calvin's candid feedback.
- Forgets sometimes that we are humans, not information technology machines.
- Should be the next CEO of National.
- Maybe Calvin should consider a career switch. Management is definitely not his field."

"As I analyze this feedback," said Haskins, "I'm concerned that I might make changes in my leadership approach that would decrease rather than increase my effectiveness."

**EXHIBIT 1**  A 360-Degree Feedback Chart for Calvin Haskins, Manager of Information Systems, National Auto Supply, Inc,

**Manager evaluated:** *Calvin Haskins*          **Ratings** *(10 is highest)*

| Behavior or Attitude | Self Rating | Average Group Rating | Gap |
|---|---|---|---|
| 1. Gives right amount of structure | 9 | 4.5 | −4.5 |
| 2. Considerate of people | 6 | 6.2 | +0.2 |
| 3. Sets a direction | 10 | 3.9 | −6.1 |
| 4. Sets high standards | 7 | 9.0 | +2.0 |
| 5. Gives frequent feedback | 10 | 8.1 | −1.9 |
| 6. Gets people pulling together | 9 | 7.1 | −2.9 |
| 7. Inspires people | 7 | 9.2 | +2.2 |
| 8. Gives emotional support | 8 | 7.7 | −0.3 |
| 9. Is a helpful coach | 10 | 4.5 | −5.5 |
| 10. Encourages people to be self-reliant | 6 | 8.4 | +2.4 |

NOTE: A negative gap means you rate yourself higher on the behavior or attitude than does your group. A positive gap means the group rates you higher than you rate yourself.

## QUESTIONS

1. What changes in leadership attitudes and behaviors do you think Haskins should make?
2. How might you explain the differences of opinion that Haskins found in the written feedback and in the ratings shown in Exhibit 1?

3. In which leadership behavior described in this chapter might Haskins particularly need improvement?

NOTE: *The names of the company and leaders have been changed to protect client confidentiality.*

# LEADERSHIP CASE PROBLEM B

## FAILURE PUMPS UP DICK ENRICO

When Dick Enrico started Scarpelli's Italian restaurant in Minneapolis in the early 1970s, he wanted to give it a 1930s-style gangster atmosphere. But with only $15,000, his budget was too tight for elaborate décor. So he persuaded a local art-school teacher to give her students an unusual assignment: create tommy guns and papier-mâché busts of gangsters for the eatery. To make the menus look authentic, he shot holes in them with a .22-caliber rifle. The restaurant started with a bang, but momentum slipped, and in the end he sold the operation at a loss.

Enrico was never short on ideas, but it has taken a long string of failures for the 64-year-old entrepreneur to learn how to create a lasting success. Throughout his forty-six years as an entrepreneur, he has started twenty businesses that have folded or been sold at fire-sale prices, including a waterbed retailer and a franchise that helped people quit smoking.

But as difficult as Enrico's startup attempts proved to be—they cost him millions of dollars and at one point drove him into depression—his string of failures eventually helped lead to success. Although some of his ideas, Enrico says, were "just ahead of my time," many of the concepts were workable. The failures helped him realize that his biggest problem was not generating new ventures, but running them.

So after Enrico opened an exercise-equipment store in 1992, he took a different route and found a manager to run the day-to-day business while he focused on big-picture ideas to build the company. The result is that 2nd Wind Exercise Equipment, Inc., has expanded into a chain of thirty-three stores that is now generating $50 million in annual revenue. It has added new equipment and now operates in five midwestern states, and it has plans to expand into two more states.

**DIFFERENT PATHS** In the past, the sting of Enrico's numerous setbacks had been compounded by the success of his younger brother. As Dick Enrico struggled to prop up ailing ventures, Roger Enrico was ascending within the ranks of PepsiCo, Inc., rising to president and then chief executive and chairman. "I probably felt so inferior," Dick Enrico says.

Dick Enrico started his career selling pots and pans door to door, and then he established a cookware sales operation of his own. Many later ventures failed. One business, United Crane, Inc., sold vending machines with tiny cranes that picked up stuffed animals. His waterbed stores, called Aqua Knight, were among his other failures. Enrico attributes his failures largely to poor management, including the need for greater oversight to prevent theft and inventory shortages. Aqua Knight went under because Enrico tried to handle everything from accounting to sales. Besides being too stretched to think, Enrico became bored and impatient with the operational work, which he considered tedious.

*(continued)*

**GOING "BROKE" AGAIN** Enrico says he financed his ventures by borrowing from banks, friends, and credit cards, although he is vague about how he continued to get backing after so many failures. "I just worked at it," he says. "A deal here, a deal there—whatever. But it was tough." He described himself as going "broke" on three separate occasions. His brother invested in two of his ideas.

Brad Krohn, chairman and chief executive of the Business Bank in Minnetonka, says that even after five of Enrico's ideas flopped, he was not hesitant to continue lending him money. "For most people I would be, but it all comes down to character," Krohn says. Enrico always paid him back.

In 1986 Enrico pulled out of a long slump by selling car phones. With cash in his pocket and spirits lifted, in 1992 he began renting and selling used exercise equipment that he found through classified advertisements in newspapers. He sold his 1986 Corvette to finance the venture, which he called 2nd Wind Exercise Equipment, and bought forty used NordicTrack machines. Demand became so strong that he could not find enough stationary bikes and treadmills to fill his stores. When he asked equipment vendors to supply him with new products, they turned him down, saying he was "an embarrassment to the industry . . . a scratch-and-dent joint," Enrico says.

Finally, though, one supplier agreed to sell him new treadmills, and the business grew more rapidly. Enrico turned to Martin Bruder, a former supervisor for a health-club chain, to take over 2nd Wind's operation. Under his management, the company has boosted earnings and grown from nine to thirty-three stores. Enrico continues to appear in the company's advertisements and scouts out new locations of new sites, but he stays out of day-to-day operations. "I realized the importance of quality people" running the operation, says Enrico.

**THE FUTURE** Dick and Roger Enrico became closer in the early 1990s when Roger Enrico began making trips to Minneapolis for meetings of Target Corporation's board, on which he serves as a director. When they ate dinner together, they talked mostly about business. Dick Enrico liked to hear about the executives he read about in the newspapers, and Roger Enrico enjoyed listening to his brother's colorful stories and new ideas.

As 2nd Wind grew bigger, Roger Enrico began listening with a more discerning ear. In May 2004 he flew a group of representatives from a private equity firm to Minneapolis to meet Dick Enrico. They wanted to know if 2nd Wind could expand to other major markets, but Enrico has not decided yet whether he is interested in such a major expansion.

"He's the quintessential man of perseverance," Roger Enrico says. "And if you think about what makes really good business leaders—people who can build and grow things—it is that quality to persevere and to stay with it."

## QUESTIONS

1. What recommendations can you offer Dick Enrico to improve his chances of staying successful for the rest of his career?

2. What does Enrico's story illustrate about the difference between leadership and management?

3. Identify several entrepreneurial traits and characteristics Dick Enrico possesses, and justify your answer.

4. Enrico was invited into a graduate business class at the University of Saint Thomas in Minneapolis to regale them with his tales of woe. What could students learn from Enrico?

SOURCE: Adapted from Janet Adamy, "Try, Try, Again," *The Wall Street Journal*, July 12, 2004, p. R9.

**LEADERSHIP-SKILL BUILDING EXERCISE 4-5**

## MY LEADERSHIP PORTFOLIO

For this addition to your leadership portfolio, identify four leadership task-oriented behaviors or relationship-oriented behaviors that you have demonstrated this week. Your list can be any combination of the two sets of behaviors. Also jot down the result you achieved by exercising these behaviors. Here is an example:

"Thursday night I applied *direction setting* and it really worked. We have a group assignment in our marketing class with each group consisting of about five people. Our assignment is to analyze how well employee self-service is working in supermarkets and home-improvement stores. The group was hitting a wall because in their Internet searches they were finding mostly advertisements for Home Depot and the like. I suggested that we each visit a supermarket or home-improvement store and make firsthand observations of the customers who were using the automated checkout system. I also suggested we ask a couple of questions of the store associate supervising the activity. The group loved my idea, and the project was a big success. We supplemented written articles with a firsthand field study. I set the group in the right direction."

## INTERNET SKILL-BUILDING EXERCISE

Apply the chapter concepts! Visit the Web and complete this Internet skill-building exercise to learn more about current leadership topics and trends.

### IDENTIFYING LEADERSHIP BEHAVIORS AND ATTITUDES

Select a business or sports leader of interest to you. If you cannot think of a leader offhand, visit web sites of a company or athletic team that might interest you. For example, if you have been a fan of Kellogg Corporation products for a long time, search the Kellogg web site to identify a key company executive. Search the site for any clues to the executive's leadership behaviors and attitudes, as perhaps revealed in statements about employee relations or management philosophy. For example, an executive might make a statement about where the company is headed in the next five years, thereby indicating *direction setting*. You will probably not get enough information on the company web site, so plug your leader's name into a search engine to find two articles about him or her.

After you have gathered your case history information, identify at least four separate leadership behaviors and attitudes practiced by the leader in question. You will have to make inferences because a leader will rarely say, "Here are my leadership behaviors and attitudes."

# 5

# Contingency and Situational Leadership

Hurricane Ivan's 105-mile-per-hour winds, capable of ripping trees out of the ground as if they were weeds, swirled toward the city of Pensacola, Florida. Meanwhile, just 10 miles away at Baptist Hospital, human resources director Celeste Norris was holed up in an office, trying unsuccessfully to ignore the screeching winds and crashing sounds outside as she began her tasks of helping the hospital survive the storm.

Norris and Teresa Kirkland, director of employee relations, and Steve Infinger, director of benefits, had brought sleeping bags to work, figuring they would be trapped overnight. As it turned out, they were stuck for the next two days on the job—without running water, plumbing, or air-conditioning to cope with the late summer Florida heat.

Norris and her colleagues juggled a series of urgent problems, from locating missing employees to arranging emergency housing and daycare services for those whose lives were in chaos. "When a big storm reaches the Gulf, it's going to hit land someplace," says Infinger. "You have to get ready, in case it's your turn."

Ivan knocked out the hospital phone system, and wrecked cell phone towers. Norris and her colleagues, however, had walkie-talkies, which they used to communicate with others inside the hospital. The network was down, preventing them from using email, but the office computer and printer still worked, so they created regular bulletins with vital information—transportation availability, where to get water, and community closings and openings, for example—and delivered them by hand.

"We made sure that everyone understood that they were part of the health care team, no matter what job they usually did," Kirkland says. "Managers, for example, might be given plebeian tasks such as moving damaged furniture or distributing supplies. But instead of resentment, it promoted camaraderie."[1]

The incident about managing through a hurricane at a hospital illustrates an increasingly important leadership task: leading people through a crisis. Leadership of this type is a special case of the general subject of this chapter—adjusting one's approach to the situation. Contingency and situational leadership further expands the study of leadership styles by adding more specific guidelines about which style to use under which circumstance.

In this chapter we present an overview of the situational perspective on leadership. We then summarize the five best-known contingency theories of leadership: Fiedler's contingency theory, path-goal theory, the situational leadership model, the normative decision model, and cognitive resource theory. We also describe a contingency model that applies mostly to CEOs. In addition, we describe crisis leadership, because leading others through a crisis has become a frequent challenge in recent years.

## Situational Influences on Effective Leadership Behavior

The situation can influence the leadership behavior or style a leader emphasizes. The essence of a **contingency approach to leadership** is that leaders are most effective when they make their behavior contingent on situational forces, including group member characteristics. Both the internal and the external environment have a significant impact on leader effectiveness. For example, the quality of the work force and the competitiveness of the environment can influence which behaviors the leader emphasizes. A manager who supervises competent employees might be able to practice consensus readily. And a manager who faces a competitive environment might find it easier to align people to pursue a new vision.

A useful perspective on implementing contingency leadership is that the manager must be flexible enough to avoid clinging to old ideas that no longer work.[2] Being stubborn about what will work in a given situation and clinging to old ideas can result in ineffective leadership. The effective leader adapts to changing circumstances, as described in the discussion of style flexibility in Chapter 4.

An example of a leader who developed a contingency approach just in time to save his firm follows:

> Derek had founded a telecom components company whose primary product was a line of batteries for mobile telephones and digital cameras. His devotion to his company, like that of many other entrepreneurs, bordered on obsessive behavior. He could not understand why his employees did not share this unswerving devotion to the firm. Derek's battle cry was, "We work as long and as hard as needed to get the job done." Living up to this belief might require seventy hours each week on the job. But many employees did not share Derek's commitment to the firm, and turnover in the professional ranks was high. As a result, sales, as well as delivery dates of batteries, began to slip.
>
> With the company in a downward spiral, Derek finally came to accept the idea that work–life balance was important to many employees—even those who were talented and hard working. He soon began to encourage his professional staff to consider a workweek of about fifty hours as acceptable, and emphasized that taking allotted vacations was acceptable behavior. Soon turnover decreased, and recruiting professional staff became easier. At a staff meeting with his management team, Derek admitted, "I guess it's no longer realistic for everybody around here to work like they owned the place. I'm making a little concession to the new view of the world."

## Fiedler's Contingency Theory of Leadership Effectiveness

Fred E. Fiedler developed a widely researched and quoted contingency model that holds that the best style of leadership is determined by the situation in which the leader is working.[3] Here we examine how the style and situation are evaluated, the overall findings of the theory, and how leaders can modify situations to their advantage.

## Measuring Leadership Style: The Least Preferred Coworker (LPC) Scale

Fiedler's theory classifies a manager's leadership style as relationship motivated or task motivated. According to Fiedler, leadership style is a relatively permanent aspect of behavior and thus difficult to modify. He reasons that once leaders understand their particular leadership style, they should work in situations that match that style. Similarly, the organization should help managers match leadership styles and situations.

The least preferred coworker (LPC) scale measures the degree to which a leader describes favorably or unfavorably his or her least preferred coworker—that is, an employee with whom he or she could work the least well. A leader who describes the LPC in relatively favorable terms tends to be relationship motivated. In contrast, a person who describes this coworker in an unfavorable manner tends to be task motivated. You can use Leadership Self-Assessment Quiz 5-1 to measure your leadership style.

**LEADERSHIP SELF-ASSESSMENT QUIZ 5-1**

### THE LEAST PREFERRED COWORKER (LPC) SCALE FOR MEASURING LEADERSHIP STYLE

Throughout your life, you will work in many groups with a wide variety of people—on your job, in social groups, in religious organizations, in volunteer groups, on athletic teams, and in many other situations. Some of your coworkers may be very easy to work with in attaining the group's goals, while others less so.

Think of all the people with whom you have ever worked, and then think of the person with whom you could work *least well*. He or she may be someone with whom you work now or someone with whom you worked in the past. This does not have to be the person you liked least well, but should be the person with whom you had the most difficulty getting a job done—the *one* individual with whom you could work *least well*.

Describe this person on the scale that follows by placing an X in the appropriate space. Look at the words at both ends of the line before you mark your X. *There are no right or wrong answers.* Work rapidly: Your first answer is likely to be the right one. Do not omit any items, and mark each item only once. Now describe the person with whom you can work least well.

**Scoring**

| | 8 | 7 | 6 | 5 | 4 | 3 | 2 | 1 | | |
|---|---|---|---|---|---|---|---|---|---|---|
| Pleasant | __ | __ | __ | __ | __ | __ | __ | __ | Unpleasant | ____ |
| Friendly | __ | __ | __ | __ | __ | __ | __ | __ | Unfriendly | ____ |
| | 8 | 7 | 6 | 5 | 4 | 3 | 2 | 1 | | |
| Rejecting | __ | __ | __ | __ | __ | __ | __ | __ | Accepting | ____ |
| | 1 | 2 | 3 | 4 | 5 | 6 | 7 | 8 | | |

*(continued)*

| | | | | | | | | | | **Scoring** |
|---|---|---|---|---|---|---|---|---|---|---|
| Tense | __ 1 | __ 2 | __ 3 | __ 4 | __ 5 | __ 6 | __ 7 | __ 8 | Relaxed | ____ |
| Distant | __ 1 | __ 2 | __ 3 | __ 4 | __ 5 | __ 6 | __ 7 | __ 8 | Close | ____ |
| Cold | __ 1 | __ 2 | __ 3 | __ 4 | __ 5 | __ 6 | __ 7 | __ 8 | Warm | ____ |
| Supportive | __ 8 | __ 7 | __ 6 | __ 5 | __ 4 | __ 3 | __ 2 | __ 1 | Hostile | ____ |
| Boring | __ 1 | __ 2 | __ 3 | __ 4 | __ 5 | __ 6 | __ 7 | __ 8 | Interesting | ____ |
| Quarrelsome | __ 1 | __ 2 | __ 3 | __ 4 | __ 5 | __ 6 | __ 7 | __ 8 | Harmonious | ____ |
| Gloomy | __ 1 | __ 2 | __ 3 | __ 4 | __ 5 | __ 6 | __ 7 | __ 8 | Cheerful | ____ |
| Open | __ 8 | __ 7 | __ 6 | __ 5 | __ 4 | __ 3 | __ 2 | __ 1 | Guarded | ____ |
| Backbiting | __ 1 | __ 2 | __ 3 | __ 4 | __ 5 | __ 6 | __ 7 | __ 8 | Loyal | ____ |
| Untrustworthy | __ 1 | __ 2 | __ 3 | __ 4 | __ 5 | __ 6 | __ 7 | __ 8 | Trustworthy | ____ |
| Considerate | __ 8 | __ 7 | __ 6 | __ 5 | __ 4 | __ 3 | __ 2 | __ 1 | Inconsiderate | ____ |
| Nasty | __ 1 | __ 2 | __ 3 | __ 4 | __ 5 | __ 6 | __ 7 | __ 8 | Nice | ____ |
| Agreeable | __ 8 | __ 7 | __ 6 | __ 5 | __ 4 | __ 3 | __ 2 | __ 1 | Disagreeable | ____ |
| Insincere | __ 1 | __ 2 | __ 3 | __ 4 | __ 5 | __ 6 | __ 7 | __ 8 | Sincere | ____ |
| Kind | __ 8 | __ 7 | __ 6 | __ 5 | __ 4 | __ 3 | __ 2 | __ 1 | Unkind | ____ |

*Total* ____

SCORING AND INTERPRETATION To calculate your score, add the numbers in the right column. If you scored 73 or higher, you are a high LPC leader, meaning that you are relationship motivated. If you scored 64 or lower, you are a low LPC leader, meaning that you are task motivated. A score of 65 to 72 places you in the intermediate range. Compare your score to your score in Leadership Self-Assessment Quiz 4-1.

In attempting to make sense of your score, recognize that the LPC scale is but one measure of leadership style and that the approach to measurement is indirect. The leadership style measure presented in Self-Assessment Quiz 4-1 is more direct. To repeat, the general idea of the LPC approach is that if you have a positive, charitable attitude toward people you had a difficult time working with, you are probably relationship oriented. In contrast, if you took a dim view of people who gave you a hard time, you are probably task oriented. The message here is that a relationship-oriented leader should be able to work well with a variety of personalities.

SOURCE: Adapted from *Improving Leadership Effectiveness,* by Fred E. Fiedler, Martin M. Chemers, and Linda Mahar, Copyright © 1976 by John Wiley & Sons. Reprinted by permission of the authors.

## Measuring the Leadership Situation

Fiedler's contingency theory classifies situations as high, moderate, and low control. The more control that the leader exercises, the more favorable the situation is for him or her. The control classifications are determined by rating the situation on its three dimensions: (1) *leader–member relations* measure how well the group and the leader get along; (2) *task structure* measures how clearly the procedures, goals, and evaluation of the job are defined; and (3) *position power* measures the leader's authority to hire, fire, discipline, and grant salary increases to group members.

Leader–member relations contribute as much to situation favorability as do task structure and position power combined. The leader therefore has the most control in a situation in which his or her relationships with members are the best.

## Overall Findings

The key points of Fiedler's contingency theory are summarized and simplified in Figure 5-1. The original theory is much more complex. Leadership effectiveness

## FIGURE 5-1  Summary of Findings from Fiedler's Contingency Theory

| Task-motivated leaders perform best when they have the most control (highly favorable). | Relationship-motivated leaders perform best when they have moderate control (moderately favorable). | Task-motivated leaders perform best when they have low control (highly unfavorable). |
|---|---|---|
| *High* | *Moderate* | *Low* |

◄———————  **AMOUNT OF SITUATIONAL CONTROL BY LEADER**  ———————►

| a. Leader-member relations are good. b. Task is well structured. c. Leader has high position power. | Both favorable and unfavorable factors are present. | a. Leader-member relations are poor. b. Task is poorly structured. c. Leader has low position power. |
|---|---|---|

depends on matching leaders to situations in which they can exercise more control. The theory states that task-motivated leaders perform the best in situations of both high control and low control. Relationship-motivated leaders perform the best in situations of moderate control. Task-motivated leaders perform better in situations that are highly favorable for exercising control because they do not have to be concerned with the task. Instead, they can work on relationships. In moderately favorable situations, the relationship-motivated leader achieves higher group productivity because he or she can work on relationships and not get involved in overmanaging. In very-low-control situations, the task-motivated leader is able to structure and make sense out of confusion, whereas the relationship-motivated leader wants to give emotional support to group members or call a meeting.

### Making the Situation More Favorable for the Leader

A practical implication of contingency theory is that leaders should modify situations to match their leadership style, thereby enhancing their chances of being effective. Consider a group of leaders who are task motivated and decide that they need to exercise more control over the situation to achieve higher work unit productivity. To increase control over the situation, they can do one or more of the following:

- Improve leader–member relations through displaying an interest in the personal welfare of group members, having meals with them, actively listening to their concerns, telling anecdotes, and in general being a "nice person."
- Increase task structure by engaging in behaviors related to initiating structure, such as being more specific about expectations, providing deadlines, showing samples of acceptable work, and providing written instructions.
- Exercise more position power by requesting more formal authority from higher management. For example, the leader might let it be known that he or she has the authority to grant bonuses and make strong recommendations for promotion.

Now imagine a relationship-motivated leader who wants to create a situation of moderate favorability so that his or her interests in being needed by the group could be satisfied. The leader might give the group tasks of low structure and deemphasize his or her position power.

### Evaluation of Fiedler's Contingency Theory

A major contribution of Fiedler's work is that it has prompted others to conduct studies about the contingency nature of leadership. Fiedler's theory has been one of the most widely researched theories in industrial/organizational psychology, and at one time it was used extensively as the basis for leadership training programs. The model has also alerted leaders to the importance of sizing up the situation to gain control. Despite its potential advantages, however, the contingency theory is too complicated to have much of an impact on most leaders. A major problem centers on matching the situation to the leader. In most situations, the amount of control the leader exercises varies from time to time. For example, if a relationship-motivated leader were to find the situation becoming too favorable for exercising control, it is doubtful that he or she would be transferred to a less favorable situation or attempt to make the situation less favorable.

## The Path-Goal Theory of Leadership Effectiveness

The **path-goal theory** of leadership effectiveness, as developed by Robert House, specifies what a leader must do to achieve high productivity and morale in a given situation. In general, a leader attempts to clarify the path to a goal for a group member so that he or she receives personal payoffs. At the same time, this group member's job satisfaction and performance increase.[4] Like the expectancy theory of motivation, on which it is based, path-goal theory is complex and has several versions. Its key features are summarized in Figure 5-2.

The major proposition of path-goal theory is that the manager should choose a leadership style that takes into account the characteristics of the group members and the demands of the task. Two key aspects of this theory will be discussed: matching the leadership style to the situation and steps the leader can take to influence performance and satisfaction.

**FIGURE 5-2  The Path-Goal Theory of Leadership**

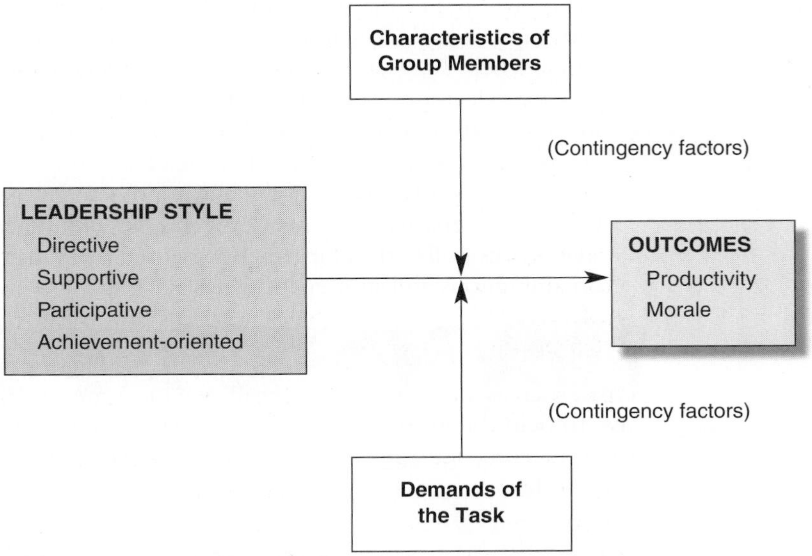

To achieve the outcomes of productivity and morale, the manager chooses one of four leadership styles, depending on (a) the characteristics of the situation, and (b) the demands of the task.

## Matching the Leadership Style to the Situation

Path-goal theory emphasizes that the leader should choose among four leadership styles to achieve optimum results in a given situation. Two important sets of contingency factors are the type of subordinates and the tasks they perform (a key environmental factor). The type of subordinates is determined by how much control they think they have over the environment (locus of control) and by how well they think they can do the assigned task.

Environmental contingency factors are those that are not within the control of group members but influence satisfaction and task accomplishment. Three broad classifications of contingency factors in the environment are (1) the group members' tasks, (2) the authority system within the organization, and (3) the work group.

To use path-goal theory, the leader must first assess the relevant variables in the environment. Then she or he selects the one of the four styles listed next that fits those contingency factors best:

1. *Directive style.* The leader who is directive (similar to task motivated) emphasizes formal activities such as planning, organizing, and controlling. When the task is unclear, the directive style improves morale.
2. *Supportive style.* The leader who is supportive (similar to relationship motivated) displays concern for group members' well-being and creates an emotionally supportive climate. He or she enhances morale when group members work on dissatisfying, stressful, or frustrating tasks. Group members who are unsure of themselves prefer the supportive leadership style.
3. *Participative style.* The leader who is participative consults with group members to gather their suggestions, and then considers these suggestions seriously when making a decision. The participative leader is best suited for improving the morale of well-motivated employees who perform nonrepetitive tasks.
4. *Achievement-oriented style.* The leader who is achievement oriented sets challenging goals, pushes for work improvement, and sets high expectations for team members, who are also expected to assume responsibility. This leadership style works well with achievement-oriented team members and with those working on ambiguous and nonrepetitive tasks.

A leader can sometimes successfully combine more than one of the four styles, although this possibility is not specified in path-goal theory. For example, during a crisis, such as a major product recall, the marketing manager might need to be directive to help the group take fast action. After the initial emergency actions are taken, the leader, recognizing how stressed the workers must be, might shift to a supportive mode.

## Steps Leaders Can Take to Influence Performance and Satisfaction

In addition to recommending the leadership style to fit the situation, the path-goal theory offers other suggestions to leaders. Most of them relate to motivation and satisfaction, including the following:

1. Recognize or activate group members' needs over which the leader has control.
2. Increase the personal payoffs to team members for attaining work goals. The leader might give high-performing employees special recognition.
3. Make the paths to payoffs (rewards) easier by coaching and providing direction. For instance, a manager might help a team member be selected for a high-level project.
4. Help group members clarify their expectations of how effort will lead to good performance and how performance will lead to a reward. The leader might say, "Anyone who has gone through this training in the past came away knowing how to implement an ISO 9000 (quality standards) program. And most people who learn how to meet these standards wind up getting a good raise."
5. Reduce frustrating barriers to reaching goals. For example, the leader might hire a temporary worker to help a group member catch up on paperwork and email.
6. Increase opportunities for personal satisfaction if the group member performs effectively. The "if" is important because it reflects contingent behavior on the leader's part.
7. Be careful not to irritate people by giving them instructions on things they already can do well.
8. To obtain high performance and satisfaction, the leader must provide structure if it is missing and supply rewards contingent on adequate performance. To accomplish this, leaders must clarify the desirability of goals for the group members.[5]

As a leader, you can derive specific benefit from path-goal theory by applying these eight methods of influencing performance. Chemers points out that although research interest in path-goal theory has waned in recent years, the basic tenets of the theory are on target. Any comprehensive theory of leadership must include the idea that the leader's actions have a major impact on the motivation and satisfaction of group members.[6] Despite the potential contributions of path-goal theory, it contains so many nuances and complexities that it has attracted little interest from managers.

## Situational Leadership® II (SLII)

The two contingency approaches to leadership presented so far take into account collectively the task, the authority of the leader, and the nature of the subordinates. Another explanation of contingency leadership places its primary emphasis on the characteristics of group members. **Situational leadership II (SLII),** developed by Kenneth H. Blanchard and his colleagues, explains how to match leadership style to the capabilities of group members on a given task.[7] For example, you might need less guidance from a supervisor when you are skilled in a task than when you are performing a new task.

SLII is designed to increase the frequency and quality of conversations about performance and professional development between managers and group members so that competence is developed, commitment takes place, and turnover among talented workers is reduced. Leaders are taught to use the leadership style that matches or responds to the needs of the situation.

Before delving further into the situational leadership model, do Leadership Self-Assessment Quiz 5-2. It will help alert you to the specific behaviors involved in regarding the characteristics of group members as key contingency variables in choosing the most effective leadership style.

## MEASURING YOUR SITUATIONAL PERSPECTIVE

INSTRUCTIONS Indicate how well you agree with the following statements, using the following scale: DS = disagree strongly; D = disagree; N = neutral; A = agree; AS = agree strongly. Circle the most accurate answer.

| | | | | | | |
|---|---|---|---|---|---|---|
| 4 | **1.** Workers need to be carefully trained before you can place high expectations on them. | DS | D | N | (A) | AS |
| 2 | **2.** The more knowledgeable the worker is, the less he or she needs a clear statement of objectives. | DS | (D) | N | A | AS |
| 4 | **3.** "Hand holding" is an ineffective leadership technique for anxious group members. | DS | (D) | N | A | AS |
| 4 | **4.** The same well-delivered pep talk will usually appeal to workers at all levels. | DS | (D) | N | A | AS |
| 5 | **5.** As a manager, I would invest the least amount of time supervising the most competent workers. | DS | D | N | A | (AS) |
| 3 | **6.** It is best not to put much effort into supervising unenthusiastic staff members. | DS | D | (N) | A | AS |
| 4 | **7.** An effective leader delegates equal kinds and amounts of work to group members. | DS | (D) | N | A | AS |
| 3 | **8.** Even the most effective workers need frequent reassurance and emotional support. | DS | D | (N) | A | AS |
| 4 | **9.** If I noticed that a group member seemed insecure and anxious, I would give him or her especially clear instructions and guidelines. | DS | D | N | (A) | AS |
| 4 | **10.** Many competent workers get to the point where they require relatively little leadership and supervision. | DS | D | N | (A) | AS |

*Total score:* 37

SCORING AND INTERPRETATION

**1.** DS = 1, D = 2, N = 3, A = 4, AS = 5

**2.** DS = 1, D = 2, N = 3, A = 4, AS = 5

**3.** DS = 5, D = 4, N = 3, A = 2, AS = 1

**4.** DS = 5, D = 4, N = 3, A = 2, AS = 1

**5.** DS = 1, D = 2, N = 3, A = 4, AS = 5

**6.** DS = 5, D = 4, N = 3, A = 2, AS = 1

**7.** DS = 5, D = 4, N = 3, A = 2, AS = 1

**8.** DS = 5, D = 4, N = 3, A = 2, AS = 1

**9.** DS = 1, D = 2, N = 3, A = 4, AS = 5

**10.** DS = 1, D = 2, N = 3, A = 4, AS = 5

- 45–50 points: You have (or would have) a strong situational perspective as a leader and manager.
- 30–44 points: You have (or would have) an average situational perspective as a leader and manager.
- 10–29 points: You rarely take (or would take) a situational perspective as a leader and manager.

SKILL DEVELOPMENT For the vast majority of leadership and management assignments, it pays to sharpen your situational perspective. If you scored lower than you want, sharpen your insights into situations by asking yourself, "What are the key factors in this situation that will influence my effectiveness as a leader-manager?" Study both the people and the task in the situation.

## Basics of SLII

college.hmco.com/pic/
dubrin5e

**@ KNOWLEDGE BANK:** contains a description of the original situational model of leadership.

Situational Leadership II stems from the original situational model. The major premise of SLII is that the basis for effective leadership is managing the relationship between a leader and a subordinate on a given task. The major concepts of the SLII model are presented in Figure 5-3 on page 148. According to SLII, effective leaders adapt their behavior to the level of *commitment* and *competence* of a particular subordinate to complete a given task. For example, team member Tanya might be committed to renting some empty office space by year-end and also highly skilled at such an

**FIGURE 5-3** Situational Leadership II (SLII)

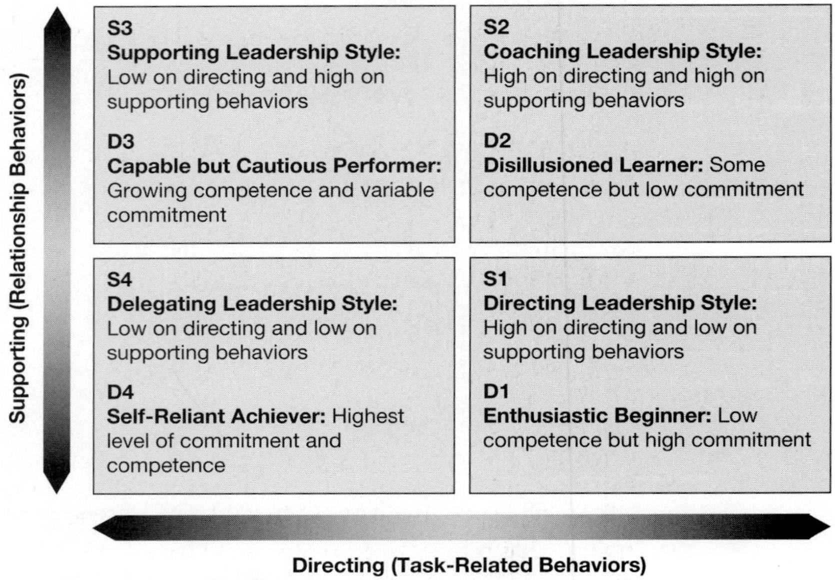

activity. Or she might feel that the task is drudgery and not have much skill in selling office space. The combination of the subordinate's commitment and competence determines his or her *developmental level,* as follows:

**D1**—Enthusiastic Beginner. The learner has low competence but high commitment.

**D2**—Disillusioned Learner. The individual has gained some competence but has been disappointed after having experienced several setbacks. Commitment at this stage is low.

**D3**—Capable but Cautious Performer. The learner has growing competence, yet commitment is variable.

**D4**—Self-Reliant Achiever. The learner has high competence and commitment.

SLII explains that effective leadership depends on two independent behaviors: *supporting* and *directing.* (By now, you have read about this dichotomy several times in this chapter as well as in Chapter 4.) Supporting refers to relationship behaviors such as the leader's listening, giving recognition, communicating, and encouraging. Directing refers to task-related behaviors such as the leader's giving careful directions and controlling.

As shown in Figure 5-3, the four basic styles are:

**S1**—Directing. High directive behavior/low supportive behavior.

**S2**—Coaching. High directive behavior/high supportive behavior.

S3—Supporting. Low directive behavior/high supportive behavior.

S4—Delegating. Low directive behavior/low supportive behavior.

For best results on a given task, the leader is required to match his or her style to the developmental level of the group member. Each quadrant in Figure 5-3 indicates the desired match between leader style and subordinate development level.

A key point of SLII is that no one style is best: an effective leader uses all four styles depending on the subordinate's developmental level on a given task. The most appropriate leadership style among S1 to S4 corresponds to the subordinate developmental levels of D1 to D4, respectively: enthusiastic beginners (D1) require a directing (S1) leader; disillusioned learners (D2) need a coaching (S2) leader; capable but cautious performers (D3) need a supporting (S3) style of leader; and self-reliant achievers (D4) need a delegating (S4) style of leader.

### Evaluation of SLII

Situational leadership represents a consensus of thinking about leadership behavior in relation to group members: competent people require less specific direction than do less competent people. The model is also useful because it builds on other explanations of leadership that emphasize the role of task and relationship behaviors. As a result, it has proved to be useful as the basis for leadership training. At least 3 million managers have been trained in situational leadership, covering various stages of the model, so we can assume that situational leadership makes sense to managers and companies. The situational model also corroborates common sense and is therefore intuitively appealing. You can benefit from this model by attempting to diagnose the readiness of group members before choosing the right leadership style.

A challenge in applying SLII is that the leader has to stay tuned into which task a group member is performing at a given time and then implement the correct style. Because assignments can change rapidly and group members are often working on more than one task in a day, the leader may have to keep shifting styles.

SLII presents categories and guidelines so precisely that it gives the impression of infallibility. In reality, leadership situations are less clear-cut than the four quadrants suggest. Also, the prescriptions for leadership will work only some of the time. For example, many supervisors use a coaching style (S2) with a disillusioned learner (D2) and still achieve poor results. A major concern is that there are few leadership situations in which a high-task, high-relationship orientation does not produce the best results.

Leadership Skill-Building Exercise 5-1, on page 150, provides you with the opportunity to practice implementing the situational leadership model. The same exercise also supports other contingency and situational models.

## The Normative Decision Model

Another contingency viewpoint is that leaders must choose a style that elicits the correct degree of group participation when making decisions. Since many of a leader's interactions with group members involve decision making, this perspective is

### APPLYING SITUATIONAL LEADERSHIP II

You are playing the role of a team leader whose team is given the responsibility of improving customer service at a consumer electronics megastore. Before jumping into this task, you decide to use SLII. Today you are going to meet with three team members individually to estimate their developmental level with respect to performing the customer-service-improvement task. You will want to estimate both their *competence* and *commitment* to perform the task. (Three different people will play the role of group members whose readiness is being assessed.) After the brief interviews (about five minutes) are conducted, you will announce which leadership style you intend to use with each of the people you interviewed. Class members not directly involved in the role-play will offer feedback on how well you assessed the team members' readiness.

sensible. The **normative decision model** views leadership as a decision-making process in which the leader examines certain factors within the situation to determine which decision-making style will be the most effective. Here we present the latest version of the model that has evolved from the work of Victor Vroom and his associates over thirty years, based on research with more than 100,000 managers.[8]

### *Decision-Making Styles*

The normative model (formerly known as the leader-participation model) identifies five decision-making styles, each reflecting a different degree of participation by group members:

1. *Decide.* The leader makes the decision alone and either announces or sells it to the group. The leader might use expertise in collecting information from the group or from others who appear to have information relevant to the problem.
2. *Consult (Individually).* The leader presents the problem to the group members individually, gathers their suggestions, and then makes the decision.
3. *Consult (Group).* The leader presents the problem to group members in a meeting, gathers their suggestions, and then makes the decision.
4. *Facilitate.* The leader presents the problem, then acts as a facilitator, defining the problem to be solved and the boundaries in which the decision must be made. The leader wants concurrence and avoids having his or her ideas receive more weight based on position power.
5. *Delegate.* The leader permits the group to make the decision within prescribed limits. Although the leader does not directly intervene in the group's deliberations unless explicitly asked, he or she works behind the scenes, providing resources and encouragement.

## Contingency Factors and Application of the Model

The leader diagnoses the situation in terms of seven variables, or contingency factors, that contribute to selecting the most appropriate decision-making style. Based on answers to those variables, the leader or manager follows the path through decision matrices to choose one of five decision-making styles. The model has two versions: one when time is critical, and one when a more important consideration is developing group members' decision-making capabilities. When development of group members receives higher priority, the leader or manager relies more on the group to make a decision even if the process is time consuming.

Figure 5-4, on page 152, depicts the matrix for time-driven group problems, a situation in which a decision must be reached rapidly. The situational factors, or problem variables, are listed at the top of the matrix. Specifying these factors makes the model a contingency approach. The decision-making style chosen depends on these factors, which are defined as follows:

*Decision Significance:* The significance of the decision to the success of the project or organization

*Importance of Commitment:* The importance of team members' commitment to the decision

*Leader Expertise:* Your knowledge or expertise in relation to the problem

*Likelihood of Commitment:* The likelihood that the team will commit itself to a decision you might make on your own

*Group Support:* The degree to which the team supports the organization's objectives at stake in the problem

*Group Expertise:* Team members' knowledge or expertise in relation to the problem

*Team Competence:* The ability of the team members to work together in solving problems

Accurate answers to these seven situational factors can be challenging to obtain. The leader may have to rely heavily on intuition and also minimize distorted thinking, such as believing he or she has some expertise but in fact does not.

To use the model, the decision maker begins at the left side of the matrix in Figure 5-4, at the "Problem Statement." At the top of the matrix are the seven situational factors, each of which may be present (H for high) or absent (L for low) in that problem. You begin by ascertaining if the decision is significant. If it is, you select H and answer the second question, concerning the importance of gaining group commitment. If you continue the process without crossing any horizontal line on the matrix, you will arrive at one of the five recommended decision styles. Sometimes a conclusive determination can be made based on two factors, such as L, L. Others require three (such as L, H, H), four (such as H, H, H, H), or as many as seven factors (such as H, H, L, L, H, H, H).

Different people giving different answers to the situational factors will arrive at different conclusions about the recommended decision style in the situation. The leader needs sufficient information to answer each of seven questions accurately. To help

**FIGURE 5-4  The Time-Driven Model for Choosing a Decision-Making Style**

Instructions: The matrix operates like a funnel. You start at the left with a specific decision problem in mind. The column headings denote situational factors which may or may not be present in that problem. You progress by selecting High or Low (H or L) for each relevant situational factor. Proceed down from the funnel, judging only those situational factors for which a judgment is called for, until you reach the recommended process.

| Problem Statement | Decision Significance | Importance of Commitment | Leader Expertise | Likelihood of Commitment | Group Support | Group Expertise | Team Competence | Recommended Process |
|---|---|---|---|---|---|---|---|---|
| P R O B L E M   S T A T E M E N T | H | H | H | H | — | — | — | Decide |
| | | | | L | H | H | H | Delegate |
| | | | | | | | L | Consult (Group) |
| | | | | | | L | — | Consult (Group) |
| | | | | | L | — | — | Consult (Group) |
| | | | L | H | H | H | H | Facilitate |
| | | | | | | | L | Consult (Individually) |
| | | | | | | L | — | Consult (Individually) |
| | | | | | L | — | — | Consult (Individually) |
| | | | | L | H | H | H | Facilitate |
| | | | | | | | L | Consult (Group) |
| | | | | | | L | — | Consult (Group) |
| | | | | | L | — | — | Consult (Group) |
| | | L | H | — | — | — | — | Decide |
| | | | L | L | H | H | H | Facilitate |
| | | | | | | | L | Consult (Individually) |
| | | | | | | L | — | Consult (Individually) |
| | | | | | L | — | — | Consult (Individually) |
| | L | H | H | — | — | — | — | Decide |
| | | | L | — | — | — | H | Delegate |
| | | | | | | | L | Facilitate |
| | | L | — | — | — | — | — | Decide |

Source: Victor H. Vroom's Time-Driven Model, reproduced from *A Model of Leadership Style.* Copyright 1998. Reprinted by permission of the author.

you apply the model, Leadership Skill-Building Exercise 5-2 presents a scenario that Vroom developed.

The normative model provides a valuable service to practicing managers and leaders. It prompts them to ask questions about contingency variables in decision-making situations. It has been found that for previous versions of the model, managers who follow its procedures are likely to increase their decision-making effectiveness. Furthermore, managers who make decisions consistent with the model (again, based on previous versions) are more likely to be perceived as effective.[9] These same good results are probable for Vroom's later model because it incorporates most of the concepts in the previous models but is easier to follow. As with other contingency approaches, however, the model does not deal with the charismatic and inspirational aspects of leadership.

When the leader concludes that group decision making is appropriate, morale will often be elevated. Lois Juliber, a Colgate-Palmolive executive, implemented a program of encouraging people throughout the organization to make decisions. She

**LEADERSHIP SKILL-BUILDING EXERCISE 5-2**

↗

### APPLYING THE TIME-DRIVEN MODEL

The exercise presented here can be done individually or in small groups.

The bank examiners have just left, having insisted that many of your commercial real estate loans be written off, which will deplete your already low capital. Along with the many other banks in your region, your bank is in serious danger of being closed by the regulators. As the financial problems surfaced, many of the top executives left to pursue other interests, but fortunately you were able to replace them with three highly competent, younger managers. Although they had no prior acquaintance with one another, each is a product of a fine training program with one of the money center banks, in which they rotated through positions in all of the banking functions.

Your extensive experience in the industry leads you to the inevitable conclusion that the only hope is a two-pronged approach involving the reduction of all but the most critical expenses and the sale of assets to other banks. The task must be accomplished quickly because further deterioration of the quality of the loan portfolio could result in a negative capital position and force regulators to close the bank.

The strategy is clear to you, but you have many details that will need to be worked out. You believe that you know what information will be needed to get the bank on a course for future prosperity. You are fortunate in having three young executives to help you. Although they have had little or no experience in working together, you know that each is dedicated to the survival of the bank. Like you, they know what needs to be done and how to do it.

The suggested path is found on page 489 in the references to Chapter 5.

SOURCE: Victor H. Vroom's Time-Driven Model, reproduced from *A Model of Leadership Style*. Copyright 1998. Reprinted by permission of the author.

noted, "All of a sudden, people got the sense that they could really make a decision, and no one was going to second-guess them. And for morale, it was just fantastic. Second-guessing is the absolute paralyzer of an organization, and not what you do in a turnaround when you need speed."[10]

## Cognitive Resource Theory: How Intelligence, Experience, and Stress Influence Leadership

Another contingency theory describes how a leader's intelligence and experience can influence performance when the stress level of the people is considered. The general thrust of **cognitive resource theory** is that stress plays a key role in determining how a leader's intelligence is related to group performance.[11] The theory, as developed by Fiedler and his colleagues, also explains how directive behavior is tied in with intelligence. Several of the many predictions made by cognitive resource theory are as follows:

1. Because experienced leaders have a larger variety of behaviors to fall back on, those with greater experience but lower intelligence are likely to have higher-performing groups under high-stress conditions. The veteran leader-manager has acquired the necessary skills and knowledge to guide the group through a difficult situation, such as dealing with a competitive threat. Under low-stress conditions, leader experience is less relevant.
2. Because experience leads to habitual behavior patterns, highly experienced leaders often use traditional solutions to problems when instead a creative approach is necessary. Leaders with high intelligence are more valuable than experienced leaders when innovation is needed and stress levels are low. The highly intelligent leader relies on intellectual ability to analyze the problem and find an optimal solution. (Leader experience helps under high-stress conditions but is not a significant factor when stress levels are low.)
3. The intellectual abilities of a leader who is experiencing stress will be diverted from the task at hand. As a result, measures of leader intelligence and competence do not correlate with group performance when the leader is stressed.
4. The intellectual abilities of directive leaders will correlate more highly with group performance than will the intellectual abilities of nondirective leaders. This is true because the directive leader provides more ideas and suggestions to the group.[12] The nondirective leader is more likely to urge the group member to be more self-reliant.
5. A leader's intellectual abilities will be related to group performance to the degree that the task requires the use of intellectual ability.[13] Cognitive resource theory assumes that intelligent leaders devise better plans for doing the work than less intelligent leaders, especially when the plan is complex. (How does this finding fit your observations about the role of intelligence in problem solving?)

Cognitive resource theory highlights how intelligence, experience, and stress can influence both leader and group performance. However, it neglects the utility of a combination of an experienced *and* intelligent leader in low-stress and high-stress situations. In reality, leaders who are both intelligent and experienced will perform the best in most situations.

## Contingency Leadership in the Executive Suite

An investigation of how top-level executives lead their organizations provides additional insight into contingency leadership.[14] The approach these leaders take lies on the borderline between style and strategy. We include the information here under contingency leadership because each approach is chosen based on an analysis of the requirements of the situation. A leadership approach is defined as a coherent, explicit style of management, not a personal style. However, the style of management centers on leadership behaviors.

Charles M. Farkas, Philippe DeBacker, and Suzy Wetlaufer interviewed 163 top executives on six continents to learn how these leaders delivered consistently extraordinary results. After scrutinizing 12,000 pages of interview transcripts, they identified five distinct approaches that were revealed by the analysis: strategic, human assets, expertise, box, and change agent. The overriding conclusion from the study is that successful CEOs assess their companies' needs, then adapt their leadership style to fit the particular situation. We will summarize each approach, including its associated contingency factors and leadership behaviors. Table 5-1 provides an outline of the approaches and accompanying contingency factors.

The *strategic approach* is a systematic, dispassionate, and structured analysis of a company's strengths and weaknesses and of its mission. CEOs using this approach perceive their major contribution as creating, testing, and designing the implementation of a long-term business strategy. Much of their workday is devoted to activities intended to analyze their organization's current situation and the most advantageous business position in the future. CEOs using this approach devote about 80 percent of their time to external factors such as customers, competitors, technological advances, and market trends.

**TABLE 5-1**  Contingency Factors for Five Approaches to CEO Leadership

| CEO LEADERSHIP APPROACH | CONTINGENCY FACTORS |
|---|---|
| Strategic (create, test, and design long-term strategy) | Unstable environment, high rate of change, complexity. |
| Human assets (add value through hiring, retention, and development programs) | Business units are better positioned than headquarters to make strategy. |
| Expertise (design and implement programs around significant specific expertise such as technology) | Certain expertise can be the source of competitive advantage. |
| Box (add value through controls that set boundaries for employee performance) | Presence of government examiners who insist on strict controls to protect consumer and company. |
| Change agent (create an environment of continual reinvention) | Company wants to remain a leader in the field, and status quo is unacceptable. |

Source: From Charles M. Farkas and Suzy Wetlaufer, "The Ways Chief Executive Officers Lead," *Harvard Business Review*, May–June 1996, pp.110–122; Farkas and Philippe DeBacker, *Maximum Leadership: The World's Leading CEOs Share Their Five Strategies for Success* (New York: Holt, 1996).

An example of a successful user of the strategic approach is Michael Dell of Dell Inc. Dell logs on to the Internet each day to track information and opinions about market trends and reactions to his company's products and those of competitors. Day-to-day operation of the business is delegated extensively to trusted subordinates.

CEOs should use the strategic approach in unstable environments in which the volume and pace of change are high. Significant complexity in terms of technology, geography, or functions is another contingency factor calling for the strategic approach. For example, the CEO of Coca-Cola uses a strategic approach because the company has 32,000 employees in approximately 200 countries worldwide. CEOs who must frequently make decisions of enormous consequence often choose the strategic approach.

In the *human assets approach,* the CEO and the corporate staff add value to the organization through hiring, retention, and development programs. CEOs using this approach believe that strategy formulation belongs in the business units. They see their most important job as imparting selected values, behaviors, and attitudes by managing the growth and development of individuals. To implement this approach, they travel extensively and spend most of their time in human resource activities such as recruiting, performance evaluation, and career planning. An important goal of the human assets approach is to develop business unit managers to the point at which they act and make decisions the way the CEO would. The human assets CEO believes that good employees should do things the *company way.* Herb Kelleher, the former CEO of Southwest Airlines, said, "We hire great attitudes, and we'll teach them any functionality they need."[15]

The human assets approach is most frequently used when a company has such far-flung operations that managers in the business units are better equipped than those in the corporate group to formulate strategy. Consistency in running the geographically remote businesses is achieved by the CEO's imparting corporate values to employees worldwide. Consistency in values is also enhanced when the CEO is involved in hiring key people. Another contingency factor favoring the human assets approach is if key executives strongly believe that the company values and standards of behavior are necessary for the success of the business.

Executives who use the *expertise approach* believe that the CEO's key responsibility is selecting and disseminating throughout the organization an area of expertise that will give the firm a competitive advantage. The majority of their working time is devoted to activities that foster the cultivation and continual improvement of this expertise. Among these activities are studying new technological research, analyzing competitors' products, and meeting with engineers and customers. Areas of expertise include marketing, manufacturing, technology, and distribution. Organizational members who have good technical expertise and share it across organizational units are rewarded. A key contingency factor for favoring the expertise approach is if a certain expertise can give the firm a significant competitive advantage. A representative example took place when Stuart Shapiro, an executive and physician, was appointed chief executive of VirtualScopics, a provider of advanced medical imaging technology. Shapiro's expertise in dealing with the Food and Drug Administration and other agencies was regarded as an asset in helping VirtualScopics as the FDA and pharmaceutical companies increase the application of medical imaging to determine if a drug is effective.[16]

A *box approach* occurs when the corporate group adds value by creating, communicating, and overseeing an explicit set of controls. The controls can take a variety of forms, including financial measures, rules, procedures, and values that define boundaries for the performance of all employees. The purpose of these controls is to ensure uniform and predictable experiences for employees and customers, and to lower risk. CEOs who use the box approach devote much of their workday to attending to deviations from standard, such as quarterly results that are below forecast. They also devote time to rewarding employees whose behavior and performance match the control standards.

The key contingency factor favoring the box approach is a regulated environment such as banking or nuclear power plants in which the government insists on strict controls to protect employees and customers. The purpose of the controls is to strive for consistency. A pharmaceutical executive is likely to implement the box approach because of the need for consistency in testing new drugs.

CEOs who use the *change agent approach* believe that their most critical role is to create an environment of continual reinvention, even if such an emphasis on change creates short-term disturbances such as anxiety, confusion, and poorer financial results. Change agent CEOs spend up to 75 percent of their time using speeches, meetings, and other forms of communication to motivate members to embrace change. They meet regularly with a variety of stakeholders to beat the drums for change. Change agent executives regularly visit factories, create and answer email, and attend company picnics. (It is a good thing these CEOs have a strong internal staff to run the business!) Employees who embrace change receive the biggest rewards. At the investment bank Goldman Sachs, a talented young banker was promoted to partner two years ahead of others in his class because he was willing to accept an assignment in Asia at a time when few U.S. employees were willing to work abroad.

The change agent approach appears to be triggered when the CEO believes that the status quo will lead to the company's undoing, such as when a software development company is content with its current lineup of products. The contingency factor is not obvious, such as a troubled organization needing change; rather, the CEO has the vision to recognize that trouble lies ahead unless changes are made now.

These five leadership approaches are not mutually exclusive, and sometimes a CEO will emphasize more than one approach. For example, the change agent approach might be needed to implement a radical business strategy. Yet in the most effectively run organizations, the CEO usually has a dominant approach or style that serves as a compass and rudder for all corporate decisions. In general, emphasizing one of these approaches, at least for a period in a firm's history, can help a CEO lead with clarity, consistency, and commitment.

The Leader in Action profile describes a deal maker who emphasizes the five leadership approaches just described.

## LEADER IN ACTION

### BIG EDDIE KNOWS HOW TO DEAL

Few people would be surprised that security is tight at Eddie Lampert's office: in 2003 he was kidnapped at gunpoint while leaving work and held for ransom for two days before talking his way free. In fact, there is no sign on the low-rise building in Greenwich, Connecticut, that his $9 billion private investment fund, ESL Investments, Inc., is even there at all. There is also no sign on ESL's door upstairs—and certainly no indication that the man sitting there might be the next Warren E. Buffett.

Since he started ESL in 1988 with a grubstake of $28 million, he has racked up returns averaging 29 percent a year. His top-drawer clients include media mogul David Geffen and Dell Inc. founder Michael Dell. Only forty-two years old, Lampert has amassed a fortune estimated at nearly $2 billion. He is so focused on his goals that he was back at work negotiating a big deal two days after his kidnappers released him.

### LAMPERT'S INVESTMENT STRATEGY AND DEALS

Lampert has built his success on companies that are seriously undervalued. He will even risk jumping into ones that are reeling from bad management or poor strategies because the potential returns are far greater.

The key to Lampert's ambitions is the merger between Kmart and Sears. Before pulling off the merger, ESL held 14.6 percent of Sears, Roebuck & Co. and a 53 percent stake in Kmart holdings. Kmart disclosed in August 2003 that the board had given Lampert authority to invest its "surplus cash" in other businesses. "There is no question he will turn Kmart into an investment vehicle like Warren Buffett's," says legendary value investor Martin Whitman (*BusinessWeek*, November 22, 2004).

In November 2004, Lampert swooped in and launched an $11 billion purchase of Sears. The new company, called Sears Holding Corp., owned Sears and Kmart after the merger. After the deal, many investors bought Kmart and Sears stock, because they saw Kmart not as a retailer trying to move product but as a springboard for lucrative deals. However, several critics feared that Lampert would get bogged down for several years trying to turn the two struggling retailers around rather than using the formidable cash pile Kmart is amassing to move quickly into more promising investments.

Lampert has made it clear that more than superior returns on investment are riding on Kmart. He also wants to earn respect as a businessman who provides expertise in how a company is run. Like Buffett, he wants chief executives to open their arms and partner with him. Dressed in a hand-tailored suit with a subtle pinstripe and an open-collared blue-striped shirt, he acknowledges that his role model is a tough comparison. Lampert notes that Buffett's investments have stood the test of time.

Kmart is a classic example of how Lampert works. He seized control of a $23 billion retail chain, the nation's third largest discounter, for less than $1 billion in bankruptcy court. He emerged as the largest shareholder and became chairman as part of a reorganization in which virtually all of its debt was converted into shares. Lampert wants to keep Kmart humming as long as it can continue throwing off cash as part of Sears.

Before the merger, Lampert was milking Kmart for cash. He imposed a program of keeping the lid on capital spending, holding inventory down, and stopping the endless clearance sales. He sold sixty-eight stores to Home Depot and Sears, raising almost $850 million in cash. With the help of outside advisers, Lampert added four upmarket brands to Kmart's clothing line and also broadened its consumer electronics selection. These moves resulted in a stock market capitalization of

$8.6 billion, on a par with Federated Department Stores. Robert Miller said the increased valuation occurred "because Lampert is a smart cookie. Essentially he is transforming the assets into a more valuable state" (*BusinessWeek*, November 22, 2004, p. 147).

There is nothing Lampert likes to control more than how money is spent. He is obsessed with making sure that every dollar he invests in a company earns the highest return. That means his companies have often used cash to buy back shares rather than boost capital spending. The CEOs of his companies say a big part of their conversations with Lampert focuses on how best to allocate the capital. "He will always want to work through, at a pretty high level of detail, what we are going to spend our money on and what the business benefits will be," says Julian C. Day, who was Kmart's CEO for a while (*BusinessWeek*, November 22, 2004, p. 148).

## LAMPERT THE MANAGER AND LEADER

Lampert can be quite assertive with management. He played rough at AutoZone, where he started amassing shares in 1997. After his stake reached 15.7 percent, he obtained a board seat in 1999. Lampert runs a tight ship at ESL too. Not a penny gets invested without his approval, say former employees. Gavin Abrams, a former ESL analyst, says Lampert has an uncanny ability to see how the pieces of an investment fit together. "When an art critic looks at a piece of art, he can talk to you not just about the color and technique but the history and where it fits into art in gen-

eral," he says. "Eddie talks about investments the same way" (*BusinessWeek*, November 22, 2004, p. 148). Once ESL has invested, it stays in close touch with the company. Lampert is sometimes in daily touch with the top executive in the company in which ESL holds a stake.

Lampert runs his fund with just fifteen employees, mostly research analysts. As he walks the floor, ESL president William C. Crowley is locked on the phone in his office. Lampert's is next door, a corner suite whose central focus is a dual set of black, flat-paneled computer screens perched on his desk. He spends much more time analyzing his investments and dealing with company outsiders than in working with the analysts on his own staff.

Whatever he does next, Lampert is full of surprises. When he was kidnapped, he managed to talk his way out of captivity by offering a small fraction of the $1 million his captors wanted. Investors are betting these deal-making skills will keep making him—and them—lots of money.

## QUESTIONS

1. Explain which one or two of the five CEO leadership approaches Eddie Lampert emphasizes.
2. How would you characterize Lampert's leadership style?
3. Based on evidence presented in this profile, how would you rate Lampert's charisma?

SOURCE: Robert Berner, "Eddie's Master Stroke," *BusinessWeek*, November 29, 2004, pp. 34–36; Berner, "The Next Warren Buffet" *BusinessWeek*, November 22, 2004, pp. 144–154.

## *Leadership During a Crisis*

Among the potential crises facing organizations are a drastic revenue decline; pending bankruptcy; homicide in the workplace; scandalous or criminal behavior by executives; natural disasters, such as hurricanes, floods, or earthquakes; and bombings and other terrorist attacks. Leading during a crisis can be regarded as contingency leadership because the situation demands that the leader emphasize certain behaviors, attitudes, and traits. **Crisis leadership** is the process of leading group members through a sudden and largely unanticipated, intensely negative, and emotionally draining circumstance. Here we describe six leadership attributes and behaviors associated with successfully leading an organization or organizational unit through a crisis.

*Be Decisive* The best-accepted principle of crisis leadership is that the leader should take decisive action to remedy the situation. After the plan is formulated, it should be widely communicated to help reassure group members that something concrete is being done about the predicament. After their physical facilities were destroyed in the terrorist attacks on the World Trade Center on September 11, 2001, several leaders announced the next day that their firms would move to nearby backup locations. Communicating plans helps reduce uncertainty about what is happening to the firm and the people in it. A leader who takes highly visible action to deal with a crisis is likely to be viewed as competent.[17]

*Lead with Compassion* Displaying compassion with the concerns, anxieties, and frustrations of group members is a key interpersonal skill for crisis leadership. The type of compassionate leadership that brings about organizational healing involves taking some form of public action that eases pain and inspires others to act as well. Compassionate leadership encompasses two related sets of actions. The first is to create an environment in which affected workers can freely discuss how they feel, such as a group meeting to talk about the crisis or disaster. The second is to create an environment in which the workers who experience or witness pain can find a method to alleviate their own suffering and that of others. The leader might establish a special fund to help the families of workers who were victims of the disaster or give workers the opportunity to receive grief counseling.

The two-pronged approach to leading with compassion is illustrated by TJX Companies, Inc., president and CEO Edmond English, who lost seven employees aboard one of the airplanes that struck the World Trade Center. He assembled his staff members together shortly after the attacks to confirm the names of the victims, encouraging his workers to express their feelings. English called in grief counselors that same day and chartered a plane to fly in victims' relatives from Europe and Canada to company headquarters in Massachusetts.[18]

*Reestablish the Usual Work Routine* Although it may appear callous and counterintuitive, an effective way of helping people deal with a workplace crisis is to encourage them to return to their regular work. It is important for workers to express their feelings about the crisis before refocusing on work, but once they have, returning to work helps ground them in reality and restores purpose to their lives. Randall Marshall, director of trauma studies for the New York State Office of Mental Health, said after 9/11, "A healthy response to this type of situation is to get back into a routine."[19]

*Avoid a Circle-the-Wagons Mentality* One of the worst ways to lead a group through a crisis is to strongly defend yourself against your critics or deny wrongdoing. The same denial approach is referred to as maintaining a bunker mentality or stonewalling the problem. Instead of cooperating with other stakeholders in the crisis, the leader takes a defensive posture. A case in point is Yoichiro Kaizaki, the former chairman of Bridgestone Corporation, the Japanese owner of Firestone tires. Rather than act promptly to control the damage when the news of faulty Firestone tires on Ford Explorers first surfaced, he refused to face critics until the controversy was raging. His stubborn behavior appears to have worsened the publicity for Firestone and Bridgestone.[20]

*Display Optimism* Pessimists abound in every crisis, so an optimistic leader can help energize group members to overcome the bad times. The effective crisis leader draws action plans that give people hope for a better future. John Chambers of Cisco has been successful in leading his company through difficult times, in part by continuously reinforcing the idea that the Internet has a glorious future. Barbara Baker Clark contends that the role of a leader during a crisis is to encourage hopefulness. She states:

> I'm not saying that you have to plaster a stupid grin on your face even if the bottom line is tanking or people are dying in battle. I am saying don't wallow in pessimism. Believe it or not, it matters to your employees that you remain reasonably optimistic. It will reduce anxiety and keep everyone motivated. That's the power of leadership.[21]

*Prevent the Crisis Through Disaster Planning* It is better to combat a computer virus by preventing the virus from attacking your system rather than dealing with the crisis of a wrecked computer system. Similarly, the ideal form of crisis leadership is to prevent a crisis through disaster planning. A key part of planning for a physical disaster, for example, is to anticipate where you would go, how you would get in touch with employees, and where you might set up a temporary workplace. Having a list of backup vendors in case they are hit by a physical disaster is also important. Arranging in advance for support groups, such as grief counselors, is another key element of disaster planning. Even the fact of letting employees know that a disaster plan is in place can be an effective leadership act because it may lower worker anxiety.[22]

*Be a Transformational Leader* During times of large and enduring crisis, transformational leadership may be the intervention of choice. The transformational leader can often lead the organization out of its misery. You may recall the case problem at the end of Chapter 3 about Ed Zander being recruited to lead Motorola out of the troubled times it faced several years ago. Transformational leadership is likely to benefit the troubled organization both in dealing with the immediate crisis and in performing better in the long run.

**READER'S ROADMAP**

So far in this book we have examined the nature of leadership, the inner qualities of leaders, and leadership styles, including contingency leadership. In the next chapter, we focus on a topic that incorporates many of these ideas: leadership ethics and social responsibility.

# Summary

college.hmco.com/pic/dubrin5e

Theories of contingency and situational leadership build on the study of leadership style by adding more specific guidelines about which style to use under which circumstances. Leaders are most effective when they make their behavior contingent on situational forces, including group member characteristics.

Fiedler's contingency theory states that the best style of leadership is determined by the situation in which the leader is working. Style, in Fiedler's theory, is measured by the least preferred coworker (LPC) scale. If you have a reasonably positive attitude toward your least preferred coworker, you are relationship motivated. You are task motivated if your attitude is negative. Situational control, or favorability, is measured by a combination of the quality of leader–member relations, the degree of task structure, and the leader's position power.

The key proposition of Fiedler's theory is that in situations of high control or low control, leaders with a task-motivated style are more effective. In a situation of moderate control, a relationship-motivated style works better. Leaders can improve situational control by modifying leader–member relations, task structure, and position power.

The path-goal theory of leadership effectiveness specifies what the leader must do to achieve high productivity and morale in a given situation. Effective leaders clarify the paths to attaining goals, help group members progress along these paths, and remove barriers to goal attainment. Leaders must choose a style that best fits the two sets of contingency factors—the characteristics of the subordinates and the tasks. The four styles in path-goal theory are directive, supportive, participative, and achievement oriented.

Situational Leadership II (SLII) developed by Blanchard explains how to match leadership style to the capabilities of group members on a given task. The combination of the subordinate's commitment and competence determines the four developmental levels: enthusiastic beginner, disillusion learner, capable but cautious performer, and self-reliant achiever. The model classifies leadership style according to the relative amounts of supporting and directing the leader engages in. The four styles are different combinations of task and relationship behavior, both rated as high versus low: directing, coaching, supporting, and delegating. The most appropriate leadership style corresponds to the subordinate developmental levels. For example, enthusiastic beginners require a directing leader.

The normative decision model explains that leadership is a decision-making process. A leader examines certain contingency factors in the situation to determine which decision-making style will be the most effective in either a time-driven or developmental situation. The model defines five decision-making styles: two individual and three group. By answering a series of seven diagnostic questions in a matrix, the manager follows the path to a recommended decision style.

Cognitive resource theory describes how a leader's intelligence and experience can influence performance under conditions of stress. A major prediction of the theory is that leaders with high intelligence are more valuable than experienced leaders when innovation is needed and stress levels are low. The highly intelligent leader relies on intellectual ability to analyze the problem and find an optimal solution. Also, the intellectual abilities of directive leaders will correlate more highly with group performance than will the intellectual abilities of nondirective leaders.

CEOs who are successful assess their companies' needs, then adapt their leadership style to fit the situation. The five approaches or styles are strategic, human assets, expertise, box (emphasis on controls), and change agent. Each approach is emphasized under different circumstances; for example, the human assets approach is used when business units are better positioned than headquarters to make strategy.

Leading others through a crisis can be considered a form of contingency leadership because the leader adapts his or her style to the situation. In a crisis, leaders should (a) be decisive, (b) lead with compassion, (c) reestablish the usual work routine, (d) avoid a circle-the-wagons mentality, (e) display optimism, (f) prevent the crisis through disaster planning, and (g) be a transformational leader.

## Key Terms

Contingency approach to leadership

Path-goal theory

Situational leadership II (SLII)

Normative decision model

Cognitive resource theory

Crisis leadership

 ## Guidelines for Action and Skill Development

1. To apply contingency and situational theory, a leader typically has to achieve the right balance between a task and a relationship orientation. Unless there is strong evidence to the contrary, the leader should strive to emphasize both tasks and relationships.
2. Consider four factors as a shortcut to deciding whether a decision is best made by a group. The stronger the need for *buy-in* or *commitment* is, the more important group participation is. When a *creative solution* is important, group input is valuable because varied viewpoints ordinarily enhance creativity. When *time is scarce,* it is better for the leader to make the decision. When a decision is needed that *reflects the bigger picture,* the leader is often in the best position to make it.
3. An effective way to develop your leadership skills is to look for opportunities to exert a small amount of helpful leadership rather than wait for opportunities to accomplish extraordinary deeds. The "little leadership" might be mentoring a struggling team member, coaching somebody about how to use a new high-tech device, or making a suggestion about improving a product. In the words of Michael E. McGill and John W. Slocum, Jr., "For those who want to stand atop the dugout, dance with the elephants, fly with the buffaloes, soar with eagles, or perform other mystical and heroic acts of large leadership, our little leadership may seem all too managerial, too modest, and too mundane."[23] Nevertheless, many situations call for a modest amount of leadership.

## Discussion Questions and Activities

1. Describe how it might be possible for a manager to be charismatic yet also practice contingency leadership.
2. Identify a personality trait you think would help a manager function as a contingency leader. Also identify a trait you think might detract from a manager's ability to function as a contingency leader.
3. Ed Whitacre, the top executive at SBC Communications Inc., said that sometimes he is a strategic manager and at other times a hands-on manager. In what way does his comment reflect the contingency approach to leadership?
4. In what ways do contingency theories go beyond stating that the best leadership approach depends on the situation?
5. How would a manager know which variables in a given situation should influence which approach to leadership he or she should take?
6. Which of the four path-goal styles do you think would be the best for managing a professional football or professional soccer team? Justify your answer.
7. Suppose that you are a first-level supervisor with responsibility for the physical relocation of your company's office. How would you assess the developmental level of your group members?
8. According to the situational model of leadership, which style is likely to be the most effective for leading a strongly motivated group of e-commerce specialists?
9. Why might a transformational leader be helpful in a crisis?
10. Show the normative decision model to an experienced leader. Obtain his or her opinion on its practicality, and be ready to discuss your findings in class.

## LEADERSHIP CASE PROBLEM A

## HECTOR ALVAREZ, THE MULTIFACETED TEAM LEADER

Hector Alvarez is the team leader for fleet operations of Belasco, an American tire and battery manufacturer. His major responsibility is to manage the company's fleet of trucks and the team members who deliver tires to distributors and large customers. Top-level management recognizes that timely delivery of tires and batteries is a major success factor for its business. One of the major challenges Belasco faces is that distributors and retailers want to minimize inventory on their premises. The problem becomes particularly acute after the first winter snowstorm in the North, which creates a spike in demand for snow tires.

**ALVAREZ REFLECTS ON HIS JOB** When asked about the major demands of his position as team leader, Alvarez responded: "Managing a truck fleet is a much more demanding job than most people think. My team members and I deal with a gaggle of problems every day. Our trucks have to be in good shape. We have to deliver the right products to the customers on time when they need it. We work on very short lead times. If we don't do our job right, the company doesn't get paid. So the efforts of manufacturing and marketing go down the drain.

"I just mentioned some of the business challenges. Yet I think the people challenges can be even greater. You get a wide range of personalities in the tire-and-battery industry. Some of the people working on our team are the dirty-fingernail types who can be crude and rude toward each other. Then you get some of the business-grad types who are dead serious about their careers and want to grab as much responsibility as they can. Sometimes they are a little unrealistic in what they want to do. One Boston University grad we hired wants to develop a new business model for Belasco that would enable us to bypass distributors by selling over the Net."

**ALVAREZ IN ACTION** One Friday morning Ashley Cohen (the Boston University graduate) met with Alvarez to discuss some ideas she had been working on at night and on the weekends. She said she had been developing a new business model that would enable Belasco to compete successfully in the twenty-first century. By shifting most of the company business to e-commerce, she said, Belasco could vaporize the distributors, allowing the company to enjoy greater profit margins. She wanted the company to support a pilot project.

Alvarez thought for a moment, then told Cohen, "What you are saying makes a lot of sense. The general idea that we should be doing more business over the Net sounds plausible. We are already getting a lot of our orders by computer. As the team leader, I applaud your efforts. We need some advanced thinking here. For now, I can authorize you to work on this project every Friday afternoon. I will try to arrange a meeting for you with top management. I would like to attend also.

"Maybe top management will grant you the funds to develop your project further. I want to encourage you, Ashley, but I have to work within the limits of my authority."

Cohen felt excited and elated by this response. She told him, "This is really great. I appreciate your confidence in me, and I know I can make this team proud by coming up with a business model that will prove useful for the company."

The following Monday morning, Alvarez was touring the garage so he could get a firsthand look at operations. Mary, a truck dispatcher, rushed up to him in tears, and said, "Please, let's get outside right away. We've got to talk."

Alvarez suggested that the two walk over to the benches by the gas pumps. "What's bothering you?" he asked Mary as they sat down.

"It's Bill, my creep of a supervisor. For the fifth consecutive day, he has grabbed my buttocks and asked me to go out for a drink with him after work. I was polite the first time he grabbed me, but the next few times I told him to never touch me again.

"It's not just me either. Bill has been hitting on Jill, the new office assistant, something terrible."

Alvarez told Mary he would investigate the problem immediately. Within ten minutes, he visited with Jill, asking her if Bill had in any way made her feel uncomfortable or conducted himself inappropriately. Jill explained that Bill hugged her at least once a day and had asked her for a date three times.

"Worst of all," said Jill, "he knows I'm a respectable married woman."

Soon after his meeting with Jill, Alvarez located Bill and told him to drop what he was doing and follow him to his office. With a stern look on his face and an angry tone in his voice, Alvarez said to Bill, "I have heard two complaints about you this morning that could very well be sexual harassment. As a supervisor, you know that Belasco has zero tolerance for sexual harassment. What do you have to say for yourself?"

Fidgeting, Bill responded, "Hector, please don't be so trigger happy. These days you wink at a lady, and she cries sexual harassment. A guy can't even act natural these days."

"That's a pathetic defense," said Hector. "Go home right now. You are suspended with pay pending a complete investigation. If you are guilty of sexual harassment, I will recommend that you be fired. From my standpoint, you will have no second chance."

"Okay," said Bill, "I'll leave right now, but you are not giving me a fair chance to tell my side of the story."

## QUESTIONS

1. In what way does the case illustrate contingency leadership and management?
2. How effective was Alvarez in dealing with Cohen?
3. How effective was Alvarez in dealing with Mary, Jill, and Bill?

SOURCE: *The company in question has chosen to remain anonymous.*

## LEADERSHIP CASE PROBLEM B

### JOE EBERHARDT WANTS TO SHIFT CHRYSLER OUT OF REVERSE

When Joe Eberhardt, chief of Daimler-Chrysler AG's United Kingdom operations, was vacationing with his wife in Italy and heard his cell phone ringing during a visit to a church, he turned it off. The respite was brief. When Eberhardt reactivated his phone, he learned that the missed call was from the Chrysler Corporation president, Dieter Zetsche, who wanted him to take on one of the toughest jobs at the German–American automaker: fixing problems in Chrysler's sales and marketing strategy that in the previous month derailed the No. 3 Detroit auto group's turnaround. Eberhardt accepted the challenge.

Because of soaring marketing costs, Daimler-Chrysler said that Chrysler would just about break even in 2003 instead of earning $2 billion as originally forecast. Previously one of the most profitable automakers in the world, Chrysler was taken over by DaimlerChrysler in 1998 and ever since has been battered by unexpectedly tough competition. Top managers have warned staffers that Chrysler is showing signs of the kind of decline that decimated the U.S. steel industry. Employees have

*(continued)*

been shown presentations that point out import brands are beating the Big Three in quality, productivity, and pricing and are gaining market share in areas that used to be U.S. strongholds: minivans, big pickup trucks, and sport utility vehicles.

The company's efforts to reposition Chrysler as a premium brand are being undermined by a reputation for mediocre quality. Jeep, the storied sport utility brand, is losing market share to softer-riding rivals and faces a growing threat from General Motor's Hummer brand. The Dodge Division's popular minivans are also facing intense competitive pressures.

A native of Stuttgart, Germany, the thirty-nine-year-old Eberhardt joins a growing cadre of relatively young managers with significant expertise outside of Germany whom DaimlerChrysler chairman Jürgen Schrempp is relying on to repair broken elements of the No. 5 automaker's global strategy. Having joined Daimler-Benz AG as a student in 1982, Eberhardt held a series of sales and marketing jobs in Mercedes-Benz's U.S. marketing arm from 1988 to 1999—a time when the Germany luxury marque was battling an assault by Toyota's then upstart Lexus brand.

Eberhardt says he learned a lot from that combat, which went badly at first for Mercedes. When Lexus launched the original LS 400 in 1990, many executives at German luxury-make automakers dismissed it as a copy of the Mercedes E-Class. But American consumers saw the LS 400 as a car every bit as good as or better than an E-Class and priced thousands of dollars lower. Soon Mercedes developed new model lines and features targeted at American tastes, such as the new $30,000 C-Class and M-Class sport utility vehicle. The company even started putting cup holders in its cars, a feature long disdained by German engineers. Mercedes tripled its sales in the United States between 1988 and 1999. Eberhardt suggests Chrysler could emulate lessons from Toyota's success at launching Lexus at a lower-than-expected price.

One of Chrysler's most immediate challenges is to invigorate the slow launch of the Chrysler Pacifica, the family wagon that company executives had hoped would begin to establish a premium image for the Chrysler brand. Dealers have complained that initial advertising for the vehicle, which featured Canadian diva Céline Dion, missed the mark, and prices in the high $30,000 range for many Pacificas sent customers looking for better choices elsewhere.

"Maybe it would have been more effective to establish the vehicle at the mid-$20,000 range as opposed to over $30,000," Eberhardt says. Although he believes that Chrysler can become a premium brand, he says, "it doesn't happen overnight."

Eberhardt has experience in another issue facing him at Chrysler: dealing with a jumbled dealer network. From about a hundred different dealers or dealer groups in the United Kingdom, DaimlerChrysler worked down to twenty-eight. The company itself took over dealerships in the key London, Manchester, and Birmingham regions. Surviving dealers were given larger and separate sales territories. Both sales and market share increased for Mercedes U.K.

By trimming dealerships, Eberhardt says, the remaining retailers have higher sales volumes, make more money, and are thus willing to invest in improving customer service and showrooms. "Our whole industry is not rocket science," he says. "But it's so hard to deliver."

## QUESTIONS

1. In what way is Eberhardt acting as a crisis leader?
2. In what way is he acting as a transformational leader?
3. What suggestions can you offer Eberhardt to be an even more effective leader in the situation he faces?
4. Based on whatever industry information you can find, how successful have Eberhardt's leadership efforts been?
5. What suggestions can you offer DaimlerChrysler for increasing market share in the United States and Canada?

SOURCE: Joseph B. White and Neal E. Boudette, "His Mission: Shift Chrysler Out of Reverse," *The Wall Street Journal*, July 16, 2003. Copyright 2003 by DOW JONES & COMPANY, INC. Reproduced with permission of DOW JONES & COMPANY, INC. in the format Textbook via Copyright Clearance Center.

## MY LEADERSHIP PORTFOLIO

For this chapter entry in your leadership portfolio, visualize two different leadership scenarios that you witnessed directly, read about, or saw on television or in a movie. Think through how you would have used a different leadership approach for each one if you had been the leader. To illustrate, suppose you had passed a construction site for a skyscraper and noticed that the crane operator seemed confident and competent. You might conclude, "In this situation, I would have used a *delegating* style of leadership with the crane operator because she was so self-sufficient. Yet I would still have given her some recognition for a job well done at the end of her shift."

Another scenario might be that you witnessed a bloody fight at a professional hockey match. You might conclude, "In this situation, I would be as directive as possible. I would suspend and fine the players, with no room for negotiation. Decisive action must be taken to help quell violence in professional sports."

## INTERNET SKILL-BUILDING EXERCISE

Apply the chapter concepts! Visit the Web and complete this Internet skill-building exercise to learn more about current leadership topics and trends.

### CRISIS MANAGEMENT

How would you like to listen to fourteen leading management scholars and consultants speak about managing in a crisis? The participants include three of the best-known management gurus: Kenneth Blanchard, Tom Peters, and Steven Covey. To do this assignment, you will need Windows Media Player, which is available as a free download. Visit *www.masie.com/perspectives*, and follow the instructions. You will be able to choose from among fourteen leading thinkers, each making a five-minute presentation about crisis management. Listen to at least five of these contributors. Write down at least six points you have learned from this Internet audio experience.

1. How does this crisis management advice compare to what you learned in this chapter?
2. Which of these ideas are you the most likely to use the next time you face a crisis?

# Leadership Ethics and Social Responsibility

Kowalski's Markets, based in Woodbury, Minnesota, was built on the principles of great customer service and plenty of community-minded good deeds. Founders Mary Anne and Jim Kowalski had an opportunity to flex their civic muscle when they purchased four store locations in 2002. One of the stores was located in Minneapolis's Camden neighborhood, a lower- to middle-class community unlike the typical upscale customer demographic for the business. The Kowalskis decided they had an obligation to provide a neighborhood grocery store to that community since the former tenant had failed to do so, and the civic experiment began.

The Kowalskis shared their vision of a community institution and their desire to create a neighborhood market during a Camden community meeting. Residents of the neighborhood were offered the power to name the store and spend all the store profits as they wished. The Kowalskis promised a clean, safe store with good lighting and security and removed cigarettes and lottery tickets from all of their stores. In the spirit of partnership, the community was asked to show support by shopping there. The neighbors astounded the couple by stating they would rather have the store prosper and remain than take any profits, and they also felt using the Kowalski's name would attract more stores and restaurants to the area.

Members of the Camden community placed voter-style placards on their lawns and businesses urging others to "shop your neighborhood grocer." The Kowalskis give the usual sponsorships and donations to athletic teams and church groups in the area, they are active in community festivals, and they publish a "recipe of the week." Although the location has cash flowing in, after two years it was still not profitable. The other eight Kowalski's markets have helped push projected total sales for the year to around $120 million. However, the Kowalskis still see the Camden store as a success because it has fostered a sense of community. City council member Barbara Johnson says Kowalski's well-kept storefront has increased the attractiveness of the community: "It's considered an amenity. Realtors use it to promote homes, and it has definitely increased property values. It's been a great thing for us."[1]

---

Mary Anne and Jim Kowalski exemplify the generosity, thoughtfulness, ethical behavior, and social consciousness shown by many business leaders. However, the "good side" of business leaders rarely receives as much publicity as the "bad side." In this chapter, we examine leadership ethics and social responsibility from several major perspectives: principles of ethical and moral leadership, an ethical decision-making guide, examples of ethical violations, examples of social responsibility, how leaders develop an ethical and socially responsible culture, and the link between business ethics and organizational performance.

## Principles of Ethical and Moral Leadership

Enough attention has been paid to what leaders at all levels *should* do that some principles of ethical and moral leadership have emerged. Since terms dealing with the ideal behavior of leaders are used so loosely, it is helpful to define what these terms have generally come to mean in the business community. **Ethics** is the study of moral obligations, or of separating right from wrong. *Ethics* can also be a plural noun meaning the accepted guidelines of behavior for groups or institutions.[2] In this sense it means much the same as **morals,** which are an individual's determination of what is right or wrong; morals are influenced by a person's values. Values are tied closely to ethics because ethics become the vehicle for converting values into action. A leader who values fairness will evaluate group members on the basis of their performance, not personal friendships. And a moral leader will practice good ethics. Many business leaders are moral, and many others are not, just as with other professional groups such as physicians and lawyers. Barbara Kellerman of the Center for Public Leadership argues that it is unrealistic to expect that all leaders are moral. Leadership morality is an ideal, yet not all leaders are moral.[3]

In this section, we present a sampling of ethical and moral behaviors, all centering on the idea that a leader should do the *right* thing, as perceived by a consensus of *reasonable* people. Note that all of these terms cannot be pinned down with great precision. We also present a brief explanation of why the ethical and moral behavior of leaders differs so widely. Before studying these principles, do Leadership Self-Assessment Quiz 6-1 to think through your work-related ethics and morality.

LEADERSHIP SELF-ASSESSMENT QUIZ 6-1

### THE LEADER INTEGRITY SCALE

**INSTRUCTIONS** Circle the numbers to indicate how well each item describes your current attitudes and behavior or how you would behave in a group situation. Response choices: 1 = not at all; 2 = somewhat; 3 = very much; 4 = exactly.

| | | | | |
|---|---|---|---|---|
| 1. I use other people's mistakes to attack them personally. | 1 | 2 | 3 | 4 |
| 2. I always get even. | 1 | 2 | 3 | 4 |
| 3. As a leader, I would give special favors to my favorite employees. | 1 | 2 | 3 | 4 |
| 4. I lie to group members if it fits my purposes. | 1 | 2 | 3 | 4 |
| 5. I would let a group member take the blame to protect myself. | 1 | 2 | 3 | 4 |
| 6. I would deliberately fuel conflict among group members. | 1 | 2 | 3 | 4 |
| 7. People who know me well consider me to be evil. | 1 | 2 | 3 | 4 |
| 8. I would use a performance evaluation to criticize an individual as a person. | 1 | 2 | 3 | 4 |
| 9. I hold grudges against people. | 1 | 2 | 3 | 4 |
| 10. I would allow coworkers to be blamed for my mistakes. | 1 | 2 | 3 | 4 |
| 11. I would falsify records to help my work situation. | 1 | 2 | 3 | 4 |

| | | | | |
|---|---|---|---|---|
| **12.** My morals are low. | 1 | 2 | 3 | 4 |
| **13.** I would make fun of someone's mistakes rather than coach the person on how to do the job better. | 1 | 2 | 3 | 4 |
| **14.** I would exaggerate someone's mistakes to make him or her look bad to my superiors. | 1 | 2 | 3 | 4 |
| **15.** I am vindictive. | 1 | 2 | 3 | 4 |
| **16.** I would blame a group member for my mistakes. | 1 | 2 | 3 | 4 |
| **17.** I would avoid coaching an employee so that he or she could fail. | 1 | 2 | 3 | 4 |
| **18.** A person's ethnic group influences how I treat him or her. | 1 | 2 | 3 | 4 |
| **19.** I would deliberately distort what another person said to make me look good. | 1 | 2 | 3 | 4 |
| **20.** I would deliberately make employees angry with each other. | 1 | 2 | 3 | 4 |
| **21.** I am a hypocrite. | 1 | 2 | 3 | 4 |
| **22.** I would limit the training opportunities of others to prevent them from advancing. | 1 | 2 | 3 | 4 |
| **23.** I would blackmail an employee if I thought I could get away with it. | 1 | 2 | 3 | 4 |
| **24.** I enjoy turning down the requests of group members. | 1 | 2 | 3 | 4 |
| **25.** If an employee were to get on my bad side, I would make trouble for him or her. | 1 | 2 | 3 | 4 |
| **26.** I would take credit for the ideas of others. | 1 | 2 | 3 | 4 |
| **27.** I would steal from the organization. | 1 | 2 | 3 | 4 |
| **28.** I would engage in sabotage against the organization just to get even. | 1 | 2 | 3 | 4 |
| **29.** I would fire a person I did not like if I could get away with it. | 1 | 2 | 3 | 4 |
| **30.** I would do things that violate organizational policy, and then expect employees to cover for me. | 1 | 2 | 3 | 4 |

*(continued)*

SCORING AND INTERPRETATION Add up your responses to all thirty items. The interpretation of the score is given below. In interpreting your score, recognize that people tend to overrate themselves on ethical behavior because it is painful to admit to being devious and unethical.

- 30–35   very ethical: If you scored in this range, your self-image is that you are trustworthy and highly principled. If your answers are accurate, it could mean that your high ethics could be an asset to you as a leader.

- 36–61   moderately ethical: Scores in this range mean that your impression is that you sometimes engage in slightly unethical behavior. You might strive to be more consistently ethical.

- 62–120   very unethical: This range describes leaders who may be perceived as engaging in practices that are unethical, dishonest, unfair, and unprincipled. Although many unethical leaders are successful for a while, your unethical attitudes and behavior could be career-limiting factors. It is time to reflect on your values and start taking corrective action. Studying ethics can also help.

SOURCE: Adapted from S. B. Craig and S. B. Gustafson, "Perceived Leader Integrity Scale: An Instrument for Assessing Employee Perceptions of Leader Integrity," *Leadership Quarterly*, vol. 9 (2), 1998, pp. 143–144.

## Five Ethical Leadership Behaviors

### Be Honest and Trustworthy and Have Integrity in Dealing with Others

Despite the importance of leaders who are trustworthy, evidence suggests that trust in business leaders is now low. As part of an ongoing study of employee attitudes and opinions, 1,200 workers were surveyed across a variety of industries. Only 60 percent said they believed that coworkers acted with integrity, with only 56 percent indicating that top management acted with integrity. Nevertheless, 72 percent believed their immediate boss behaved with honesty and integrity.[4] Furthermore, two studies found that most Asian employees have a low level of trust and confidence in their business leaders and that business leaders have too much power.[5]

An ethical leader is honest and trustworthy and therefore has integrity. According to ethics researcher Thomas E. Becker, this quality goes beyond honesty and conscientiousness. **Integrity** refers to loyalty to rational principles; it means practicing what one preaches regardless of emotional or social pressure.[6] For example, a leader with integrity would believe that employees should be treated fairly, and the pressure to cut costs would not prompt him or her to renege on a commitment to reimburse an employee for relocation expenses. As another example, a leader who preaches cultural diversity would assemble a diverse team.

### Pay Attention to All Stakeholders

An ethical and moral leader strives to treat fairly all interested parties affected by his or her decision. To do otherwise creates winners and losers after many decisions are made. The widely held belief that a CEO's primary responsibility is to maximize shareholder wealth conflicts with the principle of paying attention to all stakeholders. A team of management scholars observes, "We used to recognize corporations as both economic and social institutions—as organizations that were designed to serve a balanced set of stakeholders, not just the narrow interests of the shareholder."[7] A leader interested in maximizing shareholder wealth might attempt to cut costs and increase profits in such ways as (1) laying off valuable employees to reduce payroll costs, (2) overstating profits to impress investors, (3) overcharging customers, and (4) reducing health benefits for retirees. Although these practices may be standard, they all violate the rights of stakeholders.

Jim Goodnight, the CEO of software company SAS, is among the business leaders who contend that there is a strong link between employee satisfaction and increased productivity and profits. He explains, "Because we put employee-oriented measures in place long ago, we have the benefit of years of experience to show that the long-term benefits far outweigh the short-term costs. Most companies don't know how to represent that kind of return in their annual reports."[8]

*Authentic leader* is the new term for managers who perceive their role to include having an ethical responsibility to all of their shareholders. The welfare of others takes precedence over their own personal welfare (as in servant leadership). Authentic leaders have a deep commitment to their personal growth as well as to the growth of other stakeholders.[9]

**Build Community** A corollary of taking into account the needs of all stakeholders is that the leader helps people achieve a common goal. Leadership researcher Peter G. Northouse explains that leaders need to take into account their own and their followers' purposes and search for goals that are compatible to all.[10] When many people work toward the same constructive goal, they build a community. A business leader who works with many people to help poor schoolchildren is an ideal example of someone who builds community.

The Global Compact, an initiative of the United Nations to ensure that business practices conform with human rights, labor, and environmental standards, seeks to build community on an international scale. The common goal is equitable treatment of workers. More than 1,700 multinational companies have joined, and the pact has become the world's largest voluntary corporate citizenship group. Some groups, however, are concerned that the Global Compact is essentially a corporate public relations exercise.[11]

**Respect the Individual** Respecting individuals is a principle of ethical and moral leadership that incorporates other aspects of morality. If you tell the truth, you respect others well enough to be honest. If you keep promises, you also show respect. And if you treat others fairly, you show respect.[12] Showing respect for the individual also means that you recognize that everybody has some inner worth and should be treated with courtesy and kindness. An office supervisor demonstrated respect in front of his department when he asked a custodian who entered the office, "What can we do in this department to make your job easier?"

**Accomplish Silent Victories** According to Joseph L. Badaracco, Jr., modesty and restraint are largely responsible for the achievements of the most effective moral leaders in business. The ethical and moral leader works silently, and somewhat behind the scenes, to accomplish moral victories regularly. Instead of being perceived as a hero or heroine, the moral leader quietly works on an ethical agenda. Quite often he or she will work out a compromise to ensure that a decision in process will have an ethical outcome.

A case in point is the middle manager at a telecommunications company whose senior managers decided to outsource the manufacture of a product line to China. As a result the small U.S. community was to lose about 200 jobs. The middle manager lobbied for months for the company to establish its new call center in the same town, thereby enabling about sixty-five of the workers to continue employment with the company.[13]

## Factors Contributing to Ethical Differences

There are many reasons for differences in ethics and morality among leaders. One is the leader's *level of greed, gluttony, and avarice.* Many people seek to maximize personal returns, even at the expense of others. Former Federal Reserve chairman and economist Alan Greenspan commented publicly on the problem of executive greed. He said that "an infectious greed" had contaminated the business community in the late 1990s, as one executive after another manipulated earnings or resorted to fraudulent accounting to capitalize on soaring stock prices.[14]

Another key contributor to a leader's ethics and morality is his or her *level of moral development.* Some leaders are morally advanced, while others are morally challenged—a mental condition that often develops early in life. People progress through three developmental levels in their moral reasoning. At the *preconventional level,* a person is concerned primarily with receiving external rewards and avoiding punishment. A leader at this level of development might falsify earnings statements for the primary purpose of gaining a large bonus. At the *conventional level,* people learn to conform to the expectations of good behavior as defined by key people in their environment and societal norms. A leader at this level might be moral enough just to look good, such as being fair with salary increases and encouraging contributions to the United Way campaign. At the *postconventional level,* people are guided by an internalized set of universal principles that may even transcend the laws of a particular society. A leader at the postconventional level of moral behavior would be concerned with doing the most good for the most people, without regard for whether such behavior brought him or her recognition and fortune.[15] The servant leader described in Chapter 4 would be at this advanced level of moral development.

A third factor contributing to the moral excesses of business leaders is that many of them have developed a sense of *entitlement.* In the opinion of several psychiatrists and corporate governance experts, some CEOs lose their sense of reality and feel entitled to whatever they can get away with or steal. For example, Conrad Black, the CEO of Hollinger International Inc., felt entitled to have the company pay for his personal servants. Also, many executives feel entitled to healthy compensation. The average CEO pay at major corporations is now 301 times as high as the lowest-paid employees.[16]

A fourth factor contributing to unethical and immoral leadership behavior is the *situation,* particularly the organizational culture. If leaders at the top of the organization take imprudent, quasi-legal risks, other leaders throughout the firm might be prompted to behave similarly. The risk-taking culture at Enron Corporation is said to have contributed to firm leaders' engaging in questionable financial transactions such as creating false profit statements.

A *person's character* is a fifth factor that contributes to ethical differences. The higher the quality of a person's character, the more likely he or she will behave ethically and morally. For example, a leader who is honest and cooperative will tend to behave more ethically than a leader who is dishonest and uncooperative. Leadership Self-Assessment Quiz 6-2 digs into the behavioral specifics of good character as perceived by the U.S. Air Force.

LEADERSHIP SELF-ASSESSMENT QUIZ 6-2

## THE AIR FORCE CHARACTER ATTRIBUTES CHECKLIST

**INSTRUCTIONS** Listed and defined next are character attributes the U.S. Air Force wants to see among the ranks of its leaders. For each attribute, note your standing as being high (H), average (A), or low (L). A checklist of this nature lends itself to self-serving bias, so work extra hard to be objective. When applicable, visualize an example of how you have exhibited, or have not exhibited, a particular character attribute.

| Factor | Description | My Standing | | |
|---|---|---|---|---|
| | | H | A | L |
| Integrity | Consistently adhering to a moral or ethical code or standard. A person who consistently chooses to do the right thing when faced with alternative choices. | ☐ | ☐ | ☐ |
| Honesty | Consistently being truthful with others. | ☐ | ☐ | ☐ |
| Loyalty | Being devoted and committed to one's organization, supervisors, coworkers, and subordinates. | | | |
| Selflessness | Genuine concern about the welfare of others and a willingness to sacrifice one's personal interest for others and the organization. | ☐ | ☐ | ☐ |
| Compassion | Concern for the suffering or welfare of others and providing aid or showing mercy for others. | ☐ | ☐ | ☐ |
| Competency | Capable of excelling at all tasks assigned. Is effective and efficient. | ☐ | ☐ | ☐ |
| Respectfulness | Shows esteem for and consideration and appreciation of other people. | ☐ | ☐ | ☐ |
| Fairness | Treats everyone in an equitable, impartial, and just manner. | ☐ | ☐ | ☐ |
| Responsibility and self-discipline | Can be depended on to make rational and logical decisions and to do tasks assigned. Can perform tasks assigned without supervision. | ☐ | ☐ | ☐ |

*(continued)*

| | | | | |
|---|---|---|---|---|
| Decisiveness | Capable of making logical and effective decisions in a timely manner. Makes good decisions promptly after considering data appropriate to the decision. | ☐ | ☐ | ☐ |
| Spiritual appreciation | Values the spiritual diversity among individuals with different backgrounds and cultures and respects all individuals' rights to differ from others in their beliefs. | ☐ | ☐ | ☐ |
| Cooperativeness | Willing to work or act together with others in accomplishing a task toward a common end or purpose. | ☐ | ☐ | ☐ |

INTERPRETATION: The more of the attributes you rated as "high," the more likely it is that others perceive you as having good character. The list may provide some clues to leadership development. For example, if you are perceived to be low on integrity and cooperativeness, you are less likely to be able to influence others.

NOTE: Although competency and decisiveness are not ordinarily considered character traits, being competent and decisive contributes to having good character.

SOURCE: U.S. Air Force, as reprinted in Cassie B. Barlow, Mark Jordan, and William H. Hendrix, "Character Assessment: An Examination of Leadership Levels," *Journal of Business and Psychology*, Summer 2003, p. 568.

## Guidelines for Evaluating the Ethics of a Decision

Several guidelines, or ethical screens, have been developed to help leaders or other influence agents decide whether a given act is ethical or unethical. The Center for Business Ethics at Bentley College has developed six questions to evaluate the ethics of a specific decision:[17]

- *Is it right?* This question is based on the deontological theory of ethics that there are certainly universally accepted guiding principles of rightness and wrongness, such as "thou shall not steal."

- *Is it fair?* This question is based on the deontological theory of justice that certain actions are inherently just or unjust. For example, it is unjust to fire a high-performing employee to make room for a less competent person who is a relative by marriage.

- *Who gets hurt?* This question is based on the utilitarian notion of attempting to do the greatest good for the greatest number of people.

- *Would you be comfortable if the details of your decision or actions were made public in the media or through email?* This question is based on the universalist principle of disclosure.

■ *What would you tell your child, sibling, or young relative to do?* This question is based on the deontological principle of reversibility, which evaluates the ethics of a decision by reversing the decision maker.

■ *How does it smell?* This question is based on a person's intuition and common sense. For example, counting a product inquiry over the Internet as a sale would "smell" bad to a sensible person.

Ethical issues that require a run through the guide are usually subtle rather than blatant, a decision that falls into the gray zone. An example is the business plan of Krispy Kreme Doughnuts. Profits from company-owned stores are not large enough to cover corporate expenses. The company's real profits derive from dealing with its franchisees, which pay royalties of 4.5 to 6 percent of sales, plus 1 percent for advertising and public relations. All supplies must be purchased from the parent. After all the payments to the parent, it is exceedingly difficult for the franchisees to earn a profit. So is Krispy Kreme leadership being ethical?

Leaders regularly face the necessity of running a contemplated decision through an ethics test. Leadership Skill-Building Exercise 6-1 provides an opportunity to think through the ethics of a decision facing a telecom firm.

**LEADERSHIP SKILL-BUILDING EXERCISE 6-1**

### DIALING FOR DOLLARS

Imagine that you and several other classmates are Lucent Technologies executives and that you are reviewing the following case history related to your consumer sales group:

Roberta Sweetow, 67, keeps the hulking black rotary telephone, the one she has had in her possession since 1964, on her nightstand in case her husband, Herb, 74, receives an early-morning call to substitute-teach in a Skokie, Illinois, high school. Sweetow purchased the phone for $9 last year, after finally noticing a charge buried in her bill every three months: $18 to lease a telephone. "I realized I've paid more than $1,000 for a phone I hardly use," she says. "Who in the world rents a telephone?"

Lawyers representing approximately 44 million customers in a $10 billion class action lawsuit believe that many consumers still use rotary phones. The suit is filed against AT&T, which administered the post–Ma Bell leasing program from 1984 to 1996, and Lucent, its consumer products spinoff. Lucent administers the rotary phone leasing program today. The suit alleges that after the Bell breakup, AT&T failed to adequately inform customers of their options to lease, purchase, or return their old telephones.

Customers who took no action continued to be charged for renting the phones, a fee recorded on their bill in vague line items like TRAD ROT DSK MISC (traditional desktop rotary). Several former AT&T Lucent employees contend that the companies pressured them to keep leasing. At the time these facts were collected, some 860,000 households still leased nearly 1 million rotary phones.

*(continued)*

Your assignment as part of the Lucent team is to first decide whether leasing rotary phones is ethical by running the decision through the ethical decision-making guide presented in this chapter. Second, decide what plans Lucent should make for the program. For example, should it cease the leasing, begin a marketing campaign to sell more rotary phones, sell the phones to the remaining customers, or something else? Keep in mind that Lucent needs all the revenue it can find because the turnaround is not yet complete.

This exercise is important because it helps alert you to consider the ethics of contemplated decisions. In the current climate, many companies are seeking to promote into leadership positions at any level those individuals with a track record of making ethical decisions.

SOURCE: Based on Sean Gregory, "How'd You Like to Rent This Baby?" *Time*, July 8, 2002, p. 18.

The question of ethics arises when a person conducts a job search. The job seeker might want to size up the ethical climate established by company leaders. The wave of corporate scandals that took place a few years ago prompted more job seekers than in the past to examine prospective employers' ethical standards and practices.[18] Table 6-1 presents a list of ethics-related questions a job seeker might ask before joining a firm. In this way, the prospective leader would have a chance of finding an ethical and moral climate compatible with his or her values.

## A Sampling of Unethical Leadership Behaviors

We have been alluding to unethical behavior in this and previous chapters. Here we present a sampling of unethical behaviors from the past and present. A statement often

---

**TABLE 6-1**   **A Job Seeker's Ethics Audit**

**SOME PROBING QUESTIONS TO ASK ABOUT A PROSPECTIVE EMPLOYER:**

- Is there a formal code of ethics? How widely is it distributed? Is it reinforced in other formal ways such as through decision-making systems?

- Are workers at all levels trained in ethical decision making? Are they also encouraged to take responsibility for their behavior or to question authority when asked to do something they consider wrong?

- Do employees have formal channels available to make their concerns known confidentially? Is there a formal committee high in the organization that considers ethical issues?

- Is misconduct disciplined swiftly and justly within the organization?

- Is integrity emphasized to new employees?

- How are senior managers perceived by subordinates in terms of their integrity? How do such leaders serve as models for ethics-related behavior?

Source: Linda K. Treviño, chair of the Department of Management and Organization, Smeal College of Business, Pennsylvania State University (as reprinted in Kris Maher, "Wanted: Ethical Employer," *The Wall Street Journal*, July 9, 2002, p. B1).

made is that about 95 percent of business leaders are ethical and that the 5 percent of bad apples (mostly senior executives) get all the publicity. However, the impact of unethical leadership has been enormous. Unethical behavior has thrown companies into bankruptcy, led to the layoffs of thousands of workers, diminished trust in stock investments, and discouraged many talented young people from embarking on a business career.

Table 6-2 presents some unethical, immoral, and often illegal behaviors engaged in by business leaders whose acts have been publicly reported. Thousands of other unethical acts go unreported, such as a business owner who places a family member, friend, or lover on the payroll at an inflated salary for work of limited value to the firm.

college.hmco.com/pic/
dubrin5e
🏦 **@ KNOWLEDGE BANK:** summarizes two other business scandals.

**TABLE 6-2**    ## Examples of Unethical Behavior by Leaders

| EXECUTIVE AND COMPANY | CHARGES OR COMPLAINTS | DEFENSES AGAINST THE CHARGES | CURRENT STATUS OF EXECUTIVE AND COMPANY |
|---|---|---|---|
| FRANK P. QUATTRONE, FORMER INVESTMENT BANKER AT CREDIT SUISSE FIRST BOSTON (CSFB) | Accused of handing out hot initial public offering shares to some 300 "Friends of Frank" to get business for CSFB. Quattrone accused of pressuring analysts to write favorable reports on clients and of linking analysts' compensation to investment banking revenue. Accused of encouraging employees to destroy documents after he knew that CSFB was under investigation by authorities. | Quattrone said he did nothing wrong, but nevertheless resigned under pressure in March 2003, after earning $200 million in three years with CSFB. | In U. S. District Court, Quattrone was convicted of obstructing a government investigation into how stocks were allocated, particularly in relation to destroying documents. Sent to prison for eighteen months. |
| SANJAY KUMAR, FORMER CHIEF EXECUTIVE OF COMPUTER ASSOCIATES (CA) INTERNATIONAL, INC. | Charged with securities fraud, conspiracy, and obstruction of justice in connection with a multi-billion dollar accounting scandal, including improperly booking $2.2 billion in revenue. | Kumar's boss, CA chairman Lewis Ranieri, agreed that some former members of the CA management team engaged in illegal activity. | Federal prosecutors indicted Kumar, stating that he was an active participant in widespread accounting fraud at CA and lied to investigators about his role. |

*Continued*

| TABLE 6-2 | Examples of Unethical Behavior by Leaders (continued) |

| EXECUTIVE AND COMPANY | CHARGES OR COMPLAINTS | DEFENSES AGAINST THE CHARGES | CURRENT STATUS OF EXECUTIVE AND COMPANY |
|---|---|---|---|
| SANJAY KUMAR, FORMER CHIEF EXECUTIVE OF COMPUTER ASSOCIATES (CA) INTERNATIONAL, INC. *(continued)* | | Kumar said he was cooperating fully with investigators. | Faces charges of securities fraud and obstruction of justice. The company will pay $225 million in restitution to shareholders who lost money in CA investments. Two other CA executives were also indicted. |
| JEFFREY W. GREENBERG, CHAIRMAN AND CHIEF EXECUTIVE OF MARSH & MCCLELLAN COMPANIES, INC. (INSURANCE BROKERS) | Charged with bid rigging and price fixing, including received payments from insurance companies to which Marsh & McClellan referred business. | Greenberg resigned under pressure from investigators. The company ended incentive fees and receiving any contingent commissions (fees paid for more business) from insurance companies. Greenberg remained silent. | New York State Attorney General Eliot Spitzer filed a civil suit against Marsh & McClellan accusing the company of using illegal kickbacks, bid rigging, and price fixing. The company's willingness to reform helped it avoid criminal charges. |
| KENNETH LAY, FORMER CHAIRMAN AND CEO OF ENRON | Company executive under investigation for creating and approving outside partnerships that kept millions of dollars in losses off Enron's books. Enron sold phony assets to these partnerships at high prices to create bogus income. Lay unloaded $100 million in company stock before the price tumbled. | Lay said he was not fully informed of the executive-run partnerships. Asserted Fifth Amendment right not to testify before Congress. | Lay resigned and told Congress of his profound sadness about what happened to the company. Enron declared bankruptcy in 2002 and later continued to operate on a smaller scale. Lay later pleaded guilty to 11 criminal charges. If convicted, Lay |

| TABLE 6-2 | Examples of Unethical Behavior by Leaders (continued) |

| EXECUTIVE AND COMPANY | CHARGES OR COMPLAINTS | DEFENSES AGAINST THE CHARGES | CURRENT STATUS OF EXECUTIVE AND COMPANY |
|---|---|---|---|
| KENNETH LAY, FORMER CHAIRMAN AND CEO OF ENRON *(continued)* | | | would face 175 years in jail and $5.75 million in fines. |
| BERNARD EBBERS OF MCI/ WORLDCOM | Investigators are looking into whether he was aware of the $3.8 billion classified as capital expenses rather than operating costs. Later investigation revealed that MCI/WorldCom executives misclassified about $9 billion in expenses. Ebbers is being asked to explain why the company lent him $408 million to cover margin calls on loans secured by company stock. May still owe banks and brokerage firms about $1 billion, borrowed using WorldCom stock as collateral. Company is also accused of overcharging customers by up to 10 percent. | Ebbers said he was not directly involved in the accounting error. Has sold a boat and a few other possessions to help pay back the money. | Ebbers was forced out by the board. WorldCom stock was almost worthless in 2002. Company laid off thousands of workers to reduce costs. Was negotiating with potential buyers, but remains in business as MCI. In July 2005, Ebbers was sentenced to 25 years in prison for leading the largest business corporation fraud in U. S. history. |
| L. DENNIS KOZLOWSKI, FORMER CEO OF TYCO INTERNATIONAL LTD. | Accused of failing to pay more than $1 million in sales taxes on artwork by shipping it to an office in another state. Company is probing whether he used company funds for real estate and other expenses. Apparently borrowed hundreds of millions of dollars from Tyco, then secretly found a way to forgive these | Entered a plea of not guilty on avoiding sales tax. | Kozlowski resigned to "pursue other interests." Tyco is still functioning, and prospering under new leadership. The Securities and Exchange Commission (SEC) found no wrongdoing in earnings manipulations. As |

*Continued*

| TABLE 6-2 | Examples of Unethical Behavior by Leaders (continued) |

| EXECUTIVE AND COMPANY | CHARGES OR COMPLAINTS | DEFENSES AGAINST THE CHARGES | CURRENT STATUS OF EXECUTIVE AND COMPANY |
|---|---|---|---|
| L. DENNIS KOZLOWSKI, FORMER CEO OF TYCO INTERNATIONAL LTD. *(continued)* | loans. Is accused of padding earnings growth of acquisitions by making the acquisitions prepay expenses and forgo new revenue. | | the SEC investigation continued, Tyco faced criminal charges. Kozlowski and his chief financial officer Mark Swartz were convicted of first-degree (grand) larceny and falsifying records in relation to stealing $180 million dollars directly and making $430 million by manipulating Tyco stock value. In September 2004 Kozlowski and Swartz were sentenced to eight and one-third to twenty-five years in prison. Kozlowski and Swartz were ordered to pay a total of $134 million in restitution, and were fined a total of $105 million ($70 million for Kozlowski). |
| GARY WINNICK, FORMER CEO AND CHAIRMAN OF GLOBAL CROSSING LTD. | Company boosted profits by swapping network capacity with another carrier. Global booked the sales revenue immediately yet spread costs over time. | Winnick has said nothing about dumping stock. Work continued on his $95 million home in | Winnick has left the company and has not been charged with a crime. Company is bankrupt and listening to offers |

| TABLE 6-2 | Examples of Unethical Behavior by Leaders (continued) | | | |

| EXECUTIVE AND COMPANY | CHARGES OR COMPLAINTS | DEFENSES AGAINST THE CHARGES | CURRENT STATUS OF EXECUTIVE AND COMPANY |
|---|---|---|---|
| GARY WINNICK, FORMER CEO AND CHAIRMAN OF GLOBAL CROSSING LTD. *(continued)* | Winnick sold more than $735 million in stock just before the company downfall. | California while the firm struggled through bankruptcy proceedings. | to sell its fiber-optic network. Thousands of employees are left with worthless stock in their pension plans. Winnick later offered to distribute $25 million of personal funds to help former employees left with pensions of no value. Global Crossing still operates but on a smaller scale. |

Source: Mike France, "Who Will Fastow Implicate?" *BusinessWeek*, January 26, 2004, p. 41; Linda Himmelstein, "Frank's Life in the Rough," *BusinessWeek*, March 31, 2003, p. 89; Kara Scannell, "Quattrone Receives Support of Silicon Valley Who's Who," *The Wall Street Journal,* September 13, 2004, p. C3; "High Profiles in Hot Water," *The Wall Street Journal*, June 28, 2002, p. B1; Clifton Leaf, "Enough Is Enough," *Fortune,* March 18, 2002 p. 64; Charles Forelle and Mark Maremont, "U.S. Indicts Sanjay Kumar for Fraud, Lies," *The Wall Street Journal*, September 23, 2004, p. 1A; "Software Firm Will Pay $225 Million to Investors," Associated Press, September 23, 2004; Eileen Alt Powell, "With New Chairman, Marsh Announces 'Significant Reforms,'" Associated Press, October 27, 2004. "Eron's Ken Lay: I Was Fooled," *CBS News* (*www.cbsnews*), March 13, 2005.

## Leadership and Social Responsibility

One way of being ethical and moral is to guide the firm, or a unit within, toward doing good deeds. **Social responsibility** is having obligations to society beyond the company's economic obligations to owners or stockholders and also beyond those prescribed by law or contract. Both ethics and social responsibility relate to the goodness or morality of organizations, but social responsibility relates to an organization's impact on society and goes beyond doing what is ethical.[19] Being socially responsible fits into the "Thou Shalt" approach, or finding out better ways for leaders to make a positive contribution to society. In contrast, the "Thou Shalt Not" approach focuses on avoiding the kind of wrongdoing depicted in Table 6-2.[20] To behave in a socially responsible way, leaders must be aware of how their actions influence the environment.

Our focus here is on several illustrative actions that leaders can take to enhance social responsibility: creating a pleasant work environment, guarding the environment, engaging in philanthropy, and working with suppliers to improve working conditions. The accompanying Leader in Action vignette describes a CEO who regards social responsibility as a major aspect of his leadership.

## LEADER IN ACTION

### CEO JEFF IMMELT WANTS TO MAKE GE VIRTUOUS

In fall 2004, Jeffrey R. Immelt, the chairman and chief executive officer of one of the world's most valuable and most admired company, stood before General Electric's 200 corporate officers and said it would take four things to keep the company on top. Three of those were predictable: execution, growth, and great people. The fourth was not: virtue. And it was at the top of his list.

Virtue is not the first thing that comes to mind when people think about GE. Under Jack Welch, GE was known for hard-driving management and delivering market-beating shareholder returns. Immelt wants GE to be all that and more. To be a great company today, he likes to say, you almost have to be a good company. "The reason people come to work for GE is that they want to be about something that is bigger than themselves. People want to work hard, they want to get promoted, they want stock options. But they also want to work for a company that makes a difference, a company that's doing great things in the world."

Immelt became CEO on September 7, 2001— four days before the terrorist attacks in New York City and Washington, D.C., shortly after the stock market bubble burst, and just as Enron's collapse began what, even today, feels like an unending parade of corporate wrongdoing. "The world's changed," Immelt says. "Businesses today aren't admired. Size is not respected. There's a bigger gulf today between haves and have-nots than ever before. It's up to us to use our platform to be a good citizen. Because not only is it a nice thing to do, it's a business imperative."

GE has changed too. In 2002, Immelt appointed a trusted ally, Bob Corcoran, as GE's first vice president for corporate citizenship. Corcoran has spread the gospel to the company's far-flung business units. Today GE audits its suppliers in the developing world to make sure they comply with labor, environmental, health, and safety standards. It has performed 3,100 audits since the program began in 2002.

Immelt has moved the ball forward on diversity. In 2004, the company won high-profile awards for promoting women and African Americans into its executive ranks. It granted domestic partner benefits to gay and lesbian employees. Meanwhile, GE has set out to globalize its philanthropy, notably by launching an ambitious health care project in rural Ghana. And GE published its first corporate citizenship report in spring 2005.

In the past, GE tended to view environmental rules as a cost or burden. Now Immelt sees growth opportunities in cleaning up the planet. He wants GE to be known as one of the few companies with the scale and know-how to tackle the world's toughest problems. GE has purchased a water-purification company, a maker of solar energy equipment, and a wind energy business. The company signed an agreement to supply wind turbines to the first two utility-scale wind energy projects in China.

"Wind, water, lowering emissions, having an environmental service business . . . are going to drive lots of technological innovation over the next 10, 20, 30 years," Immelt says. "This is an approach to growing the company faster."

## QUESTIONS

1. How realistic do you think Immelt is in his belief that people come to work for GE because "they want to be about something bigger than themselves"?

2. What impact do you think GE's social responsibility initiatives will have on company profits and the stock price?

3. After reading about GE's social responsibility initiatives, are you more likely to purchase a GE product such as a light bulb or refrigerator than something similar from a different manufacturer?

SOURCE: Marc Gunther, "Money and Morals at GE," *Fortune*, November 15, 2004, pp. 176–179. © 2004 Time, Inc. All rights reserved.

### Creating a Pleasant Workplace

A social responsibility initiative that directly affects employees' well-being is to create a comfortable, pleasant, and intellectually stimulating work environment. Because many people invest about one-third of their time at work, a pleasant work environment increases the chances that their life will be enriched. Robert Levering and Milton Moskowitz, of the Great Place to Work® Institute, in cooperation with *Fortune,* have institutionalized the idea of being a "best company to work for." Employers nominate themselves, and two-thirds of the score is based on how randomly selected employees respond to the Great Place to Work Trust Index©, a survey measuring organizational culture. An evaluation of the Culture Audit by staff members at the Great Place to Work Institute determines the rest of the score. The focus is on employee satisfaction, yet the firms that fall into the "the 100 best companies to work for" are also typically profitable. Among the benefits these companies offer are flexible working hours; on-site day care; concierge services, such as dry cleaning pickup; domestic-partner benefits to same-sex couples; and fully paid sabbaticals. Following are the three most highly rated companies:[21]

*Wegmans Food Markets, Inc., Rochester, New York:* The foundation belief of this privately held grocery chain is, "Employees first, customers second." The Wegman family believes that when employees are happy, customers will be too. Most Wegmans employees develop expertise in a few foods and share this expertise with customers who inquire. The average annual pay for the salaried staff is $92,319 and $23,576 for the hourly staff.

*Starbucks Coffee Company, Seattle, Washington:* The café giant is renowned for its generous benefits. For example, part-timers and their opposite- or same-sex partners receive comprehensive health coverage, and stock options abound. The average annual pay for salaried workers is $44,790 and $35,294 for the hourly staff.

*Valero Energy Corporation, San Antonio, Texas:* In business for twenty-five years, this oil refiner and gas retailer has never had a layoff. Lower-level workers as well as higher-level workers receive bonuses. Executives receive bonuses only if every other worker at Valero does. The average annual pay for salaried workers is $40,326, and $17,067 for the hourly staff.

The employee programs that qualify a company as a best place to work focus on employee benefits. However, the leaders of these companies also emphasize stimulating work.

## Guarding the Environment

Socially responsible leaders influence others to preserve the external environment through a variety of actions that go beyond mandatory environmental controls such as managing toxic waste. Many companies sponsor team-building events in which participants build a playground or refurbish an old house in a declining neighborhood. Brenda L. Flannery and Douglas R. May studied individual and situational factors associated with corporate leaders who make ethical (or socially responsible) environmental decisions. The group studied was executives in the metal finishing business. The research task was for the executives to put themselves in the shoes of environmental engineers in wastewater treatment scenarios. The various scenarios described consequences to both human and nonhuman victims. For example, an overflow of wastewater might cause cancer in people and kill fish. Managers' treatment of wastewater was found to depend on three factors, according to the respondents:

1. *Attitudes toward wastewater treatment.* If managers believe strongly in treating wastewater, they will plan to do a careful job of taking care of hazardous wastewater.
2. *Assessment of support from others.* If managers believe key people will support their efforts, they are more likely to take corrective action against hazardous wastewater.
3. *Perception of financial costs.* Being green depends to some extent on how much green money it takes.[22] Sometimes ethics gives way to the bottom line.

The study also found that the magnitude of the consequences moderated (or influenced) the managers' attitudes toward dealing with the environment. The more serious the potential negative consequences were, the more likely it is that the leader will take decisive action to protect the environment.

## Engaging in Philanthropy

A standard organizational leadership approach to social responsibility is to donate money to charity and various other causes. Most charities are heavily dependent on corporate support. Colleges, universities, and career schools also benefit from corporate donations. Many of the leading philanthropists donate money during their lifetime rather than giving through their estates. Examples include Bill and Melinda Gates of Microsoft, who have donated or pledged $22.9 billion, and Michael and Susan Dell (Dell), who have donated or pledged $1.2 billion.[23] Another is Jim Barksdale, the former Netscape CEO. He donated $100 million to the University of Mississippi for a program to help students from kindergarten to grade 3 learn to read. Barksdale believed that because the child literacy rate in Mississippi was below average, the potential rate of social return on his investment was high.[24]

Many corporate donors want their charitable investments to benefit the end consumer, not get lost in red tape and overhead, and show measurable results. The new breed of philanthropist studies each charitable cause as he or she would a potential business investment, seeking maximum return in terms of social impact. This philanthropist might also seek follow-up data, for example, on how many children were taught to read or by what percentage new cases of AIDS declined.

The new breed of philanthropist is sometimes actively involved in the cause receiving the funding. For example, John R. Alm, the president of Coca-Cola Enterprises Inc., provides ongoing, intensive support to at-risk youths living in inner-city Los Angeles, from middle school through college. Alm's immediate efforts are supported by a broader plan for helping the young people, and he devotes a large portion of his discretionary time to implementing the plan.[25]

## Working with Suppliers to Improve Working Conditions

An opportunity for practicing social responsibility is for company leaders to work with suppliers to improve physical and mental working conditions. Instead of refusing to deal with a supplier who operates a sweatshop, management might work with the supplier to improve plant working conditions. The justification for helping the supplier improve conditions is that the supplier's employees are often in dire need of a paying job. Almost any job is better than no job to a person facing extreme poverty or who is dependent on modest wages for food and shelter.

Gap Inc. took a major initiative to begin improving working conditions at suppliers. Company leadership issued a report conceding that working conditions are far from perfect at many of the 3,000 factories worldwide that manufacture clothing for Gap. Among the working-condition violations were that between 10 and 25 percent of its Chinese factories used psychological coercion or verbal abuse. More than 50 percent of the factories visited in sub-Saharan Africa operated machinery without proper safety devices. Gap representatives now invest more time in training and helping factories develop programs for compliance with working-condition codes.[26]

college.hmco.com/pic/
dubrin5e

🏦 @ **KNOWLEDGE BANK:** contains another way business leaders can be socially responsible.

## Initiatives for Achieving an Ethical and Socially Responsible Organization

The initiatives described in the preceding section are designed specifically to enhance social responsibility. Here we look at five other initiatives that executive leadership can take to help create an ethical and socially responsible culture.

### Providing Strategic Leadership of Ethics and Social Responsibility

The most effective route to an ethical and socially responsible organization is for senior management to provide strategic leadership in that direction. In this way, senior managers become ethics leaders: their policies and actions set the ethical and social responsibility tone for the organization. If high ethics receive top priority, workers at all levels are more likely to behave ethically. When Paul O'Neil became CEO and chairperson at Alcoa years ago, he believed that plant safety was an ethical obligation. He visited Alcoa plants, communicating with managers and workers about the necessity of workplace safety. O'Neil tied promotions, evaluations, and firing to workplace safety. After twelve years of this safety climate, the annual lost workday rate was reduced from 1.87 to .014 (a reduction of 99.3 percent).[27]

Strategic leadership of ethics and social responsibility includes leading by example. If workers throughout the firm believe that behaving ethically is "in" and behaving unethically is "out," ethical behavior will prevail. A curious instance of unethical leadership by example took place at Oracle Corporation under the leadership of flamboyant CEO Larry Ellison. The Oracle chief hired private investigators to go through the dumpsters of groups that were defending his rival Microsoft in its antitrust case. Ellison defended his actions, noting that his investigators had uncovered evidence that Microsoft was secretly funding "front groups" to manipulate public opinion in its favor. Ellison insisted that his dumpster diving was a "civic duty" against Bill Gates, a "convicted monopolist."[28] Stunts like this by senior management encourage questionable ethical behavior throughout the organization.

Ethical behavior that is rewarded is likely to endure. Linda Klebe Treviño and Michael E. Brown observe that ethical behavior can be rewarded by promoting and compensating people who perform well and have developed a reputation of integrity with managers, coworkers, and customers. In addition, workers who perform unethically should not be rewarded, and perhaps disciplined.[29] A sales manager who uses a "35-day month" might not be rewarded for sales booked during those five days borrowed from the next month just to look good in the previous months.

**Establishing Written Codes of Ethical Conduct**  Many organizations use written codes of conduct as guidelines for ethical and socially responsible behavior. Such guidelines continue to grow in importance because workers in self-managing teams have less leadership than previously. Regardless of the industry, most codes deal with quite similar issues. Patricia Breeding, integrity compliance officer for Covenant Heath, in Knoxville, Tennessee, says, "They all address conflicts of interest, gifts and things like vendor relationships. They use the word 'customer' in one and 'patient' in another but they're all about doing the right thing."[30] The Sarbanes-Oxley Act, triggered by the financial scandals around the year 2000, requires public companies to disclose whether they have adopted a code of ethics for senior financial officers. In some firms, such as Boeing Company, workers at all levels are required to sign the code of conduct.

A written code of conduct is more likely to influence behavior when both formal and informal leaders throughout the firm refer to it frequently. Furthermore, adherence to the code must be rewarded, and violation of the code should be punished.

**Developing Formal Mechanisms for Dealing with Ethical Problems**  Many large employers have ethics programs of various types. Large organizations frequently establish ethics committees to help ensure ethical and socially responsible behavior. Top-level leadership participation in these formal mechanisms gives them more clout. Committee members include a top management representative plus other managers throughout the organization. An ethics and social responsibility specialist from the human resources department might also join the group. The committee establishes policies about ethics and social responsibility and may conduct an ethical audit of the firm's activities. In addition, committee members might review complaints about ethical problems.

United Technologies Corp. (UTC) has developed an advanced program for reporting ethical issues. The Ombudsman/DIALOG program is designed to provide a confidential method for UTC's 203,000 employers, as well as suppliers and customers, to report problems and wrongdoings, make suggestions, and ask questions. The communication can be done in person, by telephone, in hard copy, or online. Commentary can include accusations of wrongdoing, potential violations of ethical codes, safety problems, human resources issues, and suggestions for training programs. Complaints are confidential. Of the nearly 60,000 DIALOGs dealt with since the program's inception in the mid-1980s, 41 percent resulted in an organizational change, 23 percent did not request or require any change, and 36 percent received a reply from management saying the complaint was incorrect or could not be rectified. Administrators in the Ombudsman/DIALOG collect information and then pass it along to the appropriate company official for action.

An example of a complaint brought to the program would be an employee reporting that he or she thinks the boss is stealing from the company. Because employees with complaints are not identified to the suspected ethical violator, they are more likely to come forth with a concern about unethical behavior.[31]

### Accepting Whistleblowers

A **whistleblower** is an employee who discloses organizational wrongdoing to parties who can take action. It was a whistleblower who began the process of exposing the scandalous financial practices at Enron Corporation, such as hiding losses. Sherron Watkins, a vice president, wrote a one-page anonymous letter exposing unsound, if not dishonest, financial reporting: Enron had booked profits for two entities that had no assets. She dropped the letter off at company headquarters the next day.

Whistleblowers are often ostracized and humiliated by the companies they hope to improve. For example, they may receive no further promotions or poor performance evaluations. The Sarbanes-Oxley Act includes some protection for whistleblowers. Employees who report fraud related to corporate accounting, internal accounting controls, and auditing have a way of gaining reinstatement, as well as back pay and legal expenses.

Nevertheless, more than half of the pleas of whistleblowers are ignored. Former Coca-Cola Co. manager Matthew Whitley claimed he was fired in retaliation for reporting instances of fraud and accounting irregularities to top-level management. Among Whitley's many allegations were that Coke rigged a marketing test about preference for Coke at Burger King restaurants in 2000 and made false and misleading statements or omissions related to sales volume.[32] So it is important for leaders at all levels to create a comfortable climate for legitimate whistleblowing. The leader needs to sort out the difference between a troublemaker and a true whistleblower.

### Providing Training in Ethics and Social Responsibility

Forms of ethics training include messages about ethics and social responsibility from company leadership, classes on ethics at colleges, and exercises in ethics. These training programs reinforce the idea that ethically and socially responsible behavior is both morally right and good for business. Much of the content of this chapter reflects the type of information communicated in such programs. Leadership Skill-Building Exercise 6-2 gives you the opportunity to engage in a small amount of ethics training.

**LEADERSHIP SKILL-BUILDING EXERCISE 6-2**

### DEALING WITH DEFINING MOMENTS

The toughest ethical choices for many people occur when they have to choose between two rights. The result is a defining moment, because we are challenged to think in a deeper way by choosing between two or more ideals. Working individually or in teams, reach a decision about the two following defining moments. Explain why these scenarios could require choosing between two rights, and explain the reasoning behind your decisions.

1. You are the manager of a department in a business firm that assigns each department a fixed amount of money for salary increases each year. An average-performing member of the department asks you in advance for an above-average increase. He explains that his mother has developed multiple sclerosis and requires the services of a paid helper from time to time. You are concerned that if you give this man an above-average increase, somebody else in the department will have to receive a below-average increase.

2. You are the team leader of a group of packaging scientists at a large consumer products company. Two years ago, top management decided that any employee who is late to work more than 10 percent of the time over the course of a year should be fired. At about the same time, top management began incorporating a measure of *diversity success* into managers' performance evaluations. Managers who hired and retained targeted groups would receive a high rating on *diversity success*. Poor hiring and retention of targeted groups would result in a low performance rating. It is now mid-December, and Tim, the only employee over age 60, has been late 11 percent of the time. Several former employees have recently charged your company with age discrimination. Firing Tim will enable you to comply with the lateness policy, yet your diversity performance will suffer. Also, top management does not want to deal with any more employment discrimination suits.

Getting started dealing with defining moments is useful practice because so many leadership issues are in the gray zone—neither completely right nor completely wrong. Part of dealing with defining moments is doing some soul searching.

***Placing Company Interests over Personal Interests*** Many ethical violations, such as senior managers' voting themselves outrageous compensation, stem from managers' placing their personal interests over the welfare of the company and other employees. Jonathan M. Tish, the chairman and CEO of Loews Hotels, says that success in today's interdependent world demands "We" leaders, or people who look beyond self-interest to build partnerships in pursuit of a greater good. "We" leaders unify rather than divide, collaborate rather than compete, and believe that it is possible to "do well" and "do good" at the same time. A major requirement for building a partnership is fairness. Everyone must benefit from a partnership. Along these lines, some people question whether it is fair for Eddie Lampert (the deal maker behind merging Kmart and Sears) to be worth more than $2 billion while many Kmart suppliers were not paid after the company declared bankruptcy. Also, how fair is it for Lampert to accumulate a personal fortune from the deal when so many Kmart employees are paid close to the minimum wage?

David Neeleman, the founder and CEO of JetBlue Airways, qualifies as a "We" leader. Neeleman invests in community-building efforts in the cities JetBlue serves, employees receive stock options and profit sharing, and he donates much of his CEO salary to a crisis fund for employees.[33]

## Ethical Behavior and Organizational Performance

High ethics and social responsibility are apparently related to good financial performance. According to the International Business Ethics Institute, socially responsible behavior does enhance profits. The overall financial performance of the 2001 list of the 100 Best Firms was significantly better than that of the remaining companies in the S&P 500. The study in question took into account measures of responsibility reflecting quality service to seven stakeholder groups: community, minorities, women, employees, environment, foreign stakeholders, and customers.[34]

The relationship between social responsibility and profits can also work in two directions: more profitable firms can better afford to invest in social responsibility initiatives, and these initiatives can lead to more profits. Sandra A. Waddock and Samuel B. Graves analyzed the relationship between corporate social performance and corporate financial performance for 469 firms, spanning thirteen industries, for a two-year period. They used many different measures of social and financial performance. An example of social performance would be helping to redevelop a poor community.

The researchers found that financial success creates enough money left over to invest in corporate social performance. The study also found that good corporate social performance contributes to improved financial performance as measured by return on assets and return on sales. Waddock and Graves concluded that the relationship between social and financial performance may be a **virtuous circle,** meaning that corporate social performance and corporate financial performance feed and reinforce each other.[35]

Being ethical also helps avoid the costs of paying huge fines for being unethical, including charges of discrimination and class action lawsuits because of improper financial reporting. Being accused of unethical and illegal behavior can also result in a sudden drop in customers and clients, as well as extreme difficulty in obtaining new customers and clients. When Arthur Andersen was accused of shoddy auditing practices in relation to Enron, clients exited in droves. Telemarketers for telecommunications firms involved in major financial scandals met with much more resistance than usual when soliciting new business. As one irate consumer said, "Why should I shift my long-distance business to you? You laid off my neighbor and thousands of other employees, and you don't even pay your bills."

In short, a leader who is successful at establishing a climate of high ethics and social responsibility can earn and save the company a lot of money. Yet there are times when being socially responsible can eat into profits and lower a stock price. A case in point is Costco Wholesale Corporation, a warehouse club retailer that offers compensation above the industry average, including covering 82 percent of its employees with health insurance. (In contrast, Wal-Mart provides health insurance for 48 percent of workers.) The unusually high benefits and wages lead to investors' concerns that profit margins are not high enough. Jim Sinegal, the president and chief executive of Costco, defends his practice in these words: "I happen to believe that in order to reward the shareholder in the long term, you have to please your customers and workers."[36]

## Summary

college.hmco.com/pic/dubrin5e

Principles of ethical and moral leadership all center on the idea that a leader should do the right thing, as perceived by a consensus of reasonable people. Key principles of ethical and moral leadership are as follows: (1) be honest and trustworthy and have integrity in dealing with others, (2) pay attention to all stakeholders, (3) build community, (4) respect the individual, and (5) accomplish silent victories. Differences in ethics and morality can be traced to five factors: (1) the leader's level of greed, gluttony, and avarice; (2) the leader's level of moral development; (3) a sense of entitlement; (4) situational influences; and (5) a person's character.

Before reaching a decision about an issue that is not obviously ethical or blatantly unethical, a leader or manager should seek answers to questions such as: Is it right? Is it fair? Who gets hurt? Before joining a company, a job seeker should search for answers to ethics-related questions, such as "Is there a formal code of ethics?"

Unethical behavior has brought companies into bankruptcy, led to layoffs of thousands of workers, diminished trust in stock investments, and discouraged many talented young people from embarking on a business career.

Another way a leader can be ethical and moral is to spearhead the firm, or a unit within it, toward doing good deeds—toward being socially responsible. Among the many possible socially responsible acts are (1) creating a pleasant workplace, (2) guarding the environment, (3) engaging in philanthropy, and (4) working with suppliers to improve working conditions.

Initiatives for achieving an ethical and socially responsible organization include (1) providing strategic leadership of ethics and social responsibility, (2) establishing written codes of conduct, (3) developing formal mechanisms for dealing with ethical problems, (4) accepting whistleblowers, (5) providing training in ethics, and (6) placing company interests over personal interests.

High ethics and social responsibility are related to good financial performance, according to research evidence and opinion. Also, more profitable firms have the funds to invest in good social programs. Being ethical helps avoid big fines for being unethical, and ethical organizations attract more employees. Yet above-average compensation to employees can discourage investors.

## Key Terms

Ethics

Morals

Integrity

Social responsibility

Whistleblower

Virtuous circle

## ✔ Guidelines for Action and Skill Development

A provocative explanation of the causes of unethical behavior emphasizes the strength of relationships among people.[37] Assume that two people have close ties to each other—they may have worked together for a long time or have known each other both on and off the job. As a consequence, they are likely to behave ethically toward one another on the job. In contrast, if a weak relationship exists between two people, either party is more likely to treat the other badly. In the work environment, the people involved may be your work associates, your contacts, or your internal and external customers.

## Discussion Questions and Activities

1. If the president of the United States, George W. Bush, engaged in questionable ethical behavior while he was an energy company executive, why should you worry about being ethical?
2. The majority of business executives accused of unethical behavior have studied ethics either as a subject in a business course or as an entire course. So what do you think went wrong?
3. Based on what you have read, heard, or seen, at which level (or levels) in the organization are highly ethical leaders the most likely to be found?
4. How can consumers use the Internet to help control the ethical behavior of business leaders?
5. In what ways are many retail customers quite unethical?
6. An increasing number of critics are demanding that no executive should receive total compensation of $100 million or more in one year. What is your position on the ethics of a business leader's receiving so much compensation?
7. Companies that make and sell alcoholic or tobacco products are an easy target for individuals demanding social responsibility. Should leaders of companies that produce fattening food that can lead to cardiac problems and obesity also be targeted for being socially irresponsible?
8. In your opinion, are companies that target their athletic shoe advertising to poor teenagers being socially responsible? Explain your answer.
9. Approximately 3,500 deaths from automobile accidents in the United States each year are attributed to speaking on cell phones while driving. What social responsibility obligations should cell phone manufacturers and cell phone service providers have for dealing with this problem?
10. What is the explanation for the fact that many profitable business corporations are also socially responsible?

## LEADERSHIP CASE PROBLEM A

### THE BIG STEEL COMEBACK

Workers at an International Steel Group (ISG), Inc., mill do not seem to mind machines that roar like jets or temperatures that soar to near 1,400 degrees. The sweat pouring from their brows and the coal-black grime under their fingernails are good things for a group that thought their steel-making careers were over when LTV Corporation closed.

Workers like Eddie Reust, 50, of Cleveland, Ohio, have experienced the rarity of being hired by a U.S. steelmaker as the industry is shrinking. About 12,000 ISG employees got their jobs after the company bought bankrupt steel makers, shed retiree costs, and consolidated several expensive operations into a few cost-effective ones. "I didn't think we would even make steel here again," said Reust, who had 29½ years in when the LTV pink slip came three years ago. Donald Jenkins of South Highland, Illinois, recalled the day he lost his LTV job: "I was devastated. I had worked 30-some years of my life and all of a sudden the doors were closed."

Six months later, ISG restarted the plant near where Jenkins lived, and the company wanted him back. Gary Grimes was more than three decades into his career and six months from a pension when LTV shut down in Cleveland in 2001. The next year, he was called back to work at ISG's Cleveland hot strip mill, then part of the plant where freshly rolled steel is rung through a bath of molten coating. "They reopened with less people," Grimes said. "But there were zero people when it was shut down."

Richfield-based ISG bought LTV in 2002 and rose to become the nation's largest integrated steel maker by buying and revamping operations in several states. It shed the costs associated with more than 82,000 retirees and came up with a strategy to make the steel cheaper with fewer workers, with whom the profits were shared.

ISG says its growth will continue. The company announced it will expand its Cleveland Works plant with a hot-dipping line to make specialty steel for automakers, part of ISG's business that also produces steel for food cans, construction, and other uses. The company also restarted a second blast furnace at its newly acquired plant in West Virginia, recalling nearly 100 steelworkers from the former Weirton Steel Corporation and raising employment to 1,900. In May 2004, ISG reopened some of its west side Cleveland Works mill, bringing back 140 people.

### QUESTIONS

1. In what way is leadership at the International Steel Group being socially responsible?
2. In what way is leadership at the International Steel Group being socially irresponsible?
3. What is your evaluation of the ethics of shedding retiree costs in order to help reduce operating costs?

## LEADERSHIP CASE PROBLEM B

## BAD CREDIT? NO CREDIT? COLLEGE STUDENT? PROVIDIAN LOVES YOU.

For more than ten years, Providian Financial Corporation outdistanced the competition under the leadership of chairman Shailesh J. Mehta. By using every medium from cable TV to the Internet to troll for business from students and other consumers, Providian became the nation's fifth-biggest credit card company. But soon its fortunes took a downturn, including being forced to stop selling credit cards to consumers with poor credit ratings.

The company pioneered the business of issuing credit cards to risky, or *subprime,* customers. Lenders like Providian seek out customers with spotty credit histories or no credit histories at all—typically low-income people—and often charge them exorbitant rates and fees to compensate for the possibility of a loan default. Personal finance companies were built on subprime loans made during the Great Depression. After credit cards became part of American life and companies learned how to use demographics to target potential borrowers, the business began to flourish.

Providian's expertise was in segmenting people based on financial behavior. The company created a system that made it possible to find the "ideal" credit card customer: a person who cared more about low minimum monthly payments than high interest rates and who would pile up debt but rarely default. Mehta was one of the people who helped develop its trade-secret mathematical model for finding the ideal customer. "We found the best of the bad," said a former executive (*Fortune,* March 4, 2002, p. 144).

At first, Providian had the subprime credit card market to itself. It charged some customers an application fee, in addition to an annual fee, for a card with a limit between $300 and $500. Interest rates often reached 24 percent. A marketing technique was to send checks to potential customers. When the check was cashed, interest fees would be immediately charged to the customer. Prospects who declined to cash the check did not receive credit cards because they did not fit the profile of a person who embraced debt.

When earnings began to slow, the company attempted to compensate by generating more and more subprime customers. To find them, Providian lowered its standards and handed out credit cards to people whom its mathematical models would have rejected in the past. Providian is more troubled than most of its competitors because its charge-offs for noncollectible loans climbed from 7.6 percent of assets to 10.3 percent in one year, and are approaching 12 percent. For most companies, noncollectible loans are below 5.5 percent.

Providian has been troubled for a while. One concern is that Providian's hard sell to high-risk customers at times has been hucksterism. Several years ago, Providian paid $300 million to settle charges by the comptroller of the currency and the San Francisco district attorney that it had misled and deceived consumers with less-than-candid marketing. Investigators said that the company's telemarketers refused to specify promised "great savings" on interest rates and failed to spell out extra charges on "no annual fee" cards. Providian settled without admitting or denying the charges.

As problems mounted, Providian's share price plunged. The company then revised its practices for writing off bad accounts, delaying the impact of the customer bankruptcies for up to thirty days. To keep earnings growth looking good, Providian management deferred about $30 million in credit losses to another quarter without informing Wall Street. The analysts were angry, and Providian lost its credibility with investors.

As the company started a nosedive, Mehta and his number 2 executive began liquidating their personal stock. Shortly after, lawyers began filing class action suits against the company and its top executives for fraudulently misleading investors and having used insider knowledge to sell their stock at inflated

*(continued)*

prices. When consumer protection advocates criticized Providian, Mehta said his company was providing a valuable service in offering credit to customers whom other banks refused to serve. Yet as pressures continued to mount, Mehta resigned, though he stayed on until a successor was appointed.

In 2001, Providian pulled in its horns. In March, it stopped running television ads with 800 numbers to call to apply for credit cards. The company also phased down a TV campaign to reach a web site that offered cards with rates as high as 27.99 percent.

While Providian was growing rapidly, Mehta profited substantially: in October 2000, his stockholdings in the company were worth more than $300 million. Says a former Providian board member: "He was more motivated by money than anyone I've ever met" (*Fortune*, March 4, 2002, p. 144).

In 2004, federal regulators ordered the company to stop issuing subprime cards. Joseph Saunders, the new CEO and chairman, is now focusing Providian on the middle market, a notch higher than subprime. Although this market has a lower default rate, the competition is intense. As a stopgap measure, Saunders has sold off some of Providian's best loans to another financial company, and he has also attained other funding for a relief fund of about $11 billion.

## QUESTIONS

1. In what ways has Providian been unethical and socially irresponsible?
2. What argument can you present that Providian has been socially responsible?
3. What could company leadership have done to guide Providian in a better direction?

SOURCE: Suzanne Koudski, "Sleazy Credit," *Fortune,* March 4, 2002, pp. 143–147; Joseph Weber, "Let the Bidding Begin for Providian," *BusinessWeek,* November 5, 2001, p. 96; "Providian Financial Corporation," *www.hoovers.com, accessed November 28, 2004.*

---

**LEADERSHIP SKILL-BUILDING EXERCISE 6-3**

## MY LEADERSHIP PORTFOLIO

For this chapter's entry into your leadership journal, reflect on any scenario you have encountered recently that would have given you the opportunity to practice ethical or socially responsible behavior. The scenario could have taken place in relation to employment, an interaction with fellow students, or being a customer of some type. Write down the scenario, and how you responded to it. Indicate what you learned about yourself. An example follows:

I had been thinking of purchasing advanced software to manage and edit photos on my computer. The software I needed would cost several hundred dollars. The other day, while going through my email, I came upon an advertisement offering the exact photo software I wanted for $50. At first, I thought this would be a real money saver. After thinking through the ethical issues, I came to realize that the person selling this software was probably a pirate. If I purchased from this character, I would be supporting a software pirate. Besides, buying stolen goods might even be a crime. I learned from this incident that there are many opportunities in everyday life to practice good—or bad—ethics. I want to become a moral leader, so practicing good ethics will help me.

P.S.: By being ethical I probably avoided buying some virus-infected software that could have played havoc with my computer.

## INTERNET SKILL-BUILDING EXERCISE

Apply the chapter concepts! Visit the Web and complete this Internet skill-building exercise to learn more about current leadership topics and trends.

### CAREER CONSEQUENCES OF UNETHICAL LEADERSHIP BEHAVIOR

In this chapter and at other places in the text, you have read about business executives accused of unethical, illegal, or socially irresponsible behavior. An important issue is to understand the career consequences to these individuals stemming from their misbehavior. Use the Internet to find the current status of four executives whose unethical behavior has been cited in this chapter. Verify this status, looking for potential consequences such as (1) new employment in a corporation, (2) self-employment, (3) loss of employment, (4) working as a consultant, (5) elected as a public official, or (6) incarceration. Based on your findings, draw a conclusion about the career consequences of unethical leadership behavior.

**Chapter**

# 7

# Power, Politics, and Leadership

Tony Ronzone, the director of international scouting for the Detroit Pistons, is considered the world's best international scout. John Hammond, the Pistons' vice president of basketball operations, says that Ronzone travels to obscure places and builds lasting relationships with all kinds of people. Most people think of scouting as the ability to recognize talent. This—it turns out—is relatively easy. Good basketball players are usually quite tall, quite fast, and quite adept at shooting a basketball. The difficult part in a world of 6 billion people is actually finding those who are tall, fast, and coordinated, and the extremely difficult part is finding them before the competition does. Ronzone has conquered this problem by building a global network of coaches, journalists, and friends who tip him off to the location of the world's most gifted young players.

This network explains how, without his knowing a single word of Turkish, Ronzone was delivered to the remote island home of Mehmet Okur, an unknown even in his home country, who became a burgeoning star for the Pistons. It also explains how, while knowing little more than *qiu* (the Chinese word for "ball"), he wrangled an invitation to a cramped Shanghai apartment for the 18th birthday party of a 7-foot, 6-inch kid named Yao Ming, who is now one of professional basketball's superstars.

In order to stay in touch with 400 people on five continents in a meaningful way, one has to have a certain natural exuberance. "An uptight guy would not succeed at this job," says Pistons president Joe Dumars. "Tony will try every single food and drink. He'll smile. He'll laugh. He's easy to like."

After playing professional basketball around the globe for a few years, Ronzone joined the Dallas Mavericks in 1997 and based himself in China. Later he joined the Pistons and was given carte blanche to travel around the world looking for talent. Ronzone later discovered he could cut back on flying. "If I'm going to three normal countries—say, Italy, Spain, and France—I now have friends I call in advance who direct me to players. A trip that used to take two weeks now takes four days."

This allows Ronzone to tack on what he calls a "random country," a Kazakhstan or a Congo, to the end of each journey. When he arrives, friendless and unannounced, his strategy for expanding his network frequently consists of walking up to people, saying hello, and starting to talk about basketball. More often than not, they talk back. In Kazakhstan, a conversation with a hotel bellman led to the discovery of three raw but promising players at a club team.[1]

---

Tony Ronzone's success as a professional basketball scout can be partially attributed to his extraversion and his "ordinary-guy" personality. More specifically, however, it can be attributed to his ability to develop contacts, which gives him the power he needs to accomplish his mission. This chapter covers the nature of power, the ways leaders acquire power and empower others, and the use and control of organizational politics. Chapter 8 continues the discussion of organizational (or office) politics by examining influence tactics.

## Sources and Types of Power

To exercise influence, a leader must have **power**, the potential or ability to influence decisions and control resources. Organizational power can be derived from many sources. How a person obtains power depends to a large extent on the type of power he or she seeks. Therefore, to understand the mechanics of acquiring power, one must also understand what types of power exist and the sources and origins of these types of power. The seven types or sources of power are described in the following sections.

### Position Power

Power is frequently classified according to whether it stems from the organization or the individual.[2] Four bases of power—legitimate power, reward power, coercive power, and information power—stem from the person's position in the organization.

*Legitimate Power* The lawful right to make a decision and expect compliance is called **legitimate power**. People at the highest levels in the organization have more power than do people below them. However, organizational culture helps establish the limits to anyone's power. Newly appointed executives, for example, are often frustrated with how long it takes to effect major change. A chief financial officer (CFO) recruited to improve the profitability of a telecommunications firm noted: "The company has been downsizing for three years. We have more office space and manufacturing capacity than we need. Yet whenever I introduce the topic of selling off real estate to cut costs, I get a cold reception."

*Reward Power* The authority to give employees rewards for compliance is referred to as **reward power**. If a vice president of operations can directly reward supervisors with cash bonuses for achieving quality targets, this manager will exert considerable power.

*Coercive Power* **Coercive power** is the power to punish for noncompliance; it is based on fear. A common coercive tactic is for an executive to demote a subordinate manager if he or she does not comply with the executive's plans for change. Coercive power is limited, in that punishment and fear achieve mixed results as motivators. The leader who relies heavily on coercive power runs the constant threat of being ousted from power. Nevertheless, coercive power is widely practiced. The chief executive of Merrill Lynch and Company, Inc., E. Stanley O'Neal, exercises considerable coercive power. He has presided over one of the most intense restructurings in Wall Street history, eliminating more than 23,000 jobs, closing more than 300 offices, and ousting 19 senior executives. In the process he has purged an entire generation of key people to strengthen his own power grip.[3]

*Information Power* **Information power** is power stemming from formal control over the information people need to do their work. A sales manager who controls the leads from customer inquiries holds considerable power. As the branch manager of a real estate agency put it: "Ever since the leads were sent directly to me, I get oodles of cooperation from my agents. Before that they would treat me as if I were simply the office manager."

## Personal Power

Three sources of power stem from characteristics or behaviors of the power actor: expert power, referent power, and prestige power. All are classified as **personal power** because they are derived from the person rather than the organization. Expert power and referent power contribute to charisma. Referent power is the ability to influence others through one's desirable traits and characteristics (see Chapter 3). Expert power is the ability to influence others through specialized knowledge, skills, or abilities. An example of a leader with substantial expert power is automotive executive Bob Lutz. For many years he had spearheaded new car development at Chrysler Corporation. At age 69 he was recruited to General Motors as vice chairman for product development. His mission was to work with designers and engineers to give new GM models sex appeal.[4] Lutz has achieved some successes, but so far not enough to revitalize GM.

Another important form of personal power is **prestige power**, the power stemming from one's status and reputation.[5] A manager who has accumulated important business successes acquires prestige power. Integrity is another contributor to prestige power because it enhances a leader's reputation.[6] Executive recruiters identify executives who can readily be placed in senior positions because of their excellent track records (or prestige).

Manager Assessment Quiz 7-1 provides a sampling of the specific behaviors associated with five of the sources of power—three kinds of position power and two kinds of personal power.

MANAGER ASSESSMENT QUIZ 7-1

### RATING A MANAGER'S POWER

INSTRUCTIONS If you currently have a supervisor or can clearly recall one from the past, rate him or her. Circle the appropriate number of your answer, using the following scale: 5 = strongly agree; 4 = agree; 3 = neither agree nor disagree; 2 = disagree; 1 = strongly disagree. (The actual scale presents the items in random order. They are classified here according to the power source for your convenience.)

**My manager can (or former manager could) . . .**

| | Strongly Agree | | | | Strongly Disagree |
|---|---|---|---|---|---|

**Reward Power**

| | | | | | |
|---|---|---|---|---|---|
| 1. increase my pay level. | 5 | 4 | 3 | 2 | 1 |
| 2. influence my getting a pay raise. | 5 | 4 | 3 | 2 | 1 |
| 3. provide me with specific benefits. | 5 | 4 | 3 | 2 | 1 |
| 4. influence my getting a promotion. | 5 | 4 | 3 | 2 | 1 |

**Coercive Power**

| | | | | | |
|---|---|---|---|---|---|
| 5. give me undesirable job assignments. | 5 | 4 | 3 | 2 | 1 |
| 6. make my work difficult for me. | 5 | 4 | 3 | 2 | 1 |

*(continued)*

| | | | | | |
|---|---|---|---|---|---|
| 7. make things unpleasant here. | 5 | 4 | 3 | 2 | 1 |
| 8. make being at work distasteful. | 5 | 4 | 3 | 2 | 1 |

**Legitimate Power**

| | | | | | |
|---|---|---|---|---|---|
| 9. make me feel that I have commitments to meet. | 5 | 4 | 3 | 2 | 1 |
| 10. make me feel like I should satisfy my job requirements. | 5 | 4 | 3 | 2 | 1 |
| 11. make me feel I have responsibilities to fulfill. | 5 | 4 | 3 | 2 | 1 |
| 12. make me recognize that I have tasks to accomplish. | 5 | 4 | 3 | 2 | 1 |

**Expert Power**

| | | | | | |
|---|---|---|---|---|---|
| 13. give me good technical suggestions. | 5 | 4 | 3 | 2 | 1 |
| 14. share with me his or her considerable experience and/or training. | 5 | 4 | 3 | 2 | 1 |
| 15. provide me with sound job-related advice. | 5 | 4 | 3 | 2 | 1 |
| 16. provide me with needed technical knowledge. | 5 | 4 | 3 | 2 | 1 |

**Referent Power**

| | | | | | |
|---|---|---|---|---|---|
| 17. make me feel valued. | 5 | 4 | 3 | 2 | 1 |
| 18. make me feel that he or she approves of me. | 5 | 4 | 3 | 2 | 1 |
| 19. make me feel personally accepted. | 5 | 4 | 3 | 2 | 1 |
| 20. make me feel important. | 5 | 4 | 3 | 2 | 1 |

*Total score:* _____

SCORING AND INTERPRETATION Add all the circled numbers to calculate your total score. You can make a tentative interpretation of the score as follows:

- 90+      High power
- 70–89     Moderate power
- below 70   Low power

Also, see if you rated your manager much higher in one of the categories.

SKILL DEVELOPMENT This skill development rating can help you as a leader because it points to specific behaviors you can use to be perceived as high or low on a type of power. For example, a behavior specific for establishing referent power is to "make people feel important" (No. 20).

SOURCE: Adapted from "Development and Application of New Scales to Measure the French and Raven (1959) Bases of Social Power," by Timothy R. Hinkin and Chester A. Schriescheim, *Journal of Applied Psychology*, August 1989, p. 567. Copyright © 1989 by the American Psychological Association. Adapted with permission of the American Psychological Association and Timothy R. Hinkin.

## Power Stemming from Ownership

Executive leaders accrue power in their capacity as agents acting on behalf of shareholders. The strength of ownership power depends on how closely the leader is linked to shareholders and board members. A leader's ownership power is also associated with how much money he or she has invested in the firm.[7] An executive who is a major shareholder is much less likely to be fired by the board than one without an equity stake. The CEOs of high-technology firms are typically company founders who later convert their firm into a publicly held company by selling stock. After the public offering, many of these CEOs own several hundred million dollars worth of stock, making their position quite secure. The New Golden Rule applies: The person who holds the gold, rules.

## Power Stemming from Providing Resources

A broad way to view power sources is from the **resource dependence perspective**. According to this perspective, the organization requires a continuing flow of human resources, money, customers and clients, technological inputs, and materials to continue to function. Organizational subunits or individuals who can provide these key resources accrue power.[8]

When leaders start losing their power to control resources, their power declines. A case in point is Donald Trump. When his vast holdings were generating a positive cash flow and his image was one of extraordinary power, he found many willing investors. The name *Trump* on a property escalated its value. As his cash-flow position worsened, however, Trump found it difficult to find investment groups willing to buy his properties at near the asking price. However, by mid-1993, Trump's cash-flow position had improved again and investors showed renewed interest. By 1996 Trump had regained all of his power to control resources, and money from investors flowed freely in his direction. In 2004, the Trump casino business filed for bankruptcy, mostly to refinance debt. Trump's equity in the casinos diminished, but he still controlled enough resources to remain powerful. You can study more about Trump and his power in one of the case problems at the end of this chapter.

## Power Derived from Capitalizing on Opportunity

Power can be derived from being in the right place at the right time and taking the appropriate action. It pays to be "where the action is." For example, the best opportunities in a diversified company lie in one of its growth divisions. A person also needs to have the right resources to capitalize on an opportunity.

## Power Stemming from Managing Critical Problems

The **strategic contingency theory** of power suggests that units best able to cope with the firm's critical problems and uncertainties acquire relatively large amounts of power.[9] The theory implies, for example, that when an organization faces substantial lawsuits, the legal department will gain power and influence over organizational decisions. Another important aspect of the strategic contingency theory concerns the power a subunit acquires by virtue of its centrality. **Centrality** is the extent to which a unit's activities are linked into the system of organizational activities. A unit has high centrality when it is an important and integral part of the work done by another unit. The second unit is therefore dependent on the first subunit. A sales department would have high centrality, whereas an employee credit union would have low centrality.

### Power Stemming from Being Close to Power

The closer a person is to power, the greater the power he or she exerts. Likewise, the higher a unit reports in a firm's hierarchy, the more power it possesses. In practice, this means that a leader in charge of a department reporting to the CEO has more power than one in charge of a department reporting to a vice president. Leaders in search of more power typically maneuver toward a higher-reporting position in the organization.

One justification for studying bases of power is that they have direct application to understanding and applying leadership.

college.hmco.com/pic/ dubrin5e

**KB @ KNOWLEDGE BANK:** provides information about bases of power and leadership.

## Tactics for Becoming an Empowering Leader

A leader's power and influence increase when he or she shares power with others. As team members receive more power, they can accomplish more—they become more productive. And because the manager shares credit for their accomplishments, he or she becomes more powerful. A truly powerful leader makes team members feel powerful and able to accomplish tasks on their own. A similar rationale for empowerment is that in a competitive environment that is increasingly dependent on knowledge, judgment, and information, the most successful organizations will be those that effectively use the talents of all players on the team.[10] As Steven Covey notes, empowerment and leadership distribution are happening among progressive companies throughout the world. Also, the more trusting the culture is, the more likely it is that employees will be empowered.[11]

Here we look briefly at the nature of empowerment before describing a number of empowering practices and two cautions about empowerment.

### The Nature of Empowerment

In its basic meaning, **empowerment** refers to passing decision-making authority and responsibility from managers to group members. Almost any form of participative management, shared decision making, and delegation can be regarded as empowerment. Gretchen M. Spreitzer conducted research in several work settings to develop a psychological definition of empowerment.[12] Four components of empowerment were identified: meaning, competence, self-determination, and impact. Full-fledged empowerment includes all four dimensions along with a fifth one, internal commitment.

*Meaning* is the value of a work goal, evaluated in relation to a person's ideals or standards. Work has meaning when there is a fit between the requirements of a work role and a person's beliefs, values, and behaviors. A person who is doing meaningful work is likely to feel empowered. *Competence*, or *self-efficacy*, is an individual's belief in his or her capability to perform a particular task well. The person who feels competent feels that he or she has the capability to meet the performance requirements in a given situation, such as a credit analyst saying, "I've been given the authority to evaluate credit risks up to $10,000 and I know I can do it well."

*Self-determination* is an individual's feeling of having a choice in initiating and regulating actions. A high-level form of self-determination occurs when a worker feels that he or she can choose the best method to solve a particular problem. Self-determination also involves such considerations as choosing the work pace and work site. A highly empowered worker might choose to perform the required work while on a cruise rather than remain in the office. *Impact* is the degree to which the worker can influence strategic, administrative, or operating outcomes on the job. Instead of feeling there is no choice but to follow the company's course, he or she might have a say in the future of the company. A middle manager might say, "Here's an opportunity for recruiting minority employees that we should exploit. And here's my action plan for doing so."

Another dimension of true empowerment is for the group member to develop an *internal commitment* toward work goals. Internal commitment takes place when workers are committed to a particular project, person, or program for individual motives. An example would be a production technician in a lawn mower plant who believes he is helping create a more beautiful world.

The focus of empowerment as just described is on the changes taking place within the individual. However, groups can also be empowered so the group climate contributes to these attitudes and feelings. An example of a statement reflecting an empowering climate would be "People in our organization get information about the organization's performance in a timely fashion."[13] Being part of an empowered group can help a group member become committed to achieving group goals.

## Empowering Practices

The practices that foster empowerment supplement standard approaches to participative management, such as conferring with team members before reaching a decision. The practices, as outlined in Figure 7-1, page 207, are based on direct observations of successful leaders and experimental evidence. Before reading about these practices, do Leadership Self-Assessment Quiz 7-1 on page 206.

**Foster Initiative and Responsibility** A leader can empower team members simply by fostering greater initiative and responsibility in their assignments. For example, one bank executive transformed what had been a constricted branch manager's job into a branch "president" role. Managers were then evaluated on the basis of deposits because they had control over them. After the transformation, branch managers were allowed to stay with one branch rather than being rotated every three years.[14]

**Link Work Activities to Organizational Goals** Empowerment works better when the empowered activities are aligned with the strategic goals of the organization. Empowered workers who have responsibility to carry out activities that support the major goals of the organization will identify more with the company. At the same time,

## BECOMING AN EMPOWERING MANAGER

INSTRUCTIONS To empower employees successfully, the leader has to convey appropriate attitudes and develop effective interpersonal skills. To the best of your ability, indicate which skills and attitudes you now have, and which ones require further development.

|  | Can Do Now | Would Need to Develop |
|---|---|---|
| **Empowering Attitude or Behavior** | | |
| 1. Believe in team members' ability to be successful | ____ | ____ |
| 2. Have patience with people and give them time to learn | ____ | ____ |
| 3. Provide team members with direction and structure | ____ | ____ |
| 4. Teach team members new skills in small, incremental steps so they can easily learn those skills | ____ | ____ |
| 5. Ask team members questions that challenge them to think in new ways | ____ | ____ |
| 6. Share information with team members, sometimes just to build rapport | ____ | ____ |
| 7. Give team members timely feedback and encourage them throughout the learning process | ____ | ____ |
| 8. Offer team members alternative ways of doing things | ____ | ____ |
| 9. Exhibit a sense of humor and demonstrate care for workers as people | ____ | ____ |
| 10. Focus on team members' results and acknowledge their personal improvement | ____ | ____ |

SKILL DEVELOPMENT If, as a leader or manager, you already have most of these attitudes and have engaged in most of these behaviors, you will be good at empowerment. Most of the above attitudes and practices can be developed without transforming your personality.

SOURCE: *Supervisory Management* by Stone, Florence. Copyright 1991 by *American Management Association (J)*. Reproduced with permission of *American Management Association (J)* in the format Textbook via Copyright Clearance Center.

they will develop a feeling of being a partner in the business.[15] Imagine a scenario in which a company auditor is authorized to spend large sums of travel money to accomplish her job. She is given this authority because a strategic goal of top-level management is to become a company admired for its honest business practices.

### FIGURE 7-1  Effective Empowering Practices

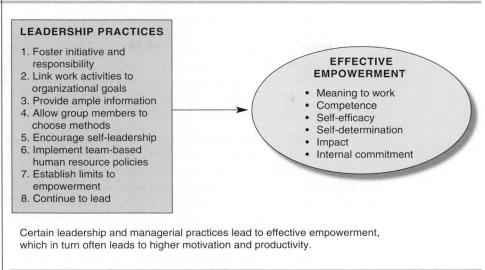

**LEADERSHIP PRACTICES**

1. Foster initiative and responsibility
2. Link work activities to organizational goals
3. Provide ample information
4. Allow group members to choose methods
5. Encourage self-leadership
6. Implement team-based human resource policies
7. Establish limits to empowerment
8. Continue to lead

**EFFECTIVE EMPOWERMENT**

- Meaning to work
- Competence
- Self-efficacy
- Self-determination
- Impact
- Internal commitment

Certain leadership and managerial practices lead to effective empowerment, which in turn often leads to higher motivation and productivity.

***Provide Ample Information*** For empowerment to be effective, employees should have ample information about everything that affects their work. Especially important is for workers to fully understand the impact of their actions on the company's costs and profits. Armed with such information, employees are more likely to make decisions that have a positive influence on the bottom line. Consultant Thomas J. McCoy poses these questions about the importance of information for empowerment:

- How can employees know the impact of their actions on the bottom line, if they do not have the kinds of financial scorecards that senior management routinely receives to run the business?

- If employees do not have full understanding of how their actions affect the whole operation, how can they act effectively?

When employees have answers to questions of the nature just described, they are more likely to use empowerment to make decisions that contribute to business success.[16] As an example, an empowered sales representative, armed with cost information, is less likely to grant discounts that lose money for the company.

***Allow Group Members to Choose Methods*** Under ideal conditions the leader or manager explains to the individual or group what needs to be done (sets a direction) and lets the people involved choose the method. Explaining why the tasks need to be performed is also important. One of the roles of a true professional is to choose the method for accomplishing a task, such as a tax consultant deciding how to prepare the taxes for a business owner. Norman Bodek explains: "What irks people the most is to be told how to do something. Allowing people to determine the most efficient work technique is the essence of empowerment."[17]

***Encourage Self-Leadership*** Encouraging team members to lead themselves is the heart of empowerment. When employees practice self-leadership, they feel empowered. At W. L. Gore and Associates, Inc., a manufacturer of insulated material including GORE-TEX®, there are no bosses or managers but many leaders. An example of self-leadership takes place during salary reviews. A compensation team drawn from individuals at the associate's work site periodically reviews each associate's (employee's) salary. Each associate has a sponsor who acts as his or her advocate during the reviews. The sponsor gathers data about the associate's performance by speaking to internal and external customers.

***Implement Team-Based Human Resource Policies*** A study conducted in four organizations found that teams are more likely to feel empowered when the organization implements a variety of team-based human resource policies. Among these policies are basing pay in part on team performance and allowing team members to participate in decisions about the selection, training, discipline, and performance evaluation of other team members. This study focused on empowering *teams,* in contrast to empowering individuals within the team.[18]

***Establish Limits to Empowerment*** One of the major situations in which empowerment creates disharmony and dysfunctions is when workers lack a clear perception of the boundaries of empowerment. Empowered group members may feel that they can now make decisions unilaterally without conferring with managers, team leaders, or other team members.[19] Limits to empowerment might mean explaining to employees that they have more authority than before, but still they cannot engage in such activities as the following:

- Set their own wages and those of top management
- Make downsizing decisions
- Hire mostly friends and relatives
- Work fewer than forty hours for full pay

Many employees justify dysfunctional actions by saying, "I'm empowered to do what I want." It is management's responsibility to guide employment activities that support the organization.

***Continue to Lead*** Although leaders empower group members, they should still provide guidance, emotional support, and recognition. Mark Samuel helps companies organize into teams to enhance accountability for results, yet at the same time he emphasizes the leader's role: "Empowerment often becomes an abdication of leadership. In other words, if I empower you, I don't have to guide you. People need guidance. Leadership cannot abdicate the role of providing guidance."[20] Because employees are empowered does not mean that they should be abandoned.

## Cultural Differences

All of the empowering practices described above can be influenced by cross-cultural factors. A group member's cultural values might lead to either an easy acceptance of empowerment or reluctance to be empowered. Americans are stereotyped as individualists. Nevertheless, they are so accustomed to working in teams (sports included) that being part of an empowered team would seem natural.

But not all cultures support empowerment. In one study, data from employees of a single firm with operations in the United States, Mexico, Poland, and India were used to test the fit of empowerment and continuous improvement practices with national culture. The company was engaged in light manufacturing, and data were collected from about forty sites. Empowerment was negatively associated with job satisfaction in the Indian plants but positively associated in the other three samples. The underlying cultural reason is that Indians (at least those working in India) expect the leader or manager to make most of the decisions.[21] Continuous improvement was positively related to satisfaction in all four samples.

## Effective Delegation and Empowerment

A major contributor to empowerment is **delegation**, the assignment of formal authority and responsibility for accomplishing a specific task to another person. Delegation is narrower than empowerment because it deals with a specific task, whereas empowerment covers a broad range of activities and a mental set about assuming more responsibility. Delegation, like empowerment, is motivational because it offers group members the opportunity to develop their skills and demonstrate their competence. It is usually discussed more in management studies than in leadership studies.

college.hmco.com/pic/
dubrin5e

**KB** @ **KNOWLEDGE BANK:** describes guidelines for effective delegation.

You are invited to gain some practice in the realities of empowerment by doing Leadership Skill-Building Exercise 7-1. Keep in mind the importance of delegation when doing the exercise. To gain more insight into empowerment, also read the accompanying Leader in Action.

**LEADERSHIP SKILL-BUILDING EXERCISE 7-1**

### CONDUCTING AN EMPOWERMENT SESSION

The description of empowering practices has given you some useful ideas to get started empowering others if you are already a manager. The role-assuming exercise described here gives you a chance to practice your empowering skills. One person plays the role of a leader, and six other people play the role of group members. You are meeting with your group today to get them started on the road toward empowerment. You will need to engage in dialogue with the group to begin the empowerment process. The empowerment scenarios described next should be staffed by different groups of students:

**Information Technology Customer-Service Center**

You are in charge of an information technology call center whose primary activity is to respond to telephone inquiries from around the country from customers who are having problems in using the company's software. The workers who answer the phone are full-time professionals, many of whom are recent college graduates. A major goal of yours is to empower your workers to do as

*(continued)*

much as they can to satisfy the demands of the callers. You want your staff to take more personal responsibility for customer problems.

**Vision-Care Proprietors**

You are the CEO of a nationwide chain of vision-care stores that sell both eyeglasses and contact lenses. You believe strongly that one of the constraining forces in your business is that your store managers, as well as franchise owners, do not take enough responsibility for running their operations. They rely too heavily on the corporate group for guidance and problem resolution. Today you are holding an empowerment meeting with the seven vision-care proprietors in your region. If your approach to empowerment works well, you will expand to other regions. Six other students play the role of store managers and franchise owners who generally believe that the corporate group should take the initiative to lead the stores toward greater prosperity. After all, why be a manager within a corporation or a franchise owner? Without corporate assistance, you might as well open your own vision-care store.

Doing this exercise is useful because it helps you develop the right mental set for a leader who empowers group members. Another advantage is that it sensitizes you to the importance of looking for signs of hesitation and ambivalence when you attempt to empower group members.

## LEADER IN ACTION

### MEG WHITMAN, THE ENABLING CEO OF eBAY

When *Fortune* introduced its 50 Most Powerful Women in Business in 2004, for the first time Meg Whitman of eBay, Inc., topped the list. A major reason for the honor is that she helped build the world's largest online marketplace, the world's most valuable Internet brand, and the fastest-growing large company in history.

Despite the *Fortune* accolade, Whitman emphasizes sharing her power as a leader. She describes eBay as a dynamic, self-regulating economy because the people who trade on eBay help regulate its activities. More than 150,000 small-business owners earn a full-time living selling everything from diet pills to automobiles on eBay.

eBay began as a trading site for nerds, the newly jobless, and bored homebound parents to sell subprime goods: collectibles and attic trash. But it quickly grew into a teaming metropolis of over 100 million people with its own laws and norms, such as a feedback system in which buyers and sellers rate each other on each transaction. When that was not quite enough, eBay formed its own police force to patrol the listings for fraud and to kick out offenders. The company also has an educational system that offers classes around the country on how to sell on eBay. Many companies have formed to act as intermediaries between consumers and eBay by collecting goods directly from people and then doing the work necessary to sell.

Meg Whitman takes a laissez-faire approach to managing eBay, in terms of both customers and employees. She emphasizes cooperation and finesse, not coercion and force. To make sure eBay does not do something that incurs the wrath of its citizens and incites a revolt, eBay executives work more like civil servants than corporate managers. They poll the populace through online town hall meetings and provide services to keep them happy—and business humming.

The collaborative approach that Whitman has spearheaded has benefited the company. As buyers and sellers flock to the site, they not only feed on it, but they also nourish it. By rating each other on transactions, they set a standard of behavior they then strive to maintain. Nevertheless, there are an increasing number of criminals who sell on eBay, including those who ship grossly defective merchandise or do not ship goods after receiving payment.

Whitman says it often takes six months for new managers to adjust to the democratic regime. "Some of the terms you learn in business school—*drive, force, commit*—don't apply," says William C. Cobb, senior vice president in charge of international operations. "We're over here listening, adapting, enabling" (*BusinessWeek*, p. 127).

Whitman adds, "I think it takes a little while to understand this dynamic, self-regulating economy. Most business people want to control, and they want to drive. eBay is much more of an enabler. We say here, 'We enable, we don't direct.' And that's the fundamental thing that people have to understand" (*The Wall Street Journal*, p. B1).

This process is clear in eBay's Voice of the Customer program. Every couple of months,

eBay brings in as many as a dozen sellers and buyers to ask them questions about how they work and what else eBay needs to do. And at least twice a week, it holds hourlong teleconferences to poll users on almost every new feature or policy, no matter how small.

Whitman, who sits in a cubicle, as do her senior managers, views her job as helping other people to succeed rather than achieving personal success herself. eBay board member Tom Tierney says, "From a leadership perspective, her most striking attribute is to enable other people and other groups to get things done." Whitman's collaborative style has had a big impact on eBay's culture, he adds. "She is not trying to control the community. She is trying to respond to the needs of the community" (*CRN.com*).

## QUESTIONS

1. Who is being empowered or enabled by Whitman and other eBay managers?
2. How might the enabling approach of eBay leaders be applied to eBay employees?
3. In what way might Whitman be classified as a servant leader?

SOURCE: Robert D. Hof, "The eBay Economy," *BusinessWeek*, August 25, 2003, pp. 124–128; Ann Harrington and Petra Bartosiewicz, "America's 50 Most Powerful Women in Business," *Fortune*, October 18, 2004, pp. 181–182; Nick Wingfield, "Auctioneer to the World," *The Wall Street Journal*, August 5, 2004, pp. B1, B6; "Whitman: Meg Whitman/President and CEO eBay," *CRN.com*, November 15, 2004.

## Factors That Contribute to Organizational Politics

As used here, the term **organizational politics** refers to informal approaches to gaining power through means other than merit or luck. Politics are played to achieve power, either directly or indirectly. The power may be achieved in such diverse ways as by being promoted, by receiving a larger budget or other resources, by obtaining more resources for one's work group, or by being exempt from undesirable assignments. The meaning of *organizational politics* continues to shift in a positive, constructive direction. A group of researchers concluded: "Political skill is an interpersonal style that combines social awareness with the ability to communicate well."[22] Nevertheless, many writers still regard organizational politics as emphasizing self-interest at the expense of others, engaging in mysterious activities, or "kissing up."

Organizational politics is an old subject that is still highly relevant in the Internet age. Teacher and consultant John Elrod was asked, "Isn't the promise of the new economy that we can all just get down to work" (and therefore ignore politics)? He replied that the biggest political mistake is to assume that organizational politics does not exist. "It's often a question of language. When we win on an issue, we call it leadership. When we lose, we call it politics. Practicing politics simply means increasing your options for effective results."[23]

People want power for many different reasons, which is why political behavior is so widespread in organizations. By definition, politics is used to acquire power. A number of individual and organizational factors contribute to political behavior, as described next.

### Pyramid-Shaped Organization Structure

The very shape of large organizations is the most fundamental reason why organizational members are motivated toward political behavior. A pyramid concentrates power at the top. Only so much power is therefore available to distribute among the many people who would like more of it. Each successive layer on the organization chart has less power than the layer above. At the very bottom of the organization, workers have virtually no power. Since most organizations today have fewer layers than they previously had, the competition for power has become more intense. Although empowerment may be motivational for many workers, it is unlikely to satisfy the quest to hold a formal position of power. Workers still struggle to obtain a corner office or cubicle.

### Subjective Standards of Performance

People often resort to organizational politics because they do not believe that the organization has an objective and fair way of judging their performance and suitability for promotion. Similarly, when managers have no objective way of differentiating effective people from the less effective, they will resort to favoritism. The adage "It's not what you know but who you know" applies to organizations that lack clear-cut standards of performance.

### Environmental Uncertainty and Turbulence

When people operate in an unstable and unpredictable environment, they tend to behave politically. They rely on organizational politics to create a favorable impression because uncertainty makes it difficult to determine what they should really be accomplishing.

The uncertainty, turbulence, and insecurity created by corporate downsizings are a major contributor to office politics. Many people believe intuitively that favoritism plays a major role in deciding who will survive the downsizing. In response to this perception, organizational members attempt to ingratiate themselves with influential people.

### Emotional Insecurity

Some people resort to political maneuvers to ingratiate themselves with superiors because they lack confidence in their talents and skills. A pension fund manager who has directed the firm toward investments with an annualized 15 percent return does not have to be overly political because he or she will have confidence in his or her capabilities. A person's choice of political strategy may indicate emotional insecurity. For instance, an insecure person might laugh loudly at every humorous comment the boss makes.

## Machiavellian Tendencies

Some people engage in political behavior because they want to manipulate others, sometimes for their own personal advantage. The term *Machiavellianism* traces back to Niccolo Machiavelli (1469–1527), an Italian political philosopher and statesman. His most famous work, *The Prince*, describes how a leader may acquire and maintain power. Machiavelli's ideal prince was an amoral, manipulating tyrant who would restore the Italian city-state of Florence to its former glory. Three hundred and sixty years later, a study by Gerald Biberman showed a positive relationship between Machiavellianism and political behavior, based on questionnaires that measured these tendencies.[24] Leadership Self-Assessment Quiz 7-2 presents an updated version of the political behavior questionnaire used in the study just mentioned.

LEADERSHIP SELF-ASSESSMENT QUIZ 7-2

### THE ORGANIZATIONAL POLITICS QUESTIONNAIRE

INSTRUCTIONS Answer each question "mostly agree" or "mostly disagree," even if it is difficult for you to decide which alternative best describes your opinion.

| | Mostly Agree | Mostly Disagree |
|---|---|---|
| 1. The boss is always right. | ____ | ____ |
| 2. It is wise to flatter important people. | ____ | ____ |
| 3. If you do somebody a favor, remember to cash in on it later. | ____ | ____ |
| 4. Given the opportunity, I would cultivate friendships with powerful people. | ____ | ____ |
| 5. I would be willing to say nice things about a rival in order to get that person transferred from my department. | ____ | ____ |
| 6. If it would help me get ahead, I would take credit for someone else's work. | ____ | ____ |
| 7. Given the chance, I would offer to help my boss build some shelves for his or her den. | ____ | ____ |
| 8. I laugh heartily at my boss's jokes, even if I do not think they are funny. | ____ | ____ |

*(continued)*

9. Dressing for success is silly. Wear clothing to work that you find to be the most comfortable.     _____ _____

10. Never waste lunchtime by having lunch with somebody who cannot help you solve a problem or gain advantage.     _____ _____

11. I think using email to zap somebody for his or her mistakes is a good idea (especially if you want to show that person up).     _____ _____

12. If somebody higher up in the organization offends you, let that person know about it.     _____ _____

13. Honesty is the best policy in practically all cases.     _____ _____

14. Power for its own sake is one of life's most precious commodities.     _____ _____

15. If I had a legitimate gripe against my employer, I would air my views publicly (such as by writing a letter to the editor of a local newspaper or posting my gripe on the Internet).     _____ _____

16. I would invite my boss to a party at my home, even if I did not like him or her.     _____ _____

17. An effective way to impress people is to tell them what they want to hear.     _____ _____

18. Having a high school or skyscraper named after me would be an incredible thrill.     _____ _____

19. Hard work and good performance are usually sufficient for career success.     _____ _____

20. Even if I made only a minor contribution to a project, I would get my name listed as being associated with that project.     _____ _____

21. I would never publicly correct mistakes made by the boss.     _____ _____

22. I would never use my personal contacts to gain a promotion.     _____ _____

23. If you happen to dislike a person who receives a big promotion in your firm, do not bother sending that person a congratulatory note.     _____ _____

24. I would never openly criticize a powerful executive in my organization.     _____ _____

25. I would stay in the office late just to impress my boss.     _____ _____

SCORING AND INTERPRETATION Give yourself a plus 1 for each answer that agrees with the keyed answer. Each question that receives a score of plus 1 shows a tendency toward playing organizational politics. The scoring key is as follows:

| | | |
|---|---|---|
| 1. Mostly agree | 10. Mostly agree | 19. Mostly disagree |
| 2. Mostly agree | 11. Mostly agree | 20. Mostly agree |
| 3. Mostly agree | 12. Mostly disagree | 21. Mostly agree |
| 4. Mostly agree | 13. Mostly disagree | 22. Mostly disagree |
| 5. Mostly agree | 14. Mostly agree | 23. Mostly disagree |
| 6. Mostly agree | 15. Mostly disagree | 24. Mostly agree |
| 7. Mostly agree | 16. Mostly agree | 25. Mostly agree |
| 8. Mostly agree | 17. Mostly agree | |
| 9. Mostly disagree | 18. Mostly agree | |

Based on a sample of 750 men and women managers, professionals, administrators, sales representatives, and business owners, the mean score is 10.

- 1–7         Below-average tendency to play office politics
- 8–12       Average tendency to play office politics
- 13 and above    Above-average tendency to play office politics; strong need for power

SKILL DEVELOPMENT Thinking about your political tendencies in the workplace is important for your career because most successful leaders are moderately political. The ability to use politics effectively and ethically increases with importance in the executive suite. Most top players are effective office politicians. Yet being overly and blatantly political can lead to distrust, thereby damaging your career.

SOURCE: Reproduced with permission of the publisher from DuBrin, A. J., "Career Maturity, Organizational Rank, and Political Behavioral Tendencies: A Correlational Analysis of Organizational Politics and Career Experience." *Psychological Reports*, 1988, 63, 531–537. © Psychological Reports 1988. Also from Andrew J. DuBrin, "Sex Differences in Endorsement of Influence Tactics and Political Behavior Tendencies," *Journal of Business and Psychology*, Fall 1989, pp. 3–14. Reprinted by permission.

## Encouraging Admiration from Subordinates

Most organizational leaders say they do not encourage kissing up and that they prefer honest feedback from subordinates. Yet without meaning to, these same managers and leaders encourage flattery and servile praise. Managers, as well as other workers, send out subtle signals that they want to be praised, such as smiling after receiving a compliment and frowning when receiving negative feedback. Also, admirers are more likely to receive good assignments and high performance evaluations. Executive coach Marshall Goldsmith explains that, without meaning to, many managers create an environment where people learn to reward others with accolades that are not completely warranted. People generally see this tendency in others but not in themselves.[25]

# Political Tactics and Strategies

To make effective use of organizational politics, leaders must be aware of specific political tactics and strategies. To identify and explain the majority of political tactics would require years of study and observation. Leaders so frequently need support for their programs that they search for innovative types of political behaviors. Furthermore, new tactics continue to emerge as the workplace becomes increasingly competitive. Here we look at a representative group of political tactics and strategies categorized as to whether they are ethical or unethical. (Several of the influence tactics described in Chapter 8, such as ingratiation, might also be considered political behaviors.)

## Ethical Political Tactics and Strategies

So far we have discussed organizational politics without pinpointing specific tactics and strategies. This section describes a sampling of ethical political behaviors, divided into three related groups: tactics and strategies aimed at (1) gaining power, (2) building relationships with superiors and coworkers, and (3) avoiding political blunders.

All of these political approaches help the leader gain or retain power. Using them can also help the leader succeed in and manage stressful work environments. As defined by a group of researchers, political skill is a constructive force. It is an interpersonal style that manifests itself in being socially astute and engaging in behaviors that lead to feelings of confidence, trust, and sincerity.[26] For example, a middle manager with political skill might be able to defend her group against an angry CEO looking for a scapegoat.

**Strategies Aimed at Gaining Power** All political tactics are aimed at acquiring and maintaining power, even the power to avoid a difficult assignment. Tom Peters says that although power can often be abused, it can also be used to benefit many people. "And as a career building tool, the slow and steady (and subtle) amassing of power is the surest road to success."[27] Here are seven techniques aimed directly at gaining power.

1. *Develop power contacts.* Cultivating friendly, cooperative relationships with powerful organizational members and outsiders can make the leader's cause much easier to advance. These contacts can benefit a person by supporting his or her ideas in meetings and other public forums. One way to develop these contacts is to be more social, for example, by throwing parties and inviting powerful people and their guests. Some organizations and some bosses frown on social familiarity, however. And power holders receive many invitations, so they might not be available.
2. *Control vital information.* Power accrues to those who control vital information, as indicated in the discussion of personal power. Many former government or military officials have found power niches for themselves in industry after leaving the public payroll. Frequently such an individual will be hired as the Washington representative of a firm that does business with the government. The vital information they control is knowledge of whom to contact to shorten some of the complicated procedures in getting government contracts approved.

3. *Stay informed.* In addition to controlling vital information, it is politically important to stay informed. Successful leaders develop a pipeline to help them keep abreast, or ahead, of developments within the firm. For this reason, a politically astute individual befriends the president's assistant. No other source offers the potential for obtaining as much information as the executive administrative assistant.

4. *Control lines of communication.* Related to controlling information is controlling lines of communication, particularly access to key people. Administrative assistants and staff assistants frequently control an executive's calendar. Both insiders and outsiders must curry favor with the conduit in order to see an important executive. Although many people attempt to contact executives directly through email, some executives delegate the responsibility of screening email messages to an assistant. The assistant will also screen telephone calls, thus being selective about who can communicate directly with the executive.

5. *Bring in outside experts.* To help legitimate their positions, executives will often hire a consultant to conduct a study or cast an opinion. Consciously or unconsciously, many consultants are hesitant to "bite the hand that feeds them." A consultant will therefore often support the executive's position. In turn, the executive will use the consultant's findings to prove that he or she is right. This tactic might be considered ethical because the executive believes he or she is obtaining an objective opinion.

6. *Make a quick showing.* A display of dramatic results can help gain acceptance for one's efforts or those of the group. Once a person has impressed management with his or her ability to solve that first problem, that person can look forward to working on problems that will bring greater power. A staff professional might volunteer to spruce up a company web site to make it more appealing. After accomplishing that feat, the person might be invited to join the ecommerce team.

7. *Remember that everyone expects to be paid back.* According to the Law of Reciprocity, everybody in the world expects to be paid back.[28] If you do not find some way to reimburse people for the good deeds they have done for you, your supply of people to perform good deeds will run short. Because many of these good deeds bring you power, such as by supporting your initiative, your power base will soon erode. As a way of paying back the person who supported your initiative, you might mention publicly how the person in question provided you with expert advice on the technical aspects of your proposal.

8. *Be the first to accept reasonable changes.* A natural inclination for most people is to resist change, so the person who steps forward first to accept reasonable changes will acquire some political capital. The team member who welcomes the changes exerts a positive influence on group members who may be dragging their heels about the change. An example might be that the company is attempting to shift to an online system of performance evaluation, thereby eliminating paper filing. It is politically wise to be an early adopter of the new system.

**Strategies and Tactics Aimed at Building Relationships** Much of organizational politics involves building positive relationships with network members who can be helpful now or later. This network includes superiors, subordinates, other lower-ranking people, coworkers, external customers, and suppliers. The following are several representative strategies and tactics:

1. *Display loyalty.* A loyal worker is valued because organizations prosper more with loyal than with disloyal employees. Blind loyalty—the belief that the organization cannot make a mistake—is not called for; most rational organizations welcome constructive criticism. An obvious form of loyalty to the organization is longevity. Although job-hopping is more acceptable today than in the past, tenure with the company is still an asset for promotion. Tenure tends to contribute more to promotability in a traditional industry such as automobile manufacturing than in high-technology firms.

2. *Manage your impression.* Impression management includes behaviors directed at enhancing one's image by drawing attention to oneself. Often the attention of others is directed toward superficial aspects of the self, such as clothing and grooming. Yet impression management also deals with deeper aspects of behavior, such as speaking well and presenting one's ideas coherently. Bad speech habits are recognized as a deterrent to advancement in organizations.[29]

   Another part of impression management is to tell people about your success or imply that you are an "insider." Email is used extensively today to send messages to others for the purpose of impressing them with one's good deeds. Displaying good business etiquette has received renewed attention as a key part of impression management, with companies sending staff members to etiquette classes to learn how to create favorable impressions on key people. Many management scholars take a dim view of impression management, yet the topic has been carefully researched.[30]

3. *Ask satisfied customers to contact your boss.* A favorable comment by a customer receives considerable weight because customer satisfaction is a top corporate priority. If a customer says something nice, the comment will carry more weight than one from a coworker or subordinate. The reason is that coworkers and subordinates might praise a person for political reasons. Customers' motivation is assumed to be pure because they have little concern about pleasing suppliers.

4. *Be courteous, pleasant, and positive.* Courteous, pleasant, and positive people are the first to be hired and the last to be fired (assuming they also have other important qualifications). Polite behavior provides an advantage because many people believe that civility has become a rare quality.

5. *Ask advice.* Asking advice on work-related topics builds relationships with other employees. Asking another person for advice—someone whose job does not require giving it—will usually be perceived as a compliment. Asking advice transmits a message of trust in the other person's judgment.

6. *Send thank-you notes to large numbers of people.* One of the most basic political tactics, sending thank-you notes profusely, is simply an application of sound human relations. Many successful people take the time to send handwritten notes to employees and customers to help create a bond with those people. In the words of Tom Peters, "The power of a thank you (note or otherwise) is hard—make that impossible—to beat."[31]

7. *Flatter others sensibly.* Flattery in the form of sincere praise can be an effective relationship builder. By being judicious in your praise, you can lower the defenses of work associates and make them more receptive to your ideas. A survey of 1,012 managers found that ingratiatory behavior toward the chief

executive plays a bigger role in receiving a board appointment than does having attended an elite school or having elite social connections. James D. Westphal concluded "The most efficient way to get more board appointments is to engage in more political behavior."[32] The type of political behavior focused on flattery. An effective, general-purpose piece of flattery is to tell another person that you are impressed by something he or she has accomplished. Leadership Skill-Building Exercise 7-2 will help you enhance your skills in flattery.

### FLATTERY ROLE-PLAY

One student plays the role of a team leader who wants to build alliances with important people in the organization. The company is a major player in consumer electronics, including plasma-screen television receivers. One day the team leader is waiting in line to board an airplane, and he or she figures the wait will be about ten minutes. Another student plays the role of the corporate vice president of marketing who unexpectedly is standing next to the team leader in the boarding line. The marketing vice president is middle age, a family person, and has been with the company for twenty-five years. The alliance-building team leader figures he or she has about seven minutes available to make an initial contact with the senior executive and perhaps start a good working relationship. So the team leader decides to engage in appropriate flattery. The marketing vice president seems at least willing to converse with the team leader. Run the scenario for about six minutes in front of the class. The rest of the class members will observe and provide some feedback on the effectiveness of the flattery techniques.

The potential contribution of this exercise is that it may help raise your awareness of the opportunity to engage in constructive political behavior. Recognizing opportunities to gain political advantage can be helpful to a leader's career.

***Strategies Aimed at Avoiding Political Blunders*** A strategy for retaining power is to refrain from making power-eroding blunders. Committing these politically insensitive acts can also prevent one from attaining power. Several leading blunders are described next.

1. *Criticizing the boss in a public forum.* The oldest saw in human relations is to "praise in public and criticize in private." Yet in the passion of the moment, we may still surrender to an irresistible impulse to criticize the boss publicly.
2. *Bypassing the boss.* Protocol is still highly valued in a hierarchical organization. Going around the boss to resolve a problem is therefore hazardous. You might be able to accomplish the bypass, but your career could be damaged and your recourses limited. Except in cases of outrageous misconduct such as blatant

sexual harassment or criminal misconduct, your boss's boss will probably side with your boss.

3. *Declining an offer from top management.* Turning down top management, especially more than once, is a political blunder. You thus have to balance sensibly managing your time against the blunder of refusing a request from top management. Today, an increasing number of managers and corporate professionals decline opportunities for promotion when the new job requires geographic relocation. For these people, family and lifestyle preferences are more important than gaining political advantage on the job.

4. *Putting your foot in your mouth* (being needlessly tactless). To avoid hurting your career, it is important to avoid—or at least minimize—being blatantly tactless toward influential people. An example would be telling the CEO that he should delegate speech making to another person because he or she is such a poor speaker. "You don't get to be a senior person if you are repeatedly tactless," advises the head of a New York recruiting firm.[33] When you feel you are on the verge of being critical, delay your response, and perhaps reword it for later delivery. Use your emotional intelligence! If you are needlessly tactless, compensate the best you can by offering a full apology later.

5. *Not conforming to the company dress code.* Although some degree of independence and free thinking is welcome in many organizations, violating the dress code can block you from acquiring more power. Conforming to the dress code suggests that you are part of the team and you understand what is expected. Dress codes can be violated by dressing too informally *or* formally, and by wearing clothing that symbolizes a cultural identity.[34]

## Unethical Political Tactics and Strategies

Any technique of gaining power can be devious if practiced in the extreme. A person who supports a boss by feeding him or her insider information that could affect the price of company stock is being devious. Some approaches are unequivocally unethical, such as those described next. In the long run they erode a leader's effectiveness by lowering his or her credibility. Devious tactics might even result in lawsuits against the leader, the organization, or both.

**Backstabbing** The ubiquitous back stab requires that you pretend to be nice but all the while plan someone's demise. A frequent form of backstabbing is to initiate a conversation with a rival about the weaknesses of a common boss, encouraging negative commentary and making careful mental notes of what the person says. When these comments are passed along to the boss, the rival appears disloyal and foolish. Email has become a medium for the backstab. The sender of the message documents a mistake made by another individual and includes key people on the distribution list. A sample message sent by one manager to a rival began as follows, "Hi, Ted. I'm sorry you couldn't make our important meeting. I guess you had some other important priorities. But we need your input on the following major agenda item we tackled. . . ."

**Embrace or Demolish** The ancient strategy of "embrace or demolish" suggests that you remove from the premises rivals who suffered past hurts through your efforts; otherwise, the wounded rivals might retaliate at a vulnerable moment. This kind of strategy is common after a hostile takeover; many executives lose their jobs because they opposed the takeover. A variation of embrace or demolish is to terminate managers from the acquired organization who oppose adapting to the culture of the new firm. For example, a freewheeling manager who opposes the bureaucratic culture of the acquiring firm might be terminated as "not able to identify with our mission."

**Setting a Person Up for Failure**  The object of a setup is to place a person in a position where he or she will either fail outright or look ineffective. For example, an executive whom the CEO dislikes might be given responsibility for a troubled division whose market is rapidly collapsing. The newly assigned division president cannot stop the decline and is then fired for poor performance.

**Divide and Rule**  An ancient military and governmental strategy, this tactic is sometimes used in business. The object is to have subordinates fight among themselves, therefore yielding the balance of power to another person. If team members are not aligned with one another, there is an improved chance that they will align with a common superior. One way of getting subordinates to fight with one another is to place them in intense competition for resources. An example would be asking them to prove why their budget is more worthy than the budget requested by rivals.

**Playing Territorial Games**  Also referred to as turf wars, **territorial games** involve protecting and hoarding resources that give one power, such as information, relationships, and decision-making authority. Territorial behavior, according to Annette Simmons, is based on a hidden force that limits peoples' desire to give full cooperation. People are biologically programmed to be greedy for whatever they think it takes to survive in the corporate environment.

The purpose of territorial games is to vie for the three kinds of *territory* in the modern corporate survival game: information, relationships, or authority. A relationship is "hoarded" through such tactics as not encouraging others to visit a key customer or blocking a high performer from getting a promotion or transfer.[35] For example, the manager might tell others that his star performer is mediocre to prevent the person from being considered for a valuable transfer possibility. Other examples of territorial games include monopolizing time with clients, scheduling meetings so someone cannot attend, and shutting out coworkers from joining you on an important assignment.

**Creating and Then Resolving a False Catastrophe**  An advanced devious tactic is for a manager to pretend a catastrophe exists and then proceed to rescue others from the catastrophe, thereby appearing to be a superhero.[36] The political player rushes in and declares that everything is a mess and the situation is almost hopeless; shortly thereafter, he or she resolves the problem. An example would be for a newly appointed information technology manager to inform top management that the system he inherited is antiquated and approaching the point of severely damaging the company's operations. One week later, he claims to have miraculously overhauled the information system, such as by ordering new equipment and hiring a few key personnel.

## Exercising Control over Dysfunctional Politics

Carried to excess, organizational politics can hurt an organization and its members. Too much politicking can result in wasted time and effort, thereby lowering productivity. A study of 1,370 employees in four organizations investigated how the perception of political behavior was related to certain outcomes. Among the many findings were the following:

- Perceptions of political behavior taking place in the work group were associated with less commitment to the organization and a stronger turnover intention (planning to leave the firm voluntarily).

- Perceptions of political behavior taking place throughout the organization were also associated with less commitment to the organization and a stronger turnover intention.[37]

The human consequences of excessive negative and unethical politics can also be substantial. Examples include lowered morale and loss of people who intensely dislike office politics. To avoid these negative consequences, leaders are advised to combat political behavior when it is excessive and dysfunctional. Table 7-1 presents some symptoms of dysfunctional office politics.

| TABLE 7-1 | Symptoms of Dysfunctional Office Politics (the DOOP Scale) |
| --- | --- |

The ten statements below concern ethics in interpersonal relationships on the job. The more frequently any of these actions take place, the more likely the organizational or organizational unit is beset with dysfunctional office politics.

1. A conflict between two or more persons or groups was resolved on the basis of who held the most power rather than on what would have made sense and would have worked better.

2. A person or group "got even" in some way with another person or group.

3. Information about what was going on at work was withheld from a person or group.

4. Information was reported about a person or group that was intentionally exaggerated, misconstrued, and/or made mostly untrue by some other person or group.

5. A person or group was led to believe one thing, when the other was clearly true.

6. A person or group agreed with another person or group solely to "keep the boat from rocking."

7. A person or group's worthwhile efforts or initiatives were intentionally undermined.

8. A person reported confidential or unfavorable information about a person or group in order to gain a special advantage.

9. A person or group who looked at things differently and had different points of view was punished and/or silenced by another person or group.

10. An organizational decision was based on self-interest rather than on what made sense and would have worked better.

Source: From Thomas P. Anderson, "Creating Measures of Dysfunctional Office and Organizational Politics: The DOOP and Short Form DEEP Scales," *Psychology: A Journal of Human Behavior*, Vol. 31, No. 2, 1994, p. 34. Reprinted by permission of the author.

In a comprehensive strategy to control politics, *organizational leaders must be aware of its causes and techniques.* For example, during a downsizing the CEO can be on the alert for instances of backstabbing and transparent attempts to please him or her. Open communication also can constrain the impact of political behavior. For instance, open communication can let everyone know the basis for allocating resources, thus reducing the amount of politicking. If people know in advance how resources are allocated, the effectiveness of attempting to curry favor with the boss will be reduced. When communication is open, it also makes it more difficult for some people to control information and pass along gossip as a political weapon.

*Avoiding favoritism*—that is, avoiding giving the best rewards to the group members you like the most—is a potent way of minimizing politics within a work group. If group members believe that getting the boss to like them is much less important than good job performance in obtaining rewards, they will kiss up to the boss less frequently. In an attempt to minimize favoritism, the manager must reward workers who impress him or her through task-related activities.

*Setting good examples at the top of the organization* can help reduce the frequency and intensity of organizational politics. When leaders are nonpolitical in their actions, they demonstrate in subtle ways that political behavior is not welcome. It may be helpful for the leader to announce during a staff meeting that devious political behavior is undesirable and unprofessional.

Another way of reducing the extent of political behavior is for *individuals and the organization to share the same goals,* a situation described as *goal congruence.* If political behavior will interfere with the company and individuals achieving their goals, workers with goal congruence are less likely to play office politics excessively. A project leader is less likely to falsely declare that the boss's idea is good just to please the boss if the project leader wants the company to succeed.

L. A. Witt conducted a study with 1,200 workers in five organizations that lends support to the importance of goal congruence in combating politics. Witt concluded that one way to approach the negative impact of organizational politics is for the manager to ensure that group members hold the appropriate goal priorities. In this way they will have a greater sense of control over and understanding of the workplace and thus be less affected by organizational politics.[38]

Politics can sometimes be constrained by a *threat to discuss questionable information in a public forum.* People who practice devious politics usually want to operate secretly and privately. They are willing to drop hints and innuendoes and make direct derogatory comments about someone else, provided they will not be identified as the source. An effective way of stopping the discrediting of others is to offer to discuss the topic publicly.[39] The person attempting to pass on the questionable information will usually back down and make a statement closer to the truth.

Finally, *hiring people with integrity* will help reduce the number of dysfunctional political players. References should be checked carefully with respect to the candidate's integrity and honesty.[40] Say to the reference, "Tell me about _____'s approach to playing politics." Leadership Skill-Building Exercise 7-3 provides an opportunity to practice the subtle art of discouraging excessive political behavior on the job.

LEADERSHIP SKILL-BUILDING EXERCISE 7-3

## CONTROLLING OFFICE POLITICS

One student plays the role of a corporate executive visiting one of the key divisions. Six other students play the roles of managers within the division, each of whom wants to impress the boss during their meeting. The corporate executive gets the meeting started by asking the managers in turn to discuss their recent activities and accomplishments. Each division-level manager will attempt to create a very positive impression on the corporate executive. After about fifteen minutes of observing them fawning over him or her, the executive decides to take action against such excessive politicking. Review the information on political tactics and their control before carrying out this role-assuming exercise.

### READER'S ROADMAP

So far in this book we have examined the nature of leaders, their ethics, and how they acquire power. The next chapter explains influence tactics, or ways of converting power into action.

## Summary

college.hmco.com/pic/dubrin5e

Organizational power is derived from many sources, including position power (legitimate, reward, coercive, and information) and personal power (expert, reference, and prestige). Power also stems from ownership, control of resources, capitalizing on opportunity, managing critical problems, and being close to power.

Full-fledged empowerment includes the dimensions of meaning, self-determination, competence, impact, and internal commitment. Actions that can be taken to become an empowering leader include the following: foster initiative and responsibility, link work activities to the goals of the organization, provide ample information, allow group members to choose methods, encourage self-leadership, implement team-based human resource policies, establish limits to empowerment, and continue to lead. Also, take into account cultural differences in how

empowerment is accepted. Delegation is another important part of empowerment.

To acquire and retain power, a leader must skillfully use organizational politics. The meaning of *politics* continues to shift in a positive, constructive direction. Contributing factors to organizational politics include the pyramidal shape of organizations, subjective performance standards, environmental uncertainty, emotional insecurity, Machiavellianism, and encouraging admiration from subordinates.

To make effective use of organizational politics, leaders must be aware of specific political tactics and strategies. Ethical methods can be divided into those aimed directly at gaining power, those aimed at building relationships, and those aimed at avoiding political blunders. Unethical and devious tactics, such as the embrace-or-demolish strategy, constitute another category of political behavior.

Carried to extremes, organizational politics can hurt an organization and its members. Being aware of the causes and types of political behavior can help leaders deal with the problem. Setting good examples of nonpolitical behavior is helpful, as is achieving goal congruence and threatening to publicly expose devious politicking. It is also good to hire people with integrity.

## Key Terms

Power

Legitimate power

Reward power

Coercive power

Information power

Personal power

Prestige power

Resource dependence perspective

Strategic contingency theory

Centrality

Empowerment

Delegation

Organizational politics

Territorial games

##  Guidelines for Action and Skill Development

To enhance your interpersonal effectiveness at the outset of joining a firm, it is helpful to size up the political climate. Even if you are new to the firm, it will often be helpful to ask the following seven diagnostic questions during meetings:

1. What method do people use here to offer new ideas?
2. How do staff members offer opposing ideas or disagreement?
3. How much evidence is required, and what type of evidence is required, to persuade other staff members?
4. What responses does assertive behavior elicit? What facial expressions do you see around the table when someone presents a strong idea? Whose words elicit nods from the meeting leader? Whose words prompt the reaction "Let's move on"?
5. How much personal reference is tolerated?
6. How much display of emotional intensity is tolerated?
7. Who gets heard? Promoted? Passed over?[41]

## Discussion Questions and Activities

1. Why do so many people think that possessing power is a good thing?
2. How can a leader occupy a top-level executive position and still have relatively little power?
3. It is not unusual for a new CEO to receive a signing bonus of around $10 million. Which kind of power or powers do these executives have to command such a large signing bonus?
4. What can you do this week to enhance your power?
5. Many business leaders say something to the effect, "We practice empowerment because we

don't expect our employees to leave their brains at the door." What are these leaders talking about?

6. Empowerment has been criticized because it leaves no one in particular accountable for results. What is your opinion of this criticism?

7. Why are entrepreneurial leaders often poor delegators?

8. Many people have asked the question "Isn't office politics just for incompetents?" What is your answer to this question?

9. Ask an experienced worker to give you an example of the successful application of organizational politics. Which tactic was used, and what was the outcome?

## LEADERSHIP CASE PROBLEM A

### THE POWERFUL MR. TRUMP

The occasion was an interview by a veteran *Fortune* reporter. Donald Trump wasted no time being Donald Trump. "I've brought some things for you," he said, handing the reporter a sheaf of papers as he boarded his private 727. (Trump was on his way to Minnesota, where he was to meet with Governor Jesse Ventura to discuss running for president on the Reform Party Ticket.) These included some glossy brochures and a copy of *New York Construction News*, which had named Trump owner and developer of the year for 1999. "Owner *and* developer of the year," he pointed out, "which is unusual" (*Fortune*, April 3, 2000, p. 189). Four years later during a flight on the same airplane, talking with another *Fortune* reporter, Trump proclaimed, "See I don't view myself as a great promoter. People say I'm a great promoter. People say I'm the greatest promoter that there is. Anywhere" (*Fortune*, April 19, 2004, p. 72).

At age 57, Trump is the most famous businessman in America. According to the Gallup Organization, fully 98 percent of Americans know who he is. Roger Stone, Trump's political adviser, says, "I think people say, 'If I won the lottery, that's how I'd want to live.' The plane, the boat, the estate in Florida, the beautiful girls (women supermodels)— our polling showed that people identified with it" (*Fortune*, April 3, 2000, p. 192). Trump is now married to Melania Knauss. Trump's hit reality television show, *The Apprentice*, has contributed immensely to his name and face recognition.

The web site *AskMen.com* offers a similar perspective on Trump. The site explains why the editors like him: "Not like him, we *love* him. He is funny, smart, and unlike seemingly every other billionaire in the world, he lives the privileged life that we can only dream of."

Trump said on the plane, "I was a little surprised *Fortune* hadn't done a cover on me in the last year and a half, because I'm the biggest developer in New York. Now I'm getting story not because I'm the biggest real estate developer but because I'm running for president. There's something about that that I don't really like" (*Fortune*, April 3, 2000, p. 192). Trump believes that what he is great at is building buildings, inside and out.

**THE TRUMP EMPIRE** The Trump enterprise has complex deals that make it difficult for an outsider to estimate the true worth of Trump's holdings. One problem is that Trump puts an exaggerated positive spin on what he owns. When he says he is building a ninety-story skyscraper next to the United Nations, he means a seventy-two-story building that has extra-high ceilings. And when he says his casino company is the "largest employer in the state of New Jersey," he actually means to say it is the eighth largest (*Fortune*, April 3, 2000, p. 194). Trump places the value of his holdings at $6 billion, and his company has 22,000 employees.

Not all of Trump's success is exaggerated, however. Trump is regarded as an enormously skilled developer. Associates describe an unfailing knack for spotting and ferreting out waste; a memory like a Zip drive; and a grasp of complex zoning laws that he uses to exploit opportunities. Trump is also familiar with technical details of construction, such as the energy efficiency of window glass. He negotiates with subcontractors himself instead of relying on a purchasing department, and he will sometimes use his celebrity status to attain better terms. "He has the ability to relate to the doorman, to the guy who's carrying the iron or steel, and make that guy feel important," says the CEO of a real estate financing firm (*Fortune*, April 3, 2000, p. 194).

Trump's self-promotion works. He has created a nationally known luxury real estate brand. Condos in Trump-branded buildings in 2004 sold for 39 percent above New York's $853-per-square-foot average. In Chicago, he singled-handedly raised the average condo price for the entire city by 25 percent at the end of 2003 based on his sale of high-price condo units while they were still in the planning stage.

Trump now refrains from putting up large sums of his own money. Instead, he forms a partnership with financial backers who want to tap the power of his name and retain him as sort of a jungle guide. Investors can be readily found because people pay more to live in a Trump building. His condos command an 80 percent premium. Trump's rivals accuse him of being a mere front man for financial interests—a brand slapped on buildings he does not own. Trump denies the charges, saying that he owns at least 50 percent of all the deals he does.

Trump's partners are pleased with his accomplishments. A financier who hired Trump to convert the Mayfair Regent Hotel into condos said: "Bottom line is, the project came in under budget four months ahead of schedule and at prices that were 40 percent above what we had pro forma'd. We didn't have one work stoppage, not one strike, not one red city tag. Everything was perfect." Even former New York Mayor Ed Koch, a Trump hater if there ever was one, said he is a great builder (*Fortune*, April 3, 2000, p. 196).

Trump found six Chinese companies to foot the bill for Trump Place, a series of rental and condo properties along a nearly mile-long parcel of land on Manhattan's West Side. During a game of golf in Hong Kong, Trump worked out the complex deal: the Chinese would put up all the money, and Trump would receive management fees, plus a big bonus when major parcels were complete and after the investors got their money back, plus a preferred return. Several years back Trump persuaded the massive Korean *chaebol* Daewoo to put up almost all the money to build the $360 million Trump World Tower, a seventy-two-story condo complex across the street from the United Nations Building in New York.

In describing his negotiating advantage, Trump reflects: "One of the advantages I have by being a superstar is that when I call people, no matter who they are, they're honored to be my partner. And I've done a great job. . . . When Donald Trump calls, you say, 'Oh great!' I get to the top immediately. And if he's not in, they call me back in five minutes" (*Fortune*, April 19, 2004, p. 76.).

**TRUMP PROBLEMS** Despite these successes, Trump has some problems. The Trump organization faces difficulty with its casino company, Trump Hotels & Casino Resorts, Inc. The company was originally taken public to help Trump stave off bankruptcy in the early 1990s. The money from selling stock could be used to pay debts when Trump began to default on his loans and had $1 billion in debt that he had personally guaranteed. The strategy worked, and the company was considered a remarkable business turnaround at the time. The hotels and casinos generate substantial cash, but debt servicing eats up $216 million in cash flow. At one point the casino company handed over 20 percent of its net revenue in interest payments.

Another problem is that Trump tends to use the casino company as his personal piggy bank. One year he voted himself a $5 million bonus from the company, the pilots of his personal 727 are on the casino company's payroll, and he borrowed $26 million from the company to pay off a personal loan. Trump denies misusing company

*(continued)*

funds. A related problem is that some investors shy away from Trump stock because of Donald Trump's flamboyance.

In November 2004, Trump Hotels & Casino Resorts filed for Chapter 11 protection from creditors in federal bankruptcy court in New Jersey. The filing is part of a broad refinancing plan aimed at reducing the casino company's $1.8 billion debt load and, ultimately, sprucing up the casinos to make them more competitive. (As mentioned above, the Trump casinos had also filed for bankruptcy in 1992.) Under the new plan, Trump's ownership interest will drop to 27 percent. Bondholder groups will have to accept lower interest payments, and the stock will be delisted from the New York Stock Exchange. Investors will lose money on the deal, but the company is paying all of its casino vendors. In addition to refinancing the debt, Trump Hotels has arranged to borrow up to $100 million from the Beal Bank in Texas. The loan will be used to renovate the Trump Taj Mahal Casino Resort in Atlantic City.

Unphased by any setback in part of his empire, Trump and his organization continue to expand on a grand scale. For example, in early 2006, showrooms were available for Trump International Hotel and Tower in Chicago, a combined residential and hotel condominium with the highest priced units selling for $8 million. The building was designed to become one of the most prominent Chicago buildings.

## QUESTIONS

1. Which sources of power does Trump use?
2. What steps can Donald Trump take to be perceived more positively by outside observers, such as reporters and business professors?
3. What is your evaluation of the ethics of the Trump casinos declaring bankruptcy when the Trump organization owns so much property and Donald Trump is so wealthy?
4. How would you describe Trump's interpersonal skills?

SOURCE: Jerry Useem, "What Does Donald Trump® Really Want?" *Fortune*, April 3, 2000, pp. 188–200; *www.AskMen.com*; Daniel Roth, "The Trophy Life," *Fortune*, April 19, 2004, pp. 70–83; Christina Binkley, "Donald Trump Files Chapter 11: Donald Trump's Stake Will Drop," *The Wall Street Journal*, November 23, 2004, p. C3.

## LEADERSHIP CASE PROBLEM B

### EMPOWERMENT AT SECONDS FOR YOU

Jenny Parsons was raised in a family of retailers. Her mom and dad owned several different retail stores, including a hardware store, and a home-improvement business. As her parents approached their mid-sixties, they were operating two home-improvement stores that competed directly with national chains such as Home Depot and Lowe's. By that time, Jenny had worked for the family business for five years.

Parsons and her parents decided to revamp their business model. Instead of competing for the same market as traditional home-improvement stores, they would aim at a market one notch lower. The stores were to be named Seconds for You and would feature manufacturer rejects or "seconds," along with inventory manufacturers could not sell at their usual profit margins. The store would also purchase merchandise from other hardware and home-improvement stores that had gone out of business for one reason or another. Representative Seconds for You specials included cinder blocks at 45 cents each, 13-inch black-and-white television sets for $49, and folding tables for $27.95.

The Parsons family recognized that to operate the two Seconds for You stores profitably, operating costs would have to be reduced substantially. Mom and Dad would become the buyers for the store, at a salary of $17,000 per year each; Jenny would draw a salary of $42,000 and operate the stores. Any new employees would be paid close to the minimum wage, even if it meant hiring workers who had probably been rejected by other retail stores. Among the reject factors could be lack of a high school diploma, limited verbal skills, or an unprofessional appearance.

Dad said to Jenny, "Our planned operating budget sure does cut expenses to the bone, but you are taking on too much responsibility. Each store is about 15,000 square feet, and the merchandise assortment will be enormous. You might need a store manager for each outlet, especially for such matters as approving customer checks."

"Have no fear, Mom and Dad, I have a plan. I'll organize the staff into teams, appoint a few team leaders, and pay them $1.00 more per hour than the other associates. And then, I will *empower* the team leaders and the associates to make managerial decisions. Have you read about empowerment in the business pages?"

Mom replied, "Oh yes, I've read about empowerment, but we're not Wal-Mart or Target. We may not be able to get away with empowering associates who have no interest in retailing as a career."

Jenny responded, "Don't be so sure. Seconds for You might be ready for a modern approach to managing a retail store."

When Jenny met with the store associates to explain the empowerment plan, she encountered a range of reactions. One of the seniors hired primarily to answer customer questions and give advice about home-improvement projects said, "Suits me fine, Jenny. I've been fixing things around the house for forty years, so I think I can handle the responsibility. I won't need much help from a boss."

A newly hired 18-year-old cashier said, "Sounds to me like you're asking us to do the work of a supervisor, yet still pay us the minimum wage. I don't think I'm ready to work without supervision." Jenny assured her that the team leader would be available to help, even though the team leader's primary responsibilities were dealing with customers and organizing the merchandise.

Six months after the empowerment program was implemented, Jenny began to wonder if she had made the right decision. The two stores were generally operating smoothly, and Jenny even took off several Sunday afternoons, the busiest day for Seconds for You. Yet several problems did surface. One of the cashiers let three customer checks get past her that bounced. In each case, the cashier had not obtained the three points of identification required for accepting a check. The cashier's plea to Jenny was "It wasn't my fault—each customer had a good story, and they all looked honest. You told me I had the power to accept a check. Besides, you or your parents weren't around to give me any help."

Another problem was inventory shrinkage. Some customers appeared to be loading into their vehicles more merchandise than they paid for, especially with bulk items like lumber, cinder blocks, and topsoil. One of the team leaders explained, "It's tough organizing the merchandise, helping customers, and trying to supervise the loadings all at the same time. I'm supposed to be doing everything at once."

Jenny told the associates, "It looks like we have a couple of holes to plug. But I have too much faith in you to give up on empowerment yet."

## QUESTIONS

1. How applicable is empowerment to Seconds for You?
2. How might Jenny Parsons become a more effective empowering leader?
3. What is your evaluation of the business model (basic idea for a business) at Seconds for You?

## MY LEADERSHIP PORTFOLIO

For this insert into your leadership portfolio, think through all the recent opportunities you might have had to use political tactics. How did you deal with the situation? Did you capitalize on any opportunities? Did you use an ethical approach? Did you use any unethical tactics? Did you commit any political blunders? Here would be an example:

> I saw a flyer indicating that our Business Management Association was having a guest speaker, an executive from Merrill Lynch. I had been pretty busy with studies, my job, and social life, yet I decided to invest the time and attend. As it worked out, the meeting was a wonderful opportunity to make a couple of good contacts. After the talk, I spoke to the speaker and complimented her. We had a brief conversation about how I was looking for a career in investment banking, and she gave me her business card. I sent her an email message the next day thanking her for the time she gave me. I also met a couple of important people at the meeting, and got their cards also.

## INTERNET SKILL-BUILDING EXERCISE

Apply the chapter concepts! Visit the Web and complete this Internet skill-building exercise to learn more about current leadership topics and trends.

### ADVICE ABOUT OFFICE POLITICS

Here is an opportunity to get some free advice about a problem of office politics. Go to *www.office-politics.com* and post an office politics problem you might be facing, and then receive an answer about how to deal with the problem. Or, you might simply want to ask about a problem of office politics. Here are several examples of problems other people have submitted to *www.office-politics.com*:

- "We recently lost a highly intelligent, highly motivated executive to another firm."
- "People in the office are making off-the-wall comments like 'What does she do all day" or 'she does nothing.'"
- "I have just learned that I am the most 'hated' person in my office."

# Influence Tactics of Leaders

Outside Colgate-Palmolive, president William C. Shanahan, age 64, is not well known. Inside, as the man who oversees the company's $10.5 billion global operations, he wields great influence. Known by his employees as extremely hard working and as having an encyclopedic knowledge of Colgate's products, processes, and marketing strategies, Shanahan is a globetrotter whose "heaviest pieces of luggage are two briefcases filled with data," says an executive who has worked with him. "When he travels, he usually isn't going to world capitals like Paris, but to company operations in remote places in developing nations. And all the way there he's reading and absorbing information," the executive adds.

Hard driving, Shanahan is known for giving explicit directions to subordinates, but he also expects them to voice their own opinions. He also feels free to disagree with his boss, chairman and CEO Reuben Mark. But Shanahan avoids the limelight and never contradicts Mark publicly.

"Reuben gives Bill huge leeway in running Colgate, and always reminds shareholders at annual meetings that he couldn't run the company without him," says another executive who knows both men well.

Over the years, recruiters have often asked Shanahan if he would be interested in taking a CEO position at another company. But he has chosen to continue as number 2 at Colgate. "Apart from helping to build a successful global company," adds Shanahan, "what's been so fulfilling and exciting has been the opportunity to work with and help our businesses and people around the world."[1]

---

William C. Shanahan works quietly as the number 2 person in a major company, using a variety of influence tactics (such as giving explicit directions and consulting with employees) to achieve important goals. Without effective influence tactics a leader is similar to a soccer player who has not learned to kick a soccer ball, or a newscaster who is unable to speak.

Leadership, as oft repeated, is an influence process. To become an effective leader, a person must be aware of the specific tactics leaders use to influence others. Here we discuss a number of specific influence tactics, but other aspects of leadership also concern influence. Being charismatic, as described in Chapter 3, influences many people. Leaders influence others through power and politics, as described in Chapter 7. Furthermore, motivating and coaching skills, as described in Chapter 10, involve influencing others toward worthwhile ends.

The terms *influence* and *power* are sometimes used interchangeably, whereas at other times power is said to create influence, and vice versa. In this book, we distinguish between power and influence as follows: **Influence** is the ability to affect the behavior of others in a particular direction,[2] whereas power is the potential or capacity to influence. Keep in mind, however, that defining power as the ability to influence others will not interfere with learning how to use influence tactics. Former Secretary of State Colin Powell says that power is the capacity to influence and inspire.[3] Leaders are influential only when they exercise power. A leader therefore must acquire power to influence others.

This chapter presents a model of power and influence, a description and explanation of influence tactics (both ethical and less ethical), and a summary of the research about the relative effectiveness and sequencing of influence tactics. We also present a theory about the characteristics group members expect in a leader in order to be influenced by him or her.

## A Model of Power and Influence

The model shown in Figure 8-1 illustrates that the end results of a leader's influence (the outcomes) are a function of the tactics he or she uses. The influence tactics are in turn moderated, or affected by, the leader's traits, the leader's behaviors, and the situation.

Looking at the right side of the model, the three possible outcomes are commitment, compliance, and resistance. **Commitment** is the most successful outcome: the target of the influence attempt is enthusiastic about carrying out the request and makes a full effort. Commitment is particularly important for complex, difficult tasks because these require full concentration and effort. If you were influencing a technician to upgrade your operating system software, you would need his or her commitment. **Compliance** means that the influence attempt is partially successful: the target person is apathetic (not overjoyed) about carrying out the request and makes only a modest effort. The influence agent has changed the person's behavior but not his or her attitude. A long-distance truck driver might comply with demands that he sleep certain hours between hauls, but he is not enthusiastic about losing road time. Compliance for routine tasks—such as wearing a hard hat on a construction site—is usually good enough. **Resistance** is an unsuccessful influence attempt: the target is opposed to carrying out the request and finds ways to either not comply or do a poor job. Resistance includes making excuses for why the task cannot be carried out, procrastinating, and outright refusing to do the task.[4]

Going to the left side of the model, the leader's personality traits affect the outcome of influence tactics. An extroverted and warm leader who has charisma can more readily use some influence tactics than a leader who is introverted and cold. For example, he or she can make an inspirational appeal. A highly intelligent leader would be able to influence others because he or she has built a reputation as a subject matter expert.

### FIGURE 8-1  A Model of Power and Influence

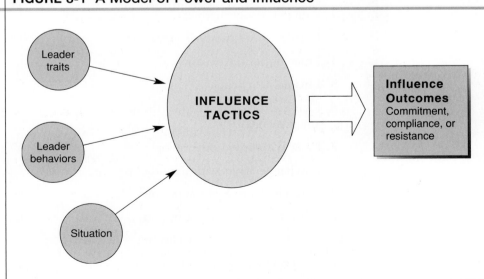

The leader's behaviors also affect the outcome of influence tactics in a variety of ways, particularly because influence tactics *are* actions or behaviors. For example, setting high standards facilitates making an inspirational appeal. As another example, the leader who performs well consistently is better able to lead by example because he or she is a good role model.

Finally, the situation partly determines which influence tactic will be effective. The organizational culture or subculture is one such key situational factor. For example, in a high-technology environment, inspirational appeal and emotional display are less likely to be effective than rational persuasion and being a subject matter expert, because high-tech workers are more likely to be impressed by facts than by feeling.

The rest of this chapter identifies and describes influence tactics, including some mention of situational variables. Leader traits and power have been described in previous chapters. Leadership Self-Assessment Quiz 8-1 will give you an opportunity to think about which influence tactics you tend to use.

## LEADERSHIP SELF-ASSESSMENT QUIZ 8-1

### SURVEY OF INFLUENCE TACTICS

INSTRUCTIONS Indicate how frequently you use the influence tactics listed below. VI = very infrequently or never; I = infrequently; S = sometimes; F = frequently; VF = very frequently. The VI to VF categories correspond to a 1-to-5 scale.

|  | 1 | 2 | 3 | 4 | 5 |
|---|---|---|---|---|---|
|  | VI | I | S | F | VF |
| 1. I am a team player. | ☐ | ☐ | ☐ | ☐ | ☐ |
| 2. I am personally charming. | ☐ | ☐ | ☐ | ☐ | ☐ |
| 3. I make a good personal appearance. | ☐ | ☐ | ☐ | ☐ | ☐ |
| 4. I manipulate the situation. | ☐ | ☐ | ☐ | ☐ | ☐ |
| 5. I manipulate people. | ☐ | ☐ | ☐ | ☐ | ☐ |
| 6. I am assertive (open and forthright in my demands). | ☐ | ☐ | ☐ | ☐ | ☐ |
| 7. I joke with or kid other people. | ☐ | ☐ | ☐ | ☐ | ☐ |
| 8. I exchange favors with the other person. | ☐ | ☐ | ☐ | ☐ | ☐ |
| 9. I promise to reward the person. | ☐ | ☐ | ☐ | ☐ | ☐ |
| 10. I threaten to punish the person. | ☐ | ☐ | ☐ | ☐ | ☐ |
| 11. I get the other person to like me. | ☐ | ☐ | ☐ | ☐ | ☐ |
| 12. I make an appeal to logic or reason. | ☐ | ☐ | ☐ | ☐ | ☐ |

**13.** I form an alliance with the other person.  ☐ ☐ ☐ ☐ ☐

**14.** I threaten to go over the person's head to the boss.  ☐ ☐ ☐ ☐ ☐

**15.** I compliment the other person.  ☐ ☐ ☐ ☐ ☐

**16.** I offer to compromise with the other person.  ☐ ☐ ☐ ☐ ☐

---

SCORING AND INTERPRETATION The more of the above tactics you use frequently or very frequently, the more influential you probably are. You might also want to compare your scores to normative data. Listed below are the mean scores on each tactic for a group of 523 working adults (292 men and 231 women). The sample was composed of mostly managers and professionals. You will recall that the scale runs from 1 for *very infrequently* to 5 for *very frequently*.

| Influence Tactic | Men | Women |
|---|---|---|
| 1. Team play | 4.1 | 4.2 |
| 2. Charm | 3.3 | 3.5 |
| 3. Appearance | 3.3 | 3.5 |
| 4. Manipulation of situation | 3.1 | 2.7* |
| 5. Manipulation of person | 2.6 | 2.3* |
| 6. Assertiveness | 3.9 | 3.9 |
| 7. Joking or kidding | 3.7 | 3.5 |
| 8. Exchange of favors | 2.9 | 3.0 |
| 9. Promise of reward | 2.5 | 2.2* |
| 10. Threat of punishment | 1.8 | 1.5* |
| 11. Ingratiation | 3.2 | 3.2 |
| 12. Logic or reason | 4.3 | 4.1* |
| 13. Alliances | 3.3 | 3.5 |
| 14. Threat of appeal | 1.5 | 1.6 |
| 15. Compliments | 3.6 | 3.5 |
| 16. Compromise | 3.4 | 3.5 |

---

SKILL DEVELOPMENT In comparing your profile to the norms, it could be apparent that you are neglecting to use, or are overusing, one or more influence tactics. For example, men and women use being a team player "frequently." If you are not using team play to influence others, you could be at a competitive disadvantage. Observe also that both men and women make "very infrequent" use of threats of appeal. If you are making threats of appeal very frequently, you could be perceived as using an unacceptable influence tactic.

*Differences between the means are significant at or beyond the 1 percent level of significance.

SOURCE: Reproduced with permission of the publisher from: DuBrin, A. J., "Sex and Gender Differences in Tactics of Influence," *Psychological Reports*, 1991, 68, 635–646. © *Psychological Reports* 1991.

## Description and Explanation of Influence Tactics

Influence tactics are often viewed from an ethical perspective. Following this perspective, the influence tactics described here are classified into those that are essentially ethical and honest and those that are essentially manipulative and dishonest. The categorization presented here is far from absolute. Except for the extremes, most of the tactics could conceivably be placed in either category, depending on how they are used. For example, one can use the tactic "joking and kidding" in either a well-meaning or mean-spirited way. Joking and kidding could therefore be classified as "essentially ethical" or "essentially manipulative."

### Essentially Ethical and Honest Tactics

This section describes essentially ethical and honest tactics and strategies for influencing others, as outlined in Table 8-1. Used with tact, diplomacy, and good intent, these strategies can help you get others to join you in accomplishing a worthwhile objective. Because these influence tactics vary in complexity, they also vary with respect to how much time is required to develop them.

**Leading by Example and Respect** A simple but effective way of influencing group members is by **leading by example,** or acting as a positive role model. The ideal approach is to be a "do as I say and do" manager—that is, one whose actions and words are consistent. Actions and words confirm, support, and often clarify each other. Being respected facilitates leading by example because group members are more likely to follow the example of leaders they respect.

Bob Nardelli, the CEO of The Home Depot, Inc. (and former GE executive) is an extreme case of leading by example. Out of bed at 5:00 A.M., he is in the office by 6:15 A.M. and usually works until at least 9:00 P.M. Saturdays and Sundays are typically workdays for him, and he calls in his executives for weekend meetings. "It's not a job," he says. "It's a life."[5]

---

**TABLE 8-1** **Essentially Ethical and Honest Influence Tactics**

| |
|---|
| 1. Leading by example and respect |
| 2. Using rational persuasion |
| 3. Developing a reputation as a subject matter expert (SME) |
| 4. Exchanging favors and bargaining |
| 5. Legitimating a request |
| 6. Making an inspirational appeal and emotional display |
| 7. Consulting |
| 8. Forming coalitions |
| 9. Being a team player |
| 10. Practicing hands-on leadership |

***Using Rational Persuasion*** Rational persuasion is an important tactic for influencing people. It involves using logical arguments and factual evidence to convince another person that a proposal or request is workable and likely to achieve the goal.[6] Assertiveness combined with careful research is necessary to make rational persuasion an effective tactic. It is likely to be most effective with people who are intelligent and rational. Chief executive officers typically use rational persuasion to convince their boards that an undertaking, such as product diversification, is mandatory.

A major moderating variable in rational persuasion is the credibility of the influence agent. Credibility helps an individual be more persuasive in two ways. First, it makes a person more convincing. Second, it contributes to a person's perceived power, and the more power one is perceived to have, the more targets will be influenced.[7]

Bob Nardelli also includes rational persuasion in his tool kit of influence tactics. During staff meetings, he hammers away at the logic behind having efficient business processes in place. Nardelli says, "What I'm known for is transferring best practices. That's particularly important in this economic environment, when you have to maximize revenues through existing assets."[8]

***Developing a Reputation as a Subject Matter Expert*** Becoming a subject matter expert (SME) on a topic of importance to the organization is an effective strategy for gaining influence. Being an SME can be considered a subset of rational persuasion. Managers who possess expert knowledge in a relevant field and who continually build on that knowledge can get others to help them get work accomplished.[9] Many of the leaders described throughout this text use expert knowledge to influence others. Small-business owners, in particular, rely on being subject matter experts because they founded the business on the basis of their product or technical knowledge. For example, the leader of a software company is usually an expert in software development.

***Exchanging Favors and Bargaining*** Offering to exchange favors if another person will help you achieve a work goal is another standard influence tactic. By making an exchange, you strike a bargain with the other party. The exchange often translates into being willing to reciprocate at a later date. It might also be promising a share of the benefits if the other person helps you accomplish a task. For example, you might promise to place a person's name on a report to top management if that person will help you analyze the data and prepare the tables.

A recommended approach to asking for a favor is to give the other person as much time as feasible to accomplish the task, such as by saying, "Could you find ten minutes between now and the end of the month to help me?" Not pressing for immediate assistance will tend to lower resistance to the request. Giving a menu of options for different levels of assistance also helps lower resistance. For example, you might ask another manager if you can borrow a technician for a one-month assignment; then, as a second option, you might ask if the technician could work ten hours per week on the project.[10] To ensure that the request is perceived as an exchange, you might explain what reciprocity you have in mind: that you will mention your coworker's helpfulness to his or her manager.

***Legitimating a Request*** To legitimate is to verify that an influence attempt is within your scope of authority. Another aspect of legitimating is showing that your request is consistent with the organizational policies, practices, and expectations of professional people. Making legitimate requests is an effective influence tactic because most workers are willing to comply with regulations. A team leader can thus exert influence with a statement such as this one: "Top management wants a 25 percent reduction in customer complaints by next year. I'm therefore urging everybody to patch up any customer problems he or she can find." According to research conducted by Gary Yukl, behavior intended to establish the legitimacy of a request includes the following:

Providing evidence of prior precedent

Showing consistency with the organizational policies that are involved in the type of request being made

Showing consistency with the duties and responsibilities of the person's position or role expectations

Indicating that the request has been endorsed by higher management or by the person's boss[11]

Legitimating sometimes takes the form of subtle organizational politics. A worker might push for the acceptance of his or her initiative because it conforms to the philosophy or strategy of higher management. At Ford Motor Company, for example, it is well known that Chairman Bill Ford is "green" in the sense of wanting to preserve the external environment. A plant manager might then encourage workers to put all scrap in recycling bins because "It's something 'Bill' would want us to do."

**Making an Inspirational Appeal and Emotional Display** A leader is supposed to inspire others, so it follows that making an inspirational appeal is an important influence tactic. As Jeffrey Pfeffer notes, "Executives and others seeking to exercise influence in organizations often develop skill in displaying, or not displaying, their feelings in a strategic fashion."[12] An inspirational appeal usually involves displaying emotion and appealing to group members' emotions. A moderating variable in the effectiveness of an inspirational appeal or emotional display is the influence agent's **personal magnetism,** or the quality of being captivating, charming, and charismatic. Possessing personal magnetism makes it easier for the leader to inspire people.

For an emotional appeal to be effective, the influence agent must understand the values, motives, and goals of the target. Often this means that the leader must explain how the group efforts will have an impact outside the company. On the basis of one study, Cynthia G. Emrich concluded: "Business leaders tend to think in terms of bottom-line goals, like boosting revenues or profits. But they need to speak about their goals in terms of how they will make a positive difference in the world. If you can see a goal—if you can touch, feel, and smell it—it seems more doable."[13]

**Consulting** Consulting with others before making a decision is both a leadership style and an influence technique. The influence target becomes more motivated to follow the agent's request because the target is involved in the decision-making process. Consultation is most effective as an influence tactic when the objectives of the person being influenced are consistent with those of the leader.[14] An example of such goal congruity took place in a major U.S. corporation. The company had decided to shrink its pool of suppliers to form closer partnerships with a smaller number of high-quality vendors. As a way of influencing others to follow this direction, a manufacturing vice president told his staff, "Our strategy is to reduce dealing with so many suppliers to improve quality and reduce costs. Let me know how we should implement this strategy." The vice president's influence attempt met with excellent reception, partially because the staff members also wanted a more streamlined set of vendor relationships.

*Forming Coalitions* At times it is difficult to influence an individual or group by acting alone. A leader will then have to form coalitions, or alliances, with others to create the necessary clout. A **coalition** is a specific arrangement of parties working together to combine their power. Coalition formation works as an influence tactic because, to quote an old adage, "there is power in numbers." Coalitions in business are a numbers game—the more people you can get on your side, the better. However, the more powerful the leader is, the less he or she needs to create a coalition.

*Collaborative influence* is one of IBM's ten new leadership traits and behaviors. The company now emphasizes forming coalitions with other members of the company community; therefore, it is desirable that a leader "creates interdependence, building genuine commitment across organizational boundaries to a common purpose."[15]

*Being a Team Player* Influencing others by being a good team player is an important strategy for getting work accomplished. In one study, men and women endorsed team play more frequently than six other tactics (personal charm, manipulation, personal appearance, assertiveness, exchange of favors, and appeal to a higher authority).[16] A leader might be a team player by doing such things as pitching in during peak workloads. An example would be a supermarket or department store manager bagging groceries or packages when the checkout lines become clogged. Another example would be an information technology team leader working through the night with team members to combat a virus attack on the company's computer network.

*Practicing Hands-On Leadership* A **hands-on leader** is one who gets directly involved in the details and processes of operations. Such a leader has expertise, is task oriented, and leads by example. By getting directly involved in the group's work activities, the leader influences subordinates to hold certain beliefs and to follow certain procedures and processes. For example, the manager who gets directly involved in fixing customer problems demonstrates to other workers how he or she thinks such problems should be resolved. An example of a hands-on leader is Darryl B. Moody, the senior vice president of homeland security and intelligence for BearingPoint, a global systems integration firm. Moody enjoys meeting clients and handling business development. He says, "I like to roll up my sleeves and get my hands dirty doing technical work on the products that my team is delivering."[17] At the same time, Moody does not neglect his leadership responsibilities.

college.hmco.com/pic/
dubrin5e

**KB** @ **KNOWLEDGE BANK:** includes information about the influence tactics of having personal magnetism and getting network members to support your position.

## Essentially Dishonest and Unethical Tactics

The tactics described in this section are less than forthright and ethical, yet they vary in intensity with respect to dishonesty. Most people would consider the first four strategies presented here as unethical and devious, yet they might regard the last three tactics as still within the bounds of acceptable ethics, even though less than fully candid. The tactics in question are outlined in Figure 8-2.

***Deliberate Machiavellianism*** Niccolo Machiavelli advised that princes must be strong, ruthless, and cynical leaders because people are self-centered and self-serving. People in the workplace who ruthlessly manipulate others have therefore come to be called **Machiavellians**. They tend to initiate actions with others and control the interactions. Machiavellians regularly practice deception, bluffing, and other manipulative tactics.[18] A current example of deliberate Machiavellianism is the practice of forcing managerial and professional employees into working many extra hours of uncompensated overtime. The employees are told that if they refuse to work extra hours, they will not be considered worthy of promotion or good team players. Even when positions in other companies are readily available, most career-minded people will stay because they want to preserve a good reputation.

***Gentle Manipulation of People and Situations*** Some people who attempt to influence others are manipulative, but to a lesser extent than an outright Machiavellian. They gain the compliance of another person by making untrue statements or faking certain behaviors. For example, a leader might imply that if a colleague supports his position in an intergroup conflict, the person *might* be recommended for promotion. A widely used manipulative approach is the **bandwagon technique**, in which one does something simply because others are doing likewise. An example is a manager who informs the vice president that she wants an enlarged budget for attendance at the latest technology seminars because "all other companies are doing it."

The bandwagon technique can be combined with peer pressure to influence a group member. If one person is not stepping forward to work well as a team member, the manager will say, "Bob, everyone in the department is committed to developing a team atmosphere and we'd like you to be a part of it."[19]

***Undue Pressure*** Effective leaders regularly use motivational techniques such as rewards and mild punishments. Yet when rewards become bribes for compliance and

## FIGURE 8-2  Essentially Dishonest and Unethical Influence Tactics

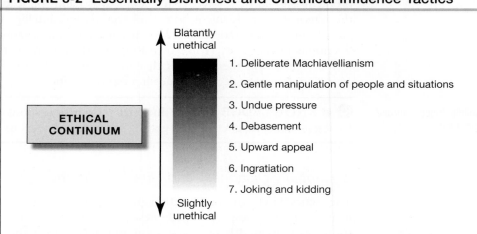

Blatantly unethical

1. Deliberate Machiavellianism
2. Gentle manipulation of people and situations
3. Undue pressure
4. Debasement
5. Upward appeal
6. Ingratiation
7. Joking and kidding

**ETHICAL CONTINUUM**

Slightly unethical

threats of punishment become severe, the target person is subjected to undue pressure or coercion. An example of a bribe by a manager might be, "If you can work eighty hours on this project this week, I'll recommend you for the highest pay grade." Two specific behaviors labeled coercive in a research study were as follows: "I demand that she do it," and "I threaten her with something if she doesn't do it."[20]

*Debasement* A subtle manipulative tactic is **debasement**, demeaning or insulting oneself to control the behavior of another person. For example, a security manager might say, "I realize our department just contributes to overhead, but we do need more cell phones and pagers to get our job done." Richard Parsons, chief executive and chairman of AOL Time Warner Inc., the media giant, uses debasement to disarm people. A long-time friend says of Parsons, "Richard's ability to get people to underestimate him is a great skill. If you are obvious, they know where to hit you. Who wins between the bull and matador?"[21] Specific debasing tactics revealed by research include the following: "I lower myself so she'll do it," and "I act humble so she'll do it."[22]

*Upward Appeal* In **upward appeal,** the leader exerts influence on a team member by getting a person with more formal authority to do the influencing. An example: "I sent the guy to my boss when he wouldn't listen to me. That fixed him." More than occasional use of upward appeal weakens the leader's stature in the eyes of group members and superiors, thus eroding his or her effectiveness. Leaders can apply upward appeal in other ways. A leader might attempt to persuade another staff member that higher management approved his or her request. The target of the influence event is thus supposed to grant acceptance automatically. Or the leader can request higher management's assistance in gaining another person's compliance with the request. The influence target thus feels pressured.[23]

*Ingratiation* Getting somebody else to like you can be considered a mildly manipulative influence tactic—particularly if you do not like the other person. Frank P. Quattrone, the high-tech investment banker imprisoned for obstructing justice, was a master of ingratiation. More than 300 high-tech executives and venture capitalists received shares in hot IPOs (initial public offerings), allegedly for giving investment-banking business to Quattrone's firm, Credit Suisse First Boston. Quattrone also invited his high-tech pals to play golf with him at exclusive courses, and he entertained them lavishly in his palatial home.[24] Ingratiating tactics identified in a study about influence tactics included the following:

Made him or her feel important (for example, "Only you have the brains and talent to do this")

Acted very humbly toward him or her while making my request

Praised him or her

Asked in a polite way

Pretended I was letting him or her decide to do what I wanted (acted in a pseudo-democratic manner)[25]

Leaders who ordinarily are the opposite of ingratiating will sometimes go out of their way to be humble and agreeable to fit an important purpose. A case in point is Bill Gates, who is often sarcastic and cutting. When Gates and Microsoft Corporation were being sued by the U.S. Department of Justice for possible monopolistic practices, Gates went on a goodwill tour, an events-packed trip around San Francisco and Silicon Valley. During his meetings with the public, Gates was modest and at times self-deprecating, even praising the competition. He shook hands, signed autographs, and smiled frequently. Gates was so convincing that a schoolgirl said, "You can tell he's not in it for the money. He wants to make software better."[26]

Leadership Self-Assessment Quiz 8-2 provides you an opportunity to measure your own ingratiating tendencies and to think through further what ingratiating yourself to your boss means in practice. Remember that being liked helps you get promoted, receive more compensation, and avoid being downsized, yet you should avoid being dishonest.

## MEASURE OF INGRATIATING BEHAVIOR IN ORGANIZATIONAL SETTINGS (MIBOS)

INSTRUCTIONS Indicate how frequently you use (or would use) the tactics for pleasing your boss listed below. N = never do it; S = seldom do it; Oc = occasionally do it; Of = often do it; A = almost always do it. The N-to-A categories correspond to a 1-to-5 scale.

| | 1 | 2 | 3 | 4 | 5 |
|---|---|---|---|---|---|
| | N | S | Oc | Of | A |
| 1. Impress upon your supervisor that only he or she can help you in a given situation mainly to make him or her feel good. | ☐ | ☐ | ☐ | ☐ | ☐ |
| 2. Show your supervisor that you share enthusiasm about his or her new idea even when you may not actually like it. | ☐ | ☐ | ☐ | ☐ | ☐ |
| 3. Try to let your supervisor know that you have a reputation for being liked. | ☐ | ☐ | ☐ | ☐ | ☐ |
| 4. Try to make sure that your supervisor is aware of your success. | ☐ | ☐ | ☐ | ☐ | ☐ |
| 5. Highlight the achievements made under your supervisor's leadership in a meeting he or she does not attend. | ☐ | ☐ | ☐ | ☐ | ☐ |
| 6. Give frequent smiles to express enthusiasm and interest about something your supervisor is interested in even if you do not like it. | ☐ | ☐ | ☐ | ☐ | ☐ |
| 7. Express work attitudes that are similar to your supervisor's as a way of letting him or her know that the two of you are alike. | ☐ | ☐ | ☐ | ☐ | ☐ |

8. Tell your supervisor that you can learn a lot from his or her experience.

9. Exaggerate your supervisor's admirable qualities to convey the impression that you think highly of him or her.

10. Disagree on trivial or unimportant issues but agree on those issues in which he or she expects support from you.

11. Try to imitate such work behaviors of your supervisor as working late or occasionally working on weekends.

12. Look for opportunities to let your supervisor know your virtues and strengths.

13. Ask your supervisor for advice in areas in which he or she thinks he or she is smart to let him or her feel that you admire his or her talent.

14. Try to do things for your supervisor that show your selfless generosity.

15. Look out for opportunities to admire your supervisor.

16. Let your supervisor know the attitudes you share with him or her.

17. Compliment your supervisor on his or her achievement, however it may appeal to you personally.

18. Laugh heartily at your supervisor's jokes even when they are really not funny.

19. Go out of your way to run an errand for your supervisor.

20. Offer to help your supervisor by using your personal contacts.

21. Try to persuasively present your own qualities when attempting to convince your supervisor about your abilities.

22. Volunteer to be of help to your supervisor in matters like locating a good apartment, finding a good insurance agent, etc.

*(continued)*

**23.** Spend time listening to your supervisor's personal problems even if you have no interest in them.

☐ ☐ ☐ ☐ ☐

**24.** Volunteer to help your supervisor in his or her work even if it means extra work for you.

☐ ☐ ☐ ☐ ☐

SCORING AND INTERPRETATION The more of these ingratiating behaviors you use frequently or almost always, the more ingratiating you are. A score of 40 or less suggests that you do not put much effort into pleasing your manager, and you may need to be a little more ingratiating to achieve a good relationship with your supervisor. A score between 41 and 99 suggests a moderate degree of ingratiating behavior. A score of 100 or more suggests that you are too ingratiating and might be perceived as being too political or insincere. So some honesty is called for, providing you are tactful.

SKILL DEVELOPMENT Leaders or future leaders should remember that a moderate amount of ingratiating behavior is the norm in relationships with superiors. Ingratiating yourself to people who report to you can also be a useful influence tactic.

SOURCE: Adapted from Kamalesh Kumar and Michael Beyerlein, "Construction and Validation of an Instrument for Measuring Ingratiatory Behaviors in Organizational Settings," *Journal of Applied Psychology*, October 1991, p. 623. Copyright © by the American Psychological Association. Adapted with permission.

***Joking and Kidding*** Good-natured kidding is especially effective when a straight-forward statement might be interpreted as harsh criticism. Joking or kidding can thus get the message across and lower the risk that the influence target will be angry with the influence agent. Joking and kidding might be interpreted either as dishonest or as extraordinarily tactful because the criticizer softens the full blow of the criticism. A vice president of manufacturing successfully used joking and kidding to influence his team to improve quality. After examining what he thought were low-quality components for the company's power tools, he commented, "I appreciate your effort, but I'm afraid you misinterpreted my message. I wanted you to produce a component we could use as a positive model of quality. You went out of your way to produce a negative model. Otherwise you did a great job."

In studying the most severe unethical influence (and political) tactics, it is important to recognize that the use of these influence approaches can bring about human suffering. For example, bullying and intimidating tactics may not be illegal, but they are unethical. Cruelty in the organization creates many problems. As one observer notes, "Cruelty is blatantly unethical and erodes the organizational character through intellectual, emotional, moral, and social vices that reduce the readiness of groups to act ethically."[27] Examples of cruelty include insulting a group member's physical appearance or belittling him or her.

The accompanying Leader in Action describes a celebrity CEO who uses a variety of influence tactics.

🔘 @ **KNOWLEDGE BANK** presents two more mildly unethical influence tactics: game playing and the silent treatment.

Leadership Skill-Building Exercise 8-1 on pages 247–248 will help you recognize several of the influence tactics described in this chapter. Another tactic mentioned in the exercise, assertiveness, was described in Chapter 2.

## LEADER IN ACTION

### "CARLY'S" TERM WIELDED INFLUENCE FOR A WHILE AT HEWLETT-PACKARD

Carleton (Carly) S. Fiorina, the chair and CEO of Hewlett-Packard Company (HP), was designated by *Fortune* magazine as the most powerful woman in business for six consecutive years. The criteria for being designated a powerful woman include the size and importance of the woman's business in the global economy, her clout outside the company, her career accomplishments (past, present, and potential), as well as her influence on mass culture and society.

#### THE RISE OF FIORINA

Fiorina holds an M.B.A. from the University of Maryland and an M.S. from the Massachusetts Institute of Technology. Before joining HP, she had a remarkable run as president of the Global Services division at Lucent Technologies Inc., where she shared responsibility for reengineering Lucent into a technology high flyer from what was once the telephone manufacturing division of AT&T. During her twenty years of technology experience, Fiorina had developed a track record of growing large businesses.

In 1999, Carly Fiorina was hired by HP's board of directors to transform a company in dire need of change. The company had failed to capitalize on the personal computer and Internet revolutions. Expectations were high for Fiorina, who, unlike her predecessors, was not an engineer or an HP insider. Instead, she was a goal-oriented, market-focused executive skilled at bringing about large-scale organizational change. Her charismatic personality and engaging smile enhanced her other qualifications. From the start, however, Fiorina's polished market-savvy focus conflicted with the company's relaxed, engineering culture, despite efforts to work out the cultural differences.

#### THE MERGER WITH COMPAQ COMPUTER

Fiorina's most powerful act was orchestrating the merger with Compaq Computer Corporation, the biggest tech merger in history. Fiorina staked her job on the merger, which cost $19 billion. To accomplish it, she had to stave off opposition from company insiders and outsiders, including the founders of Hewlett-Packard. For two years she traveled 250,000 miles per year selling the merger to shareholders to win enough of their votes. The controversial merger was completed in May 2002 and ultimately resulted in the layoff of 17,900 employees. An HP veteran said, "Employees are now treated as assets or tools, no different than machines or buildings" (*Workforce*, p. 31). The layoffs led to increased workloads for the remaining employees, with many managers putting in sixty-hour workweeks.

#### SOME FIORINA INITIATIVES

Fiorina also saw a need for modifying Hewlett-Packard's culture. HP's emphasis on teamwork and respect for coworkers had translated into a bureaucratic, consensus-style culture that had a sharp disadvantage in the Net-speed era. Fiorina believed that disposing of the counterproductive habits while retaining the good habits would not be a problem.

Fiorina was intent on transforming HP by inspiring employees to change their ways of thinking and working. At the top of her agenda, Fiorina said, was promoting eservices: technologies that

*(continued)*

help companies with their own ecommerce initiatives. As Fiorina assumed her new responsibilities, she said HP needed to reinvigorate its sense of speed and urgency. At the same time, she wanted to retain Hewlett-Packard's greatest organizational strengths: its deep engineering roots and its dependability.

Another task Fiorina assumed was to craft a vision of HP as an Internet company that could pull together a vast range of products, from inkjet cartridges to supercomputers, for any customer that had to compete in the online and offline worlds. Fiorina emphasized that Hewlett-Packard must innovate at a rapid rate. In addition to giving top customer service, employees under Carly were being asked to perform at a higher level. Fiorina instituted firing the bottom 5 percent of performers.

As a leader, Fiorina sometimes uses a personal touch that inspires intense loyalty. She's known for giving balloons and flowers to employees who land big contracts. When the wife of a senior executive fell ill, Fiorina helped make sure she got medical service, doctors, and medical support.

"Carly" has been described as brilliant and visionary but also as arrogant and self-serving. A unanimous opinion, however, is that Fiorina is an intensely driven executive who arises at 4:30 A.M. and routinely works fourteen hours a day. Her leadership slogan is "Demand more," and she expected the very best from herself and HP's 141,000 employees.

## CHANGES IN STRUCTURE AND DECISION MAKING

When Fiorina arrived, HP was a flat, decentralized company, and individual departments were given considerable autonomy. Decisions were made by consensus, or not made at all. Carly converted HP into a tightly coordinated corporate entity in which the most important decisions were made at the top. "Before we never talked about members of the executive council" (a team of senior vice presidents who report directly to Fiorina), said the general manager of product recycling solutions.

"Now we not only know who they are and what they do, we know they have 'super votes' that can override others" (*Workforce*, p. 30).

Some workers welcomed the move to centralization. One opinion was that the consensus style at HP may have worked well when the company was small, but as it grew, it was taking too long to get things done. One HP veteran said, "It was difficult to get any large-scale programs off the ground because all the power was concentrated at lower levels" (*Workforce*, p. 32).

The same veteran said that decisions under Carly were now made more quickly. "Before, people were reluctant to make decisions until they had all the facts. Carly has changed that. She's made it okay for people to take risks and go with just 80 percent of the data. For example, I work in product recycling, and our work is leading edge. Instead of making us churn out a business case for everything we do, Carly says just go ahead because recycling inherently makes sense" (*Workforce*, p. 32).

## THE FALL OF FIORINA

By the end of 2004, analysts were still debating whether Fiorina's initiatives had really paid off for the company. HP badly missed projections, but it rebounded in November. Analysts suggested that Fiorina hire a chief operating officer or break up the company's vast operations to help the far-flung company operate more efficiently. Spinning off the highly successful printer business was one frequent suggestion. Fiorina responded to the suggestion about hiring a COO as follows:

> No. If I did think that, I'd get one. There are very few companies that have a chief operating officer. IBM doesn't have one, GE doesn't have one, Tyco doesn't have one. Most companies don't have chief operating officers because you cannot separate strategy from execution. You can't separate the outside job from the inside job. In an industry as competitive as ours, with the magnitude of challenges we have, a CEO better have his or her hands on the wheel. (*The Wall Street Journal*, November 30, 2004, p. B2)

Another concern was that much of the company's profit growth stemmed from cuts in research and development and a lower tax rate. Despite these concerns, HP's profits for 2005 were projected at $4.5 based on sales of $85 billion.

By February 2005, however, the Hewlett-Packard board decided that Fiorina had not attained the ambitious goals she had set out for the company, and they asked for her resignation. Fiorina accepted gracefully, and she was given a $21 million severance package. Patricia A. Dunn, a director at HP, told industry analysts and investors, "This is not a change related to strategy. This is a change based on a desire to accelerate that strategy. We think that requires hands-on execution" (*www.nytimes*, February 9, 2005). Dunn also pointed out that the board had been deliberating the company's performance as well as that of the CEO for a long time. Part of the board's concern was that HP stock was down more than 50 percent since Fiorina began, and profits were not healthy.

Another major concern was that Fiorina had centralized too much of the company's vast operation in her office, thereby slowing down decision making. Many people also thought that she invested too much energy in being a celebrity with grand visions, and not enough energy in running the company properly.

## QUESTIONS

1. Which influence tactics did Fiorina appear to be using?
2. What improvements can you suggest Fiorina make in her use of influence tactics?

SOURCE: Ben Elgin, "Carly's Challenge," *BusinessWeek*, December 13, 2004, pp. 98–108; Pui-Wing Tam, "Carly Fiorina's Rough Ride," *The Wall Street Journal*, November 30, 2004, pp. B1, B2; Ann Harrington and Melanie Shanley, "The 50 Most Powerful Women in American Business, *Fortune*, October 13, 2003, p. 104; Patricia Sellers, "The 50 Most Powerful Women in Business: Secrets of the Fastest-Rising Stars," *Fortune*, October 16, 2000, pp. 131–132; Patricia Sellers, "Power: Do Women Really Want It? *Fortune*, October 13, 2003, pp. 80, 86; Shari Caudron, "Don't Mess with Carly," *Workforce*, July 2003, pp. 28–33; Peter Burrows, "HP's Woes Are Deeper Than the Downturn," *BusinessWeek*, May 7, 2001, p. 48; Gary Rivlin and Mark Glassman, "Hewlett-Packard's Chief Resigns, Ending Rocky Tenure," *www.nytimes*, February 9, 2005.

**LEADERSHIP SKILL-BUILDING EXERCISE 8-1**

### IDENTIFYING INFLUENCE TACTICS

INSTRUCTIONS After reading each tactic listed here, label it as being mostly an example of one of the following: I = ingratiation; E = exchange of favors; R = rationality; A = assertiveness; U = upward appeal

**Tactic Code**

1. I sympathized with the person about the added problems that my request caused. _____

2. I offered to help if the person would do what I wanted. _____

3. I set a time deadline for the person to do what I asked. _____

4. I obtained the informal support of higher-ups. _____

5. I used logic to convince him or her. _____

6. I made a formal appeal to higher levels to back up my request. _____

*(continued)*

7. I had a showdown in which I confronted the person head-on. _____

8. I offered to make a personal sacrifice if the person would do what I wanted (for example, work late or harder). _____

9. I made him or her feel good about me before making my request. _____

10. I explained the reasons for my request. _____

ANSWERS:

| | |
|---|---|
| 1. I | 6. U |
| 2. E | 7. A |
| 3. A | 8. E |
| 4. U | 9. I |
| 5. R | 10. R |

SKILL DEVELOPMENT Being able to identify influence tactics raises your awareness of how to influence others and which tactics others are using to influence you.

SOURCE: Based on information in Chester A. Schriescheim and Timothy R. Hinkin, "Influence Tactics Used by Subordinates: A Theoretical and Empirical Analysis and Refinement of the Kipnis, Schmidt, and Wilkinson Subscales," *Journal of Applied Psychology*, June 1990, p. 246. Copyright © 1990 American Psychological Association. Adapted with permission.

## Relative Effectiveness and Sequencing of Influence Tactics

Although we have described influence tactics separately, they must also be understood in relation to one another. Two ways of comparing influence tactics are to examine their relative effectiveness and to study the order in which they might be used to achieve the best result.

### Relative Effectiveness of Influence Tactics

Since influence tactics are a major component of leadership, research about their relative effectiveness is worth noting. A study by Gary Yukl and J. Bruce Tracey provides insights into the relative effectiveness of influence tactics.[28] One hundred and twenty managers participated in the study, along with 526 subordinates, 543 peers, and 128 superiors, who also rated the managers' use of influence tactics. Half the managers worked for manufacturing companies, and half worked for service companies.

The people who worked with the managers completed a questionnaire to identify which of nine influence tactics the managers used. As defined for the participants, the tactics were as follows:

1. Rational persuasion
2. Inspirational appeal
3. Consultation
4. Ingratiation
5. Exchange
6. Personal appeal
7. Coalition
8. Legitimating
9. Pressure

Another question asked how many influence attempts by the agent resulted in complete commitment by the target respondent. Respondents were also asked to rate the overall effectiveness of the manager in carrying out his or her job responsibilities. The item had nine response choices, ranging from "the least effective manager I have ever known" to "the most effective manager."

The results suggested that the most effective tactics were rational persuasion, inspirational appeal, and consultation. (An effective tactic was one that led to task commitment and that was used by managers who were perceived to be effective by the various raters.) In contrast, the least effective were pressure, coalition, and appealing to legitimate authority (legitimating). Ingratiation and exchange were moderately effective for influencing team members and peers. The same tactics, however, were not effective for influencing superiors. A related interpretation of the data would be that noncoercive tactics that provide a rational and justifiable basis for attitude change are more effective in gaining compliance than are threatening or manipulative attempts.[29]

Inspirational appeal, ingratiation, and pressure were used primarily in a downward direction, that is, toward a lower-ranking person. Personal appeal, exchange, and legitimating were used primarily in a lateral direction. It was also found that coalitions were used most in lateral and upward directions and that rational persuasion was used most in an upward direction.

The researchers concluded that some tactics are more likely to be successful. Yet they caution that the results do not imply that these tactics will always result in task commitment. The outcome of a specific influence attempt is also determined by other factors, such as the target's motivation and the organizational culture. Also, any tactic can trigger target resistance if it is not appropriate for the situation or if it is applied unskillfully. Tact, diplomacy, and insight are required for effective application of influence tactics.

Which influence tactic a manager might consider effective, and therefore choose, depends to some extent on how much group members are trusted. When we distrust people, we are likely to attempt to control their actions. Carole V. Wells and David Kipnis conducted a survey about trust involving 275 managers and 267 employees. The managers answered questions about subordinates, and subordinates answered questions about their managers. The two groups, however, were not describing each other. A key finding was that both managers and employees used strong tactics of influence when they distrusted the other party—either a manager or a subordinate. The strong influence tactics studied were appeals to higher authority, assertiveness, coalition building, and sanctions.[30]

A recent study suggests that gender differences can moderate the effectiveness of downward influence tactics. A sample of 254 employees at a midwestern life insurance company rated the influence tactics used by their direct supervisors. The results suggested that, for certain situations, managers alter their influence tactics based on the gender of the group member. Overall, followers reported that male managers used significantly more personal appeal and consultation (soft tactics) with their subordinates than did female managers. Female group members reported that their managers (both male and female) used consultation and inspirational appeal (soft tactics) more frequently. In contrast, male followers reported that their managers use the exchange tactic more frequently. The authors of the study caution that because the sample was predominantly female, the organization culture encourages the use of soft influence tactics.[31] However, one can conclude from this study that personal appeal and consultation might work more effectively with women workers, and exchange tactics might work more effectively with men.

## Sequencing of Influence Tactics

Another important consideration in using influence tactics is the sequence or order in which they should be applied. In general, you should begin with the most positive, or least abrasive, tactic. If you do not gain the advantage you seek, proceed to a stronger tactic. For example, if you want a larger salary increase than that initially assigned you, try rational persuasion. If persuasion does not work, move on to exchanging favors. Use a more abrasive tactic such as upward appeal only as a last resort. The reason is that abrasive tactics trigger revenge and retaliation. Many people who have brought their complaints to an outside agency such as a governmental office have found themselves with a limited future in their organization. Although the appeal is legally justified, it is politically unwise.

The sequencing of tactics can also be considered in terms of cost and risk. A sensible approach is to begin with low-cost, low-risk tactics. If the outcome is important enough to the influence agent, he or she can then proceed to higher-cost and higher-risk influence tactics. An example of a low-cost, low-risk tactic would be joking and kidding. An accounting manager who was disappointed with the budget offered her group might say to her boss, "Does the new budget mean that our group will have to pay for our own CDs and green eyeshades?" It would be much more costly in terms of time and potential retaliation to form a coalition with another underbudgeted group to ask for an enlarged budget.

In addition to the sequencing of tactics, the influence agent must also consider the direction of the influence attempt as a contingency factor. In general, the more position power an individual exerts over another, the less the need for being cautious in the use of influence tactics. For example, a vice president can more readily use undue pressure against a supervisor than vice versa. When you have more power, there are likely to be fewer negative consequences from using more powerful tactics.

Leadership Skill-Building Exercise 8-2 provides an opportunity to practice implementing various influence tactics. As with any other skill, influence skills need to be practiced under field conditions.

### APPLYING INFLUENCE TACTICS

Divide the class into small teams. Each group assigns one leadership influence tactic to each team member. During the next week or so, each team member takes the opportunity to practice the assigned influence tactic in a work or personal setting. Hold a group discussion with the same class teams after the influence attempts have been practiced. Report back the following information: (1) under what circumstances the influence tactic was attempted; (2) how the influence target reacted; and (3) what results, both positive and negative, were achieved.

Practicing influence tactics directly contributes to your leadership effectiveness because leadership centers on influence. If you want to exert leadership as a nonmanager, you will have to be particularly adept at using influence tactics because your formal authority will be quite limited.

## Implicit Leadership Theories and Leadership Influence

A final perspective on influence tactics is that people are more likely to be influenced by leaders who match their expectations of what a leader should be. **Implicit leadership theories** are personal assumptions about the traits and abilities that characterize an ideal organizational leader. These assumptions, both stated and unstated, develop through socialization and past experiences with leaders. The assumptions are stored in memory and activated when group members interact with a person in a leadership position. Our assumptions about leaders help us make sense of what takes place on the job. Assume that Reggie was raised in a household and neighborhood in which business leaders are highly respected and thought to be dedicated and intelligent. When Reggie later works in a full-time professional job, he is most likely to be influenced by a supervisor he perceives to be dedicated and intelligent because this person fits Reggie's preconceived notion of how a leader should behave.

According to implicit leadership theory, as part of making assumptions and expectations of leader traits and behaviors, people develop leadership prototypes and antiprototypes. *Prototypes* are positive characterizations of a leader, whereas *antiprototypes* are traits and behaviors people do not want to see in a leader. People have different expectations of what they want in a leader, yet research conducted with 939 subordinates in two different samples in British companies shows there is some consistency in implicit leadership theories. The study showed that these theories are consistent across different employee groups and are also stable trait-based stereotypes of leadership.[32]

| **TABLE 8-2** | **Implicit Leadership Theory Dimensions** |
|---|---|

| LEADERSHIP PROTOTYPE | LEADERSHIP ANTIPROTOTYPE |
|---|---|
| 1. Sensitivity (compassion, sensitive) | 1. Tyranny (dominant, selfish, manipulative) |
| 2. Intelligence (intelligent, clever) | 2. Masculinity (male, masculine) |
| 3. Dedication (dedicated, motivated) | |
| 4. Charisma (charismatic, dynamic) | |
| 5. Strength (strong, bold) | |
| 6. Attractiveness (well dressed, classy) | |

Source: Gathered from information in Olga Epitropaki and Robin Martin, "Implicit Leadership Theories in Applied Settings: Factor Structure, Generalizability, and Stability over Time," *Journal of Applied Psychology*, April 2004, pp. 297–299.

Table 8-2 lists the six traits group members want to see in a leader (prototypes), as well as the two traits they do not want to see in a leader (antiprototypes). Your study of leadership traits in Chapters 2 and 3 will reinforce these leadership attributes. The antiprototype of *masculinity* suggests that followers prefer a compassionate and relationship-oriented leader to a command-and-control leader (see Chapter 4). An implication of these data is that a leader who fits group members' prototypes is more likely to influence them than a leader who fits their antiprototype.

**READER'S ROADMAP**

So far we have studied considerable information about the nature of leadership; the attributes, behaviors, and styles of leaders; the ethics and social responsibility of leaders; and how leaders exert power and use politics and influence. The next chapter explains a variety of techniques for developing teamwork.

## Summary

college.hmco.com/pic/dubrin5e

To become an effective leader, a person must be aware of specific influence tactics. Influence is the ability to affect the behaviors of others in a particular direction. Power, in contrast, is the potential or capacity to influence. A model presented here indicates that a leader's influence outcomes are a function of the influence tactics he or she uses. The influence tactics are in turn moderated, or affected by, the leader's traits and behaviors and also by the situation. The outcomes of influence attempts are commitment, compliance, or resistance, all of which influence end results such as group success or failure.

Influence tactics are often viewed from an ethical perspective. Some tactics are clearly ethical, but others are clearly unethical. Used with tact, diplomacy, and good intent, ethical influence tactics can be quite effective. The essentially ethical tactics described here are leading by example and respect, using rational persuasion, being a subject matter expert, exchanging favors and bargaining, legitimating a request, making an inspirational appeal and emotional display, consulting, forming coalitions, being a team player, and practicing hands-on leadership.

Essentially dishonest and unethical tactics presented here were divided into two groups: clearly unethical and borderline. The more clearly unethical and devious tactics are deliberate Machiavellianism, gentle manipulation of people and situations, undue pressure, and debasement. The three borderline influence tactics are upward appeal, ingratiation, and joking and kidding (hardly devious at all).

A study of influence tactics concluded that the most effective were rational persuasion, inspirational appeal, and consultation. The least effective were pressure, coalition, and appealing to legitimate authority. Certain tactics are more effective for exerting influence upward, whereas others are better suited for downward influence. For example, inspirational appeal, ingratiation, and exchange are moderately effective for influencing subordinates and peers. Yet the same tactics are not effective for influencing superiors. When we distrust people we tend to think that stronger influence tactics, such as an appeal to higher authority, will be effective.

Gender differences can moderate the effectiveness of downward influence tactics. For example, personal appeal and consultation might work more effectively with women workers, and exchange more effectively with men.

Sequencing of influence tactics is another important consideration. In general, begin with the most positive, or least abrasive, tactic. If you do not gain the advantage you seek, proceed to a stronger tactic. Also, begin with low-cost, low-risk tactics.

Implicit leadership theories are personal assumptions about the traits and abilities that characterize an ideal organizational leader. Prototypes are positive characterizations of a leader, whereas antiprototypes are negative. Subordinates are more likely to be influenced by leaders who fit their prototypes, and do not fit their antiprototypes, of a leader.

## Key Terms

influence

commitment

compliance

resistance

leading by example

personal magnetism

coalition

hands-on leader

Machiavellians

bandwagon technique

debasement

upward appeal

implicit leadership theories

## Guidelines for Action and Skill Development

If you want to exert political influence, you will usually need a more advanced tactic than sending an email message stating your demands. A memo to the boss will sometimes work, but more often it is a sign of being politically naïve. Instead, Harvard Business School leadership professor John Kotter recommends four basic steps for exercising political influence:

1. Identify relevant relationships (figure out who needs to be led).

2. Evaluate who might resist, why they might resist, and how strongly the resistance will be. Figure out where the leadership challenges will be.

3. Develop, wherever possible, relationships with potential opponents to facilitate communication, education, or negotiation.

4. If step three fails, carefully select and implement more subtle or more forceful methods (such as the influence tactics described in this chapter).[33]

## Discussion Questions and Activities

1. Which influence tactic described in this chapter do you think would work the best for you? Why?
2. Which influence tactic do you think would work the most poorly for you? Why?
3. What differences have you observed among the influence tactics used by technically oriented versus people-oriented people?
4. How can email be used to implement any of the influence tactics described in this chapter?
5. Identify two exchanges of favor you have seen or can envision on the job.
6. In what way is being a subject matter expert (SME) a source of power as well as an influence tactic?

7. How might a business owner use the bandwagon technique to get his or her employees to lead a healthier lifestyle?
8. Which of the influence tactics described in this chapter is a charismatic leader the most likely to use? Explain your answer.
9. Which influence tactics have been the most effective in influencing you? Support your answer with an anecdote.
10. Get the opinion of an experienced leader as to the most effective influence tactics. Share your findings with class members.

 ## LEADERSHIP CASE PROBLEM A

### RESTORING TRUST AT AMERICAN AIRLINES

Union leader Campbell Little felt a jolt of pain. To keep the world's largest airline carrier from bankruptcy, employees at American Airlines, Inc., had agreed to $1.8 billion in cuts to wages, benefits, and thousands of jobs. The next morning Little received a phone call from one of his representatives, who told Little to grab a copy of *The Wall Street Journal* because it contained a shocking story about the airline.

Little, whose union represented mechanics and ground workers, bought a copy of the newspaper and read the headline: "Carrier Created Protections for Executives in Event of Reorganization Filing." The lavish protections included funding a pension trust for forty-five American Airlines executives and lucrative bonuses for six of the company's top executives, including its chief executive officer, Don Carty. All of these protections were granted without informing the unions.

"I just couldn't believe what I was reading," says Little, with a mixture of anger and shock in his voice. "My first reaction was this void. Our members had struggled to prevent American from going into bankruptcy and then to find out about significant increases for senior management on the back of workers. I believe our members were duped."

Later it was revealed that the company had delayed filing the Securities and Exchange Commission report disclosing the management perks until after negotiations with its unions had been completed. In those negotiations, the union had granted costly concessions to help save jobs. This move by Carty and the rest of top management appeared to be the final blow.

But then an event took place that no one anticipated: a new CEO was appointed, and management and employees began talking to each other.

American Airlines avoided Chapter 11 and, while still losing money, ended its most recent quarter with more than $3.5 billion in reserves, including $500 million in readily available cash.

The company also saved millions of dollars because of employee cost-cutting suggestions.

Labor leaders began to have a new idea about management. "We have cautious optimism for the new generation of leadership," says Tommie Hutto-Blake, president of the Association of Professional Flight Attendants. Union leaders agree that a major reason for the positive mood at American is new CEO Gerard Arpey, who assumed the post in May 2003 following Carty's departure. Little said, "I believe Gerard to be a sincere person, compassionate, and someone who wants American to turn around."

"The only way to build trust professionally or personally is by being trustworthy," Arpey says. "I hope I'm living up to that standard."

"We hit bottom and had to figure out what to do differently," says Mark Burdette, vice president of employee relations for American.

With Arpey, the company's former chief financial officer, in charge, American initiated a movement to disclose all financial matters to unions. At the same time, workers were encouraged to submit their ideas to make the airline more productive. Arpey says, "I think you will make better decisions and execute better on these decisions if you involve all the people doing the work. You certainly won't always agree, but the process of listening to each other can't help but lead to better outcomes, no matter which way you go."

Arpey, the 46-year-old CEO, had impressed labor leaders even before he accepted the top position. John Darrah, the former head of the Allied Pilots Association who led the union during the transition, says Arpey had approached him and other labor officials to request their approval. "He said he wouldn't take the position unless he had our support," Darrah says. Having worked with Arpey for several years, Darrah was confident that Arpey recognized the company could not succeed without the full cooperation of workers. He notes that Arpey began his career as a baggage handler with Delta Airlines and had more than twenty years of experience in the airline business.

After accepting the CEO position, Arpey visited cities about every two weeks where American had operations to conduct town hall meetings. He got rid of the expensive art in the office and replaced it with American Airlines memorabilia, a move that sent a very positive message to the flight attendants. He also implemented an open-door policy with union officials, returning phone calls, soliciting their advice on critical company issues, and constantly emphasizing the importance of getting the rank and file involved in helping the company.

In July 2004, Arpey declined a board-approved 22 percent raise, or more than $110,000 annually. He said accepting the salary increase would have sent the wrong messages to workers.

**THE FLIGHT TEAM** Arpey took another initiative to help save the airline. At the urging of the employee relations and human resources staff, the company hired a consulting firm, the Overland Resource Group. The Group has an established record of success in helping companies achieve a high degree of employee involvement and engagement. The mechanism selected to improve employee relations included establishing a Joint Leadership Team (JLT) that would be chaired by the CEO and the national presidents of the airline's three organized labor groups: flight attendants, pilots, and ground workers.

The JLT team holds a meeting once a month to discuss company issues, which could include everything from strategic plans to labor grievances. Typically two people from Overland are on hand to act as facilitators. The same type of meeting is spreading to other sites throughout American Airlines. A quarterly review of company-wide finances is included in the meetings.

American Airlines management contends that the Overland project is just one segment of a strategy to mend fences with labor and bring about efficiencies. One component of the approach was a customer strategy meeting in Dallas with 100 employees from throughout the company. At this

*(continued)*

meeting, two days were spent brainstorming about how to improve customer service.

**EVERYONE ABOARD** According to Burdette, a key component of cutting costs and improving morale is pushing useful worker ideas up the chain of command so they can be implemented. The key is encouraging managers to take the rank and file's ideas seriously, a concept Arpey is promoting throughout the company. Although American Airlines does not track the number of ideas that are implemented, top management estimates that the company saved about $100 million in 2004 because of employee-identified cost savings ideas. Most of these ideas were developed by workers, who then took them directly to their supervisors. For example, each month American went through thousands of drill bits—each costing $20 to $200—to service its fleet of aircraft. Two mechanics in Tulsa, Oklahoma, invented a drill-bit sharpening tool that allows the bits to be refurbished and reused.

Thanks to Arpey's leadership, Wall Street views American as among the most likely of the legacy (early entrant into the field) carriers to survive intact. Arpey says the company is working on all fronts to improve results. "The best way to do that is to continue driving American to be more competitive by working together, collaboratively with our union and nonunionized employees, and jointly confront the reality that's before us."

Workers believe they are making big concessions, such as reduced wages and salary increases. Ultimately, no matter how gently and cooperatively bad news is shared, if the news is still bad, that is a problem, Mitchell observes. "The biggest question is: How much sacrifice are the workers willing to make?"

## QUESTIONS

1. What is Arpey attempting to influence American Airlines employees to accomplish?
2. Which influence tactics is Arpey using to influence American Airlines employees?
3. What else might Arpey do as a leader to help American survive?

SOURCE: From Eve Tahmincioglu, "Back from the Brink." Reprinted with permission. *Workforce*, December 2004. Copyright Crain Communications, Inc. *www.workforce.com*.

## LEADERSHIP CASE PROBLEM B

### TOO MUCH GENEROSITY AT BOEING

Darleen Druyun of Vienna, Virginia, a former top Air Force procurement official, pleaded guilty in April 2004 to conspiracy to violate federal conflict-of-interest regulations. She was sentenced to nine months in prison after admitting for the first time that she helped The Boeing Company obtain an inflated price on a $23 billion contract while she was seeking an executive job at the company.

Druyun and former Boeing chief financial officer Michael Sears were subjects of a federal grand jury investigation of the Air Force's plan to acquire 100 refueling tankers from the Chicago-based jet maker. Prosecutors said Sears improperly contacted Druyun about a possible top-level company job in 2002, when she still was at the Air Force and playing a key role in deciding whether Boeing should get the tanker contract, which could be worth up to $23 billion. Druyun retired from the Air Force in November 2002 and joined Boeing in January 2003 as deputy general manager of its Missile Defense Systems unit. After learning of the incident, Boeing fired Druyun and Sears for what the company termed unethical behavior.

When Druyun pleaded guilty in April, she had admitted only technical violations of the conflict-of-interest rules. Specifically, she said she had negotiated a deal to become a vice president of the giant aircraft manufacturer and defense contractor while she was still an Air Force officer with influence over Boeing contracts. After failing government polygraph tests, however, she conceded that her conflict produced substantive benefits for Boeing and that she altered journals provided to the government to cover up the story. She was ordered to spend nine months in prison and seven months in a halfway house. Prosecutors had sought sixteen months in prison. Druyun's attorney, John Dowd, said he was pleased with the sentence handed down by U.S. District Judge T. S. Ellis III. "She had difficulty coming to grips with some matters," Dowd told Ellis, referring to Druyun's initial lies about the scope of her wrongdoing. "But she did, she finally did."

The $23 billion tanker deal is currently under review by the Defense Department. In court documents, Druyun admitted providing assistance to Boeing on other contracts as well. Among them was a $4 billion contract to provide upgrades to the Air Force C-130 fleet. She admitted that Boeing gained an advantage because it was helping her daughter's boyfriend get a job, and she said that Boeing might not have received the contract on a level playing field.

She also said she helped Boeing obtain an inflated deal on a $100 million NATO AWACS contract in 2002 at the same time she successfully intervened to keep Boeing from firing her daughter, who worked for the company, for poor performance.

Druyun offered a tearful apology "to my nation, to my Air Force" at her sentencing. "I deeply regret any damage I have done—to the integrity of the procurement process," she said.

In February 2005, Sears was sentenced to four months for illegally negotiating the $250,000 contract for Druyun. Sears had pleaded guilty to a single count of aiding and abetting illegal employment negotiations. The judge also imposed a $250,000 fine and 200 hours of community service for Sears.

## QUESTIONS

1. Which influence tactics did Darleen Druyun use to help her obtain the contract for Boeing?
2. What is your judgment of the fairness of the sentence given Druyun, given that so many procurement officials are granted special favors by vendors?
3. What might Druyun have done to help Boeing obtain a large profit margin on the contract in question?
4. What responsibility should Boeing leadership, including Michael Sears, take for the incident involving Druyun, the Air Force official?

SOURCE: "Ex–Air Force Official Sentenced in Boeing Probe," Associated Press, October 1, 2004; "Ex-Boeing Exec Receives 4-Month Term," Associated Press, February 19, 2005.

## ETHICAL INFLUENCE TACTICS

One student plays the role of Darleen Druyun while she was an Air Force procurement officer. Another student plays the role of Michael Sears, the former Boeing chief financial officer. The two are discussing at lunch a possible $23 billion deal for Boeing. Sears desperately wants the contract for Boeing, and Druyun sees this as an opportunity to gain some personal advantage from the deal: she might advance her career and help her daughter's boyfriend get a job at Boeing. But despite Druyun's hints about gaining some personal advantage, Sears decides to use ethical influence tactics to win the contract. The two role players conduct the interview for about ten minutes. Later, the class observers will provide feedback about the effectiveness of the influence tactics used by both players.

*LEADERSHIP SKILL-BUILDING EXERCISE 8-3*

## MY LEADERSHIP PORTFOLIO

Influence is to leadership as an egg is to an omelet, so you need to practice your influence tactics to enhance your leadership effectiveness. In this chapter's entry to your leadership journal, describe any influence tactic you implemented recently. Describe what you did, and how the influence target reacted. Comment on how you might use the tactic differently in your next influence attempt. Also describe which influence tactic or combination of tactics you plan to use in the upcoming week. Here might be an example:

> I coach a youth basketball team called the "West Side Indians." The kids are great, and I am enjoying the experience. Yet the name "Indians" really bothers me because it is so behind the times, and a lot of people think using the term "Indian" for sport is racist. So I tried to influence the league director that we needed a name change. I presented my argument using a bunch of facts about how "Indian" has become passé for sports team. (My technique was rational persuasion.) I did get a listen, but I didn't get approval for the name change. So next, I combined my logical argument with an inspirational appeal. I asked the league directors how they would like it if our team were called "The West Side Chinese" or the "West Side Jews." Finally, my influence tactics worked, and for next season my team will be the "West Side Rattlers."

*LEADERSHIP SKILL-BUILDING EXERCISE 8-4*

## INTERNET SKILL-BUILDING EXERCISE

Apply the chapter concepts! Visit the Web and complete this Internet skill-building exercise to learn more about current leadership topics and trends.

### HOW MACHIAVELLIAN ARE YOU?

Go to *www.humanlinks.com/personal/power_orientation.htm*, and follow the instructions for taking the Power Orientation Test. Your score will be compared to a national average. Compare your score on this test with the Organizational Politics Questionnaire you took in Chapter 7.

1. Do you think the two tests measure similar tendencies?
2. If the range of your scores on the two tests is quite different, such as high on the Power Orientation Test and low on the Organizational Politics Questionnaire, how do you explain these differences?
3. How does your score on the Power Orientation Test compare with your score on the Leader Integrity Scale from Chapter 6? What do you see as the relationship between ethical behavior and Machiavellianism?

# Developing Teamwork

Chesapeake Habitat for Humanity (CHH) is a non-profit organization that renovates vacant houses and sells them at no-interest mortgage rates to low-income home buyers. Several years ago, CHH launched its own for-profit venture, TeamBuilds, where corporate teams pay $7,500 for an all-day team-building session with an organizational development consultant while they work together to rebuild an old house. Amid nail guns and drywall, teams work out their problems and increase their competitiveness.

In the experience of Coldwell Banker real estate agent Jan Hayden, nothing promotes teamwork better than picking up a sledgehammer and reducing the interior of a house to rubble. "If you've ever been to a Habitat home-build where you get to do the demolition, it's awesome because you get rid of all your frustrations," said Hayden, taking a break from helping to frame a wall in a vacant row house.[1]

The Chesapeake Habitat for Humanity anecdote illustrates the importance business firms attach to building better teamwork, whether or not such outdoor training is the ultimate answer to enhancing teamwork. Developing teamwork is such an important leadership role that team building is said to differentiate successful from unsuccessful leaders.[2] Furthermore, leaders with a reputation as teamwork builders are often in demand. A case in point is the former fast-food restaurant executive Aylwin Lewis who became CEO of Kmart Holding Corporation (now part of Sears). A major reason Lewis was selected for the position was his strong reputation for brand expansion and team building.[3]

A difficulty in understanding teams is that the words *teams* and *teamwork* are often overused and applied loosely. For some people, *team* is simply another term for *group*. As used here, a **team** is a work group that must rely on collaboration if each member is to experience the optimum success and achievement.[4] **Teamwork** is work done with an understanding and commitment to group goals on the part of all team members. All teams are groups, but not all groups are teams. Jon R. Katzenbach and Douglas K. Smith, on the basis of extensive research in the workplace, make a clear differentiation between teams and groups.[5] A team is characterized by a common commitment, whereas the commitment within a group might not be as strong. A team accomplishes many collective work products, whereas group members sometimes work slightly more independently. A team has shared leadership roles, whereas members of a group have a strong leader. In a team there is individual and mutual accountability; in contrast, a group emphasizes individual accountability.

Team members produce a collective work product, whereas group members sometimes produce individual work products. A team leader is likely to encourage open-ended discussion and active problem-solving meetings, whereas a group leader is more likely to run an efficient meeting. Also, teams discuss, decide, and do real work together, whereas a group is more likely to discuss, decide, and delegate.

Although the distinction between a group and a team may be valid, it is difficult to cast aside the practice of using the terms *group* and *team* interchangeably. For example, a customer service team is still a team even if its teamwork is poor.

As background for this chapter, we first examine how team leadership is different from more traditional leadership. The central focus of this chapter is a description of specific leader actions that foster teamwork. We also describe outdoor training, a widely used method of teamwork development. In addition, we summarize a leadership theory that provides insight into how teamwork emerges within a work group.

## Team Leadership Versus Solo Leadership

Various writers have touted the importance of team leadership. Meredith Belbin, for one, contrasts the team leader and the solo leader (see Figure 9-1).[6] Team leaders share power and deemphasize individual glory. They are flexible and adaptable, thus welcoming change. They function as facilitators who bring out the best in others, and they are inspirational. The team leader conforms closely to the consensus style.

William D. Hitt has observed related characteristics and behaviors of team leaders. In his analysis, team leaders place considerable emphasis on team building and then evaluate their own performance on the basis of how well they have developed the team. Team leaders intuitively recognize that the whole is greater than the sum of the parts. Based on this belief, they look for linkages (members working closely with each other) among team members to help multiply productivity.[7] Team leaders understand that sharing power with group members multiplies their own power. As the team members become stronger, so does the leader. A related attitude is that team leaders are not threatened by sharing power. They are therefore willing to surround themselves with capable people in order to multiply the effectiveness of the team.

The solo leader is the traditional leader in a bureaucracy. Basically an autocrat, the solo leader receives much of the credit for the success of his or her firm. Frequently some of the credit is undeserved. The solo leader may not recognize how dependent he or she is on the team. For example, a manufacturing manager might brag about how under his leadership, the division became a top-rated supplier to a large customer. The same manager neglects to mention how attaining this high-quality status was really a collective effort.

**FIGURE 9-1  The Solo Leader and the Team Leader**

| SOLO LEADER | TEAM LEADER |
|---|---|
| 1. Plays unlimited role (interferes) | 1. Chooses to limit role (delegates) |
| 2. Strives for conformity | 2. Builds on diversity |
| 3. Collects acolytes | 3. Seeks talent |
| 4. Directs subordinates | 4. Develops colleagues |
| 5. Projects objectives | 5. Creates mission |

Source: From Meredith Belbin, "Solo Leader/Team Leader: Antithesis in Style and Structure," in Michel Syrett and Clare Hogg, *Frontiers of Leadership*, p. 271, Copyright © 1992, Blackwell Publishers, Oxford, England. Reprinted by permission of Blackwell Publishers.

college.hmco.com/pic/
dubrin5e

**KB** **@ KNOWLEDGE BANK:** To provide background information on team functioning, the Knowledge Bank describes some of the advantages and disadvantages of group activity.

To evaluate how well any work team or group familiar to you is functioning as a team, do Leadership Self-Assessment Quiz 9-1. The quiz will help sensitize you to important dimensions of team effectiveness.

---

**LEADERSHIP SELF-ASSESSMENT QUIZ 9-1**

### THE TEAMWORK CHECKLIST

**INSTRUCTIONS** This checklist serves as an informal guide to diagnosing teamwork. Base your answers on the experiences you have in leading a team, at work or outside work. Indicate whether your team has (or had) the following characteristics:

| | Mostly Yes | Mostly No |
|---|---|---|
| 1. Definite goals each member knows and understands | ____ | ____ |
| 2. Clearly established roles and responsibilities | ____ | ____ |
| 3. Members who work together very well without strong egos or personalities that create problems | ____ | ____ |
| 4. Well-documented guidelines for behavior and ground rules | ____ | ____ |
| 5. After a consensus is reached, support from every team member | ____ | ____ |
| 6. Awareness of team members that they have achieved success | ____ | ____ |
| 7. Open communication in an atmosphere of trust | ____ | ____ |
| 8. Continuous learning and training in appropriate skills | ____ | ____ |
| 9. Flexible, open-minded, and dependable team members | ____ | ____ |
| 10. Patient and supportive higher management | ____ | ____ |
| 11. Individual member pride in own work | ____ | ____ |
| 12. Rewards tied to individual as well as team results | ____ | ____ |
| 13. Team members who automatically provide backup and support for one another without the team leader's stepping in | ____ | ____ |

*(continued)*

SCORING AND INTERPRETATION The more statements are answered "mostly yes," the more likely it is that good teamwork is present. The answers will serve as discussion points among team members for improving teamwork and group effectiveness. Negative responses to the statements can be used as suggestions for taking action to improve teamwork in your group.

SOURCE: Based on material gathered from Mark Kelly, *The Adventures of a Self-Managing Team* (San Diego, Calif.: Pfeiffer, 1991); "Team Leadership: How to Inspire Commitment, Teamwork and Cooperation," brochure, Seminars International, Olathe, Kans., 1996.

## The Leader's Role in the Team-Based Organization

Although an important goal of a team-based organization is for group members to participate in leadership and management activities, leaders still play an important role. In fact, they learn to lead in new ways. Team-based organizations need leaders who are knowledgeable in the team process and can help with the interpersonal demands of teams, for example, by giving feedback and resolving conflict. Quite often the leader is a facilitator who works with two or three teams at a time. He or she helps them stay focused when personality and work-style differences create problems. Without effective leadership, teams can get off course, go too far or not far enough, lose sight of their mission, and become blocked by interpersonal conflict. Effective leadership is particularly important early in the history of a group to help it reach its potential. Key roles of a leader in a team-based organization include the following:

- Building trust and inspiring teamwork
- Coaching team members and group members toward higher levels of performance
- Facilitating and supporting the team's decisions
- Expanding the team's capabilities
- Creating a team identity
- Anticipating and influencing change
- Inspiring the team toward higher levels of performance
- Enabling and empowering group members to accomplish their work
- Encouraging team members to eliminate low-value work[8]

Several of these roles have already been noted in this book, and several others, such as building trust and coaching, are described later. All of these roles contribute to effective leadership in general. The enabling role, for example, centers on empowerment. Yet properly motivating team members also enables, or facilitates, work accomplishment. The empowering processes described in Chapter 7 are a major part of enabling. Group members who are empowered are enabled to accomplish their work. The leader behavior and attitudes that foster teamwork, described in the next section, might also be interpreted as part of the leader's role in a team-based organization.

## Leader Actions That Foster Teamwork

Sometimes a leader's inspiring personality alone can foster teamwork. An experiment with Dutch business students showed that leaders who were perceived as charismatic and fair facilitated cooperation among group members.[9] Yet inspirational leaders, as well as less charismatic ones, can also encourage teamwork through their attitudes and what they do. Table 9-1 lists the teamwork-enhancing actions that are described in the following pages. For convenience, the actions are divided into two types: actions leaders can take using their own resources (informal techniques) and actions that generally require organizational structure or policy (formal techniques).

Most of the actions for improving teamwork are subsets of having effective interpersonal skills. Several examples from the table are numbers 2, 6, and 11 in the left column, and 2 and 5 in the right.

### Actions Leaders Can Take Using Their Own Resources

**Defining the Team's Mission**  A starting point in developing teamwork is to specify the team's mission. Commitment to a clear mission is a key practice of a highly effective team. The mission statement for the group helps answer the question, "Why are we doing this?" To answer this question, the mission statement should set out a specific goal, purpose, and philosophical tone. Any goal contained within the mission statement should be congruent with organizational objectives. If a team wants to cut

**TABLE 9-1**  **Leader Actions That Foster Teamwork**

| ACTIONS LEADERS CAN TAKE USING THEIR OWN RESOURCES | ACTIONS GENERALLY REQUIRING ORGANIZATION STRUCTURE OR POLICY |
|---|---|
| 1. Defining the team's mission | 1. Designing physical structures that facilitate communication |
| 2. Establishing a climate of trust | 2. Emphasizing group recognition and rewards |
| 3. Developing a norm of teamwork, including emotional intelligence | 3. Initiating ritual and ceremony |
| 4. Emphasizing pride in being outstanding | 4. Practicing open-book management |
| 5. Serving as a model of teamwork, including power sharing | 5. Selecting team-oriented members |
| 6. Using a consensus leadership style | 6. Using technology that facilitates teamwork |
| 7. Establishing urgency, demanding performance standards, and providing direction | 7. Developing a team book |
| 8. Encouraging competition with another group | |
| 9. Encouraging the use of jargon | |
| 10. Minimizing micromanagement | |
| 11. Practicing e-leadership | |

back on its number of suppliers, the organization should have the same intent also. Here are two examples of team mission statements:

- To plan and implement new manufacturing approaches to enhance our high-performance image and bolster our competitive edge
- To enhance our web site development capability so we can provide decision makers throughout the organization with assistance in developing web sites that exceed the state of the art

The leader can specify the mission when the team is formed or at any other time. Developing a mission for a long-standing team breathes new life into its activities. Being committed to a mission improves teamwork, as does the process of formulating a mission. The dialogue necessary for developing a clearly articulated mission establishes a climate in which team members can express feelings, ideas, and opinions. Participative leadership is required in developing a mission, as in most other ways of enhancing teamwork.

**Establishing a Climate of Trust** If team members do not trust each other or the leader, it is unlikely that they will work cooperatively together. As Kouzes and Posner note, trust is at the heart of collaboration. Unless team members trust each other, they will not be dependent on each other and therefore will not work well as a team.[10] A starting point in establishing a climate of trust is for the leader to be credible and engage in the many other trustworthy behaviors described in Chapter 2. Encouraging open communication about problems and sharing information are two specific ways the leader can help promote a climate of trust.

**Developing a Norm of Teamwork, Including Emotional Intelligence** A major strategy of teamwork development is to promote the attitude among group members that working together effectively is expected. Developing a norm of teamwork is difficult for a leader when a strong culture of individualism exists within a firm. Nokia Inc., the telecommunications firm based in Finland, illustrates the teamwork type of organizational culture. Part of the culture of collegiality can be traced to the Finnish character. It is natural for Nokia employees to work together and iron out differences of opinion.[11]

A belief in cooperation and collaboration rather than competitiveness as a strategy for building teamwork has been referred to as **cooperation theory.**[12] Individuals who are accustomed to competing with one another for recognition, salary increases, and resources must now collaborate. Despite the challenge of making a culture shift, the leader can make progress toward establishing a teamwork norm by doing the following:

- Encourage team members to treat one another as if they were customers, thus fostering cooperative behavior and politeness.
- Explicitly state the desirability of teamwork on a regular basis both orally and in writing.
- Communicate the norm of teamwork by frequently using words and phrases that support teamwork. Emphasizing the words *team members* or *teammate,* and deemphasizing the words *subordinates* and *employees,* helps communicate the norm of teamwork.

Normative statements about teamwork by influential team members are also useful in reinforcing the norm of teamwork. A team member might take a leadership role by saying to coworkers: "I'm glad this project is a joint effort. I know that's what earns us merit points here."

The leader's role in developing teamwork can also be described as helping the group develop emotional intelligence. The leader contributes to the group's emotional intelligence by creating norms that establish mutual trust among members. It is also important for members to have a sense of group identity as defined in their mission statement. Group efficacy, or feeling competent to complete the group task, also contributes to emotional intelligence. Ensuring that the group has the right skills can enhance such efficacy. These three conditions—mutual trust, group identity, and group efficacy—are the foundation of cooperation and collaboration.

The leader can also promote group emotional intelligence by bringing emotions to the surface in both group and one-on-one meetings. The leader then discusses how these emotions might be affecting the group's work.[13] For example, team members might discuss how they feel about their perceived importance to the organization. One maintenance group said that they felt entirely unappreciated until a key piece of equipment broke down, and this underappreciation was adversely affecting their morale. The team leader helped the group develop an internal public relations campaign about their contribution to productivity.

Another example of dealing with emotions is encouraging group members to speak up when they feel the group is being either unproductive or highly productive. Expressing positive emotion can be an energizer.

Table 9-2 presents additional rules and thoughts that are likely to bring about cooperation within the group. Additional insights about cooperation are important because teamwork and cooperation are almost synonymous.

| TABLE 9-2 | How to Generate Cooperation Within the Group |
|---|---|

1. The sensitive and effective leader knows how to obtain cooperation. He or she must understand that he or she probably does not have all the facts and opinions in a given situation.

2. The dynamic leader understands that he or she is able to work with any group member.

3. The effective leader acquires the capacity to empathize with others. Rather than demand the cooperation of others, he or she knows how to sell the advantages of cooperating.

4. The organized leader carefully plans projects and chooses the moment and the place where his or her ideas have the best chance of being accepted. He or she then presents these ideas clearly and concisely.

5. The successful leader recognizes that the other person is probably at least partially correct. Consequently, he or she does not let personal prejudices prevent him or her from accepting counterpropositions and valuable ideas. The leader knows that the group members are a little preoccupied with the ideas they think of, or use. So he or she keeps an open mind to these ideas, and gains the cooperation of others.

SOURCE: Translated from Serge Rioux, "Avez-Vous du Leadership en Tant Que Gestionnaire?" *Réunions*, Vol. 4, No. 3, 2004, p. 8. (Group Americor Inc., 2160 de la Montagne, bureau 740, Montréal, Québec, Canada, H3G 2T3, reunions@ca.inter.net.)

*Emphasizing Pride in Being Outstanding* A standard way to build team spirit, if not teamwork, is to help the group realize why it should be proud of its accomplishments. Most groups are particularly good at some task. The leader should help the group identify that task or characteristic and promote it as a key strength. A shipping department, for example, might have the best on-time shipping record in the region. Or a claims-processing unit might have the fewest overpayments in an insurance company.[14]

To try your hand at being part of an outstanding team, do Leadership Skill-Building Exercise 9-1.

**LEADERSHIP SKILL-BUILDING EXERCISE 9-1**

### SHELTERS FOR THE HOMELESS

This exercise should take about thirty-five minutes; it can be done inside or outside class. Organize the class into teams of about six people. Each team takes on the assignment of formulating plans for building temporary shelters for the homeless. The dwellings you plan to build, for example, might be two-room cottages with electricity and indoor plumbing. During the time allotted to the task, formulate plans for going ahead with Shelters for the Homeless. Consider dividing up work by assigning certain roles to each team member. Sketch out tentative answers to the following questions: (1) How will you obtain funding for your venture? (2) Which homeless people will you help? (3) Where will your shelters be? (4) Who will do the construction?

After your plan is completed, evaluate the quality of the teamwork that took place within the group. Review the chapter for techniques you might have used to improve it.

The same kind of teamwork skills you use in this exercise can be readily applied to most teamwork assignments on the job. Note carefully that although some types of teams call for members to be generalists, dividing up the tasks is still a basic principle of collective effort.

*Serving as a Model of Teamwork, Including Power Sharing* A powerful way for a leader to foster teamwork is to be a positive model of team play. And one way to exemplify teamwork is to reveal important information about ideas and attitudes relevant to the group's work. As a result of this behavior, team members may follow suit. A leader's self-disclosure fosters teamwork because it leads to shared perceptions and concerns.[15]

Interacting extensively with team members serves as a model of teamwork because it illustrates the mechanism by which team development takes place—frequent informal communication. While interacting with team members, the team leader can emphasize that he or she is a team member. For example, he or she might say, "Remember the deadline. We must all have the proposal in the mail by Thursday." A less team-member-oriented statement would be, "Remember the deadline. I need the proposals in the mail by Thursday."[16]

Another way of being a model of teamwork is to share power with group members because a good team player avoids hogging power and making all of the decisions. As each team member takes the opportunity to exert power, he or she feels more like a major contributor to team effort. Jon Gruden, the youngest coach in NFL history to win a Super Bowl, uses power sharing to build teamwork. He says he realizes the players "get a little sick of hearing from me all the time," so he breaks up the monotony by letting one assistant coach address the team before each week's game. Each coach is required to develop a metaphor and the keys to winning that game. For one game, the defensive line coach began by talking about a rock: "That rock is your opponent and you've got to keep pounding on it with a hammer."[17] As a result of sharing power, the coaches feel even more strongly that they are an integral part of Gruden's team.

To be a model of team play as a leader, you need the attitudes of a team player. Leadership Self-Assessment Quiz 9-2 gives you an opportunity to measure such attitudes.

LEADERSHIP SELF-ASSESSMENT QUIZ 9-2

### TEAM PLAYER ATTITUDES

Describe how well you agree with each of the following statements, using the following scale: disagree strongly (DS); disagree (D); neutral (N); agree (A); agree strongly (AS).

|  | DS | D | N | A | AS |
|---|---|---|---|---|---|
| 1. I am at my best when working alone. | 5 | 4 | 3 | 2 | 1 |
| 2. I have belonged to clubs and teams since I was a child. | 1 | 2 | 3 | 4 | 5 |
| 3. It takes far too long to get work accomplished with a group. | 5 | 4 | 3 | 2 | 1 |
| 4. I like the friendship of working in a group. | 1 | 2 | 3 | 4 | 5 |
| 5. I would prefer to run a one-person business than to be a member of a large firm. | 5 | 4 | 3 | 2 | 1 |
| 6. It is difficult to trust others in the group on key assignments. | 5 | 4 | 3 | 2 | 1 |
| 7. Encouraging others comes to me naturally. | 1 | 2 | 3 | 4 | 5 |
| 8. I like the give-and-take of ideas that is possible in a group. | 1 | 2 | 3 | 4 | 5 |
| 9. It is fun to share responsibility with others in the group. | 1 | 2 | 3 | 4 | 5 |

*(continued)*

**10.** Much more can be accomplished by a team than by the same number of people working alone    1    2    3    4    5

*Total score:* _____

SCORING AND INTERPRETATION Add the numbers you circled to obtain your total score.

- 41–50 You have strong positive attitudes toward being a team member and working cooperatively with other members.
- 30–40 You have moderately favorable attitudes toward being a team member and working cooperatively with other members.
- 10–29 You much prefer working by yourself to being a team member. To work effectively in a company that emphasizes teamwork, you may need to develop more positive attitudes toward working jointly with others.

***Using a Consensus Leadership Style*** Teamwork is enhanced when a leader practices consensus decision making. Contributing to important decisions helps group members feel that they are valuable to the team. Consensus decision making also leads to an exchange of ideas within the group, with group members supporting and refining each other's suggestions. As a result, the feeling of working jointly on problems is enhanced. Generation X managers (those who were born in 1965 or later) are likely to practice consensus leadership. Part of the reason is that many of these people have taken leadership courses. Bonnie Stedt, who holds the job title of senior relationship leader and executive vice president for American Express in New York City, makes this analysis of Gen-X managers:

> I look at them as a very promising generation. They bring so much to the work force especially as managers. Xers tend to be flexible, good at collaboration and consensus building and mature beyond their years. They are also capable of multitasking. Gen X managers are very team oriented, and they absolutely want everyone on the team to get credit.[18]

Another way of framing the consensus leadership style is saying that it reflects a belief in shared governance and partnerships instead of patriarchal caretaking.[19] (This is essentially the same idea as power sharing.) The team, rather than hierarchical departments, becomes the focus of organizational activity. As with the other tactics and techniques for enhancing teamwork, people have to participate in a cultural shift to fully accept shared governance.

Striving for consensus does not mean that all conflict is submerged to make people agree. Disagreements over issues are healthy, and team members are more likely to be committed to the consensus decision if their voice has been heard. An example of a conflict over an issue would be the marketing team of an automotive company debating whether dealer discounts improve sales in the long run.

***Establishing Urgency, Demanding Performance Standards, and Providing Direction*** Team members need to believe that the team has urgent, constructive purposes. They also want a list of explicit expectations. The more urgent and relevant the rationale is, the more likely it is that the team will achieve its potential. A customer service team was told that further growth for the corporation would be impossible without major improvements in providing service to customers. Energized by this information, the team met the challenge.

To help establish urgency, it is helpful for the leader to challenge the group regularly. Teamwork is enhanced when the leader provides the team valid facts and information that motivate them to work together to modify the status quo. New information prompts the team to redefine and enrich its understanding of the challenge it is facing. As a result, the team is likely to focus on a common purpose, set clearer goals, and work together more smoothly.[20]

***Encouraging Competition with Another Group*** One of the best-known methods of encouraging teamwork is rallying the support of the group against a real or imagined threat from the outside. Beating the competition makes more sense when the competition is outside your organization. When the enemy is within, the team spirit within may become detrimental to the overall organization, and we–they problems may arise. When encouraging competition with another group, the leader should encourage rivalry, not intense competition that might lead to unethical business practices, such as making false charges against them. Various groups at Dell have delighted and united in their competition with Hewlett-Packard and IBM.

***Encouraging the Use of Jargon*** Lee G. Bolman and Terrence E. Deal contend that the symbolic and ritualistic framework of a group contributes heavily to teamwork. An important part of this framework is a specialized language that fosters cohesion and commitment. In essence, this specialized language is in-group jargon that creates a bond among team members; sets the group apart from outsiders; reinforces unique values and beliefs, thus contributing to corporate culture; and allows team members to communicate easily, with few misunderstandings.[21] Examples of in-group jargon at Microsoft Corporation are to label an intelligent person as having "bandwith," and a serious person as being "hardcore."

***Minimizing Micromanagement*** A strategic perspective on encouraging teamwork is for the leader to minimize **micromanagement,** the close monitoring of most aspects of group member activities. To be a good team leader, the manager must give group members ample opportunity to manage their own activities. Avoiding micromanagement is a core ingredient of employee empowerment because empowered workers are given considerable latitude to manage their own activities.

United Auto Workers president Ronald A. Gettelfinger is an example of how a hands-on manager can often slip into the micromanagement mode. Gettelfinger values firsthand knowledge rather than filtered summaries. Part of his role is to be actively involved in union–management negotiations. But Gettelfinger is accused of being a micromanager because he has been known to pore over group members' telephone bills looking for personal phone calls.[22]

The contingency leader recognizes the fine line between avoiding micromanagement and not providing the guidance and accountability that team members may need to function well as a unit. Consultant Bruce Tulgan of consultancy RainmakerThinking, Inc.® reports, "When we asked employees what they want from the people above them, the first thing they mention is never a raise. It's always more coaching, more guidance, clearer goals, more constructive criticism, and more recognition for achievement."[23] An implication is that a manager tinged with a little micromanagement is likely to engage in these constructive behaviors.

Leadership Self-Assessment Quiz 9-3 provides some assistance in helping you avoid becoming a micromanager. This skill is important because in most leadership situations, being perceived as a micromanager is a liability.

**LEADERSHIP SELF-ASSESSMENT QUIZ 9-3**

### OVERCOMING MICROMANAGEMENT

This brief self-quiz and accompanying suggestions provide some useful insights into avoiding micromanagement. Keeping micromanagement tendencies under control is important because the team is likely to feel more empowered, and the most capable team members will feel less like quitting. Furthermore, holding on to unimportant tasks cuts dramatically into a leader's productivity and that of staff. Is micromanagement impeding your progress?

**INSTRUCTIONS** Ask yourself these four questions, and circle the appropriate answer:

| | | |
|---|---|---|
| **1.** I sign off on all projects, from large to small. | Yes | No |
| **2.** Most decisions end up in my lap. | Yes | No |
| **3.** I feel overwhelmed by administrative tasks. | Yes | No |
| **4.** Staff turnover is high and morale is low. | Yes | No |

INTERPRETATION If you answered "Yes" two or more times, you need to learn how to modify your death-grip management style.

SKILL DEVELOPMENT The following three steps can help you feel more comfortable delegating and also encourage employee growth.

1. **Establish a trust level for each staffer.** For example, Helen has excellent judgment, so give her project authority. Although Tim is an excellent worker, you need to supervise him closely.
2. **Make sure staffers understand your instructions.** Ask them to repeat assignments verbally and confirm complex tasks with a follow-up email message.
3. **Open multiple avenues of communication.** Establish check-in, interim, and deadline dates. Follow up faithfully. Tell employees that your door is always open, but give them a good sense of how much authority they have and when they should consult you. Ask staffers, "How's it going?" occasionally. Then let them get on with their work.

SOURCE: From "Power Productivity: Stop Micromanaging and Spur Productivity," in *Manager's Edge*, July 2002, p. 6. Adapted from *The Organized Executive*, Briefings Publishing Group, (800) 722-9221.

***Practicing E-Leadership*** In organizations today, the Internet, including email, influences a leader's work to some extent. If team leader Jennifer based in Seattle sends a note of congratulations to team member Surinda based in Bombay, she is practicing e-leadership. Jennifer and Surinda are part of a virtual team: they work with each other yet do not share the same physical facility. **E-leadership** is a form of leadership practiced in a context where work is mediated by information technology. The focus of leadership shifts from individuals to networks of relationships because the Internet facilitates connecting so many people.[24] E-leadership could, therefore, encompass any activity undertaken by a leader when the Internet connects people. Our concern here is how e-leadership facilitates building teamwork.

When team members are geographically dispersed, a leader's communication with team members takes place using information technology, including the dissemination of information needed for task accomplishment. A participative leader may establish chatrooms to solicit opinions from members of a cross-border virtual team before reaching a final decision. The leader might also conduct an electronic poll to attain consensus on a controversial issue. The leader can foster team spirit (and therefore teamwork) by sending congratulatory email messages for a job well done. In short, the e-leader improves teamwork by staying connected electronically to team members—although not to the point of blitzing them with so many messages that he or she becomes an annoyance.

college.hmco.com/pic/
dubrin5e

**KB** @ **KNOWLEDGE BANK:** contains two additional suggestions for improving teamwork through actions the leader can take on his or her own.

## Actions Generally Requiring Organization Structure or Policy

***Designing Physical Structures That Facilitate Communication*** Group cohesiveness, and therefore teamwork, is fostered when team members are located close together and can interact frequently and easily. In contrast, people who spend most of their time in their private offices or cubicles are less likely to interact. Frequent interaction often leads to camaraderie and a feeling of belongingness. A useful tactic for achieving physical proximity is to establish a shared physical facility, such as a conference room, research library, or beverage lounge. This area should be decorated differently from other areas in the building, and a few amenities should be added, such as a coffeepot, microwave oven, and refrigerator. Team members can then use this area for refreshments and group interaction.

Recognizing the contribution of a shared physical facility to promoting teamwork, many organizations have incorporated more open working space into the workplace, often eliminating private offices. Many people express dissatisfaction with this lack of privacy, but no information has been published to date about the productivity loss and morale problems stemming from limited opportunity for quiet reflection on the job.

***Emphasizing Group Recognition and Rewards*** Giving rewards for group accomplishment reinforces teamwork because people receive rewards for what they have achieved collaboratively. The recognition accompanying the reward should emphasize the team's value to the organization rather than that of the individual. Recognition promotes team identity by enabling the team to take pride in its contributions and progress. The following are examples of team recognition:

- A display wall for team activities such as certificates of accomplishment, schedules, and miscellaneous announcements
- Team logos on items such as identifying T-shirts, athletic caps, mugs, jackets, key rings, and business cards
- Celebrations to mark milestones such as first-time activities, cost savings, and safety records
- Equipment painted in team colors
- Athletic team events such as softball, volleyball, and bowling
- Team-of-the-Month award, with gifts from the organization to team members or to the entire team

An extensive study of high-performing work teams concluded that financial rewards for teams should take the following form: pay for skills, team performance pay, gain sharing, and profit sharing. The last two of these practices require the organization to modify traditional reward systems that reinforce individual accomplishment. A caution is that many employees may view switching to a team-based pay plan that places much of their pay at risk as an unnerving proposition.[25]

***Initiating Ritual and Ceremony*** Another way to enhance teamwork is to initiate ritual and ceremony.[26] Ritual and ceremony afford opportunities for reinforcing values, revitalizing spirit, and bonding workers to one another and to the team. An example is holding a team dinner whenever the group achieves a major milestone, such as making a winning bid on a major contract. Another formal ritual is to send a team on a retreat to develop its mission and goals and to build camaraderie. When the team is working and socializing closely together during the retreat—even one long day—teamwork is reinforced.

***Practicing Open-Book Management*** An increasingly popular method of getting the company working together as a team is to share information about company finances and strategy with large numbers of employees. In **open-book management** every employee is trained, empowered, and motivated to understand and pursue the company's business goals. In this way employees become business partners and perceive themselves to be members of the same team. In a full form of open-book management, workers share strategic and financial information as well as responsibility. The company also shares risks and rewards based on results, so workers are likely to pull together as a team so that the company can succeed.[27] The idea is to have a well-informed, partner-oriented, high-performance company. Part of keeping workers well informed is for company leaders to host roundtable discussions about company financial information. Another approach is to regularly disseminate by email information about the company's financial progress.[28] The accompanying Leader in Action illustrates how a business owner uses open-finance (book) management to facilitate teamwork.

## LEADER IN ACTION

### OPEN-BOOK MANAGEMENT AT ZINGERMAN'S

Foodies love Zingerman's zest for the finer things in culinary life. Entrepreneurs can envy its knack for creating new businesses, evidence of the twenty-two-year-old deli and food company's ability to marry innovation, high standards, and obsessive customer service without the attitude to match. The latest example: The Zingerman's Roadshow, a 1952 Spartan trailer acquired off eBay that's peddling trademark sandwiches, soups, and drinks in a parking lot.

Business heads could respect how cofounders Ari Weinzweig and Paul Saginaw use the discipline of open-book finance to give everyone who works in the Zingerman's Community of Businesses the feeling of being an owner. From dishwashers at the Roadhouse to the management partner of the Bakehouse, they all see the books. Every week.

Managing costs and watching net operating profit margins is just as important (and difficult) in the nine Zingerman businesses as it is in autos, airlines, and steel. And up-to-date information tied to the bottom line can be as crucial to deciding which olive oil to reorder as it is in deciding how much cold-rolled steel to purchase. It is all business, and information makes it run.

Zingerman's aspires to grow to between twelve and fifteen businesses around Ann Arbor, Michigan, by 2009. To support this growth, management's attitude is not us-versus-them as much as it is "we," and the commitment to the bottom line is really a commitment to three bottom lines: food, service, and profitability.

"Who's responsible for financial performance? Everybody," says Weinzweig. His wiry build belies a daily life surrounded by artisanal breads and the finest-quality cheeses, olive oils and sea salts.

"Do I have more responsibility? Sure. So what?" he says. "To not know [the numbers] is to play the game for five years and you don't know the score but you're supposed to go out and give 100 percent."

Who's most attuned to waste in a restaurant? The dishwashers who scrape leftovers from the plates, not line cooks or the executive chef. Yet big decisions are made by the partners' group, now fourteen strong, with Weinzweig and Saginaw holding the veto power. They've yet to exercise it.

The Zingerman recipe works: the food, the retail goods, the service, and the story of financial growth. It's about attention to detail, harnessing the wits of employees, listening to customers, and unapologetically charging people what a product or service is worth because enough people will pay it.

### QUESTIONS

1. How might open-book finance contribute to teamwork at Zingerman's?
2. What does "harnessing the wits of employees" have to do with teamwork?

SOURCE: "Zingerman's Open Concept Serves Up Sweet Success," by Daniel Howes, *Detroit News*, July 1, 2004. Reprinted with permission from the *Detroit News*.

***Selecting Team-Oriented Members*** A heavy-impact method of building teamwork is to select team members who are interested in and capable of teamwork. A starting point is self-selection. It is best for the team leader to choose workers who ask to be members of a team. A person's record of past team activity can also help one determine whether that person is an effective team player. Many managers believe that those who participate in team sports now or in the past are likely to be good team players on the job. Many female executives contend that the sports they played while growing up helped prepare them for the team aspects of corporate life. In one study, 81 percent of the 401 businesswomen surveyed agreed that sports helped them function better on a team. In addition, 69 percent said that sports promoted the leadership skills that contributed to professional success.[29]

***Using Technology That Enhances Teamwork*** Workers can collaborate better when they use information technology that fosters collaboration, often referred to as *groupware*. For example, the straightforward act of exchanging frequent email messages and instant messages can facilitate cooperation. Electronic brainstorming is another example of groupware. An important new development is web sites where workers can collaborate to save time and money on activities as varied as product design and mergers. Companies can now make products more cheaply and quickly by using the Web to synchronize the various aspects of design with suppliers. For example, by using a system of collaborative software at General Motors Corporation factories, management has cut the time it takes to complete a vehicle mockup from twelve weeks to two weeks.[30]

The link to teamwork is that members of different groups work more smoothly as a team with members outside the group. This is somewhat different from the emphasis in this chapter on teamwork *within* the group.

***Developing a Team Book*** Using only a modest amount of company resources, a leader can often enhance teamwork by developing and distributing a team book that can be distributed in hard copy or by email with the book attached. The book contains a one-page biography of each team member, along with at least one photo, a list of hobbies and interests, and family information. It also can contain a comment page for other team members to make serious or light-hearted comments. As group members flip through the book, they become better acquainted with their coworkers, and perhaps they develop more camaraderie as they get to know each other better.[31]

## Outdoor Training and Team Development

Cognitive information about strategies and tactics for improving teamwork is potentially valuable. The person reading such information can selectively apply the concepts, observe the consequences, and then fine-tune his or her approach. Another approach to developing teamwork is to participate in experiential activities (several are presented throughout this text).

The most popular experiential approach to building teamwork and leadership skills is outdoor training, also referred to as offsite training. Wilderness training is closely associated with outdoor training, except that the setting is likely to be much rougher—perhaps in the frozen tundra of northernmost Minnesota. Some forms of outdoor training take place in city parks.

Both outdoor and wilderness training are forms of learning by doing. Participants are supposed to acquire leadership and teamwork skills by confronting physical challenges and exceeding their self-imposed limitations. The goals of outdoor training are reasonably consistent across different training groups. The Big Rock Creek Camp, which offers team building and leadership training, specifies these representative goals:

- Discover your strengths and weaknesses.
- Test your limits (they are far broader than you imagine).
- Work together as a team.
- Have fun.
- Face the essence of who you are and what you are made of.
- Have the opportunity to break through barriers within yourself.
- Have the opportunity to break through barriers between yourself and others.

## Features of Outdoor and Offsite Training Programs

Program participants are placed in a demanding outdoor environment, where they rely on skills they did not realize they had and on one another to complete the program. The emphasis is on building not only teamwork but also self-confidence for leadership. Sometimes lectures on leadership, self-confidence, and teamwork precede the activity. The list of what constitutes a team-building activity continues to grow and now includes tightrope walking, adventure racing, treasure hunts (such as finding a store mannequin with red hair), cooking, as well as banging drums and shaking maracas. Building or repairing houses for people in need is gaining in popularity, as described in the chapter introduction. Another recent approach is for participants to work with horses in a stable to simulate the role of the boss and employee (played by the horse). In one of these team-building activities, blindfolded individuals mount the horses and rely on coworkers to guide them through an obstacle course.[32] Some of the editorial and art staff at *Entrepreneur* magazine

> participated in a team-building workshop run by the Center for Strategic Leadership at Irvine Valley College in Irvine, California. The event included maneuvering a wooden A-frame across a field (to teach teamwork); cramming seven people on three squares of carpet remnants while moving toward a finish line (to teach closeness, presumably); and grabbing hands to form a human knot, then untangling [themselves] (to teach creative problem solving).[33]

Outward Bound is the best-known and largest outdoor training program. It offers more than 500 courses in wilderness areas in twenty states and provinces. The courses typically run from three days to four weeks. Worldwide, Outward Bound runs about forty-eight schools on five continents. The Outward Bound Professional Development Program, geared toward organizational leaders, emphasizes teamwork, leadership, and risk taking. The wilderness is the classroom, and the instructors draw analogies between each outdoor activity and the workplace. Among the courses offered are dog-sledding, skiing and winter camping, desert backpacking, canoe expeditions, sailing, sea kayaking, alpine mountaineering, mountain backpacking and horsetrailing, and cycling.

Rope activities are typical of outdoor training. Participants are attached to a secure pulley with ropes; then they climb up a ladder and jump off to another spot.

Sometimes the rope is extended between two trees. Another activity is a "trust fall," in which each person takes a turn standing on a platform and falling backward into the arms of coworkers. The trust fall can also be done on ground level. To examine a trust fall firsthand, do Leadership Skill-Building Exercise 9-2. A similar activity used in offsite training is presented in Leadership Skill-Building Exercise 9-3.

**LEADERSHIP SKILL-BUILDING EXERCISE 9-2**

### THE TRUST FALL

Perhaps the most widely used team-building activity is the trust fall, which may be familiar to many readers. Nevertheless, each application of this exercise is likely to produce new and informative results. The class organizes itself into teams. In each team, each willing member stands on a chair and falls backward into the arms of teammates. A less frightening alternative to falling off a chair is to simply fall backward standing up. Team members who for whatever physical or mental reason would prefer not to fall back into others or participate in catching others are unconditionally excluded. However, they can serve as observers. After the trust falls have been completed, a team leader gathers answers to the following questions and then shares the answers with the rest of the class.

**1.** How does this exercise develop teamwork?

**2.** How does this exercise develop leadership skills?

**3.** What did the participants learn about themselves?

Outdoor training enhances teamwork by helping participants examine the process of getting things done through working with people. Participants practice their communication skills in exercises such as rappelling down a cliff by issuing precise instructions to one another about how to scale the cliff safely. At the same time, they have to learn to trust one another because their survival appears to depend on trust.

### *Evaluation of Outdoor Training for Team Development*

Many outdoor trainers and participants believe strongly that they derived substantial personal benefits from outdoor training. Among the most important are greater self-confidence, appreciating hidden strengths, and learning to work better with others. Strong proponents of outdoor training believe that those who do not appreciate the training simply do not understand it. Many training directors also have positive attitudes toward outdoor training. They believe that a work team that experiences outdoor training will work more cooperatively back at the office.

### TRUST ME

Part of trusting team members is to trust them with your physical safety. The trust builder described here has been incorporated into many team-building programs. Proceed as follows:

- *Step 1:* Each group member takes a turn being blindfolded, perhaps using a bandanna.
- *Step 2:* The remaining team members arrange between five and eight chairs into a formation of their choosing, using a different formation for each blindfolded member.
- *Step 3:* At the appropriate signal from a team member, the blindfolded person starts to walk. The rest of the team gives instructions that will enable the blindfolded person to get past the formation of chairs without a collision.
- *Step 4:* At the end of the blindfolded person's experience, he or she immediately answers the following questions: (a) How did you feel when blindfolded in this exercise? (b) Explain why you either trusted or did not trust your team members. (c) What did you need from your team members while you were blindfolded?
- *Step 5:* After each person has taken a turn, discuss in your team (a) the impact of this exercise on the development of trust in teams and (b) what you learned about teamwork from the exercise.

Many people have legitimate reservations about outdoor training, however. Although outdoor trainers claim that almost no accidents occur, a threat to health and life does exist. (To help minimize casualties, participants usually need medical clearance.) Another concern is that the teamwork learned in outdoor training does not spill over into the job environment. As Jay Conger explains, the workplace is a different environment from the wilderness. And real workplace teams tend to gain and lose their members rapidly as teammates are transferred, promoted, terminated, or quit. This mobility often negates all the team-building efforts that take place during the experience. Another problem is that when teams return to work, they often revert to noncollaborative behavior.[34] Based on his research, management professor Chris Neck concludes that there is little compelling evidence of long-term benefits for entire teams, but there is evidence that individuals' attitudes and teamwork skills improve immediately after the exercises.[35]

An insightful perspective on the pros and cons of outdoor training comes from the *Entrepreneur* work group mentioned earlier:

The verdict? Mixed. Some participants had fun. "It was a field trip," was a common phrase. Others, those not keen on their personal space being invaded, left feeling unhappy rather than inspired. Did we return to the office a better team? Not really.

The lessons about every person being integral to the larger mission and the need for flexibility rang true but, um, we sort of already knew that.

Still, we probably could have gotten more out of the session if time constraints hadn't kept us from attending the pre- and post-training meetings typically held. The pre-training meetings would have identified areas we needed to work on: the post-training meeting would have helped us translate what we accomplished to the office.[36]

One way to facilitate the transfer of training from outdoors to the office is to hold debriefing and follow-up sessions. Debriefing takes place at the end of outdoor training. The participants review what they learned and discuss how they will apply their lessons to the job. Follow-up sessions can then be held periodically to describe progress in applying the insights learned during outdoor training.

## The Leader–Member Exchange Model and Teamwork

Research and theory about the development of teamwork lag research and theory about many other aspects of leadership. Nevertheless, the leader–member exchange model, developed by George Graen and associates, helps explain why one subgroup in a unit is part of a cohesive team but another group is excluded.[37] The **leader–member exchange model (LMX)** proposes that leaders develop unique working relationships with group members. One subset of employees, the in-group, is given additional rewards, responsibility, and trust in exchange for their loyalty and performance. The in-group becomes part of a smoothly functioning team headed by the formal leader. In contrast, the out-group employees are treated in accordance with a more formal understanding of leader–group member relations. Out-group members are less likely to experience good teamwork.

Figure 9-2 depicts the major concept of the leader–exchange model. Here we look at several aspects of LMX as it relates most closely to teamwork. Leader–member exchange has also been researched in relationship to many other aspects of workplace behavior.

### Different-Quality Relationships

Graen and his associates argue that leaders do not typically use the same leadership style in dealing with all group members. Instead, they treat each member somewhat differently. The linkages (relationships) that exist between the leader and each individual team member probably differ in quality. In theory, the differences lie on a continuum of low quality to high quality. With group members on the top half of the continuum, the leader has a good relationship; with those on the lower half of the continuum, the leader has a poor relationship. Each of these pairs of relationships, or dyads, must be judged in terms of whether a group member is "in" or "out" with the leader. The positive regard that leaders and members have for each other is a major contributor to the quality of their relationship, as documented by a study conducted in the marketing division of an electric company.[38]

Members of the in-group are invited to participate in important decision making, are given added responsibility, and are privy to interesting gossip. Members of the out-group are managed according to the requirements of their employment contract. They receive little warmth, inspiration, or encouragement. Robert

**FIGURE 9-2** The Leader–Member Exchange Model

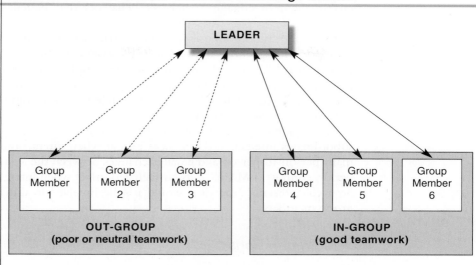

Source: From Gregory Moorhead and Ricky W. Griffin, *Organizational Behavior: Managing People and Organizations*, Fourth Edition, p. 314. Copyright © 1995 by Houghton Mifflin Company. Reprinted by permission of Houghton Mifflin Company.

Vecchio explains that an in-group member is elevated to the unofficial role of trusted assistant.[39] An out-group member is treated much like a hired hand. In-group members tend to achieve a higher level of performance, commitment, and satisfaction than do out-group members. Furthermore, they are less likely to quit. A study conducted in a retail setting found that when the quality of the leader–member exchange is high, group members are more strongly committed to company goals.[40] In turn, this commitment leads to stronger teamwork because the workers pull together to pursue goals.

The in-group versus out-group status also includes an element of reciprocity or exchange. The leader grants more favors to the in-group member, who in response works harder to please the leader, a contributor to being a good team player. Two studies provide more specific information about the consequences of a positive exchange between a supervisor and group members. In a hospital setting, positive exchanges involved group members' engaging in increased good citizenship behavior and in-group role behaviors such as putting extra effort into performing their duties.[41] As a result, the leader would feel justified in granting the in-group members more resources, such as a larger salary increase or a larger budget.

A study conducted in diverse industrial settings also found that high-quality exchanges between supervisors and employees contribute to employees' engaging in extra-role behavior, or being cooperative in ways that were not expected of them. Supervisory ratings of employee altruism were used to measure helping behaviors, as when an accountant helps a sales representative prepare a sales forecast. The researchers concluded that through the development of high-quality relationships with group members, supervisors are able to motivate the group members and enable them to engage in helping behaviors that benefit them as well as their coworkers.[42]

One contribution of positive LMXs is that they facilitate good safety performance, an important aspect of teamwork in many work environments. Sixty-four group leaders in a manufacturing plant participated in a study. A major finding of the study was that positive leader–member exchanges were associated with more communication about safety. The enhanced communication led to more commitment to safety, which in turn led to fewer accidents on the job.[43]

New evidence suggests that LMX depends on how frequently supervisors and subordinates interact. LMX is most potent when interactions are frequent, such as many person-to-person and email exchanges between the leader and the group member. In contrast, LMX has substantially less effect when interactions are infrequent.[44] So a cold, distant supervisor would not be involved in different relationships with group members.

## First Impressions

The leader's first impression of a group member's competency plays an important role in placing the group member in the in-group or the out-group. Another key linking factor is whether the leader and team member have positive or negative chemistry. We can assume that group members who make effective use of influence and political tactics increase their chances of becoming members of the in-group.

A field study seems to confirm that first impressions make a difference. The researchers gathered ratings of six aspects of the manager–group member dyad. One measure was the group members' perceived similarity with the leader. For example, "My supervisor and I are alike in a number of ways." A second measure was feelings about the manager, such as, "I like my supervisor very much as a friend." A third rating dealt directly with the member's view of the LMX: for example, "I can count on my supervisor to 'bail me out,' even at his or her expense, when I really need it."

A fourth rating measured the leader expectation of the member, such as, "I think my new employee will be an excellent employee." A fifth rating measured leader liking of the member, such as, "I like my subordinate very much as a person." A sixth rating was the leader's view of the LMX, including a rating of the statement, "I would be willing to 'bail out' my subordinate, even at my own expense, if he or she really needed it."

Results showed that the initial leader expectations of members and member expectations of the leader were good predictors of the leader–member exchanges at two weeks and at six weeks. Member expectations of the leader also accurately predicted member assessments of the quality of the leader–member exchange at six months. An important interpretation of these results is that the leader–member exchange is formed in the first days of the relationship.[45] As the adage states, "You have only one chance to make a first impression."

In summary, the leader–member exchange model provides a partial explanation of teamwork development. Members of the in-group work smoothly together and with the leader because they feel privileged. Being a member of the out-group may not diminish teamwork, but it certainly does not make a positive contribution.

READER'S ROADMAP

So far we have studied considerable information about the nature of leadership; the attributes, behaviors, and styles of leaders; the ethics and social responsibility of leaders; and how leaders exert power and use politics and influence. The techniques for developing teamwork are part of a leader's relationship with the group, as is the subject of the next chapter, motivational skills.

## Summary

college.hmco.com/pic/dubrin5e

Leaders are required to build teamwork because it is needed for such key activities as group problem solving and achieving high quality. Teamwork is an understanding of and commitment to group goals on the part of all group members. Team leaders share power, deemphasize individual glory, and understand that power sharing increases their own power. The solo style of leader is the traditional autocratic leader in a bureaucracy.

Leaders still play an important role in a team-based organization, such as being expert in the team process, being facilitators, building trust and inspiring teamwork, and enabling and empowering group members to accomplish their work. The enabling role centers on empowerment.

A wide range of leader actions foster teamwork. Measures leaders can take using their own resources include (1) defining the team's mission; (2) establishing a climate of trust; (3) developing a norm of teamwork, including emotional intelligence; (4) emphasizing pride in being outstanding; (5) serving as a model of teamwork, including power sharing; (6) using a consensus leadership style; (7) establishing urgency, demanding performance standards, and providing direction; (8) encouraging competition with another group; (9) encouraging the use of jargon; (10) minimizing micromanagement; and (11) practicing e-leadership.

Techniques to foster teamwork that require relying on organizational structure or policy include the following: (1) designing physical structures that facilitate communication; (2) emphasizing group recognition and rewards; (3) initiating ritual and ceremony; (4) practicing open-book management; (5) selecting team-oriented members; (6) using technology that facilitates teamwork; and (7) developing a team book.

In outdoor (or offsite) training, a popular experiential approach to building teamwork and leadership skills, building self-confidence is the focus. Outdoor training enhances teamwork by helping participants examine the process of collaboration. The Outward Bound Professional Development Program is geared toward organization leaders. Opinion about the effectiveness of outdoor training for developing teamwork and leadership skills is mixed. Concern has been expressed that the skills learned in the field do not carry over to the workplace.

The leader–exchange model helps explain why one subgroup in a work unit is part of a cohesive team and another unit is excluded. According to the model, leaders develop unique working relationships with subordinates. As a result, in-groups and out-groups are created. Members of the in-group tend to perform better, have higher satisfaction, and exhibit more teamwork than members of the out-group. The leader's first impression of a group member's competency plays an important role in placing that person into the in-group or the out-group.

## Key Terms

Team

Teamwork

Cooperation theory

Micromanagement

E-leadership

Open-book management

Leader–member exchange model (LMX)

## ✔ Guidelines for Action and Skill Development

Improving teamwork through the design of offices is receiving considerable attention. Texas Professional Training Associates explains how to customize your (you being the leader/manager) space to promote teamwork:

1. **Create common areas.** Have ample space, accessible from throughout your office, for the team to meet formally and informally. Leave your team-meeting tools—flip charts, whiteboards—in place even when the team is not meeting.

2. **Put yourself in the center.** Instead of reserving the back office, try to put yourself in the middle. You can be close to day-to-day action and more accessible to your team.

3. **Set up multipurpose rooms.** The back office can be used as a well-equipped workroom or library whenever team members—individually or in groups—feel they would be more productive away from their desks.

4. **Insert "activity generators."** Lively activity depends on having "generators" to draw traffic and bring people together. In your office, this could be the coffeepot, the mailboxes, or the reception desk. Turn these areas into places for team members to gather and interact comfortably and productively.[46]

## Discussion Questions and Activities

1. What would be the potential disadvantages of selecting a team leader who is highly charismatic and visionary?

2. Identify several collective work products from any group in which you have worked.

3. Identify and describe any team you have been a member of, or know about otherwise, that has a strong norm of teamwork.

4. Is there a role for independent-thinking, decisive, and creative leaders in a team-based organization? Explain.

5. What forces for and against being a good team player are embedded in American culture?

6. You have probably been told many times to minimize jargon in speech and writing in order to enhance communication, yet this chapter advocates using jargon to encourage teamwork. How do you reconcile the difference between the two pieces of advice?

7. In what way is e-leadership different from any other form of leadership?

8. What is your opinion of the value of experience in team sports for becoming a good team player in the workplace?

9. Why would the team-building activity of preparing a gourmet meal lead to enhanced teamwork back on the job?

10. How can political skill help a person avoid being adversely affected by the leader–member exchange model?

## LEADERSHIP CASE PROBLEM A

## WHY CAN'T WE WORK LIKE A REAL TEAM?

Crystal Motors is a new car dealer representing two U.S.-made luxury vehicles. Following the traditional organization structure of an automobile dealership, the company is divided into three segments: sales, service, and the office. The credit department is considered part of the office. Charlie Ventura is the president and owner of Crystal Motors, Marcie Magellan is manager of the service department, and Rob Waters is the office manager.

Crystal Motors has been profitable for ten consecutive years despite heavy competition from luxury foreign vehicles. About 10 percent of the company's profits stem directly from the sale of vehicles, 5 percent from commissions on financing, and about 85 percent from the service department. When asked about this imbalance in profits, Ventura explained, "It's the nature of the beast. When consumers see the sticker price on our vehicles, they think we're making a bundle on each one that we sell. The truth nationwide is that it is very difficult to make money on car sales alone. Commissions on vehicles financed through us help a little with profits, but our real margins come from service."

Ventura is looking to boost profits for the upcoming year. He thinks that it will be difficult to squeeze much more profit from sales. Ventura notes that his marketing budget is already quite high and that his sales staff is well trained and effective. He worries that the escalating cost of fuel and all the publicity about the negative impact of large vehicles on the environment will constrain sales for the next few years. As a consequence, Ventura thinks that his best chance for improving profit margins is to increase the efficiency of the service department. "Marcie and I agree that we have a long way to go to get our service department to get its act together," says Ventura.

The service department is divided into teams, each assigned a different color: green, blue, red,

orange, and purple. After a customer purchases a vehicle, he or she is assigned to one of the color-coded teams. Magellan explains that each team is assigned a team leader who represents the face to the public and is also responsible for making sure the vehicle in question is serviced properly. All of the teams use the same centralized body shop.

When asked about the inefficiencies in the service department, Magellan's eyebrows rose. "My take is that a team is supposed to work together," she said. "Our technicians and general helpers work on their own without acting as if they are part of a true team. Just last week I got this ticked-off customer screaming at me. She told me that she found grease stains on the white leather seats of her $50,000 convertible. I asked Jason, the Green Team leader, what happened. He said it wasn't the team's fault because the person who is supposed to put protective paper inside the car before the vehicle is serviced didn't show up for work that day.

"I remember several times that a car wasn't cleaned and polished in time for the scheduled customer pickup. It's not too cool when you pick up a new $40,000 vehicle when there is caked mud on the bottom of the fenders. That time the Red Team leader told me that car wash gal was overloaded the day the car was to be picked up by the customer."

Ventura commented that he has heard about instances in which poor cooperation has resulted in lost opportunities to generate revenues from repairs. "Here let me show you a customer complaint card," said Ventura:

Last week I had my car in for a lube, oil change, and tire rotation. I assumed that when I picked up my car, everything was okay. But two days later, I had this terrible vibration when I stepped on the brakes. I was so angry with Crystal

*(continued)*

Motors for not having found this problem that I went to Midas to get the brake work done.

"We found out later that the person who switched the tires on the car in question did see a bent rod under the car, but figured that the team leader was responsible for finding problems. So he didn't report the problem."

Magellan agreed that teamwork could stand improvement in the service department. She said, "I guess we need to work more like a pit crew, and less like a bunch of guys and gals just coming to work and doing their jobs."

## QUESTIONS

1. What do you recommend that leadership at Crystal Motors do to enhance teamwork in the service department?
2. What different contributions might Ventura and Magellan make in enhancing teamwork in the service department?
3. What do you recommend that the team leaders do to get the service technicians and general workers to cooperate better with each other?
4. In what way is a pit crew an effective team?

# LEADERSHIP CASE PROBLEM B

## SHOWBOAT BRENT

Mary Tarkington, CEO of one of the major dot-com retailers, became concerned that too many employees at the company were stressed out and physically unhealthy. Tarkington said, "I have walked through our distribution center at many different times of the day and night, and I see the same troublesome scene. The place is littered with soft drink cans and fast-food wrappers. Loads of our workers have stomachs bulging out of their pants. You always see a few workers huddled outside the building smoking. The unhealthiness around the company is also reflected in high absenteeism rates and health insurance costs that are continually rising.

"I want to see a big improvement in the health of our employees. It makes sense from the standpoint of being a socially responsible company and from the standpoint of becoming more profitable. With this in mind, I am appointing a project team to study how we can best design and implement a company wellness program. Each member of the team will work about five hours per week on the project. I want to receive a full report in forty-five days, and I expect to see progress reports along the way."

Five people were appointed to the wellness task force: Ankit, a programmer; Jennifer, a web site designer; Brent, a systems analyst; Derek, a logistics technician; and Kristine, a human resource specialist. During the first meeting, the group appointed Kristine head of the Wellness Task Force because of her professional specialty. Ankit, Jennifer, and Derek offered Kristine their congratulations and wished her the best. Brent offered a comment with a slightly different tone: "I can see why the group chose you to head our task force. I voted for you also, but I think we should be starting with a blank tablet. We are making no assumptions that anybody's ideas carry more professional weight than anybody else's ideas."

The next time the group met, each member reported some preliminary findings about wellness programs they had researched. Ankit summarized a magazine article on the topic; Jennifer reported on a friend's experience with his company wellness program; Derek presented some data on how wellness programs can boost productivity and morale; Kristine reported on *www.workforce.com*, a human resources web site that carries information about wellness programs. Each spent about six minutes on the presentation.

Brent then walked up to the front of the conference room, and engaged his laptop computer. He began a twenty-five minute PowerPoint presentation about what he thought the committee should be doing, along with industry data about wellness programs. At the end of Brent's presentation, Kristine commented with a quizzical look, "Thanks Brent, but I thought we agreed to around a five-minute presentation this first time around."

Brent replied, "Good point, Kristine, yet I'm only doing what I considered best for getting our mission accomplished."

Ten days later, CEO Tarkington visited the task force to discuss its progress. Kristine, as the task force head, began the progress report. She pointed out that the group had gathered substantial information about corporate wellness programs. Kristine noted that so far, establishing one at the company looked feasible and worthwhile. The group was beginning to assemble data about the physical requirements for having a wellness program and the cost of implementation.

With a frown, Brent said, "Not so fast, Kristine. Since we last met, I have taken another look at the productivity figures about wellness centers. People who run wellness programs apparently supplied these figures, so the information could be tainted. I say that we are rushing too fast to reach a decision. Let's get some objective data before making a recommendation to the company."

Kristine inwardly groaned as she looked at Mary Tarkington and the task force members. She whispered to Jennifer to her right, "There goes Brent, showboating again."

## QUESTIONS

1. What steps should Mary Tarkington take to develop better teamwork among the members of her task force?
2. What actions, if any, should the other task force members take to make Brent a better team player?
3. What kind of power is Brent attempting to establish for himself?

LEADERSHIP SKILL-BUILDING EXERCISE 9-4

### MY LEADERSHIP PORTFOLIO

Now that you have studied a basketful of ideas about enhancing teamwork, you can add to your skill repertoire by implementing a few of these tactics. The next time you are involved in group activity, as either the leader or a group member, attempt to enhance cooperation and teamwork within the group. Make specific use of at least two of the recommended tactics for improving teamwork. Make an entry in your journal after your first attempts to enhance teamwork. Here is an example:

I am the head of the Hispanic Business Club at our college. Attendance hasn't been too great in recent meetings, and the club seems headed nowhere. So at our last meeting, I suggested that we devote the entire meeting to building a mission statement. I explained that if we knew what our purpose was, maybe we would pull together better. We are still working on the mission, but so far it has to do with enhancing the impact and reputation of Hispanic business leaders. I also suggested that we invest in T-shirts with a logo we could be proud of. This idea may sound hokey, but the group really rallied around the idea of building unity through new T-shirts.

## INTERNET SKILL-BUILDING EXERCISE

Apply the chapter concepts! Visit the Web, and complete this Internet skill-building exercise to learn more about current leadership topics and trends.

### ARE YOU CUT OUT FOR TEAMWORK?

Monster Career Center offers a quiz to indicate how suited you are to being an effective team member. Visit *http://content.monster.com/tools/quizzes/teamplayer*. Compare your score on this test with your standing on Leadership Self-Assessment Quiz 9-1 about suitability for teamwork. The web site also offers suggestions from online experts on how to improve your teaming skills.

# Motivation and Coaching Skills

Patrick Keyes, a senior partner and director for business development at Ogilvy & Mather Worldwide, an advertising agency in New York City, enjoys acting as a mentor to his young staff members. Keyes, 40, says it is a powerful substitute when he cannot agree to their demands for raises or bonuses. "After we complete a pitch for new business," he said, "there are always opportunities to tell them what they did right, or explain how they might have done it better."

Keyes's coaching can be quite specific, particularly when young people are too casual in communicating with senior executives. "I had to explain," he said, "that it wasn't the best idea for a junior person to conclude an e-mail to the president of Oglivy with, 'Thoughts?'"[1]

---

This vignette about a senior advertising executive who coaches young professionals illustrates that coaching is both an important leadership technique and something that motivates the people coached because it helps them grow. Effective leaders are outstanding motivators and coaches. They influence others in many of the ways previously described. In addition, they often use specific motivational and coaching skills. These techniques are important because not all leaders can influence others through formal authority or charisma and inspirational leadership alone. Face-to-face, day-by-day motivational skills are also important. Good coaching is a related essential feature of management because motivating workers is an important part of coaching them.

In this chapter we approach motivation and coaching skills from various perspectives. We examine first how leaders make effective use of expectancy theory, recognition, and goal setting to motivate group members. Second, we describe coaching as a leadership philosophy, followed by a description of specific coaching skills and the role of the executive coach.

Before reading about several approaches to worker motivation, you are invited to take Leadership Self-Assessment Quiz 10-1, which deals with your understanding of motivation.

## MY APPROACH TO MOTIVATING OTHERS

INSTRUCTIONS Describe how often you act or think in the way indicated by the following statements when you are attempting to motivate another person. Scale: very infrequently (VI); infrequently (I); sometimes (S); frequently (F); very frequently (VF).

|  | VI | I | S | F | VF |
|---|---|---|---|---|---|
| 1. I ask the other person what he or she is hoping to achieve in the situation. | 1 | 2 | 3 | 4 | 5 |
| 2. I attempt to figure out if the person has the ability to do what I need done. | 1 | 2 | 3 | 4 | 5 |
| 3. When another person is heel dragging, it usually means he or she is lazy. | 5 | 4 | 3 | 2 | 1 |

4. I explain exactly what I want to the person
I am trying to motivate.                     1  2  3  4  5

5. I like to give the other person a reward up
front so he or she will be motivated.        5  4  3  2  1

6. I give lots of feedback when another person is
performing a task for me.                    1  2  3  4  5

7. I like to belittle another person enough so that
he or she will be intimidated into doing what
I need done.                                 5  4  3  2  1

8. I make sure that the other person feels fairly
treated.                                     1  2  3  4  5

9. I figure that if I smile nicely, I can get the other
person to work as hard as I do.              5  4  3  2  1

10. I attempt to get what I need done by instilling
fear in the other person.                    5  4  3  2  1

11. I specify exactly what needs to be accomplished.  1  2  3  4  5

12. I generously praise people who help me get my
work accomplished.                           1  2  3  4  5

13. A job well done is its own reward. I therefore
keep praise to a minimum.                    5  4  3  2  1

14. I make sure to let people know how well they
have done in meeting my expectations on a task.  1  2  3  4  5

15. To be fair, I attempt to reward people similarly
no matter how well they have performed.      5  4  3  2  1

16. When somebody doing work for me performs
well, I recognize his or her accomplishments
promptly.                                    1  2  3  4  5

17. Before giving somebody a reward, I attempt to
find out what would appeal to that person.   1  2  3  4  5

18. I make it a policy not to thank somebody for
doing a job he or she is paid to do.         5  4  3  2  1

19. If people do not know how to perform a task,
motivation will suffer.                      1  2  3  4  5

20. If properly laid out, many jobs can be self-
rewarding.                                   1  2  3  4  5

*Total score:* _____

*(continued)*

SCORING AND INTERPRETATION Add the circled numbers to obtain your total score.

- 90–100: You have advanced knowledge and skill with respect to motivating others in a work environment. Continue to build on the solid base you have established.
- 50–89: You have average knowledge and skill with respect to motivating others. With additional study and experience, you will probably develop advanced motivational skills.
- 20–49: To effectively motivate others in a work environment, you will need to greatly expand your knowledge of motivation theory and techniques.

SOURCE: The general idea for this quiz comes from David Whetton and Kim Cameron, *Developing Management Skills*, 5th ed. (Upper Saddle River, N.J.: Prentice Hall, 2002), pp. 302–303.

## Expectancy Theory and Motivational Skills

Expectancy theory is a good starting point in learning how leaders can apply systematic explanations of motivation, for two major reasons. First, the theory is comprehensive: it incorporates and integrates features of other motivation theories, including goal theory and behavior modification. Second, it offers the leader many guidelines for triggering and sustaining constructive effort from group members.

The **expectancy theory** of motivation is based on the premise that the amount of effort people expend depends on how much reward they expect to get in return. In addition to being broad, the theory deals with cognition and process. Expectancy theory is cognitive because it emphasizes the thoughts, judgments, and desires of the person being motivated. It is a process theory because it attempts to explain how motivation takes place.

The theory is really a group of theories based on a rational, economic view of people.[2] Expectancy theory as applied to work has recently been recast as a theory called *motivation management*. In any given situation, people want to maximize gain and minimize loss. The theory assumes that they choose among alternatives by selecting the one they think they have the best chance of attaining. Furthermore, they choose the alternative that appears to have the biggest personal payoff. Given a choice, people will select the assignment they think they can handle the best and will benefit them the most.

### Basic Components of Expectancy Theory

Expectancy theory contains three basic components: valence, instrumentality, and expectancy. Because of these three components, the theory is often referred to as VIE theory. Figure 10-1 presents a basic version of expectancy theory. All three elements must be present for motivation to take place. To be motivated, people must value the reward, think they can perform, and have reasonable assurance that their performance will lead to a reward.

*Valence* The worth or attractiveness of an outcome is referred to as **valence**. As shown in Figure 10-1, each work situation has multiple outcomes. An **outcome** is anything that might stem from performance, such as a reward. Each outcome has a

## FIGURE 10-1 The Expectancy Theory of Motivation

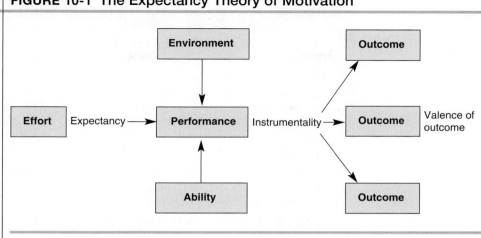

valence of its own. And each outcome can lead to other outcomes or consequences, referred to as *second-level outcomes*. A person who receives an outstanding performance appraisal (a first-level outcome) becomes eligible for a promotion (a second-level outcome). Second-level outcomes also have valences. The sum of all the valences must be positive if the person is to work hard. If the sum of all of the valences is negative, the person might work hard to avoid the outcome.

Valences range from −100 to +100 in the version of expectancy theory presented here. (The usual method of placing valences on a −1.00 to +1.00 scale does not do justice to the true differences in preferences.) A valence of +100 means that a person intensely desires an outcome. A valence of −100 means that a person is strongly motivated to avoid an outcome such as being fired or declaring bankruptcy. A valence of zero signifies indifference to an outcome and is therefore of no use as a motivator.

*Instrumentality* An individual's assessment of the probability that performance will lead to certain outcomes is referred to as **instrumentality.** (An instrumentality is also referred to as a *performance-to-outcome expectancy* because it relates to the outcome people expect from performing in a certain way.) When people engage in a particular behavior, they do so with the intention of achieving a desired outcome or reward. Instrumentalities range from 0 to 1.0, where 0 is no chance of receiving the desired reward and 1.0 is a belief that the reward is certain to follow. For example, an hourly worker might say, "I know for sure that if I work overtime, I will receive overtime pay."

*Expectancy* An individual's assessment of the probability that effort will lead to correct performance of the task is referred to as **expectancy.** (The same concept is also referred to as *effort-to-performance expectancy*.) An important question people ask themselves before putting forth effort to accomplish a task is, "If I put in all this work, will I really get the job done properly?" Expectancies range from 0 to 1.0, where 0 is no expectation of performing the tasks correctly, and 1.0 signifies absolute faith in being able to perform the task properly. Expectancies thus influence whether a person will even strive to earn a reward. Self-confident people have higher expectancies than do less self-confident people. Being well trained increases a person's subjective sense that he or she can perform the task.

The importance of having high expectancies for motivation meshes well with a current thrust in work motivation that emphasizes the contribution of **self-efficacy,** the confidence in your ability to carry out a specific task. If you have high self-efficacy about the task, your motivation will be high. Low self-efficacy leads to low motivation. Some people are poorly motivated to skydive because they doubt they will be able to pull the ripcord while free-falling at 120 mph. A more technical definition and explanation will help you appreciate the contribution of self-efficacy to motivation:

> Self-efficacy refers to an individual's convictions (or confidence) about his or her abilities to mobilize the motivation, cognitive resources, and course of action needed to successfully execute a specific task within a given context.[3]

In short, if you are confident about your task-related skills, you will get your act together to do the task. This is one reason that you should give people the skills and confidence they need to put forth effort.

An apparent contradiction in expectancy theory requires explanation. Some people will engage in behaviors with low expectancies, such as trying to invent a successful new product or become the CEO of a major corporation. The compensating factor is the large valences attached to the second-level outcomes associated with these accomplishments. The payoffs from introducing a successful new product or becoming a CEO are so great that people are willing to take a long shot.

*A Brief Look at the Evidence* The application of expectancy theory, especially the VIE version, to work motivation has been the subject of research for more than thirty-five years. Two researchers performed a meta-analysis of seventy-seven studies examining how well various aspects of expectancy theory were related to workplace criteria such as performance and effort. Although the results were not consistent, the general conclusion reached was that the three components of expectancy theory are positively related to workplace criteria. For example, job performance showed a positive correlation with valence, instrumentality, expectancy, and the total VIE model. The total VIE model typically refers to a multiplication of the values for valence, instrumentality, and expectancy. Another finding was that effort expended on the job was positively correlated with valence, instrumentality, expectancy, the VIE model, and performance.[4] The last correlation helps verify the justification for leaders' and managers' concern about motivating employees: People who try harder perform better!

## Leadership Skills and Behaviors Associated with Expectancy Theory

Expectancy theory has many implications for leaders and managers with respect to motivating others.[5] Some of these implications also stem from other motivational theories, and they fit good management practice in general. As you read each implication, reflect on how you might apply the skill or behavior during a leadership assignment.

1. *Determine what levels and kinds of performance are needed to achieve organizational goals.* Motivating others proceeds best when workers have a clear understanding of

what needs to be accomplished. At the same time, the leader should make sure that the desired levels of performance are possible. For example, sales quotas might be set too high because the market is already saturated with a particular product or service.

2. *Make the performance level attainable by the individuals being motivated.* If the group members believe that they are being asked to perform extraordinarily difficult tasks, most of them will suffer from low motivation. A task must generally be perceived as attainable to be motivational.

3. *Train and encourage people.* Leaders should give group members the necessary training and encouragement to be confident they can perform the required task. (We will return to the encouragement aspect of leadership in the discussion of coaching.) Some group members who appear to be poorly motivated simply lack the right skills and self-confidence.

4. *Make explicit the link between rewards and performance.* Group members should be reassured that if they perform the job to standard, they will receive the promised reward.

5. *Make sure the rewards are large enough.* Some rewards that are the right kind fail to motivate people because they are not in the right amount. The promise of a large salary increase might be motivational, but a 1 percent increase will probably have little motivational thrust for most workers.

6. *Analyze what factors work in opposition to the effectiveness of the reward.* Conflicts between the leader's package of rewards and other influences in the work group may require the leader to modify the reward. For example, if the work group favors the status quo, a large reward may be required to encourage innovative thinking.

7. *Explain the meaning and implications of second-level outcomes.* It is helpful for employees to understand the value of certain outcomes, such as receiving a favorable performance evaluation. (For example, it could lead to a salary increase, assignment to a high-status task force, or promotion.)

8. *Understand individual differences in valences.* To motivate group members effectively, leaders must recognize individual differences or preferences for rewards. An attempt should be made to offer workers rewards to which they attach a high valence. One employee might value a high-adventure assignment; another might attach a high valence to a routine, tranquil assignment. Cross-cultural differences in valences may also occur. For example, many (but not all) Asian workers prefer not to be singled out for recognition in front of the group. According to their cultural values, receiving recognition in front of the group is insensitive and embarrassing. Leadership Skill-Building Exercise 10-1 deals with the challenge of estimating valences.

9. *Recognize that when workers are in a positive mood, high valences, instrumentalities, and expectancies are more likely to lead to good performance.* An experiment with college students indicated that participants in a positive mood performed better, were more persistent, tried harder, and reported higher levels of motivation than those in a neutral mood. The positive affect made awards appear more attractive (higher valence). Being in a good mood also strengthened the link between performance and outcome (instrumentality), as well as between effort and performance (expectancy).[6] A note of caution is that the mood elevator in this experiment was a bag of candy. A manager might need more sustainable methods of increasing positive

affect. Being able to keep employees in a good mood is an advanced application of emotional intelligence.

Despite the utility of expectancy theory, leaders need to supplement it with other approaches to motivating group members. Two applied approaches to motivation—goal theory and giving recognition—are presented next.

LEADERSHIP SKILL-BUILDING EXERCISE 10-1

## ESTIMATING VALENCES FOR APPLYING EXPECTANCY THEORY

INSTRUCTIONS A major challenge in applying expectancy theory is estimating what valence attaches to possible outcomes. A leader or manager also has to be aware of the potential rewards or punishment in a given work situation. Listed are a group of rewards and punishments, along with a space for rating the reward or punishment on a scale of −100 to +100. Work with about six teammates, with each person rating all of the rewards and punishments.

| Potential Outcome | Rating (−100 to +100) |
|---|---|
| 1. Promotion to vice president | _____ |
| 2. One-step promotion | _____ |
| 3. Above-average performance rating | _____ |
| 4. Top-category performance rating | _____ |
| 5. $6,000 performance bonus | _____ |
| 6. $2,000 performance bonus | _____ |
| 7. $75 gift certificate | _____ |
| 8. Employee-of-the-month plaque | _____ |
| 9. Note of appreciation placed in file | _____ |
| 10. Luncheon with boss at good restaurant | _____ |
| 11. Lunch with boss in company cafeteria | _____ |
| 12. Challenging new assignment | _____ |
| 13. Allowed to accumulate frequent flyer miles for own use | _____ |
| 14. Allowed to purchase software of choice | _____ |
| 15. Assigned new equipment for own use | _____ |
| 16. Private corner office with great view | _____ |
| 17. Assigned a full-time administrative assistant | _____ |

**18.** Documentation of poor performance    _____

**19.** Being fired    _____

**20.** Being fired and put on industry "bad list"    _____

**21.** Demoted one step    _____

**22.** Demoted to entry-level position    _____

**23.** Being ridiculed in front of others    _____

**24.** Being suspended without pay    _____

**25.** Being transferred to undesirable location    _____

After completing the ratings, discuss the following issues:

**1.** Which rewards and punishments received the most varied ratings?

**2.** Which rewards and punishments received similar ratings?

Another analytical approach would be to compute the means and standard deviations of the valences for each outcome. Each class member could then compare his or her own valence ratings with the class norm. To add to the database, each student might bring back two sets of ratings from employed people who are not in the class.

To apply this technique to the job, modify the above form to fit the outcomes available in your situation. Explain to team members that you are attempting to do a better job of rewarding and disciplining and that you need their thoughts. The ratings made by team members might provide fruitful discussion for a staff meeting.

## Goal Theory

Goal setting is a basic process that is directly or indirectly part of all major theories of work motivation. Leaders and managers widely accept goal setting as a means to improve and sustain performance. A vision, for example, is really an exalted goal. A representative example of how leaders use goals to organize their efforts is the annual meeting of Linus Torvalds, the inventor of Linux, with his "maintainers," or programmers whose work has impressed Torvalds. Members discuss their goals for the operating system.[7]

The core finding of goal theory is that individuals who are provided with specific hard goals perform better than those who are given easy, nonspecific, "do your best" goals or no goals. At the same time, however, the individuals must have sufficient ability, accept the goals, and receive feedback related to the task.[8] Our overview of goal theory elaborates on this basic finding.

### Basic Findings of Goal Theory

The premise underlying goal theory (or goal-setting theory) is that behavior is regulated by values and goals. A **goal** is what a person is trying to accomplish. Our values create within us a desire to behave in a way that is consistent with them. For example, a leader who values honesty will establish a goal of hiring only honest employees. The leader would therefore have to make extensive use of reference checks and honesty testing. Edwin A. Locke and Gary P. Latham have incorporated hundreds of studies about goals into a theory of goal setting and task performance.[9] Figure 10-2 summarizes some of the more consistent findings, and the information that follows describes them. A leader should keep these points in mind when motivating people through goal setting.

To begin, remember that *specific goals lead to higher performance than do generalized goals.* Telling someone to "do your best" is a generalized goal. A specific goal would be, "Increase the number of new hires to our management training program to fifteen for this summer." Another key point is that *performance generally improves in direct proportion to goal difficulty.* The harder one's goal is, the more one accomplishes. An important exception is that when goals are too difficult, they may lower performance. Difficulty in reaching the goal leads to frustration, which in turn leads to lowered performance (as explained in relation to expectancy theory).

The finding about effective goals being realistic has an important exception for the accomplishment of high-level complex tasks. Effective leaders often inspire constituents by setting outrageous (or audacious) goals, or visions. Nicholas Lore writes that you can set reasonable, attainable goals for yourself and your staff. However, reasonable goals rarely inspire; instead, they lead to dull, comfortable lives. Here are two suggestions for developing powerful goals:

- Create a big, comprehensive goal: an ideal accomplishment for your group.
- Break the goal down into smaller steps, such as hiring two top-notch workers for the group. Treat each step (or subgoal) as a project designed to get you to your destination.[10] The same approach has been referred to as "running sprints rather than marathons."

*For goals to improve performance, the group member must accept them.* If a group member rejects a goal, he or she will not incorporate it into planning. This is why it is often helpful to discuss goals with group members rather than impose goals on them. More recent research, however, suggests that the importance of goal commitment may be overrated. A meta-analysis of mostly laboratory studies about the

**FIGURE 10-2 Goal Theory**

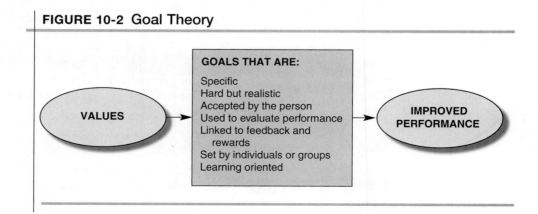

effect of goal commitment on performance concluded that commitment had a small impact on performance. Goals appeared to improve performance whether or not people participating in the studies felt committed to them.[11] Despite these recent findings, many managers and leaders think employee commitment to goals is important.

Participating in goal setting has no major effect on the level of job performance except when it improves goal acceptance. Yet the leader should recognize that participation is valuable because it can lead to higher satisfaction with the goal-setting process. *Goals are more effective when they are used to evaluate performance.* When workers know that their performance will be evaluated in terms of how well they attain their goals, the impact of goals increases.

Keep in mind the key principle that *goals should be linked to feedback and rewards.* Rewarding people for reaching goals is the most widely accepted principle of management. Another goal-setting principle is that *group goal setting is as important as individual goal setting.* Having employees work as teams with a specific team goal, rather than as individuals with only individual goals, increases productivity. Furthermore, a combination of compatible group and individual goals is more effective than either individual or group goals alone.

A final goal-setting principle is that a *learning goal orientation* improves performance more than a *performance goal orientation does.* A person with a learning (or mastery) goal orientation wants to develop competence by acquiring new skills and mastering new situations. In contrast, the person with a performance goal orientation wants to demonstrate and validate his or her competence by seeking favorable judgments and avoiding negative judgments. In support of the distinction being made, a study with medical supply sales representatives found that a learning goal orientation had a positive relationship with sales performance. In contrast, a performance goal orientation was unrelated to sales performance.[12]

## Underlying Mechanisms and Concerns

Despite their contribution to performance, goals are not motivational in themselves. Rather, the discrepancies created by what individuals do and what they aspire to creates self-dissatisfaction, which in turn creates a desire to reduce the discrepancy between the real and the ideal.[13] A person who has a desire to attain something is in a state of arousal. The tension created by not having already achieved a goal spurs the person to reach the goal. As a leader, you can sometimes create this tension by suggesting possibilities that group members might strive for.

A major concern about using goals to motivate performance is that leaders, as well as other workers, will take unethical and dysfunctional shortcuts to attain their goals. For example, a CEO might drastically reduce investment in research and development and lay off too many valuable workers to meet a profit goal such as earnings per share. Also, managers have been known to engage in unethical behavior such as shipping unfinished products to reach sales goals.[14]

Goal setting is widely practiced by leaders and managers, but they typically do not give careful consideration to goal-setting theory. Leadership Skill-Building Exercise 10-2 gives you an opportunity to apply what you have learned about goal setting.

LEADERSHIP SKILL-BUILDING EXERCISE 10-2

## THE APPLICATION OF GOAL THEORY

In a group of about five to six people, visualize your group as a task force whose mission is to make and implement suggestions for reducing water consumption in your company, a manufacturer of camping equipment. Water is a major company expense, and there is a distinct possibility that the county in which you are located will soon be rationing water. One of the group members plays the role of the task force leader. The leader must help the group establish goals that are likely to be motivational, following the principles of goal theory.

The goal of today's meeting is to establish four goals that are likely to lead to high performance. After each team has established its goals, present them to other class members. Students listening to the goals of the other groups should be willing to offer constructive feedback.

Practice in setting effective goals is useful because leaders and managers are frequently expected to set goals. When the goal follows at least some of the major findings of goal theory, there is a greater likelihood that productivity will increase.

---

college.hmco.com/pic/
dubrin5e

⟨KB⟩ @ **KNOWLEDGE BANK:** describes how behavior modification is used to motivate workers. Many of you who have studied organizational behavior, human relations, or the first course in psychology have some knowledge of behavior modification.

---

## Using Recognition and Pride to Motivate Others

Motivating others by giving them recognition and praise can be considered a direct application of positive reinforcement, that is, reinforcing the right behavior by giving a reward. Nevertheless, recognition is such a potentially powerful motivator that it merits separate attention. Also, recognition programs to reward and motivate employees are a standard practice in business and nonprofit firms. An example is rewarding high-performing employees with a crystal vase (company logo inscribed) or designating them "employee of the month." Pride, as described below, is related to recognition. People who are proud of their work like to be recognized for their good deeds.

Recognition is a strong motivator because it is a normal human need. To think through the strength of your own need for recognition, take Leadership Self-Assessment Quiz 10-2. Recognition is also effective because most workers feel they do not receive enough recognition. Several studies conducted over a fifty-year time span have indicated that employees welcome praise for a job well done as much as they welcome a regular paycheck. This finding should not be interpreted to mean that praise is an adequate substitute for salary. Employees tend to regard compensation as an entitlement, whereas recognition is perceived as a gift.[15] Workers, including your coworkers, want to know that their output is useful to somebody.

LEADERSHIP SELF-ASSESSMENT QUIZ 10-2

## HOW MUCH DO I CRAVE RECOGNITION?

Respond to the following statements on the following scale: disagree strongly (DS), disagree (D), neutral (N), agree (A), and agree strongly (AS).

| | DS | D | N | A | AS |
|---|---|---|---|---|---|
| 1. I keep (or would keep) almost every plaque, medal, trophy I have ever received on display in my living quarters. | 1 | 2 | 3 | 4 | 5 |
| 2. I feel a nice warm glow each time somebody praises my efforts. | 1 | 2 | 3 | 4 | 5 |
| 3. When somebody tells me, "nice job," it makes my day. | 1 | 2 | 3 | 4 | 5 |
| 4. When I compliment someone, I am really looking for a compliment in return. | 1 | 2 | 3 | 4 | 5 |
| 5. I would rather win an "employee-of-the-month" award than receive a $50 bonus for my good work. | 1 | 2 | 3 | 4 | 5 |
| 6. If I had the resources to make a large donation to charity, I would never make the donation anonymously. | 1 | 2 | 3 | 4 | 5 |
| 7. Thinking back to my childhood, I adored receiving a gold star or similar acknowledgment from my teacher for my good work. | 1 | 2 | 3 | 4 | 5 |
| 8. I would rather be designated as *Time* magazine's Person of the Year than be one of the world's richest people. | 1 | 2 | 3 | 4 | 5 |
| 9. I love to see my name in print. | 1 | 2 | 3 | 4 | 5 |
| 10. I do not receive all the respect I deserve. | 1 | 2 | 3 | 4 | 5 |

*Total score:* _____

SCORING AND INTERPRETATION Add the circled numbers to obtain your total score.

- 45–50: You have an above-average recognition need. Recognition is therefore a strong motivator for you. You will be happiest in a job where you can be recognized for your good deeds.
- 25–44: You have an average need for recognition and do not require constant reminders that you have done a good job.
- 10–24: You have a below-average need for recognition and like to have your good deeds speak for themselves. When you do receive recognition, you would prefer that it be quite specific to what you have done, and not too lavish. You would feel comfortable in a work setting with mostly technical people.

### Appealing to the Recognition Need of Others

To appeal to the recognition need of others, identify a meritorious behavior, and then recognize that behavior with an oral, written, or material reward. Three examples of using recognition to sustain desired behavior (a key aspect of motivation) follow:

- As the team leader, you receive a glowing letter from a customer about Kent, one of your team members, who solved the customer's problem. You have the letter laminated and present it as a gift to Kent. (The behavior you are reinforcing is good customer service.)

- One member of your department, Jason, is a mechanical engineer. While at a department lunch taking place during National Engineers Week, you stand up and say, "I want to toast Jason in celebration of National Engineers Week. I certainly would not want to be sitting in this office building today if a mechanical engineer had not assisted in its construction." (Here the only behavior you are reinforcing is the goodwill of Jason, so your motivational approach is general, not specific.)

- A sales manager of a real estate firm in Florida distributes to employees a file folder labeled Success File. Whenever employees accomplish something special, she writes them a letter of appreciation and suggests that they file it in their Success File. Later, if they encounter rough spots in their work, they can reread the letters to remind themselves how much they are appreciated. (Recognition here is being used to both reward people for what they have accomplished and to reenergize people based on previous recognition.)[16]

An outstanding advantage of recognition, including praise, as a motivator is that it is no cost or low cost yet powerful. Reward expert Bob Nelson reminds us that while money is important to employees, thoughtful recognition motivates them to elevate their performance.[17] Recognition thus has an enormous return on investment in comparison to a cash bonus. A challenge in using recognition effectively is that not everyone responds well to the same form of recognition. A good example is that highly technical people tend not to like general praise like, "Great job" or "Awesome, baby." Instead, they prefer a laid-back, factual statement of how their work made a contribution. According to one study, the more highly a person sees himself or herself as having a technical orientation, the more the person wants praise to be quite specific and task oriented.[18] The tech center worker who just conquered a virus on your desktop would prefer a compliment such as, "I appreciated your having disabled the virus and restored my computer to full functioning." This type of compliment would be preferable to, "Fantastic, you are a world-class virus fighter."

In addition to incorporating recognition into the process of leadership, leaders and managers rely on formal recognition programs. Kenneth Hain states that an effective recognition award possesses at least one of the following qualities:[19]

- *It has symbolic meaning.* Hugh McColl, CEO of Bank of America, awards his performing employees crystal replicas of hand grenades. McColl is a former Marine who believes in a take-no-prisoners style of management. (Would you suspect that employees perceive McColl as having a militaristic leadership style?)

- *It inspires pride of ownership.* Sales consultants who attain prescribed goals at Mary Kay Cosmetics are permitted to purchase specific outfits for their wardrobes. Once a consultant becomes a director, for example, she is invited to attend Mary Kay's management conference. While there, the sales consultant is fitted for a director's suit. (Kay is deceased but the tradition continues.)

■ *It helps to reinforce the philosophy or identity of the giver.* A company that practiced the quality standard Six Sigma (3.4 errors in 1 million opportunities) might give recognition awards that were inscribed with a mention of the firm having products of outstanding quality.

### Appealing to Pride

Wanting to feel proud motivates many workers, and giving recognition for a job well done helps satisfy this desire to feel proud. Being proud of what you accomplish is more of an internal (intrinsic) motivator than an external (extrinsic) motivator such as receiving a gift. Giving workers an opportunity to experience pride can therefore be a strong internal motivator yet they simultaneously receive recognition.

Imagine that you are the assistant service manager at a company that customizes recreational vehicles to meet the requirements of individual clients. Your manager asks you to prepare a PowerPoint presentation of trends in customization for people who live most of the year in their RVs. You make your presentation to top management, the group applauds, executives shake your hand, and later you receive several congratulatory email messages. One of the many emotions you experience is likely to be pride in having performed well. You are motivated to keep up the good work.

Workers can also experience pride in relation to recognition symbols. For example, a worker might receive a floor clock for having saved the company thousands of dollars in shipping costs. The clock might be more valuable to the worker as a symbol of accomplishment than as a household decoration. The feeling of pride stems from having accomplished a worthwhile activity (saving the company money) rather than from being awarded a floor clock.

According to consultant Jon R. Katzenbach, managers and leaders can take steps to motivate through pride. A key tactic is for the manager to set his or her compass on pride, not money. It is more important for workers to be proud of what they are doing day by day than for them to be proud of reaching a major goal. The manager should celebrate "steps" (or attaining small goals) as much as the "landings" (the major goal). The most effective pride builders are masters at identifying and recognizing the small achievements that will instill pride in their people.[20]

Before moving on to the section about coaching, read the Leader in Action profile about a successful leader who uses motivational techniques.

## LEADER IN ACTION

### THE MOTIVATIONAL KEN CHENAULT OF AMEX

Back in his college days, Ken Chenault argued that African Americans could best rise to power by working within the establishment instead of attacking it from the outside.

Today he is chairman and CEO of American Express Company, the owner of one of the world's premier consumer brands. Chenault is also a member of the board of directors of IBM Corporation.

*(continued)*

After graduating from Bowdoin College, Chenault earned a degree from Harvard Law School. A member of a law firm for several years, he later worked as a management consultant before joining AmEx. He rose rapidly at the consulting firm and was regarded as having the potential to become a corporate CEO, partly because of his strategic thinking and his ability to work with and motivate others.

Chenault makes an impressive physical appearance; he is also quietly charismatic, is even-tempered, and has exceptional drive. His admirers lavish him with praise. The chairman of the leading advertising agency for AmEx offers this description: "Ken radiates such a depth of belief that people would do anything for him" (*BusinessWeek*, December 21, 2001, p. 61).

Chenault has a quiet warmth that puts people at ease and makes them want to be on his team. At the same time he is a tough-minded risk taker who demands results. A former competitor for the top job at AmEx said of Chenault: "He's impossible to dislike, even when you're competing for the top job. If you work around him, you feel like you'd do anything for the guy" (*Fortune*, January 22, 2001, p. 62).

Work associates regard Chenault as hard driving and pragmatic. Yet at the same time he is able to engage the emotions of his colleagues as well as their intellects. Another former AmEx executive said, "Ken has the hearts and minds of the people at the TRS company" (the travel-related services unit of AmEx) (*BusinessWeek*, December 21, 2001, p. 63). A survey of work associates indicates that Chenault lacks the rough edges and impatience that usually accompany highly ambitious people. None of the people interviewed could recall his losing his temper or even raising his voice. He takes the time to make small talk with secretaries when he telephones their bosses. Chenault has taken the initiative to mentor dozens of high-potential AmEx managers. He has also contributed to making lay-off decisions during difficult times for the company.

Chenault is a methodical decision maker who collects input from others, encourages candor, and leaves his door open to direct reports. A veteran AmEx executive said, "With Ken, there is no game-playing, no politics whatsoever" (*BusinessWeek*, December 21, 2001, p. 63). When involved in a marketing strategy debate with other executives, "Ken would stand up for what he believed in, present his argument effectively—and forcefully when necessary," says former AmEx CEO James Robinson. "But it was always done in a professional way rather than in a stubborn way. He wasn't political; he was just someone you listened to" (*Fortune*, January 22, 2001, p. 64). Yet despite his even temper, Chenault has fired managers he thought lacked the skills he needed for his organization. While AmEx was going through substantial changes to stop the slide in American Express card use, he fired most of a group of managers who resisted the changes.

An important part of Chenault's managerial approach is to interact directly with rank-and-file employees. He regularly conducts a monthly "meet the CEO" session over lunch and says that he has picked up some of his best ideas this way. An example is a promotion that enabled Platinum card members to purchase two business-class airline tickets for the price of one.

In Chenault's opinion, the role of the leader is to define reality and give hope. He prefers to occupy the role of team leader rather than of boss. He says it is critical to share the credit. He openly acknowledges staff members who have contributed useful ideas, often mentioning them in meetings.

Chenault is a strong self-motivator as well as a motivator of others. "My father used to tell me that whatever happens, there is one thing I can control, and that's the quality of my performance," he says. "Regardless of the attitude of others, personal fortitude could overcome the odds" (*Emerge*, 1999).

The terrorist attacks of September 11, 2001, presented new challenges for Chenault as he and 3,000 other employees were driven from the American Express Tower across the street from the World Trade Center. Eleven AmEx employees died in the neighboring towers. Chenault shifted operations to a cramped and windowless office in

Jersey City only ten months after being appointed as CEO. During his first ten months as CEO, Chenault faced another crisis: he had to announce to the public that the firm was forced to write off more than $1 billion on some high-yield junk bonds in the Minneapolis money management operation. The cutback on business and personal travel in the months following September 11 created even more pressures on AmEx.

Chenault told the 3,000 employees evacuated from company headquarters: "The values of this brand are real, far more real than the bricks and mortar of our headquarters building. The tower does not represent American Express. You represent American Express. All the people of American Express are what this company is about" (*BusinessWeek*, October 29, 2001, p. 70).

Chenault assembled 5,000 American Express employees at the Paramount Theatre in New York on September 20 for an emotionally charged townhall meeting. He told employees he had been filled with such despair, sadness, and anger he had seen a counselor. Twice, he rushed to spontaneously embrace grief-stricken employees. Chenault said he would donate $1 million of the company's profits to the families of the eleven AmEx employees who died during the attack. "I represent the best company and the best people in the world," he concluded. "In fact, you are my strength, and I love you" (*BusinessWeek*, October 29, 2001, p. 66). An AmEx board member said of Chenault, "The manner in which he took command, the comfort and the direction he gave to what was obviously an audience in shock . . . was of a caliber one rarely sees" (*BusinessWeek*, October 29, 2001, p. 66).

Six weeks after the World Trade Center attacks, Chenault said, "I don't feel like we're a dispirited group. We are going to emerge a stronger and better company" (*BusinessWeek*, October 29, 2001, p. 70). Since the dark days of fall 2001, American Express has made considerable progress, including gaining relative advantage over competitors. During 2003, for example, sales grew 8.6 percent and net income 11.8 percent. Chenault identified three key areas that have made these results possible.

First, the company made key changes in the business model, emphasizing more modest growth, yet diversifying its sources of revenues, such as encouraging the payment of cable, phone, and other monthly bills by the AmEx card. The company is also working to have American Express credit cards issued through banks, as are MasterCard and Visa, thereby expanding its customer base. Second, he has worked to reinforce the values and identity of the company. He boasted that on 9/11 the employees of American Express took care of any person in need who used an AmEx card. Third is leadership of the people, in terms of giving hope to employees yet grounding that hope in reality. Trust and concern for people are also part of effective leadership during difficult times.

Part of Chenault's recovery plan for the company also involved cost reduction of $4 billion through 2004. He slashed 14,500 jobs, or 16 percent of the workforce, and outsourced 2,000 tech jobs to IBM. "Investors were doubtful that the company could recover," says analyst David A. Hendler of CreditSights. "Chenault has done an awesome job" (*BusinessWeek*, August 9, 2004, p. 54).

## QUESTIONS

1. What indicators do you find that Kenneth Chenault is a motivational leader?
2. When Chenault informed employees that he sought counseling for his grief, what effect might this have had on his leadership image?
3. How does the fact that Chenault spearheaded the layoff of 14,500 employees influence your evaluation of his leadership capability?
4. How would you like working for Ken Chenault?

SOURCE: Based on facts reported in Anthony Bianco, "The Rise of a Star," *BusinessWeek*, December 21, 1998, pp. 60–68; Ernest Holsendolph, "Beating the Odds in the Fortune 500: New Black CEOs," *Emerge* (July–August 1999), *www.msbet.com/content/live/2770.asap*; Carrie Shook, "Leader, Not Boss," *Forbes Magazine*, December 1, 1997; John A. Byrne and Heather Timmons, "Tough Times for a New CEO," *BusinessWeek*, October 29, 2001, pp. 63–70; Nelson D. Schwartz, "What's in the Cards for Amex?" *Fortune*, January 22, 2001, pp. 58–70; "Black History Month 2002," Jennifer Kattula, "Kenneth Chenault on Managing in Volatile Times," *themsj.com*, December 13, 2004, pp. 1–2; Mara Der Hovanesian, "Charge!" *BusinessWeek*, August 9, 2004, pp. 48–54.

## Coaching as a Leadership Philosophy

Effective leaders are good coaches. The coaching demands are much less rigorous for leaders who have little face-to-face contact with organization members, such as financial deal makers, CEOs, and chairpersons of the board. Nevertheless, there is a coaching component at all levels of leadership. CEO Bill Ford (of Ford Motor Company) says, "I see myself as a coach, and my job is to set the direction of the company, to make sure we have the right players and eliminate the politicking."[21] Do you think Ford took the same leadership course as you? Studies conducted by Rainmaker Thinking, Inc., indicate that many managers are falling down by failing to coach employees, particularly in the form of specific feedback on performance with guidance for improvement.[22]

The quality of the relationship between the coach and the person or persons coached distinguishes coaching from other forms of leader–member interactions. The person being coached trusts the leader's judgment and experience and will listen to advice and suggestions. Similarly, the coach believes in the capacity of the group member to profit from his or her advice. The coach is a trusted superior, and the person being coached is a trusted subordinate.

Coaching is a way of enabling others to act and build on their strengths. To coach is to care enough about people to invest time in building personal relationships with them. The organization also benefits from coaching because of the elevated productivity of many of the workers who are coached.[23]

### Key Characteristics of Coaching

Roger D. Evered and James C. Selman regard coaching as a paradigm shift from traditional management, which focuses heavily on control, order, and compliance. Coaching, in contrast, focuses on uncovering actions that enable people to contribute more fully and productively. Coaching is also seen as a partnership for achieving results. At the same time, it represents a commitment to collaborating in accomplishing new possibilities rather than holding on to old structures.[24] Figure 10-3 depicts coaching as a philosophy of management.

Coaching in the workplace might ordinarily be explained as the art of management. Because of the uniqueness of a coaching relationship, the person being coached is better motivated to accomplish goals for the good of the organization. Coaching is an interaction between two people, usually the manager and an employee. The purpose of the interaction is to help the employee learn from the job in order to help his or her development.[25] The interaction of the two personalities influences the coaching outcome. Some leaders, for example, can successfully coach certain people but not others. An executive vice president of finance was highly regarded as a good coach. Yet a newly appointed special assistant asked to be transferred after she worked for him for several months. The explanation she offered was, "My working relationship with Marty [the executive vice president] is just flat."

Coaching requires a high degree of interpersonal risk and trust on the part of both people in the relationship. The coach might give the person being coached wrong advice. Or the person being coached might reject the coach's encouragement. Think of the risk involved when a basketball player asks the coach for advice on how to

**FIGURE 10-3  Coaching Versus the Traditional Way of Thinking
About Management**

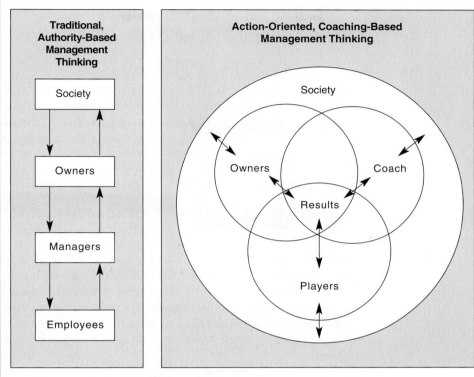

(Arrows indicate benefits)

correct a shot that is not working well. As a result of the coaching, the player might shoot more poorly, to the embarrassment of both. Similarly, an organizational leader might coach a team member in a direction that backfires—for example, that results in even fewer sales than before.

A key advantage of coaching is that it generates new possibilities for action and facilitates breakthroughs in performance. A vice president might say to a lower-ranking manager, "Have you thought of getting your people more involved in setting objectives? If you did, you might find greater commitment and follow-through." The middle manager begins to involve managers more in setting objectives, and performance increases. Coaching in this situation has achieved substantial results.

Despite all the exalted statements made about coaching as a philosophy of leadership, it is still useful to specify a few concrete contributions of coaching. One advantage is higher motivation. An effective coach keeps up the spirit and offers praise and recognition frequently. Good coaching also leads to personal development. Group members are encouraged to cross-train and serve as backups for each other. Good coaching also improves group performance. The effective coach makes team members aware of one another's skills and how these skills can contribute to attaining the group's goals.

### Fallacies About Coaching

Another approach to understanding the coaching function of leadership is to examine certain common misperceptions about coaching. Several of these false stereotypes, as explained by Ian Cunningham and Linda Honold, are presented next.[26] One false belief is that *coaching applies only in one-to-one work.* In reality, the team or other group can also be coached. As a team leader, you might make a suggestion to the group, such as, "Why are you rushing through such an important issue?"

A major misperception is that *coaching is mostly about providing new knowledge and skills.* The truth is that people often need more help with underlying habits than with knowledge and skills. A good example is coaching another person about work habits and time management. You can provide the individual with loads of useful knowledge and techniques; however, if the person is a procrastinator, he or she must reduce procrastination before time management skills will help.

Another stereotype deals with an important ethical issue: *if coaches go beyond giving instruction in knowledge and skills, they are in danger of getting into psychotherapy.* The counterargument is that coaches should simply follow the model of effective parents: listening to the other person, attempting to understand his or her real concerns, and offering support and encouragement. Another stereotype particularly resistant to extinction is that *coaches need to be expert in something in order to coach.* To use a sports analogy, a good coach does not have to be or have been an outstanding athlete. An important role for the coach is to ask pertinent questions and listen. Questioning and listening can help the other person set realistic learning goals.

An understandable stereotype is that *coaching has to be done face-to-face.* The face-to-face approach facilitates coaching. Nevertheless, telephone and email are useful alternatives when time and distance create barriers. A worker on a field trip, for example, might send his manager an email message asking, "The customer says that if I make a mistake with this installation, he'll never do business with us again. Any suggestions?"

## Coaching Skills and Techniques

Leaders and managers have varied aptitudes for coaching. One way to acquire coaching skill is to study basic principles and suggestions and then practice them. Another is to attend a training program for coaching that involves modeling (learning by imitation) and role playing. Here we examine a number of suggestions for coaching. If implemented with skill, the suggestions will improve the chances that coaching will lead to improved performance.

1. *Communicate clear expectations to group members.* For people to perform well and to continue to learn and grow, they need a clear perception of what is expected of them. The expectations of a position become the standards by which performance will be judged, thus serving as a base point for coaching. If a team member is supposed to contribute three new ideas each month for

improving operations, coaching is justified when an average of only one idea per month is forthcoming.

2. *Build relationships.* Effective coaches build personal relationships with team members and work to improve their interpersonal skills.[27] Having established rapport with team members facilitates entering into a coaching relationship with them. The suggestions that follow about active listening and giving emotional support are part of relationship building.

3. *Give feedback on areas that require specific improvement.* To coach a group member toward higher levels of performance, the leader pinpoints what specific behavior, attitude, or skills require improvement. An effective coach might say, "I read the product-expansion proposal you submitted. It's okay, but it falls short of your usual level of creativity. Our competitors are already carrying each product you mentioned. Have you thought about . . . ?" Another important factor in giving specific feedback is to avoid generalities and exaggerations such as, "You never come up with a good product idea" or "You are the most unimaginative product development specialist I have ever known." To give good feedback, the leader or manager has to observe performance and behavior directly and frequently, such as by watching a supervisor dealing with a safety problem.

To make the feedback process less intimidating, it is helpful feedback to ask permission before you start coaching, indicate your purposes, and explain your positive intentions: for example, "Jack, do you have a few minutes for me to share my thoughts with you?" (permission); "I'd like to talk to you about the presentation you just made to the venture capitalists" (purpose); "I liked your creativity, yet I have some ideas you might use in your next presentation" (positive intentions).[28]

Feedback is also likely to be less intimidating when the coach explains which behaviors should decrease and which should increase. This approach is a variation of combining compliments with criticism to avoid insulting the person being coached. You might say, "Tanya, I need you to place more emphasis on quality and less on speed."

4. *Listen actively.* Listening is an essential ingredient in any coaching session. An active listener tries to grasp both facts and feelings. Observing the group member's non-verbal communication is another part of active listening. The leader must also be patient and not poised for a rebuttal of any difference of opinion between him or her and the group member. Beginning each coaching session with a question helps set the stage for active listening. The question will also spark the employee's thinking and frame the discussion: for example, "How might we use the new computer system to help our staff generate more sales?

Part of being a good listener is encouraging the person being coached to talk about his or her performance. Asking open-ended questions facilitates a flow of conversation: for example, ask, "How did you feel about the way you handled conflict with the marketing group yesterday?" A close-ended question covering the same issue would be, "Do you think you could have done a better job of handling conflict with the marketing group yesterday?"

5. *Help remove obstacles.* To perform at anywhere near top capacity, individuals may need help in removing obstacles such as a maze of rules and regulations and rigid

budgeting. An important role for the leader of an organizational unit is thus to be a "barrier buster." A leader or manager is often in a better position than a group member to gain approval from a higher-level manager, find money from another budget line, expedite a purchase order, or authorize hiring a temporary worker to provide assistance. Yet if the coach is too quick to remove obstacles for the group member, the latter may not develop enough self-reliance.

6. *Give emotional support.* By being helpful and constructive, the leader provides much-needed emotional support to the group member who is not performing at his or her best. A coaching session should not be an interrogation. An effective way of giving emotional support is to use positive rather than negative motivators. For example, the leader might say, "I liked some things you did yesterday, and I have a few suggestions that might bring you closer to peak performance."

   Displaying empathy is an effective way to give emotional support. Indicate with words that you understand the challenge the group member faces with a statement such as, "I understand that working with a reduced staff has placed you under heavy time pressures." The genuine concern you show will help establish the rapport useful in working out the problem together.

   Another facet of giving emotional support is for the leader or manager to be a *toxic handler,* a person who shoulders the sadness, frustration, bitterness, anger, and despair of group members so they can work productively.[29] Being available as a sympathetic and empathic listener is a major part of being a toxic handler, and coming forth with creative solutions to vexing problems is also helpful.

7. *Reflect content or meaning.* An effective way of reflecting meaning is to rephrase and summarize concisely what the group member is saying. A substandard performer might say, "The reason I've fallen so far behind is that our company has turned into a bureaucratic nightmare. We're being hit right and left with forms to fill out for customer satisfaction. I have fifty email messages that I haven't read yet." You might respond, "You're falling so far behind because you have so many forms and messages that require attention." The group member might then respond with something like, "That's exactly what I mean. I'm glad you understand my problem." (Notice that the leader is also giving the group member an opportunity to express the feelings behind his or her problem.)

8. *Give some gentle advice and guidance.* Too much advice giving interferes with two-way communication, yet some advice can elevate performance. The manager should assist the group member in answering the question "What can I do about this problem?"[30] Advice in the form of a question or suppositional statement is often effective. One example is, "Could the root of your problem be insufficient planning?" A direct statement, such as, "The root of your problem is obviously insufficient planning," often makes people resentful and defensive. By responding to a question, the person being coached is likely to feel more involved in making improvements.

   Part of giving gentle guidance for improvement is to use the word *could* instead of *should.* To say, "You should do this," implies that the person is currently doing something wrong, which can trigger defensiveness. Saying, "You could do this," leaves the person with a choice: accept or reject your input and weigh the consequences.[31] (You *could* accept this advice to become a better coach!)

9. *Allow for modeling of desired performance and behavior.* An effective coaching technique is to show the group member by example what constitutes the desired behavior. Assume that a manager has been making statements to customers that stretch the truth, such as falsely saying that the product met a zero-defects standard. In coaching him, the manager's boss might allow the manager to observe how she handles a similar situation with a customer. The manager's boss might telephone a customer and say, "You have been inquiring about whether we have adopted a zero-defects standard for our laser printers. Right now we are doing our best to produce error-free products. Yet so far we do not have a formal zero-defects program. We stand by our printers and will fix any defect at no cost to you."

10. *Gain a commitment to change.* Unless the leader receives a commitment from the team member to carry through with the proposed solution to a problem, the team member may not attain higher performance. An experienced manager develops an intuitive sense for when employees are serious about performance improvement. Two clues that commitment to change is lacking are (1) overagreeing about the need for change and (2) agreeing to change without display of emotion.

11. *Applaud good results.* Effective coaches on the playing field and in the workplace are cheerleaders. They give encouragement and positive reinforcement by applauding good results. Some effective coaches shout in joy when an individual or team achieves outstanding results; others clap their hands in applause.

Leadership Self-Assessment Quiz 10-3 will help you think through the development you need to be an effective coach. If you are already an effective coach, look for ways to improve. Leadership Skill-Building Exercise 10-3 gives you a chance to practice coaching.

**LEADERSHIP SELF-ASSESSMENT QUIZ 10-3**

### CHARACTERISTICS OF AN EFFECTIVE COACH

**INSTRUCTIONS** Below is a list of traits, attitudes, and behaviors characteristic of effective coaches. Place a check mark next to each trait, attitude, or behavior that you need to develop along those lines (for example, whether you need to become more patient). On a separate sheet of paper, design an action plan for improvement for each trait, attitude, or behavior that you need to develop. An example of an action plan for improving patience might be, "I'll ask people to tell me when I appear too impatient. I'll also try to develop self-control about my impatience."

**Trait, Attitude, or Behavior**

1. Empathy (putting self in other person's shoes)      _____

2. Listening skill      _____

3. Insight into people      _____

4. Diplomacy and tact      _____

*(continued)*

5. Patience toward people     _____

6. Concern for welfare of people     _____

7. Low hostility toward people     _____

8. Self-confidence and emotional security     _____

9. Noncompetitiveness with group members     _____

10. Enthusiasm for people     _____

11. Satisfaction in helping others grow     _____

12. Interest in development of group members     _____

13. High expectations for each group member     _____

14. Ability to give authentic feedback     _____

15. Interest in people's potential     _____

16. Honesty and integrity (or trustworthiness)     _____

17. Friendliness     _____

SOURCE: Items 1–10 adapted with permission from Andrew J. DuBrin, *Participant Guide to Module 10: Development of Subordinates*, p. 11. Copyright © 1985. Items 11–15 gathered from information in William D. Hitt, *The Leader–Manager: Guidelines for Action* (Columbus, Ohio: Battelle Press, 1988), pp. 183–186.

**LEADERSHIP SKILL-BUILDING EXERCISE 10-3**

## COACHING FOR IMPROVED PERFORMANCE

Jennifer is a financial consultant (stockbroker) at a branch office of an established financial services firm. Her manager, Derek, is concerned that Jennifer is 25 percent below quota in sales of a new commodities mutual fund offered by the company. Derek schedules a late-afternoon meeting in his office to attempt to help Jennifer make quota. He has told Jennifer, "I want to talk about your sales performance on the new commodities fund and see if I can be helpful." Jennifer is concerned that the meeting might be a discipline session in disguise.

Have one member of the class assume the role of Derek, and another the role of Jennifer. Derek, of course, will attempt to implement recommended coaching techniques. Other class members will watch and then provide constructive feedback.

This exercise is a key skill builder because so much of face-to-face leadership involves working out performance problems with group members. If every employee were an outstanding, independent performer, we would have less need for managers and leaders.

## Executive Coaching and Leadership Effectiveness

A form of coaching in vogue is for managers to consult professional coaches to help them become more effective leaders and to guide them in their careers. An **executive (or business) coach** is an outside or inside specialist who advises a person about personal improvement and behavioral change. A major role of the coach is to give the leader an impartial perspective and help brainstorm solutions to problems. Executive coaches provide such a variety of services that they have been described as a combination of "a counselor, adviser, mentor, cheerleader, and best friend."[32] In the past, management psychologists were typically hired as outside coaches to help managers become more effective leaders. Today, people from a wide variety of backgrounds become executive coaches, as well as career coaches and life coaches. Executive coaches help managers become more effective leaders by helping them in ways such as the following:

- Counseling the leader about weaknesses that could interfere with effectiveness, such as being too hostile and impatient.
- Helping the leader understand and process feedback from 360-degree surveys. The coach will also solicit feedback by interviewing coworkers and subordinates, and then distill the feedback to help the executive.
- Serving as a sounding board when the leader faces a complex decision about strategy, operations, or human resource issues.
- Making specific suggestions about self-promotion and image enhancement, including suggestions about appearance and mannerisms.
- Helping the leader achieve a better balance between work and family life, thereby having more focused energy for the leadership role.
- Helping the leader uncover personal assets and strengths he or she may not have known existed.(for example, discovering that the leader has untapped creativity and imagination).
- Serving as a trusted confidante to discuss issues the leader might feel uncomfortable talking about with others: for example, talking about feeling insecure in his or her position.
- Pointing out a blind spot in the leader's decision making, such as neglecting part of the human consequences of a decision.
- Giving advice about career management, such as developing a career path.
- Strengthening the executive's strategic decision-making skills by helping him or her think more broadly about issues and appreciate how his or her actions will affect the organizational system.

Note that the coach works as an adviser about behavior but does not explicitly help the leader with functional details of the job, such as how to develop a new product strategy or design an organization.

The leader/manager's employer usually hires the executive coach. The purpose of engaging the coach could be to accelerate the development of a star player or assist an executive who is having soft-skill problems. For example, the direct reports of a manager at a consulting firm referred to her as a "weed whacker," so an executive coach was hired to help the executive develop more emotional intelligence. The executive soon learned that employees perceived in her tone and body language that she was attacking them. Coaching helped her soften her approach and work better with others.[33]

Many managers and professional people hire their own coach, much as they might hire a personal trainer. Typically the coach spends about one hour a week with the client. Many coaches rely on the telephone and email to conduct much of their coaching. For example, the leader might send an email message to the coach asking advice about how to handle an upcoming meeting. The coach would respond within twenty-four hours.

A refinement of individual coaching is for the coach to work with both the individual and his or her work associates. The coach solicits feedback from the group members, as well as involves them in helping the manager improve. For example, the coach might tell team members to assert their rights when the manager throws a temper tantrum or makes unreasonable demands. The coach might also work with the superiors or peers of the person being coached. Coach Marshall Goldsmith says, "My success rate as a coach has improved dramatically as I've realized that people's getting better is not a function of me; it's a function of the person and the people around the person."[34]

Executive coaching may frequently accomplish several of the ends specified in the above list. Company evidence about the contribution of business coaching is sometimes impressive. A huge global services company offered coaching to 127 senior managers and then observed the results. The coached executives scored higher than a contrast group of executives on a long list of measures, including "results obtained," "builds relationships," and "applies integrative thinking."[35] In another study, about 1,200 managers received multisource feedback, similar to a 360-degree survey. Measurements were taken at one-year intervals. The 404 managers who worked with a coach were more likely to set specific rather than vague goals and to solicit ideas for improvement from their superiors. In addition, they showed slightly more improvement in terms of ratings by direct reports and superiors.[36]

Executive coaching, however, has some potential drawbacks for the leader. A major problem is that a coach may give advice that backfires because he or she does not understand the particular work setting. A coach told a manager in an information technology firm that she should become more decisive in her decision making and less dependent on consensus. The advice backfired because the culture of the firm emphasized consensus decision making. A lengthy analysis found that many executive coaches do not listen well, and imposed directive advice on their clients.[37] Furthermore, many people who present themselves as executive coaches may not be professionally qualified or may not have much knowledge about business.[38]

An ethical problem is that many coaches delve into personal and emotional issues that should be reserved for mental health professionals. Psychotherapist Steven Berglas contends that executive coaches can make a bad situation worse when they ignore psychological problems they do not understand.[39] The leader who is performing poorly because of a deep-rooted problem such as hostility toward others is given superficial advice about "making nice." Another potential ethical problem is that the leader/manager may become too dependent on the coach, checking with him or her before making any consequential decision.

**READER'S ROADMAP**

So far we have studied considerable information about the nature of leadership; the attributes, behaviors, and styles of leaders; the ethics and social responsibility of leaders; and how leaders exert power and use politics and influence. The techniques for developing teamwork are part of a leader's relationship with the group, as is the subject of this chapter: motivation and coaching skills. In the next chapter we describe creativity and innovation as part of leadership.

## Summary

college.hmco.com/pic/dubrin5e

Effective leaders are outstanding motivators and coaches, and the role of the leader and manager today emphasizes coaching. The expectancy theory of motivation is useful for developing motivational skills because it is comprehensive, building on other explanations of motivation.

Expectancy theory has three major components: valence, instrumentality, and expectancy. *Valence* is the worth or attractiveness of an outcome. Each work situation has multiple outcomes, and each outcome has a valence of its own. Valences range from −100 to +100 in the version of expectancy theory presented here. Zero valences reflect indifference and therefore are not motivational. Very high valences help explain why some people persist in efforts despite a low probability of payoff. *Instrumentality* is the individual's assessment of the probability that performance will lead to certain outcomes. (An outcome is anything that might stem from performance, such as a reward.) *Expectancy* is an individual's assessment of the probability that effort will lead to performing the task correctly.

Expectancy theory has implications and provides guidelines for leaders, including the following: (1) determine necessary performance levels; (2) make the performance level attainable; (3) train and encourage people; (4) make explicit the link between rewards and performance; (5) make sure the rewards are large enough; (6) analyze factors that oppose the effectiveness of the reward; (7) explain the meaning and implications of second-level outcomes; (8) understand individual differences in valences; and (9) recognize

that when workers are in a good mood, valences, instrumentalities, and expectancies will more likely enhance performance.

Goal setting is a basic process that is directly or indirectly part of all major theories of motivation. Goal theory includes the following ideas: (1) specific and difficult goals result in high performance (yet outrageous goals can inspire); (2) goals must be accepted by group members; (3) goals are more effective when they are linked to feedback and rewards; (4) the combination of individual and group goals is very effective; and (5) a learning goal orientation is effective.

Motivating others by giving them recognition and praise can be considered a direct application of positive reinforcement. Recognition programs to reward and motivate employees are standard practice. Recognition is a strong motivator because it is a normal human need to crave recognition, and workers often do not feel they receive enough recognition. To appeal to the recognition need, identify a meritorious behavior and then recognize that behavior with an oral, written, or material reward. Formal recognition programs are also useful. Recognition and praise are no-cost or low-cost motivators that are powerful.

Giving workers an opportunity to experience pride can be a strong internal motivator, yet workers still receive recognition. To motivate through pride, it is best for the manager to set the compass on pride, not money, and for workers to be proud of daily accomplishments.

A major purpose of coaching is to achieve enthusiasm and high performance in a team setting. Coaching can also be regarded as a paradigm shift from traditional management, which focuses heavily on control, order, and compliance. Coaching is a partnership for achieving results. Several characteristics of coaching contribute to its close relationship with leadership. Coaching is a two-way process, suggesting that being a great coach requires having a talented team. Coaching requires a high degree of interpersonal risk and trust on the part of both sides in the relationship.

The coaching function can also be understood by recognizing several common misperceptions: (1) coaching applies only to one-on-one work; (2) coaching is mostly about providing new knowledge and skills; (3) coaching easily falls into psychotherapy; (4) coaches need to be experts in what they are coaching; and (5) coaching has to be done face-to-face.

Suggestions for improving coaching are as follows: (1) communicate clear expectations, (2) build relationships, (3) give feedback on areas that require specific improvement, (4) listen actively, (5) help remove obstacles, (6) give emotional support including empathy, (7) reflect content or meaning, (8) give gentle advice and guidance, (9) allow for modeling of desired performance and behavior, (10) gain a commitment to change, and (11) applaud good results.

Managers frequently consult executive (or business) coaches to help them be more effective leaders. Such coaches provide a variety of services, including counseling about weaknesses, helping achieve balance in life, helping the leader uncover hidden assets, and giving career advice. Studies show that executive coaching is effective, yet there are potential problems: executive coaches can give bad advice, the coach might be unqualified in general or to deal with mental health issues, and the leader may become too dependent on the coach.

## Key Terms

Expectancy theory

Valence

Outcome

Instrumentality

Expectancy

Self-efficacy

Goal

Executive (or business) coach

 ## Guidelines for Action and Skill Development

Given that recognition can be such a relatively low-cost yet highly effective motivator, the leader/manager should keep in mind available forms of recognition. In addition to considering those in the following list, use your imagination to think of other forms of recognition. For the recognition technique to work well, it should have high valence for the person or group under consideration.

- Compliments
- Encouragement for a job well done
- Comradeship with the boss
- Access to confidential information

- A pat on the back or a handshake
- Public expression of appreciation
- A meeting of appreciation with the executive
- Team uniforms, hats, T-shirts, or mugs
- A note of thanks to the individual (handwritten or email)
- A flattering letter from a customer distributed over email
- Employee-of-month award
- A wall plaque indicating accomplishment
- A special commendation placed in employee file
- A gift from the company recognition program, such as a watch, a clock, or a pin

## Discussion Questions and Activities

1. Identify several outcomes you expect from occupying a leadership position. What valences do you attach to them?
2. How can the influence exerted by a charismatic leader tie in with expectancy theory?
3. Explain how valence, instrumentality, and expectancy could relate to job performance.
4. What is a potential second-level outcome a person could gain from receiving an A in this course? From receiving an F?
5. What does goal theory tell managers that they probably do not already know about using goals to motivate people?

6. In what way might giving group members frequent recognition contribute to a leader's being perceived as charismatic?
7. Which forms of recognition are likely to be the most effective in motivating professional-level workers?
8. In what ways is coaching related to hands-on leadership?
9. How might a leader use coaching to help increase ethical behavior among group members?
10. Ask a manager or coach to describe the amount of coaching he or she does on the job. Be prepared to bring your findings back to class.

## LEADERSHIP CASE PROBLEM A

### EX-MILITARY OFFICERS DON ORANGE APRONS

Madeline Toft used to fly an attack helicopter and jump out of planes. As a captain in the U.S. Army, she led soldiers as they trained for war. Today she's a hardware store manager-in-training, one of more than 360 ex-military officers enrolled in Home Depot's Store Leadership program.

These recruits do not know all the power tools and paints, but that is almost beside the point. Home Depot CEO Robert Nardelli discovered junior military officers (JMO) when he ran General Electric's transportation business in the 1990s. They were intense, smart, and hard working, and with four to eight years in the military, they had leadership experience, often under challenging circumstances. Nardelli explains the company policy in these terms:

> The U.S. military community offers the Home Depot a talent pool of highly skilled individuals who have unique knowledge and character from their military experience, making them ideal for our national hiring initiative. We view our support of the military as our responsibility to our country and a valuable asset to our company's future. In short,

it is good for America, and it is good for our business" (*ir.homedepot.com*, p. 1).

The positive characteristics of former junior military officers are exactly what Home Depot needs. In the face of intense competition from Lowe's and Wal-Mart, the chain's sales growth has flagged since 2000. Its shares were down by nearly 50 percent in 2004. Nardelli wants to improve customers' experiences, overhaul information technology, and expand overseas. And to do all that, Home Depot needs leaders.

Traditionally, Home Depot store managers were experts in hardware. Now "we look for people who deliver results, act strategically, and drive excellence," says Dennis Donovan, Home Depot's executive vice president for human resources. "Leaders excel in customer service, they inspire achievement, they live with integrity, they build relationships, and they create an environment of inclusion; they build strong relationships. JMOs have these essentials" (*Fast Company*, p. 37).

More than half of the participants in Home Depot's two-year-old Store Leadership program

*(continued)*

are JMOs, often recruited at military outplacement fairs. Over two years, they are grounded in business skills and corporate culture. They are trained in stores at forums taught by senior managers, including Nardelli. Upon graduation they may run a store with, on average, more than $40 million in sales and 150 employees.

Home Depot is ranked as the most military-friendly employer in the United States, followed by Sprint and General Electric by *G.I. Jobs* (a newsletter/employment bulletin), and this includes all ranks of military workers. The company also helps the spouses of ex-military people hired by Home Depot find jobs at the company. The company hired more than 10,000 veterans in 2004 and has two full-time recruiters dedicated to hiring military veterans. A Home Depot spokesperson considered the ranking to be an honor.

When Larry Chang, a business administration major, was informed about Home Depot's quest for former military officers, he reacted, "Hold on. I detect discrimination here. I'm not knocking military experience, but I've got leadership capability also. I've been an assistant manager at Applebee's, I was an Eagle Scout, and I've studied leadership at college. You mean a guy or gal with a few years of experience as an army officer gets preferential treatment over me? Maybe I could see that if a Home Depot were looking for store managers to work at a location next to a military base."

## QUESTIONS

1. What problems with respect to leadership style might Home Depot encounter by hiring so many ex-military officers into the Store Leadership program?
2. How accurate is Donovan's description of the behaviors of leaders?
3. What do you recommend that Home Depot management do about potential complaints of job discrimination against nonmilitary people, such as those voiced by Larry Chang?

SOURCE: Rebecca Zicarelli, "Home Depot's Hardware Warriors," *Fast Company*, September 2004, p. 37; "Home Depot Is Top Firm for Hiring Vets," *The Atlanta Journal-Constitution*, November 11, 2004; "The Home Depot Joins Forces with U. S. Departments of Defense, Veterans Affairs to Launch National Hiring Initiative," *http://ir.homedepot.com*, Copyright © 2004 PR Newswire. All rights reserved; personal interviews with Home Depot customers, and business students, December 2004.

## LEADERSHIP CASE PROBLEM B

### THE REALITY COACH

Steve Randall was concerned that his managerial career had hit a plateau regarding his impact on others and his career progress. Pondering what to do, he made an appointment with Lorie LeBrun, an executive coach he heard being interviewed on a local talk show. After an initial interview, Randall signed a one-year contract with LeBrun. She would meet with Randall personally once a month. The two would also exchange a maximum of three email messages per week related to job problems and career concerns. Following are selected excerpts from their face-to-face meetings and email exchanges:

**Steve:** After listening to you on the talk show, I came away with the impression that you can make a person a better leader. That's why I came to see you. If I were a heavy-impact leader, I would be more successful.

**Lorie:** What is a "heavy-impact leader"?

**Steve:** What I'm getting at is a leader who impresses people, who is seen as a powerhouse, who gets others to bend over backward for him.

**Lorie:** Hold on, Steve. I don't like what I'm hearing. It sounds as if you want to win friends and influence people, but what about doing well for the company? What about helping people achieve goals that are important to them?

**Steve:** Whose side are you on, Lorie? Are you representing me? Or are you representing my company?

**Lorie:** I'm trying to represent the truth. I want you to grow, and you can't grow unless you get some honest feedback. It sounds as if you are more of a glory seeker than a results-focused manager.

**Steve:** Maybe there is a grain of truth in what you say. But if I didn't have a problem looking and acting like a leader, I wouldn't be here.

**Lorie:** I hear you Steve, but I have an assignment for you. For the next five times you interact with your group, focus more on them and less on yourself. Act like a servant leader. You serve the group. Help them achieve what they want. Then see what happens. I think you are too self-centered right now.

## ONE MONTH LATER

**Steve:** I did pay more attention to what the group wanted to accomplish. My team said they were afraid that we would lose funding for next year. So I am working on getting a straight answer from higher management about where the group is headed. As a result, the group seems a little bit more positive toward me.

**Lorie:** Hats off to you, Steve. It sounds as if you are making progress as a true leader.

**Steve:** The progress is really quite modest. I still need to make a big impact on key people. Toward that end, I'm thinking of going for Botox treatments. This way I could get rid of most of the wrinkles in my face. It would give me a more youthful, positive appearance.

**Lorie:** Right, Steve. You would have a frozen face like a fading Hollywood star who made one trip too many to the plastic surgeon. You're not getting the point, Steve. In terms of leadership, it's what is inside that counts. Is Bill Gates a glamour boy? Was Jack Welch [the legendary GE chief] a beautiful physical specimen? I don't think so!

**Steve:** I get your point, and I will give it some consideration. There is something else on my mind I want to discuss with you. My boss has turned out to be a backstabbing jerk, so I'm thinking about complaining about him to his boss.

**Lorie:** Those are pretty harsh words. In what way is your boss a "backstabbing jerk"?

**Steve:** He befriends me when he is with me, but he appears to be bad-mouthing me to the managers in the company. Two different reliable sources gave me that feedback.

**Lorie:** Grow up, Steve. Fight your own battles. Are you an adult person? Or are you a mouse? Get a face-to-face appointment with your boss, and share the vicious feedback with him. A true leader must confront problems head on.

**Steve:** I'll give what you said some thought, and I will email you with the results.

## QUESTIONS

1. What do you think of Lorie LeBrun's coaching techniques?
2. How literally should Steve Randall accept LeBrun's advice?
3. What would you advise Randall about the Botox treatments?

LEADERSHIP SKILL-BUILDING EXERCISE 10-4

### MY LEADERSHIP PORTFOLIO

One of the easiest and most powerful ways of motivating people is to recognize their efforts, as described in this chapter. Like any other interpersonal skill, being effective at giving recognition takes practice. During the next week, find three people to recognize, and observe how they react to your recognition. For example, if a server gives you fine service, after the meal explain how much you enjoyed the service and leave a larger-than-average tip. If your hair stylist does a fine job, similarly provide a compliment and a good tip. Or find some helper to recognize with a compliment but without a tip. Observe the responses of these people—both their facial expressions and what they say. Of even more importance, observe if any of these people appears eager to serve you the next time you interact with them.

As with other parts of your leadership portfolio, keep a written record of what happened to you and how much skill you think you developed.

### INTERNET SKILL-BUILDING EXERCISE

Apply the chapter concepts! Visit the Web and complete this Internet skill-building exercise to learn more about current leadership topics and trends.

### DREAM JOB COACHING

Visit *www.dreamjobcoaching.com* and find answers to the following questions:

1. According to the Internal Coach Federation, what does coaching entail?
2. How does Dream Job Coaching help you find an ideal position?
3. How could the principles of Dream Job Coaching help you be a more effective coach?

# Creativity, Innovation, and Leadership

## LEARNING OBJECTIVES

After studying this chapter and doing the exercises, you should be able to

- Identify the steps in the creative process.

- Identify characteristics of creative problem solvers.

- Be prepared to overcome traditional thinking in order to become more creative.

- Describe both organizational and individual approaches to enhance creative problem solving.

- Explain how the leader and the organization can establish a climate that fosters creativity.

- Identify several leadership practices that contribute to organizational innovation.

## CHAPTER OUTLINE

According to legend, it was melting ice cream that helped launch Fudgie the Whale and Cookie Puss. In 1934, Thomas Carvel was a young Greek immigrant in the New York suburbs who sold ice cream created from the back of a truck. On Memorial Day weekend, the truck broke down and the ice cream softened, and people loved it. Mr. Carvel soon invented equipment to produce soft ice cream and designed a glass-fronted building to sell it from. He started franchising in 1947 and quickly sold 100 franchises.

The franchise network grew to over 800 stores. In addition to making their own ice cream, franchises also reproduced Mr. Carvel's novelty cakes, of which Fudgie the Whale and Cookie Puss were kids' birthday-party favorites. Even after selling his company to international investment group Investcorp in 1989, Mr. Carvel, then in his 80s, remained active until his death a year later.[1]

The story about the birth of American icon Carvel tells us a lot about creativity applied to business. The creative leader recognizes a good opportunity that others might miss. Instead of saying, "I'm ruined, my ice cream is melting," Carvel probably said, "Wow, there are marketing possibilities in soft ice cream." By thinking creatively (such as by developing a new product based on a mishap), a person can form a new enterprise that can keep many people engaged in productive activity. However, the creative idea has to be executed properly for innovation to take place. Although the terms *creativity* and *innovation* are often used interchangeably, **innovation** refers to the creation of new ideas and *their implementation.*[2]

Creative thinking enables leaders to contribute novel insights that can open up new opportunities or alternatives for the group or the organization. The role of a creative leader is to bring into existence ideas and things that did not exist previously or that existed in a different form. Leaders are not bound by current solutions to problems. Instead, they create images of other possibilities. Leaders often move a firm into an additional business or start a new department that offers another service.

This chapter emphasizes the development of creativity in the leader. It also explains the nature of creativity and creative people and examines the leader's role in establishing an atmosphere that helps group members become more creative, along with leadership practices conducive to innovation.

## Steps in the Creative Process

An important part of becoming more creative involves understanding the stages involved in **creativity**, which is generally defined as the production of novel and useful ideas. An attempt has been made to understand creativity more specifically as it pertains to the workplace. As defined by Richard Woodman, John Sawyer, and Ricky Griffin, **organizational creativity** is the "creation of a valuable, useful new product, service, idea, procedure, or process by individuals working together in a complex social system."[3]

An old but well-accepted model of creativity can be applied to organizations. This model divides creative thinking into five stages,[4] as shown in Figure 11-1. Step 1 is *opportunity or problem recognition:* a person discovers that a new opportunity exists or a problem needs to be resolved. Thirty-eight years ago an entrepreneurial leader, Robert Cowan, recognized a new opportunity and asked, "Why do business meetings have to be conducted in person? Why can't they connect through television images?"[5]

Step 2 is *immersion.* The individual concentrates on the problem and becomes immersed in it. He or she will recall and collect information that seems relevant, dreaming up alternatives without refining or evaluating them. Cowan grabbed every fact he could about teleconferencing. At one point he helped NASA and the University of Alaska produce the first videoconference by satellite. He then synthesized all his information into a book about teleconferencing.

Step 3 is *incubation.* The person keeps the assembled information in mind for a while. He or she does not appear to be working on the problem actively, but the subconscious mind is still engaged. While the information is simmering, it is being arranged into meaningful new patterns. Cowan did not actively pursue his business videoconferencing idea for several years.

Step 4 is *insight.* The problem-conquering solution flashes into the person's mind at an unexpected time, such as on the verge of sleep, during a shower, or while running.

**FIGURE 11-1  Steps in the Creative Process**

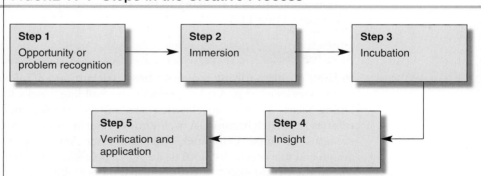

Creative problem solvers often go through these steps below the level of conscious awareness. Yet being aware of these steps (such as immersing yourself in knowledge) when faced with a challenging problem will often increase the probability of finding a creative solution.

Insight is also called the *Aha! experience:* all of a sudden something clicks. At one point Cowan suddenly thought of forming a teleconferencing business to exploit the potential of his idea.

Step 5 is *verification and application.* The individual sets out to prove that the creative solution has merit. Verification procedures include gathering supporting evidence, using logical persuasion, and experimenting with new ideas. Application requires tenacity because most novel ideas are first rejected as being impractical. When banks refused to finance Cowan's startup business, Cowan and his wife raised $45,000 from friends and obtained a second mortgage on their house. Cowan did start his business, but he faced financial trouble. When Cowan's company was on the verge of folding, Charles Schwab, the brokerage firm, hired it to connect its 100 branch offices.

The end product of Cowan's creative thinking was a business possibility rather than an invention. Nevertheless, businesspeople typically follow the same five steps of creative thought as do inventors. Even though creativity usually follows the same steps, it is not a mechanical process that can be turned on and off. Much of creativity is intricately woven into a person's intellect and personality.

## Characteristics of Creative Leaders

Creative leaders, like creative workers of all types, are different in many ways from their less creative counterparts. They are devoted to their fields and enjoy intellectual stimulation, and they challenge the status quo, which leads them to seek improvements. For example, someone questioned why listening to music on the go needed to involve a device as big as a CD player, and the result was the MP3 player. Above all, creative people are mentally flexible and can see past the traditional ways of looking at problems.

As described next, the specific characteristics of creative people, including creative leaders, can be grouped into four areas: knowledge, intellectual abilities, personality, and passion for the task and the experience of flow.[6] These characteristics are highlighted in Figure 11-2. In addition, we present a theory of creativity that helps explain how these characteristics lead to creative output. Before studying this information, compare your thinking to that of a creative person by doing Leadership Self-Assessment Quiz 11-1.

### Knowledge

Creative problem solving requires a broad background of information, including facts and observations. Knowledge provides the building blocks for generating and combining ideas. Most creative leaders are knowledgeable, and their knowledge contributes to their charisma. A well-known case in point is Steven P. Jobs, the chief executive of Apple Computer, Inc., and Pixar Animation Studios. He contributes design and marketing decisions to most of Apple's key products, and he played a major role in the development of the popular iPod portable music player. A contributor to Jobs's creativity is his in-depth technical knowledge of computer hardware and software. As with most creative people, Jobs has had his share of failed innovations, including the cube-shaped Mac. However, a few failures along the way rarely discourage a creative person.

### FIGURE 11-2 Characteristics of Creative Leaders

**Knowledge**
Knowledgeable about
wide range of information

**Personality**
Nonconformist
Self-confident
Thrill-seeking
Energetic
Persistent

**Intellectual Abilities**
Highly intelligent
Intellectually curious
Able to think divergently

**Passion for the Task
and Flow**

Having the right characteristics improves the chances of a person being a creative
problem solver and a creative leader.

**LEADERSHIP SELF-ASSESSMENT QUIZ 11-1**

## THE CREATIVE PERSONALITY TEST

INSTRUCTIONS Describe each of the following statements as "mostly true"
or "mostly false."

| | Mostly True | Mostly False |
|---|---|---|
| 1. It is generally a waste of time to read magazine articles, Internet articles, and books outside my immediate field of interest. | _____ | _____ |
| 2. I frequently have the urge to suggest ways of improving products and services I use. | _____ | _____ |
| 3. Reading fiction and visiting art museums are time wasters. | _____ | _____ |

*(continued)*

4. I am a person of very strong convictions. What is right is right; what is wrong is wrong. _____ _____

5. I enjoy it when my boss hands me vague instructions. _____ _____

6. Making order out of chaos is actually fun. _____ _____

7. Only under extraordinary circumstances would I deviate from my To-Do list (or other ways in which I plan my day). _____ _____

8. Taking a different route to work is fun, even if it takes longer. _____ _____

9. Rules and regulations should not be taken too seriously. Most rules can be broken under unusual circumstances. _____ _____

10. Playing with a new idea is fun even if it does not benefit me in the end. _____ _____

11. Some of my best ideas have come from building on the ideas of others. _____ _____

12. In writing, I try to avoid the use of unusual words and word combinations. _____ _____

13. I frequently jot down improvements in the job I would like to make in the future. _____ _____

14. I prefer to stay with technology devices I know well rather than frequently updating my equipment or software. _____ _____

15. I prefer writing personal notes or poems to loved ones rather than relying on greeting cards. _____ _____

16. At one time or another in my life I have enjoyed doing puzzles. _____ _____

17. If your thinking is clear, you will find the one best solution to a problem. _____ _____

18. It is best to interact with coworkers who think much like you. _____ _____

19. Detective work would have some appeal to me. _____ _____

20. Tight controls over people and money are necessary to run a successful organization. _____ _____

SCORING AND INTERPRETATION Give yourself a score of 1 for each answer that matches the answer key:

| | | |
|---|---|---|
| **1.** Mostly false | **8.** Mostly true | **15.** Mostly true |
| **2.** Mostly true | **9.** Mostly true | **16.** Mostly true |
| **3.** Mostly false | **10.** Mostly true | **17.** Mostly false |
| **4.** Mostly false | **11.** Mostly true | **18.** Mostly false |
| **5.** Mostly true | **12.** Mostly false | **19.** Mostly true |
| **6.** Mostly true | **13.** Mostly true | **20.** Mostly false |
| **7.** Mostly false | **14.** Mostly false | |

*Total score* _____

Extremely high or low scores are the most meaningful. A score of 15 or more suggests that your personality and attitudes are similar to those of creative people, including creative leaders. A score of 8 or less suggests that you are more of an intellectual conformist at present. Do not be discouraged. Most people can develop in the direction of becoming more creative.

How does your score compare to your self-evaluation of your creativity? We suggest you also obtain feedback on your creativity from somebody familiar with your thinking and your work.

## Intellectual Abilities

Intellectual abilities comprise such abilities as general intelligence and abstract reasoning. Creative problem solvers, particularly in business, tend to be bright but are not at the absolute top end of the brilliance scale. Extraordinarily high intelligence is not required to be creative, although creative people are facile at generating creative solutions to problems in a short period of time. Creative people also maintain a youthful curiosity throughout their lives, and the curiosity is not centered just on their own field of expertise. Instead, their range of interests encompasses many areas of knowledge, and they are enthusiastic about puzzling problems. These mental workouts help sharpen a person's intelligence.

Creative people show an identifiable intellectual style: being able to think divergently. They are able to expand the number of alternatives to a problem, thus moving away from a single solution. Yet the creative thinker also knows when it is time to narrow the number of useful solutions. For example, the divergent thinker might think of twenty-seven ways to reduce costs, but at some point he or she will have to move toward choosing the best of several cost-cutting approaches.

## Personality

The noncognitive aspects of a person heavily influence creative problem solving. Creative people tend to have a positive self-image without being blindly self-confident. Because they are self-confident, they are able to cope with criticism of their ideas, and they can tolerate the isolation necessary for developing ideas. Talking to others is a good way to get ideas, yet at some point the creative problem solver has to work alone and concentrate.

A study with production workers and office workers suggests that believing in one's ability to be creative facilitates a person solving problems creatively, as judged by supervisory ratings. Workers with **creative self-efficacy** received higher ratings than did workers who were less confident of their ability to solve problems creatively. Creative self-efficacy is an employee's belief that he or she can be creative in a work role.[7]

Creative people are frequently nonconformists and do not need strong approval from the group. Nonconformity can also mean being a maverick. Richard E. Cheverton observes: "The maverick is really the person who is the focus of creativity in a company, but a lot of people perceive them as jerks because they like to stir the pot. But these are just people driven to accomplish things anonymously. They just want to get things done, and they do not care about office politics or organizational charts. They like to spread the credit around."[8] A maverick personality who is not granted the freedom to develop new ideas is likely to join another firm or start a business.

Many creative problem solvers are thrill seekers who find that developing imaginative solutions to problems is a source of thrills. Creative people are also persistent, which is especially important for the verification and application stage of creative thinking. Selling a creative idea to the right people requires considerable follow-up. Finally, creative people enjoy dealing with ambiguity and chaos. Less creative people become quickly frustrated when task descriptions are unclear and disorder exists.

## *Passion for the Task and the Experience of Flow*

A dominant characteristic of creative people that is closely related to personality is a passion for the work. More than twenty years of research in industry conducted by Teresa M. Amabile and her associates led to the *intrinsic motivation principle of creativity:* people will be at their creative best when they feel motivated primarily by the interest, satisfaction, and challenge of the work itself—and not by external pressures.[9]

Passion for the task and high intrinsic motivation contribute in turn to a total absorption in the work and intense concentration, or the **experience of flow**. It is an experience so engrossing and enjoyable that the task becomes worth doing for its own sake regardless of the external consequences.[10] Perhaps you have had this experience when completely absorbed in a hobby or some analytical work, or when you were at your best in a sport or dance. (Flow also means *being in the zone.*) The highly creative leader, such as a business owner developing a plan for worldwide distribution of a product, will often achieve the experience of flow.

One of the problems with attempting to be creative under high-pressure conditions is that the pressure may interfere with the intense concentration required for high creativity. Based on her analysis of nearly 12,000 journal entries of workers engaged in creative tasks, Amabile discovered that time pressures may block people from deeply engaging with the problem. People can be creative when they are under heavy time pressures, but only when they can focus on the work.[11]

To fully understand the contribution of personal characteristics to creativity, we note the basic formula of human behavior : $B = f(P \times E)$ (behavior is a function of a person interacting with the environment). In this context, certain personal characteristics may facilitate a leader's being creative, but the right environment is necessary to trigger creative behavior. Greg R. Oldham and Anne Cummings conducted a study with 171 employees from two manufacturing facilities. Creativity was measured by patent disclosures, contributions to an employee suggestion program, and supervisory ratings. It was found that the participants who produced the most creative work had creativity-relevant characteristics such as self-confidence and tolerance of ambiguity. It was also important, however, for employees to work on complex, challenging jobs and to be supervised in a supportive, noncontrolling fashion.[12] The combination of the right personal characteristics with the right environmental conditions yielded the most creative output.

## The Componential Theory of Individual Creativity

The *componential theory of individual creativity* developed by Amabile integrates some of the information presented so far about the contribution of personal characteristics to creativity. According to this theory, creativity takes place when three components join together: expertise, creative-thinking skill, and task motivation.[13] *Expertise* refers to the necessary knowledge to put facts together (the knowledge required for creativity, as already explained). *Creative-thinking skill* refers to the ability to imaginatively approach problems. If you know how to keep digging for alternatives and to avoid getting stuck in the status quo, your chances of being creative multiply. The exercises to be presented in this chapter foster this type of mental flexibility. Finally, *task motivation* refers to persevering, or sticking with a problem to a conclusion, which is essential for finding creative solutions. A few rest breaks to gain a fresh perspective may be helpful, but the creative person keeps coming back until a solution emerges.

The combined forces of the three factors lead to individual creativity as follows: expertise × creative-thinking skill × task motivation = creativity. Because there are substantial individual differences for each factor, such as wide variation in domain-relevant expertise, not all leaders are equally creative.

# Overcoming Traditional Thinking as a Creativity Strategy

A unifying theme runs through all forms of creativity training and suggestions for creativity improvement: creative problem solving requires an ability to overcome traditional thinking. The concept of *traditional thinking* is relative, but it generally refers to a standard and frequent way of finding a solution to a problem. A traditional solution to a problem is thus a modal or most frequent solution. For example, traditional thinking suggests that to increase revenue, a retail store should conduct a sale. Creative thinking would point toward other solutions. As an example, a retail store might increase sales by delivering goods for a small fee, or providing for online shopping (of the store's products) in the store.

The creative person looks at problems in a new light and transcends conventional thinking about them. A historically significant example is Henry Ford, who was known for his creative problem-solving ability. A meatpacking executive invited Ford to visit his Chicago plant and observe how employees processed beef. The automotive executive noticed that at one end of the plant whole carcasses of steers were placed on a giant conveyor belt. As the meat traveled through the plant, workers carved it into various cuts until the carcass was consumed. A flash of whimsical insight hit Ford: What if the process were reversed, and all the pieces would become a whole steer again? Ford asked himself, "Why can't an automobile be built that way?" He took his creative idea back to the Ford Motor Company in Detroit and constructed the world's first manufacturing assembly line.[14]

The central task in becoming creative is to break down rigid thinking that blocks new ideas. At the same time, the problem solver must unlearn the conventional approach.[15] Henry Ford unlearned the custom approach to building autos so he could use an assembly line. (In the current era, people who have unlearned the assembly-line approach and switched to customization are considered to be creative!) A conventional-thinking leader or manager might accept the long-standing policy that spending more than $5,000 requires three levels of approval. A creative leader might ask, "Why do we need three levels of approval for spending $5,000? If we trust people enough to make them managers, why can't they have budget authorization to spend at least $10,000?"

college.hmco.com/pic/
dubrin5e

**KB @ KNOWLEDGE BANK:** provides more depth on the topic of creative thinking.

Overcoming traditional thinking is so important to creative thinking that the process has been characterized in several different ways. The most familiar is that a *creative person thinks outside the box*. A *box* in this sense is a category that confines and restricts thinking. Because you are confined to a box, you do not see opportunities outside the box. For example, if an insurance executive thinks that health insurance is only for people, he or she might miss out on the growing market for domestic animal health insurance. Inside the accompanying box insert, you will find several business examples of thinking outside the box. The Leader in Action describes how thinking outside the box helped launch an enterprise.

## CURRENT BUSINESS EXAMPLES OF THINKING OUTSIDE THE BOX

- Conventional wisdom says that to rent videos or DVDs you have to visit a physical video or DVD store. Netflix shot out of nowhere to create a new segment in the movie rental business with a simple business model that allows consumers to rent popular DVDs online and have the movies arrive quickly in the mail, all for a monthly fee. Netflix's success spawned com-

petitors, but so far the company still has about a 95 percent market share.

- Conventional wisdom says that ATM monitors are used only to display bank-statement-related information. Not Bank of America: they started a program of selling advertising space on ATMs.

- Who says companies have to sign long-term, fixed-price contracts to use hardware and software that is dedicated only to that customer? IBM Corporation introduced a service that will allow customers to run their own software applications on mainframes in IBM's data centers and pay rates based mostly on the amount of computing power they use. The pay-for-use model follows the logic of paying for utilities.

- Everybody knows that the best way to promote athletic shoes is to pay megabucks to professional basketball superstars. Nike, however, has departed from conventional wisdom by attempting to create heroes out of no-names. As part of a new marketing strategy, Nike and several other sneaker makers have hired "street ballers" to be their pitch persons. For beginners, Nike hired Luis Dasilva (aka "Trickz") for around $50,000. He shows off his playground moves on television commercials. He never played professional basketball, was an average high school player, and was working as a clerk in an Athlete's Foot store. In the ad, Trickz wears a flimsy pair of orange hot pants and an Afro wig and slides the ball up and down his arms to a funk beat.

- Conventional wisdom says that banks cannot make home loans to devout Muslims because,

according to the Koran (Islam's sacred book), Muslims are forbidden to pay or receive interest. As a consequence, a potential segment of the market was shut out from receiving home mortgages. The University Bank of Ann Arbor, Michigan, developed a unique interest-free program designed for people whose religious beliefs forbid paying interest. The bank developed a mortgage alternative loan transaction (MALT) program that replaces a traditional home loan with a redeemable lease. The bank holds the home in trust, and the customer makes monthly payments to that trust. Each rent payment includes a set amount of savings that builds equity in the property. After the savings account equals the home's original price, the customer owns the home free and clear.

SOURCE: Christopher Stern, "Netflix Braces for Amazon: DVD Rental Company Cuts Fees to Compete," *The Washington Post,* October 16, 2004 p. 1E; Sally Beatty, "Bank of America Puts Ads in ATMs," *The Wall Street Journal,* July 25, 2002, p. B8; William M. Bulkeley, "New IBM Service Will Test Vision of Computing Power as Utility," *The Wall Street Journal,* July 1, 2001, p. B4; Maureen Tkacik, "Hoop Dreams: In Search of Stars. Shoe Makers Turn to the Playground," *The Wall Street Journal,* July 3, 2002, p.1; Karen Dybis, "Banks Offer No-Interest Options for Muslims," *The Detroit News,* December 21, 2004 (*detnews.com*).

## Organizational Methods to Enhance Creativity

To enhance creative problem solving, most organizations regularly engage in brainstorming. We focus here on new developments in brainstorming and other creativity-enhancing methods. Programs of this nature are applied to actual problems, while at the same time they provide an opportunity to improve creative thinking.

**KB** **@ KNOWLEDGE BANK:** provides more information on brainstorming and other creativity-enhancing methods.

college.hmco.com/pic/
dubrin5e

The leader has a dual role in implementing creative problem-solving techniques: he or she facilitates group interaction and also provides a fair share of creative output. The six creativity-enhancing, problem-solving techniques described here are (1) systematically collecting fresh ideas; (2) brainstorming; (3) using the pet-peeve technique; (4) using the forced-association technique; and (5) equipping a kitchen for the mind. The Knowledge Bank presents a sixth method.

## LEADER IN ACTION

### THINKING OUTSIDE THE (SHOE) BOX

Kenneth Cole grew up in the shoe business. His father owned a Brooklyn-based company called El Greco that became known for producing the Candies line of women's shoes. In 1982, he left to start his own company, called Kenneth Cole Inc. He designed a line of shoes and hired an Italian factory to make them. That fall, he wanted to show off his wares at the industry's main trade show at a Hilton hotel in midtown Manhattan.

Designers had two options for showing off their products, Cole says. "You could be one of about 1,100 companies that took a little room at the Hilton. But that wasn't a great way to define yourself. Or you could set up a fancy showroom near the hotel. I clearly didn't have the money for that." So he hit upon the idea of borrowing a friend's tractor-trailer, parking it in front of the Hilton, and peddling shoes from there. Unfortunately, that required a permit, which only the city could issue.

"I called the mayor's office and said, 'How does someone get permission to park a 40-foot trailer on the street in New York?' And a representative said, 'The answer, son, is that they don't. This is New York. There are only two exceptions: if you are a utility company doing service or a production company shooting a full-length motion picture.'"

The next day, Cole changed his company's name to Kenneth Cole Productions Inc. and filed for a permit to shoot a movie called *The Birth of a Shoe Company*. "With the mayor's blessing, I opened for business on December 2, 1982," Cole says. "I had two New York policemen as my doormen, compliments of the city. I sold 40,000 pairs of shoes in less than three days."

"I tell this story often because we need to remind ourselves that in business and in life, the best solution isn't necessarily the most expensive one, but it's almost always the most creative one," Cole says.

### QUESTIONS

1. In what way was Cole thinking nontraditionally when he launched his shoe business?
2. In what way did Cole link together two previously unlinked sets of knowledge or facts to arrive at his creative idea?
3. How might the story about the launch of his shoe company contribute to the charisma of Kenneth Cole?

SOURCE: The title is from "Thinking Outside the (Shoe) Box," *Executive Leadership*, April 2004, p. 8. The story is from "Kenneth Cole: How the King of Sole Got Soul." Reprinted with permission from "Innovation and Entrepreneurship," *Knowledge @ Wharton*, January 28, 2004, pp. 1–2. For more information, contact http://knowledge.wharton.upenn.edu/

### Systematically Collecting Fresh Ideas

Creativity is often referred to as a numbers game, because the more ideas you try, the greater the probability of finding one that works. A notable way of collecting fresh ideas is for employees to furnish them to a company database so that when somebody needs a fresh idea it can be accessed through a company search engine. Google, the search-engine company, uses an internal web site to collect and retrieve ideas. Many of the ideas are used to improve the company's enormously popular search engine. Google's idea search begins with a company-use-only web page. Using a program called Sparrow, Google employees can readily create a page of ideas. This enables company leaders (such as a product manager) to cast a net across the company's 300 employees. Using this method, every Google staff member invests a fraction of the workday on research and development. Employees are encouraged to invest 20 percent of their time working on whatever they think will have the biggest payoff for the company.[16]

To facilitate having fresh ideas, the leader or manager can establish idea quotas, such as by asking staff members to bring one new idea to each meeting. Although the vast majority of these ideas may not lead to innovation, a few good ones will emerge. One reason idea quotas work is that they are a goal. Another is that an environmental need (in this case, the idea quota) is an excellent creativity stimulant.

A major leadership accomplishment is to obtain widespread participation in contributing innovative thinking. A.G. Lafley, the Procter & Gamble CEO, explains this approach:

> The P&G of five years or six years ago depended on 8,000 scientists and engineers for the vast majority of innovation. The P&G we're trying to unleash today asks all 100,000-plus of us to be innovators. We actively solicit good ideas, and if the concept is promising we put it into development. For example, we are now selling a line of hair care for women of color called Pantene Pro-V Relaxed and Natural. A few African-American employees came to me and said we're missing out: The stuff that's on the market really doesn't work, and we can do better.[17] [The line is doing well.]

### Brainstorming

The best-known method for creativity improvement is brainstorming, which most of you have already done. As a refresher, do Leadership Skill-Building Exercise 11-1. Because the vast majority of employers use brainstorming, it is helpful to have some advanced knowledge of the topic other than that it is simply shouting out ideas.

college.hmco.
com/pic/
dubrin5e

**LEADERSHIP SKILL-BUILDING EXERCISE 11-1**

### BRAINSTORMING AND *www.GETRICH.com*

**KB** **@ KNOWLEDGE BANK:** contains rules for brainstorming.

INSTRUCTIONS To refresh your memory, first study the rules for brainstorming presented in the Knowledge Bank. Then do the brainstorming exercise.

Organize into groups to play *"www.GetRich.com."* Assume the role of a small group of friends who want to launch an Internet business. Develop an appropriate Net address, such as www.surfing.com for a company that sells surfing equipment. You must also explain the nature of the business, not necessarily restricting yourself to the same business model as many others have used. Think in terms of a business that might be successful enough to eventually sell stock to the public—an initial public offering (IPO). This is why the exercise is called *"www.GetRich.com."* The brainstorming team leader will then present the team's solution to the rest of the class.

A key aspect of brainstorming is that all ideas can be steppingstones and triggers for new and more useful ideas. Any idea might lead to other associations and connections. Thus, during the idea-generating part of brainstorming, potential solutions are not criticized or evaluated in any way, so that spontaneity is encouraged. The idea for an antitheft device for automobiles, The Club, is reported to have stemmed from brainstorming. One marketing person suggested that cars should have a portable steering wheel that the driver could remove after the car is parked. Somebody else suggested that the steering wheel be made inoperative, which led to the idea of an ultrastrong bar to lock the steering wheel in place. The Club and its imitators have become highly successful products; a version of The Club has been developed for securing doors.

Brainstorming continues to evolve as a method of creative problem solving. A recent variation is the *6–3–5 method*. Six people take five minutes to write down three ideas each on a sheet of paper or large index card. After five minutes, the participants pass their papers or cards clockwise and add their own ideas to each new sheet. They continue passing along and writing down ideas until the sheets or cards get back to the people who originated them. Next, they hold a group discussion of the merits of the various ideas.[18] During the discussion, it is likely that some members will modify their ideas or think of new ones because they will be stimulated by the list of eighteen ideas. Often, however, the list will contain many duplicate or similar ideas.

Brainstorming can be conducted through email as well as through group discussion. In brainstorming by email, group members simultaneously enter their suggestions into a computer. The ideas are distributed to the monitors of other members. Or ideas can be sent back at different times to a facilitator who passes the contributions along to other members. In either approach, although group members do not talk to each other, they are still able to build on each other's ideas and combine ideas. Brainstorming via email can increase both the quantity and quality of ideas. When participants do not face each other directly, they can concentrate on the creativity task at hand and less on the interpersonal aspects of interaction.[19]

Brainstorming, much like other creative problem-solving techniques, works best in an organizational culture that fosters innovation. It is an integral part of the famous design firm IDEO, Inc., whose employees believe passionately in innovation. As a result they are able to argue about alternative solutions to problems yet still unite to produce an effective design.[20]

## Using the Pet-Peeve Technique

An important part of leadership is for organizational units to find ways to continuously improve their service to external and internal customers. The **pet-peeve technique** is a method of brainstorming in which a group identifies all the possible complaints others might have about the group's organizational unit.[21] Through brainstorming, group members develop a list of complaints from any people who interact with their group. Sources of complaints include inside customers, outside customers, competitors, and suppliers.

Group members can prepare for the meeting by soliciting feedback on themselves from the various target groups. In keeping with the informal, breezy style of the pet-peeve group, feedback should be gathered informally. Rather than approach target groups with a survey, members might tell others about the upcoming pet-peeve session and then ask, "What complaints can you contribute?"

During the no-holds-barred brainstorming session, group members throw in some imaginary and some humorous complaints. Humorous complaints are especially important, for humor requires creative thinking. After all complaints have been aired, the group can process the information during a later session, when they can draw up action plans to remedy the most serious problems.

A pet-peeve session in the human resources department of a manufacturer of small electronic appliances generated the following complaints:

> "A lot of people wonder what we are doing. They think we just fill out forms and create work for ourselves."

> "Some line managers think our job is to find good reasons why they shouldn't hire their best job candidates."

> "A lot of employees think we're the corporate ax carriers. We tell line management whom to fire and whose job to eliminate."

> "They call us the happiness people. They think our purpose is to keep everybody happy and create a big happy family."

> "Job candidates from the outside think our job is to shred résumés. They think we throw away or delete 90 percent of the résumés that arrive at the company."

As a result of these penetrating, albeit exaggerated, self-criticisms, the human resources department developed an effective action plan. The department leader arranged brief meetings with units throughout the organization to discuss the department's role and to answer questions.

The pet-peeve technique is potentially valuable for a leader because it can help the group improve its work processes. Because it has a good-spirited touch, it is not likely to be perceived as threatening. Leadership Skill-Building Exercise 11-2 presents an opportunity to practice the pet-peeve technique.

---

**LEADERSHIP SKILL-BUILDING EXERCISE 11-2**

### THE PET-PEEVE TECHNIQUE

Review the description of the pet-peeve technique given in the text. Break into groups of about five contributors each. Each group assumes the role of an organizational unit. (Pick one that is familiar to the group, either through direct contact or through secondhand knowledge. For example, you might assume the role of the auditing group of an accounting firm, the financial aid office at your school, or the service department of an automobile dealer.) Generate a number of real and imagined criticisms of your group. Take the two most serious criticisms and develop an action plan to move your group to a higher plane.

### Using the Forced-Association Technique

A widely used method of releasing creativity is the **forced-association technique**, in which individuals or groups solve a problem by making associations between the properties of two objects. An individual (working alone or in a group) selects a word at random from a dictionary. Next, the person (or group) lists all of the properties and attributes of this word.

Assume you randomly chose the word *pickle*. Among its attributes are "tasty," "green," "oblong," and "moderately priced." You then force-fit these properties and attributes to the problem you are facing. If you were trying to improve sunglasses, for example, making them "green" and "moderately priced" could be useful. The forced association is supposed to help solve the problem. A link is found between the properties of the random object and the properties of the problem object. An additional, supposedly true, example will help clarify this abstract process.

### Equipping a Kitchen for the Mind

According to Mike Vance, the former dean of Disney University (the training program for The Walt Disney Company), every business needs a *kitchen for the mind*, a space designed to nurture creativity. The supplies can be ordinary items such as a chalkboard, flip charts, a coffeepot, a refrigerator, a pencil sharpener, and a personal computer with graphics software. Creativity rooms are also sometimes supplied with children's toys, such as dart guns, Frisbees, Nerf balls, and stuffed animals. The purpose of the toys is to help people loosen up intellectually and emotionally, thus stimulating creative thinking. Many large corporations, including General Electric and Motorola, have established creative kitchens, which they often supply with VCRs, DVD players, and multimedia computers.

More important than the equipment within the kitchen for the mind is the existence of a communal meeting place where people can get together to think creatively. Vance contends that even when people's resources are limited, they can still use their ingenuity to produce creative ideas.[22]

college.hmco.com/pic/
dubrin5e

**KB @ KNOWLEDGE BANK:** Physical activities are yet another way of enhancing creativity, as presented in the Knowledge Bank.

## Self-Help Techniques to Enhance Creative Problem Solving

Leaders and others who want to solve problems more creatively can find hundreds of methods at their disposal, all of them aiming to increase mental flexibility. Five strategies and specific techniques for enhancing creative problem solving are presented below and outlined in Table 11-1. These strategies and techniques support and supplement the organizational programs described previously. An underlying contribution of these techniques is that they facilitate flexible thinking, or viewing the world with open and curious eyes.[23] With such a mental stance, almost anything can spark a new idea. As a warehouse manager you might observe young people Rollerblading

| **TABLE 11-1** | **Self-Help Techniques for Creativity Improvement** |
|---|---|
| | 1. Practicing creativity-enhancing exercises |
| | 2. Staying alert to opportunities |
| | 3. Maintaining an enthusiastic attitude, including being happy |
| | 4. Maintaining and using an idea notebook or computer file |
| | 5. Playing the roles of explorer, artist, judge, and lawyer |

in the park. With a creative attitude, you might conclude that your logistic workers would be more efficient if they used Rollerblades rather than walked.

## Practicing Creativity-Enhancing Exercises

An established way to sharpen creative thinking is to regularly engage in activities that encourage flexible thinking. If you enjoy photography, put yourself on assignment to take a photograph illustrating a theme. You might, for example, take photographs illustrating the proper use of your company's product. Puzzles of all types are useful in stretching your imagination; many creative people regularly do crossword puzzles. Another mind stretcher is to force yourself to write jokes around a given theme. Can you create a joke about the creativity of a leader?

Learning a second language, including sign language, can facilitate creativity because you are forced to shift mental sets. For example, your second language may require you to remember the gender of every noun and to match the spelling of each adjective to the gender and number (singular versus plural) of the noun.

Leadership Skill-Building Exercise 11-3 gives you an opportunity to practice creative thinking. Doing exercises of this nature enhances creative problem solving.

---

**LEADERSHIP SKILL-BUILDING EXERCISE 11-3**

### WORD HINTS TO CREATIVITY

Find a fourth word that is related to the other three words in each row.

*Example:* poke               go                    molasses              _____

The answer is *slow:* slow poke, go slow, and slow as molasses. Now try these words:

| | | | |
|---|---|---|---|
| **1.** surprise | line | birthday | _____ |
| **2.** base | snow | dance | _____ |
| **3.** rat | blue | cottage | _____ |
| **4.** nap | litter | call | _____ |
| **5.** golf | foot | country | _____ |

*(continued)*

| | | | |
|---|---|---|---|
| **6.** house | weary | ape | _____ |
| **7.** tiger | plate | news | _____ |
| **8.** painting | bowl | nail | _____ |
| **9.** jump | sea | priest | _____ |
| **10.** maple | beet | loaf | _____ |
| **11.** oak | show | plan | _____ |
| **12.** light | village | golf | _____ |
| **13.** merry | out | up | _____ |
| **14.** jelly | green | kidney | _____ |
| **15.** bulb | house | lamp | _____ |

SCORING AND INTERPRETATION Answers appear on page 496. If you were able to think of the "correct" word, or another plausible one, for ten or more of these words, your score compares favorably to that of creative individuals. More important than the score is the fact that you acquired some practice in making remote associations—a characteristic talent of creative people.

SOURCE: Updated and adapted from "Ideas: Test Your Creativity," by Eugene Raudsepp, *Nation's Business* (June 1965), p. 80.

## Staying Alert to Opportunities

A characteristic of creative leaders is that they can spot opportunities that other people overlook. Opportunity seeking is associated with entrepreneurial leadership because the entrepreneur might build an organization around an unmet consumer need. The idea behind the international chain of Starbucks coffee shops began when Howard Schultz, the director of a four-store retail operation called Starbucks Coffee, Tea, and Spice, was attending a housewares convention in Milan, Italy. Schultz noticed the coffee-bar phenomenon. Milan alone had 1,500 of them, all serving trendy beverages such as espresso. Believing that coffee bars would also prosper in the United States, Schultz convinced Starbucks to open one. Schultz left the company to form his own small chain of coffee bars, and then he bought out Starbucks's two founding partners and merged Starbucks with his firm.[24] (What unmet consumer need did Schultz identify?)

## Maintaining an Enthusiastic Attitude, Including Being Happy

The managerial leader faces a major hurdle in becoming a creative problem solver. He or she must resolve the conflict between being judicial and being imaginative.

In many work situations, being judicial (or judgmental) is necessary. Situations calling for judicial thinking include reviewing proposed expenditures and inspecting products for quality or safety defects. Imaginative thinking is involved when searching for creative alternatives. Alex F. Osburn, a former advertising executive and the originator of brainstorming, notes how judgment and imagination are often in conflict:

> The fact that moods won't mix largely explains why the judicial and the creative tend to clash. The right mood for judicial thinking is largely negative. "What's wrong with this?. . . . No this won't work." Such reflexes are right and proper when trying to judge.
>
> In contrast, our creative thinking calls for a positive attitude. We have to be hopeful. We need enthusiasm. We have to encourage ourselves to the point of self-confidence. We have to beware of perfectionism lest it be abortive.[25]

The action step is therefore to project oneself into a positive frame of mind when attempting to be creative. The same principle applies when attempting to be creative about a judicial task. For instance, a leader might be faced with the task of looking for creative ways to cut costs. The manager would then have to think positively about thinking negatively!

Closely related to enthusiasm as a contributor to creativity is the finding that being in a good mood facilitates creativity. The finding comes from an analysis of diaries or journals, as described above. The journal entries showed that people are happiest when they come up with a creative idea. However, they are more likely to have a breakthrough idea if they were happy the day before. One day's happiness is often a predictor of the next day's creative idea.[26]

## Maintaining and Using an Idea Notebook or Computer File

It is difficult to capitalize on creative ideas unless you keep a careful record of them. A creative idea trusted to memory may be forgotten in the press of everyday business. An important suggestion kept on your daily planner may become obscured. Creative ideas can lead to breakthroughs for your group and your career, so they deserve the dignity of a separate notebook or computer file. A cautious or forgetful person is advised to keep two copies of the idea book or computer file: one at home and one in the office.

## Playing the Roles of Explorer, Artist, Judge, and Lawyer

Another creativity-improvement method incorporates many of the preceding methods. Say you want to enhance your creativity on the job. This method calls for you to adopt four roles in your thinking.[27] First, be an *explorer*. Speak to people in different fields and get ideas that can bring about innovations for your group. For example, if you manage a telecommunications group, speak to salespeople and manufacturing specialists.

Second, be an *artist* by stretching your imagination. Strive to spend about 5 percent of your day asking what-if questions. For example, the leader of a telecommunications group might ask, "What if some new research suggests that the extensive use of telecommunications devices is associated with high rates of cancer?" Also remember to challenge the commonly perceived rules in your field. A bank manager, for example, asked why customers needed their cancelled checks returned each month. The questioning led to a new bank practice: returning cancelled checks only if the customer pays an additional fee.

Third, know when to be a *judge*. After developing some imaginative ideas, at some point you have to evaluate them. Do not be so critical that you discourage your own imaginative thinking. Be critical enough, however, so that you do not try to implement weak ideas. A managing partner in an established law firm formulated a plan for opening two storefront branches that would offer legal services to the public at low prices. The branches would advertise on radio, on television, and in newspapers. After thinking through her plan for several weeks, however, she dropped the idea. She decided that the storefront branches would most likely divert clients away from the parent firm, rather than create a new market.

Fourth, achieve results with your creative thinking by playing the role of *lawyer*. Negotiate and find ways to implement your ideas within your field or place of work. The explorer, artist, and judge stages of creative thought might take only a short time to develop a creative idea. Yet you may spend months or even years getting your breakthrough idea implemented. For example, many tax-preparation firms now loan clients instant refunds in the amount of their anticipated tax refunds. It took a manager in a large tax-preparation firm a long time to convince top management of the merits of the idea.

college.hmco.com/pic/ dubrin5e

**(KB) @ KNOWLEDGE BANK:** Two more self-help techniques to enhance creative problem solving are described in the Knowledge Bank.

## Establishing a Climate for Creative Thinking

Leaders need to develop creative ideas of their own to improve productivity and satisfaction. Establishing a climate, or culture, conducive to creative problem solving is another requirement of effective leadership. A foundation step in fostering organizational creativity is to establish a vision and mission that include creativity, such as "We will become the most innovative provider of automobile care (mufflers, brakes, etc.) products and services in North America" (Monro Muffler Brake, Inc.). Vision statements and mission statements set the pace, but they must be supported by the right climate and extensive use of the techniques described throughout this chapter.

Information about establishing a climate for creativity can be divided into (1) leadership and managerial practices for enhancing creativity and (2) methods for managing creative workers. To become sensitized to this vast amount of information, do Leadership Diagnostic Activity 11-1. The instrument gives you an opportunity to ponder many of the management and leadership practices that encourage or discourage creative problem solving.

LEADERSHIP DIAGNOSTIC ACTIVITY 11-1

## ASSESSING THE CLIMATE FOR INNOVATION

INSTRUCTIONS Respond "mostly yes" or "mostly no" as to how well each of the following characteristics fits an organization familiar to you. If you are currently not familiar with an outside organization, respond to these statements in regard to your school.

|  | Mostly Yes | Mostly No |
|---|---|---|
| 1. Creativity is encouraged here. | _____ | _____ |
| 2. Our ability to function creatively is respected by the leadership. | _____ | _____ |
| 3. Around here, people are allowed to try to solve the same problems in different ways. | _____ | _____ |
| 4. The main function of members of this organization is to follow orders that come down through channels. | _____ | _____ |
| 5. Around here, a person can get into a lot of trouble by being different. | _____ | _____ |
| 6. This organization can be described as flexible and continually adapting to change. | _____ | _____ |
| 7. A person cannot do things that are too different around here without provoking anger. | _____ | _____ |
| 8. The best way to get along in this organization is to think the way the rest of the group does. | _____ | _____ |
| 9. People around here are expected to deal with problems in the same way. | _____ | _____ |
| 10. This organization is open and responsive to change. | _____ | _____ |
| 11. The people in charge around here usually get credit for others' ideas. | _____ | _____ |
| 12. In this organization, we tend to stick to tried and true ways. | _____ | _____ |
| 13. This place seems to be more concerned with the status quo than with change. | _____ | _____ |
| 14. Assistance in developing new ideas is readily available. | _____ | _____ |
| 15. There are adequate resources devoted to innovation in this organization. | _____ | _____ |

*(continued)*

16. There is adequate time available to pursue creative ideas here.        ___    ___

17. Lack of funding to pursue creative ideas is a problem in this organization.        ___    ___

18. Personnel shortages inhibit innovation in this organization.        ___    ___

19. This organization gives me free time to pursue creative ideas during the workday.        ___    ___

20. The reward system here encourages innovation.        ___    ___

21. This organization publicly recognizes those who are innovative.        ___    ___

22. The reward system here benefits mainly those who do not rock the boat.        ___    ___

SCORING AND INTERPRETATION The score in the direction of a climate for innovation is "mostly yes" for statements 1, 2, 3, 6, 10, 14, 15, 16, 19, 20, and 21, and "mostly no" for statements 4, 5, 7, 8, 9, 11, 12, 13, 17, 18, and 22. A score of 16 or higher suggests a climate well suited for innovation, 9 to 15 is about average, and 8 or below suggests a climate that inhibits innovation.

SOURCE: From Susanne G. Scott and Reginald Bruce, "Determinants of Innovative Behavior: A Path Model of Individual Innovation in the Workplace," *Academy of Management Journal*, by Hitt, Michael A., June 1994, p. 593. Copyright 1994 by Academy of Management. Reproduced with permission of Academy of Management in the format Textbook via Copyright Clearance Center.

## Leadership Practices for Enhancing Creativity

Eight leadership and managerial practices are particularly helpful in fostering creative thinking, as revealed by the work of Amabile and her associates, as well as by other researchers and observers.[28]

1. *Intellectual challenge.* Matching people with the right assignments enhances creativity because it supports expertise and intrinsic motivation. The amount of stretch is consistent with goal theory; too little challenge leads to boredom, but too much challenge leads to feelings of being overwhelmed and loss of control. The leader or manager must understand his or her group members well to offer them the right amount of challenge. Moderate time pressures can sometimes bring about the right amount of challenge.

2. *Freedom to choose the method.* Workers tend to be more creative when they are granted the freedom to choose which method is best for attaining a work goal (as described in our study of empowerment in Chapter 7). Stable goals are important because it is difficult to work creatively toward a moving target.

3. *Ample supply of the right resources.* Time and money are the most important resources for enhancing creativity. Deciding how much time and money to give to a team or project is a tough judgment call that can either support or stifle creativity. Under some circumstances setting a time deadline will trigger creative thinking because it represents a favorable challenge. An example would be hurrying to be first to market with a new product. False deadlines or impossibly tight ones can create distrust and burnout. To be creative, groups also need to be adequately funded.

4. *Effective design of work groups.* Work groups are the most likely to be creative when they are mutually supportive and when they have a diversity of backgrounds and perspectives. Blends of gender, race, and ethnicity are recognized today as contributing to creative thought, similar to cross-functional teams with their mix of perspectives from different disciplines. The various points of view often combine to achieve creative solutions to problems. Homogeneous teams argue less, but they are often less creative. Putting together a team with the right chemistry—just the right level of diversity and supportiveness—requires experience and intuition on the leader's part.

5. *Supervisory encouragement.* The most influential step a leader can take to bring about creative problem solving is to develop a permissive atmosphere that encourages people to think freely. Praising creative work is important because, for most people to sustain their passion, they must feel that their work matters to the organization. Creative ideas should be evaluated quickly rather than put through a painfully slow review process.

6. *Organizational support.* The entire organization as well as the immediate manager should support creative effort if creativity is to be enhanced on a large scale. The company-wide reward system should support creativity, including recognition and financial incentives. Organizational leaders should encourage information sharing and collaboration, which lead to the development of the expertise so necessary for creativity and to more opportunities for intrinsic motivation. Executives who combat excessive politics can help creative people focus on work instead of fighting political battles. In a highly political environment, a worker would be hesitant to suggest a creative idea that was a political blunder, such as replacing a product particularly liked by the CEO.

7. *Have favorable exchanges with creative workers.* Another insight into encouraging a creative climate is for leaders to have favorable exchanges with group members, as defined by LMX theory (see Chapter 9). A study with 191 research and development specialists found a positive relationship between LMX ratings and creativity of workers as measured by supervisory ratings.[29] When group members have positive relationships with their manager, they may have a more relaxed mental attitude that allows the imagination to flow. A useful strategy for enhancing creativity throughout the organization is to emphasize the importance of working with a sense of heightened awareness, of being alert to new possibilities.

8. *Leaders as talent magnets.* An indirect way for a leader to encourage innovation is to attract talented people to work on his or her team. At W. L. Gore and Associates, Inc. (makers of Gore-Tex® fabrics along with hundreds of other innovations, including synthetic blood vessels) people become natural leaders by recruiting followers. Given that there is no chain of command, the leaders become

talent magnets who attract other people who want to work with them. The talent magnet approach led to the development of Elixir®, the top-selling acoustic guitar string.[30] In sum, the passionate and credible leader enhances creativity by attracting talented people to work together on an innovative product.

## Methods of Managing Creative Workers

Closely related to establishing organizational conditions favoring creativity is choosing effective methods for managing creative workers. One estimate is that approximately 30 percent of the work force is employed in a creative occupation.[31] The suggestions that follow supplement effective leadership and management practices in general.[32]

1. *Give creative people tools and resources that allow their work to stand out.* Creative workers have a high degree of self-motivation and therefore want to achieve high-quality output. To achieve such high quality, they usually need adequate resources, such as state-of-the-art equipment and an ample travel budget for such purposes as conducting research.

2. *Give creative people flexibility and a minimum amount of structure.* Many creative workers regard heavy structure as the death knell of creativity. "Structure" for these workers means rules and regulations, many layers of approval, strict dress codes, fixed office hours, rigid assignments, and fill-in-the-blank Web forms or paperwork (Typically, the leader/manager will have to achieve a workable compromise in this area that stays within the framework of organizational policy. Regular office hours, for example, are a must for team assignments. Also, creative people may need help with meeting deadlines because many creative people do not manage time well.)

3. *Give gentle feedback when turning down an idea.* Creative employees are emotionally involved with their work. As a result, they are likely to interpret criticism as a personal attack on their self-worth. (Students often feel the same way about their term papers and projects.)

4. *Employ creative people to manage and evaluate creative workers.* Managers of creative workers should have some creative ability of their own so that they can understand creativity and be credible as leaders. Understanding the creative process is important for evaluating the creative contribution of others. What constitutes creative output is somewhat subjective, but the output can be tied to objective criteria. At Hallmark Cards, Inc., for example, creativity is measured by such factors as how well the creative work sold and how well it performed in a consumer preference test. In general, a manager's intuition about the potential contribution of a creative idea or product still weighs heavily in the evaluation.

# Additional Leadership Practices That Enhance Innovation

Creativity in organizations leads to innovations in products, services, and processes (such as a billing system or safety improvement). All leadership and management practices that enhance creative problem solving therefore also enhance innovation. Here we describe four additional leadership initiatives that enhance innovation.

1. *Continually pursue innovation.* A major characteristic of the Most Admired Companies, as compiled by the Hay Group consultancy for *Fortune*, is constant innovation. Translated into practice, this means that company leaders stay alert to innovative possibilities. Innovation is important because a new technology can make an industry obsolete or place it in grave danger. What will happen to petroleum refineries when (and if) the fuel cell takes hold?

2. *Take risks and encourage risk taking.* "No risk, no reward" is a rule of life that applies equally well to the leadership of innovation. Even in a slow-growth economy, companies cannot win big in the marketplace by doing things just a teeny bit better than the competition. It is necessary to gamble intelligently, shrewdly, and selectively even during a period of insecurity and instability.[33] Because most new ideas fail, part of taking risks is being willing to go down blind alleys. Jeffrey P. Bezos, founder of Amazon.com, Inc., says, "But every once in a while you go down an alley and it opens up into this huge, broad avenue. That makes all the blind alleys worthwhile."[34]

3. *Acquire innovative companies.* The innovation process takes a long time as it proceeds from a creative idea, through initial experimentation, to feasibility determination, and then to final application. To shorten the process and reduce the risk of a failed innovation, many companies acquire smaller companies that have the innovation they seek. Cisco Systems, Inc., spearheaded by chief executive John Chambers, has been a model of innovation through acquisition. During an eight-year period Cisco gobbled up more than seventy companies, mostly because each one offered a technology Cisco needed for its product mix. For example, it would buy a company that produced a specialty router. Largely because of the slide in its stock price, which made buying other companies more difficult, by 2002 Cisco was shifting more toward in-house innovation.[35] Within two years, however, Cisco resumed its acquisition strategy while still developing innovations internally.

4. *Avoid innovation for its own sake.* Leaders also have to exercise good judgment: innovation just because it is innovation is not always valuable. Many gadgets are scientific marvels, yet they have limited market appeal. An example is the robot lawnmower, which arouses the curiosity of many people but does not appeal much to consumers. Most companies have loads of interesting ideas floating to the surface, but very few will even translate into a profitable product or service. The information presented earlier about playing the role of a judge in creativity is particularly relevant here. Jennifer Brown, the executive vice president of ebusiness at Fidelity Investments, says, "We have more good ideas than we can handle. We have so many good ideas here—truly innovative ideas—that sometimes our people get a little frustrated that we can't act on most of them."[36]

5. *Loose–tight leadership enhances creativity and innovation. Looseness* refers to granting space for new ideas and exploration, whereas the tight approach means finally making a choice among the alternatives. When The Gillette Company was exploring various alternatives for a breakthrough razor, many potentially useful ideas surfaced. The management group in charge said, "Let's go for it" when the idea to add flexible blades to the Trac II razor was presented (it became the Sensor razor).[37] Innovation is also enhanced when workers throughout the organization are able to pursue absurd ideas without penalty for being wrong or for having

wasted some resources. An axiom of creativity is that many ideas typically have to be tried before a commercially successful one emerges.

6. *Integrate development and production.* Innovation may suffer when the people who develop ideas do not work closely with the people responsible for their production or manufacture. For many years Japanese companies had moved manufacturing to low-cost countries to save money. Leadership at Canon Inc., however, has found that the key to creating new products quickly is for the production team to physically work close to the product developers. The result is more input and communication. Although the cost of the product, such as an advanced digital camera, may be higher, its high quality leads to higher consumer demand.[38]

7. *Encourage people across divisions to share ideas.* Leaders in multiunit organizations are at an advantage for innovation because workers from the various units can share ideas that would be useful for many different products. For example, if one unit of a medical company developed a patch for delivering medicine to the body, other units might be able to profit from the same technology. Management at Procter & Gamble encourages idea sharing: "We don't exist in silos," says Susan Arnold, P&G's beauty-care and feminine-care chief. She gathers ideas when she roams the internal trade shows in which each business unit displays a storyboard describing recent successes and best ideas.[39] The topic of encouraging idea sharing will be reintroduced in Chapter 13.

> **READER'S ROADMAP**
>
> So far we have studied considerable information about the nature of leadership; the attributes, behaviors, and styles of leaders; the ethics and social responsibility of leaders; and how leaders exert power and use politics and influence. We then studied techniques for developing teamwork as well as motivation and coaching skills. After having studied creativity and innovation as part of leadership, we focus next on communication skills as they relate to leadership.

## Summary

 college.hmco.com/pic/dubrin5e

A creative idea becomes an innovation when it is implemented or commercialized. A creative leader brings forth ideas or things that did not exist previously or that existed in a different form. The creative process has been divided into five steps: opportunity or problem recognition; immersion (the individual becomes immersed in the idea); incubation (the idea simmers); insight (a solution surfaces); and verification and application (the person supports and implements the idea).

Distinguishing characteristics of creative people fall into five areas: knowledge, intellectual abilities, personality, and passion for the task and the experience of flow. Creative people possess extensive knowledge, good intellectual skills, intellectual curiosity, and a wide range of interests. Personality attributes of creative people include a positive self-image, tolerance for isolation, creative self-efficacy, nonconformity, and the ability to tolerate ambiguity and chaos. Passion for the work and flow are related to intense intrinsic motivation. Creative people also enjoy interacting with others. The right personal characteristics must interact with the right environment to produce creative problem solving. The componential theory of creativity focuses on the expertise, creative-thinking skills, and task motivation of creative people.

A major strategy for becoming creative is to overcome traditional thinking, or a traditional mental set. Also, it is necessary to break down rigid thinking that blocks new ideas.

Creative thinking can be enhanced by systematically collecting fresh ideas and brainstorming. A spin-off of brainstorming is the pet-peeve technique, in which a group thinks of all the possible complaints others might have about their unit. Another technique to facilitate creative thinking is to force associations between the properties of two objects. Some organizations also equip a kitchen for the mind, or a space designed for creativity.

Self-help techniques to enhance creative problem solving include (1) practicing creativity-enhancing exercises, (2) staying alert to opportunities, (3) maintaining enthusiasm and being happy, (4) maintaining and using an idea notebook or computer file, and (5) playing the roles of explorer, artist, judge, and lawyer.

Establishing a climate conducive to creative problem solving is another requirement of effective leadership. A foundation step is to establish a vision statement and mission that include creativity. Specifically, leaders should (1) provide intellectual challenge, (2) allow workers freedom to choose their own method, (3) supply the right resources, (4) design work groups effectively, (5) have supervisors encourage creative workers, (6) give organizational support for creativity, (7) have favorable exchanges with creative workers, and (8) act as a talent magnet.

Special attention should be paid to managing creative workers. One should provide excellent tools and resources, give creative people flexibility, turn down ideas gently, and employ creative people to manage and evaluate creative workers.

Seven additional leadership initiatives that enhance innovation are the following: continually pursue innovation, take risks, acquire innovative companies, avoid innovation for its own sake, use loose–tight leadership, integrate development and production, and encourage the sharing of ideas across units.

## Key Terms

Innovation

Creativity

Organizational creativity

Creative self-efficacy

Experience of flow

Pet-peeve technique

Forced-association technique

## Guidelines for Action and Skill Development

To encourage creative problem solving among team members, the leader should avoid certain creativity dampeners and inhibitors, as implied in this chapter. Ten more of these creativity blockers are as follows:

1. Expressing attitudes that preserve the status quo by using such clichés as "Don't rock the boat"; "Don't make waves"; and "If it ain't broke,

   don't fix it." Also, quickly dismissing creative suggestions as being "not feasible."
2. Policing team members by every device imaginable.
3. Saying yes to new ideas but not doing anything about them.
4. Being the exclusive spokesperson for everything in the area of responsibility.

5. Putting every idea through formal channels.
6. Responding to most suggestions for change with a pained look and saying, "But that will cost *money*."
7. Promoting the "not-invented-here" syndrome (if the manager did not invent it, the manager will not consider it).
8. Being suspicious of any idea from below, because it is new and because it is from below.
9. Treating problems as signs of incompetence and failure.
10. Being free and open with criticism but stingy with praise.[40]

## Discussion Questions and Activities

1. Give an example of creativity in business that does *not* relate to the development or marketing of a product or service.
2. How might you use information about the five stages of creative thought to become a more creative problem solver?
3. In many companies, it is expected for managerial and professional workers to wear formal business attire to work (such as suits and high heels). What effect do you think this dress code has on creativity?
4. In what way does your current program of study contribute to your ability to solve problems creatively?
5. The opinion has often been expressed that too much emphasis on teamwork inhibits creativity. What do you think of this argument?
6. What is the underlying process by which creativity-building exercises, such as the forced-association technique, are supposed to increase creativity?
7. How might a manager physically lay out an office to improve the chances that creative problem solving will take place?
8. What is your opinion of the computer mouse as a major innovation? The iPod?
9. Critics of Dell Computer claim that the company is not innovative, even calling Dell the Wal-Mart of technology companies. In what way do you think Dell is innovative, or not innovative?
10. Speak to the most creative person you know in any field, and find out if he or she uses any specific creativity-enhancing technique. Be prepared to bring your findings back to class.

## LEADERSHIP CASE PROBLEM A

### WILL INNOVATION SURVIVE AT 3M?

At 3M, stories are an important part of the culture. Every employee knows about the 3M scientist who spilled chemicals on her tennis shoe—and came up with Scotchgard. Everyone knows about the researcher who wanted a better way to mark the pages of his hymnal—and invented the Post-it® Note. Collectively these stories help explain the greatness of 3M. In the last several years, however, a new story has been unfolding. This one involves no heroic innovators, just terms like *cost controls, Six Sigma,* and *sourcing effectiveness,* not exactly the stuff of company lore. But it does indicate how 3M is changing under CEO James McNerney, the first outside leader in the company's 100-year history.

Since he arrived from General Electric in December 2000, McNerney has given 3M's free-wheeling culture a dose of GE's management science. He has slashed costs, rationalized purchasing, introduced a companywide process-improvement program, and challenged 3M to amp up its growth. Furthermore, McNerney has brought more centralized direction to a company that has always favored laissez-faire experimentation and doodling.

Fears of management's heavy hand have deep roots in 3M mythology. Since its inception as the Minnesota Mining and Manufacturing Company, the company has followed a simple formula for growth: hire good scientists, give them ample resources, and get out of their way. The company remains a model of decentralization and small government, with dozens of product laboratories scattered across forty autonomous business units. Researchers can spend 15 percent of their time on any project of their choosing. If management denies them funding, they can apply for a Genesis Grant, awarded by fellow scientists, or pitch their idea elsewhere in the company. Nothing is considered too small or too zany. One-third of 3M's $16 billion in revenues comes from products that did not exist four years ago. However, before McNerney came on board 3M had produced several years of mediocre growth of earnings per share.

Diplomatic and affable, McNerney, 52, looked like a dream candidate for 3M. Besides having degrees from Yale and Harvard Business School, he had worked in a variety of business units at GE. In his most recent assignment, he had revived a sagging commercial jet engine project. He also had two years of overseas experience running GE's Asian operations.

In some ways, the company McNerney joined resembled the one he had left: it was diversified, industrial, and roughly a century old. Yet for the most part the two companies contrasted sharply. GE gave its managers a toolbox; 3M functioned more like a sandbox. GE was organized into eleven giant business units; 3M had 50,000 niche products scattered across a bewildering organizational chart organized around seven business units. Most important, GE's corporate headquarters drove earnings growth across the whole organization; 3M's corporate group placed less emphasis on financial growth standards.

**McNERNEY'S CHANGES AND INITIATIVES** In assessing the challenges facing 3M, McNerney explains that "in today's world, our overall business objectives are to be simultaneously strong in operating excellence *and* unusually strong in organic growth. In the slow-growth environment, particularly the one the manufacturing world faces, you've got to do both well" (*IndustryWeek.com*, p. 1) To ensure that 3M both operates efficiently and grows from within, McNerney is depending on innovation, international strength, leadership development, and Six Sigma.

Some early moves by McNerney were not well received, such as his announcement of the layoff of 6,500 of 3M's 75,000 workers (*Fortune*, August 12, 2002). Yet other initiatives have been well received. 3M scientists particularly like the data-driven nature of Six Sigma. By the end of 2004, virtually every member of the salaried work force at 3M had received Six Sigma training.

"More people told me to change things than told me not to change things," says McNerney. "I think the story here is rejuvenation of a talented group of people rather than replacement of a mediocre group of people" (*Fortune*, p. 130).

One of McNerney's most urgent problems was overhead: costs had grown at twice the rate of sales in recent years. After several years of implementation, Six Sigma, together with four other corporate initiatives, was reducing annual costs by about $300 million. 3M is also moving more manufacturing to lower-wage sites overseas. A longer-term priority has been leadership development. McNerney opened a leadership development institute modeled after GE's famous Crotonville Center. He also blew up 3M's seniority-based pay structure, forcing managers to grade every employee on a curve and to promote emerging stars faster.

McNerney's plan to acquire other companies has engendered controversy. He wants to use acquisitions to increase sales by 10 percent a year, nearly double the rate of the past decade. 3M has the money to purchase other companies, but it has limited experience integrating them. Some insiders feel the task could distract management from

*(continued)*

the core task of innovating. As McNerney strengthens the corporate center, he also wants it to play a more active role in allocating resources. Cash from mature businesses, like adhesives and abrasives, will be diverted to growth businesses like pharmaceuticals. McNerney has eliminated the 3M requirement that each division get 30 percent of sales from products introduced in the past four years. To make that number, some managers were resorting to rather dubious "innovations" such as pink Post-it Notes.

*Acceleration* is the name McNerney has chosen for one of his major initiatives. At any given time, 3M has about 1,500 products in the development pipeline. He thinks that is too many. His idea is to funnel more R&D spending—such as $100 million or more per year—toward the ideas with the biggest market potential while culling the weaker ones earlier. "I've got to make it culturally okay to say no," he says. "A no means you can get back onto something that has a greater chance of success" (*Fortune*, p. 132). In addition to specifying where research and development dollars are spent, McNerney and his team are establishing uniform performance standards across 3M. In the past, individual business heads had free rein. An executive with thirty-three years of tenure at the company says, "The most important thing about 3M—the single most important thing—is you get to do things your own way" (*BusinessWeek*, January 21, 2002, p. 51). This is now changing.

To facilitate innovation, McNerney and his team created a corporate research laboratory that focuses on advanced materials, processes, and systems. Also, 400 technical employees were transferred into the R&D operations of 3M's seven diverse business groups. McNerney believes that retaining and nurturing the culture of innovation is a big part of what he and his team are attempting to accomplish. In this way organic (internal) growth will be supported while at the same time 3M will acquire other companies that fit a technology niche.

McNerney believes strongly that 3M must find new avenues for growth. Part of his reasoning is that the brand could support a company perhaps five times as big, and a global infrastructure to match. (He admits to exaggeration here.)

McNerney is known as a numbers guy. He establishes quantitative goals for the heads of each of 3M's seven business units, and he regularly monitors their performances. Charles Reich, the executive vice president of the health care business, believes that McNerney has brought discipline to the company and has sharpened up 3M as a result.

**McNERNEY'S ANALYSIS OF 3M CONCERNS** Some 3M watchers are concerned about McNerney's changes because it is difficult to tell which of today's tiny projects will become tomorrow's home runs. No one predicted that Scotchgard or the Post-it Note would earn millions. They began as little experiments—solutions to a problem that people did not know they had—on the 3M principle that "no market, no end product is so small as to be scorned" (*Fortune*, p. 132). Yet McNerney insists he simply wants to stop people from spending so much money before they know if they have a product of potential value. For example, it is important to speak to a marketing representative about the market potential of a product idea early in the product-development cycle.

In slowing down spending on product development, McNerney knows he is going up against decades of 3M stories in which naysaying management is always the villain. He says that the mythology at 3M is: "'Against all odds, I ended up with Post-it Notes.' Mythology supports a lot of important and good behavior. But when it becomes apocryphal, it becomes dysfunctional. You want to get people onto a more reality-based way of looking at the world" (*Fortune*, p. 132).

McNerney has praised the 3M culture at every turn, making it clear that he wants to give employees tools, not orders. "This is a fundamentally strong company. The inventiveness of the people here is in contrast with any other place I've seen. Everybody wakes up in the morning trying to figure out how to grow. They really do" (*Fortune*, p. 130). He also says he understands the balancing act facing him: "My job is to add scale in a fast-moving entrepreneurial environment. If I end up killing that entrepreneurial spirit, I will have failed" (*BusinessWeek*, January 21, 2002, p. 51).

Two years after McNerney was at the helm of 3M, consultant Ken Taormina commented, "He's driven 3M to a more process-oriented model and high quality using Six Sigma. Yet he hasn't hurt the culture of coming up with the new ideas" (*IndustryWeek.com*, p. 1). On the financial side, 3M posted seven consecutive quarters of record earnings.

A challenge still facing McNerney and his team is to return 3M to its historical role as one of corporate America's most inventive and innovative companies. Scotch tape, Scotchgard, molds and glues for orthodontia, and floppy disks all stemmed from 3M. The company devotes $1.1 billion to research annually and has 1,000 scientists and engineers around the world searching for the next Big Thing. McNerney has three major initiatives for stepping up new product development: first, beef up R&D with the centralized laboratory; second, stop pouring big bucks into research that fails to result in commercial products; third, foster more collaboration between scientists and marketers at early stages in new product development.

Meanwhile, 3M is waiting for the next Post-it Notes.

. . . McNerney's success at 3M further enhanced his reputation as one of America's premier executives. When the Boeing Company urgently needed a CEO in 2005, McNerney accepted a lucrative offer to accept the position of chairman, president, and chief executive officer. Boeing board members knew McNerney well because he was a fellow board member for many years.

## QUESTIONS

1. To what extent might McNerney's leadership and management approach damage the culture of innovation that has been characteristic of 3M?
2. How well does McNerney appear to be managing the delicate balance between the company's center and its periphery—between efficiency and innovation?
3. What else might McNerney and his team do to enhance new product development?
4. The observation was made in the case that "GE gave its managers a toolbox; 3M functioned more like a sandbox." How does this statement relate to creativity and innovation?

SOURCE: Jerry Useem, "Can McNerney Reinvent GE?" *Fortune,* August 12, 2002, pp. 127–132; Michael Arndt, "3M: A Lab for Growth?" *BusinessWeek,* January 21, 2002, pp. 50–51; "Q&A with 3M's James McNerney," *www.businessweek.com/magazine/content/02_03/b3766086.htm;* John S. McClenahen, "New World Leader," *IndustryWeek.com,* January 1, 2004; Michael Arndt, "3M's Rising Star," *BusinessWeek,* April 12, 2004, pp. 62–74.

# LEADERSHIP CASE PROBLEM B

## HOW DO WE GET THE FIZZ BACK IN COKE?

Up until 1998 The Coca-Cola Company was considered a crown jewel of corporate America, the owner of the world's biggest, best-known brand. Since then, the company has slipped so badly that a *Fortune* writer has called Coca-Cola a case study in corporate dysfunction. The biggest public embarrassment has been an ineffective board. During a six-year period, the group installed one CEO, ousted him, and then installed another so inexperienced that he needed constant shoring up. The same CEO was insulting and abrasive toward the company's primary partners, the Coca-Cola bottlers. He also alienated European regulators and executives at big companies like Wal-Mart and Disney. Finally, after a well-publicized search that found no outside takers, a

*(continued)*

third CEO was named—a retired Coke executive who had been passed over for the top job earlier.

Many company outsiders and insiders believe that the board meddles too much in the operations of the company. The board has developed the reputation of being aged and overbearing, although it includes several of America's best-known executives. Board members have often opposed product diversification and mergers with other companies.

Despite all the confusion about leadership, the company continues to perform well financially. Coca-Cola has made considerable progress in strengthening its bottlers, cutting costs, boosting profit margins, and increasing cash flow. In the first quarter of 2004, for example, the company earned a record $1.1 billion. Despite the rosy financials, however, broad market forces were working against Coke, and its management and board were bouncing from one strategic fix to another. Worldwide volume growth slowed to 4 percent in 2003, down from a recent peak of 9 percent in 1997. Per capita consumption of soft drinks in the United States had been in steady decline for five years because of health concerns and increased competition from water and other drinks. In addition, other brands were developing more cachet, such as Starbucks coffee and the Red Bull energy drink. And after a big global push in the 1990s, Coke had fewer emerging markets to tap for growth.

To add to its troubles, in 2003 Coke faced the revelation that its middle-level managers had tried to trick Burger King into promoting a new Frozen Coke product in 2000. Coke had apparently fabricated data about consumer attitudes toward the new product. As a result, it had to apologize to one of its biggest customers and agreed to pay up to $21 million to Burger King and its franchisees.

"The whole Coke model needs to be re-thought," says Tom Pirko, the president of a beverage consulting firm. "The carbonated soft-drink model is 30 years old and out of date" (*BusinessWeek*, p. 76). Another concern is that a succession of managers at Coke has focused on trying to do what Coke has always done, only better. The new CEO, E. Neville Isdell, says the company's salvation lies in simply tuning up the soda operations and capitalizing on existing brands. He believes that the company needs to execute better but that its basic strategy is basically sound. Isdell is adamant that growth remains in carbonated soft drinks.

To stem the tide of slower growth, Coca-Cola management turned to a couple of modest innovations. Vanilla Coke was introduced in 2002, as well as a new 12-pack for cans called Fridgepak that fits conveniently in refrigerators. The Fridgepak is 15½ inches long and 4¾ inches wide, so it takes up little room in a refrigerator yet makes dispensing the cans natural and fun. Coke says it has also become the leading provider of noncarbonated, nonalcoholic beverages worldwide, with a 7 percent market share.

Overall, however, the company has had trouble finding new brands to stoke growth. Two small but high-profile acquisitions in 2001, Planet Java coffees and Mad River juices and teas, flopped, and the company phased out those drinks in 2003. Coke's iFountain dispenser, which was supposed to improve drink quality, was a bust with restaurants. The key Coke brands remain Coca-Cola, Diet Coke, Sprite, and Fanta. Coke's plans to make Dasani bottled water into a global brand were slowed when the launch in Europe was aborted after elevated levels of bromate, which can cause cancer after long-term exposure, were detected in bottles in Great Britain.

Coke still lacks a popular entry in the highly profitable energy-drink category to compete with market leader Red Bull. A drink called KMX made with ginseng continues to sputter. Coke was planning to roll out another energy drink in 2004 called Full Throttle, but the introduction has been delayed. Some frustrated Coke bottlers have resorted to selling energy drinks made by other companies to preserve shelf space in stores.

"I am convinced that a lot of the slowdown in soft-drink volume is because we forgot we had to innovate in soft drinks and keep consumers interested," says Gary Fayard, Coke's chief financial officer. "We want to be the best marketing company in the world. We're not there yet" (*The Wall Street Journal*, p. A10).

More than once, Coke has successfully overcome brand fatigue. Two decades ago, the flagship cola showed signs of running out of gas, and the company came up with the infamous reformulated New Coke. It flopped, but the nostalgia it triggered among consumers reinvigorated the original Coke for another decade.

To help boost sales, Coke gave more power to regional marketers several years ago. Some very un-Coke-like ads resulted. In a 2000 commercial in the United States, a grandmother angry that Coke is not being served at a family reunion yells at a relative and knocks down a table with her wheelchair. A German commercial for Coca Cola showed a scantily clad couple groping. The ads were pulled, and the company reversed the "act local" policy.

After studying company operations, a business reporter concluded, "In the U.S. market, Coke hasn't created a best-selling new soda since Diet Coke in 1982. In recent years, Coke has been outbid by rival PepsiCo, Inc., for faster-growing, noncarbonated beverages like SoBe and Gatorade" (*BusinessWeek*, p. 70).

## QUESTIONS

1. With Coke still generating about $5 billion in annual profit, why should company leadership worry about product innovation?
2. What steps do you recommend Coca-Cola take to enhance product innovation?
3. What is your evaluation of the likelihood that Isdell, the Coke CEO, will spearhead innovation at the company?
4. Do you have any specific new product (or service) recommendations for The Coca-Cola Company?
5. Have you consumed a Coca-Cola product in the last forty-eight hours? If not, why not?

SOURCE: Chad Terhune and Betsy McKay, "Behind Coke's CEO Travails: A Long Struggle over Strategy," *The Wall Street Journal*, May 4, 2004, p. A 10; Dean Foust, "Coke Gone Flat," *BusinessWeek*, December 20, 2004, pp. 76–82; Bettsy Morris, "Coke: The Real Story," *Fortune*, May 31, 2004, pp. 84–98.

## LEADERSHIP SKILL-BUILDING EXERCISE 11-4

## MY LEADERSHIP PORTFOLIO

You guessed it. For this chapter's entry into your leadership portfolio, record any creative or innovative idea you have had lately in relation to organizational activity, including school. After recording the idea, ask yourself what prompted you to develop it. If you have not contributed a creative idea recently, your assignment is to develop a creative idea within the next ten days. If possible, make plans to implement the idea; otherwise, it will not lead to innovation. Here is an example of a creative community initiative taken by Alexis, a marketing major:

> In my neighborhood there is a ten-story high-rise building, with practically all of the tenants being senior citizens who live on limited pensions. Some of the folks in the building are in their eighties, and even nineties. The building is old, and not particularly warm, especially for people with poor blood circulation. I've often heard friends and family members say that we should do something to help the seniors in the high rise, but nobody seems to go beyond expressing a little sympathy.

*(continued)*

Then I got a brainstorm. I thought, "Why not organize a 'Socks for Seniors' program?" My friends and I would buy dozens of pairs of socks that usually sell for about $2.00 a pair from deep discounters like dollar stores. We could raise some of the money by returning bottles and cans with deposits. A few friends of mine made a bunch of telephone calls, and we raised $175 in no time for our project. Then one cold night we visited the high rise, rang a few doorbells, and told the residents what we were up to. We were allowed in to start distributing the socks. The smiles and words of appreciation we received were enormous. My idea is *soooo* good, I plan to do it every year. My friends are with me, and we think that if we post this idea on a web site, it might spread around the country.

## INTERNET SKILL-BUILDING EXERCISE

Apply the chapter concepts! Visit the Web and complete this Internet skill-building exercise to learn more about current leadership topics and trends.

### CREATIVITY IN BUSINESS

Here is an opportunity to interact with the work of creativity guru Michael Ray of Stanford University. Visit *www.michael-ray.com*. Look over the site, and then go to "take our survey." The survey gives you the opportunity to examine your creative process and the type of work that brings meaning to your life. Your questionnaire will be scored, and you will be provided with comparative results from work done at Stanford. After you have completed the experience, reflect on these questions:

1. What did you learn about your creative process?
2. How does the feedback about your creativity that you acquired on this site compare to the feedback you received from the exercises in this chapter?

# Communication and Conflict Resolution Skills

## LEARNING OBJECTIVES

After studying this chapter and doing the exercises, you should be able to

- Explain why good communication skills contribute to effective leadership.

- Describe the basics of inspirational and emotion-provoking communication.

- Describe key features of a power-oriented linguistic style.

- Describe the six basic principles of persuasion.

- Describe the elements of supportive communication.

- Be sensitive to the importance of overcoming cross-cultural barriers to communication.

- Identify basic approaches to resolving conflict and negotiating.

## CHAPTER OUTLINE

Michael Daly's staff told him he needed to hire another dining room helper to pour coffee at breakfast. But Daly, 38, the chief executive officer of a small chain of upscale retirement rental residences, was not buying it. Why hire someone else when the nursing aides could pitch in and serve? "I'm the CEO. I've got a big ego. I didn't believe it," he said.

That is until Daly, president of Sterling Glen Communities, ditched his suit and cell phone for a day on the job, following a work schedule set by the staff at Chancellor Park, a Philadelphia retirement home.

So far he has done his "Walking in Your Shoes" program at two other of the company's nine facilities. When Daly reports for duty at 7:00 A.M., he has no idea what will be in store. "They want me to have the most difficult day they can," he said. Typically he works in the kitchen, handles a stint on the reception desks, empties trash, makes repairs, and cleans apartments. "They give me the dirtiest room, and I don't know how to clean a room," he said.

Daly said the work gives him a grass-roots knowledge of the facility, particularly when he manages to penetrate layers of middle management. His favorite spot for picking up knowledge is the laundry room, where he folds laundry with the housekeeping staff. Daly said it takes the crew about half an hour to loosen up enough to give him the lowdown.

At Chancellor Park, Daly's day started in the dining room, and that was when he saw how frantic it was. "I realized the aides were barely able to keep with the shower schedule. They couldn't pour coffee," he said. "We'll have to do something."

William Brown, executive director of Chancellor Park, said he would like Daly to authorize an additional maintenance worker. The last maintenance worker got so backed up that he left a big stack of work orders when he quit. Brown assigned Daly to complete four repair jobs in one hour and twenty minutes. It took Daly an hour longer, and he did not get everything done.

Daly visited Edith Creskoff, 94, who wanted a television moved into her apartment. "You're pretty efficient for a president," she said. Then it was on to Ron Polenz, a man in his 60s, who needed the hinges on his refrigerator door switched so he could open it from his wheelchair. "I had no idea they were reversible," Daly said. "I have to order 166 refrigerators, and now that I know, I'll make sure I order reversible ones." Polenz watched Daly struggle to turn the refrigerator on its side as Daly muttered under his breath about not having the right tools for the job. "You're seeing my first bead of sweat of the day," Daly said.

"I thought you were hot stuff already with that tool kit," Polenz joked before delivering his opinion of Daly's "Walking in Your Shoes" program. "The man's the CEO, and he comes down and sees for himself rather than wait for somebody to report to somebody else," said Polenz. "The more I think about it, the more I like the idea."[1]

---

The "Walking in Your Shoes" program implemented by the retirement community CEO illustrates how an effective leader invests time and effort to develop empathy for his or her workers. The empathy, in turn, serves as a way of communicating supportively.

Effective communication between leaders and other workers is characteristic of highly regarded and very successful companies. Effective managers and leaders listen to employees, and open communications contribute to leadership effectiveness. Peter de la Billiere reminds us that no leader is effective unless he or she is skillful at communication, which includes being able to transmit and receive messages.[2] Effective communication skills contribute to inspirational leadership. Chapter 3 describes how charismatic leaders are masterful oral communicators. This chapter expands on this theme and also covers the contribution of nonverbal, written, and supportive communication. In addition, it describes how the ability to overcome cross-cultural communication barriers enhances leadership effectiveness. Finally, because leaders spend a substantial amount of time resolving conflicts, the chapter also discusses conflict resolution skills.

## Evidence About Communication and Leadership

Research evidence supports the conventional wisdom that effective leaders are also effective communicators. Based on his synthesis of studies, Bernard M. Bass found substantial evidence of a positive relationship between competence in communicating and satisfactory leadership and management performance. An interview study of two hundred successful organizational leaders indicated that they had similar communication patterns. The leaders expanded their thinking regularly by actively soliciting new ideas and feedback from others. Furthermore, they continuously sought fresh information. They also possessed the persuasive skills necessary to convince others of the quality of their ideas.[3]

Research has also been conducted on the contribution of nonverbal behavior to leadership effectiveness. One study suggested that when nonverbal messages contradict verbal messages, the listener tends to place more reliance on the nonverbal messages. A manager who talks about wanting to empower employees but looks bored during the discussion will be regarded as insincere and manipulative. To be effective, the leader must synchronize verbal and nonverbal behavior.[4]

Technology has had a meaningful impact on leaders' communication and coordination. By relying on information technology, leaders and managers can be in frequent contact with group members without being physically present. Managers can also be part of a **virtual office** in which employees work together as if they are part of a single office despite being physically separated. Although frequent contact with company employees, customers, and suppliers enhances coordination, the manager can exercise leadership by inspiring, motivating, and persuading people more readily with this technology than by telephone and in-person contacts alone. Many leaders regularly send email messages to motivate and inspire their constituents—locally, regionally, and internationally. The discussion of e-leadership in Chapter 9 also described how leaders use information technology to stay in touch with network members. Despite these findings, many companies are not communicating their mission, vision, and values as well as they might.

college.hmco.com/pic/
dubrin5e

🔘 @ **KNOWLEDGE BANK:** provides some evidence supporting the conclusion that many companies are not communicating their mission, vision, and values as well as they might.

To focus your thinking on your communication effectiveness, complete Leadership Self-Assessment Quiz 12-1.

**LEADERSHIP SELF-ASSESSMENT QUIZ 12-1**

## A SELF-PORTRAIT OF MY COMMUNICATION EFFECTIVENESS

**INSTRUCTIONS** The statements below relate to various aspects of communication effectiveness. Indicate whether each of the statements is mostly true or mostly false, even if the most accurate answer would depend somewhat on the situation. Asking another person who is familiar with your communication behavior to help you answer the questions may improve the accuracy of your answers.

|  | True | False |
|---|---|---|
| 1. When I begin to speak in a group, most people stop talking, turn toward me, and listen. | ____ | ____ |
| 2. I receive compliments on the quality of my writing. | ____ | ____ |
| 3. The reaction to the outgoing message on my answering machine has been favorable. | ____ | ____ |
| 4. I welcome the opportunity to speak in front of a group. | ____ | ____ |
| 5. I have published something, including a letter to the editor, an article for the school newspaper, or a comment in a company newsletter. | ____ | ____ |
| 6. I have my own web site. | ____ | ____ |
| 7. The vast majority of my written projects in school have received a grade of B or A. | ____ | ____ |
| 8. People generally laugh when I tell a joke or make what I think is a witty comment. | ____ | ____ |
| 9. I stay informed by reading newspapers, watching news on television, or logging on to news information. | ____ | ____ |
| 10. I have heard such terms as *enthusiastic, animated, colorful,* or *dynamic* applied to me. | ____ | ____ |

*Total score* _____

SCORING AND INTERPETATION If eight or more of the above statements are true in relation to you, it is most likely that you are an effective communicator. If three or fewer statements are true, you may need substantial improvement in your communication skills. Your scores are probably highly correlated with charisma.

SKILL DEVELOPMENT The behaviors indicated by the ten statements in the self-assessment exercise are significant for leaders because much of a leader's impact is determined by his or her communication style. Although effective leaders vary considerably in their communication style, they usually create a positive impact if they can communicate well. Observe some current business leaders on CNBC news or a similar channel to develop a feel for the communication style of successful business leaders.

# Inspirational and Powerful Communication

Information about communicating persuasively and effectively is extensive. Here we focus on suggestions for creating the high-impact communication that contributes to effective leadership. Both formal and informal leaders must be persuasive and dynamic communicators. Effective communication often helps informal leaders be selected for formal leadership positions. In this section, suggestions for becoming an inspirational and emotion-provoking communicator are divided into the following two categories: (1) speaking and writing, and (2) nonverbal communication. We also discuss six basic principles of persuasion.

## Speaking and Writing

Most of you are already familiar with the basics of effective spoken and written communication. Yet the basics—such as writing and speaking clearly, maintaining eye contact, and not mumbling—are only starting points. The majority of effective leaders have an extra snap or panache in their communication style, both in day-by-day conversations and when addressing a group. The same energy and excitement is reflected in both speaking and writing. Kouzes and Posner underscore the importance of colorful language in communicating a vision (one of the leader's most important functions) in these words:

> Language is among the most powerful methods for expressing a vision. Successful leaders use metaphors and figures of speech; they give examples, tell stories, and relate anecdotes; they draw word pictures; and they offer quotations and recite slogans.[5]

Group members and other constituents have reasonable exposure to the spoken word of leaders. Nevertheless, with the increased use of email and instant messaging, the written word exerts considerable influence. Suggestions for dynamic and persuasive oral and written communication are presented below and outlined in Table 12-1.

| **TABLE 12-1** | **Suggestions for Inspirational Speaking and Writing** |
| --- | --- |

**A. A VARIETY OF INSPIRATIONAL TACTICS**

1. Be credible.
2. Gear your message to the listener.
3. Sell group members on the benefits of your suggestions.
4. Use heavy-impact and emotion-provoking words.
5. Use anecdotes and metaphors to communicate meaning.
6. Back up conclusions with data (to a point).
7. Minimize language errors, junk words, and vocalized pauses.
8. Write crisp, clear memos, letters, and reports, including a front-loaded message.

**B. THE POWER-ORIENTED LINGUISTIC STYLE**

Included here are a variety of factors such as downplaying uncertainty, emphasizing direct rather than indirect talk, and choosing an effective communication frame.

***Be Credible*** Attempts at persuasion, including inspirational speaking and writing, begin with the credibility of the message sender. It has long been recognized that source credibility is a powerful element in the persuasive process. If the speaker is perceived as highly credible, the attempt at persuasive communication is more likely to be successful. The perception of credibility is influenced by many factors, including those covered in this entire section. Being trustworthy heavily influences being perceived as credible. A leader with a reputation for lying will have a difficult time convincing people about the merits of a new initiative such as outsourcing. Being perceived as intelligent and knowledgeable is another major factor contributing to credibility.

***Gear Your Message to the Listener*** An axiom of persuasive communication is that a speaker must adapt the message to the listener's interests and motivations. The company president visiting a manufacturing plant will receive careful attention—and build support—when he says that jobs will not be outsourced to another country. The same company president will receive the support of stockholders when he emphasizes how cost reductions will boost earnings per share and enlarge dividends.

A review of the evidence concludes that the average intelligence level of the group is a key contingency factor in designing a persuasive message. People with high intelligence tend to be more influenced by messages based on strong, logical arguments. Bright people are also more likely to reject messages based on flawed logic.[6]

***Sell Group Members on the Benefits of Your Suggestions*** A leader is constrained by the willingness of group members to take action on the leader's suggestions and initiatives. As a consequence, the leader must explain to group members how they can benefit from what he or she proposes. For example, a plant manager attempting to sell employees on the benefits of recycling supplies as much as possible might say, "If we can cut down enough on the cost of supplies, we might be able to save one or two jobs."

Selling group members is quite often done more effectively when the persuader takes the time to build consensus. Instead of inspiring the group in a flash, the leader wins the people over gradually. Persuasion guru (note the appeal to credibility) Jay Conger writes that successful persuasion often requires ongoing effort, following this pattern: (1) At the first meeting, you convince a few teammates to consider your initiative carefully. (2) At the second meeting, you win several teammates over to your viewpoint after having modified your original position slightly. (3) The following week, events outside your control weaken your efforts or strengthen them. (4) Successive meetings and discussions finally bring all the team members to consensus. Along the way, you keep adjusting your position to satisfy diverse demands.[7] One caution is that this deliberate method of persuasion through consensus is poorly suited to crises and other urgent situations.

***Use Heavy-Impact and Emotion-Provoking Words*** Certain words used in the proper context give power and force to your speech. Used comfortably, naturally, and sincerely, these words will project the image of a self-confident person with leadership ability or potential. A mortgage officer at a bank made the following progress report to her manager:

It's important that I fill you in on my recent activities. This bank's strategic plan is to get into the next generation of financial marketing. I've bought into the strategy, and it's working. Instead of simply selling commercial mortgages, I'm heavily into relationship banking. I've been building long-term symbiotic relations with some very big potential clients.

So far, the short-term results I've achieved have been modest. But the long-term results could be mind boggling. We may soon become the dominant supplier of financial services to a key player in commercial real estate.

The mortgage officer framed her accomplishments and progress in buzzwords of interest to top management. She talked about supporting the corporate strategy, relationship banking, outstanding long-term results, and her company becoming a dominant supplier. Using powerful and upbeat language of this type enhances her leadership image. Yet if she had taken the embellishment too far, she might have shown herself to be deceptive and devious.

Closely related to heavy-impact language is the use of emotion-provoking words. An expert persuasive tactic is to sprinkle your speech with emotion-provoking—and therefore inspiring—words. Emotion-provoking words bring forth images of exciting events. Examples of emotion-provoking and powerful words include "*outclassing* the competition," "*bonding* with customers," "*surpassing* previous profits," "*capturing* customer loyalty," and "*rebounding* from a downturn." It also helps to use words and phrases that connote power. Those now in vogue include *learning organization, virtual organization*, and *transparent organization*.

A large vocabulary assists using both heavy-impact and emotion-provoking words. When you need to persuade somebody on the spot, it is difficult to search for the right words in a dictionary or thesaurus. Also, you need to practice a word a few times to use it comfortably for an important occasion.

### *Use Anecdotes and Metaphors to Communicate Meaning*

*Use Anecdotes and Metaphors to Communicate Meaning* Anecdotes and metaphors are a powerful part of a leader's kit of persuasive and influence tactics, as already mentioned in this chapter and in Chapter 3 about charismatic leadership. A carefully chosen anecdote is also useful in persuading group members about the importance of organizational values. So long as the anecdote is not repeated too frequently, it can communicate an important message.

Teresa Lever-Pollary is the CEO of Nighttime Pediatric Clinics Inc. in Midvale, Utah. She noticed that as the company grew to four clinics and seventy employees, it was losing touch with the values that helped make it such a successful provider of after-hours pediatric care. Lever-Pollary collected more than eighty stories from her employees and printed them in a book that she distributes to stakeholders. One of her favorite anecdotes was a nurse's recollection of the manner in which a pediatrician lured an ant from inside a child's ear using a morsel of cake frosting. The ant crawled out, and the doctor gently released it outdoors. The story precisely illustrates Nighttime's focus on carefully and professionally caring for small living organisms.[8]

Metaphors are useful for persuasion, as described in relation to charisma. Frances Hesselbein is widely recognized for having revitalized the Girl Scouts. She advises leaders to use the power of language to inspire others. Among the metaphors she has used are "carrying a big basket," "spring house cleaning," and "a learning journey."[9]

***Back Up Conclusions with Data*** You will be more persuasive if you support your spoken and written presentations with solid data. One approach to obtaining data is to collect them yourself—for example, by conducting an email survey of your customers or group members. The sales manager of an office supply company wanted to begin a delivery service for his many small customers, such as dental and real-estate offices. He sent email messages to a generous sampling of these accounts and found they would be willing to pay a premium price if delivery were included. By using these data to support his argument, he convinced the company owner to approve the plan. He thus exercised leadership in providing a new service.

Published sources also provide convincing data for arguments. Supporting data for hundreds of arguments can be found in the business pages of newspapers, in business magazines and newspapers, and on the Internet. The *Statistical Abstract of the United States*, published annually, is an inexpensive yet trusted reference for thousands of arguments.

Relying too much on research has a potential disadvantage, though. Being too dependent on data could suggest that you have little faith in your intuition. For example, you might convey a weak impression if, when asked your opinion, you respond, "I can't answer until I collect some data." Leaders are generally decisive. An important issue, then, is for the leader to find the right balance between relying on data and using intuition alone when communicating an important point.

***Minimize Language Errors, Junk Words, and Vocalized Pauses*** Using colorful, powerful words enhances the perception that you are self-confident and have leadership qualities. Also, minimize the use of words and phrases that dilute the impact of your speech, such as "like," "y' know," "you know what I mean," "he goes" (to mean "he says"), and "uhhhhhhh." Such junk words and vocalized pauses convey the impression of low self-confidence, especially in a professional setting, and detract from a sharp communication image.

An effective way to decrease the use of these extraneous words is to tape-record or video-record your side of a phone conversation and then play it back. Many people are not aware that they use extraneous words until they hear recordings of their speech.

A good leader should be sure always to write and speak with grammatical precision to give the impression of being articulate and well informed, thereby enhancing his or her leadership stature. Here are two examples of common language errors: "Just between you and I" is wrong; "just between you and me" is correct. *Irregardless* is a nonword; *regardless* is correct.

Another very common error is using the plural pronoun *they* to refer to a singular antecedent. For example, "The systems analyst said that *they* cannot help us" is incorrect. "The systems analyst said *she* cannot help us" is correct. Using *they* to refer to a singular antecedent has become so common in the English language that many people no longer make the distinction between singular and plural. Some of these errors are subtle and are made so frequently that many people do not realize they are wrong, but again, avoiding grammatical errors may enhance a person's leadership stature.[10]

When in doubt about a potential language error, consult a large dictionary. An authoritative guide for the leader (and anyone else) who chooses to use English accurately is *The Elements of Style* by William Strunk, Jr., and E. B. White.[11]

***Write Crisp, Clear Memos, Letters, and Reports, Including a Front-Loaded Message*** Business leaders characteristically write easy-to-read, well-organized messages both in email and more formal reports. Writing, in addition to speaking, is more persuasive when key ideas are placed at the beginning of a conversation, email message, paragraph, or sentence.[12] Front-loaded messages (those placed at the beginning of a sentence) are particularly important for leaders because people expect leaders to be forceful communicators. A front-loaded and powerful message might be "Cost reduction must be our immediate priority," which emphasizes that cost reduction is the major subject. It is clearly much more to the point than, for example, "All of us must reduce costs immediately."

One way to make sure messages are front-loaded is to use the active voice, making sure the subject of the sentence is doing the acting, not being acted upon. Compare the active (and front-loaded) message "Loyal workers should not take vacations during a company crisis" to the passive (non-front-loaded) message "Vacations should not be taken by loyal company workers during a crisis."

***Use a Power-Oriented Linguistic Style*** A major part of being persuasive involves choosing the right **linguistic style**, a person's characteristic speaking pattern. According to Deborah Tannen, linguistic style involves such aspects as amount of directness, pacing and pausing, word choice, and the use of such communication devices as jokes, figures of speech, anecdotes, questions, and apologies.[13]

A linguistic style is complex because it includes the culturally learned signals by which people communicate what they mean, along with how they interpret what others say and how they evaluate others. The complexity of linguistic style makes it difficult to offer specific prescriptions for using one that is power oriented. Many of the elements of a power-oriented linguistic style are included in other suggestions made in this section of the chapter. Nevertheless, here are several components of a linguistic style that would give power and authority to the message sender in many situations, as observed by Deborah Tannen and other language specialists:[14]

- Speak loud enough to be heard by the majority of people with at least average hearing ability. Speaking too softly projects an image of low self-confidence.
- Downplay uncertainty. If you are not confident of your opinion or prediction, make a positive statement anyway, such as saying, "I know this new system will cure our inventory problems."
- Use the pronoun *I* to receive more credit for your ideas. (Of course, this could backfire in a team-based organization.)
- Minimize the number of questions you ask that imply that you lack information on a topic, such as, "What do you mean by an IPO?"
- Minimize self-deprecation with phrases such as "This will probably sound stupid, but . . ." Apologize infrequently, and particularly minimize saying, "I'm sorry."
- Offer negative feedback directly, rather than softening the feedback by first giving praise and then moving to the areas of criticism.
- Make your point quickly. You know you are taking too long to reach a conclusion when others look bored or finish your sentences for you.

■ Emphasize direct rather than indirect talk: say, "I need your report by noon tomorrow," rather than, "I'm wondering if your report will be available by noon tomorrow."

■ Weed out wimpy words. Speak up without qualifying or giving other indices of uncertainty. It is better to give dates for the completion of a project rather than say "Soon" or "It shouldn't be a problem." Instead, make a statement like "I will have my portion of the strategic plan shortly before Thanksgiving. I need to collect input from my team and sift through the information."

■ Know exactly what you want. Your chances of selling an idea increase to the extent that you have clarified the idea in your own mind. The clearer and more committed you are at the outset of a session, the stronger you are as a persuader and the more powerful your language becomes.

■ Speak at length, set the agenda for a conversation, make jokes, and laugh. Be ready to offer solutions to problems, as well as to suggest a program or plan. All of these points are more likely to create a sense of confidence in listeners.

■ Strive to be bold in your statements. As a rule of thumb, be bold about ideas, but tentative about people. If you say something like "I have a plan that I think will solve these problems," you are presenting an idea, not attacking a person.

■ Frame your comments in a way that increases your listener's receptivity. The *frame* is built around the best context for responding to the needs of others. An example would be to use the frame "let's dig a little deeper" when the other people present know something is wrong but cannot pinpoint the problem. Your purpose is to enlist the help of others in finding the underlying nature of the problem.

Despite these suggestions for having a power-oriented linguistic style, Tannen cautions that there is no one best way to communicate. How you project your power and authority is often dependent on the people involved, the organizational culture, the relative rank of the speakers, and other situational factors. The power-oriented linguistic style should be interpreted as a general guideline.

college.hmco.com/pic/
dubrin5e

**(KB) @ KNOWLEDGE BANK:** contains information about using a combination of influence tactics to persuade others.

## The Six Basic Principles of Persuasion

One way to be persuasive is to capitalize on scientific evidence about how to persuade people. Robert B. Cialdini has synthesized knowledge from experimental and social psychology about methods for getting people to concede, comply, or change. These principles can also be framed as influence principles, but with a focus on persuasion.[15] The six principles described next have accompanying tactics that can be used to supplement the other approaches to persuasion described in this chapter.

1. *Liking: People like those who like them.* As a leader, you have a better chance of persuading and influencing group members who like you. Emphasizing similarities between you and the other person and offering praise are the two most reliable

techniques for getting another person to like you. The leader should therefore emphasize similarities, such as common interests with group members. Praising others is a powerful influence technique and can be used effectively even when the leader finds something relatively small to compliment. Genuine praise is the most effective.

2. *Reciprocity: People repay in kind.* Managers can often influence group members to behave in a particular way by displaying the behavior first. The leader might therefore serve as a model of trust, good ethics, or strong commitment to company goals. In short, give what you want to receive.

3. *Social proof: People follow the lead of similar others.* Persuasion can have high impact when it comes from peers. If you as the leader want to influence a group to convert to a new procedure, such as virtually eliminating paper records in the office, ask a believer to speak up in a meeting or send his or her statement of support via email. (But do not send around paper documents.)

4. *Consistency: People align with their clear commitments.* People need to feel committed to what you want them to do. After people take a stand or go on record in favor of a position, they prefer to stay with that commitment. Suppose you are the team leader and you want team members to become more active in the community as a way of creating a favorable image for the firm. If the team members talk about their plans to get involved and also put their plans in writing, they are more likely to follow through. If the people involved read their action plans to each other, the commitment will be even stronger.

5. *Authority: People defer to experts.* As explained in our study of expert power and credibility, people really do defer to experts. The action plan here is to make constituents aware of your expertise to enhance the probability that your plan will persuade them. A leader might mention certification in the technical area that is the subject of influence. For example, a leader attempting to persuade team members to use statistical data to improve quality might mention that he or she is certified in the quality process Six Sigma (is a Six Sigma Black Belt).

6. *Scarcity: People want more of what they can have less of.* An application of this principle is that the leader can persuade group members to act in a particular direction if the members believe that the resource at issue is shrinking rapidly. They might be influenced to enroll in a course in diversity training, for example, if they are told that the course may not be offered again for a long time. Another way to apply this principle is to persuade group members by using information not readily available to others. The leader might say, "I have some preliminary sales data. If we can increase our sales by just 10 percent in the last month of this quarter, we might be the highest performing unit in the company."

The developer of these principles explains that they should be applied in combination to multiply their impact. For example, while establishing your expertise you might simultaneously praise people for their accomplishments. It is also important to be ethical, such as by not fabricating data to influence others.[16]

## Nonverbal Communication

Effective leaders are masterful nonverbal as well as verbal communicators. Nonverbal communication is important because leadership involves emotion, which words alone cannot communicate convincingly. A major component of the emotional impact of a message is communicated nonverbally—perhaps up to 90 percent.[17] The classic study behind this observation has been misinterpreted to mean that 90 percent of communication is nonverbal. If this were true, facts, figures, and logic would make a minor contribution to communication, and acting skill would be much more important for getting across one's point of view.

A self-confident leader not only speaks and writes with assurance but also projects confidence through body position, gestures, and manner of speech. Not everybody interprets the same body language and other nonverbal signals in the same way, but some aspects of nonverbal behavior project a self-confident, leadership image in many situations.[18]

- Using an erect posture when walking, standing, or sitting. Slouching and slumping are almost universally interpreted as an indicator of low self-confidence.
- Standing up straight during a confrontation. Cowering is interpreted as a sign of low self-confidence and poor leadership qualities.
- Patting other people on the back while nodding slightly.
- Standing with toes pointing outward rather than inward. Outward-pointing toes are usually perceived as indicators of superior status, whereas inward-pointing toes are perceived to indicate inferiority.
- Speaking at a moderate pace, with a loud, confident tone. People lacking in self-confidence tend to speak too rapidly or very slowly.
- Smiling frequently in a relaxed, natural-appearing manner.
- Maintaining eye contact with those around you.
- Gesturing in a relaxed, nonmechanical way, including pointing toward others in a way that welcomes rather than accuses, such as using a gesture to indicate, "You're right," or "It's your turn to comment."

A general approach to using nonverbal behavior that projects confidence is to have a goal of appearing self-confident and powerful. This type of autosuggestion makes many of the behaviors seem automatic. For example, if you say, "I am going to display leadership qualities in this meeting," you will have taken an important step toward appearing confident.

Your external image also plays an important role in communicating messages to others. People pay more respect and grant more privileges to those they perceive as being well dressed and neatly groomed. Even on casual dress days, most effective leaders will choose clothing that gives them an edge over others. Appearance includes more than the choice of clothing. Self-confidence is projected by such small items as the following:

- Neatly pressed and sparkling clean clothing
- Freshly polished shoes
- Impeccable fingernails
- Clean jewelry in mint condition
- Well-maintained hair
- Good-looking teeth with a white or antique-white color

What constitutes a powerful and self-confident external image is often influenced by the organizational culture. At a software development company, for example, powerful people might dress more casually than at an investment banking firm. Your verbal behavior and the forms of nonverbal behavior previously discussed contribute more to your leadership image than your clothing, providing you dress acceptably.

A subtle mode of nonverbal communication is the use of time. Guarding time as a precious resource will help you project an image of self-confidence and leadership. A statement such as "I can devote fifteen minutes to your problem this Thursday at 4:00 P.M." connotes confidence and being in control. (Too many of these statements, however, might make a person appear unapproachable and inconsiderate.) Other ways of projecting power through the use of time include such behaviors as being prompt for meetings and starting and stopping meetings on time. It may also be helpful to make references to dates one year into the future and beyond, such as, "By 2009 we should have a 25 percent market share."

Now that you have refreshed your thoughts on effective verbal and nonverbal communication, do Leadership Skill-Building Exercise 12-1.

**LEADERSHIP SKILL-BUILDING EXERCISE 12-1**

### FEEDBACK ON VERBAL AND NONVERBAL BEHAVIOR

Ten volunteers have one week to prepare a three-minute presentation on a course-related subject of their choice. The topics of these presentations could be as far-reaching as "The Importance of the North American Free Trade Agreement" or "My Goals and Dreams." The class members who observe the presentations prepare feedback slips on 3 × 5 cards, describing how well the speakers communicated powerfully and inspirationally. One card per speaker is usually sufficient. Notations should be made for both verbal and nonverbal feedback.

Emphasis should be placed on positive feedback and constructive suggestions. Students pass the feedback cards along to the speakers. The cards can be anonymous to encourage frankness, but they should not be mean spirited.

Persuading and inspiring others is one of the main vehicles for practicing leadership. Knowing how others perceive you helps you polish and refine your impact.

## Supportive Communication

Communicating powerfully and inspirationally facilitates influencing and inspiring people, but a more mellow type of communication is needed to implement the people-oriented aspects of a leader's role. A leader who uses supportive communication nurtures group members and brings out their best. Instead of dazzling them with a power presence, the leader is low-key and interested in the other person's agenda. **Supportive communication** is a communication style that delivers the message

| TABLE 12-2 | Principles and Characteristics of Supportive Communication |
| --- | --- |
| | 1. Problem oriented, not person oriented |
| | 2. Descriptive, not evaluative |
| | 3. Based on congruence, not incongruence |
| | 4. Focused on validating, rather than invalidating, people |
| | 5. Specific, not global |
| | 6. Conjunctive, not disjunctive |
| | 7. Owned, not disowned |
| | 8. Requires listening as well as sending messages |

accurately and that supports or enhances the relationship between the two parties. The process has eight principles or characteristics, which have emerged from the work of many researchers.[19] They are described below and outlined in Table 12-2.

1. *Problem oriented, not person oriented.* Effective leaders and managers focus more on the problem than on the person when communicating with group members. Most people are more receptive to a discussion of what can be done to change a work method than to a discussion of what can be done to change them. Many people might readily agree that more alternative solutions to a problem are needed. Fewer people are willing to accept the message "You need to be more creative."

   A helpful adjunct to problem-oriented communication is for the leader or manager to encourage the other person to participate in a solution to the problem. In the example at hand, the leader might say, "Perhaps you can find a method that will generate more alternative solutions to the problem."

2. *Descriptive, not evaluative.* A closely related principle is that when a person's worth is being evaluated, he or she often becomes defensive. If a leader says to a group member, "You are a low-quality performer," the person will probably become defensive. The descriptive form of communication—for example, "I found errors in your last two reports that created problems"—allows the person to separate the errors from himself or herself. A supervisor's "I message" ("I found errors") is less accusatory than a "you message" ("You are a low-quality performer").

3. *Congruent, not incongruent.* A superior form of communication is **congruence**, the matching of verbal and nonverbal communication to what the sender is thinking and feeling. A leader is more credible when his or her nonverbal signals mesh with his or her spoken words. A chief executive officer might say to his staff, "I'm no longer concerned about the firm having to declare bankruptcy. Sales have improved substantially, and our costs are way down." If, at the same time, the CEO is fidgeting and has a sickly, upset appearance, the message will not be convincing. In this case the leader's message does not fit; it is incongruent. If the CEO delivers the same message with a smile and a relaxed manner, his credibility will increase.

4. *Validating rather than invalidating people.* Validating communication accepts the presence, uniqueness, and importance of the other person. Whether or not the person's ideas are totally accepted, he or she is acknowledged. During a meeting, the manager of internal auditing said to a recently hired auditor, "Your suggestion of bonus pay for auditors when they have to stay away from home more than two weekends has some merit. We can't act on your suggestion now, but please bring it up again in a future meeting." The young auditor felt encouraged to make other suggestions in the future. An invalidating communication would have been for the manager to flat out ignore the auditor or to make a snide comment such as, "Your naiveté is showing. Nobody with much business experience would make such a bad suggestion."

5. *Specific, not global.* As described in Chapter 10, most people benefit more from specific than from global, or general, feedback. To illustrate, the statement "We have terrible customer service" is too general to be very useful. A more useful statement would be "Our customer satisfaction ratings are down 25 percent from previous years": It is more specific and provides an improvement target.

6. *Conjunctive, not disjunctive.* **Conjunctive communication** is linked logically to previous messages, thus enhancing communication. **Disjunctive communication** is not linked to the preceding messages, resulting in impaired communication. Conjunctive communication makes it easier for group members and other constituents to follow the leader's thoughts. David A. Whetton and Kim S. Cameron explain that communication can be disjunctive in three ways: (1) People might have unequal opportunity to speak because of interruptions and simultaneous speaking; (2) lengthy pauses are disjunctive because listeners lose the speaker's train of thought; and (3) communication is perceived as disjunctive when one person controls the topics. Many leaders, as well as group members, fail to relate their comments to the topics introduced by others.[20]

7. *Owning, not disowning, one's statements.* Effective communicators take responsibility for what they say and do not attribute the authority behind their ideas to another person. The effective leader might say, "I want everybody to work eight extra hours per week during this crisis." The less effective leader might say, "The company wants everybody to work overtime." Other ways of disowning communication include using statements such as "they say," or "everybody thinks." Using the word *I* indicates that you strongly believe what you are saying.

8. *Listening as well as sending messages.* Truly supportive communication requires active listening (as described in the discussion of coaching). The relationship between two parties cannot be enhanced unless each one listens to the other. Furthermore, leaders cannot identify problems unless they listen carefully to group members. Listening is a fundamental management and leadership skill. It also provides the opportunity for dialogue, in which people understand each other better by taking turns having their point of view understood.

Supportive communication requires considerable practice and must be integrated into one's leadership style to be implemented successfully. The coaching style of the leader finds supportive communication to be a natural way of relating to others. Leadership Skill-Building Exercise 12-2 gives you an opportunity to try out supportive communication.

## SUPPORTIVE COMMUNICATION

Six or seven students gather for a team meeting to discuss an important operational problem, such as finding new ways to reduce the cycle time required to complete their tasks, or deciding how to convince top management to expand the team budget. One person plays the role of the team leader. All of the group members take turns at making both useful and apparently not-useful suggestions. The team leader, along with team members, uses supportive communication whenever ideas surface. Students not directly involved in the group role-play will take note of the supportive (or nonsupportive) communication they observe so that they can provide feedback later. If class time allows, another team of six or seven students can repeat the group role-play.

One of many reasons that practicing supportive communication is useful is that it creates an atmosphere in which group members are more likely to contribute productive ideas. People typically shy away from making suggestions under conditions of nonsupportive communication because they fear being criticized for foolish ideas.

## Overcoming Cross-Cultural Communication Barriers

Another communication challenge facing leaders and managers is overcoming communication barriers created by dealing with people from different cultures and subcultures. In today's workplace, leaders communicate with people from other countries and with a more diverse group of people in their own country. The latter is particularly true in culturally diverse countries such as the United States and Canada. Because of this workplace diversity, leaders who can manage a multicultural and cross-cultural work force are in strong demand. Here we give some guidelines for overcoming some cross-cultural communication barriers.

college.hmco.com/pic/
dubrin5e

**@ KNOWLEDGE BANK:** describes a few mental processes that contribute to communication barriers with people of other cultures.

Before reading the Knowledge Bank material, take Leadership Self-Assessment Quiz 12-2 to help you think through your cross-cultural skills and attitudes.

The leader attempting to communicate with members of a different culture should also follow certain guidelines. Implementing these guidelines will help overcome and prevent many communication problems.

**LEADERSHIP SELF-ASSESSMENT QUIZ 12-2**

## CROSS-CULTURAL SKILLS AND ATTITUDES

**INSTRUCTIONS** Listed below are various skills and attitudes that various employers and cross-cultural experts think are important for relating effectively to coworkers in a culturally diverse environment. Indicate whether or not each statement applies to you.

| | Applies to Me Now | Not There Yet |
|---|---|---|
| 1. I have spent some time in another country. | _____ | _____ |
| 2. At least one of my friends is deaf, blind, or uses a wheelchair. | _____ | _____ |
| 3. Currency from other countries is as real as the currency from my own country. | _____ | _____ |
| 4. I can read in a language other than my own. | _____ | _____ |
| 5. I can speak in a language other than my own. | _____ | _____ |
| 6. I can write in a language other than my own. | _____ | _____ |
| 7. I can understand people speaking in a language other than my own. | _____ | _____ |
| 8. I use my second language regularly. | _____ | _____ |
| 9. My friends include people of races different from my own. | _____ | _____ |
| 10. My friends include people of different ages. | _____ | _____ |
| 11. I feel (or would feel) comfortable having a friend with a sexual orientation different from mine. | _____ | _____ |
| 12. My attitude is that although another culture may be very different from mine, that culture is equally good. | _____ | _____ |
| 13. I would be willing to (or already do) hang art from different countries in my home. | _____ | _____ |
| 14. I would accept (or have already accepted) a work assignment of more than several months in another country. | _____ | _____ |
| 15. I have a passport. | _____ | _____ |

*(continued)*

SCORING AND INTERPRETATION If you answered, "Applies to Me Now" to 10 or more of the above questions, you most likely function well in a multicultural work environment. If you answered, "Not There Yet" to 10 or more of the above questions, you need to develop more cross-cultural awareness and skills to work effectively in a multicultural work environment. You will notice that being bilingual gives you at least 5 points on this quiz.

SOURCE: Several ideas for statements on this quiz are derived from Ruthann Dirks and Janet Buzzard, "What CEOs Expect of Employees Hired for International Work," *Business Education Forum*, April 1997, pp. 3–7; Gunnar Beeth, "Multicultural Managers Wanted," *Management Review*, May 1997, pp. 17–21.

1. *Be sensitive to the fact that cross-cultural communication barriers exist.* Awareness of these potential barriers is the first step in dealing with them. When dealing with a person of a different cultural background, solicit feedback to minimize cross-cultural barriers to communication. For example, investigate which types of praise or other rewards might be ineffective for a particular cultural group. In many instances, Asians newly arrived in the United States feel uncomfortable being praised in front of others, because in Asian cultures group performance is valued more than individual performance.

   Being alert to cultural differences in values, attitudes, and etiquette will help you communicate more effectively with people from different cultures. Observe carefully the cultural mistakes listed in Table 12-3.

2. *Challenge your cultural assumptions.* The assumptions we make about cultural groups can create communication barriers. The assumption you make about another group may not necessarily be incorrect, but stopping to challenge the assumptions may facilitate communication. An American leader, for example, might assume that the norms of independence and autonomy are valued by all groups in the workplace. Trudy Milburn notes that even the concept of equality can be phrased to alienate cultural groups. A sentence from the Johnson & Johnson mission statement reads, "Everyone must be considered as an individual."

**TABLE 12-3**    **Cultural Mistakes to Avoid with Selected Cultural Groups**

| EUROPE | |
| --- | --- |
| GREAT BRITAIN | ▪ Asking personal questions. The British protect their privacy. |
| | ▪ Thinking that a businessperson from England is unenthusiastic when he or she says, "Not bad at all." English people understate positive emotion. |
| | ▪ Gossiping about royalty. |
| FRANCE | ▪ Expecting to complete work during the French two-hour lunch. |
| | ▪ Attempting to conduct significant business during August—*les vacances* (vacation time). |
| | ▪ Greeting a French person for the first time and not using a title such as *sir* or *madam* (or *monsieur, madame,* or *mademoiselle*). |

| | |
|---|---|
| **EUROPE** | |
| ITALY | ▨ Eating too much pasta, as it is not the main course. |
| | ▨ Handing out business cards freely. Italians use them infrequently. |
| SPAIN | ▨ Expecting punctuality. Your appointments will usually arrive twenty to thirty minutes late. |
| | ▨ Make the American sign for "okay" with your thumb and forefinger. In Spain (and many other countries) this is vulgar. |
| SCANDINAVIA (DENMARK, SWEDEN, NORWAY) | ▨ Being overly rank conscious in these countries. Scandinavians pay relatively little attention to a person's place in the hierarchy. |
| **ASIA** | |
| ALL ASIAN COUNTRIES | ▨ Pressuring an Asian job applicant or employee to brag about his or her accomplishments. Asians feel self-conscious when boasting about individual accomplishments and prefer to let the record speak for itself. In addition, they prefer to talk about group rather than individual accomplishment. |
| JAPAN | ▨ Shaking hands or hugging Japanese (as well as other Asians) in public. Japanese consider the practices offensive. |
| | ▨ Not interpreting "We'll consider it" as a "no" when spoken by a Japanese businessperson. Japanese negotiators mean "no" when they say, "We'll consider it." |
| | ▨ Not giving small gifts to Japanese when conducting business. Japanese are offended by not receiving these gifts. |
| | ▨ Giving your business card to a Japanese businessperson more than once. Japanese prefer to give and receive business cards only once. |
| CHINA | ▨ Using black borders on stationery and business cards. Black is associated with death. |
| | ▨ Giving small gifts to Chinese when conducting business. Chinese are offended by these gifts. |
| | ▨ Making cold calls on Chinese business executives. An appropriate introduction is required for a first-time meeting with a Chinese official. |
| KOREA | ▨ Saying "no." Koreans feel it is important to have visitors leave with good feelings. |
| INDIA | ▨ Telling Indians you prefer not to eat with your hands. If the Indians are not using cutlery when eating, they expect you to do likewise. |
| **MEXICO AND LATIN AMERICA** | |
| MEXICO | ▨ Flying into a Mexican city in the morning and expecting to close a deal by lunch. Mexicans build business relationships slowly. |
| BRAZIL | ▨ Attempting to impress Brazilians by speaking a few words of Spanish. Portuguese is the official language of Brazil. |
| MOST LATIN AMERICAN COUNTRIES | ▨ Wearing elegant and expensive jewelry during a business meeting. Most Latin Americans think American people should appear more conservative during a business meeting. |

Note: A cultural mistake for Americans to avoid when conducting business in most countries outside the United States and Canada is to insist on getting down to business too quickly. North Americans in small towns also like to build a relationship before getting down to business.

However, the word *individual* does not have positive connotations for all groups. Among many Latino cultural groups, the term *individual* is derogatory because it may connote the separation of one person from the rest of the community.[21]

3. *Show respect for all workers.* The same behavior that promotes good cross-cultural relations in general helps overcome communication barriers. A widely used comment that implies disrespect is to say to a person from another culture, "You have a funny accent." Should you be transposed to that person's culture, you too might have a "funny accent." The attitude of highest respect is to communicate your belief that although another person's culture is different from yours, it is not inferior to your culture. Showing respect for another culture can be more important than being bilingual in overcoming communication barriers.[22]

4. *Use straightforward language, and speak slowly and clearly.* When working with people who do not speak your language fluently, speak in an easy-to-understand manner. Minimize the use of idioms and analogies specific to your language. A systems analyst from New Delhi, India, left a performance review with her manager confused. The manager said, "I will be giving you more important assignments because I notice some good chemistry between us." The woman did not understand that *good chemistry* means *rapport,* and she did not ask for clarification because she did not want to appear uninformed.

   Speaking slowly is also important because even people who read and write a second language at an expert level may have difficulty catching some nuances of conversation. Facing the person from another culture directly also improves communication because your facial expressions and lips contribute to comprehension. And remember, there is no need to speak much louder.

5. *Look for signs of misunderstanding when your language is not the listener's native language.* Signs of misunderstanding may include nods and smiles not directly connected to what you are saying, a lack of questions, inappropriate laughter, and a blank expression. If these signs are present, work harder to apply the suggestions in point 4.[23]

6. *When the situation is appropriate, speak in the language of the people from another culture.* Americans who can speak another language are at a competitive advantage when dealing with businesspeople who speak that language. The language skill, however, must be more advanced than speaking a few basic words and phrases. Speaking the local language will often bring a person more insight and prevent misunderstandings. Equally important, being bilingual helps bring a person the respect that a leader needs to be fully credible.[24]

   A new twist in knowing another language has surged recently: as more deaf people have been integrated into the work force, knowing American Sign Language can be a real advantage to a leader when some of his or her constituents are deaf.

7. *Observe cross-cultural differences in etiquette.* Violating rules of etiquette without explanation can erect immediate communication barriers. A major rule of business etiquette in most countries is that the participants conducting serious business together should first share a meal. So if you are invited to a banquet that takes place the night before discussions about a major business deal, regard the banquet as a major opportunity to build a relationship. To avoid the banquet is a serious *faux pas.*

8. *Do not be diverted by style, accent, grammar, or personal appearance.* Although these superficial factors are all related to business success, they are difficult to interpret when judging a person from another culture. It is therefore better to judge the merits of the statement or behavior. A highly intelligent worker from another culture may still be learning English and thus make basic mistakes. He or she might also not yet have developed a sensitivity to dress style in your culture.

9. *Avoid racial or ethnic identification except when it is essential to communication.* Using a person's race or ethnicity as an adjective or other descriptor often suggests a negative stereotype.[25] For example, suppose a leader says, "I am proud of André. He is a very responsible (*member of his race*) customer service rep." One possible interpretation of this statement is that most customer service reps of André's race are not so responsible. Or, a leader might say, "We are happy to have Martha on our team. She is an easy-to-get-along-with (*mention of ethnicity*) lady." A possible implication is that women from Martha's particular country are usually not too easy to work with.

10. *Be sensitive to differences in nonverbal communication.* A person from another culture may misinterpret nonverbal signals. To use positive reinforcement, some managers will give a sideways hug to an employee or will touch the employee's arm. People from some cultures resent touching from workmates and will be offended. Koreans in particular dislike being touched or touching others in a work setting. A more common cross-cultural communication error is for an American to symbolize OK by making a circle with the thumb and first finger. In some other cultures, including those of Spain and India, the "OK circle" symbolizes a vulgarity.

11. *Be attentive to individual differences in appearance.* A major cross-cultural insult is to confuse the identity of people because they are members of the same race or ethnic group. An older economics professor reared in China and teaching in the United States had difficulty communicating with students because he was unable to learn their names. The professor's defense was that "so many of these Americans look alike to me." Recent research suggests that people have difficulty seeing individual differences among people of another race because they see so-called racial differences first; they might think, "He has the nose of a Chinese person." However, people can learn to search for more distinguishing features, such as a dimple or eye color, and expression (serious or not so serious).[26]

A general way to understand cross-cultural differences in nonverbal communication is to recognize that some cultures emphasize nonverbal communication more than others. People from high-context cultures are more sensitive to the surrounding circumstances or context of an event. As a result, they make extensive use of nonverbal communication. Among these high-context cultures are those of Asians, Latinos, and African Americans. People from low-context cultures pay less attention to the context of an event and therefore make less use of nonverbal communication. The Swiss are allegedly a low-context culture. Anglo Americans are from a medium-context culture.[27] Many new members of the work force are from high-context cultures. Leaders from low- and medium-context cultures must therefore learn to be extra responsive to nonverbal communication.

It is important to recognize that people from a high-context culture need to know how to place you in context in order to understand you better. In other words, they will want to know something about your background and the company you represent. Without that knowledge, it may be difficult to establish good communication.[28]

## The Leader's Role in Resolving Conflict and Negotiating

Leaders and managers spend considerable time resolving conflicts and negotiating. A frequent estimate is that they devote about 20 percent of their time to dealing with conflict. Conflict arises frequently among top executives, and it can have enormous consequences for the organization. If this conflict is ignored, the result can be an enterprise that competes more passionately with itself that with the competition.[29] An example of such competition would be two business units competing for resources.

An extensive description of conflict resolution is more appropriate for the study of managerial skills than for the study of leadership skills because it has more to do with establishing equilibrium than with helping the firm or organizational unit reach new heights. Here we focus on a basic framework for understanding conflict resolution styles, resolving conflict between two group members, and a few suggestions for negotiating and bargaining.

### Conflict Management Styles

As shown in Figure 12-1, Kenneth Thomas has identified five major styles of conflict management: competitive, accommodative, sharing, collaborative, and avoidant. Each style is based on a combination of satisfying one's own concerns (assertiveness) and satisfying the concerns of others (cooperativeness).[30] Leadership Self-Assessment Quiz 12-3 gives you an opportunity to think about your conflict management style.

**FIGURE 12-1   Conflict-Handling Styles According to the Degree of Cooperation and Assertiveness**

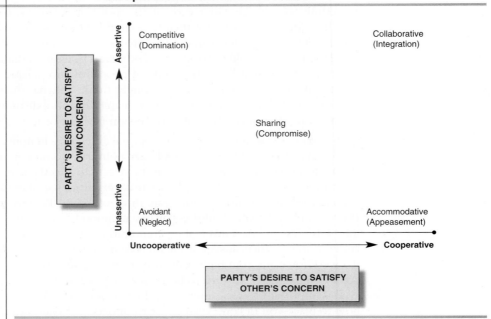

Source: Marvin D. Dunnette, ed., *Handbook of Industrial and Organizational Psychology,* p. 900 (Rand McNally). Copyright © 1976, Marvin D. Dunnette. Used by permission of Marvin D. Dunnette.

## MY CONFLICT RESOLUTION STYLE

**INSTRUCTIONS** Answer each of the following statements "mostly true" or "mostly false" with respect to how you have dealt with the situation, would deal with the situation, or how much you agree with the attitude expressed.

|  | Mostly False | Mostly True |
|---|---|---|
| **1.** I see myself as a "smash-mouth" negotiator. | _____ | _____ |
| **2.** The best way to resolve conflict is to overwhelm the other side. | _____ | _____ |
| **3.** When negotiating a price, I like to make sure that the other side walks away with at least some profit. | _____ | _____ |
| **4.** When negotiating a price, I like to start with an outrageous demand or offer so I can eventually get the price I really wanted. | _____ | _____ |
| **5.** After a successful negotiation, one side wins and one side loses. | _____ | _____ |
| **6.** After a successful negotiation, both sides walk away with something of value. | _____ | _____ |
| **7.** When I am in conflict with somebody else, I try to listen carefully to understand his or her point of view. | _____ | _____ |
| **8.** Face it: business is war, so why grant concessions when in a dispute? | _____ | _____ |
| **9.** When working out a disagreement with a workmate, I keep in mind the fact that we will have to work together in the future. | _____ | _____ |
| **10.** Nice people finish last when it comes to resolving disputes. | _____ | _____ |

*Total score* _____

SCORING AND INTERPRETATION Give yourself a score of 1 for each answer that matches the scoring key:

1. Mostly false
2. Mostly false
3. Mostly true
4. Mostly false
5. Mostly false
6. Mostly true
7. Mostly true
8. Mostly false
9. Mostly true
10. Mostly false

*(continued)*

If your score is 8, 9, or 10, you most likely use the collaborative (win–win) approach to resolving conflict and negotiating. If your score is 7 or less, you most likely use the competitive (win–lose) approach to resolving conflict and negotiating. The collaborative approach is more likely to enhance your leadership effectiveness in the long run.

**Competitive Style** The competitive style is a desire to achieve one's own goals at the expense of the other party, or to dominate. A person with a competitive orientation is likely to engage in win–lose power struggles.

**Accommodative Style** The accommodative style favors appeasement, or satisfying the other's concerns without taking care of one's own. People with this orientation may be generous or self-sacrificing just to maintain a relationship. An irate customer might be accommodated with a full refund, "just to shut him (or her) up." The intent of such accommodation might also be to retain the customer's loyalty.

**Sharing Style** The sharing style is halfway between domination and appeasement. Sharers prefer moderate but incomplete satisfaction for both parties, which results in a compromise. The term *splitting the difference* reflects this orientation, which is commonly used in such activities as purchasing a house or car.

**Collaborative Style** In contrast to the other styles, the collaborative style reflects a desire to fully satisfy the desires of both parties. It is based on the underlying philosophy of the **win–win approach to conflict resolution**, the belief that after conflict has been resolved, both sides should gain something of value. The user of win–win approaches is genuinely concerned about arriving at a settlement that meets the needs of both parties, or at least does not badly damage the welfare of the other side. When collaborative approaches to resolving conflict are used, the relationships among the parties are built on and improved.

The collaborative style of conflict management has many variations, one of which is to agree with the person criticizing you. According to Dianna Booher, when you agree with a critic, you show that you seek a solution, not a way to demonstrate that you are right. If you agree with the substance of the criticism, you show that you are aware of the situation and ready to do what is best to solve the problem.[31]

To illustrate, if a group member criticizes you for having been too harsh in your evaluation of him or her, you might say: "I agree that my evaluation was harsh, but I was harsh for a purpose. I want to be candid with you so you will be motivated to make what I think are necessary improvements." Your agreement is likely to spark further discussion about how the group member can improve. The collaborative style is the approach an effective leader is most likely to use because the outcome leads to increased productivity and satisfaction.

**Avoidant Style** The avoider combines lack of cooperation and unassertiveness. He or she is indifferent to the concerns of either party. The person may actually be withdrawing from the conflict or be relying upon fate. An example of an avoider is a manager who stays out of a conflict between two team members, leaving them to resolve their own differences.

People engaged in conflict resolution typically combine several of the five resolution styles to accomplish their purpose. For example, a generally effective approach to resolving conflict is to be competitive with regard to a cost that is important to oneself but unimportant to the opponent, and at the same time use accommodation for a cost that is unimportant to oneself but important to the opponent.[32]

Which mode or modes of conflict handling to use depends upon a number of variables, as presented in detail in Table 12-4. The major contingency factors are the importance of the conflict issue and the relative power of the opposing parties. An issue may be so important to a leader, such as preventing his or her organization unit from being outsourced, that domination may be the most effective mode. At other times a leader may use the accommodating mode of conflict management when the opposing side has much more power, and he or she may want to save domination for a more important issue in the future.

**TABLE 12-4**

## Appropriate Situations for Using the Five Modes of Conflict Resolution

| CONFLICT-HANDLING MODE | APPROPRIATE SITUATION |
| --- | --- |
| COMPETING | 1. When quick, decisive action is vital, such as in an emergency |
|  | 2. On important issues when unpopular actions need implementing, such as cost cutting, enforcing unpopular rules, or discipline |
|  | 3. On issues vital to organization welfare when you know you are right |
|  | 4. Against people who take advantage of noncompetitive behavior |
| COLLABORATING | 1. To find an integrative solution when both sets of concerns are too important to be compromised |
|  | 2. When your objective is to learn |
|  | 3. To merge insights from people with different perspectives |
|  | 4. To gain commitment by incorporating concerns into a consensus |
|  | 5. To work through feelings that have interfered with a relationship |
| COMPROMISING | 1. When goals are important but not worth the effort or potential disruption of more assertive modes |
|  | 2. When opponents with equal power are committed to mutually exclusive goals |
|  | 3. To achieve temporary settlements of complex issues |
|  | 4. To arrive at expedient solutions under time pressure |
|  | 5. As a backup when collaboration or competition is unsuccessful |

*Continued*

| TABLE 12-4 | **Appropriate Situations for Using the Five Modes of Conflict Resolution (continued)** |
|---|---|

| CONFLICT-HANDLING MODE | APPROPRIATE SITUATION |
|---|---|
| AVOIDING | 1. When an issue is trivial or more important issues are pressing |
| | 2. When you perceive no chance of satisfying your concern |
| | 3. When the potential disruption outweighs the benefits of a resolution |
| | 4. To let people cool down and regain perspective |
| | 5. When gathering information supersedes making an immediate decision |
| | 6. When others can resolve the conflict more effectively |
| ACCOMMODATING | 1. When you find you are wrong—to allow a better position to be heard, to learn, and to show your reasonableness |
| | 2. When issues are more important to others than to yourself—to satisfy others and maintain cooperation |
| | 3. To build social credits for later issues |
| | 4. To minimize the loss when you are outmatched and losing |
| | 5. When harmony and stability are especially important |
| | 6. To allow group members to develop by learning from mistakes |

Source: Slightly adapted from Kenneth W. Thomas, "Toward Multidimensional Values in Teaching: The Example of Conflict Behaviors," *Academy of Management Review* by Klimoski, Richard J., April 1977, p. 487. *Academy of Management Review* by Kenneth W. Thomas. Copyright 1997 by the Academy of Management. Reproduced with permission of the Academy of Management in the format Textbook via Copyright Clearance Center.

## Resolving Conflict Between Two Group Members

A high-level managerial skill is to help two or more group members resolve conflict between or among them. Much of the time a manager or leader invests in conflict resolution is geared toward assisting others resolve their conflict. The most useful approach is to get the parties in conflict to engage in confrontation and problem solving. (*Confrontation* refers to discussing the true problem, and *problem solving* refers to finding a way to resolve the conflict.) The manager sits down with the two sides and encourages them to talk to each other about the problem, not talk directly to him or her. This approach is preferable to inviting each side to speak with the manager or leader alone, because then each side might attempt to convince the manager that he or she is right. An abbreviated example follows:

**Leader:** I've brought you two together to see if you can overcome the problems you have about sharing the workload during a period in which one of you is overloaded.

**Stephanie:** I'm glad you did. Josh never wants to help me, even when I'm drowning in customer requests.

**Josh:** I would be glad to help Stephanie if she ever agreed to help me. If she has any downtime, she runs to the break room so she can chat on her cell phone.

**Stephanie:** Look who's talking. I have seen you napping in your SUV when you have a little downtime.

**Leader:** I'm beginning to see what's going on here. Both of you are antagonistic toward each other, and you look for little faults to pick. With a little more respect on both sides, I think you would be more willing to help each other out.

**Josh:** Actually, Stephanie's not too bad. And I know she can perform well when she wants to. Next time I see her needing help, I'll pitch in.

**Stephanie:** I know that the name "Josh" is related to joking around, but our Josh really has a warm heart. I'm open to starting with a fresh slate. Maybe Josh can ask me politely the next time he needs help.

Conflict specialist Patrick S. Nugent believes that being able to intervene in the conflicts of group members is a management skill that grows in importance. Such competencies are useful in an emerging form of management based less on traditional hierarchy and more on developing self-managing subordinates and teams.[33]

## Negotiating and Bargaining

Conflicts can be considered situations that call for negotiating and bargaining, or conferring with another person to resolve a problem. When you are trying to negotiate a fair salary for yourself, you are simultaneously trying to resolve a conflict. At first the demands of the two parties may seem incompatible, but through negotiation a salary may emerge that satisfies both parties. Two general approaches to negotiation are distributive bargaining and integrative bargaining. In *distributive bargaining*, the two sides operate under zero-sum conditions: one wins something at the expense of the other, and the purpose of bargaining is to distribute the resources. This is the common-sense approach to negotiation. *Integrative bargaining* reflects the collaborative mode of managing conflict because it assumes that win–win solutions can be found. Table 12-5 outlines the differences between distributive and integrative bargaining. Following are several negotiation techniques leaders may need to have at their disposal.

**Begin with a Plausible Demand or Offer** Most people believe that compromise and allowing room for negotiation include beginning with an extreme demand or offer. The theory is that the final compromise will be closer to the true demand or offer

---

**TABLE 12-5** ## Distributive Versus Integrative Bargaining

|  | DISTRIBUTIVE BARGAINING | INTEGRATIVE BARGAINING |
|---|---|---|
| RESOURCES TO BE DISTRIBUTED | Fixed amount | Variable amount |
| PRIMARY MOTIVATIONS OF PARTIES | To gain at the expense of the other side (I win; you lose) | To maximize gains for both sides (I win; you win) |
| PRIMARY INTERESTS | 180 degrees apart | Convergent or congruent |
| FOCUS OF RELATIONSHIPS | Short term | Long term |

than if the negotiation were opened more realistically. But a plausible demand is better because it reflects good-faith bargaining. Also, if a third party has to resolve the conflict, a plausible demand or offer will receive more sympathy than an implausible one.

***Focus on Interests, Not Position*** Rather than clinging to specific negotiating points, one should keep overall interests in mind and try to satisfy them. Remember that the true object of negotiation is to satisfy the underlying interests of both sides. As professional mediator John Heister explains, when you focus on interests, all of the disputants get on the same side of the table and say, "We have a problem to solve. Based on our common interests, we need to find a solution that meets the needs of each of the stakeholders."[34]

Here is how the strategy works: Your manager asks you to submit a proposal for increasing sales volume. You see it as an important opportunity to link up with another distributor. When you submit your ideas, you learn that management wants to venture further into ecommerce, not to expand the dealer network. Instead of insisting on linking with another dealer, be flexible. Ask to be included in the decision making for additional involvement in ecommerce. You will increase your sales volume (your true interest), and you may enjoy such secondary benefits as having helped the company develop a stronger ecommerce presence.

***Search for the Value in Differences Between the Two Sides*** Negotiation researcher and practitioner James K. Sebenius explains that according to conventional wisdom we negotiate to overcome the differences dividing the two sides. So we hope to find win–win agreements by searching for common ground. However, many sources of value in negotiation arise from differences among the parties. The differences may suggest useful ideas for breaking a deadlock and reaching a constructive agreement. Framed differently, the differences might suggest what solution will work for both sides. Here is an example:

> A small technology company and its investors were stuck in a difficult negotiation with a large acquiring company insistent on paying much less than the asking price. Exploring the differences, it turned out that the acquirer was actually willing to pay the higher price but was concerned about elevating price expectations for further companies it might purchase in the same sector. The solution was for the two sides to agree on a moderate, well-publicized purchase price. The deal contained complex contingencies that almost guaranteed a much higher price later.[35]

(So, in the end, searching for values in differences functions like win–win.)

***Be Sensitive to International Differences in Negotiating Style*** A challenge facing the multicultural leader is how to negotiate successfully with people from other cultures. Frank L. Acuff notes that Americans often have a no-nonsense approach to negotiation. Key attitudes underlying the American approach to negotiation include:

"Tell it like it is."

"What's the bottom line?"

"Let's get it out."

A problem with this type of frankness and seeming impatience is that people from other cultures may interpret such remarks as rudeness. The adverse interpretation, in turn, may lead to a failed negotiation. Acuff gives a case example: "It is unlikely in Mexico or Japan that the other side is going to answer 'yes' or 'no' to any question. You will have to discern answers to questions through the context of what is being said rather than from the more obvious direct cues that U.S. negotiators use."[36] By sizing up what constitutes an effective negotiating style, the negotiator stands a reasonable chance of achieving a collaborative solution. Other cross-cultural differences in negotiation style include these tendencies: Japanese avoid direct confrontation and prefer an exchange of information. Russians crave combat; Koreans are team players; Nigerians prefer the spoken word; and Indians the written one.[37] (We caution again, that cultural stereotypes are true much of the time, but not all of the time.)

college.hmco.com/pic/ dubrin5e

🏦 @ **KNOWLEDGE BANK:** describes an experiment about how culture can influence negotiation.

When asked to describe the essence of good negotiating in a few sentences, master negotiator Roger Fisher replied, "Be firm and friendly. Hard on the problem, soft on the people. Find out what the other side views as important and negotiate on that. Let the other side make the deal better from its point of view, at the same time that you gain what you are looking for."[38]

Negotiating and bargaining, as with any other leadership and management skill, require conceptual knowledge and practice. Leadership Skill-Building Exercise 12-3 gives you an opportunity to practice collaboration, the most integrative form of negotiating and bargaining. Practice in finding options for mutual gains is helpful for the leader because negotiating is a high-impact part of his or her job.

**READER'S ROADMAP**

So far we have studied considerable information about the nature of leadership, the attributes, behaviors, and styles of leaders, the ethics and social responsibility of leaders, and how leaders exert power and use politics and influence. We then studied techniques for developing teamwork, as well as motivation and coaching skills. After studying creativity and innovation as part of leadership, we focused on communication skills as they relate to leadership. Next, we shift our study to direction setting at the organizational level: strategic leadership.

### INTEGRATIVE BARGAINING

The class is organized into groups of six, with each group being divided into two negotiating teams of three each. The members of the negotiating teams would like to find an integrative (win–win) solution to the issue separating the two sides. The team members are free to invent their own pressing issue, or they can choose one of the following:

- Management wants to control costs by not giving cost-of-living adjustments in the upcoming year. The employee group believes that a cost-of-living adjustment is absolutely necessary for its welfare.

- The marketing team claims it could sell 250,000 units of a toaster wide enough to toast bagels if the toasters could be produced at $10 per unit. The manufacturing group says it would not be feasible to get the manufacturing cost below $15 per unit.

- Blockbuster Video would like to build in a new location that is adjacent to an historic district in one of the oldest cities in North America. The members of the town planning board would like the tax revenue and jobs that the Blockbuster store would bring, but they do not want a Blockbuster store adjacent to the historic district.

After the teams have arrived at their solutions through high-level negotiating techniques, the creative solutions can be shared with teammates.

## Summary

college.hmco.com/pic/dubrin5e

Systematic observation and empirical research support the idea that effective leaders are also effective communicators. There is substantial evidence of a positive relationship between competence in communication and leadership performance. Nonverbal skills are also important for leadership effectiveness.

Inspirational and powerful communication helps leaders carry out their roles. Suggestions for inspirational and powerful speaking and writing include the following: (1) be credible; (2) gear your message to your listener; (3) sell group members on the benefits of your suggestions; (4) use heavy-impact and emotion-provoking words; (5) use anecdotes and metaphors to communicate meaning; (6) back up conclusions with data; (7) minimize language errors, junk words, and vocalized pauses; and (8) write crisp, clear memos, letters, and reports, including a front-loaded message.

Using a power-oriented linguistic style is another way to communicate with inspiration and power. The style includes a variety of techniques, such as downplaying uncertainty, emphasizing direct rather than indirect talks, and choosing an effective communication frame. Leaders can also improve their communication skills by following the six principles of persuasion: liking, reciprocity, social proof, consistency, authority, and scarcity.

Skill can also be developed in using nonverbal communication that connotes power, being in control, forcefulness, and self-confidence. Among the suggestions are to stand erect; speak at a moderate pace with a loud, clear tone; and smile frequently in a relaxed manner. A person's external image also plays an important part in communicating messages to others. People pay more respect and grant more privileges to those they perceive as being well dressed and neatly groomed.

Supportive communication enhances communication between two people and therefore contributes to leadership effectiveness. The process has identifiable principles and characteristics. Supportive communication is (1) problem oriented, not person oriented; (2) descriptive, not evaluative; (3) based on congruence, not incongruence; (4) focused on validating, rather than invalidating, people; (5) specific, not global; (6) conjunctive, not disjunctive; (7) owned, not disowned; and (8) characterized by intense listening, including dialogue.

Overcoming communication barriers created by dealing with people from different cultures is another leadership and management challenge. Guidelines for overcoming cross-cultural barriers include the following: (1) be sensitive to the existence of cross-cultural communication barriers; (2) challenge your cultural assumptions; (3) show respect for all workers; (4) use straightforward language, and speak slowly and clearly; (5) look for signs of misunderstanding when your language is not the listener's native language; (6) when appropriate, speak in the language of the people from another culture; (7) observe cross-cultural differences in etiquette; (8) do not be diverted by style, accent, grammar, or personal appearance; (9) avoid racial or ethnic identification except when it is essential to communication; (10) be sensitive to differences in nonverbal communication; and (11) be attentive to individual differences in appearance.

A general way to understand cross-cultural differences in nonverbal communication is to recognize that some cultures emphasize nonverbal communication more than others. People from high-context cultures are more sensitive to the surrounding circumstances or context of an event.

Leaders and managers spend considerable time managing conflict. Five major styles of conflict management are as follows: competitive, accommodative, sharing, collaborative (win–win), and avoidant. Each style is based on a combination of satisfying one's own concerns (assertiveness) and satisfying the concerns of others (cooperativeness). When resolving conflict, people typically combine several of the five resolution styles to accomplish their purpose, such as dominating and accommodating. Which modes of conflict handling to use depends upon a number of variables, as presented in detail in Table 12-4.

A high-level managerial skill is to help two or more group members resolve conflict between or among them. The most useful approach is to get the parties in conflict to engage in confrontation and problem solving.

Conflicts can be considered situations calling for negotiating and bargaining. Distributive bargaining and integrative bargaining are two general approaches to negotiation. In distributive bargaining, the two sides operate under zero-sum conditions. Integrative bargaining reflects the collaborative mode of managing conflict because it assumes that win–win solutions can be found. Specific negotiating techniques include the following: (1) begin with a plausible demand or offer; (2) focus on interests, not positions; (3) search for the value in differences between the two sides; and (4) be sensitive to international differences in negotiating style.

## Key Terms

Virtual office

Linguistic style

Supportive communication

Congruence

Conjunctive communication

Disjunctive communication

Win–win approach to conflict resolution

## ✔ *Guidelines for Action and Skill Development*

Gay Lumsden and Donald Lumsden recommend a specific communications improvement program that can supplement the suggestions already made in this chapter.

1. **Seek congruity with your messages.** The information and feelings you communicate should be consistent with the verbal and nonverbal messages you use to send them.
2. **Ask for feedback from family, friends, coworkers, and managers.** Ask people who are familiar with your communication style about the congruence between your verbal and nonverbal messages.
3. **Observe others' responses.** Watch for positive, negative, and comprehending responses from others. Question how well your messages are received.
4. **Observe a videotape of yourself.** Obtain a videotape of yourself in daily conversation or making a presentation. Scrutinize your strengths and areas for development. Look for ways to appear more powerful and inspiring. Be particularly alert to voice quality, junk words, and weak expressions.
5. **Decide what to change.** Identify specific verbal and nonverbal behaviors you think you should change to enhance your communication effectiveness. Follow up by practicing the new or modified behaviors.[39]

## *Discussion Questions and Activities*

1. Now that you have studied this chapter, what are you going to do differently to improve your communication effectiveness as a leader?
2. Find an example of a powerful written or spoken message by a leader. Bring the information back to class to share with others.
3. What would be an effective *communication frame* for telling group members that they will be expected to work about seventy hours per week for the next five weeks?
4. Identify a leader who you think has a power-oriented linguistic style. How did you arrive at your conclusion?
5. Why is persuasion considered one of the leader's essential tools?
6. Given that people really do defer to experts, how might the leader establish his or her expertise?
7. Should a manager be willing to negotiate a performance standard, such as output per month, with a group member?
8. Would a powerful leader like Donald Trump ever have to negotiate anything in the workplace?
9. What concrete steps can a leader take to demonstrate that he or she respects a group member from another culture?
10. Give two examples in which it would probably be effective for a leader to use the accommodative style of conflict handling.

## LEADERSHIP CASE PROBLEM A

### SAFEWAY CEO BATTLES THE UNION AND WAL-MART

In the first quarter of 2004, Safeway Inc., Albertson's, Inc., and The Kroger Company were locked in a showdown with 71,000 unionized workers in Southern California. But as the strike that began the previous October went before a mediator, observers were worrying if the industry's aggressive stance could backfire, maybe even leading to the ouster of Safeway CEO Steven A. Burd, who has led the campaign for the three companies. The strike lasted four-and-one-half months, until worker strike funds were depleted.

The dispute inflicted serious damage on the companies, contributing heavily to a $696 million loss in the quarter ending January 3, 2004. Wall Street analysts were concerned that morale woes could persist long past the dispute's resolution. "There are people on the Street who want a change," said one analyst (*BusinessWeek*, p. 82). Yet Safeway directors said they fully support the approach that Burd and his management team took with the labor dispute.

The supermarket industry's goal is to bring its health care costs more in line with those of nonunion Wal-Mart Stores, Inc. The retail giant's medical plan covers less than half its workers, and its sales clerks earn less, on average, than the federal poverty line. To match that, Burd and his counterparts want to shift to a 402(k)-style health plan that would require current workers to bear part of the burden of future medical inflation. They also want to cut contributions for new hires' medical coverage to just $1.35 per hour worked, the union says, versus $3.85 now paid for current workers—a 65 percent cut. All this has infuriated members of the United Food & Commercial Workers (UFCW). "All I want is medical insurance to take care of my baby. Is that too much to ask?" said Cynthia Hernandez, 27, a Safeway striker and single mother (*BusinessWeek*, p. 82).

A reporter expressed the opinion that the grocery workers might not have dug in their heels so much if Burd had been savvier about playing them off against new hires. Since the industry's turnover averages roughly 10 percent a year, its new-hire demand could all but take Safeway off the hook for health coverage for up to one-third of its work force within the next three years by attrition alone. If Burd had focused on the new hires and asked less of current workers, the union probably would not have fought so hard for employees who have yet to be hired.

It was thought that with a relatively quick end to the walkout, Safeway might come out ahead. If the industry gets much of what it wants, well-

paying grocery jobs in the United States might become a thing of the past. An analyst from Morningstar, Inc., thought that Burd might have to leave to restore morale among a resentful work force.

In December 2004, the three major grocers reached a new labor agreement with the 19,000 grocery workers in Northern California, thereby averting a threatened strike and laying the foundation for a possible truce with thousands of other employees in San Francisco Bay Area stores.

Jack Loveall, the union leader who negotiated the tentative contract with the three supermarket chains, celebrated the agreement as a significant breakthrough for supermarket workers fighting management's cost-cutting efforts. "Our challenge from the start was to protect the superior wages and benefits supermarket workers have enjoyed for decades," said Loveall. "I am pleased to report that we've succeeded in that challenge" (*CNNMoney.com*, p. 1). The agreement came after ten months of negotiation, shortly before a union deadline for a strike vote.

The Bay Area talks became progressively more tense as disenchanted labor leaders stepped up efforts to organize consumer boycotts, hoping to pressure supermarket management before the workers' extended contract expired January 15, 2005.

Loveall described the agreement as a triumph for the store employees on two key battlefronts. For one, the new contract avoids a two-tier wage system that would dramatically lower the pay scale for future workers. Second, the deal ensures that workers will not have to pay insurance premiums for their medical benefits. Those issues became the flash points of a four-and-one-half month strike in Southern California that resulted in huge losses for the supermarkets and demoralizing concessions for the workers.

Although the Southern California contract also yielded long-term savings on labor expenses, such as some saving on medical insurance payments, the supermarkets are still nursing financial wounds opened by the dispute. Leaders at

*(continued)*

Safeway and the other supermarkets have insisted they need to lower costs to survive an aggressive expansion into the grocery business by Wal-Mart. Labor leaders maintain the grocers are overstating the Wal-Mart threat to finagle concessions and boost profits.

## QUESTIONS

1. Would you describe the agreement reached by management and labor as a win–win solution? Explain your reasoning.

2. How well did Burd communicate his demands to the labor union (UFCW)?
3. What do you recommend be done next to enhance the profitability of the three supermarket chains, as well as the morale and financial well-being of the workers?

SOURCE: Ronald Grover and Louise Lee, "Will Safeway's CEO Get Locked Out?" *BusinessWeek*, March 1, 2004; "Safeway, Albertson's, Kroger Reach Labor Deal in N Calif," *cnnmoney*, December 20, 2004.

## LEADERSHIP CASE PROBLEM B

### CAN HE BE THE REAL BILL GATES?

It wasn't surprising that conference attendees at the LinuxWorld trade show stopped to stare. They were probably wondering if they were gazing at the world's richest man. Only the person they were staring at was not Bill Gates. Oracle Corporation had hired a Bill Gates look-alike to hand out fliers promoting its CEO Larry Ellison's keynote speech at the San Francisco trade show. The bespectacled impersonator of the Microsoft chairman (or chief software architect) was reminding people not to miss his software rival's talk. (Readers may recall that Larry Ellison had previously hired a detective to sort through Microsoft dumpsters looking for negative information about Microsoft leaders.)

Olaf Ruehl, or "Bill," is a 20-something look-alike who offers his impersonation services part time. While he primarily dons his Gates persona, he also does general appearances for other "nerd"-type characters.

At least a dozen people commented on the irony of seeing "Bill Gates" at a Linux show this week, even though Microsoft actually does have a small booth there. Linux is the free software based on a shared computer code that is considered an alternative to Microsoft's Windows operating system franchise.

## QUESTIONS

1. What messages is Oracle sending about itself by hiring the impersonator to encourage conference attendees to attend Larry Ellison's talk?
2. How would you rate the persuasive effectiveness of this method of encouraging people to listen to Ellison's talk?
3. In what way does the incident about the Bill Gates impersonator illustrate conflict between Oracle and Microsoft?
4. What would you advise Bill Gates to do, if anything, about the Oracle stunt of hiring the impersonator?

SOURCE: Adapted from Ann Grimes, "Who Is That Geek?" *The Wall Street Journal*, August 15, 2002, p. B4 (in "Digits/Gambits & Gadgets in the World of Technology"). *The Wall Street Journal*. Eastern Edition [Only Staff-Produced Materials May Be Used] by Ann Grimes. Copyright 2002 by Dow Jones & Co. Inc. Reproduced with permission of Dow Jones & Co. Inc. in the format Textbook via Copyright Clearance Center.

## MY LEADERSHIP PORTFOLIO

For this chapter's entry into your leadership portfolio, think through how you have dealt with your opportunities to come across as a leader in your experiences. Did you have an opportunity to attempt to persuade an individual or group? Did you have an opportunity to be supportive toward another person? Did you have an opportunity to make a presentation on the job or in class? During these communication opportunities, how well did you come across as a leader? Did you impress anybody with persuasive skill or warmth? Carlos, an assistant restaurant manager, made this entry in his portfolio:

> I help manage an upscale restaurant. The wait staff has to be on top of its game when in the dining room. Without superior service, nobody is going to pay our prices even if the food and wine are good. Late one afternoon, in dragged Rick, looking in no shape to give good service to our guests. He looked worried and distracted. Instead of telling Rick to go home, I took him aside in the office. I asked him to give me a full explanation of whatever problem he was facing. We both sat down, and I poured Rick a cup of coffee. After a minute or so, Rick opened up to tell me about how he rammed the back of his car into a two-foot-high guardrail in a parking lot. His fiberglass bumper split, and he figures it will cost him $650 to replace it. I listened to his whole story without being judgmental. I said I would check with the manager to see if we could give him extra hours this month to earn more money to apply toward his repair. Rick said, "Thanks for listening," and he left our one-on-one session feeling better and looking well enough to face the guests.
>
> I give myself a gold star for having been a supportive leader. Ha! Ha!

## INTERNET SKILL-BUILDING EXERCISE

Apply the chapter concepts! Visit the Web and complete this Internet skill-building exercise to learn more about current leadership topics and trends.

### WHAT IS YOUR INFLUENCE QUOTIENT?

Visit *www.influenceatwork.com* and take the NQ test, which measures knowledge of a certain type of influence tactic. After taking the test, compare the type of influence tactic measured by the test with the influence tactics (a) mentioned in this chapter about communications and conflict, and (b) the leadership influence tactics described in Chapter 8. In a few words, how might the type of influence tactic described in the test help you be a more effective leader?

# 13

# Strategic Leadership and Knowledge Management

Toys "R" Us, battered by price wars from discounters, is considering getting out of the toy business. Top management at the giant toy retailer announced plans to restructure its toy business, but said it is considering selling the business outright as part of an effort to reduce operating and capital expenses. The $11.6 billion company is also pursuing a possible spinoff of its fast-growing Babies "R" Us, whose 200 stores sell furniture and accessories. The company will operate the toy and baby business as separate entities in the meantime.

The Babies "R" Us division has been the company's growth vehicle and has not been so vulnerable to discounters. The U.S. toy division, however, has been inconsistent since the mid-1990s, when Wal-Mart ramped up its toy department as it also dramatically expanded the number of its stores.

John Eyler, chair and chief executive officer, said the global toy and Babies "R" Us businesses are at "fundamentally different phases in their growth cycle," and separation would give the baby business more opportunity to continue its growth. The possible retreat comes after Toys "R" Us spent millions to renovate its stores and sought exclusive rights to certain toys to differentiate itself from the discounters, which it could not beat on price.[1]

T he story about Toys "R" Us contemplating getting out of the toy business may seem as bizarre as would a story about Starbucks getting out of the café business. Yet the Toys "R" Us potential move illustrates how leaders must continually think through the very nature of their business and the direction in which the firm is headed. A key leadership role is to form a **strategy,** an integrated, overall concept of how the firm will achieve its objectives.[2]

In this chapter we approach strategic leadership by emphasizing the leader's role rather than strategy and strategic planning. First, we examine the nature of strategic leadership and describe a frequently used tool for development strategy, SWOT analysis. We then examine the strategies that leaders most frequently use to bring about success. Following that is a description of a leader's contribution to a current thrust in strategy, knowledge management, and developing a learning organization.

## The Nature of Strategic Leadership

Strategic leadership deals with the major purposes of an organization or an organizational unit, and thus differs more in level than in kind from leadership in general. We study strategic leadership separately because in practice it is the province of top-level executives. For our purposes, **strategic leadership** is the process of providing the direction and inspiration necessary to create or sustain an organization. The founder of Starbucks Corporation provided strategic leadership because he developed a concept for an organization, developed the organization, and inspired large numbers of people to help him achieve his purpose.

Strategic leadership is a complex of personal characteristics, thinking patterns, and effective management, all centering on the ability to think strategically. Do Leadership Self-Assessment Quiz 13-1 to explore your orientation toward thinking strategically.

Our approach to understanding the nature of strategic leadership will be to describe certain associated characteristics, behaviors, and practices, as outlined in

## ARE YOU A STRATEGIC THINKER?

**INSTRUCTIONS** Indicate your strength of agreement with each of the following statements: SD = strongly disagree, D = disagree, N = neutral, A = agree, SA = strongly agree.

|  | SD | D | N | A | SA |
|---|---|---|---|---|---|
| 1. Every action I take on my job should add value for our customers, our clients, or the public. | 1 | 2 | 3 | 4 | 5 |
| 2. Let top management ponder the future; I have my own job to get done. | 5 | 4 | 3 | 2 | 1 |
| 3. Strategic thinking is fluff. Somebody down the organization has to get the job done. | 5 | 4 | 3 | 2 | 1 |
| 4. A company cannot become great without an exciting vision. | 1 | 2 | 3 | 4 | 5 |
| 5. What I do on the job each day can affect the performance of the company many years into the future. | 1 | 2 | 3 | 4 | 5 |
| 6. It is rather pointless to develop skills or acquire knowledge that cannot help you on the job within the next month. | 5 | 4 | 3 | 2 | 1 |
| 7. Strategic planning should be carried out in a separate department rather than involve people throughout the organization. | 5 | 4 | 3 | 2 | 1 |
| 8. It makes good sense for top management to frequently ask itself the question, "What business are we really in?" | 1 | 2 | 3 | 4 | 5 |
| 9. If a company does an outstanding job of satisfying its customers, there is little need to worry about changing its mix of goods or services. | 5 | 4 | 3 | 2 | 1 |
| 10. Organizational visions remind me of pipe dreams and hallucinations. | 5 | 4 | 3 | 2 | 1 |

SCORING AND INTERPRETATION Find your total score by summing the point values for each question. A score of 42 to 50 suggests that you already think strategically, which should help you provide strategic leadership to others. Scores of 20 to 41 suggest a somewhat neutral, detached attitude toward thinking strategically. Scores of 10 to 19 suggest thinking that emphasizes the here and now and the short term. People scoring in this category are not yet ready to provide strategic leadership to group members.

---

SKILL DEVELOPMENT Reflecting on your ability to think strategically is useful because leaders at all levels are expected to see the big picture and point people in a useful direction.

Figure 13-1. The information about charismatic and transformational leadership presented in Chapter 3 is also relevant here.

## High-Level Cognitive Activity of the Leader

Thinking strategically requires high-level cognitive skills, such as the ability to think conceptually, absorb and make sense of multiple trends, and condense all of this information into a straightforward plan of action. The ability to process information and understand its consequences for the organization in its interaction with the environment is often referred to as *systems thinking*. In one analysis of the cognitive requirements of leadership, the work of management is divided into a system of seven levels within organizations. At each level there are qualitatively different task demands and skill requirements as one moves across higher and lower strata. A contributing factor is that the longer the time span incorporated into a manager's job, the greater the demands are on intellectual ability.[3] A CEO might work with a twenty-five-year perspective regardless of whether he or she would be with the same firm in twenty-five years.

**FIGURE 13-1** Components of Strategic Leadership

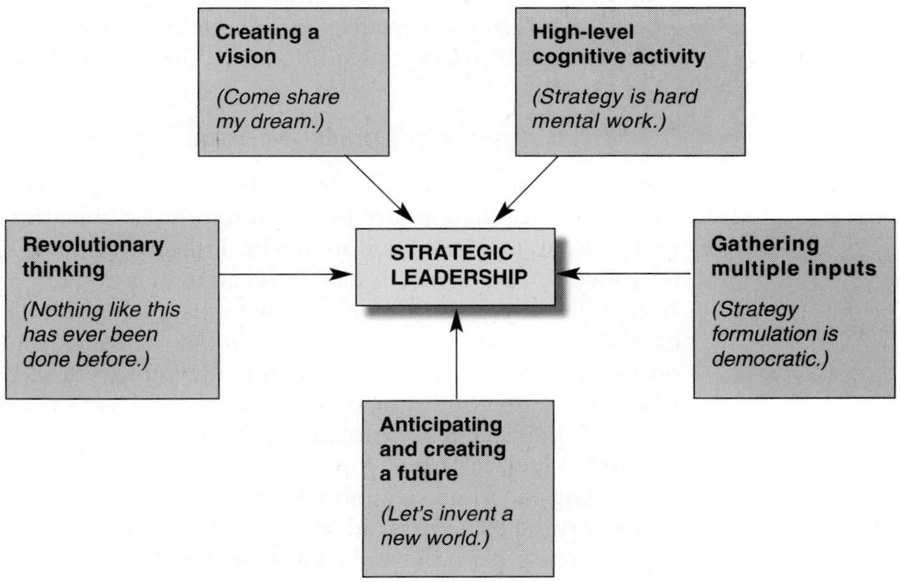

As one moves up the hierarchy, more problem-solving ability and imagination are required to handle the task environment effectively. To engage in strategic management and leadership, a person must have conceptual prowess. An organization will be successful when the cognitive abilities of its leaders are a good fit with the nature of the work. This is one of many reasons that tests of problem-solving ability correlate positively with success in managerial work.[4]

Creative problem solving is also important because the strategic leader has to develop alternative courses of action for shaping the organization. Furthermore, asking what-if questions requires imagination. To help revive the sagging fortunes of Kellogg Corporation several years ago, CEO Carlos Gutierrez asked why the company placed so much emphasis on sales volume. His new strategy, labeled Volume to Value, increased sales by shifting resources to higher-margin products such as Special K and Nutri-Grain bars.[5] Gutierrez essentially asked, "What if we shift our strategy to focusing on high-margin products instead of sales volume?"

## Gathering Multiple Inputs to Formulate Strategy

Many strategic leaders arrive at their ideas for the organization's future by consulting with a wide range of interested parties, in a process similar to conducting research to create a vision. Strategy theorist Gary Hamel reasons that imagination is scarcer than resources. As a consequence, "We have to involve hundreds, if not thousands, of new voices in the strategy process if we want to increase the odds of seeing the future."[6]

Gathering multiple inputs has the added benefit of building morale. Whirlpool Corporation earns the support of line workers by placing volunteers on strategic teams with midlevel managers and senior executives. The production workers contribute to decisions that affect Whirlpool facilities in the United States. They travel to other countries with executives to new manufacturing facilities to help top management gain a better perspective on production and workforce issues.[7] As a result Whirlpool leadership can make crisper strategic decisions about production and work force issues.

## Anticipating and Creating a Future

A major component of leadership is direction setting, which involves anticipating and sometimes creating a future for the enterprise or organizational unit. To set a direction is also to tell the organization what it should be doing. To set a productive direction for the future, the leader must accurately forecast or anticipate that future. Insight into tomorrow can take many forms, such as a leader's making accurate forecasts about consumer preferences, customer demands, and the skill mix needed to operate tomorrow's organization. A truly visionary leader anticipates a future that many people do not think will come to pass. A classic example is that in the early days of xerography, market research indicated that most people polled saw no need for a product to replace carbon paper.

Creating the future is a more forceful approach than anticipating the future. The leader, assisted by widespread participation of team members, creates conditions that do not already exist. He or she must ask questions about the shape of the industry in five to ten years and decide how to ensure that the industry evolves in a way that is highly advantageous to the company. Furthermore, the leader must recognize the skills and capabilities that must be acquired now if the company is to occupy the industry high ground in the future.

Creating the future has been conceptualized as reinventing an industry. Entrepreneurial leaders frequently engage in such activity. C. K. Prahalad explains that the shoe industry is a good example of reinvention. Nike and Reebok have fundamentally reinvented their industry and consequently are fast-growing businesses in a mature industry. One factor is that they have changed the price-performance relationship in the industry. Both companies have introduced high technology, new materials, large-scale advertising, and global brands. None of these factors was so pronounced previously in the shoe industry.[8]

## Revolutionary Thinking

Using even stronger terms than *reinventing an industry*, Gary Hamel characterizes strategy as being revolutionary.[9] According to Hamel, corporations are reaching the limits of incrementalism. Incremental improvements include squeezing costs, introducing a new product a few weeks earlier, enhancing quality a notch, and capturing another point of market share. These continual improvements enhance an organization's efficiency and are therefore vital to a firm's success, but they are not strategic breakthroughs or radical innovations.[10]

To be an industry leader, a company's leaders must think in revolutionary terms. Revolutionary companies such as Dell Computer Corporation and Netflix create the rules for others to follow. According to Hamel, any strategy that does not seriously challenge the status quo is not actually a strategy. What passes for strategy in most companies is often sterile and unimaginative.

Strategy expert Michael Porter agrees somewhat with the revolutionary aspect of business strategy by insisting that a key component of strategy is deliberately choosing to be different.[11] Although the idea that strategy focuses on revolution and differences is widely accepted, many leaders still successfully use a business strategy of imitating a product or service of proven value. The strategy of *imitation* will be described later.

## Creating a Vision

We have already mentioned vision in this book, including the description in Chapter 3 of the vision component of charismatic leadership. Here we examine the concept of vision in more depth, because visions are an integral part of strategic leadership. Although the term *vision* in relation to leadership has achieved common-use status, it is a multifaceted concept. Laurie Larwood and her associates conducted a study in which 331 chief executives in one national sample and three regional samples were asked about the content and structure of their organizational visions.

The chief executives were asked to write a one-sentence statement of their organizational vision. Participants in the study were also asked to analyze the statements by applying twenty-six descriptors from a list the researchers provided. The twenty-six descriptors were reduced to seven identifiable factors:

1. Involving far-reaching strategic planning
2. Involving sharing with others

3. Involving innovative realism
4. General
5. Detailed
6. Including risk taking
7. Profit oriented

The visions based on these factors extended from six months to more than twenty years, with an average of sixty-four months. The current visions (those in use at the time of the study) were retained between three months and twenty years, with an average of seventy-four months. Another important aspect of the study was to relate this analysis of visions to previous research. The factor results were thought to provide good support for what is known about visions. Another conclusion from the study is also relevant for strategic leadership: executives with a triple emphasis on long-term strategy, wide communication and acceptance of their visions, and operational realism or style are the most likely to be successful in creating change within their organizations.[12]

The components of a vision just described are important, but the final vision statement is relatively short. James R. Lucas, a specialist in vision formulation, writes that a carefully considered and articulated vision helps us know who we are and who we are not. The vision also points to what we do successfully and what we do not, which activities we should take on and which we should avoid.[13] (A few more specifics about developing a vision statement are presented in the Guidelines for Action and Skill Development section of this chapter.)

A vision statement of Amazon.com, Inc., fits many of the criteria of a strong vision statement, including pointing to what the organization can do well: "Our job is to accelerate access to things that inspire, educate, and entertain." With this vision as a guide, the company now sells and distributes a wide range of products and services over the Internet. Founder Jeff Bezos believes that constantly articulating the vision of what is to be achieved is one of the keys to the success of his firm.[14]

college.hmco.com/pic/
dubrin5e

🔘 @ **KNOWLEDGE BANK:** Sometimes a simple statement of intention can serve as an inspiring vision, as presented in the Knowledge Bank. One such statement by top management of a pharmaceutical firm would be, "We will find a vaccine for AIDS."

## Conducting a SWOT Analysis

Strategic planning helps a manager lead strategically. **Strategic planning** encompasses those activities that lead to the statement of goals and objectives and the choice of strategy. Under ideal circumstances, a firm arrives at its strategy after completing strategic planning. In practice, many executive leaders choose a strategy prior to strategic planning. Once the firm has the strategy, such as forming strategic alliances, a plan is developed to implement it.

Quite often strategic planning takes the form of a **SWOT analysis,** a method of considering **s**trengths, **w**eaknesses, **o**pportunities, and **t**hreats in a particular situation.

A SWOT analysis represents an effort to examine the interaction between the particular characteristics of your organization or organizational unit and the external environment, or marketplace, in which you compete.[15] The framework, or technique, is useful in identifying a niche the company has not already exploited. The four components of a basic version of SWOT are described next.

## Internal Strengths

The emphasis in this step is assessing factors within the organization that will have a positive impact on implementing the plan. (In some versions of SWOT analysis, an analysis of the external environment is included in this step.) What are the good points about a particular alternative? What are your advantages? What do you do well? Use your own judgment and intuition, and also ask knowledgeable people. As a business owner, you may have a favorable geographic location that makes you more accessible to customers than your competitor is. Another strength is that you may have invested in state-of-the art equipment that became available only recently.

## Internal Weaknesses

Here the strategy developer takes a candid look at factors within the firm that could have a negative impact on the proposed plan. Consider the risks of pursuing a particular course of action, such as subcontracting work to a low-wage country (outsourcing). What could be improved? What is done badly? What should be avoided? Examine weaknesses from internal and external perspectives. Do outsiders perceive weaknesses that you do not see? (You may have to ask several outsiders to help you identify these weaknesses.) Are there products, services, or work processes your competitors perform better than you do? You are advised to be realistic now and face any unpleasant truths as soon as possible. Again, use your judgment, and ask knowledgeable people. As a manager or business owner, you may have problems managing your inventory, or you may have employees who are not up to the task of implementing a new plan or venture.

## External Opportunities

The purpose of this step is to assess socioeconomic, political, environmental, and demographic factors among others to estimate what benefits they may bring to the organization. Think of the opportunities that await you if you choose a promising strategic alternative, such as creating a culturally diverse customer base. Use your imagination, and visualize the possibilities. Look for interesting trends. Useful opportunities can derive from such events as the following:

- Changes in technology and markets on both a broad and narrow scale
- Changes in government policy related to your field
- Changes in social patterns, population profiles, lifestyles, and so forth.

## External Threats

The purpose of this step is to assess what possible negative impact socioeconomic, political, environmental, and demographic factors may have on the organization.

There is a downside to every alternative, so think ahead, and do contingency planning. Ask people who may have tried in the past what you are attempting now. Answer questions such as:

- What obstacles do you face?
- What is your competition doing?
- Are the required specifications for your job, products, or services changing?
- Is changing technology changing your ability to compete successfully?

Despite a careful analysis of threats, do not be dissuaded by the naysayers, heel-draggers, and pessimists. To quote Nike, "Just do it."

Carrying out a SWOT analysis is often illuminating in terms of both pointing out what needs to be done and putting problems into perspective. Although much more complex schemes have been developed for strategic planning, they all include some analysis of strengths, weaknesses, and opportunities.[16] Leadership Skill-Building Exercise 13-1 gives you an opportunity to conduct a SWOT analysis.

---

**LEADERSHIP SKILL-BUILDING EXERCISE 13-1**

### CONDUCTING A SWOT ANALYSIS

In small groups, develop a scenario for a SWOT analysis, such as the group starting a chain of coffee shops, pet-care service centers, or treatment centers for online addictions. Since you will probably have mostly hypothetical data to work with, you will have to rely heavily on your imagination. Group leaders might share the results of the SWOT analysis with the rest of the class. Conducting a SWOT analysis reinforces the skill of thinking strategically about a course of action.

---

## A Sampling of Business Strategies Formulated by Leaders

We have been focusing on the process by which leaders and managers make strategic decisions. Also of interest to leaders and potential leaders is the content of such decisions. Business strategies are often classified according to their focus of impact: corporate level, business level, or functional level. Corporate-level strategy asks, "What business are we in?" Business-level strategy asks, "How do we compete?" And functional-level strategy asks, "How do we support the business-level strategy?" Some of the business strategies listed next might cut across more than one of these three levels. The first three of these strategies are the generic strategies espoused by Michael Porter.[17]

1. *Differentiation.* A differentiation strategy seeks to offer a product or service that the customer perceives as being different from available alternatives. The organization may use advertising, distinctive features, exceptional service, or new technology to gain this perception of uniqueness. The mammoth size and rugged appearance of the Hummer SUVs is part of the company's (a division of GM) differentiation strategy, despite the fact that several Hummer models are now smaller. What differentiates one of your favorite products?

2. *Cost leadership.* A basic strategy is to produce a product or service at a low cost in order to lower the selling price and gain market share. Wal-Mart is a master at cost leadership because the company's massive buying power enables it to receive huge price concessions from suppliers. A variety of general merchandise stores, such as Dollar General, implement the cost-leadership strategy.

3. *Focus.* In a focus strategy, the organization concentrates on a specific regional market or buyer group. To gain market share, the company will use either a differentiation or a cost leadership approach in a targeted market. The focus strategy is a natural, commonsense approach to business because it is difficult to serve every customer well. A sample of successful, well-planned focus marketing strategies is as follows:

   - Gap Inc. recently launched a chain of specialty stores for baby boomer women, a group of 40 million people born between 1946 and 1964. The chain focuses on selling work wear and dressy casual outfits for low- to middle-income shoppers.[18]

   - Instead of competing directly with eBay, several smaller online auctions stick to a narrow, successful niche, giving them an identity that facilitates sales. An example is StubHub Inc., which competes with eBay as a middleman for ticket sales to sporting events, concerts, and other spectator activities.[19]

   - Under CEO Henri Termeer, Genzyme has built a billion-dollar-plus business by specializing in so-called orphan drugs—those that treat ailments suffered by fewer than 200,000 persons in the United States. Patients with these rare disorders (for example, Fabry's disease) lack key enzymes that regulate the body's metabolism.[20] (Fabry's disease is a fat storage disorder caused by an enzyme deficiency in the biodegradation of lipids.)

4. *High quality.* A basic business strategy is to offer goods or services of higher quality than the competition does. Leaders continue to emphasize quality, even if there is less explicit emphasis today on formal quality programs than in the past. An important exception are the Six Sigma programs that emphasize statistical approaches to attaining quality. Leaders at GE and 3M, for example, emphasize Six Sigma. One reason that quality is classified as a strategy is that it contributes to competitive advantage in cost and differentiation. Because many customers now expect high quality, a quality strategy must be supplemented with other

points of differentiation, such as supplying customized features and services that customers desire.

5. *Imitation.* If you cannot be imaginative, why not imitate the best? Manufacturers of popular digital devices such as digital cameras and cell phones use an imitation strategy. The company waits for the right time to introduce a lower-priced competitor. Benchmarking is a form of learning by watching. One company emulates the best practices of another company, usually without outright stealing the product or service ideas of another company.

6. *Strategic alliances.* A modern business strategy is to form alliances, or share resources, with other companies to exploit a market opportunity. A strategic alliance is also known as a *virtual corporation.* Strategic alliances have become more common as the high-tech industry struggles with needed yet expensive innovation. Sometimes the alliances are between rivals. General Motors Corporation and DaimlerChrysler AG teamed up to develop fuel-saving hybrid engines in hopes of competing successfully in an expanding market already dominated by hybrid vehicle leaders Toyota Motor Corporation and Honda Motor Company. The first of the vehicles was scheduled to appear in 2007. (Hybrids draw power from two energy sources: gas or diesel, and an electric motor.)[21]

   Strategic alliances are widely used to help reduce developmental and manufacturing expenses in digital technology. Eastman Kodak Company teamed with rival Sanyo Electric Corporation to produce display screens for consumer electronic devices such as camcorders, digital cameras, and cell phones. A joint venture, SK Display Corporation, was established to make the screens.[22]

7. *Growth through acquisition.* A standard strategy for growth is for one company to purchase others. Growth in size is important, but companies may also purchase other companies to acquire a new technology or complete a product line. Buying a new technology is often less expensive than investing huge sums in R&D that might not yield a marketable product. Cisco Systems, Inc., achieved much of its growth by purchasing smaller companies, and much of General Electric's growth over the years can be attributed to acquiring other companies.

8. *High speed and first-mover strategy.* High-speed managers focus on speed in all of their business activities, including product development, sales response, and customer service. Knowing that "time is money," they choose time as a competitive resource. It is important to get products to market quickly because the competition might get there first or might deliver a product or service more rapidly. A contributing factor to Dell Computer's success has always been how rapidly it can deliver a custom computer to an office or home after receiving an order—sometimes within three or four days. Yet there are exceptions when delivery can take much longer. Getting to market first is also referred to as the *first-mover strategy.* Starbucks was the first national chain of coffee bars. The many storefronts served as marketing devices to acquire more customers.

9. *Product and global diversification.* A natural business strategy is to offer a variety of products and services and to sell across borders to enhance market opportunities. Sometimes a company with a strong reputation for delivering one product or service will branch out to capitalize on the allure of its brand. Starbucks began selling music in 2003 at its Hear Music Coffeehouse, its first fully integrated café–music

store—a joint venture with its wholly owned subsidiary, Hear Music. The cafés include CD Hear Music CD-burning stations.[23]

Another example of diversification based on reputation is when Montblanc, the century-old maker of luxury fountain pens, began marketing its own deluxe watches. The watches are the centerpiece of a bold effort to transform Montblanc, a division of Switzerland-based Richmont SA, into a leading global luxury brand. Aside from pens, the Montblanc trademark now appears on many items, from fragrances and pocket knives to sunglasses. "Watches are clearly the strategic growth area," says Jan-Patrick Schmitz, the head of U.S. operations for Montblanc.[24]

A widely practiced business strategy, especially with products, is to diversify globally in order to expand business. Major restaurant chains such as McDonald's, Burger King, and Pizza Hut, for example, employ a diversification strategy. Global diversification is such a widely accepted strategy that the burden of proof would be on a business leader who shunned globalization.

10. *Sticking to core competencies.* Many firms of all sizes believe they will prosper if they confine their efforts to the activities they perform best—their core competencies. Corporate strategist Jim Collins calls this the *Hedgehog concept:* becoming very good at one thing in a world of companies that spread themselves into many areas where they lack depth.[25] Many firms that expanded through diversification later trimmed back operations to activities on which they had built their reputation, including PepsiCo. In the late 1990s the company exited the restaurant business by divesting itself of Pizza Hut, Taco Bell, and Kentucky Fried Chicken (now part of Yum Brands). In addition, it spun off its huge bottling operation into an independent company. As a result, PepsiCo focused on its Pepsi-Cola, Frito-Lay, and Tropicana operations. The proceeds from the restaurant sales and the spinoff gave PepsiCo more money to compete better with Coca-Cola in fountain soda sales.[26]

11. *Brand leadership.* As obvious as it may appear, succeeding through developing the reputation of a brand name can be considered a business strategy. The opposite strategy is to build components for others, build products that others market under their names, or be a commodity like cinder blocks. Jeffrey Bezos of Amazon has implemented a relentless brand leadership strategy to the point that his company has become almost synonymous with etailing. The ultimate goal of the brand leadership strategy is to make Amazon the best-known destination for purchasing anything that might be for sale on the Internet.

According to *BusinessWeek*, the world's ten leading brands in order of strength of brand are (1) Coca-Cola, (2) Microsoft, (3) IBM, (4) GE, (5) Intel, (6) Nokia, (7) Disney, (8) McDonald's, (9) Marlboro, and (10) Mercedes.[27] By building the reputation of their brands, senior management (assisted by countless thousands of workers) has helped these companies succeed financially.

12. *Create demand by solving problems.* The simple idea that the best way to sell is to offer to solve a problem has become a business strategy. Cardinal Health Inc., a heath care services provider, has innovated a demand for its services. Cardinal leadership uses its unique access to drug manufacturers to identify problems in the pharmaceutical business. It then creates new products and services to solve

those problems and save customers money. For example, Cardinal workers noticed a problem of delivering medicine to patients in hospitals for such reasons as messy, handwritten prescriptions and a nurse shortage. Cardinal CEO Robert Walter detected an opportunity to deliver drugs better. His solution was to purchase a company that produced an ATM-like machine for dispensing drugs after a prescription is inserted. About 90 percent of U.S. hospitals use these machines.[28] (Note the combination of two strategies here: growth through acquisition and creating demand by solving problems.)

13. *Conducting business on the Internet.* Developing a presence on the Internet has emerged as a strategy for survival and growth for both retailers and industrial companies. Because the Internet profoundly influences many aspects of customer relations and operations, the leader must choose a specific strategy that relates to conducting business on the Internet. All Internet players are not equal: one person trading oil with an iMac from a loft apartment cannot compete successfully with Exxon. The matching Internet strategy is to capitalize on advantages of scale. Big established companies are discovering that their advantages of scale, their established brands, their loyal customer base, and their long-standing supplier relationships are as valuable online as offline.[29]

college.hmco.com/pic/ dubrin5e

🏦 @ **KNOWLEDGE BANK:** contains a few more details about the Internet and business strategy.

14. *Peoplepalooza (competitive advantage through hiring talented people.)* A powerful strategy for gaining competitive advantage is to build the organization with talented, well-motivated people at every level. According to the authors who coined the term *peoplepalooza*, the most urgent need in building great companies is to find and keep great people.[30] Microsoft and Amazon.com, along with elite business consulting firms, are examples of firms that explicitly use the peoplepalooza strategy. Talented people may need some leadership direction, but they will think of new products and services and develop effective work processes.

All of these impressive strategies have limited impact unless they are implemented properly, meaning that effective management must support strategic leadership. In Chapter 4, we noted that visions must be followed up with execution. Based on case research in many companies, Michael Beer and Russell A. Eisenstat found that strategies are sometimes not implemented correctly because top management is not aware of problems that threaten the business. In many organizations, it is difficult for leadership to hear the unfiltered truth from managers down below. Beer and Eisenstat developed a method whereby a task force of the most effective managers collects data about strategic and organizational problems. Task force members present their findings to senior managers in the format of an honest conversation. As a result of these discussions, senior managers can make the right moves to adjust strategy.[31] For example, the task force might discover that the true reason a strategy is not working well is that the top management team is not granting enough decision-making authority to the business units. If the business unit leaders were empowered more fully, they could perform better.

The Leader in Action illustrates how a company can thrive by finding an unusual niche, as well as other aspects of strategy.

## LEADER IN ACTION

### JORGE PEREZ OF THE RELATED GROUP OF FLORIDA: STRATEGIC THINKING CONDO KING

Jorge Perez explains his success with one word: Miami. The CEO of The Related Group of Florida increased his company's revenues 96.4 percent in 2004 to $2.125 billion, making Related the number 1 company on the 2005 Hispanic Business 500. Most billion-dollar companies do not double their revenue in one year; but as Perez observes, "Most markets aren't Miami." Perez says, "The stars just lined up. Miami is the dear of the international community. It was a local market fueled by New Yorkers, and suddenly it became an international market."

A developer of upscale condominiums, Related caught the South Florida real estate juggernaut at precisely the right time. According to director of sales Harold Gallo, the company doubled its inventory of condos on the market during 2004, so the revenue jump followed naturally. Demand peaked at the same time prices soared.

"The gains have been pretty incredible," says Tom Milana, CEO of Milana Real Estate Investment Group in Boca Raton, Florida. "I've had customers, including myself, see gains of 300 to 400 percent. Related is one of the main builders we follow because anything Jorge Perez builds seems to turn to gold. He's probably the Donald Trump of South Florida right now."

Like most good luck, Related's hot streak came from hard work and great intuition about the direction of the market. Several years ago, the company's management team realized Miami would become more urban and populous. "We made the decision that this trend was going to happen, so we retooled our corporate structure to go away from rentals toward condominiums," says Perez. "We gambled, and now you're seeing the results of that gamble."

Perez's vision of a new urban lifestyle, with an emphasis on build-in construction and mixed-use projects, plays to the Miami market. (Build-in construction refers to the idea that cities should repurpose centrally located land rather than building new projects on the periphery of urban sprawl.) Gentrification and new construction created a booming market for downtown residences. For years, Perez has predicted that "people are going to move away from suburbs into the city, especially the younger generation."

"With higher prices for single-family homes, many young professionals are now opting for

*(continued)*

the amenities and lower pricing available in the condominium market," a real estate analyst confirms. "With increased traffic and congestion, the condo market provides a viable alternative for those who want to live close to their workplace."

"As a city like Miami grows," he explains, "The perimeter of the city expands farther and farther out, meaning people have to drive longer distances. But also, as more people come in, the same distance takes a longer time to travel."

Perez reports that his upscale Latin American and European buyers feel comfortable with this sort of lifestyle. In architecture, these same customers like Spanish and Italian styles, but that creates a problem for Related. By definition, high-rise buildings are modern structures; trying to convert them to a Mediterranean style comes across as visually confusing. So Perez has developed a simple formula for buildings: modern on the outside, Mediterranean on the inside.

For the short term, Perez can rest easy: every condo Related will build in the next three years already has a buyer. Beyond that, he plans to diversify to other geographic areas, retaining an emphasis on the new urban lifestyle, such as in Las Vegas.

Related group's personal connection to the market is considered one of its competitive advantages. "Mr. Perez is one of those people—Latino by birth, educated in Latin America and the United States. He loves art and has traveled the world," says Gallo. "He's very sophisticated. When he develops a project, he gets involved in minuscule details, and that gives a personality to the project. . . . It makes our buildings unique and beautiful, and that is what allowed us to double our sales in one year."

### QUESTIONS

1. Which leadership strategy or strategies have Jorge Perez and his management team emphasized?
2. In what way is Perez a visionary?
3. How would you characterize Perez's leadership style?

SOURCE: Excerpted and adapted from Joel Russell, "A Cool $2 Billion," *Hispanic Business,* June 2005, pp. 32–38. Reprinted by permission. For more insight into Related construction, see *www.apogeesouthbeach.com* and *www.theloftdowntown.com.*

## Knowledge Management and the Learning Organization

Another thrust of leaders is to help their organizations better adapt to the environment by assisting workers and the organization to become better learners. To accomplish this, the leader manages knowledge and cultivates a learning organization. **Knowledge management (KM)** is the systematic sharing of information to achieve such goals as innovation, nonduplication of effort, and competitive advantage. When knowledge is managed effectively, information is shared as needed, whether it be printed, stored electronically, or rests in the brains of workers. Managing knowledge helps create a **learning organization**—one that is skilled at creating, acquiring, and transferring knowledge and at modifying behavior to reflect new knowledge and insights.[32] To develop a sensitivity toward some of the key ideas in knowledge management and the learning organization, take Leadership Self-Assessment Quiz 13-2.

LEADERSHIP SELF-ASSESSMENT QUIZ 13-2

## DO YOU WORK FOR A LEARNING ORGANIZATION?

**INSTRUCTIONS** Indicate for each of the following statements whether it is mostly true or mostly false in relation to your current, or most recent, place of work. Indicate a question mark when the statement is either not applicable or you are not in a position to judge.

|  | Mostly True | Mostly False | ? |
|---|---|---|---|
| 1. Company employees often visit other locations or departments to share new information or skills they have learned. | _____ | _____ | _____ |
| 2. Our company frequently repeats mistakes. | _____ | _____ | _____ |
| 3. We get most of our market share by competing on price. | _____ | _____ | _____ |
| 4. Loads of people in our organization are aware of and believe in our vision. | _____ | _____ | _____ |
| 5. Top management assumes the majority of employees are experts at what they do. | _____ | _____ | _____ |
| 6. Almost all of our learning takes place individually rather than in groups or teams. | _____ | _____ | _____ |
| 7. In our company, after you have mastered your job, you do not have to bother with additional learning such as training programs or self-study. | _____ | _____ | _____ |
| 8. Our firm shies away from inviting outsiders into our company to discuss our business because few outsiders could understand our uniqueness. | _____ | _____ | _____ |
| 9. If it were not for a few key individuals in our company, we would be in big trouble. | _____ | _____ | _____ |
| 10. Our new product launches go smoothly and quickly. | _____ | _____ | _____ |
| 11. Our company creates a lot of opportunities for employees to get together and share information, such as conferences and meetings. | _____ | _____ | _____ |
| 12. We are effective at pricing the service we provide to customers. | _____ | _____ | _____ |

*(continued)*

13. Very few of our employees have any idea about company sales and profits.   ___ ___ ___

14. I often hear employees asking questions about why the company has taken certain major actions.   ___ ___ ___

15. The company maintains a current database about the knowledge and skills of almost all of our employees.   ___ ___ ___

16. Having specialized knowledge brings you some status in our company.   ___ ___ ___

17. It would be stretching the truth to say that many of our employees are passionate about what our organization is attempting to accomplish.   ___ ___ ___

18. Our performance appraisal system makes a big contribution to helping employees learn and improve.   ___ ___ ___

19. Following established rules and procedures is important in our company, so creativity and imagination are not encouraged.   ___ ___ ___

20. Most of our employees believe that if you do your own job well, you do not have to worry about what goes on in the rest of the organization.   ___ ___ ___

21. We get loads of useful new ideas from our customers.   ___ ___ ___

22. I have frequently heard our managers talk about how what goes on in the outside world has an impact on our company.   ___ ___ ___

23. We treat customer suggestions with a good deal of skepticism.   ___ ___ ___

24. During breaks, you sometimes hear employees discussing the meaning and implication of the work they are doing.   ___ ___ ___

25. Employees at every level tend to rely on facts when making important decisions.   ___ ___ ___

26. If a process or procedure works well in our company, we are hesitant to experiment with other approaches to a problem.   ___ ___ ___

**27.** Our company treats mistakes as a valuable learning experience about what not to do in the future.    _____  _____  _____

**28.** Our company rarely copies ideas from the successful practices of other companies.    _____  _____  _____

**29.** Each time we face a significant problem, our company seems to start all over to find a solution.    _____  _____  _____

**30.** It is a waste of time to be reading about a learning organization, when my real interest is in learning how to prevent problems.    _____  _____  _____

*Total score* _____

SCORING AND INTERPRETATION (1) Record the number of "mostly true" answers you gave to the following questions: 1, 4, 5, 10, 11, 12, 14, 15, 16, 18, 21, 22, 24, 25, 27. (2) Record the number of "mostly false" answers you gave to the following questions: 2, 3, 6, 7, 8, 9, 13, 17, 19, 20, 23, 26, 28, 29, 30. (3) Add the numbers for **1** and **2**. (4) Add half of your (?) responses to **1** and half to **2**.

- **25 or higher:**   You are most likely a member of a learning organization. This tendency is so pronounced that it should contribute heavily to your company's success.
- **13–24:**   Your company has an average tendency toward being a learning organization, suggesting an average degree of success in profiting from mistakes and changing in response to a changing environment.

SOURCE: From A. J. Dubrin, *Looking Around Corners: The Art of Problem Prevention* (Worcester, MA: Chandler House Press, 1999), pp. 181–183. Reprinted by permission of Chandler House Press.

## Knowledge Management

Knowledge management (KM) deals with a cultural focus on knowledge sharing. Managing knowledge is an important leadership role because so few organizations make systematic use of the collective wisdom of employees. As illustrated in Figure 13-2, most knowledge in the organization resides in the brains of employees or in documents not readily accessible to others.

Knowledge management systems sometimes take the form of a computer-based system for collecting and organizing potentially useful information. Yet many effective systems rely on person-to-person exchange of information. A study of 800 managers by eePulse Inc. found that 78 percent share information through personal and informal channels, compared to 19 percent that have technology-driven systems. (Three percent pay no formal attention to knowledge sharing.) Of the companies using technology, the most frequent methods were basic, such as email, telephone, and web-based communication. In one company, employees were not making optimum use of reports placed online by the

**FIGURE 13-2** Where Corporate Knowledge Lives

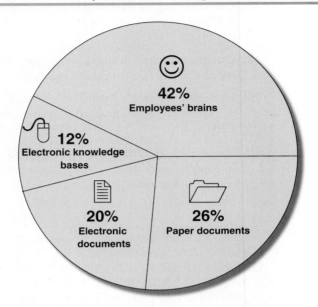

A study of more than 700 U.S. companies shows that only a small portion of corporate knowledge is in a form that can be shared readily. The majority of knowledge resides in the brains of employees and in documents not readily shared.

Source: "Knowledge Management: User Survey 97," Copyright © 1997 by *American Management Association (J)*. Adapted and published in Michael Hickins, "Xerox Shares Its Knowledge," *Management Review*, September 1999, p. 42. Reproduced with permission of *American Management Association (J)* in the format Textbook via Copyright Clearance Center.

research department, so the company made the site interactive. Employees can now ask precise questions of the scientists, and knowledge sharing is more successful.[33]

We have emphasized how important it is for leaders to use anecdotes to communicate meaning. Narratives also play a major role in knowledge sharing, as Thomas Davenport illustrates in this anecdote:

As part of its knowledge management initiative, British Petroleum rolled out some videoconferencing technology for rapidly sharing ideas. Soon after, one of their gas drills broke down in the North Slope of Alaska. BP's leading expert in gas turbines was working in the North Sea; it would have taken him 20 hours to fly to Alaska. Instead of putting him on a plane, BP patched him into the North Slope via videoconferencing, and he worked with on-site technicians to pinpoint the problem and get the drill back on-stream. They finished the job in just 30 minutes. That story quickly circulated throughout BP. In time, it found its way into other organizations. Because it gave real-world evidence of a dramatic improvement, the story became part of knowledge-sharing lore. [Note that the human touch was helpful in selling a technology-based method of knowledge sharing.][34]

An advance in knowledge management is to deliver information just in time, or at the point at which it is most needed. For example, Partners HealthCare System, Inc. embeds knowledge into the technology that physicians use so that retrieving the knowledge is no longer a separate activity. When a staff physician orders medicine or a lab test, the order-entry system automatically checks his or her decision against a huge clinical database as well as the patient's own medical record. Just-in-time delivery of knowledge is also useful in business. Customer service representatives at Hewlett-Packard and Dell work with computer systems that give them immediate access to information to help them respond to customer problems.[35] In this way, the representative does not have to have reams of information in his or her head.

Whatever advanced technology is used to implement knowledge management, it works best in an organization culture that values knowledge and encourages its dissemination. The organizational subculture shapes our assumptions about what knowledge is and which knowledge is worth managing.[36] Professional workers in the finance division of Gap Inc. might think that watching MTV on company time or surfing the Net is a waste of company time. In the merchandising division, however, watching MTV and surfing the Net might be perceived as a valuable way of understanding clothing trends.

A major challenge a leader faces in advancing knowledge sharing is the human tendency to want to keep our best ideas secret, so we can receive full credit for them. Another human factor to keep in mind is that people prefer to share information face-to-face than to enter their ideas into a database. Much of what is useful information cannot be neatly categorized. Moreover, the mere act of entering information into a database frequently robs it of the intuitive spark generated by face-to-face communication. Despite the marvels of technology, it cannot combine two bits of data stored in separate memory banks into a new insight, as can face-to-face communication.[37]

Think through your attitudes toward sharing knowledge by taking Leadership Self-Assessment Quiz 13-3.

---

LEADERSHIP SELF-ASSESSMENT QUIZ 13-3

## MY ATTITUDES TOWARD SHARING KNOWLEDGE

INSTRUCTIONS Indicate how much you agree with the following statements: disagree strongly (DA); disagree (D); neutral (N); agree (A); and agree strongly (AS).

|  | DA | D | N | A | AS |
|---|---|---|---|---|---|
| 1. I have often helped other students with their homework. | 1 | 2 | 3 | 4 | 5 |
| 2. In brainstorming sessions, I usually hold back giving my best ideas because I do not want them stolen. | 5 | 4 | 3 | 2 | 1 |
| 3. I enjoy helping another person with a work or school problem. | 1 | 2 | 3 | 4 | 5 |

*(continued)*

| | | | | | |
|---|---|---|---|---|---|
| 4. I would be willing to submit some of my best ideas to a company database, such as an intranet. | 1 | 2 | 3 | 4 | 5 |
| 5. I am concerned about submitting my most creative ideas on a term paper because these ideas could be stolen. | 5 | 4 | 3 | 2 | 1 |
| 6. I enjoy working as part of a team and sharing ideas. | 1 | 2 | 3 | 4 | 5 |
| 7. I get a little suspicious when a coworker or fellow student attempts to pick my brain. | 5 | 4 | 3 | 2 | 1 |
| 8. It upsets me if I do not receive full credit for my ideas. | 5 | 4 | 3 | 2 | 1 |
| 9. If I had a great idea for a screenplay or novel, I would not tell anyone about it before I was finished with the idea. | 5 | 4 | 3 | 2 | 1 |
| 10. I have often let other people know about a good method I developed to improve work efficiency. | 1 | 2 | 3 | 4 | 5 |

*Total score* _____

SCORING AND INTERPRETATION: Tally your score by adding the numbers you circled or checked.

- 40 or higher: You are generous with respect to knowledge sharing and would probably fit well in an organization that practices knowledge management.
- 20–39: You have average attitudes toward sharing knowledge, with a mixture of enthusiasm and skepticism about knowledge sharing.
- 1–19: You are quite cautious and guarded about sharing ideas. Unless you become more willing to share your ideas, you would not fit well in an organization that emphasized knowledge management.

NOTE: *You are authorized to share this quiz with as many people as you would like.*

## The Learning Organization

According to Peter Senge, a learning organization can be viewed as a group of people working together to enhance their capacities to create the results they value.[38] Organizational leadership, however, must usually take the initiative to create the conditions whereby such enhancement of capacities, or learning, takes place. Toward this end, many firms have created a position labeled chief knowledge officer (CKO), or its equivalent. The major justification for creating such a position is that in many companies, human skills, intuition, and wisdom are replacing capital as the most precious resource. Chief knowledge officers seek to disperse those assets throughout the firm and convert them into innovations. They are in charge of systematically collecting information and connecting people with others who might have valuable information.[39]

In order to manage organizational learning, the most effective strategic leaders function in both the transformational and transactional modes. Acting as a transformational leader, the manager might inspire workers with a vision of knowledge sharing and learning from mistakes. Acting as a transactional leader, he or she might reward workers for sharing knowledge.[40]

Here we identify major leadership initiatives that enhance a learning organization. Understanding them will help you grasp the concept of what a leader might do to enhance organizational learning.[41]

To begin, a top-level leader should *create a strategic intent to learn*. Organizational learning then becomes a vehicle for gaining competitive advantage. *Creating a shared vision* enhances learning as organization members develop a common purpose and commitment to having the organization keep learning. If workers at all levels believe that the company is headed toward greatness, they will be motivated to learn to help deliver greatness.

In a learning organization, *employees are empowered to make decisions and seek continuous improvement.* The idea is to develop a community of learning in which every worker believes that he or she can contribute to a smarter, more effective organization.

*Systems thinking* is almost synonymous with organizational learning. The leader helps organization members regard the organization as a system in which everybody's work affects the activities of everybody else. Systems thinking also means keeping the big picture foremost in everybody's mind and being keenly aware of the external environment. In addition to the big picture of systems thinking, the leader must encourage the little picture of *personal mastery of the job.* As team members gain personal mastery of their jobs, they contribute to *team learning,* an essential part of a learning organization. Team learning centers on collective problem solving in which members freely share information and opinions to facilitate problem solving.

*Action learning*, or learning while working on real problems, is a fundamental part of a learning organization. Participants in action learning are asked to work in teams to attack a significant organizational problem, such as decreasing the cycle time on a project. In the process of resolving an actual work problem, the participants acquire and use new skills, tools, or concepts. As the project progresses, new skills are applied while working with the problem. For example, if the team learned how to eliminate duplication of effort in one aspect of the work process, it would look to eliminate duplication at other points in the cycle.

*Learning from failure* contributes immensely to a learning organization. A company that diversified into an area unsuccessfully might analyze why it failed and then not repeat the same mistake. *Encouraging continuous experimentation* is another important practice for crafting a learning strategy. The leader encourages workers to learn from competitors, customers, suppliers, and other units within the organization.

For organizational learning to proceed smoothly, workers throughout the organization must have the *political skills to make connections with and influence others.* For example, if a production technician discovers an effective method of reducing water consumption, he or she must have the skill to sell an influential person on the merits of this idea.

A final perspective on the learning organization is that the leader must encourage organizational members to think creatively—to imagine possibilities that do not already exist. Instead of merely adapting to the environment, the organization engages in the type of breakthrough thinking described in our previous discussions of creativity and strategic leadership. Organizations cannot rely on CKOs alone to manage knowledge. The entire knowledge process must be embedded in the position of line manager.[42]

---

**READER'S ROADMAP**

So far we have studied the nature of leadership; the attributes, behaviors, and styles of leaders; the ethics and social responsibility of leaders; and how leaders exert power and use politics and influence. We then studied techniques for developing teamwork as well as motivation and coaching skills. After having studied creativity and innovation as part of leadership, we focused on communication skills as they relate to leadership. We then shifted to strategic leadership. Next, we examine another broad challenge facing leaders: dealing with cultural diversity with the organization and across borders.

---

## Summary

college.hmco.com/pic/dubrin5e

Strategic leadership deals with the major purposes of an organization or organizational unit and provides the direction and inspiration necessary to create, provide direction to, or sustain an organization. Strategic leadership has five important components: (1) the high-level cognitive activity by the leader, (2) gathering multiple inputs to formulate strategy, (3) anticipating and creating a future, (4) revolutionary thinking, and (5) creating a vision.

Creating a vision is an integral part of strategic leadership. One study found that visions contain seven identifiable factors: strategic planning, sharing, innovative realism, general, detailed, risk taking, and profit orientation. After formulating a vision, the leader should be involved in its communication and implementation.

A carefully considered and articulated vision helps us know who we are and who we are not. The vision also points to what we do successfully and what we do not, which activities we should take on and which to avoid.

Strategic planning quite often takes the form of a SWOT analysis, taking into account internal strengths and weaknesses and external opportunities and threats in a given situation. A SWOT analysis examines the interaction between the organization and the environment.

Strategic leaders use many different types of business strategies, including the following: (1) differentiation, (2) cost leadership, (3) focus, (4) high quality, (5) imitation, (6) strategic alliances, (7) growth through acquisition, (8) high speed and first-mover strategy, (9) product and global diversification, (10) sticking to core competencies, (11) brand leadership, (12) create demand by solving problems, (13) conducting business on the Internet, and (14) peoplepalooza—gaining competitive advantage through hiring talented people.

Another strategic thrust of leaders is to help their organizations adapt to the environment by assisting workers and the organization to become better learners. To accomplish this feat, the leader manages knowledge and cultivates a learning organization. Knowledge management focuses on the systematic sharing of information, including being able to deliver information just in time. Major leadership initiatives for creating a learning organization include creating a strategic intent to learn, creating a shared vision, and empowering employees to make decisions and seek continuous improvements. Also important is encouraging systems thinking, encouraging personal mastery of the job, and team learning. Action learning, or learning while working on real problems, learning from failures, and encouraging continuous experimentation are also part of the learning organization. Workers must have the political skills to make connections and influence others. Encouraging creative thinking is also part of the learning organization.

## Key Terms

Strategy

Strategic leadership

Strategic planning

SWOT analysis

Knowledge management

Learning organization

##  Guidelines for Action and Skill Development

To make sure that all workers understand the company's vision of where it wants to go, the vision statement should have certain key characteristics:[43]

1. **Brief.** The statement should be short enough so employees can recall it with ease. In its early days, Starbucks maintained the vision "2,000 stores by 2000."

2. **Verifiable.** A verifiable vision is one that ten people could agree that an organization has achieved. By the year 2005, Starbucks had attained approximately 9,100 cafés.

3. **Focused.** Vision statements often contain too many ideas. It is better to focus on a major goal such as the vision of Ford Motor Company: "Employee involvement is our way of life." (Notice that this vision is about human resource management, not about a product or brand.)

4. **Understandable.** A major purpose of the vision statement is that employees will know where the organization wants to go and how to help it get there. Being understandable is therefore a key quality of the vision statement. Terms such as "world class" and "leading edge" might be subject to wide interpretation. The following component of the H&R Block vision statement would be understandable by most company employees: "Quality products, excellent service, reasonable fees."

5. **Inspirational.** To inspire, a vision statement should make employees feel good about working for the organization and should focus them on measurable business goals.

## Discussion Questions and Activities

1. How might a business strategy deal with a topic other than products or services?

2. In what way can a business strategy motivate employees?

3. How could you adapt a business strategy to guide you in your own career as a leader?

4. Many top-level managers say that they want lower-ranking managers to think strategically.

How can a middle manager or a first-level manager think strategically?

5. Why is formulating business strategy likely to be a more exciting activity than disciplining workers for violating ethical codes or performing poorly?

6. Working by yourself or with several team members, provide a recent example of revolutionary thinking by a company.

7. The average age of Cadillac owners, across the various models, was about 65 until the Escalade (a luxury SUV) was introduced to the market. It had an immediate appeal to affluent rappers, professional athletes, and a variety of other young, wealthy entertainers. What is the business strategy lesson here?

8. In what way might doing a good job of knowledge management give a company a competitive advantage?

9. What steps might a leader take to help group members become systems thinkers?

10. Why do you think it has been so difficult for researchers to prove that knowledge management pays dividends to an organization?

## LEADERSHIP CASE PROBLEM A

### SAMSUNG SINGS A DIFFERENT TUNE

Samsung Electronics Co. Ltd of South Korea manufactures and sells high-tech consumer products like cell phones that are voice activated and play MP3 tunes. Like many other Samsung devices, the phone combines cutting-edge technology with award-winning design at premium prices. Yet six years ago, the company was known as a mass marketer of cheap TVs and VCRs. On the industrial products side, Samsung had become the world's largest maker of memory chips. Samsung Electronics employs approximately 75,000 people in eighty-nine offices in forty-seven countries.

For much of the past three decades, Samsung and South Korea's other massive conglomerates, known as *chaebols*, were looked down on abroad as low-end makers of refrigerators, VCRs, and sedans. Samsung ran the risk of becoming a faceless supplier of computer monitors and semiconductors to more powerful multinationals. Even that niche was under threat from low-cost producers springing up in China. So leadership at the Samsung Electronics unit agreed on a key strategic move.

**SAMSUNG'S CHANGING IMAGE** Since 1997 Samsung has rubbed shoulders with the market leaders in high-end cell phones, DVD players, elegant flat plasma TVs, and a wide range of other consumer products. These electronic devices are sometimes less expensive than those of Japanese and Finnish competitors but not inferior in quality. Samsung is approaching global recognition and has a $450 million annual advertising budget to promote its brand. The company successfully shifted from semiconductors to branded products like mobile phones. Samsung also was a sponsor of the Sydney Olympic Games and has been running heavy advertising in the United States, according to Interbrand Corporation's global director for brand valuation.

All this favorable attention to Samsung products has prompted Eric Kim, 49, executive vice president for marketing, to assert that he hopes to surpass Sony Corporation in brand recognition. At Samsung Electronics, many executives express a near obsession with outperforming Sony. Dong-Jin Oh, president of Samsung Electronics in America, says: "Sony is now only strong in audio and video, like

DVDs and TVs. We are much stronger now in other fields such as mobile phones and flat-panel screens" (*The Wall Street Journal*, June 13, 2002, p. A6).

According to the consultancy Interbrand, Samsung has the second most recognizable consumer electronics brand in the world. A researcher for the Nomura Securities Co. Ltd. says Samsung is no longer making poor equivalents of Sony products. Instead it is making products that people want.

Furthermore, during a period when most of the world's high-technology companies were shutting plants and trimming research and development to cope with the global economic slump, Samsung was extending its reach. Bolstered by the resurgent Korean economy, Samsung Electronics' worldwide revenues are running more than $30 billion per year. The company is growing fast and is the best performer in the family-controlled conglomerate that spawned it, the Samsung Group.

In addition to developing its own brand, Samsung remains an important supplier of components for other companies. Sprint executives now say Samsung Electronics is their biggest supplier of mobile phone handsets. Rival Sony is also an important customer, buying semiconductors and displays from the Korean company.

During a product showcase meeting in New York City, Jong-Yong Yun, vice chairman and CEO of Samsung Electronics Co. Ltd., revealed new plans to achieve the company's vision of becoming the leader in the digital convergence revolution. (Digital convergence is about digital devices linking with each other, such as retrieving a desktop computer file with your cell phone while sitting on a park bench.) Key changes to help achieve this convergence include home networking and wireless network products.

Yun also noted that Samsung would continue to invest in people and technology as needed to transform the company. "Business entities cannot survive without innovation as they face numerous changes and uncertainty. Samsung will continue to create solutions that vitalize and enrich your lifestyle," said Yun. "Technology spawns the future; people are key to technology" (*Clari News*, p. 2).

**KIM TAKES ACTION** Much of this success is attributable to Eric Kim. After being recruited to Samsung as executive vice president for marketing, the former Lotus Development Corporation executive overhauled Samsung Electronics' marketing arm. He consolidated fifty-five advertising agencies into one to create a global brand image for the company. Progress was swift. "Just 24 months ago, Samsung was seen as a third-tier company, but now it's broken into the top level," says Ray Brown, vice president for general merchandising, electronics, at Sears, Roebuck and Company. (*The Wall Street Journal*).

Kim started developing relationships with American's top retail chains. He explains that his company has exploited an opening created by new digital technology. Consumers are now more open to consider different brands. "That transition, and our strategy to move upmarket very aggressively, are the main reasons why our brand improved rapidly," Kim says (*BusinessWeek online*, p. 2).

The consumer electronics chain Best Buy has become a major distributor of Samsung products. CompUSA is another strong partner. Samsung dropped Wal-Mart, perceiving the mammoth retailer as incompatible with its upscale image. "During the 1980s and '90s, the Japanese and Europeans dominated the electronics industry," Kim said at a New York City meeting. "But now we believe Samsung can dominate any market, including the U.S." (*The Wall Street Journal*).

## QUESTIONS

1. Identify at least three business (or marketing) strategies Samsung uses now or used in the past.
2. What suggestions can you offer Kim and other Samsung leaders so they can become even more successful in building the Samsung brand?
3. What is your opinion of Eric Kim as a strategic leader? Explain your answer.
4. How realistic is Samsung's vision of becoming the leader in the digital convergence revolution?

(*continued*)

SOURCES: Frank Gibney, Jr., "Samsung Moves Upmarket," *Time*, March 25, 2002, pp. 49–51; Jay Solomon, "Seoul Survivors: Back from the Brink, Korea Inc. Wants a Little Respect," *The Wall Street Journal*, June 13, 2002, pp. A1, A6; Moon Ihlwan, "Samsung: No Longer Unsung," *BusinessWeek online*, August 6, 2001; "SAMSUNG Announces Major Semicon Achievements," *www.samsung.com/PressCenter/PressRelease/, 2004*; "Samsung Lifts the Veil on Global Performance, Surge in Brand Value, and Corporate Strategy," *Clari News, http://quickstart.clari.net/qs_se/webnews/wed/cb/Bny-samsung-electronics.RTG_DSG.h...*, September 15, 2003; "Samsung Rewords Strategy to Widen Focus," *www.channeltimes.com/*, accessed December 30, 2004.

## LEADERSHIP CASE PROBLEM B

### THE RELUCTANT INFORMATION SHARERS

Blueberry Capital Management specializes in managing the portfolios of individuals and small businesses with a net worth of at least $2 million. Almost all of its clients have advanced knowledge of investments themselves. Because investors have so many options, including investing through online investment firms, a major challenge to the business is attracting new clients. Blueberry earns a large share of its profits by receiving a commission on the profits it generates for clients. An important part of the Blueberry investment strategy is to seek investments for clients it usually cannot find through traditional sources. For example, some client money is invested in business startups, giving clients the opportunity to become venture capitalists.

Mike Basilio, the founder of the firm, has been concerned that his company develops ideas inefficiently. He said to Lindsay Taylor, the executive vice president, "I keep hearing the same discussions over and over about how to attract new clients or solve a client investment problem. People don't capitalize on all the good problem solving that has taken place in the past. We go through the same agonizing process of dealing with similar problems."

Taylor replied, "Are you suggesting, Mike, that we should offer canned solutions to clients so we could save lots of time?"

"Not at all," responded Mike. "We could at least save some time and offer similar types of assistance to clients that we offered to other clients in the past. I'll give you a good example. Allan Whitcomb was recently working with a restaurant owner. The client wanted to invest in a high-risk, high-yield instrument. So Allan spent a week researching interesting possibilities for his client. He finally discovered a way to invest in wine futures [betting on the future price of rare wines] that appealed to his client.

"If Allan could have picked up some ideas in-house, he could have found some good ideas a lot more quickly. Also, if he had spent less time, the client might have been willing to invest a larger sum up front. Instead, the client invested some of his money into a hedge fund."

Looking perplexed, Lindsay said, "But how would Allan have known about who had tackled a similar client problem in the past?"

Mike jumped in, "Lindsay, you have pinpointed the problem. We have done a poor job of systematically pooling all that great information in our heads. Not only do we reinvent the wheel, we reinvent the idea that a wheel would be useful. I'm proposing that we find a way of sharing knowledge that will pay big dividends for the firm. The major consulting firms have developed pretty effective systems of knowledge management and knowledge sharing in recent years. I'm not implying that we hire somebody to be our chief knowledge officer or that we invest $500,000 in sophisticated software. I just want us to do a better job of sharing ideas with each other."

"I've got an idea," said Lindsay. "Let's schedule a combination dinner and focus group for the professional staff. The subject will be why we weren't doing a better job of information sharing." Among the comments that emerged from the dinner/focus group were the following:

**Gerry:** I would like to share more of my experiences with the other financial consultants. I'm concerned, though, about the good of the firm. Suppose I give some of my best ideas to another consultant, and then he or she leaves the firm? My good ideas are fed right to the competition.

**Barbara:** Unlike Gerry, I have no hesitancy in sharing ideas. The problem is the time. We were encouraged at one time to do a write-up of how we solved unusual client problems. The task proved to be busywork. We had to follow a complicated format. Maybe we should use a briefer method of recording good ideas.

**Samantha:** Sharing ideas makes me a little self-conscious. To ask someone else for ideas suggests that I'm not so creative myself.

**Kurt:** So long as we are all being brutally honest here, let me get to the heart of the problem. Our careers are dependent on having good ideas and investment strategies. Once you share an idea with another exec, the idea becomes public knowledge. It loses its originality. So if you use that idea again, you are no longer creative because other consultants are using it.

**Amber:** Kurt has a point. Teamwork is nice, but you still have to look out for numero uno. Sure I have warm, fuzzy feelings toward top management and the other consultants. Yet I'm still evaluated by Blueberry management in terms of my originality, including ways to find new clients and finding high-yield investments.

Mike Basilio said to the group, "Lindsay and I both thank you for being so candid. I see a few glimmers of hope in terms of knowledge sharing in our firm. But this is just the start of a continuing dialogue. We have a long way to go to manage knowledge well at Blueberry Capital."

Lindsay nodded in agreement.

## QUESTIONS

1. What suggestions can you offer Mike Basilio and Lindsay Taylor to improve knowledge sharing at Blueberry Capital?
2. How valid are the points made by the financial consultants for not doing a better job sharing information?
3. What cultural changes might be needed at Blueberry to improve knowledge sharing?

LEADERSHIP SKILL-BUILDING EXERCISE 13-2

### MY LEADERSHIP PORTFOLIO

A major part of being a strategic leader is to think strategically. Entrapped by the necessities of the small tasks facing use daily, it is easy to "think little" instead of "think big" as required to be a strategic thinker. A "little thinker" might attend a leadership seminar and spend five minutes demanding a $5.00 rebate because he or she was served ill-prepared food at lunch. A "big thinker" might reflect on the same poorly prepared meal as a lesson in the importance of employees' taking care of small details to ensure customer satisfaction. For this installment in your leadership portfolio, enter into your journal how you capitalized—or did not capitalize—on the opportunity to think strategically during the last week, or so. An example follows:

My friend and I visited a large shopping mall on Saturday morning. We noticed a large number of vehicles, both autos and small trucks, circling

(*continued*)

<br>

around within a block of the mall entrance. The drivers were obviously looking for a parking spot close enough so they could avoid walking the block, or so, necessary if they parked farther from the entrance.

My friend is a fitness nut, so he said the parking space chasers could do themselves a favor by parking a long distance from the mall entrance. In this way they could get a little physical exercise. A strategic flash went through my mine. If I, or perhaps the First Lady, could launch a national campaign for parking a distance away from mall entrances, we could make some headway on two of the major problems facing our society. First, physical inactivity is becoming almost as big a killer as smoking. Second, think of all the gas people are wasting. On a national scale, think of all the gas we would save if people would stop circling around looking for spaces. Besides, those little extra blocks of gas consumption add up. My strategic brainstorm could lead to more fitness and less energy consumption in our country.

## INTERNET SKILL-BUILDING EXERCISE

Apply the chapter concepts! Visit the Web and complete this Internet skill-building exercise to learn more about current leadership topics and trends.

### PROFESSIONAL ASSISTANCE IN IMPLEMENTING KNOWLEDGE MANAGEMENT

Visit *www.knowledgebase.net* to learn about Knowledge Base, a group of engineers, scientists, and entrepreneurs whose aim is to help their clients and partners achieve corporate objectives by unlocking and leveraging the power of intelligent knowledge management. Take the PowerPoint tour (*www.knowledgebase.net/tour/tour1.html*). After your tour is complete, answer these questions: (1) What are the goals of Knowledge Base? (2) What is your opinion of the value of the service offered by the company?

# International and Culturally Diverse Aspects of Leadership

When Axcelis Technologies, Inc. outsourced some engineering jobs to India last year, the Beverly, Massachusetts, company worried that some of its workers might resent their new Indian colleagues. So Axcelis called in Bidhan Chandra. Over two days, the Indian-born Chandra taught some sixty Axcelis Technologies employees the finer points of how to shake hands with Indians and why not to get frustrated if an Indian worker makes no eye contact during a meeting. He got the group to role-play scenarios in which one person would pretend to be an Indian and the other his or her U.S.-based colleague. Indian music throbbed in the background during breaks.

"At first I was skeptical and wondered what I'd get out of the class," says Randy Longo, a human resources director at Axcelis, which makes tools for manufacturing semiconductors. "But it was enlightening for me. Not everyone operates like we do in America."

One tip Chandra gave to another client was for the team not to plunge into business talk right away during meetings but to first chat about current events and other subjects. The rationale: Indians culturally prefer to establish a connection with others before getting involved in business issues.

Even as tension over the outsourcing of jobs in India mounts, people like Chandra are preaching a gospel of understanding. As one of the country's premier "awareness trainers," the 56-year-old former mechanical engineer not only teaches at Empire State College in Saratoga Springs, New York, but also travels the United States to teach workers how to be sensitive to their counterparts abroad. His business is booming. Chandra began by teaching his sensitivity course once every two months and now conducts it once or twice a month.[1]

---

The story about the India trainer illustrates how much emphasis leaders place on workers achieving better cross-cultural understanding so they can work smoothly with cross-border colleagues. Working in another country—and thus dealing with cultural groups different from one's own—is becoming a requirement for many senior-level management positions. In addition, corporate success, profit, and growth depend increasingly on the management of a diverse work force both outside and within one's own country.

For example, the average age of the American worker is increasing, and white males now constitute less than 50 percent of the work force. An increasing number of new entrants are women and people of color. The diversity umbrella in the work force encompasses such groups as men, women, people of color, white people, able-bodied people, the physically disabled, gay males, lesbians, the old, the young, married people with children, unmarried people with children, and single parents. These groups want their leaders and coworkers to treat them with respect, dignity, fairness, and sensitivity. At the same time, these groups must work together smoothly to serve a variety of customers and to generate an array of ideas.[2]

Because the focus on diversity is including so many people in an opportunity to participate fully in the organization, the word *inclusion* is often used to replace *diversity*. Not only is the work force becoming more diverse, but business has also become increasingly global. Small and medium-size firms, as well as corporate giants, are increasingly dependent on trade with other countries. Furthermore, most manufactured goods contain components from more than one country, and global outsourcing has become a dominant trend.

Our approach to cultural diversity both within and across countries emphasizes the leadership perspective. Key topics include the ethical and competitive advantage of managing for diversity, how cultural factors influence leadership practices, and how cultural sensitivity and global leadership skills contribute to leadership effectiveness. This chapter also describes initiatives that enhance the acceptance of cultural diversity and shows how to achieve cultural diversity among organizational leaders. The underlying theme is that effective leadership of diverse people requires a sensitivity to and enjoyment of cultural differences.

## The Advantages of Managing for Diversity

The ethical and socially responsible goals of leaders and their organizations include providing adequately for members of the diverse work force. Ethical leaders should therefore feel compelled to use merit as a basis for making human resource decisions. A firm that embraces diversity is also behaving in a socially responsible manner. A leader, for example, who chose to hire five environmentally disadvantaged, unemployed people would be acting in a socially responsible manner. Hiring these people would transfer responsibility for their economic welfare from the state or private charity to the employer. (Some would argue that unless hiring these people is cost effective, the company is neglecting its responsibility to shareholders.)

The many spheres of activity that managing for diversity encompasses are shown in Figure 14-1. According to research and opinion, managing for diversity also brings the firm a competitive advantage. Such an advantage is most likely to accrue when diversity is built into the firm's strategy. Furthermore, according to long-term research conducted by Massachusetts Institute of Technology Professor Thomas A. Kochan, diversity can enhance business performance only if the proper training is provided and the organizational culture supports diversity.[3] Here we review evidence and opinion about the competitive advantage of demographic and cultural diversity.

1. *Reduction of turnover and absenteeism costs.* As organizations become more diverse, the cost of managing diversity poorly increases. Turnover and absenteeism decrease when minority groups perceive themselves as receiving fair treatment. More effective management of diversity may increase the job satisfaction of diverse groups, thus decreasing turnover and absenteeism and their associated costs. The major initiatives in managing diversity well at Allstate Corporation have substantially reduced turnover among Latinos and African Americans, both in corporate headquarters and in field locations.[4]

2. *Managing diversity well offers a marketing advantage.* A representational work force facilitates the sale of products and services. A key factor is that a multicultural group of decision makers may be at an advantage in reaching a multicultural market. At least one member of the multicultural group may be able to focus a marketing strategy to demonstrate an appreciation of the targeted audience. Pepsi-Cola North America developed a beverage specifically designed for the Latino community, Dole Aguas Frescas, a line of noncarbonated, caffeine-free juice. The idea came from Latino input within Pepsi-Cola, which revealed that Latinos typically make this type of product in their homes. Tested in the Chicago area, the brand is supported by outdoor advertising, in-store merchandising, and sampling.[5]

**FIGURE 14-1** Spheres of Activity in the Management of Cultural Diversity

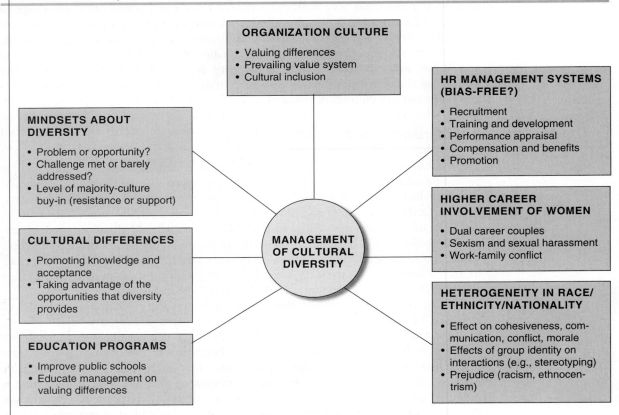

Source: Taylor H. Cox and Stacy Blake, "Managing for Cultural Diversity: Implications for Organizational Competitiveness," *Academy of Management Executive: The Thinking Manager's Source*, August 1991, p. 46. *Academy of Management Executive* by Newsom, Walter B. Copyright 1991 by Academy of Management. Reproduced with permission of Academy of Management in the format Textbook via Copyright Clearance Center.

Another marketing advantage is that many people from culturally diverse groups prefer to buy from a company with a good reputation for managing diversity. Allstate Insurance Company, Incis well known for its diversity initiatives, and the company has become the nation's leading insurer of African Americans and Latinos. The large number of agents and customer service representatives from these two groups facilitates attracting and retaining a high percentage of African Americans and Latinos as customers.

A culturally diverse work force or advertising agency also helps a company avoid costly and embarrassing bloopers. In 2004 China banned a Nike TV commercial showing basketball superstar LeBron James battling a kung fu master, saying the ad insulted national dignity. James was depicted as defeating the kung fu master, two women in traditional Chinese attire, and two dragons. (Dragons are considered a sacred symbol in traditional Chinese culture.)[6]

3. *Companies with a favorable record in managing diversity are at a distinct advantage in recruiting and retaining talented people.* Those companies with a favorable reputation for welcoming diversity attract the strongest job candidates among women and racial and ethnic minorities. Also, a company that does not welcome a diverse work force shrinks its supply of potential candidates.

4. *Managing diversity well unlocks the potential for excellence.* When companies hire culturally diverse workers and provide them with all the tools, resources, and opportunities they need to succeed, those companies are more likely to display the full talents of their workforce. A man raised in China earned an MBA from an American institute. After carefully searching for companies with an enviable record of managing diversity, he landed a position as a financial analyst with PepsiCo. After one year, his manager complimented his ability to generate ideas and asked why he tried so hard. The analyst said, "In this company, there is nothing to hold me back so long as I am a star performer."

5. *Heterogeneity in the work force may offer the company a creativity advantage, as well as improve its problem-solving and decision-making capability.* Creative solutions to problems are more likely to be reached when a diverse group attacks a problem. It is also possible that a member of a given ethnic group will add a creative touch to product development. Frank Saucedo is director of GM's design studio in North Hollywood. "I grew up in a very automotive family," he says. "My dad worked a lot on cars, and I think Latinos are generally very artistic and expressive. Growing up in this area, you're surrounded by a culture that reveres the car—most people will forgo a meal to buy that set of wheels. Your car says a lot about who you are, and I grew up in that."[7]

Diversity offers both a substantial advantage for organizations and a formidable challenge. Some research suggests that a diverse group is likely to consider a greater range of perspectives and to generate more high-quality solutions than a homogeneous group. Yet the greater the amount of diversity within an organizational subunit, the less cohesive the group. The result may be dissatisfaction and turnover. According to Frances J. Milliken and Luis L. Martins, diversity thus appears to be a double-edge sword: it increases both the opportunity for creativity and the likelihood that group members will be dissatisfied and fail to identify with the group.[8]

However, research at one of the world's largest employers substantiates many of the points already mentioned about the advantages of a culturally diverse work force. The goal of the Diversity Development Program of the U.S. Postal Service (USPS) is to build an inclusive work force to serve its diverse customer base. For five consecutive years, *Fortune* magazine identified the U.S. Postal Service as one of the "50 best companies for minorities." More than 36 percent of the USPS's approximately 729,000 employees are minorities, as well as close to 25 percent of its top-paid executives and 32 percent of its officials and managers. Furthermore, how well managers attain diversity goals is considered when decisions are made about their performance and compensation.[9]

The department in charge of the program conducted a study to determine the return on investment (ROI) from employing a diverse work force within diverse communities. Work force inclusiveness was measured in terms of the percentages of underrepresentation of ten different ethnic groups in comparison to the local civilian labor force. For example, if 15 percent of the local work force were Native American and only 8 percent of the local Postal Service employees were Native American, this group would be underrepresented by 7 percent. All eighty-five postal districts were included in the study. Work force inclusiveness (the opposite of underrepresentation) was positively correlated with more favorable levels of performance. The following criteria were used:

- Customer ratings of overall satisfaction
- Customer ratings of courteous and friendly service from clerks
- Customer ratings of the ability of clerks to explain products and services
- Employee ratings regarding not feeling excluded from the work unit
- Employee ratings regarding concern over being a victim of workplace violence
- Employee ratings regarding freedom from sexual harassment
- Employee ratings regarding the Postal Service as a place to work
- Corporate productivity rate

On the basis of these results, the researchers concluded that diversity initiatives provide a worthwhile ROI to the Postal Service. Also, when an organization embraces the communities it serves and its work force is representative of those communities, customer and employee satisfaction increase, as well as organizational productivity.[10] An important situational factor here is that the U.S. government has always been a leader in hiring a diverse work force. Employees therefore expect to be part of a culturally and demographically diverse environment.

The accompanying Leader in Action insert describes a business owner whose company is culturally diverse and who also has capitalized on the need for companies to be sensitive to cultural diversity in their marketing.

## LEADER IN ACTION

### AD AGENCY CEO DONALD COLEMAN EMBRACES CULTURAL DIVERSITY

As more and more companies abandon the one-ad-fits-all mentality of yesteryear, a Detroit-based advertising agency is riding the crest of a new wave of marketing to African Americans, Hispanics, and Asian Americans. According to *Advertising Age*, GlobalHue is the biggest multicultural advertising agency in the country. It counts DaimlerChrysler, Verizon Communications, American Airlines, and the U.S. Navy among its customers.

GlobalHue advertisements aimed at specific minority groups are often broadcast regionally or printed in specialty publications, sometimes in Spanish, Chinese, or Korean. But these targeted messages also work well for the general market because of the growing influence of minority groups on popular culture, according to founder and CEO Donald Coleman.

"It's about attitude and it's not just a black thing. People in Iowa and Nebraska want to be part of the freedom of expression and irreverence," he said. "We must hit our target market first, but a lot of people will be interested in the communication."

Coleman, 52, is a former University of Michigan linebacker who played four seasons in the National Football League. A former vice president at another advertising agency, he found the Don Coleman Agency in 1988 to focus on the African American market. In 1999 Coleman, in the process of selling a 49 percent share now owned by The Interpublic Group of Companies, Inc., merged his agency with several multicultural agencies to create New American Strategies Group.

The name was changed to GlobalHue in 2002 following mergers with Montemayor y Asociados, an Hispanic advertising agency based in San Antonio, Texas, and Innovasia Communications of Long Beach, California, which targeted Asian American communities. Billings doubled after the mergers created one-stop shopping for multicultural advertising campaigns, according to Coleman.

Chrysler started working with both Coleman and Montmayor in the early 1990s, and DaimlerChrysler remains GlobalHue's biggest client. The agency is currently involved in half a dozen campaigns for Chrysler's three nameplates.

Two years ago GlobalHue lined up Tex-Mex musician Flaco Jimenez to help launch a new line of Dodge Ram trucks to the Southwest Hispanic community. Local appearances by the tejano icon complemented the mass media advertising, according to Julie Roehm, director of marketing communications for Chrysler, Jeep, and Dodge. "They're excellent at creating relationships with consumers that drive business directly to the dealerships," Roehm said.

Chrysler also relies on GlobalHue to reach the gay–lesbian–bisexual–transsexual market. "They're unique in their ability to create campaigns for four markets," Roehm said. "Most of their competition is focused on one or two, so our competition has to use more than one agency."

According to Coleman, the key to staying ahead of advertising trends is to monitor the "early adopters," often young African Americans, who define the "urban mindset" that drives many popular culture trends. These innovators influence the lifestyle choices of many entertainers and professional athletes who serve as pop culture role models.

GlobalHue uses sampling from the Yankelovich research firm, but many insights come from staff members who belong to the minority community they are trying to reach. This gives GlobalHue an edge, according to Michele Williamson, manager of multicultural advertising at Verizon. "The team members are representative of the market segments they produce for, and I think that's the key," she said. "They are pretty passionate about their segments."

According to Coleman, his agency has to act as an advocate because only between 2 and 5 percent of advertising is directed at minority markets. African Americans, Hispanics, and Asian Americans represent 37 percent of the population, and that percentage continues to grow. Census projections show that more than half of people younger than 21 will belong to one of these three groups by 2010.

The agency is working to develop better statistical tools to measure minority spending and the impact of advertising targeting those minority segments. "Everyone wants to see the return on their investment," he said.

## QUESTIONS

1. What leadership roles does Coleman appear to be carrying out?
2. In what way is GlobalHue capitalizing on cultural diversity within the company?
3. What is your evaluation of the ethics of pitching an advertising campaign to appeal to a specific demographic market such as gay males?

SOURCE: "Ad Agency Embraces Multicultural Approach," by Eric Pope, *Detroit News*, July 9, 2004. Reprinted with permission from the *Detroit News*.

**LEADERSHIP SKILL-BUILDING EXERCISE 14-1**

### CAPITALIZING ON DIVERSITY

The class organizes into small groups of about six students each who assume the roles of the top management team of a medium-size manufacturing or service company. Each group has the following assignment: "Being socially aware, ethical, and modern in its thinking, your company already has a highly diverse work force. Yet somehow, your company is not any more profitable than the competition. As the company leaders (yourself a diverse group), today you will work on the problem of how to better capitalize on the cultural diversity within your company. Working for about fifteen minutes, develop a few concrete ideas to enable your company to capitalize on diversity." After the problem solving has been completed, the team leaders might present their ideas to the other groups.

To raise your level of awareness about how to capitalize on the potential advantages of diversity, do Leadership Skill-Building Exercise 14-1, which illustrates that diversity skills are another important subset of interpersonal skills associated with leadership.

## Cultural Factors Influencing Leadership Practice

A **multicultural leader** is a leader with the skills and attitudes to relate effectively to and motivate people across race, gender, age, social attitudes, and lifestyles. To influence, motivate, and inspire culturally diverse people, the leader must be aware of overt and subtle cultural differences. Although such culturally based differences are generalizations, they function as starting points in the leader's attempt to lead a person from another culture. For example, many Asians are self-conscious about being praised in front of the group because they feel that individual attention clashes with their desire to maintain group harmony. Therefore, a manager might refrain from praising an Asian group member before the group until he or she understands that group member's preferences. The manager is likely to find that many Asians welcome praise in front of peers, especially when working outside their homeland.

Here we examine two topics that help a leader learn how to manage in a culturally diverse workplace: (1) understanding key dimensions of differences in cultural values and (2) the influence of cultural values on leadership style.

### Key Dimensions of Differences in Cultural Values

One way to understand how national cultures differ is to examine their values. Here we examine eight different values and the ways in which selected nationalities relate to them. Geert Hofstede identified the first five value dimensions in research spanning eighteen years and involving more than 160,000 people from more than sixty countries.[11] The qualitative research of Arvind V. Phatak identified two other values.[12] The eighth value is recently formulated. A summary of these values is described next and is also outlined in Figure 14-2.

1. *Individualism/collectivism.* At one end of the continuum is **individualism**, a mental set in which people see themselves first as individuals and believe their own interests and values take priority. **Collectivism**, at the other end of the continuum, is a feeling that the group and society should receive top priority. Members of a society that value individualism are more concerned with their careers than with the good of the firm. Members of a society who value collectivism, on the other hand, are typically more concerned with the organization than with themselves. Individualistic cultures include the United States, Canada, and Great Britain; collectivistic cultures include Japan, Hong Kong, Mexico, and Greece.

2. *Power distance.* The extent to which employees accept the idea that members of an organization have different levels of power is referred to as **power distance**. In a high-power-distance culture, the boss makes many decisions simply because he or she is boss, and group members readily comply. In a low-power-distance culture, employees do not readily recognize a power hierarchy. They accept directions only

### FIGURE 14-2  Dimensions of Individual Values

| | |
|---|---|
| 1. Individualism | Collectivism |
| 2. High power distance | Low power distance |
| 3. High uncertainty avoidance | Low uncertainty avoidance |
| 4. Materialism | Concern for others |
| 5. Long-term orientation | Short-term orientation |
| 6. Formality | Informality |
| 7. Urgent time orientation | Casual time orientation |
| 8. Work orientation | Leisure orientation |

when they think the boss is right or when they feel threatened. High-power-distance cultures include France, Spain, Japan, and Mexico. Low-power-distance cultures include the United States, Israel, Germany, and Ireland.

3. *Uncertainty avoidance.* People who accept the unknown and tolerate risk and unconventional behavior are said to have low **uncertainty avoidance**. In other words, these people are not afraid to face the unknown. A society ranked high in uncertainty avoidance contains a majority of people who want predictable and certain futures. Low-uncertainty-avoidance cultures include the United States, Canada, and Australia. At the other end of the continuum, workers in Israel, Japan, Italy, and Argentina place more value on certainty and predictability.

4. *Materialism/concern for others.* In this context, **materialism** refers to an emphasis on assertiveness and the acquisition of money and material objects, and a de-emphasis on caring for others. At the other end of the continuum is **concern for others**, which refers to an emphasis on personal relationships, caring for others, and a high quality of life. Materialistic countries include the United States, Japan, and Italy, whereas "concern for others" cultures include Sweden and Denmark.

5. *Long-term orientation/short-term orientation.* Workers from a culture with a **long-term orientation** maintain a long-range perspective, and thus are thrifty and do not demand quick returns on their investments. A **short-term orientation** is characterized by a demand for immediate results and a propensity not to save. Pacific Rim countries are noted for their long-term orientation. In contrast, the cultures of the United States and Canada are characterized by a more short-term orientation.

6. *Formality/informality.* A country that values **formality** attaches considerable importance to tradition, ceremony, social rules, and rank. In contrast, **informality** refers to a casual attitude toward tradition, ceremony, social rules, and rank. Workers in Latin American countries highly value formality, such as lavish public receptions and processions. Germans are among the most formal people in Europe. American and Canadian workers are much more informal. An important note of caution is that the entire work world is becoming more informal, as indicated by the extensive use of addressing people by their first names and rarely addressing people by their title.

7. *Urgent time orientation/casual time orientation.* Long- and short-term orientations focus mostly on planning and investment. Another time-related value dimension is how much importance a person attaches to time. People with an **urgent time orientation** perceive time as a scarce resource and tend to be impatient. People with a **casual time orientation** perceive time as an unlimited and unending resource and tend to be patient. Americans are noted for their urgent time orientation. They frequently impose deadlines and are eager to "get down to business." Asians and Middle Easterners, in contrast, are patient negotiators. In fact, businesspersons in the Middle East are known to allow a business meeting to run over while another visitor waits outside the office.

8. *Work orientation/leisure orientation.* A major cultural value difference is the number of hours per week people expect to invest in work rather than in leisure or other nonwork activities. American corporate professionals typically work about fifty-five hours per week, take forty-five-minute lunch breaks, and go on two weeks of vacation. Japanese workers share similar values with respect to amount of work per week. European professionals, in contrast, are more likely to work forty hours

per week, take two-hour lunch breaks, and go on six weeks of vacation. In recent years, European countries have steadily reduced the workweek while lengthening vacations. The average German worker invests about 1,400 hours a year in work, a 17 percent decrease from 1980. Europeans, particularly Swedes, also are likely to take much more sick leave than workers from other countries. Furthermore, labor market statistics indicate that Americans ages 15 to 64, on a per-person basis, work 50 percent more than do the French.[13]

How might a manager use information about differences in values to become a more effective leader? A starting point would be to recognize that a person's national values might influence his or her behavior. Assume that a leader wants to influence a person with a low-power-distance orientation to strive for peak performance. The "low-power" person will not spring into action just because the boss makes the suggestion. Instead, the leader needs to patiently explain the personal payoffs of achieving peak performance. Another example is a leader who wants to improve quality and therefore hires people who value collectivism. A backup tactic would be to counsel people who value individualism on the merits of collective action. Leadership Self-Assessment Quiz 14-1 will help you think about how values can moderate (or influence) work performance.

---

**LEADERSHIP SELF-ASSESSMENT QUIZ 14-1**

## CHARTING YOUR CULTURAL VALUE PROFILE

**INSTRUCTIONS** For each of the eight value dimensions, circle the number that most accurately fits your standing on the dimension. For example, if you perceive yourself to be "highly concerned for others," circle the 7 on the fourth dimension.

**1.** Individualism                                         Collectivism

    1         2         3         4         5         6         7

**2.** High Power Distance                   Low Power Distance

    1         2         3         4         5         6         7

**3.** High Uncertainty Avoidance       Low Uncertainty Avoidance

    1         2         3         4         5         6         7

**4.** Materialism                                  Concern for Others

    1         2         3         4         5         6         7

**5.** Long-Term Orientation                Short-Term Orientation

    1         2         3         4         5         6         7

**6.** Formality                                      Informality

    1         2         3         4         5         6         7

*(Continued)*

7. Urgent Time Orientation                                    Casual Time Orientation

   1      2      3      4      5      6      7

8. Work Orientation                                                   Leisure Orientation

   1      2      3      4      5      6      7

SCORING AND INTERPRETATION After circling one number for each dimension, use a felt-tip pen to connect the circles; this gives you a *profile of cultural values.* Do not be concerned if your marker cuts through the names of the dimensions. Compare your profile to others in class. Should time allow, develop a class profile by computing the class average for each of the eight dimensions and then connecting the points. If the sample size is large enough, compare the cultural value profiles of Westerners and Easterners.

One possible link to leadership development is to hypothesize which type of profile would be the most responsive and which would be the least responsive to your leadership.

## Cultural Values and Leadership Style

The values embedded in a culture influence the behavior of leaders and managers as well as the behavior of other workers. As Hofstede explains, relationships between people in a society are affected by the values programmed in the minds of these people. Because management deals heavily with interpersonal relationships, management and leadership are affected by cultural values. Management and leadership processes may vary from culture to culture, but, being value based, these processes show strong continuity in each society.[14]

***French Managers*** One example of the influence of values on management and leadership style is the behavior of French managers. France has always put a strong emphasis on class. A typical manufacturing plant in France has several classes of workers. Managers and professionals are labeled the *cadres;* first-level supervisors are called the *maîtrise;* and lower-level workers are the *noncadres.* Within each of these classes there are further status distinctions such as higher and lower cadres. French managers who have attended the major business schools (*Grand Écoles*) have the highest status of all. The implication for leadership style is that French managers, particularly in major corporations, are part of an elite class, and they behave in a superior, authoritarian manner. (Of course, not every French manager follows the cultural tradition of being authoritarian.) This style of manager would expect obedience and high respect from group members.

***German Managers*** Another example of a distinctive leadership style related to culture is the stereotype of the German manager. German managers were studied as part of the GLOBE (Global Leadership and Organizational Behavior Effectiveness)

project. Data were collected on culture and leadership from 457 middle managers in the telecommunications, food processing, and finance industries. A strong performance orientation was found to be the most pronounced German cultural value. German middle managers thus tend to avoid uncertainty, are assertive, and are not terribly considerate of others. They typically show little compassion, and their interpersonal relations are straightforward and stern.[15] And the strong performance they expect must be packed into a short workweek!

***Malaysian Managers***  The characteristic leadership style of Malaysian managers is instructive because other Asian managers use a similar style. Malaysia has become important as a trading partner of both the United States and Europe, particularly because of the outsourcing movement. The following conclusions about the Malaysian leadership style were also based on the GLOBE project.[16] Malaysians emphasize collective well-being (collectivism) and display a strong humane orientation within a society that respects hierarchical differences (high power difference). The culture discourages aggressive, confrontational behavior, preferring harmonious relationships. The preferred organizational leadership style is therefore for managers to show compassion, while at the same time be more autocratic than participative. The Malaysian work group member defers to the boss and in turn is treated with respect and compassion. A Malaysian supervisor might say typically to a worker, "Here is exactly how I want this job done, but I want you to enjoy yourself and learn something valuable while doing the job."

The three highest-ranking leadership dimensions in terms of importance for Malaysian managers were as follows: (1) charismatic/transformational, (2) team oriented, and (3) human oriented. Specifically, the Malaysians emphasized the importance of being willing to act decisively, of using logic and intuition to make decisions firmly and quickly, and of being strong willed, determined, and resolute. Malaysian managers also think it is important for leaders to coordinate activities in a diplomatic style, avoiding conflict and showing consideration for team members.

***Northern U.S. Versus Southern U.S. Managers***  Differences in cultural values between regions of a large country can also have an impact. An example of a cross-regional stereotype is that managers in the southern United States are lower key and more interested in relationship building than their brusque counterparts in the North. Leaders from the North have a reputation for efficiency and getting tasks accomplished quickly. Leaders from the South perceive such behavior as rude, pushy, and short on relationship building. "If Donald Trump was from the South, he would say, 'You're fired, but bless your heart, you've tried,'" says Joe Hollingsworth, CEO of Hollingsworth Companies. in Clinton, Tennessee.[17] The point here is that Southern hospitality has worked its way into leadership style.

However, the stereotype of Southern business leaders being more laid-back and slow moving has been challenged. For one, business in the South may have moved more slowly in the days before air conditioning was widespread. Heat tends to slow people down. John Thompson, CEO of Symantec Corporation and a Florida A&M graduate, says there is nothing regional about attaining business results. "I was raised in the South and spent 27 years working for IBM all over the world. I don't think management style can be localized."[18]

college.hmco.com/pic/
dubrin5e

**K** @ **KNOWLEDGE BANK:** describes how a leader might apply the expectancy theory of motivation across cultures.

## Cultural Sensitivity, Cultural Intelligence, and Global Leadership Skills

Some managers are more effective at leading diverse groups than others. The traits and behaviors described in Chapters 2, 3, and 4 should equip a person to lead diverse groups. In addition, cultural sensitivity, cultural intelligence, and certain specific global leadership skills are essential for inspiring people from cultures other than one's own. Although they reinforce each other, here we describe cultural sensitivity and global leadership skills separately.

### Cultural Sensitivity

Leaders, as well as others, who are attempting to influence a person from a foreign country must be alert to possible cultural differences. Thus, the leader must be willing to acquire knowledge about local customs and learn to speak the native language at least passably. A cross-cultural leader must be patient, adaptable, flexible, and willing to listen and learn. All of these characteristics are part of **cultural sensitivity**, an awareness of and a willingness to investigate the reasons why people of another culture act as they do. A person with cultural sensitivity will recognize certain nuances in customs that will help build better relationships with people in his or her adopted cultures. Refer to Table 12-3 in Chapter 12 for a sampling of appropriate and less appropriate behaviors in a variety of countries. (These are suggestions, not absolute rules.) Another aspect of cultural sensitivity is being tolerant of the subtle differences between cultures. Leadership Self-Assessment Quiz 14-2 gives you an opportunity to reflect on your own toleration.

Cultural sensitivity is also important because it helps a person become a **multicultural worker**. Such an individual is convinced that all cultures are equally good and enjoys learning about other cultures. Multicultural workers and leaders are usually people who have been exposed to more than one culture in childhood. (Refer to Leadership Self-Assessment Exercise 12-2, about cross-cultural relations.) Being multicultural helps one be accepted by a person from another culture. According to Gunnar Beeth, a *multilingual* salesperson can explain the advantages of a product in other languages, but it takes a *multicultural* salesperson to motivate foreigners to buy.[19]

Sensitivity is the most important characteristic for leading people from other cultures because cultural stereotypes rarely provide entirely reliable guides for dealing with others. An American manager, for example, might expect Asian group members to accept his or her directives immediately because Asians are known to defer to authority. Nevertheless, an individual Asian might need considerable convincing before accepting authority.

Problems of cultural misunderstanding that leaders should be aware of cluster in five areas.[20] *Language* differences create problems because U.S. workers (most of whom are monolingual) can become frustrated by coworkers' accents and limited

English skills. Non-English speakers may feel that they do not fit well into the team. Differences in *religion* are the source of many misunderstandings. In many cultures, religion dominates life in ways that Americans find difficult to comprehend. *Work habits* vary enough across cultures to create friction and frustration. Employees in some cultures are unwilling to spend personal time on work. Problems can also stem from office rituals, such as having coffee or tea together during work breaks, or singing songs together at the start of the workday.

*Women's roles* may differ considerably from those in the United States. Women in many countries may not have the same independence or access to education and higher-level jobs as American women. Workers from various countries may therefore have difficulty accepting the authority of an American manager who is female. *Personal appearance and behavior* vary considerably across cultures. Grooming, office attire, eating habits, and nonverbal communication may deviate significantly from the U.S. standards. Many workers around the world may perceive American workers as overfriendly, aggressive, or rude.

Cultural sensitivity is enhanced by cultural training, and also by simply listening carefully and observing. A key principle is to be flexible when dealing with people from other cultures. An excellent example is the attitude of Zhang Xin Sheng, the mayor of Suzho, China, whose strategic goal is to make Westerners feel comfortable in his city. Zhang says in fluent English, "It's not necessary to use chopsticks. A knife and fork are okay."[21]

**LEADERSHIP SELF-ASSESSMENT QUIZ 14-2**

## MY TOLERANCE FOR CULTURAL DIFFERENCES

INSTRUCTIONS: Indicate how comfortable you would feel in the following circumstances: very uncomfortable (VU); uncomfortable (U); neutral (N); comfortable (C); very comfortable (VC).

|  | VU | U | N | C | VC |
|---|---|---|---|---|---|
| 1. Working on a team with both men and women | 1 | 2 | 3 | 4 | 5 |
| 2. Coaching a team or club when all the members are of a different sex than myself | 1 | 2 | 3 | 4 | 5 |
| 3. Having a transsexual person for a boss | 1 | 2 | 3 | 4 | 5 |
| 4. Having a person of a different race for a boss | 1 | 2 | 3 | 4 | 5 |
| 5. Having an opposite-sex person for a boss | 1 | 2 | 3 | 4 | 5 |
| 6. Answer 6a if you are heterosexual; 6b if you are homosexual: | 1 | 2 | 3 | 4 | 5 |

**6a.** Having a gay or lesbian boss
**6b.** Having a straight boss

*(Continued)*

| | | | | | |
|---|---|---|---|---|---|
| 7. Having dinner with someone who eats what I consider to be a pet | 1 | 2 | 3 | 4 | 5 |
| 8. Having dinner with someone who eats what I consider to be a repulsive animal or insect | 1 | 2 | 3 | 4 | 5 |
| 9. Working alongside a teammate who I know is HIV positive | 1 | 2 | 3 | 4 | 5 |
| 10. Working alongside a teammate who has served prison time for vehicular homicide | 1 | 2 | 3 | 4 | 5 |

Total score _____

SCORING AND INTERPRETATION

- 40–50: You are highly tolerant and flexible in terms of working with a broad spectrum of people. These attitudes should help you be an effective multicultural leader.
- 21–39: Your toleration for working with people different from yourself is within the average range. If you learn to become more tolerant of differences, you are more likely to become an effective multicultural leader.
- 10–20: You may be experiencing difficulties in working with people quite different from yourself. As a consequence, your effectiveness as a multicultural leader might be hampered. If you seek out more diverse cross-cultural experiences, you are likely to become more tolerant of differences.

## Cultural Intelligence

A refinement and expansion of cultural sensitivity, is **cultural intelligence (CQ)**: an outsider's ability to interpret someone's unfamiliar and ambiguous gestures the way that person's compatriots would.[22] For example, an American might be attending a business meeting in Europe. He or she might pick up the clue that the Europeans present prefer to discuss American politics and trade agreements (or current events) for an hour before discussing the business purpose of the meeting. So the cross-border visitor engages in a lively but nonpartisan discussion of politics and trade agreements. Cultural intelligence has three facets or components:

- *Cognitive CQ (head).* The first facet of cultural intelligence is the ability to pick up some factual clues about relevant behavior such as the importance of deadlines.
- *Physical CQ (body).* Your actions and demeanor must prove to your foreign hosts that you have entered their world by adopting people's habits and mannerisms. You might gently kiss each cheek of a French compatriot (or be kissed), and not shake hands with a Japanese work associate in Tokyo. With the latter, you might bow slightly or smile as a form of greeting.
- *Emotional/motivational CQ (heart).* Adapting to a new culture involves overcoming obstacles and setbacks. You need the self-confidence and courage to

keep trying even though your first few attempts at adapting your behavior to a group of foreign workers went poorly. You might say to yourself, "Okay, when I stood very close to the Mexican workers, they didn't like it even though they stand close to each other. Maybe I looked a little stiff. I'll practice some more."

To attain the highest level of cultural intelligence, you would need competence in all three facets, and the head, body, and heart would have to work together smoothly. You would need to gather the facts, adapt your mannerism and appearance to fit the culture, and stay motivated to make refinements.

Cultural intelligence is similar to emotional intelligence, yet it goes one step further by enabling a person to distinguish between behaviors that are (a) produced by the culture in question, (b) peculiar to particular individuals, and (c) found in all human beings. Suppose you are making a PowerPoint presentation in Germany and suddenly your presentation is attacked. You ask yourself, "Is this a German trait? Are these people just being hostile? Or are my slides so bad anyone would attack them?" Picking up on the cues, you decide that German corporate professionals find it normal to challenge ideas and that they are not being personal.

## Global Leadership Skills

*Global leadership skills* are so important that they improve a company's reputation and contribute to a sustainable competitive advantage. (These skills are especially important in dealing with workers from different companies.)[23] Excellent global leaders have a leadership style that generates superior corporate performance in terms of four criteria: (1) profitability and productivity, (2) continuity and efficiency, (3) commitment and morale, and (4) adaptability and innovation. *Behavioral complexity* is the term given to this ability to attain all four criteria of organizational performance. Excellent global leaders are able to understand complex issues from the four perspectives just mentioned and to achieve the right balance. For example, when a company is facing a mature market, it might be necessary to invest more effort into being innovative than into achieving high profits.

Global leadership skills also include *stewardship*, because excellent global leaders act as responsible stewards of human and natural resources. By being responsible, they simultaneously promote economic, social, biological, and ecological development; they act with social responsibility.

The global leader must tap into a deep, universal layer of human motivation to build loyalty, trust, and teamwork in different cultures. Universal needs are found among people in all cultures; for example, both Dominican Republicans and Inuit want to be part of a group. To get at universal needs (such as the desire for affiliation and exploration), the global leader must satisfy three metavalues: community, pleasure, and meaning.

1. *Community.* The leaders of successful multinational firms nurture good citizenship behavior, or the desire to serve the common good. In these organizations, teamwork is highly valued and workers are more concerned with the common good than with their individual concerns.
2. *Pleasure.* In successful global organizations, fun or intrinsic motivation is an important energizer. Enjoying work by engaging in new activities is an essential part of the organizational culture. The fun, in turn, facilitates productivity and creativity.

3. *Meaning.* Meaningful work is another universal motivator. As one CEO said, "People will work for money but die for a cause." Employees prefer to feel that they are contributing something to society through their efforts.[24]

What is a global leader supposed to do to satisfy these three key metavalues? In general, he or she would have to engage in the type of leadership practices and behaviors described throughout this text. A more specific action plan would be to use team development tactics, including empowerment, to promote a sense of community. Pleasure and meaning would derive from job enrichment, with its emphasis on challenging, interesting work.

A study was conducted of success factors in international management positions. Two traits were specifically related to success in conducting international business: sensitivity to cultural differences and being culturally adventurous.[25] Cultural sensitivity has already been described. The adventurous aspect refers to a willingness to take chances and experiment with a new culture. A Mexican American from Phoenix, Arizona, who volunteered for a six-month assignment in Johannesburg, South Africa, would be culturally adventurous. Another study demonstrated that deficits in emotional intelligence contributed to executive failure on assignments in Latin America, Europe, and Japan.[26] Being able to read emotions is particularly helpful when evaluating how well the person from another culture is accepting your propositions.

A confusing skill issue for many international workers is the importance of having a good command of a second language. Part of the confusion comes from the fact that English has become the standard language of business, technology, engineering, and science. For example, when Europeans from different countries assemble at a business conference, they communicate in English. However, when you are trying to influence a person from another culture, you are more influential if you can speak, read, and write well in his or her language. On the Internet, consumers are four times more likely to purchase from a web site written in their preferred language.[27] A command of a second language also enhances the person's charisma.

# Leadership Initiatives for Achieving Cultural Diversity

For organizations to value diversity, top management must be committed to it. The commitment is clearest when it is embedded in organizational strategy, as well as in the life and culture of the organization. Diversity initiatives should be deep rather than superficial.[28] A true diversity strategy should encourage all employees to contribute their unique talents, skills, and expertise to the organization's operations, independent of race, gender, ethnic background, and any other definable difference. In addition, leaders should take the initiative to ensure that dozens of activities are implemented to support the diversity strategy. Figure 14-3 lists the most frequent issues (such as race) around which diversity efforts are directed in large firms. Table 14-1 lists the five leadership initiatives for encouraging diversity that are discussed in the following text.

## Hold Managers Accountable for Achieving Diversity

A high-impact diversity initiative is for top-level organizational leaders to hold managers accountable for diversity results at all levels. If managers are held accountable

## FIGURE 14-3  Diversity Initiatives at Major Business Firms

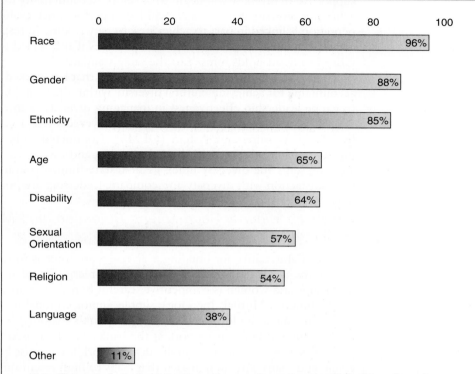

Note: Figures indicate the percentage of responding companies that address these issues through diversity initiatives.

Source: "Impact of Diversity on the Bottom Line," an SHRM/*Fortune* survey reflecting the responses of 121 human resources professionals from one thousand companies on *Fortune* magazine's list of the "100 Top Companies to Work For." Presented in Lin Grensing-Pophal, "Reaching for Diversity," *HR Magazine,* May 2002, p. 56. *Human Resource Magazine* by Lin Grensing-Pophal. Copyright 2002 by Society for Human Resource Management. Reproduced with permission of *HR Magazine* published by the Society for Human Resource Management, Alexandria, VA, in the format Textbook via Copyright Clearance Center.

---

**TABLE 14-1**    ## Leadership Initiatives for Achieving Cultural Diversity

1. Hold managers accountable for achieving diversity.
2. Establish minority recruitment, retention, and mentoring programs.
3. Conduct diversity training.
4. Conduct intercultural training.
5. Encourage the development of employee networks.
6. Avoid group characteristics when hiring for person–organization fit.

for behavior and business changes in the diversity arena, an organizational culture supportive of diversity will begin to develop. Accountability for diversity results when achieving diversity objectives is included in performance evaluations and when compensation is linked in part to achieving diversity results. In response to charges of discrimination, Wal-Mart cut executive's bonuses if they failed to meet diversity goals. CEO Lee Scott holds himself to the same standard.[29]

The Allstate Corporation exemplifies a firm that has worked hard to hold managers accountable for achieving cultural diversity within the firm. One of the methods used to gauge leadership effectiveness in managing diversity is an employee feedback survey. All 53,000 employees of Allstate are surveyed twice a year through a quarterly leadership measurement system (QLMS). Conducted online, the survey includes measures of satisfaction with both leadership and diversity accomplishment. (Table 14-2 presents the diversity index.) An Allstate human resource specialist has noted that satisfaction with diversity and company leadership are positively correlated.[30]

### Establish Minority Recruitment, Retention, and Mentoring Programs

An essential initiative for building a diverse work force is to recruit and retain members of the targeted minority group. Because recruiting talented members of minority groups and women is competitive, careful human resources planning is required. At Washington Mutual, Inc., for example, senior regional manager Ming Wong systematically hires employees who reflect the bank's customer base. For example, Ming hires Chinese Americans to work at the bank's San Francisco Chinatown branch.[31]

Efforts at recruiting a culturally diverse work force must be supported by a leadership and management approach that leads to high retention. To increase retention rates, diversity consultants advise employers to strengthen cultural training programs, recognize employees' hidden skills and talents, and give diversity committees clout with top management.[32] Retaining employees is also a function of good leadership and management in general, such as offering workers challenging work, clear-cut goals, feedback, and valuable rewards for goal attainment.

Mentoring is a key initiative for retaining minority-group members, as well as for facilitating their advancement. In a survey of successful minority executives, 48 percent

---

**TABLE 14-2**   **The Diversity Index at Allstate**

The diversity index at Allstate asks the following questions on employee surveys:

1. To what extent does our company deliver quality service to customers regardless of their ethnic background, etc.?

2. To what extent are you treated with respect and dignity at work?

3. To what extent does your immediate manager/team leader seek out and utilize diverse backgrounds and perspectives?

4. How often do you observe insensitive behavior at work: for example, inappropriate comments or jokes?

5. To what extent do you work in an environment of trust?

Source: From Allstate Insurance Company (*www.allstate.com*).

of the respondents said they had a role model who guided them toward early career goals. The role model or mentor was primarily of the same ethnic, racial, or cultural origin as the respondent. A specific finding was that successful minorities with supportive managers and coworkers have faster compensation growth and progress more rapidly in their firms. A sponsor of the survey said, "Minority executives believe that mentors are very helpful in advocating for upward mobility and teaching them how to navigate through the corporation."[33] More will be said about mentoring in Chapter 15 in relation to leadership development.

## Conduct Diversity Training

**Diversity training** has become a widely used, though controversial, method for enhancing diversity within organizations. The purpose of diversity training is to bring about workplace harmony by teaching people how to get along better with diverse work associates. Quite often the program is aimed at minimizing open expressions of racism and sexism. All forms of diversity training center on increasing people's awareness of and empathy for people who are different from themselves in some important way.

Training sessions in valuing differences focus on the ways in which men and women, or people of different races, reflect different values, attitudes, and cultural backgrounds. These sessions can vary from several hours to several days or longer. Sometimes the program is confrontational, sometimes not.

An essential part of relating more effectively to diverse groups is to empathize with their point of view. To help training participants develop empathy, representatives of various groups explain their feelings related to workplace issues. Leadership Skill-Building Exercise 14-2 gives you the opportunity to engage in an effective diversity training exercise. A useful way of framing diversity training is to say that it represents a subset of interpersonal skills: relating effectively to coworkers who are different from you in some meaningful way adds to your interpersonal effectiveness.

**LEADERSHIP SKILL-BUILDING EXERCISE 14-2**

### THE DIVERSITY CIRCLE

Some diversity trainers use the *diversity circle* exercise to help workers appreciate diversity and overcome misperceptions. The exercise adapts well for classroom use. Form a group of about ten students. Arrange your chairs into a circle, and put one additional chair in the center of the circle. A "diverse" group member volunteers to sit in the center chair and become the first "awareness subject." Because most people are diverse in some way, most people are eligible to occupy the center chair.

The person in the center tells the others how he or she has felt about being diverse or different and how people have reacted to his or her diversity. For example, an Inuit described how fellow workers were hesitant to ask him out for a beer, worrying whether he could handle alcohol.

An equally effective alternative to this procedure is for each class member to come up in front of the class to describe a significant way in which he or she is

*(Continued)*

different. After each class member has presented, a discussion might be held of observations and interpretations.

What lessons did you learn about interpersonal relations from this exercise that will help you be a more effective leader?

A frequently mentioned concern about diversity training is that it reinforces stereotypes about groups. Participants are informed about group differences, such as cultural values, and tactics might be suggested for coping with these differences—such as using more body language when relating to Latinos.

Leaders of diversity training exercises are cautioned to guard against encouraging participants to be too confrontational and expressing too much hostility. Companies have found that when employees are too blunt during these sessions, it may be difficult to patch up interpersonal relations in the work group later on. Sometimes the diversity trainer encourages group members to engage in outrageous behavior, such as by having women sexually harass men so the men "know what it feels like." Key themes of negative reactions to diversity training are charges of "political correctness" and "white-male bashing."

Based on a review of relevant studies and theory, Patricia L. Nemetz and Sandra L. Christensen concluded that diversity training is most likely to lead to behavioral and attitudinal change under three conditions: (1) participants have not yet committed to strong views of their own based on long-standing paradigms; (2) a conflicting informal influence (such as peer pressure) is not present; and (3) the organizational culture supports a well-defined ideal of multiculturalism.[34]

---

college.hmco.com/pic/
dubrin5e

🔣 **@ KNOWLEDGE BANK:** contains some comments by leadership at Progress Energy, Inc., about their diversity efforts.

---

### Conduct Intercultural Training

For many years, companies and government agencies have prepared their managers and other workers for overseas assignments. The method frequently chosen is **intercultural training**, a set of learning experiences designed to help employees understand the customs, traditions, and beliefs of another language. Foreign language training is often included in cultural training. Table 14-3 illustrates how English can be spoken differently across English-speaking countries. (The information in the table has been included in cultural training.) The multicultural leader needs to know that English is spoken differently in the United States, Great Britain, Australia, and South Africa, among other countries.

A recent development in intercultural training is to train global leaders in cultural intelligence. Following the model of cultural intelligence described earlier in this chapter, global managers receive training in the cognitive, physical, and emotional or motivational domains. The training is highly complex, with the leader being expected

| TABLE 14-3 | **English-to-English Dictionary** |
|---|---|

| BRITONS SAY . . . | AMERICANS SAY . . . |
|---|---|
| At the end of the day | The bottom line is (Many Americans now use the phrase "At the end of the day.") |
| Bank holiday | National holiday |
| Holidays or hols | Vacation |
| Scheme | Plan or program |
| Keen | Enthusiastic |
| To table (an idea) | To put (an idea) out for discussion |
| To put (an idea) aside | To table (an idea) |
| Elevenses | Late morning snack |
| Up to you, really | Do not do it/proceed with caution/have another look at it |
| To ring up | To telephone |
| To knock up* | To visit |
| Fortnight | Two weeks |
| To strike out | To go after something |
| To fail | To strike out |
| Being sent to Coventry | Being ignored |
| Made redundant | Laid off |
| Been given the sack, sacked | Fired |
| Aggro | Trouble |
| Pear-shaped | Disaster |
| To throw a wobbly | To have a tantrum |
| Taking the mickey | Making fun of |
| Car park | Parking lot |
| Lift | Elevator |
| Not bad | Very good |
| Not good | Very bad |

*A caution for Britons visiting the United States is that "to knock up" means to impregnate a woman, illustrating that everyday expressions in one language might be perceived as curious or offensive in another country.

Source: DeeDee Doke, "Perfect Strangers," *HR Magazine*, December 2004, p. 64. Copyright 2004 by the Society for Human Resource Management. Reproduced with permission of *HR Magazine* published by the Society for Human Resource Management, Alexandria, VA, in the format Textbook via Copyright Clearance Center.

to learn dozens of different concepts and behaviors, as well as insights. A sampling of what training in cultural intelligence involves is as follows:[35]

> A Canadian manager is attempting to interpret a "Thai smile." First, she needs to observe the various cues provided in addition to the smile gesture itself (for example, other facial or bodily gestures, significance of others who may be in proximity, the source of the original smile gesture) and to assemble them into a meaningful whole and make sense of what is really experienced by the Thai employee. Second, she must

have the requisite motivation (directed effort and self-confidence) to persist in the face of confusion, challenge, or apparently mixed signals. Third, she must choose, generate, and execute the right actions to respond appropriately.

If any of these elements is deficient, she is likely to be ineffective in dealing with the Thai employee. A high CQ manager has the capability with all three facets as they act in unison.

Again, cultural intelligence is a refinement of cultural sensitivity. The international leader who remains alert to cues in the environment can go a long way toward building relationships with people from different cultures.

### Encourage the Development of Employee Networks

Another leadership initiative toward recognizing cultural differences is to permit and encourage employees to form **employee network groups**. The network group is composed of employees throughout the company who affiliate on the basis of a group characteristic such as race, ethnicity, sex, sexual orientation, or physical ability status. Group members typically have similar interests and look to the groups as a way of sharing information about succeeding in the organization. Although some human resources specialists are concerned that network groups can lead to divisiveness, others believe they play a positive role.

Dan Sapper, a divisional quality leader at Eastman Kodak Company, illustrates the potential contribution of an employee network group to an employee's well-being. Sapper felt relatively isolated when he began employment at Kodak. To widen his contacts within the company, he became a charter member of Kodak's group for gay and lesbian employees. Sapper now chairs the group's board and says he wants to keep his leadership role to help employees who "might be in my shoes in the future." These are employees who "may be thinking of 'coming out'" or employees who "left something of themselves at the gate when they entered work."[36]

### Avoid Group Characteristics When Hiring for Person–Organization Fit

An important consideration in employee recruitment and hiring is to find a good *person–organization fit*, the compatibility of the individual with the organization. The compatibility often centers on the extent to which a person's major work-related values and personality traits fit major elements of the organization culture. Following this idea, a person who is adventuresome and prone to risk taking would achieve highest performance and satisfaction where adventuresome behavior and risk taking are valued. Conversely, a methodical and conservative individual should join a slow-moving bureaucracy.

Many business firms today are investing time and effort into recruiting and hiring employees who show a good person–organization fit. A selection strategy of this type can lead to a cohesive and strong organizational culture. The danger, however, is that when employers focus too sharply on cultural fit in the hiring process, they might inadvertently discriminate against protected classes of workers. Specifically, the hiring manager might focus on superficial aspects of conformity to culture, such as physical appearance and which schools the candidates attended. Selecting candidates who look alike and act alike conflicts with a diversity strategy. Elaine Fox, a labor and employment attorney, cautions that "one of the biggest problems that can occur when hiring based on culture is if the culture you're comfortable with doesn't open the way for women and minorities."[37]

Leaders can take the initiative to guard against this problem. The way to circumvent it is to avoid using group characteristics (such as race, sex, ethnicity, or physical status) in assessing person–organization fit. The alternative is to focus on traits and behaviors, such as intelligence or ability to be a team player. Leaders at Microsoft emphasize hiring intelligent people only because bright people fit their culture best. Being intelligent is an individual difference rather than a group characteristic.

## Developing the Multicultural Organization

The leadership initiatives just reviewed strongly contribute to valuing diversity. An even more comprehensive strategy is to establish a **multicultural organization**. Such a firm values cultural diversity and is willing to encourage and even capitalize on such diversity. Developing a multicultural organization helps achieve the benefits of valuing diversity described previously. In addition, the multicultural organization helps avoid problems stemming from diversity, such as increased turnover, interpersonal conflict, and communication breakdowns.

According to Taylor Cox, the multicultural organization has six key characteristics, all of which require effective leadership.[38] A seventh characteristic, having a culturally diverse group of leaders, also merits consideration.[39] These characteristics are shown in Figure 14-4 and summarized next.

1. *Creating pluralism.* In a pluralistic organization, both minority- and majority-group members are influential in creating behavioral norms, values, and policies. Diversity training is a major technique for achieving pluralism. Another useful technique is to encourage employees to be conversant in a second language spoken by many coworkers, customers, or both.

2. *Achieving leadership diversity.* To achieve a multicultural organization, firms must also practice leadership diversity—that is, have a culturally heterogeneous group of leaders. Many global firms have already achieved leadership diversity with respect to ethnicity. Sex is another key area for leadership diversity, with many organizations today having women in top executive positions. An organization with true **leadership diversity** also has a heterogeneous group of leaders in such positions as supervisors, middle managers, and team leaders.

3. *Creating full structural integration.* The objective of full structural integration is a zero correlation between culture-group identity and job status; that is, no one should be assigned to a specific job just because of his or her ethnicity or gender. One approach to achieving full structural integration is to upgrade the education of minority-group members where needed. Affirmative action programs and career development programs also help achieve integration. The firm's performance evaluation and reward systems should reinforce the importance of effectively managing for diversity.

4. *Creating full integration of informal networks.* Because minorities are often excluded from informal networks, it is difficult for them to achieve career advancement.

**FIGURE 14-4 The Multicultural Organization**

Several things can help integrate informal networks: company-sponsored mentoring programs that target minorities; company-sponsored social events that minorities are encouraged to attend; and the creation of employee networks within an organization, provided they do not foster a "minority-versus-majority" attitude. Xerox Corporation's Hispanic Professional Association is a positive example of a minority association within a company.

5. *Creating a prejudice- and discrimination-free organization.* Since bias and prejudice create discrimination, organizational efforts to reduce bias help prevent discrimination. Some companies create task forces that monitor organizational policy and practices for evidence of unfairness.

6. *Organizational identification.* In a multicultural organization, there is a zero correlation between the cultural identity group and the levels of organizational identification. This would mean, for example, that Asians would identify as strongly with the organization as would white males. All of the techniques mentioned in the other five steps help foster such strong identification.

7. *Minimizing intergroup conflict.* To achieve a multicultural organization, conflict must be at healthy levels. Taylor Cox believes that the most effective approach to minimizing conflict among cultural groups is to collect and share data about sensitive issues. Corning Incorporated, for example, at one time collected data to help white males understand that diversity programs had not adversely affected their promotion rates.

**READER'S ROADMAP**

So far we have studied the nature of leadership, the attributes, behaviors, and styles of leaders, the ethics and social responsibility of leaders, and how leaders exert power and use politics and influence. We then studied techniques for developing teamwork as well as motivation and coaching skills. After studying creativity and innovation as part of leadership, we focused on communication skills as they relate to leadership. We then shifted our attention to strategic leadership, after which we discussed another broad challenge facing leaders: dealing with cultural diversity within the organization and across borders. Next, we deal with the capstone topic of developing leaders and choosing successors for executives.

## Summary

college.hmco.com/pic/dubrin5e

The modern leader must be multicultural because corporate success, profit, and growth depend increasingly on the management of a diverse work force. The ethical and social responsibility goals of leaders and their organizations include providing adequately for the members of the diverse work force.

Managing for diversity brings a competitive advantage to the firm in several ways. Turnover and absenteeism costs may be lower because minorities are more satisfied. Marketing can be improved because a representational work force facilitates selling products and services, and a good reputation for diversity management may attract customers. Companies with a favorable record in managing diversity are at an advantage in recruiting and retaining talented minority-group members. Managing diversity also helps unlock the potential for excellence among employees who might otherwise be overlooked. A heterogeneous work force may also offer an advantage in creativity and problem solving. Research at the U.S. Postal Service documents the many advantages of diversity.

To influence, motivate, and inspire culturally diverse people, the leader must be aware of overt and subtle cultural differences. Differences in cultural values help explain differences among people. Eight of these values are as follows: degree of individualism or collectivism, power distance (how much the power hierarchy is accepted), uncertainty avoidance, materialism versus concern for others, long-term versus short-term orientation, degree of formality, time orientation, and work orientation.

Cultural values influence leadership style as well as the behavior of other workers. For example, French managers believe in a class system. Another way to understand how culture influences leadership is to compare leadership styles across cultural groups. For Malaysian managers, the preferred organizational leadership style is to show compassion while at the same time being more autocratic than participative. Cultural differences in leadership style within the same country exist also, such as the stereotype of U.S. Southern managers being more interested in building relationships than their Northern counterparts.

Cultural sensitivity is essential for inspiring people from different cultures. Part of this sensitivity is the leader's willingness to acquire knowledge about local customs and to learn to speak the native language. A person with cultural sensitivity will recognize certain nuances in customs that help him or her build better relationships with people from different cultures. Cultural misunderstandings tend to cluster in five key areas: language differences, religious differences, work habits, women's roles, and personal appearance and behavior. Cultural intelligence helps an outsider interpret someone's unfamiliar and ambiguous gestures the way that person's compatriots would. Such intelligence has three facets: cognitive (head), physical (body), and emotional/motivational (heart).

Global leadership skills help improve a company's reputation and contribute to a sustainable competitive advantage. Behavioral complexity helps a leader attain high organizational performance. Stewardship is also important. To tap into universal needs, global leaders should satisfy three metavalues: community, pleasure, and meaning.

Top management commitment to valuing diversity is clearest when valuing diversity is embedded in organizational strategy. Specific leadership initiatives for valuing diversity can be divided into five categories: (1) hold managers accountable for diversity; (2) estab-lish minority recruitment, retention, and mentoring programs; (3) conduct diversity training; (4) conduct intercultural training, (5) encourage the development of employee networks; and (6) avoid group characteristics when hiring for person–organization fit.

A comprehensive strategy for valuing diversity is to establish a multicultural organization. Such a firm values cultural diversity and is willing to encourage such diversity. A multicultural organization has seven key characteristics: pluralism, leadership diversity, full structural integration, full integration of informal networks, absence of prejudice and discrimination, no identification gap based on cultural identity groups, and low levels of intergroup conflict.

## Key Terms

Multicultural leader

Individualism

Collectivism

Power distance

Uncertainty avoidance

Materialism

Concern for others

Long-term orientation

Short-term orientation

Formality

Informality

Urgent time orientation

Casual time orientation

Cultural sensitivity

Multicultural worker

Cultural intelligence (CQ)

Diversity training

Intercultural training

Employee network groups

Multicultural organization

Leadership diversity

 ## Guidelines for Action and Skill Development

When asked for concrete advice for managers who want to do an effective job at diversity management, the human resource manager of a multicultural firm said: "Any manager starting a Diversity Program should be ready to walk the talk before embarking or the effort will backfire. The walk should be seen in communication, compensation, recruiting, committee membership, promotions, advertising, and family and work/life initiatives. Also, setting up a strong support system within the social structure of the organization is critical to success." The researchers who interviewed the manager add that using diversity solely as a public relations tool will not bring forth lasting organizational change aimed at achieving more inclusion.[40]

A caution in implementing diversity management is for managers and other interviewers not to go overboard in trying to make a minority-group member feel comfortable. "When interviewers try too hard to be black, Latin or Asian," says Martin de Campo, managing consultant with an executive search firm, "they come across as hokey." John Fujii, the president of a diversity recruiting firm, says, "The best way to make minority candidates feel comfortable is to make them feel that they have an equal opportunity to compete for a position. That's all they want."[41]

## Discussion Questions and Activities

1. Given that the U.S. work force is becoming increasingly Latino (or Hispanic), should managers all be required to speak and read Spanish?
2. How does the concept of diversity in organizations relate to *political correctness?*
3. The manager in charge of diversity is typically a minority-group member. How well do you think this practice contributes to the goal of having a culturally diverse and bias-free organization?
4. What actions might a leader take to demonstrate that his or her interest in diversity goes beyond rhetoric?
5. How does a culturally heterogeneous staff contribute to the leader's ability to make effective decisions?
6. Imagine that your company is going to establish a major facility in the Democratic Republic of the Congo, Africa. Explain whether or not you should give preference to hiring a Belgian Congo citizen to lead that operation.
7. Assume that an outstanding sales representative works for a company that considers it unethical to bribe officials to make a sale. The sales representative is about to close a major deal in a country where bribing is standard practice. Her commission will be $60,000 for a signed contract. What should the representative do if an official demands a $4,000 *gift* before closing the deal?
8. With so much business being conducted over the Internet, including email, why is it important to understand cross-cultural differences in values?
9. Suppose you are a team leader and one of your team members has a strong work ethic, based on his or her cultural values. Is it fair to assign this member much more work just because he or she is willing to work longer and harder than the other team members?
10. What can you do this week to help prepare yourself to become a multicultural leader?

## LEADERSHIP CASE PROBLEM A

### DOMINIQUE MERCIER, WHO ARE YOU REALLY?

On the job in Dakar, Senegal, she's Dominique Mercier—nattering in lilting French, working her headset eight hours a day, and hawking telephone services to Europeans. Come day's end, the accent drops, and Dominique's true identity stands revealed: Fatou Ndiaye, a 32-year-old Senegalese college graduate and one of thousands of operators dialing up the West from booming call centers in West Africa.

"When I applied for this job, I did not know what to expect," says Ndiaye, a supervisor watching over a dozen operators wearing Islamic headscarves, West African robes, and Western clothes. The women chatter away in the finest—faked—Parisian accents to consumers in France 3,700 miles to the north.

Across West Africa, varying degrees of instability, corruption, and decay long have scared outside businesses. But in countries that are managing to hold it together, low-cost African outsourcing is luring investors and jobs. The numbers, although not totaled, are clearly tiny compared with the hundreds of thousands of U.S. and European jobs migrating to India, China, Malaysia, and the Philippines, but the job figures are significant.

In Ghana, Affiliated Computer Services, Inc., of Texas has become one of the largest private employers in the English-speaking West African nation. In Accra, Ghana's capital, more than 1,700 employees process American health insurance claims around the clock. The forms are filled

*(Continued)*

out under supervision of Americans 8,000 miles away and electronically shipped to the United States via satellite.

Senegal, a bucolic former French colony boasting a rare African record of forty-four coup-free years since independence, is luring outsourcing from the Francophone world. Senegal's stability, low wages, and stock of young, educated employees attracted Ndiaye's employer, the French-Senegalese partnership of Premium Contact International. So did Senegal's infrastructure: a fiber-optic cable running from France gives the country strong telecommunications.

"Besides, here we can get the best and smoothest French accent," says call center deputy manager Abdoulaye M'boup.

Yet occasional glitches do occur with having a call center in Senegal serving European customers. One day a customer from a suburb of Paris detected that a call center representative had a slight African accent. The customer asked, "How is the weather today in Dakar, and why are you taking a job away from a French citizen?"

## QUESTIONS

1. What is your feeling about the ethics of a Senegalese worker pretending to be "Dominique Mercier"?
2. How should leadership at a European telecom company deal with the problem of the occasional complaint about the call center being located in Africa?
3. What other services do you recommend these African firms offer the rest of the world?

# LEADERSHIP CASE PROBLEM B

## RALPH LAUREN SEEKS RACIAL HARMONY

Fashion magnate Ralph Lauren says he first became aware of racial tension within his company after an incident in 1997 at a Long Island sportswear boutique. A regional manager with Polo Ralph Lauren Corporation dropped by the new Polo Sport store in anticipation of an inspection by an important visitor: Jerome Lauren, Ralph's older brother and the executive overseeing Polo menswear. The Roosevelt Field Mall where the boutique was located attracts a middle-class, racially integrated clientele. But apparently the regional manager was afraid that the store's ambiance was too "urban." He ordered two black and two Latino sales associates off the floor and back into the stock room so they would not be visible to Mr. Lauren, according to Polo ex-officials. The sales associates followed orders, but they later hired a lawyer and threatened to sue Polo for discrimination. The company reached confidential settlements.

Ralph Lauren says he learned about the incident several weeks after it happened and "was just sick" about it. The regional manager, Greg Ladley, was ordered to undergo racial-relations training but was not fired. A company spokesman says that Ladley's recollection is that some sales associates working on inventory were asked to move to the stock room because they were not "dressed appropriately."

After the episode, Ralph Lauren told subordinates, "We have to correct this. Let's make a change." But executives who worked at Polo at the time say their boss did not make clear what changes he wanted.

**AIR OF EXCLUSIVENESS** Polo, like some of its rivals, presents a multiracial face to the world, with black models in some of its ads and a following of young black consumers wearing its familiar logo of a horseman wielding a polo mallet. Yet internally, big fashion houses tend to exude an exclusiveness that is uninviting to many nonwhites. Few blacks or Latinos have penetrated the upper ranks of major clothes manufacturers and retailers.

In response to complaints that have flared up at Polo over the last five years, Lauren has met with lawyers, hired lieutenants to overhaul company personnel practices, and embraced diversity training. But he says he has left the details to others, since he is usually preoccupied with design work at his headquarters studio. "For me it has always been about the clothes," he says.

Polo is the standard-bearer for American fashion's fantasy of life-as-country-club. In much of its advertising and retailing, the company sells clothes, home furnishings, and cosmetics with images of old-money privilege: English country mansions, and prep school reunions and summers on Nantucket. British accents, even among American employees, are not rare.

This aura of Anglo-Saxon elitism is the elaborate creation of Polo's founder, Ralph Lauren, 62 years old, who remade himself as he rose from modest roots in the Bronx to become the chairman and CEO of a fashion powerhouse. As teenagers in the late 1950s, he and his brother, Jerome, 67, Americanized their last name from the Russian *Lifshitz*. Polo retail supervisors routinely tell salespeople to think Hollywood. "Ralph is the director," the instruction goes, "and you are the actors, and we are here to make a movie." But some black and Latino employees say the movie seems to lack parts for them.

In August 2001, the Equal Employment Opportunity Commission (EEOC) cleared the way for a private discrimination suit by a pair of ex-Polo employees. The agency's letter of determination said that "testimony from several witnesses suggests that [Polo] managers sought to maintain a 'blond-hair-and-blue-eyes' image of employees, who often advanced the image over more qualified and experienced minority employees." Mitchell Kosh, Polo's senior vice president for human resources, says the agency "never asked us to do anything specific." The EEOC was impressed by "the programs and diversity initiatives we had put in place," he adds. Some argue that it is not unusual for discrimination claims to crop up from time to time in a company the size of Polo, which has 10,000 employees worldwide.

**COLOR-BLIND?** Lauren says he is color-blind when it comes to hiring talent. He frequently points out the wide visibility he has given Tyson Beckford, the striking, shaven-headed, black fashion model who has appeared in Polo ads since 1994. "Tyson is not just in jeans," Lauren says. "We put him in a pinstripe suit, in our best Purple Label brand. Tyson is in the annual report, in our advertisements on TV."

However, Polo declines to provide the de facto makeup of its work force or executive ranks. At least 3 black or Latino executives hold the rank of vice president, or higher, out of a total of more than 100. In 2001, Polo appointed the firm's minority director to its ten-member board: Joyce Brown, president of the Fashion Institute of Technology in New York.

Lauren says Polo "is a leader to do the right things to bring in the people who are the best in the industry." Some of his subordinates complain, however, that it is difficult to find black and Latino applicants with the credentials for design jobs coming out of the New York fashion schools where Polo usually recruits.

A Polo staffer recommended in 1998 that Lauren meet Lacey Moore, a 20-year-old African American from Brooklyn who had taken some college-level communications courses and had

*(Continued)*

aspirations to be in the music business. Since high school, Moore had worn Polo Oxford shirts and knit tops with flashy gold chains and a hip-hop attitude: precisely the sort of hybrid image Lauren hoped would draw younger customers: "Lacey is edgy—he gets it," Mr. Lauren recalls thinking, snapping his fingers for effect. He hired the young man as a design assistant.

The new recruit's rap-influenced personal style and lingo confounded his coworkers. Moore felt isolated. He says he understood that in any competitive workplace "there are people who don't like you." But in Polo's cliquish and overwhelmingly white Madison Avenue headquarters, he says coworkers made it clear he was not welcome. "I kept getting this bad vibe," he says. He quit in 2000.

Shocked, Lauren telephoned Moore at home. "Lacey, I want you to come back," he recalls saying. After listening to Moore's complaints, Lauren says he made it clear to the young man's white coworkers, "I want you all to work this out." A couple of weeks later, Moore returned, but warily.

**ADVICE AND PRESSURE**   Polo has received advice and pressure on the race issue from a variety of outside counselors and advocates. A civil rights authority advised Lauren that achieving a truly diverse work force requires hiring more than a few black employees. A black activist minister met with Polo officials and helped some minority workers reach confidential settlements with the company.

Roger Farah was hired into the company as chief operating officer in 1999. Soon Farah introduced Polo's first formal policies for job postings and employee reviews, as well as a toll-free hot line for employee complaints. Two human resource managers were hired; one is Paul Campbell, an African American with experience in handling racial issues. Campbell soon became a company vice president. Lauren also hired diversity expert Roosevelt Thomas to conduct a series of two-day race relation seminars. A message communicated in these seminars, as well as by Lauren, is that to get along in the office, you do not have to like another person—or even abandon negative stereotypes of a person's ethnic group. But you have to be tolerant.

Today Moore (the young design assistant) says his colleagues seem friendlier. Campbell, the human resources vice president, has given Moore reassurance. "You feel there is someone looking out for you," says the young assistant, who helps prepare for fashion shows and consults on clothing design.

Lauren says he is paying more attention to what he sees at work. For example, he recalls that at a company Christmas party in 2000 he was surprised that a group of blacks and Latinos had congregated in a separate room. "Why is this happening?" he wondered. "What's not welcoming to those employees?" Lauren says he did not approach his workers to ask them, however, and is still wondering about the answers to those questions.

## QUESTIONS

1. To what extent is Ralph Lauren on the right track to developing a multicultural organization?

2. What further advice can you offer Lauren to achieve fuller workplace diversity at Polo?

3. Is the Christmas party incident a symptom of an organizational problem? Or were the black and Latino employees just behaving as they chose?

4. Does Ralph Lauren "get it" as a leader with respect to cultural diversity in the workplace?

SOURCE: Adapted from Teri Agins, "Color Line: A Fashion House with an Elite Aura Wrestles with Race," *The Wall Street Journal*, August 19, 2002, pp. A1, A9.

## MY LEADERSHIP PORTFOLIO

To be an effective cross-cultural leader you need to work effectively with people from demographic and cultural groups different from your own. Describe what experiences you have had lately in working and/or relating effectively to a person quite different from you. If you have not had such an experience, take the initiative during the next week to relate meaningfully to a person quite different from you in terms of culture or demographic group membership. Finance major Stephanie had this to say:

> Claire, a special ed teacher, lives on my block. Claire goes to work every school day in spite of being legally blind. She can read with visual assists, including reading what is on her computer screen. Yet paper forms are difficult for Claire to navigate. I telephoned Claire one night and asked her if she could use my assistance in preparing her income tax this year. Claire agreed, and it worked out well. I now feel more comfortable working side by side with a visually handicapped person. Also, I picked up some practical experience in preparing a complicated tax form.

## INTERNET SKILL-BUILDING EXERCISE

Apply the chapter concepts! Visit the Web and complete this Internet skill-building exercise to learn more about current leadership topics and trends.

### TEST YOURSELF FOR HIDDEN BIAS

To be an effective multicultural leader and to promote diversity, it is helpful to be aware of your own biases. Visit *www.tolerance.org/hidden_bias*, a web project of the Southern Poverty Law Center. Go to Test Yourself for Hidden Biases. Created by psychologists at Yale University and the University of Washington, this collection of Implicit Association Tests claims to measure unconscious bias in the following eleven areas: Native Americans; sexual orientation; six types of racial bias (Arab Muslims, weapons, black/white children, black/white adults, skin tone, Asian Americans); age bias; gender bias; body image bias. After reflecting on the results of these tests, what ideas did you gather that might help you be less biased in your dealings with other people in the workplace?

# Leadership Development and Succession

When consulting firm Deloitte & Touche LLP instituted a reverse mentoring program several years ago, 48-year-old Jim Wall, its national managing director for human resources, found himself tapping the wisdom of a 26-year-old associate consultant.

According to Wall, many participating executives were surprised by how quickly the mentoring led to valuable insights into how both younger staffers and the marketplace perceived the firm. "The big muckety-mucks sometimes lose connection with the crowd and forget what it's like to be out in the trenches," he says.

For his part, Wall says private tutoring helped him expand his Internet proficiency and get a better handle on the daily torrent of email. He even received constructive criticism on his management style. The relationship continues. "It turns into a mutual mentoring," he says.[1]

---

The anecdote about the middle-aged human resources executive being mentored by a person twenty-two years his junior, and also mentoring the junior person in return, illustrates one of the many ways in which leaders grow and develop. Because so many people are expected to exert leadership, programs to develop leadership are provided today to all levels of management, and sometimes also to staff professionals. These programs enhance leadership effectiveness and, by showing the organization's commitment to leadership development, also help organizations attract talented employees.

The previous chapters in this book have included information and activities designed to develop leaders and enhance their effectiveness. This chapter describes how self-development can enhance leadership effectiveness, as well as the processes organizations use to develop present and future leaders. Such activities and processes are typically referred to as leadership development, or management development.

In addition to describing various approaches to leadership development, this chapter also describes leadership succession. Leadership succession is included here because an important part of leadership development is being groomed for promotion. The text concludes with a glimpse of the next generation of leaders.

## Development Through Self-Awareness and Self-Discipline

Leadership development is often perceived in terms of education and training, job experience, and coaching. Nevertheless, self-help also contributes heavily to developing leadership capabilities. Self-help takes many forms, including working on one's own to improve communication skills, to develop charisma, and to model the behavior of effective leaders. Two major components of leadership self-development are self-awareness and self-discipline.

### Leadership Development Through Self-Awareness

An important mechanism underlying self-development is **self-awareness**, insightfully processing feedback about oneself to improve one's effectiveness. According to two specialists in leadership assessment, many big mistakes in careers and organizations result from gaps in self-awareness.[2] For example, a managerial leader might observe that three key group members left her group over a six-month time span. The leader might defensively dismiss this fact with an analysis such as, "I guess we just don't pay well enough to keep good people." Her first analysis might be correct. With a self-awareness orientation, however, the leader would dig deeper for the reasons behind the turnover. She might ask herself, "Is there something in my leadership approach that creates turnover problems?" She might ask for exit-interview data to sharpen her perceptions about her leadership approach.

Chris Argyris has coined the terms *single-loop learning* and *double-loop learning* to differentiate between levels of self-awareness.[3] **Single-loop learning** occurs when learners seek minimum feedback that might substantially confront their basic ideas or actions. As in the example of the high-turnover leader, single-loop learners engage in defensive thinking and tend not to act on the clues they receive. Argyris offers the example of a thermostat that automatically turns on the heat whenever the room temperature drops below 68 degrees Fahrenheit (20 degrees Celsius).

**Double-loop learning** is an in-depth type of learning that occurs when people use feedback to confront the validity of the goal or the values implicit in the situation. The leader mentioned above was engaged in double-loop learning when she questioned the efficacy of her leadership approach. To achieve double-loop learning, one must minimize defensive thinking. Many people are blind to their incompetencies and do not know their vision is blocked. Argyris explains that a double-loop learning thermostat would ask, "Why am I set at 68 degrees?" The thermostat would then ask whether another temperature might more economically achieve the goal of heating the room. Figure 15-1 illustrates the difference between single-loop and double-loop learning.

An important contribution of double-loop learning is that it enables the leader to learn and profit from setbacks. Interpreting the reason that a setback occurred may help the leader to do better the next time. Faced with a group in crisis, a leader might establish a vision of better days ahead for group members. The leader observes that

**FIGURE 15-1 Single-Loop Learning Versus Double-Loop Learning**

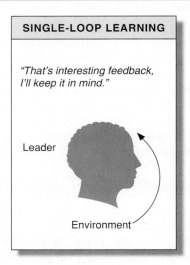

**SINGLE-LOOP LEARNING**

*"That's interesting feedback, I'll keep it in mind."*

Leader

Environment

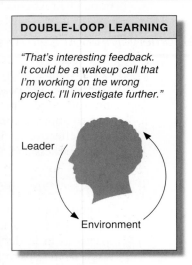

**DOUBLE-LOOP LEARNING**

*"That's interesting feedback. It could be a wakeup call that I'm working on the wrong project. I'll investigate further."*

Leader

Environment

the vision leads to no observable changes in performance and behavior. Perhaps the group was not ready for a vision. In a comparable situation in the future, the leader might hold back on formulating a vision until the group is headed out of the crisis.

## Leadership Development Through Self-Discipline

As with other types of personal development, leadership development requires considerable self-discipline. In the present context, **self-discipline** is mobilizing one's effort and energy to stay focused on attaining an important goal. Self-discipline is required for most forms of leadership development. Assume, for example, that a leader is convinced that active listening is an important leadership behavior. The leader reads about active listening and also attends a workshop on the subject. After the reading and workshop are completed, the leader will need to concentrate diligently in order to remember to listen actively. Self-discipline is particularly necessary because the pressures of everyday activities often divert a person's attention from personal development.

Self-discipline plays an important role in the continuous monitoring of one's behavior to ensure that needed self-development occurs. After one identifies a developmental need, it is necessary to periodically review whether one is making the necessary improvements. Assume that a person recognizes the developmental need to become a more colorful communicator as a way of enhancing charisma. The person would need self-discipline to make the conscious effort to communicate more colorfully when placed in an appropriate situation. Leadership Self-Assessment Quiz 15-1 contains an interpersonal skills checklist that will help you identify your own developmental needs related to interpersonal relationships.

LEADERSHIP SELF-ASSESSMENT QUIZ 15-1

### THE INTERPERSONAL SKILLS CHECKLIST

INSTRUCTIONS Below are a number of specific aspects of behavior that suggest that a person needs to improve his or her interpersonal skills related to leadership and influence. Check each statement that is generally true for you. You can add to the reliability of this exercise by asking one or two other people who know you well to rate you. Then compare your self-analysis with their analysis of you.

**Developmental Needs and Areas for Improvement**

1. I am too shy and reserved. _____

2. I bully and intimidate others too frequently. _____

3. I tell others what they want to hear rather than emphasizing the truth. _____

4. I have trouble expressing my feelings. _____

*(Continued)*

**5.** I make negative comments about group members too readily. _____

**6.** Very few people pay attention to the ideas I contribute during a meeting. _____

**7.** My personality is not colorful enough. _____

**8.** People find me boring. _____

**9.** I pay too little attention to the meaning behind what team members and coworkers are saying. _____

**10.** It is very difficult for me to criticize others. _____

**11.** I am too serious most of the time. _____

**12.** I avoid controversy in dealing with others. _____

**13.** I do not get my point across well. _____

**14.** It is difficult for me to make small talk with others. _____

**15.** I boast too much about my accomplishments. _____

**16.** I strive too much for individual recognition instead of looking to credit the team. _____

**17.** Self-confidence is my weak point. _____

**18.** My spoken messages are too bland. _____

**19.** My written messages are too bland. _____

**20.** I relate poorly to people from cultures different from my own. _____

**21.** I read people poorly. _____

**22.** I display a lot of nervous mannerisms when I am working in a group. _____

**23.** I do a poor job of making a presentation in front of others. _____

**24.** _____
(Fill in your own statement.)

Now that you (and perhaps one or two others) have identified specific behaviors that may require change, draw up an action plan. Describe briefly a plan of attack for bringing about the change you hope to achieve for each statement that is checked. Ideas might come from personal development books or from human relations and leadership development workshops. After formulating an action plan, you will need self-discipline for its successful implementation. For example, if you checked, "People find me boring," you might want to expand your fund of knowledge by extensive reading and by talking to dynamic people.

You will then need the self-discipline to continue your quest for ideas and to incorporate some of these ideas into your conversation.

Another approach to this exercise is for each student to choose one developmental need, combined with an action plan, that he or she is willing to share with others. Next, students present their developmental need and action plan to the rest of the class. After all students have presented, a class discussion is held about whatever observations and generalizations students have reached.

## Development Through Education, Experience, and Mentoring

Much of leadership development takes place through means other than self-awareness and self-discipline or leadership development programs. Leadership is such a comprehensive process that almost any life activity can help people prepare for a leadership role. The president and owner of a large residential and commercial heating and cooling company made these comments:

> One of my best preparations for running a company came from my early days as a waiter. I learned how to handle difficult people and how to accept compliments. I also learned how to persuade people to make choices on the menu that gave them pleasure and increased the restaurant's profits. Those lessons are all important in running a $45 million business.

Three important life and work experiences that contribute to leadership development are education, experience as a leader, and mentoring. In the next several pages, we look at the link between each of these three factors and leadership.

### Education

Education generally refers to acquiring knowledge without concern about its immediate application. If a potential leader studies mathematics, the logical reasoning acquired might someday help him or her solve a complex problem facing the organization. As a result, the leader's stature is enhanced. Formal education is positively correlated with achieving managerial and leadership positions. Furthermore, there is a positive relationship between the amount of formal education and the level of leadership position attained.

The correlation between education and leadership status, however, may not reflect causation. Many people get the opportunity to hold a business leadership position *only if* they have achieved a specified level of education. A more important issue than the statistical association between leadership and formal education is *how* education contributes to leadership effectiveness.

Most high-level leaders are intelligent, well-informed people who gather knowledge throughout their career. The knowledge that accrues from formal education and self-study provides them with information for innovative problem solving. Being intellectually alert also helps them exert influence through logical persuasion.

### Experience

On-the-job experience is an obvious contributor to leadership effectiveness. Without experience, knowledge cannot readily be converted into skills. For example, you will need experience to put into practice the appropriate influence tactics you studied in Chapter 8. Leadership experience also helps build skills and insights that a person may not have formally studied.

**Challenging Experiences** Based on the research of Morgan W. McCall, the best experiences for leadership development are those that realistically challenge the manager. Creating an environment for development requires that an organization first rid itself of the belief in survival of the fittest. The goal of leadership development is to provide meaningful development opportunities, not to push managers to the point where they are most likely to fail.[4] An example of a stretch experience for many managers would be to be placed in charge of an organizational unit with low productivity and morale. The manager would need to apply many leadership skills to improve the situation.

Failure is a special type of challenging experience that contributes enormously to reaching one's leadership potential. One reason is that people who have never failed have avoided taking big risks. Richard Branson, the flamboyant chairman of Virgin Atlantic Airways Limited, claims that "the best developer of a leader is failure." An effective way of capitalizing on failure is to reflect on what you might do differently in the future. Ask yourself questions such as "What would have to change inside me to enable me to do things differently?"[5] For example, perhaps the project failed because you did not provide enough guidance to the group and did not communicate a sense of urgency. In the future, you might lead with more control and assertion.

Table 15-1 lists a number of powerful learning experiences for developing leadership and managerial skills.

An important part of capitalizing on challenging experiences is for the leader or manager to be given leeway in choosing how to resolve the problem. An interview study of 80,000 managers in more than 400 companies concluded that the best way to develop talent is to define the right outcomes and then encourage each person to find his or her own route toward those outcomes.[6] A team leader, for example, might be told, "Increase productivity by 10 percent, while at the same time decreasing costs by 10 percent." The team leader would have the developmental opportunity of finding a solution to this challenge.

**Sources of Experience** The two major developmental factors in any work situation are work associates and the task itself.[7] Work associates can help a person develop in myriad ways. An immediate superior can be a positive or negative model of effective leadership. You might observe how your boss skillfully confronts a cost overrun problem during a staff meeting. You observe carefully and plan to use a similar technique when it becomes necessary for you to confront a problem with a group. In contrast, assume that your boss's confrontational approach backfires and the group becomes defensive and recalcitrant. You have learned how *not* to confront. Members of upper management, peers, and reporting staff can also help a worker profit from experience. For example, by trial and error the worker might learn which type of praise is best for influencing others.

Work-related tasks can also contribute to leadership development because part of a leader's role is to be an effective and innovative problem solver. The tasks that do

| **TABLE 15-1** | **Powerful Learning Experiences for Developing Leadership Skills** |
|---|---|

Research with managers has revealed fifteen types of powerful learning experiences that contribute to one's development as a leader and manager.

1. *Unfamiliar responsibilities*. Responsibilities are new, quite different, or much broader than previous ones.

2. *Proving yourself*. There is pressure to show others that one can get the job done.

3. *Developing new directions*. The leader is responsible for starting something new, implementing a reorganization, or responding to rapid changes in the business environment.

4. *Inherited problems*. The manager must fix problems created by a former manager or is handed the responsibility for problem employees.

5. *Downsizing decisions*. The manager must make decisions about shutting down operations or reducing staff.

6. *Dealing with problem employees*. The group members lack adequate experience, are incompetent, or are resistant.

7. *Facing high stakes*. The manager is faced with tight deadlines, pressure from senior management, high visibility, and responsibility for success and failure.

8. *Managing business complexity*. The job is large in scope, and the manager is responsible for multiple functions, groups, products, customers, or markets.

9. *Role overload*. The size of the job requires a large investment of time and energy.

10. *Handling external pressure*. The manager is forced to deal with external factors that affect the business, such as negotiating with unions or government agencies or coping with serious community problems.

11. *Having to exert influence without authority*. To accomplish the job it is necessary to influence peers, higher management, external parties, or other key people over whom one has no formal control.

12. *Adverse business conditions*. The business unit faces a drop in revenues or a drastic budget cut.

13. *Lack of top management support*. Senior management is reluctant to provide direction, support, or resources for the manager's major work activities or for a new project.

14. *Lack of personal support*. The manager is excluded from key networks and receives little encouragement from others about the work activities.

15. *Difficult boss*. A personality clash with the boss is evident, or he or she is incompetent.

Source: Adapted from C. McCauley, M. Ruderman, P. Ohlott, and J. Morrow, "Assessing the Developmental Components of Managerial Jobs," *Journal of Applied Psychology* 79, 4 (1994), 544–560. Copyright © 1994 by the American Psychological Association. Adapted with permission.

most to foster development are those that are more complex and ambiguous than a person has faced previously. Starting a new activity for a firm, such as establishing a dealer network, exemplifies a developmental experience.

***Broad Experience*** Many aspects of leadership are situational. A sound approach to improving leadership effectiveness is therefore to gain managerial experience in different settings. An aspirant to executive leadership is well advised to gain management experience in at least two different organizational functions, such as marketing and operations. **Multifunctional managerial development** is an organization's intentional efforts to enhance the effectiveness of managers by giving them experience in multiple functions within the organization.[8]

As shown in Figure 15-2, the most modest level of commitment to multifunctional management development would be for managers merely to study other functions. Studying other functions, however, is quite useful because it provides a person with the necessary background to profit from experience. Participation in multifunctional task forces indicates more commitment to the acquisition of breadth.

The highest level of commitment is complete mobility across functions. For example, an employee may begin in product design and then move on to assignments in marketing, manufacturing, customer service, purchasing, human resources, and so forth. Employees judged to have leadership potential are the most likely to be offered complete mobility.

A growing practice is to assign managers to cross-functional teams to give them experience in working with other disciplines. The more urgent the purpose of the team, the more likely meaningful leadership development will take place. A case in point is the business incubator project at Schneider Electric SA, a company of 15,000 employees. The project selects about fifty high-potential employees to join "SWAT teams" that have the authority and capability to move quickly within the organization to find new opportunities and solve problems. The team leader works full-time at the project, whereas group members devote only a quarter of their time to the project. The company believes that the incubator project will become its primary sales-growth engine while giving high-potential employees experience that helps them to develop into future leaders.[9]

Achieving broad experience fits well with the current emphasis on growth through learning new skills rather than a preoccupation with vertical mobility. In one successful manufacturing company the most promising managers receive lateral transfers, including experience in the human resources department. The company also uses its

## FIGURE 15-2 Continuum of Practical Options for Multifunctional Managerial Development

**High commitment**

- Complete mobility across functions, i.e., "career maze"

- Temporary (six-month to two-year) assignments outside the person's "home function"

- Brief, orientational rotation through functions

- Exposure to other functions on task forces project teams

- Classroom education about other functions

**Low commitment**

Source: "Continuum of Practical Options for Multifunctional Managerial Development." Reprinted from *Organizational Dynamics*, Autumn 1992, Copyright © 1992, with permission from Elsevier Science.

most innovative manufacturing facilities as "hothouses" for developing managers. The innovative units become leadership development centers for the company.[10]

*Pivotal Life Experiences*  Another perspective on how experience contributes to leadership effectiveness is that certain pivotal events—often occurring early in life—help people recognize a capacity to make things happen and gain the support of others. These transformational experiences vary from being mentored to climbing a mountain or losing an election. The pivotal experience might be an event or a relationship, sad or joyous, but it is always a powerful process of learning and adaptation. A case in point is Jack Kahl, the founder and former CEO of the company that makes the Duck® brand of duct tape. He remarks that he learned his most crucial leadership experience from his mother when he was 7 years old. Kahl's father had fallen ill with tuberculosis, and his mother informed her children that they would have to work as a team to hold the family together financially and emotionally. Kahl started a newspaper route and quickly learned the importance of doing the job well and pleasing customers.[11]

The leadership portfolio that you have been maintaining will help you capitalize on experience as a source of leadership development.

### Mentoring

Another experience-based way to develop leadership capability is to be coached by an experienced, knowledgeable leader. Quite often this person is a **mentor**, a more experienced person who develops a protégé's abilities through tutoring, coaching, guidance, and emotional support. The mentor, a trusted counselor and guide, is typically a person's manager. However, a mentor can also be a staff professional or coworker. An emotional tie exists between the protégé (or mentee) and the mentor. To personalize the subject of mentoring, test your attitudes toward the process by taking Leadership Self-Assessment Quiz 15-2.

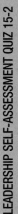

**LEADERSHIP SELF-ASSESSMENT QUIZ 15-2**

## MY ATTITUDES TOWARD MENTORING

INSTRUCTIONS: Answer "Generally Agree" or "Generally Disagree" to the ten statements below.

|  | Generally Agree | Generally Disagree |
|---|---|---|
| 1. Many times in life I have taught useful skills to younger family members or friends. | ☐ | ☐ |
| 2. Few people would be successful if somebody else had not given them a helping hand. | ☐ | ☐ |
| 3. I would enjoy (or have enjoyed) being a Big Brother or Big Sister. | ☐ | ☐ |

*(Continued)*

4. Experienced workers should be willing to show the ropes to less experienced workers.  ☐  ☐

5. I would like to be considered a good role model for others in my field.  ☐  ☐

6. I have very little concern that if I shared my knowledge with a less experienced person, he or she would replace me.  ☐  ☐

7. At least one of my teachers has been an inspirational force in my life.  ☐  ☐

8. I am willing to drop what I am doing to help somebody else with a work or study problem.  ☐  ☐

9. I am willing to share my ideas with others, even if I do not receive any credit.  ☐  ☐

10. Helping others contributes toward becoming immortal.  ☐  ☐

SCORING AND INTERPRETATION: This quiz does not have a precise scoring key. However the more of the above statements that you agree with, the more likely you have the proper mental set to be a mentor.

SOURCE: Andrew J. DuBrin, *Coaching and Mentoring Skills,* First Edition, © 2005, p. 161. Adapted with permission of Pearson Education, Inc., Upper Saddle River, NJ.

*Informal Versus Formal Mentoring* Mentoring is traditionally thought of as an informal relationship based on compatibility or spark between two personalities. In reality it is a widespread practice for employers to formally assign a mentor to a new employee to help him or her adjust well to the organization and to succeed. Belle Rose Ragins and John L. Cotton conducted a study comparing the effectiveness of informal versus formal mentoring programs for men and women.[12] Three occupations were studied: engineering (male dominated); social work (female dominated); and journalism (gender integrated). Formal mentoring programs were used in all three of these occupations.

Protégés with informal mentors received greater benefits than protégés with formal mentors. Informal mentors were also perceived as more effective. The protégés with informal mentors reported that their mentors provided more career development and psychological and social support than protégés with formal mentors. Protégés with informal mentors also reported higher incomes. A possible explanation for these findings is that people who are able to attract their own mentor are more career-driven and have the type of interpersonal skills that help one earn a higher income.

Three key human resource elements are associated with a successful mentoring program. First, the human resource department in conjunction with senior management needs to set the goals of the program and base its design on those goals. Second, the program administrators must carefully pair the mentors and protégés, set realistic expectations for both parties, and follow up with the pairs to ensure that the arrangement is satisfactory. Third, top management must be committed to the program.[13] An example of a realistic goal for a given protégé might be to develop better interpersonal and strategic leadership skills.

Another approach to mentoring is **shadowing**, or directly observing the work activities of the mentor by following the person around for a stated period of time, such as one day per month. The protégé might be invited to strategy meetings, visits with key customers, discussions with union leaders, and the like. The protégé makes observations about how the mentor handles situations, and a debriefing session might be held to discuss how and why certain tactics were used.

Ementoring is popular because sending email messages helps overcome barriers created by geography, limited time, and voice mail. The protégé might pose a career or work question to the mentor and receive back a helpful reply that day. Nevertheless, some face-to-face contact with a mentor is recommended to help keep the relationship vibrant.

*Impact on Leadership* Mentors enhance the career of protégés in many ways, such as by recommending them for promotion and helping them establish valuable contacts. A survey of large companies found that 96 percent of executives credited mentoring as an important developmental method, and 75 percent said mentoring played a key role in their career success.[14] High-level leaders sometimes use mentors as a way of obtaining useful feedback. For example, Melissa Dyrdhal, an Adobe systems executive, says she uses mentors because "they provide a mirror for me to reflect back on, presenting perspectives that I am unable or unwilling to see."[15] The roles of a coach and mentor can blur.

A high level of mentor involvement is to coach the apprentice on how he or she handles certain leadership assignments. The mentor is usually not physically present when the protégé is practicing leadership. A substitute is for the protégé to recap a leadership situation and ask for a critique. Wendy Lopez, who is the data processing manager for a payroll services firm, recounts a mentoring session with her boss about a leadership incident:

> I explained to Max [her mentor and the vice president of administration] that I had some trouble motivating my supervisors to pitch in with weekend work. We had received a surge of new clients because many firms had decided to downsize their own payroll departments. Our group was having trouble adjusting to the new workload. Instead of operations running smoothly, things were a little spastic. Although I tried to explain the importance of getting out the work, the supervisors were still dragging their heels a little.
>
> Max reviewed the incident with me. He told me that I might have helped the supervisors take a broader view of what this new business meant to the firm. Max felt I did not communicate clearly enough how the future of our firm was at stake. He also suggested that I should have been more specific about how pitching in during an emergency would benefit the supervisors financially.
>
> With Max's coaching behind me, I did a much better job of enlisting cooperation the next time an emergency surfaced.

A challenge in having a strong mentor is to at some point no longer be regarded as his or her protégé. The mentor may have given you credibility and connections for a long time, but at some point you have to get away from the mentor's shadow in order to be perceived as a leader with your own strengths. Detaching yourself from a strong mentor is often facilitated by a few accomplishments of your own, outside the jurisdiction of the mentor.[16] One mentee put it this way: "Until I joined another company, I could never overcome the reputation of being Ben's sidekick."

The accompanying Leader in Action will give you additional insight into how mentoring assists in a manager's development as a leader.

## LEADER IN ACTION

### CHARLENE BEGLEY, CEO OF GE TRANSPORTATION SYSTEMS, PROFITS FROM MENTORING

Charlene T. Begley, a 36-year-old mother of three, is president and CEO of GE Transportation Systems—the first woman to ever lead a major GE unit. She lives in Erie, Pennsylvania, and is taking on some of the biggest challenges facing General Electric Company, but she does not work weekends.

Jeffrey R. Immelt, the CEO of GE, has loudly pledged to make GE a model of diversity, especially in the senior ranks. Immelt says that Begley is just the most prominent of numerous female executives who are rising fast at the company. "We've got an excellent pipeline," he says. "But the only way I look at success in this area is [by] the percentage of women and minorities in leadership jobs."

Begley, who says she never encountered any sexism at the company en route to the top, is classic GE: impatient, smart, and driven to succeed. She even plays golf. After receiving a business degree in 1988 from the University of Vermont, Begley fought to get into the financial management program at GE. A friend's father had convinced her it was "the best company in the world."

She won the job and was sent straight to the industrial city of Erie, where she handled forecasting, accounting, and a range of other financial activities at the locomotive unit, GE Transportation

Systems, for a salary of $26,500. By 1990, she had joined the grueling but prestigious corporate audit staff. Her first assignment was to improve the methods for sourcing materials at GE Appliances in Louisville. "I had no clue what I was doing," says Begley, who recalls tears, extreme fatigue, and angst-ridden phone calls to her husband about how terribly she was handling the job. In fact, she won a management award after she completed the four-month project.

That put Begley on the fast track, which at GE means she has worked in twenty locations worldwide over fifteen years. "She is being tracked through the chairs that allowed other stars to rise," notes Peter Crist, an independent executive recruiter. The stints ranged from vice president of operations for GE Capital Mortgage Services, a job that required her to lay off nearly three-quarters of the staff shortly after she returned from a six-week maternity leave, to heading the audit staff and becoming, at age 32, the youngest corporate officer in GE history.

In that job she tried to make sure that people received better mentoring and assignments. She noticed, for example, that Japanese and Chinese employees tended to be quiet. So to build confidence she let them do initial audits in their home countries and tried to make sure "we weren't evaluating them on a style difference."

As someone who admits she often did not feel ready for the next promotion, Begley understands the value of a great mentor. Her biggest champion is David L. Calhoun, now president and CEO of GE Aircraft Engines. He recognized her talent when she worked for him on the audit staff, wooed her back to Erie to take over the Six Sigma quality initiative when he ran GE Transportation Systems, and then asked her to become its chief financial officer, despite what he calls a "skinny" background in finance. "She looked like a person with massive potential who just needed the right assignments," says Calhoun.

Begley always has been quick to seek out feedback and support. Linda Micowski, her eighth-grade teacher, recalls a girl who would linger after class to discuss everything from boys to her plan to be in the top 10 of her graduating high school class. Micowski, a mother figure who has also become one of Begley's best friends, even helped her buy a power suit for her first GE job.

GE has tried to institutionalize the same sort of assistance through its 16,000-member Women's Network. "I was initially against the network," says Begley. "I wanted no part of being treated differently because I'm a woman." She has since come to see its value in networking, mentoring, and promoting alternate routes to the top.

## QUESTIONS

1. In what way did Begley achieve broad experience on the route to the top?
2. In what way might the Women's Network help GE women advance their careers?
3. Which leadership traits and behaviors does Begley appear to possess?

SOURCE: Adapted from Diane Brady, "Crashing GE's Glass Ceiling," *BusinessWeek*, July 28, 2003, pp. 76–77.

## Leadership Development Programs

A time-honored strategy for developing prospective, new, and practicing leaders is to enroll them in leadership development programs. These programs typically focus on such topics as personal growth, strategy formulation, influence, motivation, persuasive communication, and diversity management. Outdoor and wilderness training, as described in Chapter 9, is one important type of leadership training. Many management development programs are also aimed at leadership development. The difference, however, is that management development programs offer courses that cover hundreds of topics within the functions of planning, organizing, controlling, and leading. Table 15-2 lists a sample of leadership development programs.

A term in vogue to cover company activities geared toward leadership and management development, as well as other forms of high-level training, is *corporate university*. As noted by HRevents™, corporate universities come in many forms. They range from training departments with a new sign on the door to massive organizations that strategically propel their corporate parent[17] (such as the GE facility in Crotonville, New York). Corporate universities use internal specialists as well as outside experts to conduct the training and development sessions.

Developing and training leaders is far more complex than merely sending aspiring leaders to a one-week seminar. The leadership development program has to be appropriately sponsored, carefully designed, and professionally executed.

| Table 15-2 | A Sampling of Leadership Development Programs Offered by Universities and Training and Development Firms |
|---|---|

The Executive Program (four-week program for senior executives involved in the strategic management of their firms)

Leadership: The New Challenges

Strategic Business Leadership: Creating and Delivering Value

Business Ethics for the Professional Manager

The Disney Approach to Leadership Excellence

Leading Change and Innovation

Leadership for an Uncertain Time

Leadership, Women

Implementing Successful Organizational Change

Managing People for Maximum Performance

The Essentials of Executive Decision Making

Developing Exemplary Leaders: Key Practices for Achieving Results

The Voice of Leadership: How Leaders Inspire, Influence, and Achieve Results

Outdoor Training

Note: Organizations offering such seminars and courses are the Wharton School of the University of Pennsylvania, the University of Michigan Business School, the University of Chicago Graduate School of Business, the Cornell University School of Industrial and Labor Relations, the Center for Creative Leadership, the Center for Management Research, the American Management Association, Dale Carnegie Training, the World Business Forum, the Cape Cod Institute, and the Disney Institute.

college.hmco.com/pic/
dubrin5e

**🏦 @ KNOWLEDGE BANK:** presents a description of key things that a leadership development program should do.

## Types of Leadership Development Programs

In practice, the various programs for developing leaders often overlap. For ease of comprehension, we divide these programs into seven categories: feedback-intensive programs, and those based on skills, conceptual knowledge, personal growth, socialization, action learning, and coaching and psychotherapy.

**Feedback-Intensive Programs**  As implied at many places in this text, an important vehicle for developing as a leader is to obtain feedback on various aspects of your behavior. A **feedback-intensive development program** helps leaders develop by seeing more clearly their patterns of behaviors, the reasons for such behaviors, and the impact of these behaviors and attitudes on their effectiveness. Such a program also helps leaders or potential leaders find more constructive ways of achieving their goals.

Feedback-intensive programs combine and balance three key elements of a developmental experience: assessment, challenge, and support. The program typically takes place in a classroom or conference room. At the Center for Creative Leadership, the program lasts six days. Assessment and feedback are almost constant, immersing participants in rich data about themselves and how they interact with others.[18] The amount and intensity of the feedback create intense challenges. Among them is the need to look inward, the discomfort of being observed and rated while engaging in such tasks as group problem solving, and encounters with new ideas. An example of uncomfortable feedback is being told that you are a poor delegator because you basically distrust most people.

To help participants cope with these challenges, the program provides intensive support from both the program staff and other participants. When the program goes well, a good team spirit develops among participants. Support continues after the program with follow-up letters by the staff and continued contact with program participants.

Feedback in the program comes from many sources, including interviews with the participant's boss, personality tests, leadership tests, and video tapings. Ratings by others, including 360-degree surveys, are included. The feedback is supposed to result in increased self-awareness. Combined with an explanation of the findings, the feedback often results in behavior change. For example, the person cited above may become more trustful of others and consequently a better delegator. Helping participants understand why they engage in certain behaviors contributes to the behavior change.

The Hasbro Global Leadership Development Program includes intensive feedback. (Hasbro's successes include Mr. Potato Head, G.I. Joe, Monopoly, and Scrabble.) Each participant receives a sealed envelope containing his or her individual 360-degree assessment report. No one but the participant sees the report. Each participant chooses at least one behavior he or she would like to change. The general manager of international brands at Hasbro, for example, found out that her blind spot was listening. She was a multitasker who is always doing three things at once, and therefore perceived as not listening. She said, "I learned that I need to stop what I am doing, look a person in the eye and focus on [him or her] when we talk to counteract that perception."[19]

**Skill-Based Programs** Skill training in leadership development involves acquiring abilities and techniques that can be converted into action. Acquiring knowledge precedes acquiring skills, but in skill-based training the emphasis is on learning how to apply knowledge. A typical example would be for a manager to develop coaching skills so he or she can be a more effective face-to-face leader. Skills training, in short, involves a considerable element of "how to."

Five different methods are often used in skill-based leadership training: lecture, case study, role play, behavioral role modeling, and simulations. Since the first three methods are quite familiar, only the last two are described here. *Behavioral role modeling* is an extension of role playing and is based on social learning theory. You first observe a model of appropriate behavior, and then you role-play the behavior and gather feedback. A person might observe a video of a trainer giving positive reinforcement, then role-play giving positive reinforcement. Finally, the classroom trainer and the other participants would offer feedback on performance.

*Simulations* give participants the opportunity to work on a problem that simulates a real organization. In a typical simulation participants receive a hard copy or computerized packet of information about a fictitious company. The participants are given details such as the organization chart, the company's financial status, descriptions of the various departments, and key problems facing the organization and/or organizational units. Participants then play the roles of company leaders and devise solutions to the problems. During the debriefing, participants receive feedback on the content of their solutions to problems and the methods they used. The group might be told, for example, "Your decision to form a strategic alliance was pretty good, but I would have liked to have seen more group decision making."

Anecdotal evidence suggests that skill training for leaders can have substantial pay-offs for the company. Electronic Arts Inc., a video-game developer, trains its leaders in various business skills. The vice president of human resources said, "One participant applied several newly learned business-analysis and negotiation techniques, and added millions in sales and increased profitability. This shows that the program is providing promotable, effective 'suits' who are making business contributions. And the 'creatives' are upgrading the entertainment value of products with ideas and practices from the program."[20]

*Conceptual Knowledge Programs* A standard university approach to leadership development is to equip people with a conceptual understanding of leadership. The concepts are typically supplemented by experiential activities such as role playing and cases. Non-university learning firms such as the American Management Association and the Brookings Institution also offer conceptually based leadership development programs. Conceptual knowledge is very important because it alerts the leader to information that will make a difference in leadership. For example, if a person studies how a leader brings about transformations, he or she can put these ideas into practice. The World Business Forum is a leadership development program for well-established managers that offers considerable conceptual knowledge. The presenters are well-known executives, business professors, and authors. One of the forum presenters is Jack Welch of General Electric, who offers suggestions about business strategy. Table 15-2 presents examples of the types of conceptual knowledge contained in leadership development programs.

*Personal Growth Programs* Leadership development programs that focus on personal growth assume that leaders are deeply in touch with their personal dreams and talents and that they will act to fulfill them. Therefore, if people can get in touch with their inner desires and fulfill them, they will become leaders. A tacit assumption in personal-growth training programs is that leadership is almost a calling. The executive leadership development program at PepsiCo, Inc., focuses on personal growth and business topics such as corporate strategy, ethics, and bringing about change and innovation. Jim Loehr, the psychologist heading the program, challenges the participants to reflect about their lives and identify something they want to change that will give them more energy and improved motivational skills.[21]

The Institute for Women's Leadership exemplifies a private firm that offers a program of leadership development through personal growth. (The program is also available to men.) The director, Rayona Sharpnack, guides participants through a process of unlearning what they assume to be true about what they can (or cannot) accomplish. Sharpnack emphasizes that for most people leadership is what people need to know or do, whereas her approach is learning *who you need to be*. It is the "being" part of leadership that facilitates breakthroughs in what people do and learn. The emphasis is on learning to perceive events differently, such as coming to believe that one can bring about key changes in the firm. Changing your perception is also like double-loop learning because you might challenge the validity of what you are doing. A leader might ask, "Is giving out $750 watches to employees an effective form of recognition? Or maybe a word of appreciation here and there would be more effective?"

A financial vice president who attended a Women's Leadership seminar later commented, "You walk in with a challenge, some mountain that you don't think you can climb. When you walk out, you've built a *higher* mountain that you know you *can* climb."[22]

**Socialization Programs** From the company standpoint, an essential type of leadership development program emphasizes becoming socialized—becoming acclimated to the company and accepting its vision and values. Senior executives make presentations in these programs because they serve as role models who thoroughly understand the vision and values participants are expected to perpetuate.[23] Many of the other types of programs presented so far also include a segment on socialization, particularly in the kickoff session. Quite frequently the chief executive makes a presentation of the company's vision and values.

**Action Learning Programs** A directly practical approach to leadership development is for leaders and potential leaders to work together in groups to solve organizational problems outside their usual sphere of influence. You will recall that action learning is part of the learning organization, as described in Chapter 13. Much of the development relates to problem solving and creativity, yet collaborating with a new set of people from your firm can also enhance interpersonal skills. The cross-functional teams at Schneider Electric described earlier are also a form of action learning because the managers assigned to the SWAT teams work on real company problems.

**Coaching and Psychotherapy** Executive coaching as described in Chapter 10 is clearly a form of leadership development because the managers coached receive advice and encouragement in relation to their leadership skills. A coach, for example, might advise a leader that giving more recognition for good performance would make him or her a more dynamic leader.

Another highly personal way of enhancing leadership effectiveness is to undergo treatment for emotional problems that could be blocking leadership effectiveness. For example, a leader who has difficulty giving recognition might not improve in response to coaching. The person might have underlying problems of being so hostile toward people that he or she really does not want to boost their morale. Psychotherapy might help, but positive changes are not always forthcoming. Psychiatrist Kerry Sulkowicz notes that change does not always take place quickly. However, executives are accustomed to getting quick results, which can make them highly motivated patients.[24]

In general, leaders who score low on the personality dimension of emotional stability might become more effective in their interpersonal relationships with the benefit of psychotherapy. Some of the bizarre behavior exhibited by executives, such as swearing at and belittling subordinates and arbitrarily firing workers, are symptoms of psychological problems.

A final point about leadership development is that the process continues to evolve. The content of these programs varies to fit new opinion and research as to what is the most relevant for leaders to know. For example, if the dollar is declining, seminars about dealing with the impact of this decline might be popular, as well as seminars on making the most of intuition in decision making. In the early 1990s, dealing with a strong U.S. dollar and making the most of rational decision making were popular. Although elearning may supplement more of leadership development in the future, face-to-face interaction with other leaders and course presenters will most likely remain popular.

## Evaluation of Leadership Development Efforts

A comprehensive approach to leadership development would include a rigorous evaluation of the consequences of having participated in a developmental experience. Executives and human resource professionals would ask such tough questions as the following:

Do people who receive mentoring actually become more effective leaders?

Do leaders who attend outdoor training become better team leaders than (1) those who do not attend the training, or (2) those whose "team development" consists of playing softball with the office gang?

Does the university-based executive program improve the decision-making skills of participants?

The evaluation of training and development programs is a comprehensive topic that includes such considerations as the design of experiments and the development of accurate outcome measures.[25] Here we examine the traditional approach to evaluating training and development outcomes and an approach that is better adapted to leadership development.

### The Traditional Approach to Evaluation

The traditional approach to the evaluation of leadership training and development programs would first specify the program objectives. After training was completed, measurements would be made of the extent to which those objectives were met. Two sets of outcomes are especially relevant. First, an assessment is made of the extent to which the participants acquired new skills during the program. For example, did the seminar participants acquire new skills in giving supportive feedback? Second, an assessment is made of whether the organization has become more effective as a result of this new skill acquisition. Did the bottom line improve because of the new skills? For example, has supportive feedback by leaders resulted in higher quality and profits?

Human resource specialists will often ask participants if the development program helped them perform their jobs better and how. Unit heads should be asked if the training program helped them achieve their units' business goals. Development specialists at the Boeing Leadership Center take such an objective approach to program evaluation. Data indicate that workers who report to the managers who have participated in programs at the center consistently give them higher ratings in employee satisfaction than they give managers who have not attended. Also, when answering the question "I am given a real opportunity to improve my skills at Boeing," leadership center alumni scored an 85 percent response in comparison to the 69 percent scored by managers who did not attend.[26]

A more rigorous approach to the evaluation of leadership training and development would include an experiment, as shown in Table 15-3. The experimental group would consist of the participants in the development program. Before-and-after measures of skills would be taken to determine if improvements took place. Outcome measures from the experimental group would then be compared to those from two control or contrast groups. All three groups would be composed of people similar in education, intelligence, job level, job experience, and so forth. People in one control group would receive no special development. Members of the second control group would receive a different kind of development. Instead of training in giving supportive feedback, they might be trained in business communications. The purpose of the second control (or contrast) group is to determine if training in supportive feedback has an edge over simply sending people to any sensible training program.

### Evaluation Through Domains of Impact

The traditional method of evaluation is best suited to evaluating structured, definable skills, such as running software or performing a breakeven analysis. Leadership training and development, however, involve much broader, less structured behaviors, such as inspiring others and identifying problems. Another problem is that few organizations are willing to randomly assign managers to expensive and time-consuming leadership development programs.

Following the traditional method of evaluation, a useful method of measuring the outcome of leadership development is to differentiate types of learning and to measure them separately.[27] Areas of possible changes are referred to as **domains of impact**. Competency domains have been conveniently organized into four types, all of which have been alluded to in this text:[28]

1. *Intrapersonal skills*—being effective with yourself, such as having good self-awareness
2. *Interpersonal skills*—dealing effectively with others
3. *Leadership skills*—influencing, inspiring, and persuading others, as well as visioning and many other capabilities
4. *Business skills*—cognitive skills such as planning, budgeting, forecasting, cost cutting, running meetings, preparing reports, and so forth

Understanding the domains of impact of a leadership development program may help evaluate the essence of such a program. Nevertheless, some executives who

**Table 15-3**    **Evaluating Leadership Development Through the Experimental Method**

|  | PRETRAINING MEASURES | TRAINING | POST-TRAINING MEASURES |
|---|---|---|---|
| EXPERIMENTAL GROUP | Yes | Supportive feedback | Yes |
| CONTROL GROUP I | Yes | None | Yes |
| CONTROL GROUP II | Yes | Business communications | Yes |

authorize payment for the program may want to know how improvement in the domains of impact leads to improved productivity and profits. The business skills domain is the one most obviously tied to productivity, but the other three also make a contribution.

# Leadership Succession

In a well-managed organization, replacements for executives who quit, retire, or are dismissed are chosen through **leadership succession**, an orderly process of identifying and grooming people to replace managers. Succession planning is linked to leadership development in two important ways. First, being groomed as a successor is part of leadership development. Second, the process of choosing and fostering a successor is part of a manager's own development.

Succession planning is vital to the long-term health of an organization, and therefore an important responsibility of senior leadership. Consultant Chris Pierce-Cooke observes that companies lacking succession plans are fragile enterprises. They lose the intellectual capital that goes with the people that have left. They also lose traction, momentum, productivity, morale, and customer service. In addition, when a capable leader departs and no well-regarded replacement is named, the stock price might plunge as much as 10 percent.[29]

Our approach to understanding the leadership aspects of succession focuses on four topics: (1) how the board chooses a new chief officer; (2) succession planning at GE; (3) the emotional aspects of leadership succession; and (4) developing a pool of successors.

## How the Board Chooses a Successor

A major responsibility of the board of directors is to select a successor to the chief executive, typically a CEO. The general approach is to follow standard principles of human resource selection, such as thoroughly screening candidates, including speaking to several people who have worked with the individual. Conducting a background investigation to uncover any possible scandalous or illegal behavior is also important. When the successor is an outsider, boards consistently use executive search firms (also known as *headhunters*) to locate one or several candidates. For example, both Hewlett-Packard Company and Tyco International Ltd. used an executive search firm to hire their current highest-ranking executive. Even when the board has an outside candidate in mind, a search firm might be hired to act as an intermediary.

George D. Kennedy, a person with experience on many boards, provides a few specifics of a representative approach to selecting an internal candidate for the top executive position. First, the information from a development program for successors must be carefully reviewed, including documentation of performance. Second, the board should have direct and regular contact with all of the promising candidates. Some of the contact should be formal; for example, the candidate should make regular presentations at board meetings. Informal connections are also important. Board members should invest the time to develop a feel for the personal chemistry of the candidates through such means as casual conversations over dinner and lunch.[30] (Because some of the decision making about succession is based on subjective judgments, it is imperative for CEO candidates to be skilled at organizational politics and influence tactics.)

## Succession Planning at General Electric

General Electric Company is often noted for its progressive and thorough management techniques. Its system for identifying and developing talent is considered exemplary. Much of this activity is linked closely to succession planning. Board members are closely involved in an ongoing evaluation of the company's 130 highest-ranking managers. Twice a year, directors scrutinize about 15 of these people. The information they use comes from lengthy interviews with the managers, their managers, former associates, and group members. Directors investigate the managers' strengths and weaknesses, make suggestions for leadership development, and discuss future assignments. Should the day arrive when a manager must be chosen to replace a higher-level manager, the board will be prepared to make an independent decision rather than have to give automatic approval to an insider's recommendations.[31]

Key advantages of the GE system for identifying successors are that it is based on multiple opinions and that it tracks longitudinal performance. Yet the system may still be replete with political biases. The board members, for example, are not exempt from giving high ratings to the people they like the best or to people who have personal characteristics similar to theirs.

## The Emotional Aspects of Leadership Succession

Leadership succession should not be regarded as a detached, objective management process. Even financially independent executives are likely to experience an emotional loss when they are replaced; they might yearn for the power and position they once possessed. Leadership succession in family-owned firms is a highly emotional process for many reasons. Family members may fight over who is best qualified to take the helm, or the owner and founder may not feel that any family member is qualified. An intensely emotional situation exists when the owner would like a family member to succeed him or her, yet no family member is willing. The business may therefore have to be sold or simply abandoned; in any case, its identity will be lost.

The emotional aspects of leadership succession are also evident when a business founder is replaced by another leader, whether or not the enterprise is a family business. After the sale of his or her company, the business founder often stays on in some capacity, perhaps as a consultant or chairperson. Watching the new owner manage the business can be uncomfortable for the founder. The issue transcends concerns about delegation. The entrepreneurial leader is typically emotionally involved in the firm he or she has founded and finds it difficult to look on while somebody else operates the firm.

## Developing a Pool of Successors

Developing a pool of successors goes beyond succession planning, which usually involves identifying one or two candidates for a specific job. The steps involved in developing a pool of successors (or succession management) are as follows:[32]

- Evaluate the extent of an organization's pending leadership shortage.
- Identify needed executive competencies based on the firm's future business needs, values, and strategies.

- Identify high-potential individuals for possible inclusion in the pool, and assess these individuals to identify strengths and developmental needs to determine who will stay in the high-potential pool.

- Establish an individually tailored developmental program for each high-potential candidate that includes leadership development programs, job rotation, special assignments, and mentoring.

- Select and place people into senior jobs based on their performance, experience, and potential.

- Continuously monitor the program and give it top management support.

Developing a pool of candidates, therefore, combines evaluating potential with giving high-potential individuals the right type of developmental experiences. To the extent that these procedures are implemented, a leadership shortage in a given firm is less likely to take place.

Another approach to developing a pool of successors is using the **leadership pipeline**, a model of leadership development that tightly links leadership development with management responsibilities at each level of the organization. The pipeline model has been used successfully at GE for many years, partly because it supports the company's approach to leadership succession.[33] It has six levels, each with unique management challenges: (1) managing individual contributors, (2) managing managers, (3) being a functional manager, (4) being a business manager, (5) being a group manager, and (6) being an enterprise manager. The model applies primarily to a large, hierarchical organization but can be adapted to fewer levels.

The leadership pipeline feeds succession because managers are prepared to be leaders at the next level. Each level requires the manager to develop skills, invest time in the most appropriate activities, and adjust values to perform successfully. For example, coaching is an important skill at level 1, and strategic planning at level 6. When moving from managing individual contributors to managing managers, leaders must learn to value a different type of work and have fewer quantitative measures to evaluate the results of their direct reports.

A recent analysis suggests that large, family-owned businesses often have an edge in leadership succession. The reason is that potential leaders have the benefit of years of experience under the watchful eyes of their elders. Successors are identified early and provided with all of the choice assignments and mentoring they need. An example of a large family business that emphasizes succession planning is Cintas Inc, a business uniform powerhouse that began as a rag reclamation company.[34]

Many small, family-run companies in contrast to large firms, lack clear succession plans. A survey of 38,000 small businesses indicated that of those CEOs expected to depart in five years, only 52 percent have chosen a successor. Lacking a succession plan, the family might be forced to sell the business.[35]

A concern expressed about most methods of succession planning is that minority group members are often overlooked. People whose personality type differs from those in power might also be overlooked. The problem often arises because people nominated for key leadership positions are often those who have performed well in the best opportunities and assignments. It is often likely that these high-power experiences came about because of the candidates' resemblance to those they hope to replace. According to the Mini-Me syndrome, executives feel more comfortable when critical organizational roles are given to people similar to the incumbent.[36] When top management is sensitive to the need for more diversity in choosing successors, the problem is on the way toward resolution.

## Who Will Be the New Top Business Leaders?

In the last several years, the often-neglected middle managers have come back in style as being major contributors to the success of business firms. Part of the reason is that middle managers are often perceived as having more credibility and goodwill than members of the executive suite.

The middle managers most likely to advance into top jobs are likely to have financial know-how and an ability to communicate with a range of constituents—in addition to many of the traits, attitudes, and behaviors emphasized in earlier chapters in this book. Another asset for middle managers is that they often have more frequent contact with customers, suppliers, and workers than do high-level executives, so they have a chance to show the all-important leadership trait of integrity.[37]

Public relations executive Roger Ailes believes that the class of 2006 will redefine power for the next ten years. Ailes believes that people with dynamic personalities will rise to the top. These leaders will make institutions even flatter, simpler, and faster moving, but they will not hunger for the perks of leadership. Furthermore, because people are looking for strong institutions, these leaders will bring back institutional trust.[38]

And above all, leaders at every level will need to be effective at recognizing the need for change and motivating people to accept and implement these necessary changes.[39]

Leadership Skill-Building Exercise 15-1 may give you a few good insights into the type of leader you are becoming and how well you fit the future generation of business leaders.

**LEADERSHIP SKILL-BUILDING EXERCISE 15-1**

### BUILDING FOR THE FUTURE

Our final skill-building exercise, the use of a feedback circle, encompasses many aspects of leadership covered in this and the previous fourteen chapters. Ten members of the class arrange their chairs in a circle. One person is selected as the feedback "target," and the other nine people take turns giving him or her supportive feedback. Assume it is "Ralph's" turn. Each person in the circle gives Ralph two pieces of feedback: (a) his best leadership attribute, and (b) how he needs to develop for the future. The feedback should take about thirty seconds per feedback giver. After receiving input from all of the circle members, Ralph is free to comment. It is then the next person's turn to be the feedback target.

Class members who are not in the circle observe the dynamics of what is happening and report their observations after the circle finishes. With diligence, the whole process will take about ninety minutes. If time permits, a new feedback circle can form. Alternatively, the class can break into several circles that operate simultaneously, or run just one circle with ten volunteers.

## Summary

college.hmco.com/pic/dubrin5e

Leadership and management development are widely practiced in a variety of organizations and take many forms, including self-development. Self-awareness involves the insightful processing of feedback about oneself to improve personal effectiveness. Single-loop learning occurs when learners seek minimum feedback that may substantially confront their basic ideas or actions. Double-loop learning occurs when people use feedback to confront the validity of the goal or values implicit in the situation; it enables the leader to learn and profit from failure.

Leadership development requires considerable self-discipline. For example, self-discipline is needed to monitor one's behavior to ensure that the necessary self-development takes place.

Education, leadership experience, and mentoring are all major contributors to leadership development. Most high-level leaders are intelligent, well-informed people who gather knowledge throughout their career. The best experiences for leadership development are those that realistically challenge the manager. An important part of capitalizing on challenging experiences is for the leader/manager to be given leeway in how to resolve the problem. Two important aspects of leadership experience are work associates and the task itself (such as a complex and ambiguous assignment).

Broad experience is important for leadership development, as suggested by multifunctional managerial development, and membership on a cross-functional team. Pivotal events can help people recognize a capacity to make things happen and gain the support of others.

Another experience-based way to develop leadership capability is to receive mentoring. Although usually an informal relationship, mentoring can also be assigned. A study showed that informal mentors typically were more helpful to a person's career than formal mentors, and informal mentoring is also associated with higher income. The human resource department often coordinates a formal mentoring program. Shadowing is a form of mentoring. Mentors enhance the career of protégés in many ways, such as by recommending them for promotion and helping them establish valuable contacts. Also, the mentor can serve as a model for effective (or ineffective) leadership.

Feedback-intensive development programs help leaders develop by seeing more clearly their patterns of behavior, the reasons for such behaviors, and the impact of these behaviors and attitudes on their effectiveness. Skill training in leadership development involves acquiring abilities and techniques that can be converted into action. Such training involves a considerable element of "how to." Five methods of skill-based training are lecture, case study, role play, behavior role modeling, and simulations. During simulations, participants play the role of company leaders and devise solutions to problems. Feedback on performance is provided.

A standard university approach to leadership development is to equip people with a conceptual understanding of leadership. The concepts can be applied to leadership situations. Personal growth experiences for leadership development assume that leaders are deeply in touch with their personal dreams and talents and will act to fulfill them. Another emphasis in these programs is learning who you need to be. From the company standpoint, an essential type of leadership development is becoming socialized in the company vision and values. Action learning is a directly practical approach to leadership development and may be directed at areas outside the participant's expertise. Coaching and psychotherapy are two highly personal ways of developing as a leader. Psychotherapy is called for when the leader has emotional problems that lower his or her effectiveness.

The traditional approach to the evaluation of leadership development programs includes specifying objectives and then measuring whether they were met. Measures of organizational outcomes, such as increased profits, might also be made. A more rigorous approach to evaluation would be based on an experimental design. An alternative approach to evaluation is to examine the domains of impact (ranges of possible effects) a program might have. The four types of competency domains are intrapersonal skills, interpersonal skills, leadership skills, and business skills.

Leadership succession is linked to leadership development because being groomed as a successor is part of a leader's development. Boards of directors use standard selection methods in choosing a CEO. In addition, they look for both formal and informal contact with insiders. When recruiting an outsider, organizations often employ executive search firms. General Electric is an example of a company that uses rigorous succession planning. Leadership succession is highly emotional for the leader who is being replaced, especially when a founder sells a business. The succession problem in a family business often leads to conflict among family members.

Large family-run businesses are more likely to identify leadership successors. One way to cope with potential shortages of leaders is to identify a pool of high-potential individuals and provide them with developmental experiences. The leadership pipeline, a model of leadership development, feeds succession because managers are prepared to be leaders at the next level.

Middle managers are again being perceived as major contributors to the success of business firms, and many of them will be the next top business leaders. It is predicted that financial know-how, good communication skills, and a dynamic personality will help leaders rise to the top and also be able to manage change.

## Key Terms

Self-awareness

Single-loop learning

Double-loop learning

Self-discipline

Multifunctional managerial development

Mentor

Shadowing

Feedback-intensive development program

Domains of impact

Leadership succession

Leadership pipeline

 ## Guidelines for Action and Skill Development

An important method for enhancing both the acceptance and the effectiveness of leadership development is *needs analysis*, the diagnosis of the needs for development. A needs analysis is based on the idea that there are individual differences among leaders and future leaders. For example, Jennifer might have excellent conceptual knowledge about leadership but limited team experience. She might be a good candidate for outdoor training. Jack might be an excellent team leader with limited conceptual knowledge. He might be a good candidate for a leadership development program concentrating on formal knowledge about leadership. Sources of data for assessing leadership developmental needs include the following:

1. Self-perceptions of developmental needs, including the results of many of the diagnostic instruments presented in this text
2. Perceptions by superiors, subordinates, and peers of the person's developmental needs, including 360-degree survey results
3. Psychological evaluation of developmental needs
4. A statement of organizational needs for development, such as the importance of leaders who can deal effectively with diversity (within the company, with customers, and globally)

Multiple sources of data are useful because of possible errors in perception, biases, and favoritism.

## Discussion Questions and Activities

1. Many business executives believe that playing team sports helps a person develop as a leader. Based on your knowledge of leadership development, where do you stand on this issue?

2. Where can a person get some honest feedback about his or her leadership ability?

3. Give an example from your own life in which you engaged in double-loop learning, or in which you *should* have engaged in such learning.

4. Suppose you aspired to become a senior manager in a large company. How would working as an office supervisor, production supervisor, or manager in a fast-food restaurant help you achieve your goal?

5. Why is being a member of a cross-functional team considered to be helpful experience for a future leader?

6. How will you know if the course for which you are reading this book will have helped you in your development as a leader or manager?

7. What are the advantages and disadvantages of having an outsider succeed the top executive in an organization?

8. What can you as a parent, future parent, or close relative do to help a child under 10 years old become a leader later in life?

9. Why are many CEOs who are planning to retire reluctant to identify a replacement a year or two in advance?

10. Ask an experienced leader what he or she thinks is the most effective method of developing leadership skills. Bring your findings back to class.

## LEADERSHIP CASE PROBLEM A

### THE LEADERSHIP INVENTORY CHART AT PINE GROVE

Pine Grove HealthCare is a multiservice health care company providing such services as administration of company health care plans, health maintenance organizations (HMOs), employee assistance programs, and assisted living retirement communities. Last year CEO Mandy Ming recognized that Pine Grove had grown so much that the firm needed a systematic method of identifying candidates to occupy future leaders of the company. To assist in this process, Ming hired human resources consultant Perry Watson.

After meeting with Ming and her staff for several hours, Watson recommended that Pine Grove implement a system of Leadership Inventory Charts. These charts, which are developed by the consultant working with top management, take an inventory of current and future leadership capability. The charts are based on performance information the company already has on hand as well as on the formulation of new judgments.

Ratings are made of both current performance and judgments about a candidate's potential for new responsibility. "Leadership potential" is a summary judgment based on such factors as current performance, charisma, conceptual thinking, and interpersonal skills. The Leadership Inventory Chart is supplemented with narrative descriptions backing up the ratings. A portion of the Leadership Inventory Chart for Pine Grove HealthCare is shown in Exhibit A.

**EXHIBIT A**  Pine Grove HealthCare Management Inventory Chart (Top Secret)

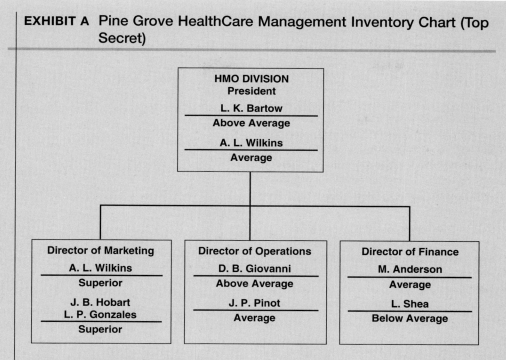

Code for ratings and names with boxes:
Rating at top of the box refers to job performance. Rating at bottom refers to potential for additional responsibility and a higher-level leadership position. Names within the boxes refer to individuals considered promotable to the position in question.

**Description of Performance Ratings**

*Superior:*           The unique, exceptional top performer.

*Above Average:*      Standards are usually exceeded. Carries out almost all responsibilities well.

*Average:*            Performs most responsibilities in a satisfactory manner. Results are acceptable.

*Below Average:*      Carries out several responsibilities unsatisfactorily. Achieves poor results. Job tenure is doubtful.

**Description of Potential Ratings**

*Superior:*           Person of general management potential. Exceptional leadership qualities.

*Above Average:*      Promotable person. Should be able to advance one or two levels.

*Average:*            With average growth and development is promotable to at least one higher level.

*Below Average:*      Has achieved a plateau. Considered to be non-promotable.

*(Continued)*

Watson repeated several times to Ming and her team that the Leadership Inventory Chart should be highly confidential, that it was a succession-planning document that was not part of a person's personnel record.

I caution you not to send this information to each other by email, or to keep several copies of the Inventory Chart at several different places in company hard-copy files. Classify the document as "Top Secret." If word gets out that such a planning document exists, all of the managers involved will want to see how they rate on the chart.

I am not recommending that you be a secretive top management team. You should be discussing your evaluation of key staffers with them during performance evaluation and more informal discussions. Yet, you can create a hornet's nest if the Leadership Inventory Chart gets out.

Within one month Ming and her staff, assisted by Watson, had prepared the Leadership Inventory Chart. Ming advised her staff, "Note that we have attached a date to this chart. The chart will be updated every quarter to reflect performance changes and perhaps any updated opinion we have about the leadership potential of our managers."

A few days before Watson, Ming, and her staff had completed the Leadership Inventory Chart, Michael Anderson, the director of finance at the HMO division, passed Perry Watson in the parking lot. After a little recollecting he recalled that Watson was a human resources consultant specializing in leadership succession issues. Watson had consulted with Anderson's previous firm.

That night Anderson searched the Internet to find out if Watson was still consulting in the area of management succession and preparing Leadership Inventory Charts. His findings were affirmative. Later that night Anderson sent email messages to several other managers at HealthCare asking them if they had heard about a Leadership Inventory

System being implemented at the company. By 10:00 A.M. the next morning all of the managers to whom Anderson sent messages had replied. Not one of them had heard about a Leadership Inventory System in place.

Within fifteen minutes, Anderson sent Ming an email message requesting an appointment as soon as possible to discuss a sensitive issue. Ming freed up time at 4:45 P.M. to meet briefly with Anderson. During the meeting, Anderson explained his concerns about a covert system of evaluating the succession potential of managers taking place in the company.

"My well-founded suspicions are that you and the other members of the top management team are making judgments about the promotion potential of key members of your staff. I understand that it is part of your job to plan for the future of Pine Grove, but I think each manager should receive honest feedback about your conclusions. I, for one, want to know if I have much of a future here."

"I am not denying that making judgments about the leadership potential of managers is part of my job," replied Ming. "Yet, I am not yet ready to discuss the specifics of our system."

Ming reflected quickly that because Anderson was thought to have below-average potential, it would be awkward to discuss the Leadership Inventory with him. At the same time, Anderson was a major contributor in his present role. After these few moments of reflection, Ming said to Anderson, "Let me get back to you in a few days about this topic."

## QUESTIONS

1. What should Ming tell Anderson at their next meeting?
2. What do you see as the advantages and disadvantages of the Leadership Inventory Chart? Comment also about the confidentiality issue.
3. What should L. Shea do from a career management standpoint if he finds out that he is considered to have below-average leadership potential at Pine Grove?

## LEADERSHIP CASE PROBLEM B

## "HELP! I'M THE NEW BOSS!"

You are the new boss, a couple of years younger than your colleagues. Shortly after your honeymoon ends, you invite a group member to your office and nicely suggest that she change her approach to improve her efficiency, bring herself in line with department changes, etc., etc. She listens. Sits back. Unblinking, she says, "Thanks, but no thanks. I'll keep doing things my way. Will that be all?"

What do you do? Go ballistic? Calmly explain to her that she will make the changes or be fired? When it happened to me, I didn't quite know how to react. I was a first-time boss, a 26-year-old free agent turned manager. No one had taught me how to react to outright disregard for my newfound authority. So finally I shrugged. I sort of mumbled, "Okay, um, I understand how you feel, and, you know, we'll talk about it another time."

As one might expect, my career as a manager at the company effectively ended that day. Word of my meekness spread, as good gossip always does.

I would go on to make every mistake imaginable, to the chagrin of most of the staff. I made Coach from *Cheers* (a television show) look masterful. My boss, who had hoped I would find my inner bossness on my own, eventually cut back the number of people who reported to me. It was a tough, but, yes, merciful call.

There is some solace in realizing now that I was not simply a young and clueless manager but one of many young and clueless managers.

### QUESTIONS

1. What type of leadership development program do you recommend for the person who wrote this case history?
2. What specific traits and behaviors does the boss in question need to work on?
3. How would you deal with the situation of a group member who refuses to act on your suggestions for improved performance?

SOURCE: Dimitry Elias Léger, "Help! I'm the New Boss," *Fortune*, May 29, 2000, p. 281.

## MY LEADERSHIP PORTFOLIO

LEADERSHIP SKILL–BUILDING EXERCISE 15-2

The final entry for your leadership portfolio deals more with the future than the present. As you build your leadership career in either a formal or informal leadership position, update your journal from time to time, perhaps once a quarter. Review what experiences you have that contribute to your development as a leader. Entries might take forms such as the following:

■ In January my company sent me to a seminar about dealing with difficult people. I came away with a few good insights about helping to turn around a difficult person, such as explaining how his or her behavior was hurting productivity and morale. I also learned that many difficult people are crying out for attention, so I will try to pay more attention to a difficult person should I encounter one.

*(Continued)*

- We had a major flood in the area last week, and our office became inundated. We had to do something quick before we were damaged so badly that we could not serve our customers. Our supervisor was out of town. I called her on her cell phone and asked for her authorization to be in charge of organizing our salvage operation. I spearheaded an effort that helped salvage a lot of equipment and computer records. I think I really polished my crisis management skills.

## INTERNET SKILL-BUILDING EXERCISE

Apply the chapter concepts! Visit the Web, and complete this Internet skill-building exercise to learn more about current leadership topics and trends.

### A SCIENTIFIC APPROACH TO SUCCESSION PLANNING

Visit *www.successionwizard.com,* a human resources consultancy located in the United Kingdom. Go to the "animated tutorials" to see a demonstration of how the Succession Wizard works. You will have a choice of six different tutorials to view. Begin with "1. Introduction," which gives a quick demonstration of the key program features. The tutorial will take you through an elaborate series of charts and dialogue boxes that help executives and human resource specialists engage in succession planning. Imagine that you are a senior executive of a company that wants to engage in serious succession planning.

1. What do you think of the potential value of the Succession Wizard?
2. Do you think it will be possible for your firm to do succession planning with such precision?
3. Why would any medium-size or large firm *not* use such a system?

# Endnotes

## Chapter 1

1. Mary Stone, "Software Firm CEO Aims to Deliver Results," *Rochester Business Journal*, June 18, 2004, pp. 12–14.
2. W. Kan Kim and Renée A. Maubourgne, "Parables of Leadership," *Harvard Business Review*, July–August 1992, p. 123.
3. Derived from a literature review in Bernard Bass, *Bass & Stogdill's Handbook of Leadership: Theory Research, and Managerial Applications* (New York: The Free Press, 1990), pp. 11–18.
4. Jeffrey Zaslow, "Joe Montana: Leadership, Says the Legendary Quarterback of Four Super Bowls, Means 'Being Willing to Take the Blame,'" *USA Weekend*, January 30–February 1, 1998, p. 15.
5. Keith M. Hammonds, "Leaders for the Long Haul," *Fast Company*, July 2001, p. 56.
6. Amy Barrett and Louis Lavelle, "It's Getting Lonely at the Top, Too Lonely," *BusinessWeek*, November 13, 2000, p. 60.
7. Peter Block, *Stewardship: Choosing Service over Self-Interest* (San Francisco: Berrett-Koehler Publishers, 1993), pp. 27–32.
8. Ibid., pp. 29–31.
9. James H. Davis, F. David Schoorman, and Lex Donaldson, "Toward a Stewardship Theory of Management," *Academy of Management Review*, January 1997, p. 20.
10. James M. Kouzes and Barry Z. Posner, *The Leadership Challenge*, 3rd ed. (San Francisco: Jossey-Bass, 2002), p. 20.
11. John P. Kotter, *A Force for Change: How Leadership Differs from Management* (New York: The Free Press, 1990); "Managing + Leading = True Leadership," *Executive Leadership*, September 2004, p. 8; Bill Leonard, "From Management to Leadership," *HR Magazine*, January 1999, pp. 34–38; Edwin A. Locke and Associates, *The Essence of Leadership: The Four Keys to Leading Successfully* (New York: Lexington/Macmillan, 1991), p. 4.
12. David A. Waldman, Gabriel G. Ramirez, Robert J. House, and Phanish Puranam, "Does Leadership Matter? CEO Leadership Attributes and Profitability Under Conditions of Perceived Environmental Uncertainty," *Academy of Management Journal*, February 2001, pp. 134–143.
13. Nitin Nohria, William Joyce, and Bruce Roberson, "What Really Works," *Harvard Business Review*, July 2003, p. 51.
14. Gary A. Yukl, *Leadership in Organizations*, 3rd ed. (Upper Saddle River, N.J.: Prentice Hall, 1994), pp. 384–387.
15. Jon P. Howell, David E. Bowen, Peter W. Dorfman, Steven Kerr, and Philip Podaskoff, "Substitutes for Leadership: Effective Alternatives to Ineffective Leadership," *Organizational Dynamics*, Summer 1990, p. 23.
16. Bass, *Bass & Stogdill's Handbook*, p. 686.
17. Shelly D. Dionne, Francis J. Yammarino, Leanne E. Atwater, and Lawrence R. James, "Neutralizing Substitutes for Leadership Theory: Leadership Effects and Common-Source Bias," *Journal of Applied Psychology*, June 2002, pp. 454–464.
18. Jeffrey Pfeffer, "The Ambiguity of Leadership," *Academy of Management Review*, April 1977, pp. 104–112.
19. Jerry Useem, "Conquering Vertical Limits," *Fortune*, February 19, 2001, p. 94.
20. Thomas H. Hout, "Are Managers Obsolete?" *Harvard Business Review*, March–April 1999, pp. 161–162. (Books in Review.)
21. Updated and expanded from Henry Mintzberg, *The Nature of Managerial Work* (New York: Harper & Row, 1973); Kenneth Graham, Jr., and William M. Mihal, *The CMD Managerial Job Analysis Inventory* (Rochester, N.Y.: Rochester Institute of Technology, Center for Management Development, 1987), pp. 132–133.
22. Christopher A. Bartlett and Sumantra Ghosal, "Changing the Role of Top Management Beyond Systems to People," *Harvard Business Review*, May–June 1995, pp. 132–133.
23. Ronald A. Heifetz and Marty Linsky, "A Survival Guide for Leaders," *Harvard Business Review*, June 2002, pp. 65–74.
24. Thomas A. Stewart, "The Nine Dilemmas Leaders Face," *Fortune*, March 18, 1996, pp. 112–113.
25. Two examples are Martin M. Chemers, *An Integrative Theory of Leadership* (Mahwah, N.J.: Lawrence Erlbaum Associates, 1997), pp. 151–173; and Francis J. Yammarino, Fred Dansereau, and Christina J. Kennedy, "A Multiple-Level Multidimensional Approach to

Leadership: Viewing Leadership Through an Elephant's Eye," *Organizational Dynamics,* Winter 2001, pp. 149–162.

26. Paul Hersey, Kenneth Blanchard, and Dewey E. Johnson, *Managing Organizational Behavior: Utilizing Human Resources* (Upper Saddle River, N.J.: Prentice Hall, 1997), pp. 418–420.

27. Stephen P. Robbins, *Managing Today!* (Upper Saddle River, N.J.: Prentice Hall, 1997), pp. 418–420.

28. Cited in "Firms Cite People Skills as Essential for Leaders," *Human Resource Management,* July 2002, p. 11.

29. Robert Goffee and Gareth Jones, "Followership: It's Personal Too," *Harvard Business Review,* November–December 1998, p. 148.

30. Robert E. Kelley, "In Praise of Followers," *Harvard Business Review,* November–December 1988, pp. 142–148.

31. Warren Bennis, "The End of Leadership: Exemplary Leadership Is Impossible Without Full Inclusion, Initiatives, and Cooperation of Followers," *Organizational Dynamics,* Summer 1999, pp. 76–78.

## Chapter 2

1. Theresa Howard, "Torre Goes to Bat for His Team," *USA Today,* August 10, 2004, p. 3B.

2. Shelley A. Kirkpatrick and Edwin A. Locke, "Leadership: Do Traits Matter?" *Academy of Management Executive,* May 1991, pp. 48–60; Daniel Goleman, "What Makes a Leader?" *Harvard Business Review,* November–December 1998, pp. 92–102.

3. George P. Hollenbeck and Douglas T. Hall, "Self-Confidence and Leader Performance," *Organizational Dynamics,* no. 3, 2004, p. 254.

4. Ibid., pp. 254–269; Rosabeth Moss Kanter, *Confidence* (New York: Crown Business, 2004).

5. Stephen G. Harrison, "Leadership and Hope Go Hand in Hand," *Executive Leadership,* June 2002, p. 8.

6. Jim Collins, "Level 5 Leadership: The Triumph of Humility and Fierce Resolve," *Harvard Business Review,* January 2001, p. 70.

7. Gareth R. Jones and Jennifer M. George, "The Experience and Evolution of Trust: Implications for Cooperation and Teamwork," *Academy of Management Review,* July 1998, pp. 531–546; Jenny C. McCune, "That Elusive Thing Called Trust," *Management Review,* August 1998, pp. 10–16.

8. Roy J. Lewicki, Daniel McAllister, and Robert J. Bies, "Trust and Distrust: New Relationships and Realities," *Academy of Management Review,* July 1998, p. 439.

9. Robert Glaser, "Paving the Road to Trust," *HRfocus,* January 1997, p. 5; Thomas A. Stewart, "Whom Can

You Trust? It's Not So Easy to Tell," *Fortune,* June 12, 2000, p. 334.

10. Kurt T. Kirks and Donald L. Ferrin, "Trust in Leadership: Meta-Analytic Findings and Implications for Research and Practice," *Journal of Applied Psychology,* August 2002, pp. 611–628.

11. Linda Tischler, "IBM's Management Makeover," *Fast Company,* November 2004, pp. 112–113.

12. Timothy A. Judge, Joyce E. Bono, Remus Ilies, and Megan W. Gerhardt, "Personality and Leadership: A Qualitative and Quantitative Review," *Journal of Applied Psychology,* August 2002, pp. 765–780.

13. Edwin A. Locke and Associates, *The Essence of Leadership: The Four Keys to Leading Successfully* (New York: Lexington/Macmillan, 1992), p. 55.

14. "The Hot Seat: Leadership in the 90s Is a Different Ball Game," *Executive Strategies,* September 1992, p. 1.

15. Sandra McElwaine, "A Different Kind of War: A Blunt Interview with the Army's First Female Three-Star General," *USA Weekend,* October 3–5, 1997, p. 6.

16. Quoted in "Leadership Concepts," *Executive Strategies,* July 9, 1991, p. 1.

17. "'The Company Is Not the Stock': Amazon's Jeff Bezos Sees a Pro Forma Profit This Year," *BusinessWeek,* April 30, 2001, p. 96.

18. "Randy Komisar: Virtual CEO," *Success,* December–January 2001, p. 29.

19. Goleman, "What Makes a Leader?" p. 94. For more research supporting the same conclusion, see Jennifer Laabs, "Emotional Intelligence at Work," *Workforce,* July 1999, pp. 68–71.

20. Daniel Goleman, Richard Boyatzis, and Annie McKee, "Primal Leadership: The Hidden Driver of Great Performance," *Harvard Business Review,* December 2001, pp. 42–51.

21. "How Coke Bottled Up Heyer's Flair," *Executive Leadership,* August 2004, p. 4.

22. Goleman, Boyatzis, and McKee, "Primal Leadership," pp. 42–51.

23. Leslie Cauley, "AT&T Rings in a New Business Strategy: Venerable Ma Bell Looks to Fork in the Road," *USA Today,* August 9, 2004, pp. 1B, 2B.

24. David C. McClelland and Richard Boyatzis, "Leadership Motive Pattern and Long-Term Success in Management," *Journal of Applied Psychology,* December 1982, p. 727.

25. Locke and Associates, *The Essence of Leadership,* p. 22.

26. Ibid.

27. John B. Miner, Normal R. Smith, and Jeffrey S. Bracker, "Role of Entrepreneurial Task Motivation in the Growth of Technologically Innovative Firms," *Journal of Applied Psychology,* August 1989, p. 554.

28. Cited in Julie Cohen Mason, "Leading the Way to the 21st Century," *Management Review,* October 1992, p. 19.

29. Timothy A. Judge, Amy E. Colbert, and Remus Ilies, "Intelligence and Leadership: A Quantitative Review and Test of Theoretical Propositions," *Journal of Applied Psychology,* June 2004, pp. 542–552.

30. Alex Taylor III, "Toyota's Secret Weapon," *Fortune,* August 23, 2004, pp. 60, 62.

31. Charles M. Farkas and Suzy Wetlaufler, "The Ways Chief Executive Officers Lead," *Harvard Business Review,* May–June 1996, p. 112.

32. From Jeffrey E. Garten, *The Mind of the C.E.O.* (Cambridge, Mass.: Perseus Publishing, 2001), as quoted in "Random Wisdom," *Executive Leadership,* April 4, 2002, p. 1.

33. "Dell Founder Asks: 'Are You Acting on Emotion?' " *Executive Leadership* (Extra), February 2003, p. 4.

34. David Tyler, "Twin Visionaries," Rochester, New York, *Democrat and Chronicle,* February 3, 2002, pp. 1E, 6E; *www.homeproperties.com,* accessed October 30, 2004.

35. Robert J. Sternberg, "WICS: A Model of Leadership in Organizations," *Academy of Management Learning and Education,* December 2003, pp. 386–401.

36. Goleman, "What Makes a Leader?" p. 97.

37. Scott Gummer, "CEO DNA," *Fortune,* November 26, 2001, pp. 259–264.

38. Kirkpatrick and Locke, "Leadership: Do Traits Matter?" p. 59.

39. Cited in Frances Hesselbein, Marshall Goldsmith, and Richard Beckhard (eds.), *The Leader of the Future* (San Francisco: Jossey-Bass, 1996).

40. Gary A. Yukl, *Leadership in Organizations,* 5th ed. (Upper Saddle River, N.J.: Prentice Hall, 2002), pp. 201–202; Martin M. Chemers, *An Integrative Theory of Leadership* (Mahwah, N.J.: Lawrence Erlbaum Associates, 1997), p. 20.

## Chapter 3

1. "Jobs's Cancer Scare Hangs Like a Cloud over Apple's Future," Associated Press, August 3, 2004.

2. Jay A. Conger, Rabindra N. Kanungo, and Associates, *Charismatic Leadership in Organizations* (Thousand Oaks, Calif.: Sage, 1998).

3. Juan-Carlos Pastor, James R. Meindl, and Margarit C. Mayo, "A Network Effects Model of Charisma Attributions," *Academy of Management Journal,* April 2002, pp. 410–420.

4. Cited in Jay A. Conger, *The Charismatic Leader: Beyond the Mystique of Exceptional Leadership* (San Francisco: Jossey-Bass, 1989).

5. William L. Gardner and Bruce J. Avolio, "The Charismatic Relationship: A Dramaturgical Perspective," *Academy of Management Review,* January 1998, pp. 32–58.

6. Eugene Schmuckler, book review in *Personnel Psychology,* Winter 1989, p. 881.

7. Robert J. House, "A 1976 Theory of Charismatic Leadership," in *Leadership: The Cutting Edge* (Carbondale: Southern Illinois University Press, 1977), pp. 189–207; Martin M. Chemers, *An Integrative Theory of Leadership* (Mahwah, N.J.: Lawrence Earlbaum Associates, 1997), pp. 80–82.

8. Jane A. Halpert, "The Dimensionality of Charisma," *Journal of Business Psychology,* Summer 1990, p. 401.

9. Jeffrey D. Kudisch et al., "Expert Power, Referent Power, and Charisma: Toward the Resolution of a Theoretical Debate," *Journal of Business and Psychology,* Winter 1995, pp. 177–195.

10. Conger, Kanungo, and Associates, *Charismatic Leadership in Organizations;* Bernard M. Bass, *Bass & Stogdill's Handbook of Leadership: Theory, Research, & Managerial Applications,* 3rd ed. (New York: The Free Press, 1990), pp. 185–186.

11. The following paragraphs are based on Jane M. Howell and Bruce J. Avolio, "The Ethics of Charismatic Leadership: Submission or Liberation?" *Academy of Management Executive,* May 1992, pp. 43–52; Patricia Sellers, "What Exactly Is Charisma?" *Fortune,* January 15, 1996, pp. 72–75; David A. Waldman and Francis J. Yammarino, "CEO Charismatic Leadership: Levels-of-Management and Levels-of-Analysis Effects," *Academy of Management Review,* April 1999, pp. 266–285.

12. Jim Collins, "Aligning Action and Values," Leader to Leader Institute, *http://leadertoleader.org,* as reported in "Actions: Louder than Vision Statements," *Executive Leadership,* May 2004, p. 8.

13. Alex Taylor III, "Schrempp Shifts Gears," *Fortune,* March 13, 2002, p. 98.

14. Howell and Avolio, "Ethics of Charismatic Leadership," p. 46.

15. Noel Tichy and Christopher DeRose, "Roger Enrico's Master Class," *Fortune,* November 27, 1995, p. 406.

16. Jay A. Conger, "Inspiring Others: The Language of Leadership," *Academy of Management Executive,* February 1991, p. 39.

17. Ibid.

18. "Management by Anecdote," *Success,* December 1992, p. 35.

19. Ibid.

20. Mark Lasswell, "Fabulists as the Firm," *The Wall Street Journal,* January 9, 2004, p. W11.

21. Dennis A. Romig, *Side by Side Leadership: Achieving Outstanding Results Together* (Marietta, Ga.: Bard Press, 2001), p. 157.

22. Karl Taro Greenfield, "Ralph's Rough Ride," *Time,* March 15, 1999, p. 50.

23. Kris Maher, "The Jungle: Focus on Recruitment, Pay and Getting Ahead," *The Wall Street Journal,* July 13, 2004, p. B6.

24. Michael Frese, Susanne Beimel, and Sandra Schoenborn, "Action Training for Charismatic Leadership: Two Evaluations of a Commercial Training Module on Inspirational Communication of a Vision," *Personnel Psychology,* Autumn 2003, pp. 671–697.

25. Marshall Sashkin and Molly G. Sashkin, *Leadership That Matters: The Critical Factors for Making a Difference in People's Lives and Organizations' Success* (San Francisco: Berrett-Koehler, 2003).

26. Bernard M. Bass, "Does the Transactional-Transformational Leadership Paradigm Transcend National Boundaries?" *American Psychologist,* February 1997, p. 130.

27. Joann S. Lublin and Steven Gray, "Burger King Set to Put Brenneman in CEO's Office," *The Wall Street Journal,* July 13, 2004, pp. A3, A6; Brian Grow, "Fat's in the Fire for This Burger King," *BusinessWeek,* November 8, 2004, pp. 69–70.

28. John J. Hater and Bernard M. Bass, "Superiors' Evaluations and Subordinates' Perceptions of Transformational and Transactional Leadership," *Journal of Applied Psychology,* November 1988, p. 65; Noel M. Tichy and Mary Anne Devanna, *The Transformational Leader* (New York: Wiley, 1990).

29. Peter Koestenbaum, *Leadership: The Inner Side of Greatness* (San Francisco: Jossey-Bass, 1991).

30. Alan J., Dubinsky, Francis J. Yammarino, and Marvin A. Jolson, "An Examination of Linkages Between Personal Characteristics and Dimensions of Transformational Leadership," *Journal of Business and Psychology,* Spring 1995, p. 316.

31. Carlos Ghosn, "First Person: Saving the Business Without Losing the Company," *Harvard Business Review,* January 2002, p. 40.

32. W. Chan Kim and Renée Mauborgne, "Tipping Point Leadership," *Harvard Business Review,* April 2003, pp. 65–66.

33. Literature reviewed in Sally A. Carless, Alexander J. Wearing, and Leon Mann, "A Short Measure of Transformational Leadership," *Journal of Business and Psychology,* Spring 2000, pp. 389–405; Joyce E. Bono and Timothy A. Judge, "Personality and Transformational and Transactional Leadership: A Meta-Analysis," *Journal of Applied Psychology,* October 2004, pp. 901–910; Taly Dvir, Dov Eden, Bruce J. Avolio, and Boas Shamir, "Impact of Transformational Leadership on Follower Development and Performance: A Field Experiment," *Academy of Management Journal,* August 2002, pp. 735–744.

34. Timothy A. Judge and Joyce E. Bono, "Five-Factor Model of Personality and Transformational Leadership," *Journal of Applied Psychology,* October 2000, pp. 751–765; Bono and Judge, "Personality and Transformational and Transactional Leadership," pp. 901–910.

35. Barbara Mandell and Shilpa Pherwani, "Relationship Between Emotional Intelligence and Transformational Leadership Style: A Gender Comparison," *Journal of Business and Psychology,* Spring 2003, pp. 387–404.

36. Nick Turner et al., "Transformational Leadership and Moral Reasoning," *Journal of Applied Psychology,* April 2002, pp. 304–311.

37. Timothy A. Judge and Ronald F. Piccolo, "Transformational and Transactional Leadership: A Meta-Analytic Test of Their Relative Validity," *Journal of Applied Psychology,* October 2004, pp. 755–768.

38. Jane M. Howell and Bruce J. Avolio, "Transformational Leadership, Transactional Leadership, Locus of Control, and Support for Innovation: Key Predictors of Consolidated-Business-Unit Performance," *Academy of Management Journal,* August 1998, pp. 387–409.

39. Warren G. Bennis and Burt Nanus, *Leaders: Strategies for Taking Charge* (New York: Harper & Row, 1985), p. 223.

40. Robert C. Tucker, "The Theory of Charismatic Leadership," *Daedalus,* Summer 1968, pp. 731–756.

41. The first six items on the list are from Roger Dawson, *Secrets of Power Persuasion: Everything You'll Need to Get Anything You'll Ever Want* (Upper Saddle River, N.J.: Prentice Hall, 1992), pp. 179–194; the last item is from James M. Kouzes and Barry Z. Posner, *The Leadership Challenge,* 3rd ed. (San Francisco: Jossey-Bass, 2002), p. 158.

## Chapter 4

1. "Unusual Route Takes Her to the Driver's Seat: Liberal Arts Grad Goes from Factory Foreman to CEO," *Associated Press,* July 18, 2004.

2. Ralph M. Stogdill and Alvin E. Coons (eds.), *Leader Behavior: Its Description and Measurement* (Columbus: The Ohio State University Bureau of Business Research, 1957); Carroll L. Shartle, *Executive Performance and Leadership* (Upper Saddle River, N.J.: Prentice Hall, 1956).

3. Margaret Littman, "Best Bosses Tell All," *Working Woman,* October 2000, p. 50.

4. Quoted in Joshua Kurlantzick, "Lead the Way," *Entrepreneur*, March 2003, p. 51.

5. Stanley Holmes, "Boeing's Favorite Supergeek," *BusinessWeek*, September 6, 2004, p. 101.

6. Timothy A. Judge, Ronald F. Piccolo, and Remus Ilies, "The Forgotten Ones? The Validity of Consideration and Initiating Structure in Leadership Research," *Journal of Applied Psychology*, February 2004, pp. 36–51.

7. Thomas J. Peters and Robert H. Waterman, Jr., *In Search of Excellence: Lessons from America's Companies* (New York: Harper & Row, 1982).

8. Desa Philadelphia, "Q&A: Larry Bossidy on Execution." *Time Global Business*, July 2002, p. B5. See also Larry Bossidy and Ram Charan, *Execution: The Discipline of Getting Things Done* (New York: Crown Business, 2002).

9. Bridget McCrea, "Hands-On Experience," *Black Enterprise*, November 2004, p. 63.

10. Shawn Tully, "Rebuilding Wall Street," *Fortune*, October 1, 2001, pp. 95–96.

11. Ronald A. Heifetz and Donald R. Laurie, "The Work of Leadership," *Harvard Business Review*, January–February 1997, pp. 124–134.

12. "A CEO on the Go: Randy Komisar on the Art of Snap Leadership," *Executive Strategies*, July 2000, p. 3.

13. John P. Kotter, "What Leaders Really Do," *Harvard Business Review*, May–June 1990, pp. 105–106.

14. Tom Lowry, "The NFL Machine," *BusinessWeek*, January 27, 2003, p. 88.

15. David S. Brown, "Manager's New Job Is Concert Building," *HR Magazine*, September 1990, p. 42.

16. James M. Kouzes and Barry Z. Posner, *The Leadership Challenge*, 3rd ed. (San Francisco: Jossey-Bass, 2002), p. 242.

17. David Kirkpatrick, "Inside Sam's $100 Billion Growth Machine," *Fortune*, June 14, 2004, p. 88.

18. Quoted in Gerald Secour Couzens, *Success*, November 1998, p. 55.

19. Don Dinkmeyer and Dan Eckstein, *Leadership by Encouragement* (Delray Beach, Fla.: St. Lucie Press, 1995).

20. "Covey Proposes Principle-Based Leadership," *Management Review*, September 1995, p. 21.

21. Quoted in David Bank, "Keeping Information Safe," *The Wall Street Journal*, November 11, 2004, p. B4.

22. Bill George, *Authentic Leadership* (San Francisco: Jossey-Bass, 2003).

23. Robert K. Greenleaf, *The Power of Servant Leadership* (San Francisco: Berrett-Koehler Publishers, 1998).

24. Based on Robert K. Greenleaf, *Servant Leadership: A Journey into the Nature of Legitimate Power and Greatness* (Mahwah, N.J.: Paulist Press, 1997); Michael Useem, "The Leadership Lessons of Mt. Everest," *Harvard Business Review*, October 2001, pp. 53–54; and "Blueprint for a Servant Leader," *WorkingSMART*, March 2000, p. 7.

25. "The Essence of Servant Leadership," *Manager's Edge*, January 2004, p. 3; Kenneth Hein, "Taking the Lead," *www.incentivemag.com*.

26. Ginka Toegel and Jay A. Conger, "360-Degree Assessment: Time for Reinvention," *Academy of Management Learning and Education*, September 2003, pp. 297–311.

27. David Kirkpatrick, "Dell and Rollins: The $41 Billion Buddy Act," *Fortune*, April 19, 2004, p. 85.

28. Bruce Pfau and Ira Kay, "Does 360-Degree Feedback Negatively Affect Company Performance?" *HR Magazine*, June 2002, pp. 58–59.

29. Joan F. Brett and Leanne E. Atwater, "360° Feedback: Accuracy, Reactions, and Perceptions of Usefulness," *Journal of Applied Psychology*, October 2001, pp. 930–942.

30. The research of Michael Useem reported in Bill Breen, "Trickle-Up Leadership," *Fast Company*, November 2001, p. 70.

31. Craig L. Pearse, "The Future of Leadership: Combining Vertical and Shared Leadership to Transform Knowledge Work," *Academy of Management Executive*, February 2004, pp. 47–57.

32. Robert Berner, "P&G: New and Improved," *BusinessWeek*, July 7, 2003, pp. 54–55.

33. Faith Arner, "Pass Go and Collect the Job of CEO," *BusinessWeek*, April 4, 2003, p. 84.

34. Hector Ruiz, "Chipping Away at Intel," *Fortune*, November 1, 2004, p. 112.

35. Robert R. Blake and Anne Adams McCarse, *Leadership Dilemmas and Solutions* (Houston, Tex.: Gulf Publishing, 1991).

36. J. Robert Baum and Edwin A. Locke, "The Relationship of Entrepreneurial Traits, Skill, and Motivation to Subsequent Venture Growth," *Journal of Applied Psychology*, August 2004, pp. 587–598; Gayle Sato Stodder, "Goodbye Mom & Pop: The Neighborhood's Not Big Enough for Today's Entrepreneur. Only the World Will Do," *Entrepreneur*, May 1999, pp. 145–151; Michael Warshaw, "The Mind-Style of the Entrepreneur," *Success*, April 1993, pp. 28–33.

37. Judy Rosener, "Ways Women Lead," *Harvard Business Review*, November–December 1990, pp. 119–125.

38. Cited in "Debate: Ways Men and Women Lead," *Harvard Business Review*, January–February 1991, p. 151.

39. Debra Phillips, "The Gender Gap," *Entrepreneur*, May 1995, pp. 110, 111.

40. Robert J. Kabacoff, "Gender Differences in Organizational Leadership," Management Research Group, Portland, ME, as reported in "Do Men and Women Lead Differently?" *Leadership Strategies*, Premier Issue, copyright 2001, Briefings Publishing Group.

41. Research reported in Michael Schrage, "Why Can't a Woman Be More Like a Man? *Fortune,* August 16, 1999, p. 184.
42. Much of the research on this topic is summarized in Mary Crawford, *Talking Difference: On Gender and Language* (London: Sage Publications, 1995).
43. Jan Grant, "Women Managers: What Can They Offer Organizations?" *Organizational Dynamics,* Winter 1988. pp. 56–63.
44. Quoted in Phillips, "The Gender Gap," p. 112.
45. Daniel Goleman, "Leadership That Gets Results," *Harvard Business Review,* March–April 2000, pp. 78–90.
46. Felix Brodbeck, Michael Frese, and Mansour Havidan, "Leadership Made in Germany: Low on Compassion, High on Performance," *Academy of Management Executive,* February 2002, pp. 16–30.
47. Ralph M. Stogdill, "Historical Trends in Leadership Theory and Research," *Journal of Contemporary Business,* Autumn 1974, p. 7.
48. "Directive Management or Not?" *WorkingSMART,* December 1992, p. 3.

## Chapter 5

1. Patrick J. Kiger, "Dealing with Disaster," *Workforce Management,* November 2004, pp. 30–38.
2. "Surprising and Effective Cure for Today's Biggest Workplace Crisis," *Executive Focus,* September 2004, p. 21.
3. For a synthesis of contingency theory by one of its key researchers, see Martin M. Chemers, *An Integrative Theory of Leadership* (Mahwah, N.J.: Erlbaum, 1997), pp. 28–38. See also Fred E. Fiedler, Martin M. Chemers, and Linda Mahar, *Improving Leadership Effectiveness: The Leader-Match Concept,* 2nd ed. (New York: Wiley, 1994).
4. Robert J. House, "A Path-Goal Theory of Leader Effectiveness," *Administrative Science Quarterly,* September 1971, pp. 321–328; Robert T. Keller, "A Test of the Path-Goal Theory with Need for Clarity as a Moderator in Research and Development Organizations," *Journal of Applied Psychology,* April 1989, pp. 208–212; Robert J. House and Terence R. Mitchell, "Path-Goal Theory of Leadership," *Journal of Contemporary Business,* Autumn 1974, pp. 81–97.
5. House and Mitchell, "Path-Goal Theory," p. 84; Bernard M. Bass, *Bass & Stogdill's Handbook of Leadership: Theory, Research, and Managerial Applications,* 3rd ed. (New York: Free Press, 1990), p. 633.
6. Chemers, *An Integrative Theory of Leadership,* p. 48.
7. Kenneth H. Blanchard, David Zigarmi, and Robert Nelson, "Situational Leadership After 25 Years: A Retrospective," *Journal of Leadership Studies,* vol. 1, 1993, pp. 22–26; Kenneth Blanchard and Robert Nelson, "Recognition and Reward," *Executive Excellence,* no. 4, 1997, p. 15; "Building Materials Leader Builds Better Leaders," *kenblanchard.com/casestudies/certainteed.pdf,* accessed November 26, 2004.
8. Victor H. Vroom, "Leadership and the Decision-Making Process," *Organizational Dynamics,* Spring 2000, pp. 82–93.
9. Richard H. G. Field and Robert J. House, "A Test of the Vroom–Yetton Model Using Manager and Subordinate Reports," *Journal of Applied Psychology,* June 1990, pp. 362–366.
10. Susan Caminiti, "Turnaround Titan," *Working Woman,* December–January 1999, p. 57.
11. Fred E. Fiedler and Joseph E. Garcia, *New Approaches to Effective Leadership: Cognitive Resources and Organizational Performance* (New York: Wiley, 1987); Robert P. Vecchio, "Theoretical and Empirical Examination of Cognitive Resource Theory," *Journal of Applied Psychology,* April 1990, p. 141; Chemers, *An Integrative Theory of Leadership,* pp. 38–40.
12. Vecchio, "Theoretical and Empirical Examination of Cognitive Resource Theory," pp. 141–147.
13. Robert Vecchio, "Cognitive Resource Theory: Issues for Specifying a Test of the Theory," *Journal of Applied Psychology,* June 1992, p. 66.
14. Charles M. Farkas and Suzy Wetlaufer, "The Ways Chief Executive Officers Lead," *Harvard Business Review,* May–June 1996, pp. 110–122; Charles M. Farkas and Philippe DeBacker, *Maximum Leadership: The World's Leading CEOs Share Their Five Strategies for Success* (New York: Holt, 1996).
15. Farkas and Wetlaufer, "The Ways Chief Executive Officers Lead," p. 116.
16. Michael Wentzel, "Imaging Firm Hires Exec," *Rochester Democrat and Chronicle,* July 20, 2004, p. 6D.
17. Research cited in Gary Yukl, *Leadership in Organizations,* 5th ed. (Upper Saddle River, N.J.: Prentice Hall, 2002), p. 344.
18. James E. Dutton et al., "Leading in Times of Trauma," *Harvard Business Review,* January 2002, p. 56.
19. Suzanne Koudsi, "How to Cope with Tragedy," *Fortune,* October 1, 2001, p. 34.
20. Chester Dawson, "What Japan's CEOs Can Learn from Bridgestone," *BusinessWeek,* January 29, 2001, p. 50.
21. Barbara Baker Clark, "Leadership During a Crisis," *Executive Leadership,* December 2001, p. 8.
22. Joyce M. Rosenberg, "Business Must Be Ready for Disasters," Associated Press, April 19, 2004.

23. Michael E. McGill and John W. Slocum, Jr., "A Little Leadership Please?" *Organizational Dynamics,* Winter 1998, p. 48.

Suggested path for Leadership Skill-Building Exercise 5-2: Applying the Time-Driven Model: H H H L H H L CONSULT GROUP.

# Chapter 6

1. April Y. Pennington, "A World of Difference," *Entrepreneur,* October 2004, pp. 80–81.

2. James G. Clawson, *Level Three Leadership: Getting Below the Surface,* 2nd ed. (Upper Saddle River, N.J.: Prentice Hall, 2002), p. 54.

3. Barbara Kellerman, "Leadership—Warts and All," *Harvard Business Review,* January 2004, pp. 40–53.

4. "Workers Lack Trust in Bosses and Colleagues," Associated Press, September 6, 2004.

5. Chris Prystay, "Most Workers in Asia Distrust Bosses," *The Wall Street Journal,* November 24, 2004, p. B8.

6. Thomas E. Becker, "Integrity in Organizations: Beyond Honesty and Conscientiousness," *Academy of Management Review,* January 1998, pp. 154–161.

7. Robert Simons, Henry Mintzberg, and Kunal Basu, "Memo to CEOs Re Five Half-Truths of Business," *Fast Company,* June 2002, p. 118.

8. Tricia Bisoux, "Corporate Counter Culture," *BizEd,* November–December 2004, p. 18.

9. Douglas R. May, Adrian Y. L. Chan, Timothy D. Hodges, and Bruce J. Avolio, "Developing the Moral Component of Authentic Leadership," *Organizational Dynamics,* no. 3, 2003, p. 248.

10. Peter G. Northouse, *Leadership: Theory and Practice,* 2nd ed. (Thousand Oaks, CA: Sage, 2001), p. 263.

11. Pete Engardio, "Global Compact, Little Impact," *BusinessWeek,* July 12, 2004, p. 86.

12. Clawson, *Level Three Leadership,* p. 57.

13. Joseph L. Badaracco, Jr., "We Don't Need Another Hero," *Harvard Business Review,* September 2001, pp. 120–126.

14. "Fed Chief Points to Cautious Recovery," Gannett News Service, July 17, 2002.

15. Research synthesized in Richard L. Daft, *Leadership: Theory and Practice* (Fort Worth, Tex.: Dryden Press, 1999), pp. 369–370.

16. Susan Chandler, "Why Do Rich CEOs Steal? Entitlement," Knight Ridder News Service, September 19, 2004; "Study Finds Greater Pay for CEOs of Outsourcers," Associated Press, September 1, 2004.

17. James L. Bowditch and Anthony F. Buono, *A Primer on Organizational Behavior,* 5th ed. (New York: Wiley, 2001), p. 4.

18. Kris Maher, "Wanted: Ethical Employer," *The Wall Street Journal,* July 9, 2002, p. B1.

19. Keith A. Lavine and Elina S. Moore, "Corporate Consciousness: Defining the Paradigm," *Journal of Business and Psychology,* Summer 1996, pp. 401–413.

20. Richard L. Schmalensee, "The 'Thou Shalt' School of Business," *Wall Street Journal,* December 30, 2003, p. B4.

21. Robert Levering and Milton Moskowitz, "The 100 Best Companies to Work For," *Fortune,* January 24, 2005, pp. 72–78.

22. Brenda L. Flannery and Douglas R. May, "Environmental Ethical Decision Making in the U.S. Metal Finishing Industry," *Academy of Management Journal,* August 2000, pp. 642–662.

23. Michelle Conlin and Jessi Hempel, "The Top Givers," *BusinessWeek,* December 1, 2003, p. 81.

24. Anamaria Wilson, "Better Reading for $100 Million," *Time,* January 31, 2000, p. 55.

25. Dayton Fandray, "The Ethical Company," *Workforce,* December 2000, p. 76.

26. Amy Merrick, "Gap Offers Unusual Look at Factory Conditions," *The Wall Street Journal,* May 12, 2004, pp. A1, A12.

27. Terry Thomas, John R. Schermerhorn, Jr., and John W. Dienhart, "Strategic Leadership of Ethical Behavior in Business," *Academy of Management Executive,* May 2004, pp. 56–66.

28. Adam Cohen, "Peeping Larry," *Time,* July 10, 2000, p. 94.

29. Linda Klebe Treviño and Michael E. Brown, "Managing to Be Ethical: Debunking Five Business Ethics Myths," *Academy of Management Executive,* May 2004, p. 79.

30. Quoted in Joanne Lozar Glenn, "Making Sense of Ethics," *Business Education Forum,* October 2004, p. 10.

31. Joanne Sammer, "United Technologies Offers a Model for Reporting Ethical Issues," *Workforce,* August 2004, pp. 64–65.

32. Harry R. Weber, "Coke Receives Grand Jury Subpoenas from Feds in Fraud Probe," Associated Press, February 28, 2004.

33. Jonathan M. Tisch, "From 'Me' Leadership to 'We' Leadership," *The Wall Street Journal,* October 26, 2004, p. B2. (The observation about Lampert is not from Tisch.)

34. Study reported in *www.business-ethics.org* and cited in Deb Koen, "Ethical Conduct Is Good for Business," *Rochester (N.Y.) Democrat and Chronicle,* June 16, 2002, p. 4E.

35. Sandra A. Waddock and Samuel B. Graves, "The Corporate Social Performance—Financial Performance Link," *Strategic Management Journal,* Spring 1997, pp. 303–319.

36. Ann Zimmerman, "Costco's Dilemma: Be Kind to Its Workers, or Wall Street?" *The Wall Street Journal*, March 26, 2004, p. B1.

37. Daniel J. Brass, Kenneth D. Butterfield, and Bruce C. Skaggs, "Relationships and Unethical Behavior: A Social Network Perspective," *Academy of Management Review*, January 1998, pp. 14–31.


## Chapter 7

1. Josh Tyrangiel, "Looking for Mr. Really Big," *Time*, October 11, 2004, pp. 83–85.

2. John R. French and Bertram Raven, "The Basis of Social Power," in Dorwin Cartwright, ed., *Studies in Social Power* (Ann Arbor, Mich.: Institute for Social Research, 1969); Timothy R. Hinkin and Chester A. Schriescheim, "Power and Influence: The View from Below," *Personnel*, May 1988, pp. 47–50.

3. Ann Davis and Randall Smith, "Merrill Switch: Popular Veteran Is in, Not out," *The Wall Street Journal*, August 13, 2003, p. C1; Landon Thomas Jr., "Dismantling a Wall Street Club," *www.nytimes.com*, November 2, 2003.

4. Frank Gibney, Jr., "Vroooom at the Top," *Time*, January 14, 2002, p. 42.

5. Sydney Finkelstein, "Power in Top Management Teams: Dimensions, Measurement, and Validation," *Academy of Management Journal*, August 1992, p. 510.

6. Michael Warshaw, "The Good Guy's (and Gal's) Guide to Office Politics," *Fast Company*, April 1998, p. 158. See also *www.fastcompany.com/online/14/politics.html*.

7. Finkelstein, "Power in Top Management Teams," p. 510.

8. Jeffrey Pfeffer, *Managing with Power: Power and Influence in Organizations* (Boston: Harvard Business School Press, 1992), pp. 100–101.

9. C. R. Hinings, D. J. Hickson, C. A. Lee, R. E. Schenck, and J. W. Pennings, "Strategic Contingencies Theory of Intraorganizational Power," *Administrative Science Quarterly*, 1971, pp. 216–229.

10. Gregory G. Dess and Joseph Picken, "Changing Roles: Leadership in the 21st Century," *Organizational Dynamics*, Winter 2000, p. 22.

11. "The Secrets of His Success," *Fortune*, November 29, 2004, p. 158.

12. Gretchen M. Spreitzer, "Psychological Empowerment in the Workplace: Dimensions, Measurement, and Validation," *Academy of Management Journal*, October 1995, pp. 1442–1465.

13. Scott E. Seibert, Seth R. Silver, and W. Alan Randolph, "Taking Empowerment to the Next Level: A Multiple-Level Model of Empowerment, Performance, and Satisfaction," *Academy of Management Journal*, June 2004, pp. 332–349.

14. Jay A. Conger, "Leadership: The Art of Empowering Others," *Academy of Management Executive*, August 1995, pp. 21–31.

15. Barbara Ettorre, "The Empowerment Gap: Hype vs. Reality," *HRfocus*, July 1997, p. 5.

16. Ibid.

17. Quoted in Phillip M. Perry, "Seven Errors to Avoid When Empowering Your Staff," *Success Workshop* (a supplement to *Manager's Edge*), March 1999, p. 3.

18. Bradley L. Kirkman and Benson Rosen, "Beyond Self-Management: Antecedents and Consequences of Team Empowerment," *Academy of Management Journal*, February 1999, p. 59.

19. Kyle Dover, "Avoiding Empowerment Traps," *Management Review*, January 1999, p. 52.

20. Dimitry Elias Léger, "Tell Me Your Problem, and I'll Tell You Mine," *Fortune*, October 16, 2000, p. 408.

21. Christopher Robert et al., "Empowerment and Continuous Improvement in the United States, Mexico, Poland, and India: Predicting Fit on the Basis of the Dimensions of Power Distance and Individualism," *Journal of Applied Psychology*, October 2000, pp. 751–765.

22. Gerald R. Ferris et al., "Political Skill at Work," *Organizational Dynamics*, Spring 2000, p. 25.

23. Polly Labarre, "The New Face of Office Politics," *Fast Company*, October 1999, p. 80.

24. Gerald Biberman, "Personality Characteristics and Work Attitudes of Persons with High, Moderate, and Low Political Tendencies," *Psychological Reports*, vol. 57, 1985, p. 1309.

25. Marshall Goldsmith, "All of Us Are Stuck on Suck-Ups," *Fast Company*, December 2003, p. 117.

26. Pamela L. Perrewé et al., "Political Skill: An Antidote for Workplace Stressors," *Academy of Management Executive*, August 2000, p. 115.

27. Tom Peters, "Power," *Success*, November 1994, p. 34.

28. Warshaw, "The Good Guy's (and Gal's) Guide," p. 160.

29. Joann S. Lublin, "To Win Advancement, You Need to Clean up Any Bad Speech Habits," *The Wall Street Journal*, October 3, 2004, p. B1.

30. A good example is Sandy J. Wayne and Robert C. Liden, "Effects of Impression Management on Performance Ratings," *Academy of Management Journal*, February 1995, pp. 232–260.

31. Peters, "Power," p. 34.

32. Research reported in Jennifer Reingold, "Suck Up and Move Up," *Fast Company*, January 2005, p. 34.

33. Quoted in Joann S. Lublin, "'Did I Just Say That?!' How You Can Recover From Foot-in-Mouth," *The Wall Street Journal*, June 18, 2002, p. B1.

34. Tracy Minor, "Office Politics: Master the Game by Making Connections," *Monster: Diversity & Inclusion,* October 30, 2002 *(monster.com).*

35. Annette Simmons, *Territorial Games: Understanding & Ending Turf Wars at Work* (New York: AMACOM, 1998); Robert J. Herbold, *The Fiefdom Syndrome* (New York: Currency Doubleday, 2004).

36. Jared Sandberg, "Office Superheroes: Saving the Rest of Us from Unseen Dangers," *The Wall Street Journal,* December 10, 2003, p. B1.

37. John M. Maslyn and Donald B. Fedor, "Perceptions of Politics: Does Measuring Foci Matter?" *Journal of Applied Psychology,* August 1998, p. 650.

38. L. A. Witt, "Enhancing Organizational Goal Congruence: A Solution to Organizational Politics," *Journal of Applied Psychology,* August 1998, pp. 666–674.

39. Robert P. Vecchio, *Organizational Behavior,* 4th ed. (Fort Worth, Tex.: Dryden Press, 2000), p. 136.

40. "Throw Politics Out of Your Office," *Manager's Edge,* July 2001, p. 8.

41. Adapted from Sarah Myers McGinty, *Power Talk: Using Language to Build Authority* (New York: Warner Books, 2001), as cited in "6 Ways to Judge Internal Dynamics," *Executive Leadership,* August 2001, p. 7.

## Chapter 8

1. Carol Hymowitz, "Often the Go-To Person for Company Insiders Isn't Known Outside," *The Wall Street Journal,* November 23, 2004, p. B1.

2. Allan R. Cohen, Stephen L. Fink, Herman Gadon, and Robin D. Willits, *Effective Behavior in Organizations: Cases, Concepts, and Student Experiences,* 5th ed. (Homewood, Ill.: Irwin, 1992), p. 139.

3. Colin Powell, "A Leadership Primer," PowerPoint presentation for Department of the Army, United States of America, undated.

4. Gary Yukl, *Leadership in Organizations,* 5th ed. (Upper Saddle River, N.J.: Prentice Hall, 2002), p. 143.

5. Patricia Sellers, "Something to Prove," *Fortune,* June 24, 2002, p. 94.

6. Gary Yukl and J. Bruce Tracey, "Consequences of Influence Tactics Used with Subordinates, Peers, and the Boss," *Journal of Applied Psychology,* August 1992, p. 526.

7. Mitchell S. Nesler, Herman Aguinis, Brian M. Quigley, and James T. Tedeschi, "The Effect of Credibility on Perceived Power," *Journal of Applied Social Psychology,* vol. 23, no. 17, 1993, pp. 1407–1425.

8. Patricia Sellers, "Exit the Builder, Enter the Repairman," *Fortune,* March 19, 2001, p. 87.

9. Bernard Keys and Thomas Case, "How to Become an Influential Manager," *Academy of Management Executive,* November 1990, p. 44.

10. "You Scratch My Back—Tips on Winning Your Colleague's Cooperation," *Working Smart,* October 1999, p. 1.

11. Gary Yukl, *Skills for Managers and Leaders: Texts, Cases, and Exercises* (Upper Saddle River, N.J.: Prentice Hall, 1990), pp. 58–62.

12. Jeffrey Pfeffer, *Managing with Power: Power and Influence in Organizations* (Boston: Harvard Business School Press, 1992), p. 224.

13. Cited in "Choose Words That Inspire," *Executive Leadership,* March 2001, p. 2.

14. Yukl, *Skills for Managers,* p. 65.

15. Linda Tischler, "IBM's Management Makeover," *Fast Company,* November 2004, p. 113.

16. Andrew J. DuBrin, "Sex Differences in the Endorsement of Influence Tactics and Political Behavior Tendencies," *Journal of Business and Psychology,* Fall 1989, p. 10.

17. Bridget McCrea, "Hands-On Experience," *Black Enterprise,* November 2004, p. 63.

18. Bernhard M. Bass, *Bass & Stogdill's Handbook of Leadership: Theory, Research, & Managerial Applications,* 3rd ed. (New York: The Free Press, 1990), p. 134.

19. "Create an Arsenal of Influence Strategies," *Manager's Edge,* March 2003, p. 1.

20. David M. Buss, Mary Gomes, Dolly S. Higgins, and Karen Lauterbach, "Tactics of Manipulation," *Journal of Personality and Social Psychology,* December 1987, p. 1222.

21. Anthony Bianco and Tom Lowry, "Can Dick Parsons Rescue AOL Time Warner?" *BusinessWeek,* May 19, 2003, p. 89.

22. Buss et al., "Tactics of Manipulation," p. 1222.

23. Gary Yukl and Cecilia M. Falbe, "Influence Tactics and Objectives in Upward, Downward, and Lateral Influence Attempts," *Journal of Applied Psychology,* April 1990, p. 133.

24. Linda Himelstein, "Frank's Life in the Rough," *BusinessWeek,* March 31, 2003, pp. 88–89.

25. David Kipnis and Stuart Schmidt, "Intraorganizational Influence Tactics: Explorations in Getting One's Way," *Journal of Applied Psychology,* August 1980, p. 445.

26. Amy Cortese, "I'm Humble, I'm Respectful," *BusinessWeek,* February 9, 1998, p. 40.

27. Comment contributed anonymously to author by a professor of organizational behavior, September 1996.

28. Yukl and Tracey, "Consequences of Influence Tactics," pp. 525–535.

29. Martin M. Chemers, *An Integrative Theory of Leadership* (Mahwah, N.J.: Lawrence Erlbaum Associates, 1997), p. 76.

30. Carole V. Wells and David Kipnis, "Trust, Dependency, and Control in the Contemporary Organization," *Journal of Business and Psychology,* Summer 2001, pp. 593–603.

31. Jennifer Moss Reimers, John E. Barbuto Jr., Gina S. Matkin, and Tzu-Yun Chin, "Gender Differences in Downward Influence," *Psychological Reports,* vol. 96, 2005, pp. 499–510.

32. Olga Epitropaki and Robin Martin, "Implicit Leadership Theories in Applied Settings: Factor Structure, Generalizability, and Stability over Time," *Journal of Applied Psychology,* April 2004, pp. 297–299.

33. Cited in Lee G. Bolman and Terrence E. Deal, *Reframing Organizations,* 3rd ed. (San Francisco: Jossey-Bass, 2003).

## Chapter 9

1. Chris Penttila, "Heart of Gold: Nonprofits Are Reaping the Rewards of Starting For-Profit Ventures," *Entrepreneur,* September 2004, pp. 19–20; Paul Adams, "Home-Building Charity to Offer Businesses Teamwork Training Sessions for Fee," *The Baltimore Sun Knight-Ridder/Tribune Business News,* August 1, 2004.

2. Edwin A. Locke and Associates, *The Essence of Leadership: The Four Keys to Leading Successfully* (New York: Lexington/Macmillan, 1991), p. 94.

3. Sonia Alleyne, "Kmart Makes Branding Pro Its New Chief," *Black Enterprise,* December 2004, p. 33.

4. W. Dyer, *Team Building: Issues and Alternatives* (Reading, Mass.: Addison-Wesley, 1977), as cited in Lynn R. Offerman and Rebecca K. Spiros, "The Science and Practice of Team Development: Improving the Link," *Academy of Management Journal,* April 2001, p. 380.

5. Jon R. Katzenbach and Douglas K. Smith, "The Discipline of Teams," *Harvard Business Review,* March–April 1993, p. 112.

6. Meredith Belbin, "Solo Leader/Team Leader: Antithesis in Style and Structure," in Michel Syrett and Clare Hogg (eds.), *Frontiers of Leadership* (Oxford, England: Blackwell Publishers, 1992), p. 271.

7. William D. Hitt, *The Leader–Manager: Guidelines for Action* (Columbus, Ohio: Battelle Press, 1988), pp. 68–69.

8. Shari Caudron, "Teamwork Takes Work," *Personnel Journal,* February 1994, p. 45; Andrew J. DuBrin, *The Reengineering Survival Guide: Managing and Succeeding in the Changing Workplace* (Mason, Ohio: Thomson Executive Press, 1996), pp. 129–144.

9. David De Cremer and Daan van Knippenberg, "How Do Leaders Promote Cooperation? The Effects of Charisma and Procedural Fairness," *Journal of Applied Psychology,* October 2002, pp. 858–866.

10. James M. Kouzes and Barry Z. Posner, *The Leadership Challenge,* 3rd ed. (San Francisco: Jossey-Bass, 2002), p. 244.

11. Stephen Baker, "Nokia: Can CEO Ollila Keep the Cellular Superstar Flying High?" *BusinessWeek,* August 10, 1998, p. 56.

12. Dean Tjosvold and Mary M. Tjosvold, *The Emerging Leader: Ways to a Stronger Team* (New York: Lexington Books, 1993).

13. Vanessa Urch Druskat and Steven B. Wolff, "Building the Emotional Intelligence of Groups," *Harvard Business Review,* March 2001, pp. 80–90.

14. William A. Cohen, *The Art of the Leader* (Upper Saddle River, N.J.: Prentice Hall, 1990).

15. Paul S. George, "Teamwork Without Tears," *Personnel Journal,* November 1987, p. 129.

16. Clive Goodworth, "Some Thoughts on Creating a Team," in Syrett and Hogg, *Frontiers of Leadership,* p. 472.

17. "How Jon Gruden Pounds the Rock," *Executive Leadership,* November 2004, p. 4, as adapted from Jon Gruden with Vic Carducci, *Do You Love Football?* (New York: HarperCollins, 2004).

18. Quoted in Nancy Hatch Woodward, "The Coming of the X Managers," *HR Magazine,* March 1999, pp. 75, 76.

19. Susan Sonnesyn Brooks, "Managing a Horizontal Revolution," *HR Magazine,* June 1995, p. 56.

20. Katzenbach and Smith, "The Discipline of Teams," pp. 118–119.

21. Lee G. Bolman and Terrence E. Deal, "What Makes a Team Work?" *Organizational Dynamics,* Autumn 1992, p. 6.

22. Joann Muller, "Next Up: A No-Nonsense Hoosier," *BusinessWeek,* June 10, 2002, p. 80.

23. Anne Fisher, "In Praise of Micromanaging," *Fortune,* August 23, 2004, p. 40.

24. Buce J. Avolio and Surinder S. Kahai, "Adding 'E' to E-Leadership: How It May Impact Your Leadership," *Organizational Dynamics,* Vol. 31, No. 4, 2003, p. 325; Mary Lynn Pulley, John McCarthy, and Sylvester Taylor, "E-Leadership in the Networked Economy," *Leadership in Action,* vol. 20, July–August 2000.

25. Dale E. Yeatts and Cloyd Hyten, *High Performing Self-Managed Work Teams: A Comparison of Theory and Practice* (Thousand Oaks, Calif.: Sage, 1998).

26. Bolman and Deal, "What Makes a Team Work?" pp. 41–42.

27. Thomas J. McCoy, *Creating an "Open Book" Organization—Where Employees Think and Act Like Business Partners* (New York: AMACOM, 1999); John Case, "HR Learns How to Open the Books," *HR Magazine,* May 1998, pp. 71–76.

28. "Open the Books to Educate Your Team: Motivate Your Employees with Bottom-Line Figures," *WorkingSMART*, May 1999, p. 7.

29. Study cited in "Poll Says Sports Helps Women's Career Paths," *Rochester (N.Y.) Democrat and Chronicle*, March 3, 2002, p. 1E.

30. Faith Keenan and Spencer E. Ante, "The New Teamwork," *BusinessWeek e.biz*, February 18, 2002, pp. EB12–EB16.

31. "Easy Ways to Build Team Spirit," *Executive Leadership*, August 2003, p. 5.

32. Joyce Gannon, "Horses Help People Learn to Work Better with Others," *Pittsburgh Post-Gazette*, June 4, 2004.

33. Adapted from Nichole L. Torres, "Go, Team!" *Entrepreneur*, July 2002, p. 22.

34. Jay A. Conger, *Learning to Lead: The Art of Transforming Managers into Leaders* (San Francisco: Jossey-Bass, 1992), p. 159.

35. Cited in Michael P. Regan, "Radical Steps to Help Build Teamwork," Associated Press, February 20, 2004.

36. Torres, "Go, Team!" p. 22.

37. George Graen and J. E. Cashman, "A Role Making Model of Leadership in Formal Organizations: A Developmental Approach," in J. G. Hunt and L. L. Larson (eds.), *Leadership Frontiers* (Kent, Ohio: Kent State University Press, 1975), pp. 143–165; Robert P. Vecchio, "Leader–Member Exchange, Objective Performance, Employment Duration, and Supervisor Ratings: Testing for Moderation and Mediation," *Journal of Business and Psychology*, Spring 1998, p. 328.

38. Elaine M. Engle and Robert G. Lord, "Implicit Theories, Self-Schemas, and Leader–Member Exchange," *Academy of Management Journal*, August 1997, pp. 988–1010.

39. Robert P. Vecchio, "Are You IN or OUT with Your Boss?" *Business Horizons*, 1987, pp. 76–78. See also Charlotte R. Gerstner and David W. Day, "Meta-Analytic Review of Leader–Member Exchange Theory: Correlates and Construct Issues," *Journal of Applied Psychology*, December 1997, pp. 827–844.

40. Howard J. Klein and Jay S. Kim, "A Field Study of the Influences of Situational Constraints, Leader–Member Exchange, and Goal Commitment on Performance," *Academy of Management Journal*, February 1998, pp. 88–95.

41. Randall P. Settoon, Nathan Bennett, and Robert C. Liden, "Social Exchange in Organizations: Perceived Organizational Support, Leader–Member Exchange, and Employee Reciprocity," *Journal of Applied Psychology*, June 1995, pp. 219–227.

42. Pamela Tierney and Talya N. Bauer, "A Longitudinal Assessment of LMX on Extra-Role Behavior," *Academy of Management Best Papers Proceedings*, 1996, pp. 298–302.

43. David A. Hofman and Frederick P. Morgeson, "Safety-Related Behavior as a Social Exchange: The Role of Perceived Organizational Support and Leader–Member Exchange," *Journal of Applied Psychology*, April 1999, pp. 286–296.

44. K. Michele Kacmar, Suzanne Zivnuska, L. A. Witt, and Stanley M. Gully, "The Interactive Effect of Leader–Member Exchange and Communication Frequency on Performance Ratings," *Journal of Applied Psychology*, August 2003, p. 770.

45. Robert C. Liden, Sandy J. Wayne, and Deal Stilwell, "A Longitudinal Study on the Early Development of Leader–Member Exchanges," *Journal of Applied Psychology*, August 1993, pp. 662–674.

46. "Promote Teamwork by Rearranging the Office," *people@work*, sample issue, 1999, published by Texas Professional Training Associates.

## Chapter 10

1. Julie Connelly, "Youthful Attitudes, Sobering Realities," *The New York Times*, October 28, 2003.

2. Thad Green, *Motivation Management: Fueling Performance by Discovering What People Believe About Themselves and Their Organizations* (Palo Alto, Calif.: Davies-Black Publishing, 2000). An original version of expectancy theory applied to work motivation is Victor H. Vroom, *Work and Motivation* (New York: Wiley, 1964).

3. Alexander D. Stajkovic and Fred Luthans, "Social Cognitive Theory and Self-Efficacy: Going Beyond Traditional Motivational and Behavioral Approaches," *Organizational Dynamics*, Spring 1998, p. 66.

4. Wendelien Van Eerde and Hank Thierry, "Vroom's Expectancy Models and Work-Related Criteria: A Meta-Analysis," *Journal of Applied Psychology*, October 1996, pp. 548–556.

5. David A. Nadler and Edward E. Lawler III, "Motivation: A Diagnostic Approach," in Richard Hackman, Edward E. Lawler III, and Lyman W. Porter (eds.), *Perspectives on Behavior in Organizations*, 2nd ed. (New York: McGraw-Hill, 1983), pp. 67–78; James A. F. Stoner and R. Edward Freeman, *Management*, 4th ed. (Upper Saddle River, N.J.: Prentice Hall, 1989), p. 448.

6. Amir Erez and Alice M. Isen, "The Influence of Positive Affect on the Components of Expectancy Motivation," *Journal of Applied Psychology*, December 2002, pp. 1055–1067.

7. "Linux's Quiet Leader Courts Success," *Executive Leadership*, February 2004, p. 2.

8. Literature reviewed in Gerard H. Seitjts, Gary P. Latham, Kevin Tasa, and Bradon W. Latham, "Goal Setting and Goal Orientation: An Integration of "Two Different Yet Related Literatures," *Academy of Management Journal*, April 2004, pp. 227–228.

9. Edwin A. Locke and Gary P. Latham, *A Theory of Goal Setting and Task Performance* (Upper Saddle River, N.J: Prentice Hall, 1990).

10. Cited in "Set Outrageous Goals," *Executive Leadership*, June 2001, p. 7.

11. John J. Donavan and David J. Radosevich, "The Moderating Role of Goal Commitment on the Goal Difficulty-Performance Relationship: A Meta-Analytic Review and Critical Reanalysis," *Journal of Applied Psychology*, April 1998, pp. 308–315.

12. Don VandeWalle, Steven P. Brown, William L. Cron, and John W. Slocum, Jr., "The Influence of Goal Orientation and Self-Regulation Tactics on Sales Performance: A Longitudinal Field Test," *Journal of Applied Psychology*, April 1999, pp. 249–259.

13. P. Christopher Earley and Terri Lituchy, "Delineating Goal and Efficacy Effects: A Test of Three Models," *Journal of Applied Psychology*, February 1991, p. 83.

14. Maurcie E. Schweitzer, Lisa Ordoñez, and Bambi Douma, "Goal Setting as a Moderator of Unethical Behavior," *Academy of Management Journal*, June 2004, p. 430.

15. Jennifer Laabs, "Satisfy Them with More Than Money," *Workforce*, November 1998, p. 43.

16. "Motivate Staffers with a Twist," *Manager's Edge*, April 2003, p. 2.

17. Leslie Gross Klaff, "Getting Happy with the Rewards King," *Workforce*, April 2003, p. 47.

18. Andrew J. DuBrin, "Self-Perceived Technical Orientation and Attitudes Toward Being Flattered," *Psychological Reports*, Vol. 96, 2005, pp. 852–854.

19. Kenneth Hain, *Incentive*, June 1999, as cited in "Reward + Performance Measurement = Success," *Executive Leadership*, January 2001, p. 2.

20. Cited in John A. Byrne, "How to Lead Now," *Fast Company*, August 2003, p. 66.

21. Frank Gibney, Jr., "Is He Built Ford Tough?" *Time*, November 12, 2001, p. 83.

22. Bruce Tulgan, "The Under-Management Epidemic," *HR Magazine*, October 2004, p. 119; "Request Permission to Coach," *Manager's Edge*, June 2003, p. 5.

23. David B. Peterson and Mary Dee Hicks, *Leader as Coach: Strategies for Coaching and Developing Others* (Minneapolis, Minn.: Personnel Decisions, 1996).

24. Robert D. Evered and James E. Selman, "Coaching and the Art of Management," *Organizational Dynamics*, Autumn 1989, p. 15.

25. James M. Hunt and Joseph R. Weintraub, *The Coaching Manager: Developing Top Talent in Business* (Thousand Oaks, Calif.: Sage, 2002).

26. Ian Cunningham and Linda Honold, "Everyone Can Be a Coach," *HR Magazine*, June 1998, pp. 63–66.

27. "Coaching—One Solution to a Tight Training Budget," *HRfocus*, August 2002, p. 7.

28. "Request Permission to Coach," p. 5.

29. Peter Frost and Sandra Robinson, "The Toxic Handler: Organizational Hero and Casualty," *Harvard Business Review*, July–August 1999, pp. 96–106.

30. Richard J. Walsh, "Ten Basic Counseling Skills," *Supervisory Management*, November 1990, p. 6.

31. "Fast Tips for Savvy Managers," *Executive Strategies*, April 1998, p. 1.

32. Amy Joyce, "Career Watch: Business Coach," *The Washington Post*, September 14, 1998.

33. Amy Joyce, "Career Coaches Nurture Executives," *Washington Post*, August 16, 2004.

34. Interview by Bob Rosner, "Team Players' Expect Real Choices," *Workforce*, May 2001, p. 63.

35. Annie Fisher, "Readers Weigh In on Coaches, Crazy Colleagues," *Fortune*, July 23, 2001, p. 272.

36. James W. Smither et al., "Can Working with an Executive Coach Improve Multisource Feedback Ratings over Time? A Quasi-Experimental Field Study," *Personnel Psychology*, Spring 2003, pp. 23–44.

37. Terry R. Bacon and Karen I. Spear, *Adaptive Coaching: The Art and Practice of a Client-Centered Approach to Performance* (Palo Alto, Calif.: Davies-Black, 2003).

38. Stratford Sherman and Alyssa Freas, "The Wild West of Executive Coaching," *Harvard Business Review*, November 2004, pp. 86–88.

39. Steven Berglas, "The Very Real Dangers of Executive Coaching," *Harvard Business Review*, June 2002, pp. 86–92.

## Chapter 11

1. Julie Bennett, "Finding Success with Franchisee-Centered Survival Strategies," *The Wall Street Journal*, April 7, 2003, p. A25.

2. Edward R. Roberts, "Managing Invention and Innovation," *Research Technology Management*, January–February 1998, pp. 1–19.

3. Richard D. Woodman, John E. Sawyer, and Ricky W. Griffin, "Toward a Theory of Organizational Creativity," *Academy of Management Review*, April 1993, p. 293.

4. G. Wallas, *The Art of Thought* (New York: Harcourt Brace, 1926).

5. Quoted in Anna Esaki-Smith and Michael Warshaw, "Renegades 1993: Creating the Future," *Success,* January–February 1993, p. 36.

6. John A. Gover, Royce Ronning, and Cecil R. Reynolds, eds., *Handbook of Creativity* (New York: Plenum Press, 1989); Teresa M. Amabile, "How to Kill Creativity," *Harvard Business Review,* September–October 1998, pp. 78–79.

7. Pamela Tierney and Steven M. Farmer, "Creative Self-Efficacy: Its Potential Antecedents and Relationship to Creative Performance," *Academy of Management Journal,* December 2002, pp. 1137–1148.

8. Cited in Anita Bruzzeset, "Seek Out Creative Free Spirit," Gannet News Service, October 31, 2000.

9. Amabile, "How to Kill Creativity," p. 79.

10. Mihaly Csikszentmihalyi, "If We Are So Rich, Why Aren't We Happy?" *American Psychologist,* October 1999, p. 824.

11. Cited in Bill Breen, "The 6 Myths of Creativity," *Fast Company,* December 2004, pp. 77–78.

12. Greg R. Oldham and Anne Cummings, "Employee Creativity: Personal and Contextual Factors at Work," *Academy of Management Journal,* June 1996, pp. 607–634.

13. Amabile, "How to Kill Creativity," pp. 78–79.

14. "Putting Creativity into Action," *Success Workshop,* supplement to *The PryorReport,* April 1996, p. 1.

15. Cynthia D. McCauley, Russ S. Moxley, and Ellen Van Velsor, *The Center for Creative Leadership Handbook of Leadership Development* (San Francisco: Jossey-Bass), p. 111.

16. Fara Warner, "How Google Searches Itself," *Fast Company,* July 2002, pp. 50, 52; Carl Hymowitz, "Google Founders Face Wealth, Resentment And a Changed Culture," *The Wall Street Journal,* May 18, 2004, p. B1.

17. "Special: CEOs on Innovation: A. G. Lafley, Procter & Gamble," *Fortune,* March 8, 2004, pages not numbered.

18. "Brainstorm Better Ideas with the 6-3-5 Method," *Manager's Intelligence Report,* undated sample distributed in September 1996, Lawrence Ragan Communication, Inc. 316 N. Michigan Avenue, Chicago, IL 60601.

19. Keng L. Siau, "Electronic Brainstorming," *Innovative Leader,* April 1997, p. 3.

20. Michael Schrage, "Playing Around with Brainstorming," *Harvard Business Review,* March 2001, pp. 149–154. [Review of Tom Kelley with Jonathan Littman, *The Art of Innovation: Lessons in Creativity from IDEO, America's Leading Design Firm* (New York: Doubleday/Currency, 2001)].

21. Anne Sagen, "Creativity Tools: Versatile Problem Solvers That Can Double as Fun and Games," *Supervisory Management,* October 1991, pp. 1–2.

22. Cited in Robert McGarvey, "Turn It On: Creativity Is Crucial to Your Business's Success," *Entrepreneur,* November 1996, p. 156.

23. Juanita Weaver, "The Mental Picture: Bringing Your Definition of Creativity into Focus," *Entrepreneur,* February 2003, p. 69.

24. Scott S. Smith, "Grounds for Success," *Entrepreneur,* May 1998, p. 120.

25. Alex F. Osburn, quoted in "Breakthrough Ideas," *Success,* October 1990, p. 38.

26. Breen, "The 6 Myths of Creativity," p. 78.

27. "Be a Creative Problem Solver," *Executive Strategies,* June 6, 1989, pp. 1–2.

28. Amabile, "How to Kill Creativity," pp. 80–81; Teresa M. Amabile, Constance N. Hadley, and Steven J. Kramer, "Creativity Under the Gun," *Harvard Business Review,* August 2002, pp. 52–61; G. Pascal Zachary, "Mighty Is the Mongrel," *Fast Company,* July 2000, pp. 270–274; Breen, "The 6 Myths of Creativity," pp. 77–80.

29. Pamela Tierney, Steven M. Farmer, and George B. Graen, "An Examination of Leadership and Employee Creativity: The Relevance of Traits and Relationships," *Personnel Psychology,* Autumn 1999, pp. 591–620.

30. Alan Deutschman, "The Fabric of Creativity," *Fast Company,* December 2004, pp. 59–60.

31. Richard Florida as cited in Chris Pentila, "An Art in Itself," *Entrepreneur,* December 2003, p. 96.

32. Shari Caudron, "Strategies for Managing Creative Workers," *Personnel Journal,* December 1994, pp. 104–113; Pentila, "An Art in Itself," pp. 96–97.

33. Keith H. Hammonds, "No Risk, No Reward," *Fast Company,* April 2002, pp. 81–93.

34. Cited in Robert d. Hof, "Building an Idea Factory," *BusinessWeek,* October 11, 2004, p. 194.

35. Ben Elgin, "A Do-It-Yourself Plan at Cisco," *BusinessWeek,* September 10, 2001, p. 52.

36. Quoted in Michael Schrage, "Getting Beyond the Innovation Fetish," *Fortune,* November 13, 2000, p. 232.

37. Robert McGarvey, "Idea Inc.," *Entrepreneur,* March 1998, pp. 127, 129.

38. Sebastian Moffett, "Separation Anxiety," *The Wall Street Journal,* September 27, 2004, p. R11.

39. Patricia Sellers, "P&G: Teaching an Old Dog New Tricks," *Fortune,* May 31, 2004, p. 174.

40. Gareth Morgan, *Creative Organization Theory: A Resource-Book* (Newbury Park, Calif.: Sage, 1990); Lee E. Meadows, "Don't Let 'No' Stop Creativity, Ideas," *detnews.com,* November 19, 2004.

Solutions to Leadership Skill-Building Exercise 11-3, Word Hints to Creativity

| | | | |
|---|---|---|---|
| 1. party | 5. club | 9. high | 13. make |
| 2. ball | 6. dog | 10. sugar | 14. bean |
| 3. cheese | 7. paper | 11. floor | 15. light |
| 4. cat | 8. finger | 12. green | |

## Chapter 12

1. "CEO Demotes Himself for a Day," *Knight Ridder*, September 23, 2002. Copyright © 2002. Distributed by Knight Ridder/Tribune. Reprinted by permission.

2. Peter de la Billiere, "Leadership," in *Business: The Ultimate Resource* (Cambridge, Mass.: Perseus Publishing, 2002), p. 226.

3. Bernard M. Bass, *Bass & Stogdill's Handbook of Leadership: Theory, Research, & Managerial Applications*, 3rd ed. (New York: The Free Press, 1990), p. 111.

4. M. Remland, "Leadership Impressions and Nonverbal Communication in a Superior–Subordinate Interaction," *Journal of Business Communication*, vol. 18, no. 3, 1981, pp. 17–29.

5. James M. Kouzes and Barry Z. Posner, *The Leadership Challenge: How to Get Extraordinary Things Done in Organizations* (San Francisco: Jossey-Bass, 1987), p. 118.

6. Stephen P. Robbins and Phillip L. Hunsaker, *Training in Interpersonal Skills: Tips for Managing People at Work* (Upper Saddle River, N.J.: Prentice Hall, 1996), p. 115.

7. Jay Conger, "The Six Myths of Persuasion," *Executive Leadership*, October 2000, p. 8.

8. Mark Hendricks, "Wag Your Tale," *Entrepreneur*, February 2001, pp. 78–81.

9. Frances Hesselbein, *Hesselbein on Leadership* (San Francisco: Jossey-Bass, 2002).

10. Several of these examples are from "Avoid These Top Ten Language Errors," *Working SMART*, October 1991, p. 8; Joann S. Lublin, "Readers Agree Speech Needs Cleaning Up, And They Provide Tips," *The Wall Street Journal*, October 19, 2004, p. B1.

11. William Struck, Jr., and E. B. White, *The Elements of Style*, 4th ed., with a forward by Roger Angell (Boston: Allyn and Bacon, 1996).

12. Sherry Sweetham, "How to Organize Your Thoughts for Better Communication," *Personnel*, March 1986, p. 39.

13. Deborah Tannen, "The Power of Talk: Who Gets Heard and Why?" *Harvard Business Review*, September–October 1995, pp. 138–148.

14. Ibid., pp. 138–148; "How You Speak Shows Where You Rank," *Fortune*, February 2, 1998, p. 156; "Speak Like You Mean Business," *Working Smart*, www.nibm.net, March 2004; "Weed Out Wimpy Words: Speak Up Without Backpedaling, Qualifying," *WorkingSMART*, March 2000, p. 2.

15. Robert B. Cialdini, "Harnessing the Science of Persuasion," *Harvard Business Review*, October 2001, pp. 72–79.

16. Ibid., p. 79.

17. Albert Mehrabian and M. Wiener, "Decoding Inconsistent Communications," *Journal of Personality and Social Psychology*, vol. 6, 1947, pp. 109–114.

18. Several of the suggestions here are from *Body Language for Business Success* (New York: National Institute for Business Management, 1989), pp. 2–29; "Attention All Monotonous Speakers," *WorkingSMART*, March 1998, p. 1.

19. The literature is reviewed in David A. Whetton and Kim S. Cameron, *Developing Management Skills*, 5th ed. (Upper Saddle River, N.J.: Prentice Hall, 2002), pp. 223–233.

20. Ibid., p. 230.

21. Trudy Milburn, "Bridging Cultural Gaps," *Management Review*, January 1997, pp. 26–29.

22. Gunnar Beeth, "Multicultural Managers Wanted," *Management Review*, May 1997, p. 17.

23. "When English Is Not Their Native Tongue," *Manager's Edge*, April 2003, p. 5.

24. Kathryn Kranhold, "Lost in Translation," *The Wall Street Journal*, May 18, 2004, p. B1.

25. "Cross Cultural Communication: An Essential Dimension of Effective Education," *Northwest Regional Educational Laboratory: CNORSE—www.nwrel.org/cnorse*.

26. Siri Carpenter, "Why Do 'They All Look Alike'?" *Monitor on Psychology*, December 2000, p. 44.

27. Jim Kennedy and Anna Everest, "Put Diversity in Context," *Personnel Journal*, September 1991, pp. 50–52.

28. Lowell H. Lamberton and Leslie Minor, *Human Relations: Strategies for Success* (Chicago: Irwin/Mirror Press, 1995), p. 124.

29. Howard M. Guttman, "Conflict at the Top," *Management Review*, November 1999, p. 50.

30. Kenneth Thomas, "Conflict and Conflict Management," in Marvin D. Dunnette, ed., *Handbook of Industrial and Organizational Psychology* (Chicago: Rand McNally, 1976), pp. 900–922.

31. Cited in "Replace Criticism with Agreement," *Manager's Edge*, May 1999, p. 50.

32. Elizabeth A. Mannix, Leigh L. Thompson, and Max H. Bazerman, "Negotiation in Small Groups," *Journal of Applied Psychology*, June 1989, pp. 508–517.

33. Patrick S. Nugent, "Managing Conflict: Third-Party Interventions for Managers," *Academy of Management Executive*, February 2002, p. 152.

34. John Heister, "Collaborate to Solve Societal Ills," Rochester, New York, *Democrat and Chronicle*, May 14, 2004, p. 18A.

35. James K. Sebenius, "Six Habits of Merely Effective Negotiators," *Harvard Business Review*, April 2001, pp. 91–92.

36. Frank Acuff, *The World Class Negotiator: An Indispensable Guide for Anyone Doing Business with Those from a Foreign Culture* (New York: AMACOM, 1992).

37. Marc Deiner, "Culture Shock," *Entrepreneur*, July 2003, p. 77.

38. "Roger Fisher: Master Negotiator and Best-Selling Author," in *In Their Own Words*, National Institute of Business Management Special Report 250, 1997, p. 7.

39. Adapted from Gay Lumsden and Donald Lumsden, *Communicating in Groups and Teams: Sharing Leadership* (Belmont, Calif.: Wadsworth, 1993), p. 233.

## Chapter 13

1. "Toys "R" Us May Exit Toy Business, Take New Focus," Associated Press, August 12, 2004.

2. Donald C. Hambrick and James W. Fredrickson, "Are Your Sure You Have a Strategy?" *Academy of Management Executive*, November 2001, p. 48.

3. Robert L. Phillips and James G. Hunt (eds.), *Strategic Leadership: A Multiorganizational-Level Perspective* (Westport, Conn.: Quorum Books, 1992).

4. Bruce J. Avolio and David A. Waldman, "An Examination of Age and Cognitive Test Performance Across Job Complexity and Occupational Types," *Journal of Applied Psychology*, February 1990, pp. 43–50.

5. Matthew Boyle, "The Man Who Fixed Kellogg," *Fortune*, September 6, 2004, p. 220.

6. Quoted in John A. Byrne, "Three of the Busiest New Strategists," *BusinessWeek*, August 26, 2002, p. 50.

7. Samuel Greengard, "Leveraging a Low-Wage Workforce," *Workforce Online*, February 2004.

8. "A Strategy Session with C. K. Prahalad, *Management Review*, April 1995, pp. 50–51.

9. Gary Hamel, "Strategy as Revolution," *Harvard Business Review*, July–August 1996, pp. 69–82; Hamel, *Leading the Revolution* (New York: Penguin/Putnam, 2002).

10. Gary Hamel, "Revolution vs. Evolution: You Need Both," *Harvard Business Review*, May 2001, p. 150.

11. Keith H. Hammonds, "Michael Porter's Big Ideas," *Fast Company*, March 2001, p. 153.

12. Laurie Larwood, Cecilia M. Falbe, Mark P. Kriger, and Paul Miesing, "Structure and Meaning of Organizational Vision," *Academy of Management Journal*, June 1995, pp. 740–769.

13. James R. Lucas, "Anatomy of a Vision Statement," *Management Review*, February 1998, p. 26.

14. Lesley Hazelton, "Jeff Bezos," *Success*, July 1998, p. 58; Alan Deutschman, "Inside the Mind of Jeff Bezos," *Fast Company*, August 2004, pp. 52–58.

15. Several ideas for this version of SWOT are from "SWOT Analysis," *Business Owner's Tool Kit*, November 8, 1999, *www.toolkit.cch.com/text/p02_4341.asp;* "Performing a SWOT Analysis," in *Business: The Ultimate Resources* (Cambridge, Mass.: Perseus Publishing, 2002), pp. 226–227.

16. A representative example of a complex strategic planning scheme is Joseph C. Picken and Gregory G. Dess, "Right Strategy–Wrong Problem," *Organizational Dynamics*, Summer 1998, pp. 35–49.

17. Michael Porter, *Competitive Strategy* (New York: Free Press, 1980), pp. 36–46.

18. Amy Merrick, "Gap's Greatest Generation?" *The Wall Street Journal*, September 15, 2004, p. B1.

19. Nick Wingfield, "Taking on eBay," *The Wall Street Journal*, September 15, 2004, p. R10.

20. Joshua Watson, "This Dutchman Is Flying," *Fortune*, June 23, 2003, pp. 89–90.

21. "GM, DaimlerChrysler Team Up on Hybrids," Associated Press, December 14, 2004.

22. Ben Rand, "Kodak's Screen Venture Grows," *Rochester (N.Y.) Democrat and Chronicle*, January 17, 2003, p. 16D.

23. Alison Overholt, "Listening to Starbucks," *Fast Company*, July 2004, pp. 51–52.

24. Matthew Karnitschnig, "Montblanc, Famed for Pens, Targets Wrists," *The Wall Street Journal*, December 23, 2004, p. B1.

25. George Anders, "Homespun Strategist." *The Wall Street Journal*, January 6, 2004, p. B1.

26. Frank Gibney, Jr., "Pepsi Gets Back in the Game," *Time*, April 26, 1999, pp. 44–46.

27. "Brands in an Age of Anti-Americanism," *BusinessWeek*, August 4, 2003, p. 69.

28. Alison Overholt, "Smart Strategies: Putting Ideas to Work," *Fast Company*, April 2004, p. 63.

29. Paul C. Judge, "Internet Strategies That Work," *Fast Company*, March 2001, p. 170.

30. Bill Breen and Anna Muoio, "Peoplepalooza," *Fast Company*, January 2001, pp. 80–81.

31. Michael Beer and Russell A. Eisenstat, "How to Have an Honest Conversation About Your Business Strategy," *Harvard Business Review*, February 2004, pp. 82–89.

32. David A. Garvin, "Building a Learning Organization," *Harvard Business Review*, July–August 1993, p. 80.

33. Pamela Babcock, "Shedding Light on Knowledge Management," *HR Magazine*, May 2004, p. 7.

34. Thomas H. Davenport and John Glaser, "Just-in-Time Delivery Comes to Knowledge Management," *Harvard Business Review,* July 2002, pp. 107–111.

35. Bill Breen, "Hidden Asset," *Fast Company,* March 2004, p. 95.

36. David W. De Long and Liam Fahey, "Diagnosing Cultural Barriers to Knowledge Management," *Academy of Management Executive,* November 2000, pp. 115–117.

37. Megan Santosus, "Information Micromanagement," *CIO Enterprise Magazine,* April 15, 1998 (*www.cio.com/archive/enterprise/041598_reality.html*).

38. Robert M. Fulmer and J. Bernard Keys, "A Conversation with Peter Senge: New Developments in Organizational Learning," *Organizational Dynamics,* Autumn 1998, p. 35.

39. Lester Thurow, "Help Wanted: A Chief Knowledge Officer," *Fast Company,* January 2004, p. 91.

40. Dusya Vera and Mary Crossan, "Strategic Leadership and Organizational Learning," *Academy of Management Review,* April 2004, p. 235.

41. Robert M. Fulmer and Philip Gibbs, "The Second Generation Learning Organizations: New Tools for Sustainable Competitive Advantage," *Organizational Dynamics,* Autumn 1998, pp. 7–20; Peter M. Senge, *The Fifth Discipline* (New York: Doubleday, 1990); Thomas P. Lawrence, Michael M. Mauws, Bruno Dyck, and Robert F. Kleysen, "The Politics of Organizational Learning: Integrating Power into the 4I Framework," *Academy of Management Review,* January 2005, pp. 180–191; Constance James, "Designing Learning Organizations," *Organizational Dynamics,* vol. 32, no. 1, pp. 46–61.

42. Neil Gross, "Mining a Company's Mother Lode of Talent," *BusinessWeek,* August 28, 2000, p. 137.

43. Cited in "Making Vision Statements 'Visionary,'" *Manager's Edge,* December 1998, p. 1.

### Chapter 14

1. Pui-Wing Tam, "'Awareness Training' Helps U.S. Workers Better Know Their Counterparts in India," *The Wall Street Journal,* May 25, 2004, p. B1.

2. Jennifer Schramm, "Acting Affirmatively," *HR Magazine,* September 2003, p. 192.

3. Cited in Fay Hansen, "Diversity's Business Case Doesn't Add Up," *Workforce,* April 2003, pp. 28–32.

4. Irwin Speizer, "Diversity on the Menu," *Workforce Management,* November 2004, pp. 41–45; Louisa Wah, "Diversity at Allstate: A Competitive Weapon," *Management Review,* July–August 1999, p. 24; Jeremy Kahn, "Diversity Trumps the Downturn," *Fortune,* July 9, 2001, pp. 114–116; Daren Fonda,

"Selling in Tongues," *Time,* November 26, 2001, pp. B12–B15.

5. Jim Kirk, "PepsiCo Wants Hispanics to Feel at Home," *Chicago Tribune* online edition, June 20, 2004, p. 1.

6. "Cleveland Cavaliers," Rochester, New York, *Democrat and Chronicle,* December 7, 2004, p. 3D.

7. Anthony Limon, "Back to the Future," *Hispanic Business,* November 2004, p. 66.

8. Frances J. Milliken and Luis L. Martins, "Searching for Common Threads: Understanding the Multiple Effects of Diversity in Organizational Groups," *Academy of Management Review,* April 1996, p. 403. See also Daan van Knippenberg, Carsten K. W. De Dreu, and Astrid C. Homan, "Work Group Diversity and Group Performance: An Integrative Model and Research Agenda," *Journal of Applied Psychology,* December 2004, pp. 1008–1022.

9. Pamela Babcock, "Diversity Down to the Letter," *HR Magazine,* June 2004, p. 91.

10. Study reported in brochure for Diversity Summit 2002, IQPC, 150 Clove Road, P.O. Box 401, Little Falls, NJ 07424-0401.

11. Geert Hofstede, *Culture's Consequences: International Differences in Work-Related Values* (Beverly Hills, Calif.: Sage, 1980); updated and expanded in Geert Hofstede "The Universal and the Specific in 21st-Century Global Management," *Organizational Dynamics,* Summer 1999, pp. 39–41.

12. Arvind V. Phatak, *International Dimensions of Management* (Boston: Kent, 1983), pp. 22–26.

13. Facts are from Christopher Broads, "Clocking Out: Short Work Hours Undercut Europe in Economic Drive," *The Wall Street Journal,* August 8, 2002, pp. A1, A6. Edward C. Prescott, "Why Do Americans Work More than Europeans?" *The Wall Street Journal* October 21, 2004, p. A18.

14. Hofstede, "The Universal and the Specific," pp. 35–37.

15. Felix C. Brodbeck, Michael Frese, and Mansour Javidan, "Leadership Made in Germany: Low on Compassion, High on Performance," *Academy of Management Executive,* February 2002, pp. 16–30.

16. Jeffrey C. Kennedy, "Leadership in Malaysia: Traditional Values, International Outlook," *Academy of Management Executive,* August 2002, pp. 15–26.

17. Del Jones, "North vs. South: Leaders from Both Sides of the Mason–Dixon Line Have Strong Opinions About the Styles of their Regionally Different Peers," *USA Today,* July 9, 2004, p. 5B.

18. Ibid.

19. Gunnar Beeth, "Multicultural Managers Wanted," *Management Review,* May 1997, p. 17.

20. Carla Johnson, "Cultural Sensitivity Adds Up to Good Business Sense," *HR Magazine,* November 1995, pp. 83–85.

21. Louis Kraar, "Need a Friend in Asia: Try the Singapore Connection," *Fortune*, March 4, 1996, p. 180.

22. P. Christopher Earley and Elaine Mosakowski, "Cultural Intelligence," *Harvard Business Review*, October 2004, pp. 139–146.

23. Joseph A. Petrick, Robert E. Scherer, James D. Bodzinski, John F. Quinn, and M. Fall Ainina, "Global Leadership Skills and Reputational Capital: Intangible Resources for Sustainable Competitive Advantage," *Academy of Management Executive*, February 1999, pp. 58–69.

24. Manfred F. R. Ket De Vries and Elizabeth Florent-Treacy, "Global Leadership from A to Z: Creating High Commitment Organizations," *Organizational Dynamics*, Spring 2002, pp. 295–309.

25. Gretchen M. Spreitzer, Morgan W. McCall, Jr., and Joan D. Mahoney, "Early Identification of International Executive Potential," *Journal of Applied Psychology*, February 1997, pp. 6–29.

26. Research cited in Douglas T. Hall, Guorong Zhu, and Amin Yan, "Developing Global Leaders: To Hold On to Them, Let Them Go," *Advances in Global Leadership*, vol. 2, 2001, p. 331.

27. Daren Fonda, "Selling in Tongues," *Time*, November 26, 2001, pp. B12–B15.

28. Todd Campbell, "Diversity in Depth," *HR Magazine*, March 2003, p. 152.

29. Ann Zimmerman, "Defending Wal-Mart," *The Wall Street Journal*, October 6, 2004, p. B1.

30. Louisa Wah, "Diversity at Allstate," *Management Review*, July–August 1999, p. 28.

31. Cora Daniels, "50 Best Companies for Minorities," *Fortune*, June 28, 2004, p. 138.

32. Marc Adams, "Building a Rainbow One Stripe at a Time," *HR Magazine*, August 1998, pp. 73–74.

33. Jerry Langdon, "Minority Executives Benefit from Mentors," Gannett News Service, December 7, 1998. See also Letty C. Hardy, "Mentoring: A Long-Term Approach to Diversity," *HRfocus*, July 1998, p. S11.

34. Patricia L. Nemetz and Sandra L. Christensen, "The Challenge of Cultural Diversity: Harnessing a Diversity of Views to Understand Multiculturalism," *Academy of Management Review*, April 1996, p. 455.

35. P. Christopher Earley and Randall S. Peterson, "The Elusive Cultural Chameleon: Cultural Intelligence as a New Approach to Intercultural Training for the Global Manager," *Academy of Management Learning and Education*, March 2004, p. 105.

36. Quoted in Lin Grensing-Pophal, "Reaching for Diversity," *HR Magazine*, May 2002, p. 54.

37. Quoted in Lin Grensing-Pophal, "Hiring to Fit Your Corporate Culture," *HR Magazine*, August 1999, p. 52.

38. Taylor Cox, Jr., "The Multicultural Organization," *Academy of Management Executive*, May 1991, p. 34.

39. Ann M. Morrison, *The New Leaders: Guidelines for Leadership Diversity in America* (San Francisco: Jossey-Bass, 1992).

40. Jacqueline A. Gilbert and John M. Ivancevich, "Valuing Diversity: A Tale of Two Organizations," *Academy of Management Executive*, February 2000, pp. 103–104.

41. Quoted in Julie Bennett, "'Corporate Angst' Can Generate Gaffes That Turn Off Coveted Candidates," *The Wall Street Journal*, October 21, 2003, p. D9.

## Chapter 15

1. Kris Maher, "The Jungle: Focus on Recruitment, Pay and Getting Ahead," *The Wall Street Journal*, November 11, 2003, p. B10.

2. Robert Hogan and Rodney Warrenfeltz, "Educating the Modern Manager," *Academy of Management Learning and Education*, March 2003, p. 74.

3. Chris Argyris, "Teaching Smart People How to Learn," *Harvard Business Review*, May–June 1991, pp. 99–109; Chris Argyris, "Double-Loop Learning, Teaching, and Research," *Academy of Management Learning and Education*, December 2002, p. 206.

4. Cynthia D. McCauley, Russ S. Moxley, and Ellen Van Velsor, *Handbook of Leadership Development* (San Francisco: Jossey-Bass, 1998), pp. 132–133. The same theme is found in Morgan W. McCall, "Leadership Development Through Experience," *Academy of Management Executive*, August 2004, pp. 127–130.

5. "How Great Leaders Benefit from Failure," *Manager's Edge*, November 2004, p. 3.

6. Marcus Buckingham and Curt Coffman, "How Great Managers Develop Top People," *Workforce*, June 1999, p. 103; Marcus Buckingham and Curt Coffman, *First Break the Rules: What the World's Greatest Managers Do Differently* (New York: Simon & Schuster, 1999).

7. Richard L. Hughes, Robert C. Ginnett, and Gordon J. Curphy, *Leadership: Enhancing the Lessons of Experience* (Burr Ridge, Ill.: Irwin, 1993) pp. 33–36.

8. Daphna F. Raskas and Donald C. Hambrick, "Multifunctional Managerial Development: A Framework for Evaluating the Options," *Organizational Dynamics*, Autumn 1992, p. 5.

9. Joe Mullich, "Warming Up for Leadership," *Workforce Management*, November 2004, p. 64.

10. Michael Beer, Russell Eisenstadt, and Bert Spector, *The Critical Path to Corporate Renewal* (Boston: Harvard Business School Press, 1995).

11. Carol Hymowitz, "Effective Leaders Say One Pivotal Experience Sealed Their Careers," *The Wall Street Journal*, August 27, 2002, p. B1; Warren Bennis and

Robert Thomas, *Geeks and Geezers* (Boston: Harvard Business School Press, 2002).

12. Belle Rose Ragins and John L. Cotton, "Mentor Functions and Outcomes: A Comparison of Men and Women in Formal and Informal Mentoring Relationships," *Journal of Applied Psychology,* August 1999, pp. 529–550.

13. Andrea C. Poe, "Establish Positive Mentoring Relationships," *HR Magazine,* February 2002, p. 65.

14. Shimon-Craig Van Collie, "Moving Up Through Mentoring," *Workforce,* March 1998, p. 36.

15. Joann S. Lublin, "Even Top Executives Could Use Mentors to Benefit Their Careers," *The Wall Street Journal,* July 1, 2003, p. B1.

16. Lublin, "Protégé Finds Mentor Gave Her a Big Boost, but Shadow Lingers," *The Wall Street Journal,* September 7, 2004, p. B1.

17. Flyer for *Corporate University Week 2002,* presented by HRevents™, p. 4.

18. Victoria A. Guthrie and Lily Kelly-Radford, "Feedback Intensive Programs," in Cynthia D. McCauley, Russ S. Moxley, and Ellen Van Velsor, eds., *Handbook of Leadership Development* (San Francisco: Jossey-Bass, 1998), pp. 66–105.

19. Ann Pomeroy, "Head of the Class," *HR Magazine,* January 2005, p. 57.

20. Maryann Hammers, "High Scores in the Leadership Game," *Workforce Management,* December 2003, p. 57.

21. Carol Hymowitz, "PepsiCo Chief Executive Asks Future Leaders to Train Like Athletes," *The Wall Street Journal,* September 9, 2003, p. B1.

22. Cheryl Dahle, "Natural Leader," *Fast Company,* December 2000, p. 270.

23. Jay A. Conger and Beth Benjamin, *Building Leaders: How Successful Companies Develop the Next Generation* (San Francisco: Jossey-Bass, 1999), p. 79.

24. Carol Hymowitz, "More CEOs Seek Psychotherapy," *The Wall Street Journal,* June 22, 2004, pp. B1, B3.

25. Dale S. Rose and Karen E. Fiore, "Practical Considerations and Alternative Research Methods for Evaluating HR Programs," *Journal of Business and Psychology,* Winter 1999, pp. 235–240.

26. Caroline Louise Cole, "Boeing U.," *Workforce,* October 2000, p. 68.

27. Ellen Van Velsor, "Assessing the Impact of Development Experiences," in McCauley, Moxley, and Van Velsor, *Handbook of Leadership Development,* pp. 264–268.

28. Robert Hogan and Rodney Warrenfeltz, "Educating the Modern Manager," *Academy of Management Learning and Education,* March 2003, pp. 78–79.

29. Sheila Anne Feeney, "Irreplaceable You," *Workforce Management,* August 2003, p. 38.

30. Jay W. Lorsch and Rakesh Khurana, "Changing Leaders: The Board's Role in CEO Succession," *Harvard Business Review,* May–June 1999, p. 100.

31. Linda Grant, "GE: The Envelope, Please," *Fortune,* June 26, 1995, pp. 89–90.

32. William C. Byham, "Grooming Next-Millennium Leaders," *HR Magazine,* February 1999, pp. 46–50.

33. Ram Charan, Steve Drotter, and Jim Noel, *The Leadership Pipeline: How to Build the Leadership Powered Company* (San Francisco: Jossey-Bass, 2001).

34. Joseph Weber, "Family, Inc.," *BusinessWeek,* November 10, 2003, p. 108.

35. Gene Colter, "Leadership Crisis Awaits Owners of Family Firms," *The Wall Street Journal,* March 3, 2003, p. B4A.

36. Martha Frase-Blunt, "Moving Past 'Mini-Me'," *HR Magazine,* November 2003, pp. 95–98.

37. Carol Hymowitz, "In the Lead: Middle Managers Find Their Skills, Integrity Now Carry More Weight," *The Wall Street Journal,* July 30, 2002, p. B1.

38. Harriet Rubin, "Power," *Fast Company,* September 2002, p. 72.

39. Linda A. Hill, "New Manager Development for the 21st Century," *Academy of Management Executive,* August 2004, p. 124.

# Glossary

*NOTE:* The number in brackets following each term refers to the chapter in which the term first appears.

**Achievement motivation** Finding joy in accomplishment for its own sake. [2]

**Assertiveness** Forthrightness in expressing demands, opinions, feelings, and attitudes. [2]

**Attribution theory** The theory of how we explain the causes of events. [1]

**Autocratic leader** A person in charge who retains most of the authority for himself or herself. [4]

**Bandwagon technique** A manipulative approach emphasizing that "everybody else is doing it." [8]

**Casual time orientation** The view that time is an unlimited and unending resource, leading toward extreme patience. [14]

**Centrality** The extent to which a unit's activities are linked into the system of organized activities. [7]

**Charisma** A special quality of leaders whose purposes, powers, and extraordinary determination differentiate them from others. [3]

**Coalition** A specific arrangement of parties working together to combine their power. [8]

**Coercive power** The power to punish for noncompliance; power based on fear. [7]

**Cognitive factors** Problem-solving and intellectual skills. [2]

**Cognitive resource theory** An explanation of leadership emphasizing that stress plays a key role in determining how a leader's intelligence is related to group performance. [5]

**Collectivisim** A belief that the group and society should receive top priority. [14]

**Commitment** The most successful outcome of a leader's influence tactic: The person makes a full effort. [8]

**Compliance** Partial success of an influence attempt by a leader: The person makes a modest effort. [8]

**Concern for others** In Hofstede's research, an emphasis on personal relationships, caring for others, and a high quality of life. [14]

**Concert building** A conception of the leader's role that involves both aligning and mobilizing in a manner similar to an orchestra leader. [4]

**Congruence** The matching of verbal and nonverbal communication to what the sender is thinking and feeling. [12]

**Conjunctive communication** Communication that is linked logically to previous messages, thus enhancing communication. [12]

**Consensus leader** The person in charge who encourages group discussion about an issue and then makes a decision that reflects general agreement and that group members will support. [4]

**Consideration** the degree to which the leader creates an environment of emotional support, warmth, friendliness, and trust. [4]

**Consultative leader** A person in charge who confers with group members before making a decision. [4]

**Contingency approach to leadership** The contention that leaders are most effective when they make their behavior contingent upon situational forces, including group member characteristics. [5]

**Cooperation theory** A belief in cooperation and collaboration rather than competitiveness as a strategy for building teamwork. [9]

**Creative self-efficacy** An employee's belief that that he or she can be creative in a work role. [11]

**Creativity** The production of novel and useful ideas. [11]

**Crisis leadership** The process of leading group members through a sudden and largely unanticipated, intensely negative, and emotionally draining circumstance. [5]

**Cultural intelligence(CQ)** An outsider's ability to interpret someone's unfamiliar and ambiguous gestures the way that person's compatriots would. [14]

**Cultural sensitivity** An awareness of and a willingness to investigate the reasons why people of another culture act as they do. [14]

**Debasement** The act of demeaning or insulting oneself to control the behavior of another person. [8]

**Delegation** The assignment of formal authority and responsibility for accomplishing a specific task to another person. [7]

**Democratic leader** A person in charge who confers final authority on the group. [4]

**Disjunctive communication** Communication that is not linked to the preceding messages, resulting in impaired communication. [12]

**Diversity training** A learning experience designed to bring about workplace harmony by teaching people how to get along better with diverse work associates. [14]

**Domains of impact** Areas of possible change in leadership development programs. [15]

**Double-loop learning** An in-depth style of learning that occurs when people use feedback to confront the validity of the goal or the values implicit in the situation. [15]

**Drive** A propensity to put forth high energy into achieving goals and persistence in applying that energy. [2]

**Effective leader** One who helps group members attain productivity including good quality, and satisfaction. [4]

**E-leadership** A form of leadership practiced in a context where work is mediated by information technology. [9]

**Emotional intelligence** The ability to do such things as understand one's feelings, have empathy for others, and regulate one's emotions to enhance one's quality of life. [2]

**Emotional stability** The ability to control emotions to the point that one's emotional responses are appropriate to the occasion. [2]

**Employee network group** A group of employees throughout the company who affiliate on the basis of a group characteristic such as race, ethnicity, sex, sexual orientation, or physical ability status. [14]

**Empowerment** Passing decision-making authority and responsibility from managers to group members. [7]

**Ethics** The study of moral obligations, or separating right from wrong. [6]

**Executive (or business) coach** An outside or inside specialist who advises a person about personal improvement and behavioral change. [10]

**Expectancy** An individual's assessment of the probability that effort will lead to correct performance of the task. [10]

**Expectancy theory** A theory of motivation based on the premise that the amount of effort people expend depends on how much reward they can expect in return. [10]

**Experience of flow** An experience so engrossing and enjoyable that the task becomes worth doing for its own sake regardless of the external consequences. [11]

**Expert power** The ability to influence others because of one's specialized knowledge, skills, or abilities. [3]

**Expertise approach** A belief that the leader's most important responsibility is providing an area of expertise that will be a source of competitive advantage. [2]

**Farsightedness** The ability to understand the long-range implications of actions and policies. [2]

**Feedback-intensive development program** A learning experience that helps leaders develop by seeing more clearly their patterns of behaviors, the reasons for such behaviors, and the impact of these behaviors and attitudes on their effectiveness. [15]

**Flexibility** The ability to adjust to different situations. [2]

**Forced-association technique** A method of releasing creativity in which individuals or groups solve a problem by making associations between the properties of two objects. [11]

**Formality** The attachment of considerable importance to tradition, ceremony, social rules, and rank. [14]

**Goal** What a person is trying to accomplish. [10]

**Hands-on leader** A leader who gets directly involved in the details and process of operations. [8]

**Implicit leadership theories** Personal assumptions about the traits and abilities that characterize an ideal organizational leader. [8]

**Individualism** A mental set in which people see themselves first as individuals and believe their own interests and values take priority. [14]

**Influence** The ability to affect the behavior of others in a particular direction. [8]

**Informality** A casual attitude toward tradition, ceremony, social rules, and rank. [14]

**Information power** Power stemming from formal control over the information people need to do their work. [7]

**Initiating structure** Organizing and defining relationships in the group by activities such as assigning specific tasks, specifying procedures to be followed, scheduling work, and clarifying expectations of team members. [4]

**Innovation** The process of creating new ideas and their implementation. [11]

**Insight** A depth of understanding that requires considerable intuition and common sense. [2]

**Instrumentality** An individual's assessment of the probability that performance will lead to certain outcomes. [10]

**Integrity** Loyalty to rational principles, thereby practicing what one preaches, regardless of emotional or social pressure. [6]

**Intercultural training** A set of learning experiences designed to help employees understand the customs, traditions, and beliefs of another culture. [14]

**Internal locus of control** The belief that one is the primary cause of events happening to oneself. [2]

**Knowledge management (KM)** The systematic sharing of information to achieve goals such as innovation, nonduplication of effort, and competitive advantage. [13]

**Leader–member exchange model (LMX)** An explanation of leadership proposing that leaders develop unique working relationships with group members. [9]

**Leadership** The ability to inspire confidence and support among the people who are needed to achieve organizational goals. [1]

**Leadership diversity** The presence of a culturally heterogeneous cadre of leaders. [14]

**Leadership effectiveness** Attaining desirable outcomes such as productivity, quality, and satisfaction in a given situation. [1]

**Leadership Grid®** A framework for specifying the concern for the production and people dimensions of leadership simultaneously. [4]

**Leadership pipeline** A model of leadership development that tightly links leadership development with management responsibilities at each level of the organization. [15]

**Leadership polarity** The disparity in views of leaders: they are revered or vastly unpopular, but people rarely feel neutral about them. [3]

**Leadership style** The relatively consistent pattern of behavior that characterizes a leader. [4]

**Leadership succession** An orderly process of identifying and grooming people to replace executives. [15]

**Leading by example** Influencing others by acting as a positive role model. [8]

**Learning organization** An organization that is skilled at creating, acquiring, and transferring knowledge and at modifying behavior to reflect new knowledge and insights. [13]

**Legitimate power** The lawful right to make a decision and expect compliance. [7]

**Linguistic style** A person's characteristic speaking pattern. [12]

**Long-term orientation** A long-range perspective by workers, who thus are thrifty and do not demand quick returns on investments. [14]

**Machiavellians** People in the workplace who ruthlessly manipulate others. [8]

**Management by anecdote** The technique of inspiring and instructing group members by telling fascinating stories. [3]

**Materialism** In Hofstede's research, an emphasis on assertiveness and the acquisition of money and material objects, and a de-emphasis on caring for others. [14]

**Mentor** A more experienced person who develops a protégé's abilities through tutoring, coaching, guidance, and emotional support. [15]

**Micromanagement** The close monitoring of most aspects of group member activities by the manager or leader. [9]

**Morals** An individual's determination of what is right or wrong influenced by his or her values. [6]

**Multicultural leader** A leader with the skills and attitudes to relate effectively to and motivate people across race, gender, age, social attitudes, and lifestyles. [14]

**Multicultural organization** A firm that values cultural diversity and is willing to encourage and even capitalize on such diversity. [14]

**Multicultural worker** A worker who is convinced that all cultures are equally good and enjoys learning about other cultures. [14]

**Multifunctional managerial development** An organization's intentional efforts to enhance the effectiveness of managers by giving them experience in multiple functions within the organization. [15]

**Normative decision model** A view of leadership as a decision-making process in which the leader examines certain factors within the situation to determine which decision-making style will be the most effective. [5]

**Open-book management** An approach to management in which every employee is trained, empowered, and motivated to understand and pursue the company's business goals. [9]

**Organizational creativity** The creation of novel and useful ideas and products that pertain to the workplace. [11]

**Organizational politics** Informal approaches to gaining power through means other than merit or luck. [7]

**Outcome** Anything that might stem from performance, such as a reward. [10]

**Participative leader** A person in charge who shares decision making with group members. [4]

**Partnership** A relationship between leaders and group members in which power is approximately balanced. [1]

**Path-goal theory** An explanation of leadership effectiveness that specifies what the leader must do to achieve high productivity and morale in a given situation. [5]

**Personal magnetism** A captivating, inspiring personality with charm and charismatic-like qualities. [8]

**Personal power** Power derived from the person rather than from the organization. [7]

**Personalized charismatic** A charismatic leader who exercises few restraints on the use of power in order to best serve his or her own interests. [3]

**Pet-peeve technique** A method of brainstorming in which a group identifies all the possible complaints others might have about the group's organizational unit. [11]

**Power** The potential or ability to influence decisions and control resources. [7]

**Power distance** The extent to which employees accept the idea that the members of an organization have different levels of power. [14]

**Prestige power** The power stemming from one's status and reputation. [7]

**Pygmalion effect** The situation that occurs when a managerial leader believes that a group member will succeed, and communicates this belief without realizing it. [4]

**Referent power** The leader's ability to influence others through his or her desirable traits and characteristics. [3]

**Resistance** The state that occurs when an influence attempt by a leader is unsuccessful: The target is opposed to carrying out the request and finds ways to either not comply or do a poor job. [8]

**Resource dependence perspective** The view that an organization requires a continuing flow of human resources, money, customers and clients, technological inputs, and materials to continue to function. [7]

**Reward power** The authority to give employees rewards for compliance. [7]

**Self-awareness** Insightfully processing feedback about oneself to improve personal effectiveness. [15]

**Self-discipline** The ability to mobilize one's efforts to stay focused on attaining an important goal. [15]

**Self-efficacy** The confidence in one's ability to carry out a specific task. [10]

**Servant leader** One who serves constituents by working on their behalf to help them achieve their goals, not the leader's own goals. [4]

**Shadowing** An approach to mentoring in which the trainee follows the mentor around for a stated period of time. [15]

**Short-term orientation** A focus by workers on immediate results, and a propensity not to save. [14]

**Single-loop learning** A situation in which learners seek minimum feedback that might substantially confront their basic ideas or actions. [15]

**Situational Leadership II (SLII)** a model of leadership that explains how to match the leadership style to capabilities of group members on a given task. [5]

**Social responsibility** The idea that organizations have an obligation to groups in society other than owners or stockholders and beyond that prescribed by law or union contract. [6]

**Socialized charismatic** A charismatic leader who restrains the use of power in order to benefit others. [3]

**Stewardship theory** An explanation of leadership that depicts group members (or followers) as being pro-organizational, collectivists, and trustworthy. [1]

**Strategic contingency theory** An explanation of sources of power suggesting that units best able to cope with the firm's critical problems and uncertainties acquire relatively large amounts of power. [7]

**Strategic leadership** The process of creating or sustaining an organization by providing the right direction and inspiration. [13]

**Strategic planning** Those activities that lead to the statement of goals and objectives and the choice of strategies to achieve them. [13]

**Strategy** An integrated, overall concept of how the firm will achieve its objectives. [13]

**Substitutes for leadership** Factors in the work environment that provide guidance and incentives to perform, making the leader's role almost superfluous. [1]

**Supportive communication** A communication style that delivers the message accurately and that supports or enhances the relationship between the two parties. [12]

**SWOT analysis** A method of considering strengths, weaknesses, opportunities, and threats in a given situation. [13]

**Team** A work group that must rely on collaboration if each member is to experience the optimum success and achievement. [9]

**Teamwork** Work done with an understanding and commitment to group goals on the part of all team members. [9]

**Territorial games** Also referred to as turf wars, political tactics that involve protecting and hoarding resources that give one power, such as information, relationships, and decision-making authority. [7]

**360-degree feedback** A formal evaluation of superiors based on input from people who work for and with them, sometimes including customers and suppliers. [4]

**Tough question** One that makes a person or group stop and think about why they are doing or not doing something. [4]

**Transformational leader** A leader who brings about positive, major changes in an organization. [3]

**Trust** A person's confidence in another individual's intentions and motives and in the sincerity of that individual's word. [2]

**Uncertainty avoidance** A dislike of—and evasion of—the unknown. [14]

**Universal theory of leadership** The belief that certain personal characteristics and skills contribute to leadership effectiveness in many situations. [2]

**Upward appeal** A means of influence in which the leader enlists a person with more formal authority to do the influencing. [8]

**Urgent time organization** A view of time as a scarce resource, leading to impatience. [14]

**Valence** The worth or attractiveness of an outcome. [10]

**Virtual office** A situation in which employees work together as if they were part of a single office despite being physically separated. [12]

**Virtuous cycle** The idea that corporate social performance and corporate financial performance feed and reinforce each other. [6]

**Vision** The ability to imagine different and better conditions and ways to achieve them. [3]

**Whistleblower** An employee who discloses organizational wrongdoing to parties who can take action. [6]

**WICS model of leadership** An explanation of leadership effectiveness that encompasses and synthesizes wisdom, intelligence, and creativity. [2]

**Win–win approach to conflict resolution** The belief that after conflict has been resolved, both sides should gain something of value. [12]

**Work ethic** A firm belief in the dignity of work. [2].

# Name Index

# Organization Index

# Subject Index